*Senator Thomas J. Walsh
of Montana*

Senator Thomas J. Walsh of Montana

Law and Public Affairs, from TR to FDR

J. Leonard Bates

Foreword by Richard Lowitt

University of Illinois Press

Urbana and Chicago

Publication of this book was supported by grants from the
Research Board of the University of Illinois at Urbana-
Champaign and the Oliver M. Dickerson Fund, established
by Mr. Dickerson (Ph.D., Illinois, 1906) to enable the
University of Illinois Press to publish selected works in
American history, designated by the executive committee
of the Department of History.

㊾ This book is printed on acid-free paper.

Library of Congress Cataloging-in-Publication Data
Bates, J. Leonard (James Leonard)
Senator Thomas J. Walsh of Montana: law and public affairs,
from TR to FDR / J. Leonard Bates ; foreword by Richard
Lowitt.
p. cm.
ISBN 0-252-02470-2 (acid-free paper)
1. Walsh, Thomas James, 1859–1933. 2. Legislators—United
States—Biography. 3. Montana—Politics and government.
4. United States—Politics and government—1865–1933.
5. United States. Congress. Senate—Biography. I. Title.
E748.W25B38   1999
978.6'031'092—DDC21   98-58022
[B]   CIP

C 5 4 3 2 1

To Dotty, Alan, and the memory of Dan

Contents

Foreword

Richard Lowitt

The progressive impulse, the American phase of a reform movement that permeated western Europe, was notable in that, unlike previous reform movements and the later New Deal, it got underway during a period of prosperity. Emerging from a decade of depression marked by political, economic, and social turmoil and a popular war that witnessed the arrival of the United States as a world power with an empire of its own, Americans, who were chiefly but not exclusively middle-class citizens, began to take stock and assess their country as it moved into the twentieth century. The shock of recognition was appalling, all but overwhelming. Literally, almost everywhere one turned, observers found conditions clamoring for reform. The rise of big business in the late nineteenth century brought in its wake trusts and monopolies, pollution, and other hazards, as well as exploited workers, who in many instances were recent immigrants living in ghettoes in rapidly expanding urban areas administered by venal bosses and political leaders. Bribery, fraud, and political corruption were all too common. Privilege seemed to control politics from the local to the national level.

In addition, reformers were becoming acutely aware of the victims of industrialization. During the last decades of the nineteenth century farmers and other rural Americans west of the Mississippi River engaged in a tremendous battle to regain control of their destiny by refusing to be incorporated into modern America. They lost that battle with the defeat of both William Jennings Bryan and the Populists in 1896. Then, in the twentieth century, urban reformers manifested concern for the plight of women and children in particular but also for exploited industrial workers, immigrants, and to a lesser degree African Americans.

People who called themselves progressives were equally concerned with ways and means of modernizing the system, promoting greater efficiency in government and business, making business more rational and government both rational and responsive to the democratic aspirations of the American people through, for example, woman suffrage, direct election of senators, the direct primary, and other procedures to give voters greater voice in public affairs. This movement affected all sectors of American life and produced a set of remarkable leaders, both men and women, many of whom were active for decades to come. In the American West, however, the impulse played itself out in ways somewhat different than the rest of the country.

In the West, reformers were not so much concerned about what was occurring in state and local governments, which exercised less power than those in the East, but with the federal government, which exercised a kind of authority it had never possessed in the East. For one thing, it still owned much of the land and resources available in the West. The federal government dispensed land grants, permits to miners, cattlemen, railroads, and developers, including homesteaders, all interested in utilizing the resources of the public domain. Acquiring water rights and utilizing streams and rivers that crossed state lines created political battles, as did many issues pertaining to land utilization that local and state governments could not resolve. The federal government had either to provide guidelines or to help arbitrate.

Some of the most important issues involving the West called for action above the state level. Federal bureaucrats employed by several cabinet-level departments and agencies wielded enormous power in areas that state and local governments did not control. Consequently, political parties in the West were relatively weak. But the region produced notable progressive U.S. senators in the early decades of the twentieth century. Aspiring public figures in the West tended to look to Washington, D.C., because it was in the nation's capital that reform and change affecting their states could occur.

Thus, it is not surprising that prominent and not so prominent western senators have attracted serious scholarly attention. Most were Theodore Roosevelt Republicans, and the most notable among them were ranked among the outstanding progressive leaders of the time. William E. Borah (1865–1940), Hiram Johnson (1866–1945), George W. Norris (1861–1944), and Gerald P. Nye (1892–1971) are all subjects of major biographies and numerous articles and monographs. So too have lesser progressive Republican senators received historical attention. Bronson Cutting (1888–1935), William Langer (1886–1959), and Peter Norbeck (1870–1936), for example, are the subjects of well-received biographies.

Democratic senators have not been as fortunate as their Republican brethren. Francis Newlands (1848–1917) and Burton Wheeler (1882–1975) have received biographical attention. In Wheeler's case there is an autobiography as well. But his Montana colleague and fellow Democrat Thomas J. Walsh (1859–1933) is the last prominent progressive senator to be the subject of a major biography. J. Leonard Bates, in the months before his death in October 1998, turned over to the University of Illinois Press his much-revised and long-awaited manuscript. Though he will not see his book in print, he died knowing that his task was accomplished and that his biography of Walsh would be published.

It was a long road to publication. After service in the U.S. Navy as a gunnery officer on merchant vessels conveying supplies through the Barents Sea to the northern Soviet port of Murmansk, Len enrolled for graduate work at the University of North Carolina at Chapel Hill. In 1952, upon the acceptance of his dissertation, "Senator Walsh of Montana, 1918–1924: A Liberal under Pressure," he was awarded a Ph.D. degree. The dissertation focused on Walsh's role in unearthing the Teapot Dome controversy. Now he was hooked. He had found his subject, and a biography became his ultimate goal. It was a most formidable challenge.

I met Len in the 1950s when we were instructors at the University of Maryland. We became fast friends and spent many hours in the Library of Congress, I in the George W. Norris papers, but Len, still interested in Walsh, began to shift his attention to Teapot Dome and conservation. In 1963 he published *The Origins of Teapot Dome: Progressivism, Parties, and Petroleum,* an important monograph that has not been superseded. It was preceded by a flurry of articles, one of which, published in the *American Historical Review* in 1955, "The Teapot Dome Scandal and the Election of 1924," emanated from his dissertation; the other, "Fulfilling American Democracy: The Conservation Movement, 1907–1921," appeared in 1957 in the *Mississippi Valley Historical Review.* It was widely reprinted and became a topic of much discussion and controversy as historians in increasing numbers began to focus attention on the conservation movement.

While conservation history and progressivism commanded much of Len's attention and that of some of his graduate students, he also continued his research on Thomas J. Walsh. In 1966 *Tom Walsh in Dakota Territory: Personal Correspondence of Senator Thomas J. Walsh and Elinor C. McClements* appeared. Walsh first held public office in Dakota Territory, and this volume was a clear indication that Bates had control over the early part of Walsh's career. But before he devoted full time to rounding out his research on Walsh,

Len prepared a text that provided the rich texture for his biography. *The United States, 1898–1928: Progressivism and a Society in Transition,* published in 1976, is a beautifully nuanced text that revealed his mastery of this period, the years in which Walsh was a significant public figure. It also suggests that Len was an impressive teacher and graduate student advisor. In all, he directed at least twenty dissertations, a significant number of which fall within the progressive era.

Prior to the publication of *The United States, 1898–1928,* Len published other articles on Walsh's career, but after its publication only one or two articles appeared. Most of his time now was devoted to finishing his research, drafting chapters, and guiding graduate students completing their dissertations. Writing soon became his passion and the Walsh biography began to take on gigantic dimensions. Len became so deeply involved with his subject that he began to lose perspective. He worked and reworked his manuscript, crafted and honed its numerous chapters. When he turned it over to Press, the manuscript ran to over a thousand pages and more than fifty chapters. Len had reached a point where he found it difficult to distinguish between the significant and the less consequential. All had received his most careful and detailed attention. At this point, the Press, aware of Walsh's stature as a prominent progressive senator, asked several readers, of which I was one, to review the manuscript and make suggestions as to how it could be reduced and therefore improved and made ready for publication. The last time I saw Len was at the Atlanta meeting of the Southern Historical Association in 1997. We enjoyed a long, leisurely lunch. He was full of enthusiasm for his project and grateful for the suggestions of his friends. He assured me that many, if not most, were acceptable. He was eager to get home and begin revising the manuscript. Clearly he had regained perspective and was ready to pare down the chapters. He spent the next several months doing just that.

Thomas J. Walsh now has the first-rate biography he merits. Our knowledge of progressive western politics, of Montana in particular, of conservation, of the Wilson years and the 1920s is enriched. J. Leonard Bates has fulfilled his scholarly mission. He did it admirably. And our knowledge and understanding of the years from Theodore Roosevelt to Franklin Roosevelt is now considerably enhanced.

Preface

The 1960s was an important decade for the completion of this book in its present form. I spent much time in the Walsh Papers in the Library of Congress and in the state of Montana, interviewing people and trying to get a grasp on the state sources. I benefited more than anticipated from the collection that had been maintained for many years by Walsh's daughter, Genevieve W. Gudger. A centerpiece of this small collection was the correspondence of T. J. Walsh and his wife, Elinor (Ellen), running most notably from the 1890s to her death in 1917.

Earlier I heard about Walsh at the University of North Carolina when Howard K. Beale of the history department mentioned that the papers of this Montanan in the Library of Congress were of high quality and could be the basis of a good study. After moving to the University of Maryland, a few miles from the Library, I was a frequent researcher there. On relocating to the University of Illinois, I often went east to use the Walsh Papers and other manuscript collections. Walsh's career intrigued me because he was an American of Irish extraction who differed from other Democrats and from Republicans of progressive views, with whom he often collaborated. He was energetic, intelligent, and never easy to categorize. The fact that he grew up in Wisconsin, lived in Dakota Territory for a time, and moved on to Montana helped to make him unique.

In addition to Professor Beale, I benefited from the knowledgeability of others at North Carolina. A. R. Newsome encouraged and guided me in my graduate program. Fletcher M. Green ultimately became my adviser and saw me through to the completion of a dissertation on Senator Walsh that focused on the years in which he first became prominent.

Colleagues at the University of Maryland and the University of Illinois, including H. Samuel Merrill, E. James Ferguson, and Richard Lowitt, often gave assistance. Robert M. Sutton, a professor of history and director of the Illinois Historical Survey (a research library) assisted, too, and presided over the creation of a Walsh manuscript collection made possible by documents received from Walsh's daughter, Genevieve Walsh Gudger. John Hoffmann, librarian of the Survey, read the manuscript and assisted in many ways.

On two occasions I received research grants from the Social Science Research Council. Also, in 1968, I gained research time by being appointed an associate member of the Center for Advanced Study at the University of Illinois. Meanwhile, I was fortunate to obtain research assistance from the University's Graduate College. Harold F. Cahalan, Richard A. Swanson, and Ralph Stone were notably helpful in this capacity; the last gave additional aid in research after he had retired from teaching to live in Missoula, Montana.

Of all libraries and research institutions, the Library of Congress and the University of Illinois Library gave the most important and sustained assistance. I would like to name all the librarians who helped but cannot do more than tell the places to which I went (or occasionally telephoned) for aid. Following is a list of those who responded: the Franklin D. Roosevelt Library at Hyde Park, the New York City Public Library, the State Historical Society of Wisconsin, the Two Rivers (Wis.) Public Library, the Denver Public Library, the Montana Historical Society Library (Helena), the Whitman College Library (Walla Walla, Wash.), the Huntington Library (San Marino, Calif.), the Bancroft Library of the University of California, and libraries of Yale University, Duke University, the University of Virginia, the University of North Carolina at Chapel Hill, Indiana University, the University of Kentucky, and the University of Montana at Missoula.

I have waited until last to mention aid that was indispensable. Senator Walsh's daughter, Genevieve W. Gudger, helped with interviews and provided invaluable family manuscripts, as noted. Clark C. Spence, a colleague at the University of Illinois, often assisted regarding my "computer problems," contributed his time and knowledge to run off drafts of the manuscript, and read the entire study. My wife, Dorothy Pettit Bates, has helped in countless ways, both personal and professional, and I can never thank her enough. Finally, while many have contributed, I assume responsibility for the manuscript in its entirety.

Senator Thomas J. Walsh
of Montana

I

An Irish-American Family

Thomas James Walsh came under the influence of a strong family heritage. His Catholicism had something to do with the circles in which he moved and with many occurrences. Learning politics from his father, he functioned at times with the skills of an Irish politico.

He was a devout Catholic who tried to keep his faith private. Like many of his generation, he was an idealist and a moralist who spoke out periodically for higher standards of public morality. Occasionally he was chided for his denunciatory role, as in the Teapot Dome affair of the 1920s. But William Hard, the journalist, who knew Walsh well, commented on the Senator's sincerity and what he described as a kind of spirituality. President Cavanaugh of Notre Dame University, writing a personal note in 1931, had a similar judgment to make: "Men like you are the pride of the priesthood and the ornament and persuasive example to the world of what the Church really means."[1]

How Walsh gained a religious heritage and found his road to fame is the story of an Irish family in Two Rivers, Wisconsin. In this village north of Milwaukee the future senator was born on June 12, 1859, the third of ten children. He was fortunate in the character and ability of his parents and the ties of affection that bound his kinfolk together. Felix and Bridget (Comer) Walsh, both natives of Ireland, came separately to Wisconsin with their families and were married in 1853. His mother never learned to read and write; soon she was busy in America taking care of her own children.[2]

To be a Catholic of Irish parents in 1859 was to start with disadvantages. The children of such parents could go far in the relatively fluid American society, but certain doors were closed. In the minds of many Americans the Irish were a brawling people doing work that even slaves were often too good to do. In politics the Irish could seldom hope to win more than local leadership. Socially, as well, there were difficulties.[3]

In Wisconsin the Irish were a substantial group with 6.4 percent (about 50,000) of the total population. They worked in lead mines of the southwest counties or variously as laborers, loggers, fishers, and farmers. A few were professionally trained. In the vicinity of Two Rivers a majority were rural.[4]

Catholics predominated in many places, including Two Rivers. German, French Canadian, and Irish Catholics mingled freely with the native Protestants. The Walsh family lived in circumstances that were almost idyllic.[5]

The Walshes' way of life and that of the community in which they lived were almost inseparable. Just a short distance from the Walsh home the Neshoto and Mishicott rivers came together, their dark waters flowing eastward into Lake Michigan. This waterway provided the site for a trading center and fishing village and a beautiful locale for the children who lived there.

Two Rivers experienced the frontier exploitation of resources that typically occurred in the Great Lakes country. Fur trading was the original activity of white men in this region of waterways, wild life, and vast, unbroken forests. Fishing soon became important, as did logging, lumbering, and tanning (using the bark of hemlock). When the population increased, farming became a mainstay of the economy. In Two Rivers, however, the early experience with lumber and wood products led to the growth of a permanent industry.[6]

The story is told that when Bridget Comer first arrived in Wisconsin with her family, Felix Walsh had a team of horses and was looking for business at the newly constructed pier which jutted into Lake Michigan. The Comers disembarked and sought transportation farther inland to an Irish settlement where relatives had taken up land. Felix conveyed the party there, meanwhile getting acquainted with Bridget, who was about 18 years old. Not long afterward they were married.

Felix had been a weaver in North Ireland, following the trade of his father. In Manitowoc County, he became essentially a skilled laborer and part-time farmer who also showed talent for public affairs. He served as trustee (alderman) of the first ward in Two Rivers, as the village and town clerk for twenty years, and as a longtime justice of the peace.

The Walshes lived on a tract of about twenty acres on the east edge of Two Rivers, where they did some farming and began to raise a family. Their residence was at first a log house in the woods and later a one-story structure of rough boards. Their first child was Mary, born in 1856. Henry was the oldest son, born in 1857, and Tom followed two years later. At intervals of one or two years came Kate, Elizer, Sarah, Bridget, Joseph Felix, John, and Lucy.

The Walshes had a supporting role in the business of commercial fishing, in which seining and the use of nets was important. As John, the youngest brother, recalled, "at night and in the winter the entire family knit fish nets by piece to add to the family income." This gave continuing associations with French-Canadian families, whose fish sheds or places of business were located on the Mishicott River.

Like others, the Walshes found time to fish for sport or food, and Tom, an inveterate fisher in later years, acquired his passion in the rivers near his home and the teeming waters of Lake Michigan.

Village records of Two Rivers reveal that Felix Walsh sold cordwood to the town, and doubtless also to individuals for private use. He and his sons cleared the timber on their little farm. Probably the father also worked at times as a logger in the woods and a raftsman on the rivers.[7]

The rivers and the great lake beyond gave life to the town. Communication with the outside world was primarily by water. Residents commented on the excitement with which they greeted the weekly passenger boat bringing news, cargo, and strange people. Such boats, for example, brought soldiers back from the Civil War when Walsh was six years old. The river added a special quality to the memories of youth.[8]

It was farming with which the people of Manitowoc County increasingly occupied their time in the 1860s and 1870s. In the summer there was a variety of fresh food, including the fish that were so plentiful, the fruits and vegetables, and the wild berries that grew in places known to children. Walsh wrote of how they "rambled" through the woods, enjoyed the lilies on the marshes, and looked for crayfish. In later years he looked to the Rocky Mountains and to Glacier Park for pleasures that equalled those of his youth.[9]

The Two Rivers area provided opportunities for a young person to learn of many things and to whet an appetite concerning the world beyond. There was little excuse in Two Rivers for a narrow provincialism, for failing to achieve something of a "social education." Felix Walsh, from Ireland, was for twenty years the village and town clerk and otherwise active in public affairs. Andrew Baetz, from Germany, was blacksmith and carriage maker. He later served as mayor. Walsh, Baetz, and H. C. Hamilton (of native stock) served together in the village government, and this was the pattern.

Germans, however, easily outnumbered the other immigrant groups by 1860, while a few native born individuals like Hamilton were the principal owners of village stores and factories. Relatively less influential were Irish families and the French Canadians.

The Walsh children played with friends of several nationalities. In this way, and by going to church where the sermons were primarily in German or French, Tom Walsh acquired a rough speaking knowledge of two foreign languages and later showed keen interest in the study of other languages such as Norwegian. As a politician decades later, seeking the foreign vote, he did not fail to use this language skill as an evidence of his personal interest and sympathy.[10]

There was a dark side to life in the village of Two Rivers. Disease, violence, and death were common. Though the Walsh family was relatively healthy, one of the daughters, Bridget, died at the age of twelve. Another, Elizer, lived to adulthood but succumbed to tuberculosis. Henry, the oldest son and a favorite of all, died at forty.

The family structure, however, provided a means of mutual aid in an individualistic society. Bridget Walsh capably and firmly managed her large and growing family with aid from a local girl who was part Indian, and from Mary, the oldest daughter. Tom Walsh remembered how good his mother had been to him, "when I was sick and always." His sister Kate added that their mother was a strong and vigorous woman. "Never was there a half way measure with her—a thing was either right or it was wrong"—an attitude her son Tom would adopt in most cases.

Probably more than Felix Walsh, the mother insisted that all the children be up early and ready for school. "No one must miss a day & no one must be late," Kate remembered. Similarly, the church must not be neglected.

The father was also firm. There is no suggestion, however, of harsh discipline or of damaged spirits. Felix Walsh was a man of talent. His qualities, in different circumstances, might have taken him to high public office. As it was, his achievements on the local level made him a respected figure.

His formal education had occurred in a school conducted by the Anglican Church in Ulster, North Ireland. Here, as his son John observed: "the reading text book was the king James (Protestant) version of the bible. He alway[s] had great familiarity with passages of the Bible." Later he served an apprenticeship with a Methodist weaver and lived in his home for three years, gaining further familiarity with Protestants and with their habit of Bible study.

In the Walsh home newspapers figured more conspicuously than books. Yet because of his work with documents as justice of the peace and his long service as village and city clerk, Felix Walsh must have seemed a bookish man. He subscribed for a time to the *Boston Pilot,* a principal source of Irish-American news, and later to the *Catholic Citizen* of Milwaukee, an Irish-American weekly; also to the *Manitowoc Pilot,* and to the *Two Rivers Chronicle.*

Such interests in their father's life were an inspiration to Henry, Tom, and John, all of whom became lawyers. John commented that their father "was the village magistrate, the Squire," probably referring to the later years of his life when he had attained his greatest prestige.

Also notable was the fact that Felix Walsh, a Democrat, often presided in the local caucuses and conventions; he knew the leaders and spoke knowingly of national affairs. The Irish in Two Rivers in decades after the Civil War joined with other voters to make the village overwhelmingly Democratic, running up majorities of three to one against the Republicans. The Walsh sons were strong Democrats, much as their father was.[11]

A parental influence may be seen in other instances. The Irish in Wisconsin supported public schools, partly because Germans controlled the parochial schools; Felix Walsh served on the local school board, working to enrich the curriculum and to achieve the construction of the high school. Meanwhile, his own children, Mary, Henry, Tom, and the others were one by one becoming school teachers. Tom proceeded, after a time, to law school at the University of Wisconsin. His youngest brother, John, also studied at Madison. Walsh in later years was a champion of the University of Wisconsin and the role such institutions could play in a democracy.

The liquor question was another that affected the Walsh family and the Irish, but not according to later stereotypes. It seemed to many in the 1920s that Senator Walsh of Montana was a strange sort of Irishman, who supported the Eighteenth Amendment and the Volstead Act. Actually the Walsh family tradition, like that of many from the old country, was strongly antiliquor. Not a few Irishmen in Wisconsin supported a temperance movement, and the *Catholic Citizen* of Milwaukee waged a fight for total abstinence. Actually Tom Walsh was not a teetotaller (perhaps because of German beer drinkers with whom he grew up).[12]

What the Walshes lacked in wealth and sophistication, they compensated for in affection. This feature of their life is remarkable. Henry and Tom were particularly close. They played together, studied together, and finally practiced law together in Dakota Territory. They even slept in the same bed in a room adjoining their law office for some five years. When Tom Walsh moved on to Helena, Montana, he received a loan from someone in his family. Almost immediately, as his law fees permitted, he began to repay the loan and to send money to John for further schooling at the University of Wisconsin and to Elizer, who was then dying of tuberculosis in California.

To some, this type of aid and support, or the acceptance of it, seemed "unmanly" and un-American. Walsh expressed, however, his profound indebtedness to Henry for all that he had done and his pride in the love of his sisters.[13]

From an early age, the future senator applied himself to his books. This was not unusual, but certain aspects of his education were, even for the mid-nine-teenth century. He learned his letters from the part-Indian girl who assisted with household chores. Since Walsh's mother could not read and his father was especially busy, the source of instruction was not so surprising. Walsh's formal schooling consisted of elementary work in the public school of Two Rivers, which had seven grades, where he learned "the fundamentals," as he described them. He also did some "post-graduate" work there and eventual-ly had one year at the University of Wisconsin Law School. Between elemen-tary school and law school came eight years of teaching. Obviously he was largely self-educated, although he was fortunate to have the guidance and inspiration of some talented and experienced instructors, in the years at Two Rivers and later.[14]

One of these teachers was James S. Anderson, a native of Glasgow, Scot-land, who emigrated to Wisconsin and served in the Union army. A gradu-ate of Lawrence College at Appleton, Wisconsin, he also became a lawyer, newspaper editor, and politician of some prominence in Manitowoc, fifteen miles down the lakeshore from Two Rivers. Walsh read law with Anderson in his Manitowoc office. Another teacher in an upper grade was John Faville, also a veteran of the Civil War, who went on from his teaching at Two Rivers to become a Congregational clergyman of national distinction. Another able man, principal of the elementary school and briefly Walsh's teacher, was John Nagle of Manitowoc, known later as editor of the *Pilot,* to which Walsh's fa-ther subscribed.

In speaking afterward of John Nagle, Walsh placed him in a "galaxy" of leaders in the Manitowoc area, who "would have added luster to any com-munity with which they identified themselves." Daily contact was possible with "cultivated minds."[15]

The Two Rivers home had many "dear associations" for Walsh, and he continued in the 1870s and early 1880s to spend his vacations there. But by 1875 he was teaching away from home, and he continued to do so every year but one. Gradually his intellectual interests and high ambitions seemed to make him distinctive. Exactly what his future would be and where he would spend it remained uncertain, even while he was teaching school with consid-erable success. But his mental abilities could not be doubted, and he harbored a "hallucination" of becoming famous.[16]

2

The Young Intellectual

T J. Walsh (as he was beginning to call himself) lacked a glamorous personality or traits of conviviality, but allusions to his mental abilities are a recurrent theme throughout his career in teaching, law, and politics. In many respects a "man of the people," Walsh also became an intellectual who moved among the highly educated; and he gained near legendary status for his prowess as a lawyer.

In a moment of exasperation in 1914, Senator "Jim" Reed of Missouri put his finger on one of Walsh's predominant traits: He knew of no man who "can more thoroughly get on one side of a case and stay there than the Senator from Montana." Even as a young man, Walsh tended to feel strongly on many questions and to mobilize his arguments accordingly. In a moment of introspection, he recognized a danger in this aspect of his personality: "I sometimes accuse myself of coming to conclusions and forming resolutions without due reflection and then afterwards endeavoring to support them by specious arguments having only possibilities for their bases."[1]

From 1875 to 1883 young Walsh taught school in a succession of places. In 1883–84 he attended law school at Madison. But the direction of his thought and the uses to which he would put his abilities were not evident. As a Christian he believed in good deeds on this earth, and personal salvation and a life hereafter were not his paramount concerns, as suggested by a short talk he gave to one group of his own faith. "The supreme duty of a Christian is charity," he began. "It is the mistress and queen of virtues. It is the lesson of the life of Christ."[2]

Walsh was an admirer of liberals in the Church, including Pope Leo XIII and James Cardinal Gibbons of Baltimore, whom he came to know well. The feeling persists that Walsh was a person of overwhelmingly secular interests even though the Church, as described, occupied a place of importance in his life. Certainly the study of law, in its ramifications, became his passion. Indicative of temporal interests is an entry in his diary, late one Sunday during a 1923 visit to the Far East, though he may have written this with a chuckle: "Mass in the morning, Golf in the afternoon, Ma-jong in the evening."

He once stated his views on the conflict between faith and reason. His faith was important to him, and he did not know what he would do if it were "shattered." At the same time, "A faith that will not bear the test of reason, that can not endure the light of truth confesses itself false." That he meant this is indicated by his support of public schools and universities, his own reading habits, and his admiration for freethinking liberals such as Thomas Jefferson.

Walsh seems to have accepted rather completely the "idea of progress" of the nineteenth century. By no means did he oppose material gains, the march of science, and the modernization of agriculture. His doubts and reservations mostly concerned the distribution of profits. Even so, he tended to be optimistic.[3]

There is no way to explain in simple terms or to pigeonhole Thomas J. Walsh. Sympathetic with the cause of Ireland and active among those seeking her relief, he was at the same time an admirer of English literature and of the British people. A product of the times in his drive for self-improvement and "success," he did not equate success with the making of money. But he was almost painfully ambitious to attain the economic wherewithal to a "better life." His starting point was teaching and the study of law.

One of Walsh's first teaching positions was close to home. This was at the tannery, about two and a half miles up the Mishicott River, where a village had developed around the tannery works.

Handicapped by the lack of library facilities, he did his best with the books available, studying to push himself up the educational ladder. The highest certificate he could obtain was an "unlimited" or life certificate requiring a knowledge of college subjects. Below this were other levels of attainment. He was trying to acquire at least an elementary knowledge of a wide range of subjects, to give himself a liberal education.

It is not accidental that Walsh gained a reputation in later years as a "thinking machine." He was motivated to think systematically and he heavily emphasized mathematics for the "valuable mental training which it affords." In a paper perhaps prepared for a teachers' meeting, he stated: "The exercise which it [mathematics] gives in exact reasoning, and in prolonged and intense attention can be supplied in no other way. These are two great results and are powers not lightly to be valued." Still another subject of importance was history. A thick sheaf of papers gives an indication of the way in which he studied, though without notation as to the books he was using at the time.

The official evidence of Walsh's successful study lies in two certificates he received. The first was a "limited" certificate, dated August 18, 1879, declaring that a state board of examiners had found him possessing "the requisite scholarship in all the branches of study required." More important was the "unlimited" certificate, dated August 23, 1881. Kate Walsh recalled how her brother had been watching the post office for some days, and how she and her mother were anxious, too. One day they waited outside the house for him to go and return home. "As he turned the corner quite a distance from the house he saw us—raised the certificate and hollered so we could hear him— 'I have it Ma—I have it.'"[4]

Even before this Walsh qualified for the position of principal in a state-aided high school. In the fall of 1880, at the age of twenty-one, he secured such a post at Glenbeulah, Wisconsin, southwest of Two Rivers in Sheboygan County. Glenbeulah, or "Glen," was a fateful place in Walsh's life. A teacher who assisted him there was Mary McClements of Sheboygan, whose sister, Elinor McClements, would be the future Mrs. Walsh.

Walsh's abilities and predilections were apparent by this time. Further evidence of mental prowess is to be found in miscellaneous papers that he prepared for delivery in the late 1870s and early 1880s. If not brilliant, they were impressive for intellectual force and boldness of interpretation and for a wide knowledge of history, public affairs, and the world of ideas. He combined his book learning with homely common sense and a dry sense of humor.

All the indications are that Walsh had sound ideas on educational practice and that he probably did give his students a good start in their intellectual life, as some testified. Many years later, in a graduation address, the former teacher expressed a thoroughly acceptable attitude toward the role in which he had worked for eight years: "He is the most successful teacher who best equips his classes for independent investigation."[5]

Important as a historical source for this period are the letters Walsh exchanged with his new friend, Elinor McClements. "Miss McClements," a school teacher in Sheboygan and later in Chicago, attracted Walsh as much by her brains and cleverness as by her good looks. They wrote frequently of their hopes, aspirations, and career developments. By the summer of 1882 Walsh was reading law and had every intention of becoming a lawyer, although he continued to teach in high school and to serve as principal for another year.

Walsh's home for the two academic years, 1881–83, was Sturgeon Bay, Wisconsin, the county seat of Door County. Up in this "Northland," as "Ellen"

McClements described it, he had probably the best experience of his teaching career. Sturgeon Bay offered a social and intellectual life that small towns of the day often afforded. Soon Walsh and others of literary interests were overhauling Thomas Moore, criticizing Byron, doing up Sheridan, and disposing of Southey. "Our literary society is thriving," said Walsh, "and is a source of much enjoyment to me." He felt even happier a little later when they turned to "historical discussion."[6]

Quite a different subject occupied the young man's thoughts in the days that followed. On March 17, 1882, he delivered an address before the Auxiliary Land League of Door County. His topic was the land problem in Ireland, with special reference to British policy and the evils of absentee ownership. This address is the best statement of Walsh's early ideas on the Irish question. It is also indicative of his later attitude toward the British government and its people, as well as other matters.[7]

As a side interest in Sturgeon Bay, Walsh wrote articles for the educational column of the local newspapers, while sometimes complaining about the lack of credit he received from the editor.[8]

Through all these months (in fact, for nine years) Tom Walsh wrote his regular "column" to Ellen McClements, off in Sheboygan or Chicago. Walsh was obviously in love, perhaps from the time when he first met Ellen in Glenbeulah and heard her sing (he was "startled"); or perhaps he was stricken on a hike when she threw burrs in his hair. Yet he had no thought of proposing marriage until he had established himself, and that would be some time in the future. As for the elegant Miss McClements, she obviously enjoyed the young man's company and his letters. She announced, in an early letter, that her ideal man "must be courteous, a model in manners and speech, and he must not have a Roman nose." Walsh may have been teasing in reply when he said that he had no "Roman" but felt condemned to "despair" by the other requirement.[9]

The Walsh-McClements correspondence was primarily an intellectual exchange. Ellen McClements showed respect for Walsh's ability and urged him to use it. She provided advice and opinions, and occasionally books that he wanted. Her strong interest in art, music, literature, drama, and "society" stimulated his own cultural curiosity.[10]

Walsh once said of himself, whether seriously or not, that he hadn't the "conversational talent of a ten-year old." Ellen replied that he possessed "the gift of talking fluently, gracefully, strongly, convincingly, and that is just what you will need as a lawyer." She continued that she had heard him debate at Glenbeulah and had seen for herself how he "relentlessly showed the opposition's want of argument in the case." Also, he had a capacity for entering "heartily into a subject, to the utter exclusion of surroundings." Such a power was necessary to a good speaker.[11]

It was true that by the time he began to study law in the summer of 1882 Tom Walsh had become a widely read man. His tastes in literature were those, in general, of his age. In later life, he said his favorite poem was Gray's "Elegy Written in a Country Church-Yard." He greatly admired the "myriad-minded" Shakespeare and appropriated not a few of his phrases. The novels of George Eliot were also among his favorites; indeed they were works of "rare merit," he thought, partly because she had a "wonderful insight into and power of analyzing human character and motives." And he found a kindred spirit in Lord Byron—the fighter, the believer in human liberty and religious toleration, the intellectual, the activist.[12]

In the summers of 1882 and 1883 Walsh turned his attention to the reading of law. The first summer he spent in Manitowoc, reading in the office of Judge J. S. Anderson, his old teacher. Walsh quickly received one admonition. When he pointed out some grammatical errors in the commentaries of Blackstone, Judge Anderson "curtly" remarked that if Walsh wanted to become a lawyer he would be "obliged to quit being a schoolmaster."

In the summer of 1883 Walsh resumed the study of law, having completed his final term as a teacher. This time he remained in Sturgeon Bay and was joined by his brother, Henry. They were having a "jolly time," he reported in late June. Several weeks later, writing about court week in Sturgeon Bay, he sounded like a lawyer. His friend, Scudder, told him that, if he wished, he could easily pass the examination and begin his practice. Walsh agreed. But he was studying law "to know it and not to pass the examination," and so he would continue for a while.

The University of Wisconsin, when Walsh arrived, was already celebrated as a liberal school where freedom of inquiry was encouraged. Doubtless Walsh had his alma mater in mind a few years later when he wrote of the vast difference it made "what kind of air there is about a college," whether a "great abundance of tolerance and liberality" pervaded it or whether, on the contrary, students had to "seek the fountain of knowledge in the icy air of Puritanic or Inquisitorial holiness."[13]

Wisconsin in the 1880s was still a small school and in some respects a poor one. Its total enrollment was about 400, while the law students numbered only 36. Of the latter, 23 were in the senior class, and T. J. Walsh was among them. According to requirements of the time, no student could graduate with a law degree until he had spent two years in legal studies, one of which had to be under supervision of the faculty. Walsh, like others, was admitted to senior standing on the basis of his independent study. Students could be admitted "at any time," and one of those who entered late was Mrs. Robert M. La Follette, wife of the young district attorney of Dane County.

The law school in the 1870s and 1880s left much to be desired. Located away from the University campus, near the state capitol, its budget was small, and practicing attorneys in Madison gave most of the lectures. Theoretically, members of the Supreme Court of Wisconsin were also on the staff, but they seldom lectured or made a genuine contribution. Indications are strong, nevertheless, that the able student could acquire what the law school promised: a "comprehensive general view" of the subject, a knowledge of books and sources of information and "the habits and methods of legal study and thought."

The sessions of moot court were probably more exciting to Walsh than his classes. "The thing I like best in the world," he once announced to a fellow senator, "is to try a law suit." Moot court provided a rigorous introduction to the experience. Writing to Ellen McClements, Walsh told of his successes, although he worried a little about his inability to convince the "jury" as readily as the "court" (the judge).[14]

Meanwhile, Walsh was serving as the law editor of *The Badger*, after election to that position by his classmates. This meant that his name was listed on the masthead and he contributed a number of items, usually brief, on recent graduates and their developing careers, along with current activities and problems of the law school.

Another activity was the Ryan Debating Club (named after the Chief Justice whom Walsh admired). Walsh was a leading organizer and an author of the club's constitution, although much wrangling ensued over the organic document, and one of his classmates saw fit to write a long letter to the "Editors Badger" assailing Walsh and pointing to alleged weaknesses in his rhetoric and in his character.[15]

The Ryan Club went on to a busy year of activities, in which the principal event seems to have been a public debate on the tariff. This occurred on two successive nights, in the law lecture hall, with six students arguing for protection and six against. Walsh was among the speakers for a low tariff. Three Madison attorneys served as the judges. According to the next issue of *The Badger*, the program "created quite a little excitement in University circles."

The timely subject and the participation of good debaters brought large audiences and a crowded hall. The low tariff speakers prevailed and, according to the columnist, "T. J. Walsh of the Senior class made the best debate, presenting the 'anti-protection' side of the labor question in a very clear, forcible and most ingenious manner." (One presumes that Walsh did not write this particular column for *The Badger.*)

As the catalog of the law school had claimed, good opportunities existed in Madison for students to observe court procedures on the local, state, and national level. Walsh put in an appearance often. During the Christmas vacation, when he went with a friend to Emmettsburg, Iowa, he spent much of his time investigating the system of courts and reflecting on whether he might start his practice there.

The wider cultural life in Madison was also irresistible to this devotee of self-improvement. Walsh was terribly excited by the University library, its pleasant reading room, and its collection of books. He saw so much to read on his first visit that he was "bewildered" and soon left. He also joined a literary club.

By May 1884, Walsh was writing his thesis (required for the law degree) and was moving to the conclusion of his university career. The subject of politics also occupied his thoughts. At the end of May the state Democratic convention met in Madison, and Walsh attended its sessions as a delegate from Door County (Sturgeon Bay). Uppermost in his mind, however, was his law career.

In high spirits, Walsh paid Ellen McClements a visit in Chicago and returned to Madison for the last events of the school year. He completed his thesis and then joined fellow students for two memorable evenings. Before members of the Ryan Club he took his turn in contributing to the "mystical lore" of legal commentary. With another group he attended a banquet at the price of $1.50 per plate, during which one of his friends served as toastmaster and Walsh delivered a speech on "The Future of the Democratic Party."

Walsh still had not decided where to begin his practice. Returning to Two Rivers for a vacation, he reported that he was about to make up his mind and that, when he had done so, he would then proceed with all the vigor at his command. True to his word, he soon announced that he was leaving for Dakota Territory—following westward the "star of empire." The first question to be answered was, Could he make a living in the practice of law?[16]

3

On the Dakota Frontier

Politicians who lived on the American frontier can be compared with presidential candidates born in a log cabin. The frontier experience could serve merely as "window dressing" in a subsequent career or it could be, in fact, a highly instructive experience. In 1913, for example, Walsh wrote to President Wilson on the subject of office holders in Alaska Territory, referring to the problem as he had observed it in Dakota Territory. To live in a territorial stage was different than to live in one of the American states. Almost inevitably an intelligent person, practicing law and participating in government affairs under the territorial organization, learned things about federalism and political realities that could be learned in no other way.

During Walsh's six years in Dakota, from 1884 to 1890, he crammed in some memorable experiences and was tested "as if by fire" in the vast reaches of the territory. He made his start as a lawyer in what became difficult times of drought and agricultural distress. He was also an "Irish Democrat," linked at times with the saloon element, against a majority overwhelmingly Republican. But by the time he moved west he had become an experienced lawyer and a veteran organizer in the Democratic party.

The territory of Dakota was much in the news in the 1880s as hundreds of thousands sought their fortunes there and the issue of statehood was everywhere discussed. Frequently pioneers went by train to a railhead in eastern Dakota, unloaded their wagons and belongings, and continued across the plains. According to one estimate the territory had about 236,000 people in 1882 but more than 400,000 two years later.[1]

When Walsh arrived in Dakota Territory he suffered from asthma, the effects of which, it was believed, could be reduced by living in a dry climate. Walsh's brother Henry was another reason for the selection of Dakota Territory. They had decided to form a partnership, and Henry was already acquainted with Redfield in the east central part of the territory. So there they hung out their shingle, to practice law. Henry, like Tom, had begun teaching school in his teens and turned in spare moments to the reading of law. Upon agreement with Tom, he became the senior member of the partnership. Cheerful and generous in disposition, Henry was popular with everyone. He would spend the rest of his life (thirteen years) in this town on the Dakota prairies.

From their new location, Tom Walsh sent a report to Ellen McClements in Chicago. Redfield, he said, was about three years old with a population of 800. He was interested in its political prospects. Two years before a commission of nine members had selected Bismarck as capital of the territory, but Redfield received three votes and had not surrendered its ambitions. One possibility was that if Dakota were divided along the 46th parallel Redfield could become the capital of South Dakota.

He looked forward to an approaching term of court, which would be the first ever held in Spink County. His law practice would begin in a county that was also beginning.[2]

Spink County was in some respects a primitive place. Almost everyone there had arrived since 1880. The sod house was a common sight, and many early arrivals lived in dugouts on the banks of the James River, five miles from Redfield. Lumber had to be imported. Public buildings did not exist or they were mere shanties. Living was far more precarious than suggested in Walsh's first letter, for rainfall was less than twenty inches in a normal year. Not only droughts, but hot winds, hail storms, and blizzards were among the natural hazards.[3]

One of the beliefs about Thomas J. Walsh was that he lacked the social graces. His experiences in Dakota suggest the exaggeration of such a picture. He was not a back-slapper or one who mixed easily with people, yet he enjoyed company; he liked to talk, to listen to people who talked well, to play card games, to play baseball, and to take the center of the stage before literary or drama groups. By October he was deeply involved in activities of the Democratic party. He and his brother lived in a hotel where political meetings often occurred on the floor just below them.

The year 1884 was so important politically that Walsh's entire stay in Dakota would be affected by it. First he was immediately drawn into political activity on the local level. Second, this was the year of the national campaign in which Grover Cleveland defeated James G. Blaine, giving the Democrats control of the White House for the first time since the Civil War.

Walsh noted that the party in power assumed a "special importance in territorial affairs," and Dakota Democrats were "suddenly lifted from insignificance to a position that the smallness of our numbers makes all the more enviable." What he had in mind was the President's appointive power. If Cleveland wished he could replace the Republican governor and other territorial officials. The new governor in turn would have various appointments at his disposal.[4]

Arguments over the seat of government, or "capital fights," assumed much importance and notoriety in Dakota history. Walsh was intimately associated with the "Spink County War," probably the most notable of the county seat controversies in Dakota history. To citizens of Spink County, the most important issue in the elections of 1884 was the location of the county seat. Business practically came to a "standstill," Walsh said, as he and his fellow citizens—of both parties—campaigned for their town, Redfield.[5]

The election of Cleveland in 1884 further contributed to Walsh's loyalty to the Democratic party and hopes for it. Among the issues that tied him closely to his party was the tariff. In his years as a teacher and law student he had studied this question, debated it publicly, and had come to think of himself as an expert. In Dakota Territory the subject of tariff reduction was not "popular doctrine," but Walsh talked it relentlessly. Walsh admired Congressman Samuel "Sunset" Cox of New York, who argued powerfully against the unfair and oppressive features of the high tariff.[6]

If Walsh found harmony in his party, he also learned of the things that divide a political organization. Democrats disagreed, as did the Republicans, over the two great questions: division of the territory into one or more states, and control of patronage. They also had trouble knowing what to do about woman's suffrage, prohibition, and complaints from the farmers.

At first Walsh was cautious on the statehood question. By the fall of 1886 he joined with the Dakota Democrats who believed in division of the territory, with South Dakota becoming a state, and who were willing to fight the Cleveland administration or its Dakota appointees on this issue. The young lawyer from Redfield was gaining recognition over the territory.

In the campaign of 1888 Walsh was caught up in the agrarian revolt then sweeping Dakota and much of the country. He was interested in farming and sympathetic to the farmers' demands. Also, self interest led him to follow anxiously the news of crops, droughts, and blizzards. Even the least discerning, he wrote, must see in Dakota that "his prosperity and that of the farmer have a common basis." Many people were heavily encumbered and would be completely ruined unless "helped out by a good crop."

In 1885 Walsh was elected treasurer of the Spink County Agricultural Society. His tendency toward political independence and his low-tariff arguments gave him something in common with agrarian leaders attacking the status quo. As a well-educated professional man, he also showed, at times, a condescension toward the "ruralities," even though able to sympathize with them and combine with them politically.

The Democrats and the farmer leaders of Spink County effected an alliance in October 1888. A joint ticket was arranged, with T. J. Walsh as nominee for the Territorial Council. The head of the territorial ticket, also jointly supported, was John W. Harden, running for delegate to Congress. Harden was a Democrat and vice president of the Farmers Alliance who had emerged in the Democratic territorial convention as a compromise choice, seemingly able to satisfy various elements of the party. Resolutions of this Democratic convention strongly supported agricultural interests, demanding, for example, government control of railroads and the telegraph.[7]

That Walsh had little chance was very clear, but he campaigned happily. This was for him a time of testing—of his physical strength, his voice, his oratorical style, and political temperament. In one exchange of letters he and Ellen McClements discussed oratorical style. They agreed that, as she put it, "the calm, logical, polished speaker" was likely to be most successful. Walsh had studied the delivery of Wendell Phillips, Thomas Erskine, and Joseph H. Choate; and he quoted Hamlet approvingly: "In the very torrent, tempest and, as I may say, whirlwind of passion, you must acquire and beget a temperance that may give it smoothness." Before this campaign was over, he probably had fashioned his own style—at once restrained and intensely earnest—for which he later was noted.[8]

The young campaigner could be pleased with many things said about him, but not with the election tally. His "eminent fitness" to sit on the Territorial Council was attested to by such Republican sources as the *Redfield Observer* and the *Ashton Argus*. He was not, however, talking a popular doctrine. He called especially for tariff reform, as did Cleveland in the national campaign and John Harden across the Territory. The *Argus,* after praising Walsh, referred to an "error" of his: He looked at most public questions "through democratic spectacles." Such an "error" left him with little chance to win. He did receive 1,110 votes to 1,870 for his Republican opponent.[9]

Notwithstanding his political and other involvements, Walsh gave most of his time to the study and practice of law. He never seems to have doubted that, for him at least, professional success must come before everything else. The lawyer and author John P. Frank, writing of Abraham Lincoln's law practice, concluded that Lincoln immersed in it, "like a fish in a lake." This was also true of T. J. Walsh. His practice on the Dakota frontier was similar to the "country practice" that Lincoln enjoyed in the new state of Illinois forty years earlier. Frank carried his point further: "Whether the law was the largest single *formative* factor in Lincoln's adult life is a matter of opinion; but that in terms of time and energy and preoccupation it was in bulk the largest single factor of his life there can be no doubt at all." The identical statement can be made about T. J. Walsh for the first twenty-five years of his law practice.[10]

The parallel with Lincoln can be carried another step. Lincoln once warned that nothing was a "more fatal error" for young lawyers than "relying too much on speech making." He believed in careful preparation. T. J. Walsh emphasized this even more heavily and once observed with some pique: "I have no love for criminal law and no ambition to be known as a criminal lawyer, . . . Extensive learning tells after a long time but it's rather useless in the business of building up a practice."[11]

His cases overwhelmingly involved contracts, mortgages, property damage, nonpayment of wages, and the like. Many originated before justices of the peace, who lacked jurisdiction when more than $100 was at issue. Less frequently he had a criminal case, or was called into one. In addition to his Redfield practice, Walsh traveled extensively—to Huron, where the territorial district court was located, to Bismarck, for sessions of the supreme court, and to various county seats. Occasionally, when no judge was available in his district, he had to go chasing after one.

This could be a trying business. Walsh lamented at one point that wealth was "so much dissipated" in Dakota that interests were small and "litigation trifling." He added: "You must try so many cases in order to make anything and then you can't devote to any one the study it might receive. Occasionally though we get something worth fighting for."

Walsh was impressive even when losing. Amazingly, he and the various lawyers with whom he was associated failed every time in six appeals to the territorial supreme court. The explanation seems to be that these were difficult cases and that Walsh was bold enough to step in and take his chances. It is also clear that he was, at times, brash in the language he employed. Thus he asserted in one instance that the law was "too plain to require any construction"; and he went on: "All discretion is taken from the court. The appeal shall be dismissed." But the court thought otherwise, deciding against him. According to one lawyer, this sort of behavior is typical of the "best of newcomers." Walsh's own judgment, some ten years later, was that he had been "inexperienced" and was not always "discerning," either in his selection of the law or evidence.[12]

Meanwhile, Walsh was handling hundreds of cases in the magistrates' courts or the district courts and winning his share. By several indices, he was doing well. He estimated the earnings of Walsh and Walsh in 1887 as something over $3,000. By the middle of 1888 he thought they would earn at least as much that year. An equal division of the profits with Henry would leave him some $1,200 after office expenses. Admittedly this was a "pittance," but he still believed it enough not only for a single man but for a married couple.

The years 1889 and 1890 were, in several respects, the most important of Walsh's life. For some time a young lady off in Chicago had been an "inspiration" to him. Now, in August 1889, he and Ellen McClements were married, the ceremony taking place in Chicago. They honeymooned in Sturgeon Bay at the home of Mrs. Nettie MacEacham, Walsh's friend and former landlady, with whom Ellen McClements had visited enjoyably. Sturgeon Bay was a place of happy associations, and Walsh loved its scenery and the famed fishing grounds. With young William MacEacham, the newlyweds went fishing, and caught string after string of northern perch and pike. Whether the bride enjoyed this as much as the bridegroom is doubtful.

Shortly before this the *Redfield Observer* had announced that T. J. Walsh was having the "old Plunkett property fitted up and remodeled within." Guessing at what was coming, they followed with congratulations on his marriage. Just a month earlier, Henry Walsh had gone to Ohio and there succumbed to the "intoxicating influences of Hymen." With both brothers married, the law partnership would necessarily undergo something of a change.[13]

This was a period of continued disappointments in politics, even though Walsh seemed to take them well. Republicans came into control of the government, both in the territory and the national capital, after the election of 1888. Furthermore, the good citizens of Redfield, who had won their county seat fight in 1886, failed in 1889 to make their community the capital of the new state of South Dakota.

Along with Dakotans generally, Walsh took satisfaction in approaching statehood. He thought for a time that he might become one of the fathers of the state constitution. Congress passed the necessary enabling act in February 1889, and a constitutional convention was scheduled for Sioux Falls on July 4, 1889. The enabling act had provided for minority representation, so that Democrats could be elected. Presumably the Republicans would choose only two of the three delegates from Spink County. In May, while Walsh was away on a trip, he was nominated by the Democrats. Elated at this honor, he

Thomas J. Walsh. (Photographer: Clinedinst, Washington, D.C. Donor: Field Enterprises, Chicago. Montana Historical Society, Helena, MHS 945-481)

Elinor ("Ellen") McClements Walsh. (Montana Historical Society, Helena, MHS 945-474)

explained it as due partly to his critical analysis of the Dakota constitution of 1885—an analysis which had appeared in the newspapers and gained him "some notoriety."[14]

The aspiring constitutional lawyer had his problem resolved when voters of Spink County elected a prohibitionist, rather than a Democrat, as the minority delegate. He received only 207 votes out of a total of about 1,200.

This defeat is noteworthy in the light of Walsh's subsequent career. The voters of Spink County turned down a man later considered one of the ablest constitutional lawyers in the Senate. Prohibitionists rejected a man later regarded as one of the staunchest friends of nationwide prohibition. Walsh's attitude on prohibition in the Dakota years is not entirely clear, but he seems to have resisted the attempt to make it a political and constitutional issue.[15]

The Dakota phase of Walsh's career was drawing to a close, though he remained in the new state until December of 1890 and continued briefly as a "wheelhorse" of the Democratic party. Many times he had considered leaving Redfield. The final decision was closely related to the difficulties that he and others were experiencing under conditions of drought and depression, affecting his law practice; and, of course, political and legal defeats inclined him toward testing the possibilities elsewhere. He recalled in 1913 that he left South Dakota after a series of bad crop years, when the place was almost destitute.[16]

In a number of letters written between 1889 and 1890 Walsh pondered the question as to where he should move—if he moved. Chicago, Minneapolis, Denver, and other places received consideration. His trouble with asthma may have prevented the selection of Chicago or some metropolitan center, where his wife really preferred to be. There was also the matter of whether to continue as an independent attorney or to join a firm. He did not want to live again where Democrats were a hopeless minority, as they had been in Dakota. He stated, for example, that the one-party system of southern states, favoring the Democrats, was almost duplicated in Dakota where "none but a Republican need apply." Public service was thus closed to many qualified men, as a result of the "tyranny of party."[17]

Although it seemed so remote as to be "out of the world," Helena, Montana, loomed as an attractive possibility. It was the capital of Montana and a thriving town of some 14,000. Walsh could read in the newspapers that the Democrats there had at least an even chance and that Joseph K. Toole, a Democrat, was elected the first governor of the new state. More important, there were big law suits with huge sums involved. In such a place he could "manage larger interests and earn larger fees," as he had long thought himself capable of doing.

In September 1890, he visited Helena and carefully appraised the situation. The business houses impressed him as "costly" or "grand" and the banks suggested "ponderous wealth." A new stone courthouse was "magnificent." He learned that the court was always in session in contrast to Dakota courts, and that it had so much business it couldn't keep up. Also, the state supreme court and the U.S. courts were located in Helena and the state library had a collection of books and reports that were excellent. Walsh talked with various lawyers and "sized up" the bar. He even got up his nerve and paid his respects to Governor Toole. Finally, with a friend, a contractor who had formerly lived in Redfield, he looked into the matter of houses.

In the next several months, Walsh and his wife made their final plans. They now had an infant daughter, Genevieve, to think of and household furnishings to sell or pack. They also had a mortgage on their house that gave them some concern and various business matters to attend to. On the day before Christmas 1890, with some $350 in cash reserve they said their goodbyes to Redfield and boarded the train west.[18]

4

A Helena Lawyer and Democrat

Roughness and refinement jostle each other," Walsh wrote of Helena, Montana, the temporary capital, in 1890. Montana had been admitted to statehood in 1889 as one of the "omnibus states." The Indian wars were over, mining for gold was in a state of decline, and the cowboy was making his last stand. But the "war of the copper kings" was just beginning. In the eastern half of the state an era of dry-land homesteading would soon begin. This was a challenging land with natural resources to be developed and services to be provided for a growing population.

Third largest of the states geographically, Montana had a population in 1890 of only 132,000. The Walshes had a view of its variety en route from South Dakota, as they traveled on a Northern Pacific car through the eastern plains and occasional badlands through the valley of the Yellowstone River, into the Rockies to Bozeman, and finally to Helena in the west central part of the state. In the Gallatin Range near Bozeman they could see forests and mountains of spectacular beauty.

Most Montanans lived in the valleys, or on the lower slopes of the mountains. South of Helena lay the towns of Butte and Anaconda; to the west across the continental divide was Missoula; to the north was Great Falls on the Missouri River. The western counties of the state had scenery and also wealth, in the form of production from the mines, from irrigated valleys, and from timbered slopes. For the time being, at least, the plains of the north and east would remain a province of cattlemen and Indians.[1]

Helena, Montana, was an exciting place in 1890. Originally a mining camp, known in the 1860s as "Last Chance Gulch," it grew rich on gold strikes and diggings that produced an estimated $80,000,000 of the precious metal by 1900. A boom occurred in the 1880s, and in various ways Helena seemed an appropriate place to be designated as the permanent capital of the "Treasure State." Other towns in the state had not been convinced, however, and that question remained to be fought over.[2]

As Walsh saw Helena for the first time: "The main street is a little wider and a little crookeder than the principal street of Deadwood. . . . The great peaks stand like sentries about the town—that is about half way around." Mountains actually encircle Helena, but in the north and east they are miles away, across a valley.

Helena had some surprising features of achievement. It claimed the highest per capita wealth of any city in the United States and had a number of wealthy residents with fine homes and carriage houses. Not only did it have a city transportation system, it had two. Steam motorcars "flitted through the streets," said one observer, "easily climbing the steep grades"; electric street cars were also available. West of town was the Broadwater Hotel with a "natatorium," or "plunge," 150 feet by 350 feet—built at a cost of half a million dollars. In its commercial establishments, public buildings, and extensive residential areas Helena had much to boast about. A new high school building, a large one of handsome gray stone, was completed in the fall of 1890. Builders used the same stone for a variety of structures and for the retaining walls that were often necessary because of steep inclines. They also used porphyry stone, of a pinkish hue, and fashioned attractive combinations of brick and stone.[3]

By the 1890s Helena was still the center of a mining district, although its own mines were declining. It was also a commercial center with transcontinental rail connections and the Montana Central Railroad that ran south to Butte and north to Great Falls. According to the census of 1890, Helena's population was 13,834. Males outnumbered females by more than four to one. Foreign born numbered more than one-fourth of the total population, including about 500 Chinese, or "Celestials," as they were often called. In the matter of a "rough element," using a phrase from the *Helena News,* the city had its share and places for them to consort. Visitors noticed the signs "Licensed Gambling House" and "Beer only five cents a glass." In some areas almost every door led to a saloon, concert hall, or dive. The Coliseum was a house of prostitution in the Wood Street District, while Harmonia Hall which opened in 1890 as a "variety theatre" soon had curtained booths with girls serving drinks. It is noteworthy that the first case won by Thomas J. Walsh in the Montana Supreme Court (1892) was that of a German-American prostitute whose paramour had taken her earnings.[4]

In spite of a surface prosperity, Helena was entering a time of economic troubles. The noted journalist Christopher P. Connolly, a friend of Walsh's, wrote of hard days following the panic of 1892–93. As early as November 1890, U.S. Representative Thomas Carter (later senator) gave a hint of Helena's instability: "New faces show up everywhere and many of the old familiar countenances are not to be seen." Years after his own arrival in Helena, Walsh remarked that the place had already seen its best days by the time he got there.[5]

The Walshes always lived on the west side of Helena, that is, west of the main street or "gulch," and this meant in the early days of their residence that they had walking to do. Walsh's law office was several blocks from home, on Main Street or nearby, while the courthouse was still farther away in an easterly direction and thus on the far side of the gulch. The distances were not great, but the hills were steep.[6]

Walsh's beginnings as a Montana lawyer have been described by Christopher Connolly, also a lawyer in Helena before he turned to journalism. He remembered Walsh stowing "himself in a cubicle of an office, putting in his spare time annotating the Montana statutes and absorbing the decisions of the State Supreme Court." At least for a year, he had few cases. Other lawyers in Helena looked upon the newcomer "as a poacher upon their own meager preserves."

But Connolly said "there was something in the character of this newcomer which everyone noticed. There was a studious aspect, as of one who had serious business and was attending to it to the exclusion of everything else."[7]

Even more revealing is a ledger that Walsh began to keep meticulously as soon as he and his family were settled in their small frame house at the foot of the mountain. On December 29, 1890, he wrote: "To cash on hand 359.30." During the next four and a half years he and his wife maintained this ledger, recording almost all items of expense, both personal and professional, and their income as well. The struggle of the first months is apparent.

Expenses were not light. House rent was $25 a month and office rent $20. Coal for heating the house was $7.15, presumably for a ton. Other necessities included the compiled statutes of Montana, an inkstand, pens, stationery, bookcases, and stamps. Finally, after two months in Helena, Walsh recorded his first income, an entry of $5. The Walshes needed reading matter and entertainment. Periodically they attended shows of one kind or another, including *Othello* in the winter of 1893. Also Mrs. Walsh had brought her piano from Redfield.

The smallness of Walsh's first fee may be misleading; there is evidence that it represented a turn in his fortunes. About this time, according to Christopher Connolly, Walsh had a case in a justice of the peace court, opposing C. B. Nolan, the county attorney. When the proceedings were over, Nolan spread the news that this T. J. Walsh was quite a lawyer. Coming from Nolan—"one of Helena's leading citizens," gifted with a rich Irish brogue—such praise was valuable indeed. Walsh and Nolan would soon know each other well, as they often battled in the courtroom and then with increasing frequency worked together. Finally in 1907 they formed a partnership.[8]

One item of expense in August 1891 was a trip "home"—back to Two Rivers, where Felix Walsh had fallen into a final illness. Tom Walsh went to his father's bedside but soon felt compelled to return to his family and his business in Helena. Then came word of Felix Walsh's death. Unable to make the trip again, Tom wrote to his youngest brother, John, eulogizing their father: "May God grant him eternal rest. . . . May we too die as he did—enjoying the undivided love of our families and the esteem of all who know us."[9]

During his trip east Walsh had suffered severely from asthma. The Helena climate was one reason for being thankful about his return, but there were other reasons too. His gross receipts month by month were uneven, but in five separate months he garnered more than $170; and in two months he did exceedingly well. January showed $391 and December brought an unheard of figure of $923.

The Walshes burst out of their bonds of "poverty." T. J. paid $50 down on a typewriter for the office and made payments periodically thereafter. He also arranged for janitorial services in his building. For the first time, starting in August 1892, they employed a maid (Maggie) and paid her $25 a month. Walsh sent money to his sister, Eliza, who was ill; to Mary McClements and his sister Mary (from whom he had probably borrowed money with which to move to Montana); and to his mother. He spent, almost with abandon, it must have seemed, for show tickets, books, a visit to the circus, and for clothing and other items.

But Walsh was not satisfied with the way his practice was going. He suffered, as most people did, from the economic distress of 1892–93. Tom Carter, soon to be one of the state's senators, observed in December 1892 that business was dull in Helena and that, in fact, a "wave of distress seems to run along the whole mountain chain." At the end of 1893 Walsh was dispirited. On a business trip in Butte, he found "as much complaint . . . about hard times as there is in Helena." Thinking back over his business of the year, he noted his embarrassment at having to draw so much money out of the bank without putting any in. Also, he was sorry to admit that he had attained less recognition in his home town than he had outside, for example, in Boulder, Montana (Jefferson County).[10]

Everyone who knew the Walshes remembered that Ellen Walsh worked in the law office with her husband. She did typing, kept the books at times, and was an indispensable assistant when he tried cases out of town, leaving behind matters requiring attention. During an extended absence in Butte, Walsh once gave Ellen the following instructions: "You will have to do the best you can to satisfy the parties who call. Don't hesitate to ask them their business and don't feel bad if they do not disclose it. That is a privilege they have. If they do, probably you will be able to answer their inquiries frequently. If not perhaps there may be time enough to report to me so I can write you."

Walsh worked hard in the office himself and had such high standards of performance that he was a difficult man to please. On one occasion he apologized to his wife for words that had obviously been upsetting to her. In years to come he was particularly demanding of his law clerks. Wellington Rankin remembered, however, that he was stimulated to his best efforts by Walsh's presence and example.[11]

In Walsh's view, the law was a grand profession worthy of all the attention he lavished upon it, and more. He identified it in one speech with the will of God, with helping to establish justice among men in so far as human abilities permitted. It was a proud and noble profession. On law and the obedience to law depended the fate of civilization, but unjust laws would fail to command obedience, and unjust or corrupt officials would undermine the confidence of those upon whom law finally depended—the people. Thus, popular participation in the lawmaking process was of utmost importance, and the role of interpreting the law was something with which citizens must be concerned. He was an ardent believer, for this reason, in the jury system. While juries erred, so also did judges. Service on a jury, moreover, was excellent for the training it afforded in the principles of justice and self-government.[12]

The cruelties and injustices of the capitalist system were matters of concern to Walsh. Like Pope Leo XIII in his *Rerum Novarum* (1891), Walsh rejected a laissez-faire theory of government, and he could not tolerate a presidential administration such as Benjamin Harrison's which allied itself with large economic interests. He believed in labor unions, collective bargaining, and the acceptance of responsibility by employers for safe conditions of employment. Having the latter view, he was more than willing to handle personal injury suits for working men or their survivors in the event of a fatal accident, and he would do so on a "contingent fee" basis, that is, with his payment contingent upon winning the case. As an independent lawyer with a sense of justice and a willingness to fight—as well as the ability to fight resourcefully—he commanded respect.[13]

To those who knew him well, T. J. Walsh seemed endowed with phenomenal legal abilities. Christopher Connolly was one admirer. Walsh, he said, had a marvelous energy and was characterized by "unremitting mental activity." After a long day in the courtroom, he was able to "return immediately to his office and take up other and unrelated matters"; routinely he did this. He was "quiet, logical, mentally penetrating, a master of legal technic [sic]." About his speeches there was a "tang of preparation and study." Connolly believed that "he had no intuitions, only cold, hard logic." Another observer, speaking of Walsh in the courtroom, said that "he was very austere, clear, cold, precise, inspiring confidence." He added: "I guess I never saw a more earnest man." In a different vein, Justice William H. De Witt of the Montana Supreme Court noted in a decision of 1896 (which went against Walsh) that he had argued the case "with his accustomed zeal." Almost paradoxically, his delivery could strike the onlookers as cold, logical, methodical—and zealous. There was a fire and passion in him, ordinarily held in check.[14]

A second judge once wrote to Walsh paying him the highest of compliments: He had an ability that was "immeasurable," superior to that of anyone who had ever practiced in his court. The year was 1893, when Walsh was only beginning his Montana practice. Still another judge, better known in the state's history, said many years after the senator's death that in the history of Montana lawyers Walsh was "up on a pinnacle, and he was all alone." The judge and Walsh's law partner, Nolan, had agreed on this point.[15]

However much these and similar compliments may be credited, Walsh was susceptible, like other professional men, to the worries and temptations of his craft. He was almost consumed, for one thing, by an ambition to succeed.

He doubtless remembered, in this connection, his early days in Helena. He had the idea then that his wife should sing in the choir to attract attention to him and to help in his business. In a few years he no longer believed this necessary, but he still wanted her to sing for her own enjoyment (which she apparently refused to do); and he hoped that generally she would stand in with those who counted. For his part, Walsh was keenly aware of judges, or "the court," and of the human feelings that influenced the decisions of judges and juries. Thus in 1895 he remarked that he must hear a certain Miss Hunt sing. She was Judge Hunt's sister and was visiting the judge at the time! On another occasion he noted that he was staying in the hotel where the "common herd" was staying; this could contribute to getting some favorable verdicts.[16]

If Walsh's ambition lagged, his wife's helped to spur him on, as indicated by some reflections in 1896: "Hope springs eternal with me yet, but perhaps it has been the blustery, blue weather and the depression which usually overtakes me on the train away from home that set me to thinking how many disappointments I suffer . . . and how hard I work . . . and how much truth there may be in the remark you made a short time ago that if a man doesn't make his mark or his stake . . . before he is forty, it's all day with him." Walsh was thirty-seven. Obviously neither he nor his wife was satisfied. Their blue moods were produced to an extent by bouts of ill health. Walsh at this point was taking a patent medicine. Mrs. Walsh also had periods of illness, mostly of suffering from headaches which began, it seems, with a severe cold followed by an attack of "la grippe" in the first year of her marriage. She continued to have headaches periodically for the rest of her life.[17]

Offsetting Walsh's ambition was the fact that he liked and respected many people. He was a good neighbor—literally speaking—who tended his lawn and flowers, watered his neighbors' lawns, enjoyed animals and pets, and appreciated the amenities of social living. His wife once remarked that women admired him. She said again that while he was not convivial, as Nolan or a lawyer friend named Richard Purcell were, people liked him just the same out of appreciation and respect. "Everyone" liked him—unless they were jealous of him. For most of his life Walsh continued to be troubled by his lack of a familiar manner and his inability to make friends quickly. Yet he had compensations as indicated in a letter to his wife when she was away in Chicago (1895): "It is a matter of gratification to me Ellen to recognize how many people here [Helena] . . . have confidence in me."[18]

Walsh was a worrier. He carried his cases home—or to his hotel room—and did much thinking about them. In 1895 he spoke of his "nervousness" and "anxiety" over a case and added that he thought "nervousness under fire" was growing on him. The "wheels got to turning" one night, and he got out of bed and wrote down some ideas. He was apprehensive about a case when it looked too easy and he couldn't figure out what line of argument the opposition would take. Once he believed that he just couldn't lose; *but,* was there something he hadn't thought of?

Typically, however, Walsh showed confidence or elation over his cases. He was a tough competitor and expected to win, whether the odds were against him or not. Thus, in one case, he was "ready for the pay." Again, he had looked up the statutes and found enough to "worry the life" out of an opposing attorney. Walsh was always searching for an idea, an angle, a "molehill," and frequently he found one, winning the case. Even in defeat, he was capable of finding satisfaction in the technically proficient argument he had made. According to a prominent lawyer, Walsh once said: "It's not whether you win that counts; it's how you argue the case."

As he traveled about the United States, back to his Wisconsin haunts, to Washington, D.C., to San Francisco, and elsewhere, he met his professional brethren, examined their libraries, considered their practice, and took satisfaction in his own. He was pleased at his freedom from corporate ties, his independence, and his record of support for the "underdog."[19]

The variety of Walsh's practice and some of the qualities that brought him success may be illustrated by cases from the 1890s. His collected briefs (which were printed), along with the *Montana Reports* and other sources, make possible a close examination and a more detailed discussion than will be attempted in this chapter. His briefs often run extremely long, showing that he tended to work hard on just this aspect of his profession. His language is forceful and lucid and sometimes highly quotable. His powers of systematic reasoning are apparent. As early as 1891 Walsh tried his first case before the Montana Supreme Court, losing that particular fight, but he proceeded to win his next two. Before the decade ended he had tried literally dozens of cases before the state's high court, not to mention those elsewhere, including the federal courts.

In 1893 Walsh and Nolan handled a mineral dispute in Boulder, Montana. They won the case, and on appeal to the State Supreme Court the decision of the lower court was affirmed. Comparatively speaking, this was a small affair, but Walsh would proceed to handle some of the biggest mining suits in the state, including a number in which the Anaconda Copper Company and F. Augustus Heinze were involved.[20]

In a personal injury suit of the same period he and Nolan again worked together. They represented one Charles Kelley, who had been severely injured in an accident in the Fourth of July Mine in 1891. They won the case for Kelley in the lower court and won again on appeal, but the company failed to pay. Walsh and Nolan then brought suit against shareholders to prove their individual liability. By the time this decision was rendered (1898) Walsh was attaining a reputation as a "personal injury lawyer."[21]

Similar in some respects to the Fourth of July case were the so-called explosion cases, which originated in Butte in an "appalling tragedy," considered the worst in the city's history. On the night of January 15, 1895, a fire broke out in the warehouse district. The fire department responded to the call, and crowds of people gathered. At eight minutes after 10:00 "a terrific explosion occurred." The burning warehouse had been "blown to atoms," along with hapless victims. The horror was heightened by the fact that the temperature stood at twenty degrees below zero, and windows in the city were shattered by the blasts. Some sixty were dead or dying with hundreds injured and many mutilated. The firemen had been killed almost to a man.[22]

Immediately there were charges of criminal negligence. It was known that powder had been stored in the warehouse by the Kenyon-Connell Company, but its spokesmen claimed only three boxes had been there—150 pounds. Under state law even this was excessive. In fact, as the evidence revealed, large quantities of Hercules powder had been kept in the warehouse for the sake of convenience, rather than in a magazine three miles outside of town where it should have been. Walsh was brought into the case. He and a Butte attorney attempted to secure damages for the victims or their heirs, but discovered that this would be difficult because the company had lost most of its assets in the holocaust. The remaining hope was to convict the directors, or trustees, of an individual liability. When the Supreme Court of Montana accepted this interpretation (1899), the defendants were compelled to arrive at settlements with victims of the Butte tragedy. One of these defendants was William A. Clark, the Butte capitalist.[23]

Early in 1894 the Montanan took his first trip to Washington, D.C. He handled a land case for a client and found it advisable to appear before the commissioner of the General Land Office to present an argument. He also found opportunities to go sightseeing and to indulge his personal, political, and professional interests. As described in letters to his wife, the trip is a revealing episode.[24]

There was much to see and do, and Walsh had enjoyable visits to the Corcoran Art Gallery, the gallery of the Capitol (watching the House in session), the Supreme Court, and the White House. Walsh fell victim to "Potomac fever." He must have seen, dimly, the possibilities that lay ahead. He also knew that the attainment of political influence demanded a willingness to make sacrifices. Already he was giving much of his time to community service and to the Democratic party of Montana.

Walsh had hardly arrived in Helena before he began attending Democratic meetings of his ward, or of Lewis and Clark County, and making himself known in party circles. Toward the end of 1891 or the early part of 1892, Walsh was an organizer of a political group calling itself the Hendricks Club (after Thomas A. Hendricks, Democrat of Indiana who had served as vice president in Cleveland's first administration). Speeches by Walsh indicate that he may have been the real leader of this group as it became active in 1891–92.

Most powerful among the local Democrats were Samuel T. Hauser and Charles Broadwater, pioneer capitalists in the economic development of

Montana, usually placed in the "Big Four" of the state's Democrats, together with the copper kings of Butte. Another celebrity was Martin Maginnis, who had served for many years as Territorial Delegate to Congress and in 1892 replaced Broadwater on the Democratic National Committee. The incumbent governor of Montana, Joseph K. Toole, was also a resident of Helena and obviously a political leader of note.[25]

At an early meeting of the Hendricks Club, Walsh congratulated his fellow members on the progress they had made and then proceeded to discuss the means by which they could become a "potent factor in political work." They had the machinery, he said, and were supported by a favorable public sentiment. "We are to be the active workers for party success," Walsh said. "Its triumphs and its defeats will be ours."

The *Helena City Directory* for 1892 reveals that R. B. Smith, a lawyer and future Populist governor of Montana, was president of the Hendricks Club. A. J. Davidson, one of the city's merchants, was vice president, while Christopher Connolly, lawyer and future muckraker, was listed as secretary. Considering that Walsh, too, was a member, this club had a distinguished leadership.[26]

In addition to his organizational work, Walsh took to the stump in the campaign. It would appear that the party leaders made use of his services primarily in laboring centers where a Democrat of his views might prevent defections to the newly organized Populist party. Thus he spoke in Marysville, a mining town north of Helena; in East Helena, a smelter town; and in Granite, another mining center. His remarks on these occasions were tailored to a labor audience. He had much to say about the level of wages in relation to tariff benefits (profits) received by employers. The Homestead Strike at the Carnegie works near Pittsburgh reached a bloody conclusion in late summer, and this tragedy demanded some attention. The rise of the Populists and their possible success in capturing the vote of laborers, farmers, and others presented a difficult problem that could not be evaded. The prominence of big capitalists in the state's Democratic party was a sore point for Walsh and others democratically inclined.[27]

What emerges from these campaign addresses is the picture of a Jeffersonian Democrat—one nurtured on the history of Democratic party battles and a liberal ideology and convinced of the rightness of his cause. The Irish-Catholic background can be detected in some of Walsh's emphases and perhaps in his political skill. Having made his home in Montana, he could not neglect the silver question, the tariff on wool, or other issues of local importance. At least for a newcomer, it was discreet not to say too much about the economic giants of Montana (though in fairness to Walsh the worst of this situation had not yet developed).

Prominent in Walsh's speeches was the idea of limited government (although he would change notably by 1916). He asked an audience: "But what particular interest have we in the question of the tariff? We have in common with all lovers of our country and its institutions a desire to see the powers of the government restricted to their legitimate channels and constitutional limits." He deplored "the amassing of gigantic law-made fortunes [as by high tariff duties]." He added to this audience, consisting predominantly of Democrats: "But there is the tariff on wool I think I hear some one say. For shame! Shall we throw away our birth-right for a mess of pottage." (Walsh would change his mind in later years and advocate some protection for Montana sheepmen.)[28]

The "Southern question" of the late nineteenth century is one on which Walsh's attitudes are not entirely clear, although he and other western Democrats had little of which to boast. In one speech he referred to slavery as having been the "nation's disgrace," and indicated that he believed that blacks should be permitted to vote. On the other hand, he would not countenance the idea of Republican interference in southern affairs, as through a "force bill," to guarantee black suffrage. He believed, in fact, that the Republicans had exploited the black vote and would do so again, and by this means they might intrench themselves in power. Walsh deplored the Republican record in the "Carpetbag" Reconstruction era.[29]

Closer to home he argued that the Democratic party was the only hope for free silver; that while a minority of men "eminent in the party" were now opposed to silver the Democrats would move toward a united front on this issue, much as they had in recent years on the tariff. Indications are that Walsh was a sincere believer in free silver coinage and apparently in the ability of the Democrats to achieve that goal—even if President Cleveland should withhold his support. Walsh said, "We want silver coinage not only for the United States but for the entire commercial world," and the result would be the entry of Montana "upon a period of prosperity of which its present greatness is only a suggestion."[30]

Grover Cleveland won the election of 1892 with the tariff as his main issue. The results otherwise were to prove bitterly disappointing to men like Walsh. It was not surprising that many Democrats in the state leaned increasingly toward the Populist cause. If the two parties had combined in 1892, they could have carried the state elections, and a policy of "fusion" seemed especially promising. Walsh became one of the architects of this strategy. By the end of 1895 he wrote to his wife that the ties that bound him to the Democrats were "frail" indeed. Nevertheless, he did not bolt the party.

The foregoing account has suggested the nucleus of Walsh's political ideas. He would change in years to come, as domestic and foreign problems virtually demanded an enlargement of the functions and services of government. A basic liberalism remained: a concern for fair play in the economy, to be attained primarily in his view by equitable taxation, of which the tariff was one form; a concern for people and their problems (especially if they were white people); and a willingness to criticize the misuses of power, whether governmental or private. He was notable for his acceptance of labor unions, for his sympathy with agriculture, and for his unhappiness with a federal judiciary that verged on tyranny. Walsh was a middle-class politician who had limitations. His viewpoint in the 1890s was heavily sectional, and he exhibited jaundiced ideas concerning the Republicans.

A beginner in Montana politics, Walsh enhanced his reputation politically as a man of energy and forensic skill. During the next decade his political reputation continued to grow, while Montana as a state experienced the most tumultuous period in its history—that of the so-called war of the copper kings.

5

Politics, Law, and the Copper Kings

I n leaving Dakota for the mining camps of Montana, Walsh moved to an uneasy situation, for he was a moralist concerning public affairs and a foe of monopolies. He knew the notoriety Dakota had gained for the economic and political influence of its railroads. To the influence of railroad men Montana added the power of mining kings—notably Marcus Daly, William A. Clark, and F. Augustus Heinze. Ultimately from this rivalry the Amalgamated Copper Company (with a Standard Oil infusion) emerged as the consolidating group. As the mining leaders struggled for commercial and political supremacy, no citizen of the state was unaffected. The economic issue was ownership and control of rich veins of ore, along with transportation facilities, timber supplies, coal, water power, and other natural resources. No less important was the fight to control the newspapers and the political institutions of the state. At issue too was the integrity of the people, now subjected to pressures and temptations such as they had never known. Christopher Connolly believed that thousands had been ruined by the long struggle. Ellen Walsh in 1898 referred to the "quagmire" of Montana politics.[1]

The principals in this affair were William A. Clark and Marcus Daly. Clark, a Pennsylvanian by birth (1839), had a good education, including law study at Iowa Wesleyan College. He demonstrated his shrewdness by going to the Columbia School of Mines for a short course. Clark's burning ambition was to take a seat in the U.S. Senate, and he seemingly had a good start in that direction by serving as president of the Montana constitutional conventions in 1884 and 1889.[2]

Marcus Daly resembled Clark in the magnitude of his business operations and a determination to extend his influence. Daly was born in Ireland of poor parents in 1842 and came to the United States at the age of fifteen. After a period in New York, he went to California as a miner. He demonstrated his talents and attracted the attention of some wealthy California businessmen, who sent him to Montana. He became convinced that the Butte mines were valuable mostly for copper deposits and was able to acquire at a low figure extremely valuable properties. Daly did not seek office personally. A genial Irish-American in his private relations, he surrounded himself in 1882 with Irish associates in the Anaconda Copper Mining Company and for occasional recreation turned to horses and horse racing. Personal traits help to explain the implacable hostility that developed between him and Clark.[3]

Whatever the reasons, the feud between the two came into the open in 1888. Clark failed in his ambition to be the delegate to Congress and was defeated by large majorities in the centers of Daly strength. In 1892 and 1894 Daly failed in his bid to make Anaconda the state capital while Clark, by successfully supporting Helena, won many friends there. Daly and his forces succeeded thereafter in denying Clark the Senate seat that he wanted so badly. Climactic struggles occurred from 1898 to 1900.

A third force in the "copper war" was F. Augustus Heinze, a younger man born in 1869. He entered Montana in 1889 after completing courses at the Columbia School of Mines, and quickly found opportunities that his predecessors had missed. In particular he took advantage of the apex law. According to this law, the owner of land on which a vein of ore apexed (or came to the surface) could follow the vein even under someone else's property. Huge, illicit profits were possible. Heinze's fights were primarily with the Daly interests (or Anaconda Copper, reorganized in 1899 as the Amalgamated Copper Company). Heinze was a popular, handsome fellow who entered politics by attacking the Amalgamated as the "big interests." He endorsed judges and others who were friendly and threatened to become a dominant force.[4]

Walsh was involved at least as a minor actor in the economic and political battles of the late nineteenth century. He and his wife were caught up in an event of much local importance—the state capital fight which finally came to a climax in 1894. As provided by the constitutional convention of 1889, the voters of Montana had to choose a permanent capital, with the winning city required to receive a majority of the votes. In 1892, Helena and Anaconda ran ahead of all contenders, and a runoff election became necessary in November 1894. Each city had to canvass the entire state. Speakers must be sent out, funds collected, and all posssible influence brought to bear. Walsh contributed financially in 1892 and in 1894; in the later year he made a number of speeches for the cause.[5]

The logic of the situation indicated that Helena should be the capital. Her location, relative to the population of the state at that time, was a central one, and there could be no serious complaints over her record as the temporary capital. But Marcus Daly resolved that Anaconda, his home town and that of the Anaconda Copper Mining Company, should win the prize, while William A. Clark threw his support to Helena.

"To sell or not to sell" was becoming a question in Montana campaigns. In the capital fight and the legislative stalemate of 1893 precedents were established for the spending of huge sums of money, mostly "legitimate," it was said, rather than the buying of votes outright. Both sides spent heavily in 1894, Daly laying out at least $1,000,000 and the Helena interests about one fourth of that (huge sums for the time).[6]

Walsh and his wife became deeply involved in the fight for Helena, as did loyal citizens en masse. Ellen Walsh was an active member of the Helena women's club, which sent out campaign literature and endeavored to establish lines of communication throughout the state. By October Walsh entered the thick of the fight, traveling and speaking in the western and southwestern part of the state. Generally his assignments were to the backwater places, for Helena had its big names to send to the cities: Tom Carter, chairman of the Republican National Committee; ex-senator and vigilante hero Col. Wilbur F. Sanders (Republican); ex-congressman and Civil War hero Major Martin Maginnis (Democrat); and others of prominence.[7]

Toward the end of the campaign Walsh had a personal triumph at Thompson Falls. He and O. W. McConnell represented Helena against two debaters espousing the cause of Anaconda. As the *Helena Independent* reported the affair, "Mr. Walsh concluded the argument by a masterful, forcible and eloquent address that swept the flimsy pretext of argument advanced in behalf of Anaconda like snow before the rays of the sun. Many votes were made for Helena as a result of the meeting."

To make an argument against Anaconda—a company town controlled by a New York corporation down in the southwestern part of the state—was not difficult. But Walsh did it with reference to the problems of democracy in an industrial age. Could it be possible, he asked, that the laborers of Montana, with a knowledge of corporate aggression and the memory of the Homestead and Pullman affairs fresh in their minds, would nevertheless vote to place the capital of Montana precisely where the great mining corporation wished it to be? Would they vote to move it away from Helena "where speech like thought is free" to Anaconda, built and owned by a corporation?[8]

The arguments of Helena prevailed, though not by a wide margin. "It is a close fit," the *Anaconda Standard* admitted, and went on to describe the victory celebrations in Helena on the night of November 7. Later came the planning for a capitol building and finally the completion of the structure, with a copper-plated dome, in 1899.[9]

In addition to his contribution in the capital fight, Walsh emerged as a Democrat of growing importance. In the party primaries of mid-September 1894, he was elected as a delegate to the Lewis and Clark County Convention, along with such Helena notables as Joseph K. Toole, Martin Maginnis, C. B. Nolan, and Christopher Connolly. When the convention met ten days later in the Helena auditorium, Walsh served as permanent chairman.[10]

In national politics the year 1894 was disastrous for Democrats, and the party in Montana fared little better. A severe economic depression and President Cleveland's repeal of the Sherman Silver Purchase Act, after a bitter struggle in Congress, left the Democrats badly divided. Defections to the Republicans or the Populists were numerous.

That Walsh would support the forces of silver in 1896, and the candidacy of William Jennings Bryan, could be taken as a foregone conclusion. Even the "Silver Republicans," including Senator Lee Mantle and Congressman Charles Hartman, gave their blessing to Bryan rather than to William McKinley and the Republicans' gold platform.[11]

Walsh was a member of the state Democratic convention which met in Missoula in September and arranged for fusion with the Populists, and with silver Republicans as well. He served in fact on the "fusion committee." In the voting that soon followed, the fusionists swept the state. Bryan received some 44,000 votes to only 10,000 for McKinley. One scholar, Thomas Clinch, has observed that the silver forces hardly bothered to campaign, knowing they would receive huge majorities. The effort was, of course, wasted so far as the national election was concerned. William McKinley's election was a painful awakening for the crusading silverites of the Treasure State.[12]

For many in Montana the election of 1896 did not come to an end when the votes were counted. The rise of the Populists and the Silver Republicans led to a number of complex election disputes, with arguments before district judges and eventual appeals to the state supreme court. This situation gave opportunities to Walsh. Since the days in Dakota Territory he had taken a special interest in disputed elections and factional disputes in political parties and had studied the subject closely. Christopher Connolly wrote of this aspect of his friend's career: "Walsh's first political prominence came through or because of his legal knowledge. . . . He thought out in advance the legal problems likely to arise in convention conflicts, studied the law, and argued it with confidence before nonplused committees. In this way he became the legal adviser of his party."[13]

In the years just before the turn of the century, Walsh was becoming a uniquely successful lawyer, as indicated in part by a growing affluence. He was earning, he said, "beyond . . . my dreams." More frequent trips to the Broadwater natatorium, extended vacation trips, and the purchase of a family carriage were indicative of a new social status. During a long visit to Wisconsin in the summer of 1898, Walsh referred pointedly to the economic independence he had attained or was in the process of attaining. He was notably proud of his law practice which he said was a genuine practice, not a hybrid of law, real estate sales, collection services, and business.[14]

But Walsh was not satisfied. With economic independence he saw the opportunity, finally, for a political career. He believed that he could enter politics and maintain his personal independence and integrity—even in the state of Montana. As usual, however, he sought the advice of his wife in so serious a matter.

The election of 1898 was imminent. That election would determine the makeup of the Montana legislature. Walsh asked his wife to "consider carefully whether in view of the impending struggle it would or would not be wise for me to make the race for the legislature." Ellen's reply at first was acquiescent: "I don't mind your running for the legislature under the circumstances if you are sure to be elected." A week later she had changed her mind. What influenced her considerably was a recent conversation with Richard Purcell, an ambitious Helena friend, in which he told her of certain political plans. She now accused her husband of asking her advice on the matter after he had already made up his mind. She suspected Purcell and Nolan of playing their own game: If they thought there was the "very r-e-m-o-t-e-s-t possibility of your coming in as a 'dark horse' they would use every effort in their power to keep you out."

Ellen Walsh proceeded to lecture her husband on the dangers and pitfalls of Montana politics. Her observations were astute: "Tom, Purcell talks the usual nonsense of their getting *better* men in the coming legislature. Their sole aim and effort will be to get men that they can manipulate. Money will be as free as air, and the man who takes and the one who does not will share alike the obloquy of the opposite faction and their friends." She wanted him to keep his hands "clean," and she concluded: "Be a candidate if you like for the Chief Justiceship, but keep out of the mire—the quagmire."[15]

Fortunately for Walsh, he did not become an office holder in this particular year. The legislative session of 1899 proved to be the most notorious of them all. Money flowed like "air," as Ellen Walsh had predicted, though most of it turned out to be Clark money. Friends and acquaintances of the Walshes were deeply involved, and few emerged from the sordid affair with reputations unblemished. What happened was incredible except for the physical presence of "corruption money," but masses of evidence accumulated in state and federal investigations, as well as in the trials. The investigation conducted by the Privileges and Elections Committee of the U.S. Senate (1900) was thorough and damaging to Clark's reputation.

Senator Fred Whiteside, a Democrat of Kalispell, made himself famous in the session of 1899. He was the exposer of Clark and his agents of corruption. Whiteside was also a personal friend of T. J. Walsh's at this time and the means by which Walsh got involved in the affair. Whiteside determined, early in the session, to expose the corruptionists by accepting their money, thus appearing to fall in with their plans. He did so, along with two cooperating members of the legislature. Whiteside then exhibited $30,000 in "purchase money" on the floor of the chamber.[16]

The fight had not ended; far from it. Daly was infuriated, according to reports, by the charges that he was the source of the $30,000. He would give Clark a chance to prove that, and the proper medium was the U.S. Senate. Whiteside was no less determined to prove the veracity of his charges and to clear his name, for he was under attack in the Clark newspapers, such as the *Butte Miner.* Walsh attempted to help Whiteside as a legal adviser.

Walsh was influenced by the longtime political factionalism in Helena and his lack of accord with Clark's men there. The powerful ex-governor, Samuel Hauser, was one such ally of Clark's, and no friend of Walsh's. One may speculate that Walsh had a greater fondness for the Irish Catholic partisans of Marcus Daly than for Clark and his associates. Also, he had a dream of going to the U.S. Senate. This made him a competitor of Clark's, while Daly had no personal ambition for a Senate seat and might conceivably give him a boost.

Whiteside's libel suit against the *Butte Miner* dragged on into 1900, when the Montana Supreme Court ruled against him in his attempt to compel the disclosure of information alleged to be privileged. Opposing Walsh and W. S. Hartman were four different law firms from Helena and Butte, including Roote and Clark. The latter, in a brief of sixty pages, referred to Walsh as an "intellectual giant." But on this occasion, they said, they could not believe in the soundness of his views. To win a libel suit in Montana was almost unheard of, and Walsh and Whiteside had no success in this effort.[17]

By 1900 a new giant had risen in the business life and politics of Montana. F. Augustus Heinze, somewhat like Clark, portrayed himself as the enemy of the big interests, that is, of Anaconda. Soon he was engaged in a succession of legal battles, claiming much of the Anaconda Company's property under the apex law. Having learned his lessons well, he boldly attempted to enhance his power by the control of public opinion, the purchase of public officials, and the formation of useful alliances. In June 1900, he and Senator Clark made an adroit move, calculated to win votes. They announced an eight-hour day in their mines.

The political campaign of 1900 was a welter of confusion in which Clark and Heinze (amazingly) were allied as "regular Democrats." Fighting them hard were the so-called independent Democrats, or the "coal-oil" Amalgamated crowd, as the hostile press designated them. These "independents" were partial to Daly. The Republicans were also divided in this campaign, as the "copper kings" fiercely contended for their vote.

T. J. Walsh pursued a course that was consistent with his recent attitudes. Between Clark and Daly, he much preferred the latter. Also, Walsh as a lawyer was pitted against the Heinze mining interests in half a dozen cases around the turn of the century. Apparently he never represented Heinze and had a low opinion of the way in which he operated. Thus, in one letter he referred to Heinze as paying his witnesses to perjure themselves and in another he commented: "The Heinze forces have a crowd of toughs here, but we have the jury under surveillance and do not allow them to separate."[18]

Not only did Walsh oppose the Clark-Heinze combination, he was, at times, the "head and front" of the opposition. Notably he provided legal brains for the independents. The Clark men were furious with him, and John Neill (editor of the *Helena Independent*) threatened him physically. His main services, however, were rendered as a lawyer for the independent candidates, seeking to get them on the ballot or to keep their opponents off. In one such case he was associated with H. L. Myers (later a U.S. senator) of Ravalli County. They succeeded in obtaining a writ of mandamus to force the county clerk and recorder of Ravalli County to print the names of independents on the ballot.[19]

Meanwhile, Walsh had taken another category of cases that tended to put him on the Daly side of things in the fight of 1900. He handled a case for Marcus Daly personally and attached considerable importance to it. He was also a friend of William Scallon, acting manager of the Amalgamated Company, and was associated with Scallon and other lawyers in pressing a series of suits against the Heinze interests. These included some of the most famous disputes over the apex law (1899–1901). Walsh's services were impressive, and at some point in 1900 he received an invitation to join the legal staff of the Amalgamated Company. He declined, with regret. Walsh was clearly on good terms with the Daly forces and believed that he had reason to hope for political preferment as a result.[20]

Everything went wrong in November. The independents suffered a crushing defeat. Clark's and Heinze's tactic of blaming everything on Standard Oil (some of whose leaders had helped form Amalgamated Copper) was a success. In Lewis and Clark County, for example, the independent gubernatorial candidate received only 200 votes in a total of some 4,000. Walsh took these results as a personal defeat, and he retreated from political life for the next three years.

Who would control the fabulously rich mines of Butte? This was the main question, to which the integrity of political parties and standards of personal morality must be sacrificed. Much of the fight revolved around the control of two district judges in Butte. At last, the Amalgamated interests had the best of this struggle. They closed down their mines and smelters, putting great pressure on the administration of Governor Toole, until he called a special session of the legislature. They then obtained the passage of a "fair trial" bill, which would permit a change of venue when the judge was considered to be biased. Soon the Amalgamated forced Heinze to sell out. He left the state a loser, although richer than when he arrived.[21]

Watching from the sidelines in September 1902, Walsh found some satisfaction in the political trends, especially in his home town. John S. M. Neill, for example, had castigated Walsh two years before in the state central committee and asserted that Walsh had been "spewed out" by the people of his ward. Now Neill had himself been repudiated. "The mills of the gods grind slowly," commented Walsh, but they eventually bring results. He was resolved to devote himself to his lawsuits. While enhancing his reputation as a lawyer, he bided his time politically and waited for an opportunity to reassert himself.[22]

6

Lawyer, Progressive, and Public Man

In the first decade of the new century T. J. Walsh was nearing the top of his profession. An era of "progressivism" had opened in which many professional men were seeking public office for the first time. Earlier the young Walsh had spoken almost despairingly of the need for rejuvenation of the party system in America. Now the Bryans, La Follettes, Roosevelts, and Wilsons were rising to positions of influence. The mood of the country had changed, and state by state, city by city, and in the national government as well, significant reforms were put into effect. The country had altered its way of thinking.[1]

Increasingly Walsh became a public man. If he had wished to confine himself to his law practice and to pile up a large fortune, there is no doubt he could have done so. Early in the twentieth century, he was overwhelmed with work including a number of lucrative cases. But money was not enough, nor was an extensive and prestigious practice. To his wife he remarked that the problem was one of getting "rid of the grind" without becoming a "back number." A partial solution was to take C. B. Nolan in as a law partner, while he devoted more attention to public affairs and politics.[2]

An antagonist of Walsh's in a law suit once referred to him as a "publicist" with a wide knowledge of sociology and economics. He was an "intellectual giant," though hardly infallible. This description probably was a trifle sarcastic, but it indicates the reputation that Walsh was beginning to enjoy. He took an active part in the bar association of Lewis and Clark County and in the state association and the American Bar Association as well, occasionally making headlines for the positions he assumed. As a legal specialist, he involved himself in arguments over railroad rate regulation, public land policy, and other matters. He attended state and regional conferences and appeared before congressional committees in Washington. By 1906, when he ran for office as a Democratic nominee for Congress, he was deeply involved in state and national politics.[3]

Both Walsh and his wife were active in civic affairs. In many respects they typified the good citizens of this era doing their utmost to apply trained intelligence and higher standards of morality to the problems of city and society. He was among the founders of a Helena Improvement Society, president of the first civic club, and a president of the public library board. His interest in municipal problems was enhanced by his close friendship with Frank Edwards, civic leader, longtime mayor of Helena, and a power in the Republican party. Edwards had a progressive viewpoint congenial to Walsh's, and at least in city affairs the two often worked together. They also enjoyed camping and bicycling excursions, as in July 1897 when they toured Yellowstone Park with Christopher Connolly.[4]

Mrs. Walsh had a distinguished career in her own right and contributed to the recognition accorded her husband. As early as 1896 she was active in the woman's suffrage movement of Montana. She served as president of the Helena Woman's Club, as president for two terms of the Montana Federation of Women's Clubs (with 1,200 members), and as president of the state antituberculosis league. She had a personal interest in city planning and park development and acquired an early passion for the remote, mountainous area that eventually became known as Glacier National Park. She was an agitator for the creation of that park.[5]

T. J. Walsh, the public man and aspirant after high office, cannot be understood apart from his legal career. When he reached the Senate he gained distinction for the same qualities he had displayed in the courtroom over a period of three decades. His most notable achievement, the Teapot Dome investigation, found him functioning essentially as a lawyer. The truism that "knowledge is power" has seldom been demonstrated more clearly than in his career as a Montana lawyer. Numbers of his cases were concerned with public policy. His mining cases are an excellent illustration. These disputes occurred primarily in U.S. public land areas. State and federal law and provisions of the U.S. Constitution were involved, not to mention complex questions of geology, physics, and engineering.

Did Walsh's "legalism" inhibit his "progressivism"? Certainly he put too much faith in laws, as his generation was prone to do, and some of his hopes were illusory. Also, as a practicing attorney, he tended to take the cases that came to him and did not ally himself with the underprivileged, to the extent that Clarence Darrow or Louis D. Brandeis did. His sympathies, however, were strongly in that direction. He handled many cases for those financially insecure and was often called a "personal injury" lawyer. He argued for the expansion of the regulatory functions of the state and occasionally served as counsel for the State of Montana. As a lawyer and student of the law, Walsh had no difficulty in supporting progressive measures, including such radical and notorious ideas as the recall of judges!

The subject of railroads and the regulation of rates was an important matter in 1906, with strong political implications. A fight occurred over the Hepburn Bill in Washington, and locally there was much agitation and discussion of the problem. Popular sentiment was running against the railroads, with calls for stricter regulation and the physical evaluation of railroad properties, in order to better determine what their rates should be. The Northern Pacific Railway Company shared in the criticism. Years before it had aroused the indignation of many Montanans by acquiring mineral lands in its federal grants, when the obvious intent of the government was not to give away such valuable lands. Also, like other great corporations of the day, it interfered regularly in politics to promote its self interest.

As the railroads came under scrutiny, T. J. Walsh stood to benefit from his extensive experience in the intricacies of their business and from his capacity for logical analysis. No better example can be found than the railroad rate convention which met in Helena on December 14, 1905, with leaders assembled from around the state. This was a bipartisan conference of men concerned over the railroad situation. For Walsh, however, it seems to have ended as a road to the election of 1906.

The morning session of Thursday, December 14, was largely for organizational purposes. On the recommendation of the committee on permanent organization, Walsh was chosen permanent chairman of the meeting. At the afternoon session he gave what the *Helena Independent* described as "an extended and forceful address."[6]

The delegates worked until midnight, adopting resolutions and preparing their platform, but the high point was the afternoon session. Among the many comments to this effect were those of Lee Mantle, Republican of Butte: "The central point of interest in the proceedings was the clean, logical and convincing address of the permanent chairman, Mr. T. J. Walsh, which evinced a profound knowledge of the entire subject, being filled with pertinent facts and figures relating [to] the entire subject, and bearing particularly upon the situation in this state." And he went on to cite some of Walsh's figures on freight rate inequities. Another person much impressed was John S. M. Neill, manager of the *Helena Independent.* Only recently he had been Walsh's bitter opponent in affairs of the state Democratic party.[7]

The rate convention was illustrative of a dilemma facing the Democrats in 1906. Those who dominated the proceedings were reform-minded men of both parties, but they looked to the example of Theodore Roosevelt in Washington and to the Hepburn Bill, by which the powers of the Interstate Commerce Commission would be significantly enlarged. How successfully could the Democrats in Montana hope to run for office, when the Rooseveltian influence seemed so pervasive, when even the Democrats had to admire his leadership and engage in a considerable amount of "me-tooism"?

Walsh had to consider this and other factors as he debated his course with reference to a possible race for high office. He was thinking not only of 1906 but of the senatorial elections to come. If 1906 turned out to be a Republican year in Montana, and he were defeated for Congress, would his position as a Democratic leader be weakened? He talked with other Democrats who might be senatorial candidates, including W. G. Conrad of Great Falls, a wealthy rancher. It seemed also that Governor Toole was willing to go to Washington. No Democrat was eager to run against Joseph M. Dixon, the congressman from Missoula, considered to be a progressive in his views and formidable on the platform. Dixon, Walsh noted, was asserting that he would run for the Senate.[8]

"Strangest of all," Walsh said, was an offer from John Neill of the *Helena Independent,* urging him to run for Congress and "promising the active support of the paper." The ostensible reason for this offer from a political enemy was that Neill was conducting a campaign on the railroad question. He believed Walsh could run a "hurrah campaign" on the railroad matters and "pull through," although the fight would be difficult.[9]

In late September Walsh entered the race, going from the county convention in Helena to the state convention in Butte, where he received the nomination for Congress by acclamation. That he would run as a progressive was apparent from his record and also from the mood of assembled Democrats. Walsh knew that he must wage a hard campaign to have any chance of victory and that, politics being what it was, personal attacks might be made on him and his record.

Walsh's speeches in both the county and state conventions sounded the notes that Joseph Folk, Robert La Follette, Theodore Roosevelt, and others had made familiar. Unable to attack the popular Theodore Roosevelt or progressive leaders of the Republican party, Walsh aimed his fire at the Republican national organization and what it represented. He argued that, after

Roosevelt, there was no "commanding figure" in the Republican party and Americans must look to the Democrats and to the "great commoner," W. J. Bryan, admired around the world as a champion of the people.[10]

Walsh closed his acceptance address in Butte with a veiled allusion to the unjustifiable power of railroads and copper interests in Montana affairs. Walsh could truthfully say that he had a strong desire "to have a part, however humble, in the work of restoring the rule of the people in legislation and in administration, and to bring its blessing, under Providence, in fullest measure to Montana."

The campaign was an interesting one, pitting Governor Toole and Congressman Dixon against each other as aspirants for the U.S. Senate (whose selection must occur in the legislature). Walsh's opponent for Congress, Charles Pray, a lawyer from Ft. Benton, would normally have been rather weak, but he benefited immensely from the mantle of Roosevelt and from the fact that Dixon campaigned with him. An odd feature of the campaign was that Walsh challenged Pray to a debate, but he refused. Whereupon Dixon, through the Republican State Committee, challenged Walsh to a debate, and he accepted. So these two relative newcomers to the political life of the state, who would soon be among the most notable of its leaders, had a confrontation even though they were running for different offices.

Democrats faced problems that were insurmountable. Their only issue, according to the Republicans, was Theodore Roosevelt and whether or not the people of Montana would support him by sending loyal Republicans to Congress. It was a strong argument, especially when coupled with "Republican prosperity" and a rehashing of the "Democratic" depression under Grover Cleveland, only ten years before.[11]

Republicans began the campaign with a surprise issue and closed it with another, each of which could be described as hitting under the belt. Early in October the *Helena Record* and other papers began to attack Walsh and Governor Toole as employers of Oriental labor. Walsh, it was true, employed a "Chinaman" to fight the dandelions, when weather permitted.[12]

Walsh hammered away on railroad questions, as expected, speaking in laboring towns around the state. From these matters the Democratic candidate easily branched off into broader questions of capital, labor, and the distribution of wealth. At Virginia City he spoke out against the Republican party nationally as a tool of the trusts, choosing to ignore the Amalgamated and allied Montana evils. At various times he denied that the Republican party deserved any particular credit for prosperity conditions. It was American labor and ingenuity and worldwide conditions of prosperity that were truly responsible.[13]

In replying to Walsh, and in trying to destroy his credibility, the Republican editors were clever. Most important were the columns of Oscar Lanstrum in the *Helena Record* and Joseph Dixon in the *Missoulian*. They started with the knowledge that Walsh had built up a reputation as lawyer, intellectual, and reformer; and, in fact, as the *Independent* noted, Republicans had themselves contributed to his image by frequent praise. Now, however, he was running for office, and they must whittle him down.

More serious were the actual weaknesses in his campaign and that of the Democrats in 1906. Some of these were clearly revealed in the debate with Congressman Dixon at Townsend.[14]

Dixon poked fun at the Democratic claims that they would support the president. It was popular to do this in the West, he said, but in the eastern part of the country Democrats were attacking Roosevelt. Then Dixon took a crack at the Montana Democrats where they were so vulnerable. He said Walsh did much talking about great corporations and their connections with the Republican party, their huge donations, and the like. "But here in Montana, the democratic party is worm-eaten and rotten with corporation money. Sometimes it was one corporation and then another. The democratic party was not consistent enough to stay with any one of the big corporations."[15]

More to the point was an observation in the *Great Falls Leader*, stressing the victory that Charles Pray had won and saying he deserved great credit because he had beaten T. J. Walsh, probably the ablest man in the Montana Democratic party. Along with his wounds, Walsh received other compliments. Ex-Senator Paris Gibson, for example, told him that his speech at Great Falls was the "best political speech he ever listened to in Montana." Walsh may have performed better in this campaign than the newspapers would indicate, with their tendency to stress railroad issues and sensational charges. Seldom, if ever, could one read the full text of his campaign addresses.[16]

In any case, Walsh seems to have come out of this election with his political stature only slightly diminished, if at all. He had run as well as other Democrats in a year of party setbacks and his name was now better known around the state. Those who expected him to spend his days sulking, or to drop out of public life, were destined for some quick surprises.

The pattern of Walsh's life was established for a time; there were no changes, except those of greater prominence and prosperity. His law practice was a thriving one which took him increasingly outside of Montana, and his peri-

odic involvement in the discussion of public issues could be expected as before. Early in 1907, for example, he went to New York on business and then
down to Washington to join a delegation of Montanans who had come to
the capital on a matter of "grave moment." The Congress was considering a
bill by the terms of which a leasing system, similar to that used in selected
forest reserve areas, would be put into effect for the public lands generally.
The subject was also under investigation by the Public Lands Commission,
which President Roosevelt had appointed earlier to study the land laws and
suggest means for their improvement. On the morning of February 11, Walsh
was among those speaking before the commission in opposition to this leasing idea.[17]

Following his appearance at the hearing, Walsh returned to New York, where
he had one case against F. Augustus Heinze and other cases as well. The number of Montana people in New York was "astonishing," he found; and as long
as he stayed ("if not too long") his services would be in demand. He was living at the Waldorf-Astoria and doing his work at the bar association library
just a few blocks from the hotel. The library was "complete as to books" and
a "charming place . . . architecturally beautiful." Walsh urged his wife to come
and join him, for he was not especially busy and would like "first rate," he
said, to spend two or three weeks in New York and Washington with her. Mrs.
Walsh quickly took up the invitation. Obviously the Walsh family was enjoying the benefits of his law practice and the reorganization of their office
in Helena, allowing more leisure.[18]

Public business, in part, took him back to Washington in October 1907.
He made a call on Attorney General Charles Bonaparte and on Secretary of
the Interior James R. Garfield, as a result of which he was authorized to "institute suit in the name of the government" against the Northern Pacific
Railroad. This was an attempt to recover for the government 1,100 acres of
coal land which the Northern Pacific had "appropriated by means of Mt.
Rainier Forest Reserve scrip under an act [Senator] Carter is charged with
having engineered for them."[19]

That Walsh's position in the Democratic party had been solidified rather
than weakened by his congressional race and subsequent activities was apparent in 1908. He wanted to go to Denver in early July as a delegate to the national convention and as a supporter of William J. Bryan. When he attended the state convention in Bozeman, where the delegates were chosen, he
polled the highest number of votes. William A. Clark, W. G. Conrad, and
three others rounded out the group. Something of a personal triumph for him
was the announcement in the Denver convention that he would be a mem-

ber of the platform committee. According to Walsh, the delegates "broke out [in applause] and kept the thing up until I was forced to bow my acknowledgements." He was gaining respect and appreciation that Clark and other leaders of the party did not command.[20]

The national convention did nothing to diminish his reputation. The *Helena Independent* noted in an editorial that he became a member of the subcommittee of sixteen on the platform committee, consisting (it said) of "the ablest men in the convention." Walsh had now initiated a career of service in the preparation of Democratic platforms and would exert his "resolutions wizardry" during five conventions in a row.[21]

He was much in evidence during the campaign. He served as chairman of the Lewis and Clark convention and later as chairman of the state convention, meeting in Anaconda. One of his contributions in the latter convention was to declaim "eloquently" for the noninterference of corporations in the governmental affairs of the state, although according to the *Montana Lookout* the corporation leaders went right on to control the convention.

There can be no question that between 1904 and 1908 T. J. Walsh had truly arrived as a Democratic leader and a public man of prominence. He suffered disappointments, as in his congressional defeat in 1906 and Bryan's loss to Taft in the presidential election of 1908. But he had established himself as a man to watch in the political affairs of the state. He looked to the elections of 1910, and to his possible selection as a U.S. Senator by the Montana legislature, with greater confidence than ever.

7

The Emergence of a Leader

I n 1910 Walsh inaugurated his campaign for the U.S. Senate against a well
entrenched Thomas Henry Carter. Still a young man, Carter had served
as territorial delegate to Congress (1889); as Montana's first representative
(1889–91); as commissioner of the General Land Office (1891–92); and as a
senator for two nonconsecutive terms, the first starting in 1895 and the second in 1905.

Of Irish extraction, Carter was a Catholic who attended the same church
in Helena as Walsh. He was a likeable person, eloquent on the speaker's platform, forceful in the expression of ideas, and never to be taken lightly. A
possible weakness is suggested by his earlier affiliation with the Republican
National Committee in the administration of Benjamin Harrison. To him,
General Grant, James G. Blaine, and others of that vintage were heroes. He
changed his ideas only slightly with the rise of progressivism in the twentieth century. At the same time, Carter, as a senator from Montana and a spokesman for its interests, had done much for farmers, ranchers, copper kings, and
others. To defeat such a servant of "the people" would not be an impossibil-
ity, but it would require a hard campaign.[1]

Walsh's own party gave him the greatest concern. If the Democrats could
win control of the legislature—and this seemed possible in 1910—what would
be the result? Would they stand together and send the majority choice of their
party to the Senate, or would they fight among themselves to an indefinite
conclusion? Would the Anaconda Company's leaders permit a free choice in
the legislature?

No one who reads the correspondence of Senator Carter, T. J. Walsh, Joseph Dixon, or other political leaders of this era can doubt the influence of
"the Company." By 1910, Heinze was no longer a factor of importance, and

the Clark interests generally collaborated with Anaconda. For practical purposes, therefore, politicians had to think of the political operations of the Company, centering on the sixth floor of the Hennessy Building in Butte or at 26 Broadway, New York City. John D. Ryan, formerly a banker, now president of the Company, pursued a policy of nonpartisan political activity to assure the dominance of his organization. Assisting him as the managing director was John G. Morony of Butte, long active in the state as a banker and politician. From their positions as officials of Anaconda and of the Montana Power Company, of railroad companies, banks, steamship companies, and an assortment of organizations, national and international, these corporate bigwigs freely dealt in Montana politics. They had friends and allies all over the state. They conducted many activities furtively and usually believed that the advancement of company interests meant the advancement of Montana.

The Anaconda and Clark forces, nominally Democratic, were primarily concerned with getting the right men into office irrespective of party. One factor above all enabled the mining interests to swing great influence. The two parties were almost evenly matched, and the vote was small. By controlling solid blocs in conventions, primaries, or the general elections, the "interests" could have their way. As one writer observed, popular allegiance to the forms of party facilitated the Company's manipulation of both parties. Anaconda strongholds were in Butte (Silver Bow County), Anaconda (Deer Lodge County), and Great Falls (Cascade County) where the mines, smelters, and water power industries were concentrated.

Political operations of the Company were subtle and mysterious. Jerre Murphy, who ran newspapers in Butte and Helena and could qualify as an expert (with a progressive bias), gave this analysis: "The organization is at once so complex and so perfect that its several parts can be made to work . . . in conflict, or together."

Most Montanans, uncertain about the status of others, sought to keep their own independence or to reassert it. Even Company leaders defected. The most notable example was William Scallon, Daly's close friend, an outstanding lawyer, who served for three years as president of the Company following Daly's death, then chose to resign. A progressive, a moralist, and a gentleman, he simply would not do what was expected of him and deliberately surrendered his lucrative position.

The Anaconda Company was not a monolithic structure, or a cruel, impersonal force. Rather, in the practical world of Montana affairs it was people—with whom the aspiring politician must have official and social relations. Montanans met in hotel lobbies, in restaurants, in bars, on trains, at private parties. They met in New York, Washington, Denver, and San Francisco, not to mention Butte, Helena, and Missoula. They talked of business and politics but also of families and personal problems.

Company leaders were friendly, even ingratiating. But an office-holder, or a seeker after office, was kept in a state of suspense. An excellent example of this was Senator Carter in 1910. In his recent career, Carter had been identified with Anaconda. As a man of influence in the Taft administration and in the Senate, he could be of service to Company interests and was. Their collaboration was facilitated by the fact that Carter was a conservative on economic matters and inclined to support virtually anything that would allegedly contribute to business stability and prosperity. He used his good offices in a smoke damage proceeding brought against Anaconda, endeavoring to insure a compromise settlement. He gave information as to pending federal appointments. When Montana appointments were at stake, he paid close attention to the wishes of the Anaconda leaders. Meanwhile, in Helena, Carter's confidante Dr. Oscar Lanstrum, editor of the *Record*, worked closely with John G. Morony and Company favorites in the legislature.

Still, Carter and Lanstrum were anxious to do more. In February 1910, Lanstrum wrote on a matter he conceived to be of utmost importance. City elections were pending in Helena, and he believed that defeat in this "preliminary struggle" would handicap them severely in the remainder of the campaign. No one could help them more at this juncture, he believed, than Cornelius (Con) Kelley of the Company. They needed to "line him up" and could do so by finding a job for his son. Soon Senator Carter had arranged for a position at the U.S. Capitol, so that young Kelley could also attend law school at night. He reported to Kelley that his son was "looking splendidly" and getting along fine and that he intended to have him up to his house for a stay and would endeavor to "interest him as well as I can."

A few months later Carter showed his anxiety about "that smoke matter," concerning which Anaconda leaders were also anxious. He had pulled wires as best he could and now wrote to the influential Senator W. Murray Crane of Massachusetts. Crane responded with several reassuring communications, the burden of which was that he had talked with President Taft, and the Justice Department would probably delay action until after the election.[2]

In the same period, T. J. Walsh revealed his concern over the copper interests. Their support outright was too much to hope for, but conceivably they would not fight him. Walsh had good relations with a number of the Anaconda people, dating back to the campaign of 1900 and to his legal assistance in the controversies with Heinze. Captain D. Gay Stivers was one of these.

In Red Lodge to try a suit (March 1910) Walsh described Stivers as his friendly antagonist in the case, and went on to say that he intended to speak to Stivers but had not had the opportunity.[3]

Most important, nationally, in the politics of 1910 was "insurgency." A small group of Republicans in Congress rebelled against the policies made notorious by Old Guard leaders such as Senator Nelson Aldrich of Rhode Island and Speaker "Joe" Cannon of Illinois. Robert M. La Follette, George W. Norris, and others arraigned the politics of "special privilege" and became increasingly critical of the Taft administration. Theodore Roosevelt was a hero to many of these insurgents. From 1910 to 1912 the divisions among Republicans became increasingly serious, with the ultimate formation of Roosevelt's Progressive Party.[4]

Montana was almost a microcosm of the national struggle. The senior senator, Thomas Carter, was a Cannon-Aldrich partisan and a loyal friend and admirer of the Taft administration. He and his associates showed no capacity to understand reform movements sweeping the country. Thus, of insurgency, he said it was "an article manufactured by self-seeking politicians."[5]

Whatever the appearances, the party was divided by insurgency. Joseph Dixon of Missoula, the junior senator, was embarked on an independent course which would take him into the Bull Moose party two years later. Ever since 1908, Dixon and some members of the Carter entourage had been at odds, although the two senators were personally friendly. By 1910, the differences were irreconcilable.[6]

Carter had not kept pace with the times and to many he was little more than an errand boy for Anaconda. They knew or suspected what his letters later revealed; that he was, in truth, allied with copper interests, the James J. Hill railroad, and large capitalistic interests generally, to whom he appealed for support in this campaign.[7]

One of the issues of the period was the direct election of U.S. senators, to be accomplished in some way by a state law pending the adoption of a constitutional amendment. Senator Dixon, T. J. Walsh, and many liberal-minded men of both parties were strongly in favor of this reform. They also advocated the primary system of nominations, generally, to supplant the old convention system. Carter, on the other hand, along with Dr. Lanstrum, John G. Morony, and others of their group were determined to prevent any meaningful legislation on this subject.[8]

By the old standards of Montana politics, Carter was doing what the clever man was supposed to do. But many had seen enough of this. About a year later Walsh looked back and assessed the public's mood: "The people distrust parties. They are prone to believe, . . . that the party management is likely to fall into the hands of men of more or less sordid motives, . . . The man who would die for his party can now be found only in a museum or in a sanitarium."[9]

Walsh had intimate knowledge of the extent to which men were crossing party lines in their attempt to escape from the old system. Without the aid of Republican independents, he could not have been a serious contender for the U.S. Senate in 1910–11, and he could not have won in 1912. In Helena itself a Democratic-Insurgent combination engaged in a struggle with Dr. Lanstrum, Thomas A. Marlowe, and others of the Carter group. As a result, Walsh's friend and confidante Frank Edwards, a Republican progressive, was five times elected mayor of Helena. In April 1910, for example, a crucial test occurred, as Walsh and the Carter forces privately indicated their anxiety over the results. To Walsh, the success of his friends in Helena meant a secure home base, without which he would have difficulty in his larger ambitions. Republican assistance there might compensate for the Democratic opposition he always faced in his home county. On April 4, he was able to send a telegram to his wife that Edwards had been reelected in a close vote.[10]

By midsummer a question of strategy had arisen. Was it wise to seek an outright endorsement of his senatorial candidacy in the Democratic state convention? Many argued that neither Walsh nor anyone else should be endorsed, so that all contenders would work harder for the party ticket. Others, including Walsh, saw the plans of the copper interests and of Senator Carter in this argument—one of seeking to keep the Democrats divided. Walsh decided to throw down the gauntlet: "we had better 'smoke them out' in the convention."[11]

Shortly after Walsh wrote this, the *Anaconda Standard* came out with an editorial attacking his candidacy. They alleged that he could not win, that he had gone down to inglorious defeat in his recent attempt at a seat in the House of Representatives. At the same time the situation looked precarious in Lewis and Clark County (Helena).[12]

Political managers of the copper interests had made their decision to block the ambitions of Walsh and his type of obstreperous Democrats. Carter heard from one of his informants in Butte: "The Amalgamated people are fearful lest T. J. Walsh should be elected in the event of a Democratic legislature. I know positively that the interests referred to are hostile to Mr. Walsh, . . . Walsh is regarded by them as a very dangerous man."[13]

The Democrats met at Livingston in early September, with some 500 delegates in attendance. Walsh made a personal argument in behalf of endorsing a senatorial candidate. The party, he said, could not honestly and consistently oppose such a course when it had already committed itself to the principle of the direct election of senators. Action by the convention was the closest they could come to popular election under the present system. Not long before this the supporters of Walsh and W. G. Conrad had agreed on the idea of convention endorsement. But, at Livingston, most of the Conrad delegates went over to the other side. Walsh's resolution was rejected by 335 to 175, and there could be no doubt where the opposition lay: Delegates from the counties of Silver Bow, Deer Lodge, Cascade, and Flathead were unanimously opposed. Silver Bow alone, with 107 delegates, made the difference. Walsh could find some satisfaction in the large vote he carried against a formidable combination, and in the unanimous vote of endorsement from his home county.[14]

Walsh's hope now was based on the general reform spirit of the United States, as it affected the voters of Montana, and on the effectiveness of his leadership. At considerable expense and personal inconvenience this "noncandidate" continued his organizing efforts around the state. Several times he escaped the scenes of political battle to visit with his family at Lake McDonald in the newly created Glacier National Park, where his wife was supervising the construction of their lodge. At crucial points in the campaign Ellen Walsh came to Helena to assist him.

Walsh's aim was clear. He intended to make inroads in a number of Republican counties, hoping the gain in Democratic legislators there would compensate for defeats he suffered in the centers of Democratic strength. He and some of his editorial admirers, such as Tom Stout of Lewistown, scathingly indicted the brand of leadership that Senator Carter represented.

Carter, in the final months, made a vigorous campaign that he expected would pull him through. The senator also lived up to his reputation for being a puller of strings. He wrote to Charles D. Norton, White House secretary, to Charles G. Dawes of the Central Trust Company in Chicago concerning "a large ditch contract" near Hamilton in Ravalli County, and to Alexander McKenzie in St. Paul, Minnesota, concerning "a large sewer contract" at Missoula in Montana.[15]

Carter made other appeals to men high in the financial world and the U.S. government, the most important of whom probably were those of the copper interests and the railroads in Montana. He was puzzled about leaders of the Northern Pacific Railroad in his state, who seemed to be "hostile, indifferent, or confused." Carter could not understand this. It seemed obvious that his defeat would contribute to financial instability; that if the Taft administration were "broken down in the center an unsettled state of thought will obtain in the country." He appealed for cooperation.[16]

It is ironic that about this time Carter felt compelled to deny that he owed anything much to the great financial interests of his state. Those forces, he said, were Democratic in their politics. His own reliance had always been placed in an "appeal to the plain, common sense of the average citizen."[17]

The common sense of these citizens seems to have dictated Carter's defeat in 1910. Other Republican candidates, such as the lackluster Congressman Charles Pray, had no difficulty in winning their races. But the legislative candidates upon whom Carter depended for his reelection did not fare well. The Montana Senate was still Republican by a margin of 16 to 12. But the House went Democratic by 42 to 32. Thus in a joint session, the Democrats should easily control the senatorial selection.

Walsh and others pointed to election matters that Carter failed to mention. Deer Lodge County (Anaconda) was of special interest. In the previous assembly, four of its House members and the single senator were Democrats. As a result of voting in 1910, all Democrats from Deer Lodge were replaced by Republicans—something that went against all the state and national trends. Walsh concluded that the event confirmed, "in the most unmistakable manner," the popular belief that Carter and his political associates were intimately allied with "the great copper company and the Hill roads."[18]

Whatever the reasons for Democratic gains in Montana, Walsh was a principal beneficiary. From the spring to the fall of 1910 he became the leading Democrat in Montana, not excluding Edwin L. Norris, the governor. Formerly considered as only one of several contenders for a place in the Senate, he had made himself the popular choice on the Democratic side.

Editorial comments reflected Walsh's rise. In late November the *Montana Lookout* noted that Walsh was the senatorial candidate "who led the party fight within the state and who unquestionably can command the support of the majority of the democratic legislators for his candidacy." The *Cutbank Pioneer Press* (northwest of Great Falls) offered a comparison of Walsh with the other Democratic possibilities saying he stood out intellectually and otherwise, "strong and unafraid": "If Walsh lands the prize we shall say Montana democracy is commencing to evince signs of taking on a sense of respectability . . . that it has never heretofore been suspected of possessing."[19]

Could Walsh, whatever his ability and claims to leadership, overcome the hard core of opposition in his own party? And was it possible that fighting among the Democrats could open the door to Tom Carter, who still commanded the loyalty of most Republicans elected to the legislature? Carter, it seemed clear, would have the backing of copper interests.

The *Lookout* noted that "combine organs in the state, labeled Democratic," gave their plans away: first, by "protracted silence" as to Walsh's leadership; and, second, by "flippant ridicule" of W. G. Conrad's aspirations. Eventually there would appear in the balloting "the compromise candidate, the dark horse candidate, the 'logical' candidate . . . an Amalgamated Company candidate."[20]

But many Montanans had not given up. Walsh and his supporters were prepared to fight, and they counted upon a rising sense of public indignation to assist in their efforts.

The twelfth legislative assembly of Montana convened on January 2, 1911. It produced, as expected, a long wearisome fight for the Senate seat but had in its end results a momentous effect upon Montana politics. This was the last Montana legislature to choose a U.S. senator. The man so honored was a Democrat, inaugurating a new era of Democratic representation in the Senate (not until 1946 would the state send another Republican to the upper chamber). T. J. Walsh, representing the new order of things, had a central role in the changes that occurred.

When the balloting began on January 10, in joint session, Walsh received 28 of the Democratic votes, while Conrad had 18 and the rest were scattered. Carter received 31 Republican votes; others were scattered. To be elected, a total of 51 votes was necessary. Carter needed the Republican votes and a few Democratic votes, but a Democrat could win easily if he garnered all the votes of his party.

Here was the dilemma. Walsh's vote climbed in the early balloting—to 29, to 30, to 32, to 33, to 34. He doubled the vote on Conrad and pushed several votes ahead of Carter, but he was short of the 51 required.[21]

The "Walsh men," as they came to be called, saw their hope as lying in a party caucus. Controlling a majority vote, they wanted a decision of the caucus which would bind the party members and push Walsh over the top. This point could be made with particular force by a Democratic legislator elected from the Republican counties of eastern Montana. Thus, Senator W. B. George of Billings (Yellowstone) stated on the floor: "We stand here representing a people that are demanding the election of Thomas J. Walsh in no uncertain terms."[22]

Early in February, the call for a caucus was blocked by ten individuals—the senator and seven representatives from Silver Bow County, and two others. The copper combine was the chief source of this opposition. As Jerre Murphy of the *Montana Lookout* assessed the situation: "The only opposition to him [Walsh] is the opposition of the corrupt corporate combine . . . with tools in the legislature who forget their oaths of office or knowingly violate them in fidelity to the dishonest policies and aims of their corporate employers."[23]

Walsh did everything he knew how to do. Directly or through intermediaries he appealed to national figures like William Jennings Bryan and Clarence Darrow, hoping they could exert some pressure in his behalf. Darrow responded directly to a letter from Walsh. He said he had tried to get the Chicago newspapers to give publicity to the Montana situation, but so far they had not. Darrow also attempted to use his influence with union officials in Denver and Butte, hoping to swing several members of the Montana legislature over to Walsh's side.[24]

Carter and his friends, meanwhile, were not idle. Carter remained in his Washington office, relying upon the political skill of Dr. Oscar Lanstrum and others in Helena. Clearly they contributed to the stop-Walsh movement and to the stalemate that possibly would create a situation in which Carter could still win.[25]

The deadlock continued from early January to the evening of March 2, the last day of the session. What finally happened is not entirely clear. There is a hint in Carter's correspondence that he could have had the election if he had been willing to accept it under the shadow of scandal. He was not willing, perhaps because the times would hardly permit it. Nor did he agree with those Republicans who preferred a failure to elect rather than the election of a Democrat. Carter said, with apparent sincerity, that the state should not be denied its right to a second senator.[26]

In the final ballots, the Walsh men switched their votes from man to man among those known to be loyal; for example, to C. B. Nolan, Walsh's law partner. Then someone suggested Henry L. Myers, a former legislator with whom Walsh had experienced cordial relations. At 7:23 in the evening of March 2, after 7½ hours of continuous session, Myers received 53 votes and was elected a U.S. senator.

Walsh had won a moral victory in this session, and he could look to the future with confidence. He expressed his pleasure at Myers's election and said he felt amply repaid for anything he had contributed to the outcome.[27]

Indicative of a new spirit in the legislature was a bill passed on March 1, the day before the session ended. If the bill worked as expected by Democratic and Republican reformers, it would make impossible a repetition of this session's deadlock and would permit, in effect, the popular election of senators.

The best men in the state, of both parties, knew that recent events had produced another scandal, that Walsh had been cheated out of an election that was rightfully his—at least by the new standards of popular democracy. They intended to prevent such a miscarriage from happening again.

One supporter was Tom Stout of Lewistown, editor of the *Fergus Democrat* and a state senator. In the aftermath of the legislative session, Stout looked to the future and made a prediction: "the people of Montana are going to demand that the next democratic state convention nominate the Hon. T. J. Walsh of Helena for the United States senate. . . . Mr. Walsh is fairly and honestly entitled to this honor at the hands of the party." It was to be expected, then, that Walsh would soon go to Washington.[28]

8

To the Senate at Last

Following his defeat in the legislature, Walsh seldom forgot the political battles just ahead, for in the spring and summer of 1912 his fate would be determined. As he looked ahead, the tide of progressivism neared its highest point, and one may well ask about this Montanan, how liberal—or possibly radical—was he? As suggested, he started as a Jeffersonian Democrat and rejected early in his career some of the antidemocratic and brutalizing aspects of the rising industrial society. He tended to find new justification for his basic idealism. Nevertheless, as the mood of the American people was altered, as they were swept along "with an ardor almost religious," in Walsh's words, his attitudes also changed. His rhetoric reflected the hopefulness of the times, and his remedies for social ills were sometimes different from those of twenty years earlier.[1]

Walsh spoke in the idiom of the time and was aware of the latest developments through his reading, his personal involvement in affairs, and his acquaintance with those in public life. Thus he entitled one speech "The Growth of Democracy in the West." He assessed in it the political situation in the western states, with special reference to the recent election of Democratic governors and senators. He referred familiarly to the work of such men as Charles Evans Hughes of New York, to the findings of muckrakers, and to the ideas of scholars like J. Allen Smith of the University of Washington.[2]

In an address at Fargo, North Dakota, on January 18, 1912, Walsh showed his grasp of public events. The occasion was a Democratic banquet, at which another speaker was Charles C. Heifner, the western campaign manager for Woodrow Wilson. Walsh placed his faith in popular government and in the restoration of that form of government where it had been "cozened" away from the people. He charged the existence of an "extra-constitutional oligarchy of wealth," a sordid alliance between corporate interests and those who made a "trade" of politics. Such an alliance had to be destroyed, and Americans had dedicated themselves to the task: "They revere the institutions under the benign influence of which this nation has grown great," and "by the grace of God," he said, they proposed "to enjoy its blessings undiminished and transmit it unimpaired to their children."[3]

To this gathering of Democrats he stressed the new propensities of the voters to which, he said, they must give attention in nominating candidates. Party ties were "dissolved" as Americans pursued their patriotic purposes. It was now the man, the leader, who was important, not the party: "No platform, however elaborate its makeup or radical its promises, will avail much without a candidate whose public life has been in harmony with its principles. . . . The people distrust parties."[4]

Not too surprisingly, this Montana lawyer next commented on legal questions and the problem of the judiciary. To conservatives in the audience he must have sounded radical, but in his own judgment he made moderate suggestions almost requiring an apology. Walsh was deeply disturbed by the criticism of American institutions, including the courts, but even more disturbed by the fact that they deserved much of it. Not just socialists, he noted, but able students and scholarly thinkers had written of the "base uses" to which great institutions had been put. This was "the legitimate fruit . . . of a policy of hidebound conservatism." Walsh referred to the economic interpretation of the Constitution, the argument that the Constitution of 1787 had been written in the interest of property-holding classes and to the idea that property interests in America had, generally speaking, enjoyed unprecedented protection. In the latter connection, bitter attacks had been made repeatedly on the federal courts.

He defended the courts as an institution, and argued in behalf of judicial review, or "judicial legislation," as some called it. He warned against an impulse to "destroy the machinery because the operators are faulty." With a "progressive democrat" in the White House they would have their chance for the "infusion of new blood in the federal judiciary," and this would be cause for "universal rejoicing."

Giving a further example of his "conservative view," Walsh noted an instance in which he could not agree with that "eminent Democrat," William J. Bryan. The great Nebraskan and others were upset by the trust situation and by rulings of the Supreme Court which seemed to emasculate the Sherman antitrust law. Walsh, however, urged a wait-and-see attitude with reference to the "rule of reason." If it played into the hands of the trusts, as asserted, there would be time enough (he believed) to agitate for changes in the law. He added: "The idea that great public wrongs ought to be tolerated because to arrest them would disturb business, has always been a most revolting one to me." But in this matter they could afford to wait a while. Speaking more generally, he said: "The abuses of a generation are not all to be uprooted in a day, nor in the course of one administration. . . . Let us not try to do it all or promise to do it all at once."[5]

Walsh did not sound moderate in another address of this same period. Directly or by implication he discussed the Amalgamated Copper Company, its economic allies, its "army of spoliation," its notorious activities, and the determination of Montanans to rid themselves of such corporate intrusion into their political affairs.[6]

As people were awakening and bestirring themselves in various states, Montanans were aware of the "malign" influences at work in the last legislature in Helena—a workman's compensation act, the recall, and other measures. Already the railroads of the state had begun to learn their lesson and had virtually left the field of politics. But the Amalgamated had not. Giving emphasis to his message in the Walla Walla address, Walsh closed with these words of warning: "If the copper corporation does not profit by their example [the railroads'] there is a day of reckoning."[7]

The boldness of Walsh's attack was an indication of his confidence. Yet he knew the resourcefulness of those who opposed his senatorial candidacy. Thus there was the necessity of controlling, if possible, the county Democratic committees, the Democratic state central committee, and the party conventions that would meet during the spring and summer. In a moment of exhilaration Walsh bubbled that Tom Stout, his friend, supporter, and a "good old scout," wanted to go as a delegate to the national convention in Baltimore; when the time came, however, Walsh could not control the selection of delegates, and Stout did not go to Baltimore.[8]

On March 17, Walsh gave a political report to his wife, commenting, "I think we boosted the game a little last night." He had attended a St. Patrick's Day banquet in Butte at which he was among the principal speakers. His effort was well received, and he had a chance to talk with Judge "Jere" Lynch (who served as toastmaster), Swede Murphy, Tin-plate Bill Brennan, and others. They thought the sentiment in Silver Bow County was for him, and that it would be difficult to select any delegation that would not support him. He heard that some Republicans of the progressive faction had decided to resuscitate a newspaper called *The Taxpayer* for the "special purpose of whacking the Amalgamated."[9]

The fight was underway for control of the party machinery in Montana. In this period occurred the beginning of difficulties between Walsh and Senator Myers, for the latter, although having the reputation of being an independent man, did not appreciate the serious divisions in the party.[10]

There was one tactical maneuver to which Walsh was vulnerable. On a statewide basis he was the acknowledged Democratic leader, but if he could be beaten in his home county his position would be undermined. Concerted efforts were made—though finally unsuccessful—to keep Walsh and C. B. Nolan off the Lewis and Clark delegation to attend the state Democratic convention. It met in Butte, and when the Helena group arrived they found that (according to Walsh) everything had been "framed up" for Purcell to become the temporary chairman. This had been accomplished by holding an early meeting of the state committee, while seven counties were still unrepresented. As a vote disclosed, Harry Gallwey and others of the Amalgamated "string" were principally backing Purcell. The plan succeeded: Purcell became temporary chairman. Walsh concluded later that Dick's "elevation" had undone him, for he made a speech that was a "whirlwind" and a failure that disillusioned many possible supporters.[11]

This convention, meeting late in May, had the principal task of choosing delegates to the national nominating convention in Baltimore. Governor Norris, Senator Myers, and Walsh were chosen by acclamation. Walsh took satisfaction in the fact that he had received applause "decidedly more vociferous" than the others. Purcell's behavior was atrocious, many thought, and Walsh believed he had been "effectually" retired from the race.[12]

Once again, Walsh was too optimistic. He went to Baltimore, served on the party's platform committee (on a subcommittee of the platform subcommittee) and further enhanced his stature as a national Democratic leader. But he gained little or nothing in Lewis and Clark County, Montana. Returning to Helena and his law practice, he soon found himself in a "nerve-wracking" situation.[13]

A fight was on for control of the county convention and the selection of delegates who would attend the all-important state nominating convention in late August. Was it possible that—having come so far—he could still be beaten by a supposed friend, in league with other supposed friends and the disreputable elements of the party, and by active opposition of the Amalgamated? Walsh virtually had to abandon his law practice for a week or two while making the rounds, "begging people" to come to the primaries. He could not even go to Lake McDonald for a rest, as his wife urged. What he most feared was that the Butte interests would send over "a wad of money" to buy up some votes, but he did not quite believe they would do this. He was right. The Walsh men prevailed, and the last major threat to his candidacy had ended.[14]

At the state convention in Great Falls the Helena man had virtually no opposition, and on August 29 he was awarded the party's nomination by acclamation. On the whole, progressivism was reflected in the party slate and platform.[15]

Meanwhile, the GOP opposition was divided. The Progressive party of Montana had been formed in July, and two months later it proceeded to nominate almost a full slate of candidates, while the Republican party nominated its own candidates. Thus the Republicans were split down the middle. Henry C. Smith received the Republican nomination, and the incumbent Senator "Joe" Dixon got the Progressives' endorsement. Frank Edwards ran as the Progressive candidate for governor.[16]

What was happening in Montana was similar to the unfolding of events nationally as Theodore Roosevelt failed to receive the Republican nomination but ran against Taft on a third party ticket, while Woodrow Wilson captured the Democratic nomination. In the senatorial race Dixon suffered several handicaps. He was out of Montana while serving as Roosevelt's national manager, and he had antagonized Montana's copper interests.

The Progressive party of Montana was organized as an out-and-out anti-Amalgamated aggregation. Their slogan stood out boldly on the stationery of the state committee: "Put the Amalgamated out of Montana Politics." Included in the platform was a plank calling for heavier taxation on the mines and railroads of the state, a topic of long and bitter contention and one which, by itself, would guarantee the relentless opposition of the "interests" to Progressive candidates.[17]

There was a chance that such a party would appeal to many Democrats, but Walsh's assessment proved correct. By nominating Walsh and assuming a generally progressive stance, the Montana Democrats closed their ranks and made victory almost inevitable.[18]

The campaign of 1912 brought few surprises. Toward the end of September Walsh delivered a major address at Billings in which he discussed both state and national issues. The Republican party, he charged, was still "ruled" by the special interests of the past, while the Democrats had purged their ranks and in the recent Baltimore convention had "named as their chieftain a man of resplendent talents and lofty character, the great governor of New Jersey, Woodrow Wilson." Walsh criticized the convention system as susceptible to the control of "privilege seeking interests," and he talked of the merits of the alternative primary system. The U.S. Senate, he continued, had become a "last refuge of predatory wealth," although lately it was divided into reactionary and progressive factions. He allied himself with the progressives on some great questions of the day: the direct election of senators, the income tax, corrupt practices legislation, physical evaluation of railroad properties, the expulsion of William Lorimer, and the admission of Arizona to statehood.[19]

All aspects of the campaign went well, and by mid-October Walsh predicted privately that he would achieve a plurality in every county of the state. Even so, he continued with a fairly vigorous effort. He called his wife home from Lake McDonald to assist in speech-writing and letter-writing and in various tasks which necessitated her working closely with members of the state Democratic committee. Once he wrote from Havre in the north-central part of the state that his telegrams might ask her to do "impossibilities" but did not require her to. His daughter also arrived to give assistance.[20]

Walsh's usual attention to detail was apparent, and he received notable assistance from the Democratic National Committee. For "special use" in his campaign, the committee sent $2,000 to Montana, while arrangements were also made to bring in prominent speakers such as Senator Francis G. Newlands of Nevada. In the general effort, various letters had to be prepared and mailed, including one to the railroad men of the state, one to University of Wisconsin alumni, one to the voters of Lewis and Clark County, and a weekly letter for the Democratic newspapers.[21]

From scattered points around the state, Walsh sent home the news of his meetings, of the hospitality of friends and activities of the opposition, along with numerous suggestions for the Helena workers and drafts of letters that might be used. Among the prosaic needs of a man on the campaign trail was clean laundry, to which his wife gave some attention. As opportunities arose, he asked her to come and join him, for example, at Fort Benton about the 20th of October, where he expected they would meet family friends. At one point, sending a letter about himself to be used with the voters in Lewis and Clark County, he commented: "Possibly it transcends what modesty would permit. Please go over it with Nolan, before you put it out."[22]

Finally it was over. Walsh had defeated Dixon by 28,421 votes to 22,161 with Henry Smith receiving 18,450. Tom Stout and John M. Evans won seats in Congress, Samuel V. Stewart was elected governor, and Democrats carried all of the statewide races. Especially satisfying to Walsh was the fact that he led the Democratic ticket, receiving nearly 500 more votes than Woodrow Wilson and 3,000 more than Samuel Stewart. Tom and Ellen Walsh were elated at the outcome, and she sent off a letter to her sister, Mary, in Weiser, Idaho: "there is no doubt of Toms election to the United States senate. His plurality will probably reach ten thousand."[23]

The letters of congratulation poured in—from friends and supporters like Burton K. Wheeler and from old friends of the days in Wisconsin and Dakota. There could be nothing sweeter for a man who had dreamed of success, and worked hard to achieve it.[24]

On the local level Walsh was involved at once in what could be considered patronage politics, but not according to his interpretation. He was determined that his supporters, the independent Democrats of 1911–12, should receive federal appointments as they became available. Thus, he tried to express to Wheeler his gratitude for the support that the Butte attorney had given him and his regret that Wheeler and others of "the boys" had not been reelected to the legislature of 1913. He felt the deepest sense of obligation to those who had dared to stay with him in spite of their residence in centers of Amalgamated strength.[25]

Walsh was engaged, meanwhile, in quietly making preparations for his career in Washington. He was lucky enough to inherit Senator Dixon's executive secretary, Miles Taylor, and through him was able to move toward the acquisition of senatorial offices and personal quarters as well. For some years he had had a secretary in his law office named Imogene Howell, and he decided to take her along as a stenographer to join the senatorial office force. From Taylor he soon learned that he would be permitted to keep Senator Dixon's space in the Senate Office Building (Dixon had made the request), and that these were choice, "outside rooms."[26]

Before leaving Helena, T. J. Walsh and his family had their occasions of triumph. On January 14, 1913, the Legislative Assembly took up the senatorial question and ratified the popular decision of November 1912.[27]

In mid-January, in a joint session, Walsh was declared duly elected. He then addressed the legislators in a speech worthy of the occasion. He said he hoped to make up for any deficiencies of talent by "assiduity in labor which 25 years of active practice as a lawyer has made a fixed habit of my life." He added that party affiliation, in his judgment, meant little to Montanans with reference to great questions such as "care of the Indians," preservation and utilization of forests, and administration of the land laws generally. He would be guided by his judgment and his conscience, rather than membership in the Democratic party. He harbored no ambition beyond that of serving with fidelity for the term to which he had been elected.[28]

That evening T. J. and Ellen Walsh were at home to friends at 343 Clark Street. Thus, at the foot of Mt. Helena, in the home of which they were so proud, the Walshes brought to a close their proudest day, receiving guests, serving refreshments, and accepting congratulations and best wishes.

Several weeks later over one hundred guests attended a dinner in Walsh's honor at the Montana Club in downtown Helena. If one may believe the menu, this was a feast, including "Caviar, Imperial Romanoff," "Broiled Montana Squab, Sur Le Canape," and "Cognac, 1875."

When Walsh rose to speak, he said that he was proud of the confidence manifested in him. He assured his audience that the "greater part" of his time in Washington would be given to "problems of government of special interest to the west." He spoke also of the Progressive movement in the United States, and he asserted that "the supremacy of the new order" was complete in the U.S. Senate as shown, for example, by the junking of the seniority system in committee assignments.[29]

One can imagine the mixed emotions with which friends, rivals, and sometime enemies listened to these remarks while trying to envision this slender, energetic man making his next address on the Senate floor. He spoke well, and none could doubt his ability, but questions undoubtedly remained as to how he would perform in the "greatest forum of them all."

In a few days T. J. Walsh was in Washington, trying to translate his words and promises into action. If devotion to duty could bring success, he would achieve it.

9

The Tariff Fight of 1913

As Walsh entered the Senate, his career was interrelated with that of the newly elected president and Democratic leader Woodrow Wilson, whose eight years in office were momentous ones for the American people. Governor Wilson of New Jersey assumed his new national responsibilities with ideas about executive leadership and party discipline. He had campaigned in 1912 on the basis of a "New Freedom" for Americans, a program of economic reform and moral rejuvenation, which he wasted little time in pressing upon his congressional leaders. To achieve what he wanted would require political leadership of a high order. He must rally Democrats from South, North, and West, inspiring and cajoling them as necessary. The first item on his agenda was tariff reform.

The Democratic platform of 1912, which Walsh had helped to write as a member of the subcommittee of eleven at Baltimore, contained a long section attacking the "high Republican tariff" and chastising the opposition for failing to accomplish needed reductions. According to the Democrats, there was no power under the Constitution to levy tariff duties for any purpose whatever, except the collection of revenues. Over the years, Republican protectionism had made "the rich richer and the poor poorer," had raised the price of commodities without commensurate benefits, and had contributed to the growth of trusts. As would be expected in a political platform, the Democrats did not say what the new level of tariff duties should be.[1]

Wilson, however, announced to party leaders that drastic reductions must be effected. He called for the elimination of duties on wool, leather, sugar, and food. Many Democrats in Congress were placed in an embarrassing situation, especially if they happened to represent "wool states" or "sugar states."

The wishes of constituents and the campaign promises made in 1912, or earlier, could not be taken lightly.[2]

Finding himself in such a predicament, T. J. Walsh acquitted himself ably and with such political finesse that he soon wrote to a friend: "The position I occupy gives me a rather unique importance so early in my [Senate] career." A little later he said: "It will be gratifying to you to know that the fight I made has earned for me the esteem of my colleagues." It was true that within a few months of his arrival in Washington the junior senator from Montana had established himself as a figure to be reckoned with.[3]

Walsh and his family came to the capital toward the end of February and moved into their rooms in the Cochran Hotel, a rather "ancient affair" recommended for its location and the high quality of its "table." That they had been misled is suggested by Mrs. Walsh's early departure, with her daughter, for an extended stay in California and Montana, while Walsh stated that the Cochran's food palled on him until it became "appalling."[4]

A circle in which Walsh moved comprised his coreligionists, including notables such as Senator James A. O'Gorman of New York, Senator Joseph E. Ransdell of Louisiana, Monsignor William T. Russell, Rector of St. Patrick's Church in Washington, and James Cardinal Gibbons of Baltimore. In early May he had dinner with a group at Mons. Russell's. He also addressed the law school graduates at Georgetown University and went to dinner at the Metropolitan Club with "the entire faculty comprising many of the leading lawyers and judges."[5]

Soon after arriving in the capital, Walsh and his family became acquainted with Secretary of the Interior Franklin Lane and his family. Walsh valued this friendship highly, and almost immediately began working with the secretary to help pass bills relating to the public lands.

Of all the issues none was so important in 1913 as tariff reform. On April 7, in response to the president's call, a special session of the Sixty-third Congress convened. Along with other freshman members, Walsh assumed his seat, and the following day in a joint session of Congress he listened to Wilson's speech calling for tariff revision. Meanwhile, the president had been in conference with members of the House Ways and Means Committee and gained their acceptance of free sugar and free wool. After two weeks of debate in the House, that body passed the Underwood bill, providing for reductions on an average of 10 percent and placing many items on the free list. It also included an income tax and a graduated surtax on income above $20,000 annually. This was a Democratic measure and a party triumph, as virtually all

Democrats were held in line in the final vote. Five defections (four from the sugar state of Louisiana) were offset by the affirmative vote of four Progressives, two Republicans, and an independent. The focus now shifted to the Senate.[6]

Even before the convening of Congress, Walsh was defining his course. The sugar question was of importance to Montana because of sugar beet farming in the irrigated valleys and the establishment of a sugar factory at Billings. A number of correspondents made known their concern that tariff protection on sugar should not be abandoned. In late January, Walsh said he would be "extremely cautious" not to do anything that would destroy this important industry but, at the same time, he would have to insist that any tariff asked for was "absolutely essential." He added that he had no intention to permit "sugar interests to write their own schedule in order to swell fortunes already vast."[7]

On the subject of wool, the junior senator from Montana was in a more sensitive position. He was himself involved, as a stock holder and a director, in three companies that operated sheep ranches, with a total investment of $35,000. Walsh observed at one point that critics had been "uncharitable enough" to refer to his owning some sheep.[8]

Immediately after the president began to insist on free sugar and free wool (April 1), Walsh helped to arrange a conference between the leader in the White House and some western Democratic senators. To a constituent he said that the sugar controversy at this time was one between the sugar refiners (and importers) of the East, who wanted free sugar, and sugar factory interests of the South and West who favored retention of the existing duty. The best policy, he argued, was a duty "about midway between the demands of these conflicting interests." He wrote to the president explaining how farming and sugar production were interrelated: "you are aware that the pulp, being the refuse of the beets in the process of manufacture, is fed to cattle."[9]

Walsh's overall argument against "free trade" was a strong one stated time and again to constituents, as well as to the Democratic caucus in the Senate and to the Senate Finance Committee. Presumably, much of this message got through to the president. For two reasons, the Montanan asserted, he was obligated to do all in his power to seek modifications in the Underwood bill. First, the House of Representatives had dealt "most unfairly" with the products of his state. To one correspondent he wrote: "Can you see any just reason why our people should be compelled to pay protective duties on everything that they buy, while practically everything they produce—wool, sugar, meats and lumber—go on the free list?"[10]

"If the President thinks that a general reduction, averaging say 25 percent, ought to be made, I shall cheerfully join with him; . . . I would not object to making a reduction of 75 percent. All I complain about is that the present duty leaves the manufacturers of woolen goods with a very substantial part of the advantages they now enjoy and takes away from the producer of wool and sugar *all* that they enjoy." He referred back to the elections of 1910 and 1912 in Montana and to Democratic campaign promises: "we assured the people upon what seemed the plain promises of the Denver platform [of 1908], that these commodities would continue to bear a revenue duty."

To offset the strength of the copper interests, it had been necessary to go into eastern counties of the state, where wool and sugar were important, and appeal for the Republican vote. These voters had been led to believe that the tariff would not be entirely eliminated. He was "simply trying to be honest," Walsh said. "I am doing the best I can to make good the promises that we all held out in the two campaigns mentioned."[11]

Walsh's position would have been strengthened if he could have prevailed upon his colleague, Senator Myers, to give assistance. He could not. It was an awkward and embarrassing situation, as Myers stood firmly with the administration, tending to undercut what Walsh was saying. To a Montana legislator Walsh wrote: "It very naturally is a most embarrassing condition, . . . to be met with the suggestion everywhere that my colleague openly announces himself as in favor of free wool and free sugar."[12]

The Democratic margin in the Senate was six votes. Acting swiftly to hold the party lines, President Wilson went to Capitol Hill on April 9 for a long conference with Democratic senators. In addition, he skillfully used his personal influence with individual members of the upper house.

Wilson's biographer, Arthur S. Link, has concluded that Walsh was largely bluffing in the position he assumed on wool and sugar. But Walsh was deadly serious about the matter and fighting for any concessions he could get, while probably intending all along to stay with his party in the final vote on the Senate floor. In mid-April he wrote to his friend Lewis Penwell, with whom he was associated in the sheep companies mentioned, earnestly soliciting Penwell's advice. At the same time, he gave an indication of his own trend of thought: "Of course, if I feel compelled to vote against the bill and thus perpetuate the Payne-Aldrich measure, I shall be in a most embarrassing situation before my party associates in the Senate and before the country, for that matter, not to speak of the White House."[13]

From the last week of April through the month of June, Walsh worked energetically on tariff problems. Partly he was attempting to resolve the disputes already mentioned, but he was also drawn into a new and crucial aspect of the Senate's work. As a member of a subcommittee of the Judiciary Committee—the famous lobby investigating group—he had a role of importance. In this capacity he was squarely in support of the Wilson administration.

Meanwhile, in appearances before the Finance Committee, which was shaping the Senate's tariff measure, he enhanced his reputation for ability and integrity. Furnifold Simmons of North Carolina was the chairman, and John Sharp Williams was another member with whom Walsh developed cordial relations. In early May Walsh claimed that he and other westerners had virtually "captured" the committee, but they still had to convince the president as to a duty on wool and sugar. In talks with him the results were "indifferent," and the outlook was not bright.

A few days later Walsh addressed the Finance Committee "with all the earnestness" he "could command," speaking for about an hour. It was gratifying to hear a report from the Senate cloakroom and pass it on to his wife: "O'Gorman told me that John Sharp Williams was telling in the cloakrooms of my argument before the committee and asserted that I was a coming man, 'the most intellectual member on the democratic side, bar none.'"[14]

Meanwhile, Walsh spoke on the Senate floor, acquitting himself well. He reported this experience: "I was congratulated by [John W.] Kern, [Thomas S.] Martin and many others on our side and by some from the opposition as well. La Follette came right over and said he was proud of me as a Wisconsin product and even old [Jacob H.] Gallinger passing by shortly after I got through reached out both of his hands to me." Walsh's friend O'Gorman added the remark: "Now that you have tried the water you may go in swimming any time."[15]

A new phase of the struggle soon developed in which the president seized the initiative, while Walsh with others was forced "into line." Alarmed by threats to the tariff measure and angered by the pressure of lobbyists in Washington, Wilson issued an appeal to the people, denouncing the tariff lobby. Soon thereafter, the Senate Judiciary Committee began its inquiry which tended to show that the president had been correct in his charges of an "insidious" lobby at work. Ironically, Walsh was one of those who conducted the inquiry, helping to destroy any remaining hope for avoiding free wool and free sugar.[16]

Labors of the subcommittee began on June 2, with Lee Overman of North Carolina as chairman and James A. Reed of Missouri as another Democrat. The two Republicans were Albert Cummins of Iowa and Knute Nelson of Minnesota. Meeting in a large hearing room of the Senate Office Building, the lobby committee conducted what one newspaper described as "the most extraordinary" investigation in the history of Congress. In its initial phase, all 96 senators were scheduled to come before the committee, take an oath, and testify as to their property holdings or business interests primarily as related to the tariff. The schedule was a rigorous one for the committee, attempting to finish the probe in one week.

The senators testified in alphabetical order, and Walsh's turn came in a night session at the end of the first week. His statement revealed that he had several small investments, including $35,000 in sheep ranches in Montana, with some cattle as well; also 1/3 ownership of 1,440 acres of Montana timberland; an interest in a gold mine where mining had been discontinued; and a plan to help establish a Portland cement plant.

The next weeks of investigation were drastically different from the first, as the committee turned its attention to the sugar lobby, the wool lobby, and to sensational charges relating to the National Association of Manufacturers. Observers in the capital had their first look at Thomas J. Walsh as an investigator. He referred in this connection to a "ridiculous kind of cartoon" of their committee, which was placed on display opposite the Willard Hotel: "I'm doing the examining. My mustache floats luxuriantly in the breeze. I'm pointing an accusing [?] finger at the 'subject' whose so scared his hair stands on end and great drops of perspiration are falling from him."[17]

In much of this interrogation of witnesses and examination of evidence, Walsh was associated with "Jim" Reed of Missouri. Gradually, Walsh was being converted by the facts that accumulated. The evidence was fortuitous, for it afforded justification for his making a change that he almost was compelled to make anyway. Using language to which the president might have objected, he said: "Wilson is a lucky dog." The disclosures had justified "the substance of every stricture he made." About a week later he wrote that Wilson had "bagged no end of game," and that it "was harder now to support even a moderate duty on sugar."[18]

Walsh noted later that his committee was engaged in a rivalry with the House of Representatives, which was trying to "capture" their star witness. He continued: "The thing gathers volume as it goes. We are making history daily. I regret that its work will deny me an opportunity to attend the tariff debates, . . . but I am sure there is no way in which I can render equal service to the country as by aiding in exposing the 'invisible government' which it is laying bare."[19]

The junior senator from Montana was sensitive about the role he had played and was anxious that his sincerity should not be impugned. He also had hopes that minor concessions could be obtained from the party majority, especially with reference to the *time* when wool and sugar would go on the free list. After making his major argument he wrote to his wife: "I got an abundance of compliments but no votes in consequence of my speech to the caucus. I have about made up my mind to call the fight ended so far as I am concerned."

Some days later the Finance Committee moved, in caucus, to bind all Democrats to its action and to prevent any amendments to the tariff bill. The two Montanans clashed again. According to Walsh, he "rather startled the meeting" in a short denunciation of the resolution, telling them "plainly that the forcing of the resolution would in view of the fight I had made, be an expression of doubt of my sincerity in declaring that I should support the bill on the floor." Myers, on the other hand, spoke in favor of the committee's resolution. To Walsh, this meant that his colleague was willing for him to be "stigmatized." When O'Gorman and several other "strong men" took Walsh's side of the argument, the resolution was so modified as to make it generally acceptable.

In the same session the matter of dating the wool schedule (that is, to delay the reductions decided upon) came up for discussion, and Walsh described how he "fought the thing out for an hour and won, holding the caucus in session until after 7 P.M.." Myers could have helped in this matter, but when Walsh looked around he had "fled."[20]

Though annoyed by the differences with his Montana colleague, Walsh was elated at the outcome generally of his caucus fight and deeply gratified by the "spirit that prevailed" among party leaders, so far as his actions were concerned. Senators Claude Swanson and Thomas S. Martin of Virginia had been considerate, and John Sharp Williams, who disagreed with him on the dating of the wool schedule, had commented generously: "We have done so many things the senator from Montana did not want us to do, he has made such a valiant fight and so chivalrously accepted the result in every instance that I'm going to vote with him on this although I think he's wrong."[21]

There were other reasons to congratulate himself. Through hard work, and by his good relations with Senator Simmons of the Finance Committee and others, Walsh succeeded in making changes of some importance in the tariff bill. He was particularly concerned to reduce the duty on products that Montanans would have to buy, since they would benefit so little from the tariff on products they sold. For example, he sought and obtained a reduction of more than 50 percent on the jute bags in which wool and grain were sacked. As Walsh pointed out to John Sharp Williams of the Finance Committee, the cost of these sacks was a matter of real expense. He also believed that the committee would wish to disarm the charge of a sectional discrimination—making the bagging for cotton duty-free, while jute bagging used in the western states would bear a heavy duty.[22]

On Saturday, August 2, the junior senator from Montana delivered an address that ran for several hours, with sporadic interruptions by Asle Gronna of North Dakota, Coe I. Crawford and Thomas Sterling of South Dakota, Joseph Bristow of Kansas, Reed Smoot and George Sutherland of Utah, and others. Secretary of State William J. Bryan was among those who congratulated Walsh on his speech. Several features of the address were indicative of Walsh's status in the "greatest forum on earth." First, he was mastering the arts of senatorial courtesy and parliamentary rhetoric, handling himself with dignity and sophistication. (Actually, in private, he noted that he had got into a "state of trepidation" about possible violation of the proprieties but that his fears proved groundless.) Second, he had done his homework, exhibiting an intimate knowledge of most subjects discussed. Some of this information he had acquired by personal experience in Montana, or more recently in the lobby investigation. He had also used the research facilities available to a knowledgeable senator. Finally, he showed his old capacity to handle ideas and maintain a forceful argument, while avoiding bombast and evincing a respect for the opinions of others.[23]

Walsh was arguing, in effect, that new land, new scientific techniques, and diverse economic factors were more important than losses that might be suffered because of the tariff. Moreover, the present bill was a general revision in which there would be various benefits for farmers and others in the form of lower prices. Some senators questioned Walsh, or baited him, with reference to his recent stand on sugar and wool. To John R. Thornton of Louisiana he replied: "I have made no argument today in favor of either free wool or free sugar. I have simply undertaken to show that neither will destroy those industries so far as my own State is concerned." Rather surprisingly, Walsh argued that the importance of the wool industry had been exaggerated and that other products of equal significance should receive greater attention. In Montana, for example, the flax crop was almost as valuable as wool; and in Ohio, known as a "wool state," poultry had a value five times greater than the wool clip. The final portion of his address was devoted to the Sugar Trust. With abundant documentation, the Montanan showed the notorious lobbying activities of sugar companies over the past twenty years, and he predicted that their present complaints and lamentations could be safely ignored.

When Walsh had taken his seat, William J. Stone of Missouri praised him for a "magnificent address." In a letter to his wife Walsh reported other reactions, along with equally vivid allusions to the hot weather in Washington: "Tom [Stout] and I are leaving in a few minutes to spend the day at Chesapeake Beach, and I'm writing to tell you that I launched my maiden speech yesterday with a measure of success reasonably satisfactory, considering that I had to work it up nights in the terrific weather we have been having. Hot? Hotter! Hottest!; and then some. . . . I am enclosing a note sent me by the Vice President. [Charles S.] Thomas [of Colorado] complimented me highly and in a way that I thought meant that in my line he felt he was not my equal."[24]

Like many senators in this final period before the vote, Walsh made a contribution as the opportunity arose, but primarily he was marking time, seeking relief from the heat, and watching the occasional controversies that erupted. Secretary Lane was out of town, so work on public land matters was delayed. The currency bill had not yet come over from the House of Representatives, and other business was less urgent than before.

One Sunday morning Walsh started his day by rising at nine o'clock, reading his newspapers, and going to church at eleven. There he was "detained" only forty minutes, so he was back in his sweltering apartment before noon, where, stripping to his underclothes, he read the latest installment of "How I found the South Pole" by Roald Amundsen, before dropping off to sleep again.

In these same weeks Walsh became a member of a senatorial golfing group, led by Senator Henry Hollis of New Hampshire, "a most charming fellow," who was also "the most polished senatorial performer." They gaily planned a game for Wednesday afternoon, September 10, following the Senate vote on the tariff, and decided to proceed from the golf course to a "stag dinner" at Key Pittman's. The latter, a senator from Nevada, and a half dozen senators from the so-called Cherokee Strip, were to be the participants. About this time, John Sharp Williams confided to Walsh that he was proposing to form a mystic society of six senators, including Pittman, Hollis, Walsh, and several others.

Democrats were feeling good, and they had reason to feel even better after the showdown votes on the tariff in late August and early September. There were some final, hectic debates and late caucuses, as the Senate moved to pass a tariff bill which, for the first time in memory, actually improved upon the House version. Walsh voted with administration forces as they beat down amendments or effected compromises. One of these compromises was an increase in the maximum income tax rate forced by Robert M. La Follette and others of both parties.[25]

On September 9 Walsh was among the 44 Democrats and 2 Republicans (La Follette and Poindexter) who voted for the tariff bill, while only the sugar Democrats from Louisiana bolted the Democratic party. The bill now went to conference. A final bit of good news reached the Montanan via Furnifold Simmons concerning action in the conference committee. As Walsh reported it: "Quite a fight was made before the conferrees to make the free wool provision effective at once but Simmons [opposed] and he says the President stood by me and the Senate amendment stays. I should have been embarrassed and disappointed had it gone out." Generally the Senate prevailed in conference, and on October 3, 1913, the Underwood-Simmons bill became law.[26]

At the end of this first session of the Sixty-third Congress, the junior senator from Montana had gained an enviable position. He was a member of the Senate "club," in good standing both legislatively and socially. He had proven himself a fighter, an intellectual force, and a man of principle who also possessed a keen sense of the political realities. His differences with the president had not resulted, as they might have, in his alienation from the White House. Rather, he had won Wilson's attention and respect. Even in Montana, where he could be regarded most critically, Walsh was considered to have made himself a success, and some thought him on his way to becoming the greatest senator in the history of the state. The months ahead, however, would present Walsh with exceedingly difficult decisions.[27]

The "New Freedom" in Montana: Hopes and Illusions

Some months after Walsh went to Washington he made a statement on the Senate floor that helped to show his aspirations toward democracy in state and national affairs. He referred to the Morgan-Guggenheim combination in Alaska and the extent of its influence in the territory, then went on to say: "We have been making a somewhat heroic struggle in the State of Montana to free our political life from the influence of a gigantic financial organization which, like that which faces us at every turn in Alaska, has its center in the city of New York." He was referring to the Amalgamated Copper Company, with its national headquarters at 26 Broadway, New York City, and its state offices in Butte, Montana. This comment by the new junior senator from Montana was not an idle one. Walsh's correspondence, like that of Joseph M. Dixon and other Montana leaders, reveals a concern that was almost morbid over the political manipulations of "the Company" and a determination on the part of liberal-minded people to make their state a better place in which to live. In some respects this was a nonpartisan movement. To the extent that party members clung to their old organizations and shibboleths of the past they lessened the chances of a "New Freedom" for the people of Montana.[1]

In a remarkable letter to the new attorney general, James C. McReynolds, Walsh explained the basic problem he and others had faced in his home state. He described "a warfare . . . for political independence" being waged against the Amalgamated Copper Company, "which has put up and pulled down governors, senators and congressmen, bossed our legislature and controlled our political conventions." He said the difficulty of what Montanans were trying to do could be understood better if it were known that "the subsidiary and allied companies referred to generally as the 'Amalgamated Interests' have in their employ at least twenty thousand men—a number equivalent to one-fourth of all the voters of our state."[2]

One of Walsh's purposes in writing at this time was to help secure the appointment of men who were not controlled by the Company. While the fight went on in Montana, it must be waged in Washington as well, even though the opposition was antagonized.

Walsh was one of a host in Montana who were determined at this time to carry forward the progressive movement. Voters of the state in 1912 gave their approval to several measures placed on the ballot through the initiative process, including a corrupt practices act, a direct primary system for nominating party candidates, and a tightening of the method for direct election of senators. Contributing to the success of this effort was the People's Power League. Headed by the journalist Miles Romney of Hamilton, it was supported by labor leaders, liberal lawyers, and other reformers of both parties. A similar organization was the Direct Legislation League, in which progressive Republicans were especially prominent. Many reformers wanted to raise the taxes on mining corporations and also favored a workmen's compensation plan which would extend help to the large number of employees injured in industrial accidents. Aiming toward farmer-labor cooperation, some also called for state loans to the farmers. Still another objective was the consolidation of the state's institutions of higher learning in order to have a single strong university less subject to political influences.[3]

Broadly based reform movements were more or less interrelated and seemed to help the general cause. There was, for example, the woman's suffrage movement dating back to the nineteenth century. Around 1910 it gained strength and found a new leader whose name would soon be well known, Jeannette Rankin of Missoula. In 1912 both the Democrats and Republicans agreed to put suffrage planks into their platforms. Other organizations gave support, including the Montana Federation of Women's Clubs (in which Ellen Walsh was active), the Woman's Christian Temperance Union, and the Men's League for Woman's Suffrage. Finally success came to Miss Rankin and her allies in the November election of 1914 when a suffrage amendment gained the necessary votes for passage. Meanwhile, the movement for statewide prohibition was picking up strength, and in 1916 the people of Montana approved this proposal by a large margin. One area of support for moralistic reforms of this type was the agricultural regions, notably in eastern Montana where homesteaders were arriving by the thousands. Farmers also began to organize more effectively in the new Society of Equity and the Nonpartisan League.[4]

The period in which Walsh campaigned for and gained his Senate seat was a boom time for Montana agriculture. He was aware of this and regarded the great influx of settlers in the state's eastern counties as an encouraging development in many respects, one of which was political. Thus he wrote to a friend in Belgrade: "I have been looking hopefully toward the appropriation and settlement of our tillable and productive lands in the expectation that as that condition came the condition of political serfdom from which we are happily emerging would be dead forever." A growing population of independent farmers in eastern Montana would offset the power of the copper interests in mining and smelter towns to the west; or so Walsh hoped.

Walsh delivered several speeches from 1910 to 1912 that showed the overly optimistic cast of his mind regarding economic and political change. One of these was a commencement address in June 1910 to the graduating class of the Montana Agricultural College. Inspirational in spirit, it also demonstrated a solid grasp of economic and scientific information. It emphasized the important developments in modern agriculture that would permit agricultural workers to live exciting lives and render important services to their state and nation. He offered his congratulations to the young people before him and he talked of the "marvels" in scientific agriculture, of the phases of agricultural education including federal aid through the land grant acts, of seed selection, of the great increase in productivity in the wheat fields, of the gasoline engine as it was now "coming into general use for traction purposes about the farm and in hauling products to market," of the growing number of automobiles in farming country. The automobile, he thought, might be an important force in the "'back to the farm' movement."

One of Walsh's more optimistic statements was this: "Thus old mother earth is continually yielding up more and more abundantly of her riches at a constantly diminishing cost. More and more farming becomes a matter of intelligence—less and less of mere physical labor." Thomas Malthus, he said, had been proven wrong. Malthus had believed that in a country like the United States the population might double every twenty-five years, and food supplies would be inadequate. How amazed Malthus would have been if he could be told, "'But the food supply doubles in eleven [years].'"

Walsh referred to the phenomenon of dry farming in areas that ten years before had been considered simply too arid for any such agriculture. The development of "drouth resisting plants" and of dry farming techniques in general had opened up a vast new acreage in eastern Montana and elsewhere. The people of their state, he noted, had witnessed with pleasure and some apprehension this "influx of land hungry settlers." What did it all mean anyway? One explanation was that these people came from the Middle West, where miracles had already been achieved through "the application of science and business methods." They obviously believed in the possibilities of successful farming in the Mountain West and the upbuilding of new communities.

The speaker from Helena went ahead to conclude with a theme of social progress, very much in accord with the spirit of the age and his own credo. In this period of extraordinary achievement and production, they must not forget their fellow men; they must take care that the benefits of science and technology be fairly distributed. "It is yours to guard the treasure that we look to spring from the scientific cultivation of the soil. It will be a blessing very largely as it is equitably shared by those who contribute to its production and conservation." Admitting that the "generality of mankind" lived better than they had in the past, Walsh still expressed his belief that the "'captains of industry,' the 'Napoleons of finance' and the 'kings of the commercial highways'" were absorbing an "inordinate share" of the national wealth.[5]

One hopeful development in Montana around the time of Walsh's election to the Senate was the movement to effect a consolidation of the state's colleges. In the 1890s the state legislature had decided for political reasons to place educational units in several aspiring cities: the university in Missoula, a mining school in Butte, the agricultural college at Bozeman, and a normal school in Dillon. They had rejected an offer from Paris Gibson, founder of the city of Great Falls, to build a single university on land which he would donate. By 1913 many were convinced that a mistake had been made in creating the separate units. Paris Gibson, Senator Walsh, President Craighead of the University in Missoula, and others were pushing for a consolidated university, with its location to be either in Missoula or Bozeman. The reason essentially was their belief that Montana had the resources to build a great consolidated university that could proudly take its place among universities of the land. If, however, these resources were scattered among a number of units, the state had no chance to benefit according to its capabilities.

Walsh gave strong support to this idea. He was influenced by his experience at the University of Wisconsin and his knowledge that a university of the type he had attended could bestow blessings on the people of a state that were simply boundless. Thus he wrote to Paris Gibson: "I recall very well your earnest advocacy of consolidation during the first working session of the state legislature, more than twenty years ago. I felt that you were right then, and I know you are right now." He went on: "The influence, materially speaking, of such an institution reaching to every community and affecting every avocation, is incalculable. If one doubts the benign effect . . . , let him study the recent history of the State of Wisconsin." The separate educational units in

Montana, he said, had made a creditable record, but they simply could not compete with universities that already had been luring so many of Montana's young people. He closed his letter by declaring he would do all that he possibly could to aid in "the establishment of a great university which will be the pride of our people."

The question of consolidation was placed on the ballot for November 1914, under the initiative amendment, but it failed to get the vote required. President Edwin Craighead of the University of Montana explained to Walsh: "You know the forces that were arrayed against us. The Amalgamated, the three great railways and the liquor interests sent out on Wednesday before [the] election to their employees an order to vote against all consolidation measures." In addition, Governor Samuel V. Stewart had tried (for reasons that are unclear) to turn the Democratic campaign "into an anti-consolidation fight." Craighead took some consolation in the fact that 30,000 citizens had voted in favor, and he thanked Walsh warmly for his "courageous" assistance.[6]

One of the most exasperating features of life in Montana was the newspapers. In the "war of the copper kings" around 1900 each combatant discovered the advantages of owning his own newspaper and using it to sway public opinion and pour abuse on the opposition. Marcus Daly ran the *Anaconda Standard* (later the *Montana Standard*), William A. Clark ran the *Butte Miner,* and Augustus Heinze ran the *Reveille.* During its fight with Heinze, the Amalgamated steadily extended its influence into daily newspapers of the major cities. In one way or another as years passed it also brought pressure to bear on the owners or editors of other papers. The situation was constantly changing, and no one could be sure which papers were controlled by, or heavily influenced by, the Company. Some papers fought the "copper-collared" press, at least briefly, or tried to engage in independent journalism. Factual reporting of public affairs was often hard to find in the state of Montana.

In 1908 Jerre Murphy, a crusading progressive formerly associated with Robert M. La Follette, began to publish in Helena the *Montana Lookout.* Soon Walsh wrote to Murphy and complimented him on this new paper. The people of Montana, he said, were a reading people, and they wanted to know the "plain truth about matters of public interest."[7]

One way to solve this problem was to acquire a newspaper or purchase a part interest. Walsh in early 1913 invited other Democrats to join him in this venture, writing as follows to one friend in Virginia City, far down in the southwestern tip of Montana: "The friends of good democratic government in the state have long regarded with the gravest concern the newspaper situation, and deplored the fact that no newspaper in the state tells those things the people are most anxious to know in relation to political and legislative activities." Walsh and his Helena friend Lewis Penwell soon led the way in buying the *Helena Independent,* and the senator-elect expressed his hopes for a "clean democratic newspaper" which would be helpful to him politically and also a stimulus to Helena's and the state's growth. He hoped the paper would be willing to "fearlessly tell what is going on."[8]

Unfortunately, the editor (and part owner) was a crusty character named Will Campbell who succeeded in running the paper as he wanted to. Formerly associated with James J. Hill's railroads, Campbell turned out to be more friendly toward business interests of the state than he was toward Walsh and the Progressives. He was also erratic and unpredictable, particularly when drinking. After several years the senator wrote in exasperation: "It is rather unfortunate to be placed in the position in which I find myself of being held responsible for every fool thing that the *Independent* does or says without being able in any effectual manner to control either." Concern over the newspaper situation continued and particularly over the city dailies including the *Butte Miner,* the *Anaconda Standard,* the *Montana Record-Herald,* the *Helena Independent,* the *Billings Gazette,* and the *Great Falls Tribune.*[9]

Of all Walsh's dreams concerning a new and better future for Montana, the wildest was that a substantial number of the Bull Moose Progressives in the state would join the Democratic party rather than return to the GOP; and, therefore, these bipartisan forces of progressivism would put the Amalgamated leaders back into the business they deserved to be in—the production and sale of copper products. Already the railroads of the Northwest and of Montana had begun to realize that they should not "thrust themselves" into political matters. The Amalgamated interests, it seemed, could be brought to the same realization if only the people of the state fought hard and persistently for the right of self-government.

For Walsh and the "Walsh men" (and women) probably no time was more crucial than that immediately following the election of 1912. Democrats now controlled the Montana legislature, the governorship (in the person of Samuel V. Stewart), both seats in the U.S. Senate, and both seats in the House of Representatives. In the optimism of victory, Montana Democrats looked to the Wilson administration for help, notably in the filling of federal positions. Progressives of the party also hoped for a degree of support in the legislature from the GOP progressives. Walsh made clear his conviction, both through words and deeds, that what had been "won in the past for good government in the state should not be lost for lack of effort to retain it."[10]

The extent to which Walsh remained involved in state politics while going off to Washington to a new career was surprising. These efforts testified to his physical and mental energy, to the depth of his commitment, and probably to the need of Montana Democrats for someone as knowledgeable and inspirational as he had been if they were to have any chance to keep their reform movement alive.

"Walsh men" were scattered around the state, but several in Helena functioned in a special advisory capacity. Foremost among these was C. B. Nolan, Walsh's law partner, and hardly less important was Lewis Penwell, a close friend and business associate. Able and well-informed on the latest developments, they wrote to Walsh often and did not hesitate to tell him frankly when they disagreed with his ideas or decisions. The Senator encouraged this straight talk. E. C. Day, a prominent lawyer and leader of progressive Democrats in the Montana House of Representatives, was another trusted friend. In Fort Benton, north of Great Falls, lived one of Walsh's strongest political supporters, once described in this manner by another loyal supporter: "Every friend of yours in the State recognizes the fact that among your friends Dave Browne stands, like Saul, head and shoulders above us all; and besides that he is the noblest Roman of them all." Browne was a power in Choteau County and also served on the Democratic State Committee, along with other "Walsh guards."[11]

In Butte there were Burton K. Wheeler, Joseph Binnard, and others; in Great Falls from 1913 to 1914 two members of the Montana House, Joseph Kirschwing and Martin Durkan, were prominent among Walsh's friends and correspondents; in western Montana, Miles Romney, editor of the *Western News,* occupied a place of special importance; and far at the other end of the state, in Glendive, was a young lawyer friend and supporter, Daniel L. O'Hern. Walsh wrote to him in rather typical fashion, with information about events in Washington, with words of encouragement, and finally with a request: "Let me hear from you frequently and particularly about how matters are going with you personally. I should like to keep informed likewise about immigration into your section and its general development." In 1913–14 Walsh wrote to countless Montanans of local importance, asking what the conditions were in their town or region, trying to get information and showing his interest. If they were involved in politics of the independent sort, he tried to stir them into greater activity. In various letters he referred openly and bluntly to his struggle with the copper interests. Many correspondents replied in kind.

Even with proven supporters, Walsh had no easy time in trying to control, or to strongly influence, the course of local politics. There was the case, for example, of H. C. Groff, a bank cashier in Victor, Montana, south of Missoula, who had given loyal support in the legislature and was "true as steel" to him. But Miles Romney of the same county opposed Groff for the Democratic nomination in 1914. Walsh believed that Romney was "blinded to the true situation" by local rivalries in Ravalli County. He pleaded, "You ought to rise above any such considerations and I am looking to you with some degree of confidence to do so."

Walsh argued also that to defeat Senator Groff or discourage him from running for another term would play into the hands of Company agents. "You know how cynical those fellows are. They teach the doctrine that it is useless to stand up for the right because neither your efforts nor your sacrifices will be either appreciated or rewarded."

The situation that faced Walsh, as leader of the progressive Democrats in Montana, was a difficult one. Samuel V. Stewart, the new governor, soon revealed his colors as a conservative and a rival to Walsh for public recognition. It seemed to many, in fact, that Stewart was working smoothly with political agents of the Company, if he was not such an agent himself. Born in Ohio and educated in Kansas, Stewart established a law practice in Virginia City, Montana, in 1898. He was active in Democratic politics and chairman of the Democratic State Central Committee before winning his race for governor in 1912. He posed a problem for the progressives of his party.[12]

U.S. Senator Henry L. Myers was another problem. Myers was not especially qualified for his high office and seemed at times to be aware of this fact. He knew also that Walsh had made possible his election in 1911 even though he (Myers) was now the senior senator. At times Myers deferred to Walsh as the nearest thing to a genuine party leader in the home state, and a man of great ability. At other times, perhaps in jealousy, he refused to be cooperative. Myers was apparently an honest, well-meaning person who intended to assert his own views on many subjects but who had no interest whatever in fighting the Amalgamated Copper Company. A mutual friend of the two Montana senators (W. B. Rhoades of Kalispell) helped to explain the differences that developed between them: "Senator Myers has not been thru the bitter fights and does not realize the extreme importance as we see it of keeping the party and appointments free from the baneful influence[s] that have been so long working in Montana and to him a Democrat is merely a Democrat."[13]

Soon after Walsh's election he was involved in fights over patronage that continued sporadically through his first term in the Senate. Essentially he tried to put into federal positions as many of his progressive friends as he reasonably could, and particularly those who had stood by him in the legislative battle of 1911. Those to whom he felt most obligated were the supporters who lived in the Company strongholds of Butte and Great Falls and had stayed with him through everything. He also hoped to reward particular blocs of his supporters in different sections of the state by choosing someone more or less suitable to them. Obviously there were not enough jobs to go around; or, as Walsh phrased the problem, they found it "impossible to meet the deserts of all." There was a great deal of commiserating among Walsh and his advisers, such as Nolan and Penwell.[14]

Of all the appointments Walsh made or was principally responsible for making the most important was that of Burton K. Wheeler as the U.S. attorney for Montana. Wheeler had been one of the Democratic legislators from Butte who boldly supported Walsh in the balloting of 1911. His ability and legal experience helped to qualify him for the duties of U.S. attorney, representing the Department of Justice in Montana. He was a progressive noted for his willingness to criticize the big interests of his state. This appointment was controversial from the start, in 1913, but the major campaign against Wheeler and the attempt to drive him from office did not come until five years later.[15]

Walsh and his friends found that the trends were against them in their attempts to control Montana's Democratic party machinery. The new senator was too far away and too busy with his duties to exercise a predominant influence over day-to-day operations of the party; and such an influence was necessary in order to win a majority, for example, in the Democratic Central Committee meeting of April 1914, or in the state convention when it met in the summer, as well as in various local and state gatherings of the brethren. Guided from the sixth floor of the Hennessey Building in Butte, the Company's politicians worked ceaselessly to maintain control, or to regain it. They benefited from the financial power at their disposal; from the newspapers they controlled; from the many politicians who were inclined to follow instructions. They benefited from rivalries among the elected officials and from the ambitions of these men, including Walsh. They profited from the party system that kept so many reform-minded people working at cross purposes.

Conservatives in the state meanwhile became adept at using progressive innovations, as Joseph Kirschwing and others discovered. Kirschwing entered the Democratic primary in August 1914, seeking renomination for another term in the legislature. After losing in his race he gave an explanation of what had happened. The big interests, he told Walsh, had arranged for a meeting of Republicans in Great Falls where they gave advice on how to beat Kirschwing. All one had to do was enter the Democratic primary and vote for his opponent. In the city of Great Falls alone 450 Republicans had entered the Democratic primary and done their dirty work, as Kirschwing saw it.

Chagrined at these results, Walsh worried over similar developments now taking place elsewhere. Conservatives were using the primary system with great success, as in Broadwater County, where GOP voters helped to renominate the Company-oriented Democrat, C. S. Muffly. The problem was also an opportunity, since progressives could employ the same tactics, but Walsh decided they had apparently made a serious mistake in providing for an open primary system that permitted this type of switchover.[16]

One shocking occurrence was a meeting of the State Central Committee in Helena, during mid-April 1914, in which Walsh and several progressive friends came under attack. Resolutions adopted by the committee also praised Governor Stewart and his services to the state, while slighting those of Senator Walsh. The secretary of the committee boldly sent the senator a copy of the resolutions adopted. Meanwhile, a vivid summary of the meeting came from one of Walsh's friends: "The old gang was out in force and easily in control. There was a deliberate and studied effort to discredit you, cropping out all through the proceedings, though they did not dare to get in the open."[17]

Walsh did not try to conceal his indignation. He sent out letters of protest, including one to Governor Stewart, who had been present at the meeting, and another to John D. Ryan, the president of Amalgamated Copper. Stewart wrote to Walsh first, denying the charges that there had been "any intention of evening up old scores." As far as he was aware, "no one had any old scores to even up." He went on: "To my mind it was sort of a ratification meeting, every man present feeling sort of at peace with the whole world."

Walsh replied in a revealing letter. He said he believed the governor was personally friendly toward him and expressed his appreciation for that. But Walsh let the governor know in no uncertain terms that "the great State Committee" was also needlessly stirring up trouble, and that credit was being given to Stewart for saving the state's reclamation projects when he (Walsh) was the one who had talked with Secretary Lane and the president and performed the principal service in this regard. Walsh continued: "I have a silly sort of a notion that the general cause would be helped along to some degree if every opportunity were seized to set forth to the people of Montana whatever may be done by any of us that ought to attract the favorable notice of the public." Instead, a "base attack" had been made on him while he was 3,000 miles away; this in spite of the fact that some of his critics owed a good deal to him as a result of his labors and sacrifices. Also, the Democratic newspapers in Montana had persisted in a "studied silence" about some of his work, failing to pick up commendatory notices about him in national publications, recently for example in *Harper's Weekly* and the *Baltimore Sun*.

"I am weary," said Walsh, "of this senseless fight against which I have been contending for nearly ten years." There was no need to fight him now. "It would be wiser, as I think, to wait three or four years yet before starting to wage a new warfare on me." If he decided to run, he would not be running for four years, but the Democrats needed to reelect their representatives Tom Stout and John Evans in a matter of months: it was vital to do so in support of the president's policies. And Governor Stewart would come up for reelection in two years.[18]

From his vantage point in Washington, Walsh followed the Montana political developments of 1914 and 1915 with interest and concern but also with a sense of equanimity. He had the luxury of four more years in Washington and the opportunity to take a long view on crucial matters at home. Undoubtedly the public official in Montana who worried him most was Governor Stewart. There was a chance that Stewart would oppose Senator Myers for reelection in 1916 or wait two more years and oppose Walsh. If all went well, however, Stewart would simply seek another term as governor in 1916, while the junior senator would have a good chance to win reelection in 1918.

By the spring of 1915, a change had occurred in Senator Walsh's attitudes. No doubt the reasons are many and complicated; but, stated simply, some of his hopes for democracy in Montana had turned out to be illusions. The task of reform in the Treasure State was more difficult than anticipated. The strength of the Company's forces, the weaknesses of human nature, the obstacles of a two-party system that divided the progressives almost irretrievably—these problems and others were a little more apparent in 1915 than they had been two years earlier.

Meanwhile, Walsh was lucky to be a U.S. senator, as he well knew, and he had much to do to live up to the responsibilities of the assignment. He also had made up his mind that he wanted another term in the Senate, if at all possible. To win that term a working relationship with Governor Stewart was necessary, as was a record of supporting the Amalgamated in its legitimate economic interests—which by 1915, after war had started in Europe, were international as well as national. Walsh's work in the Senate had become his interest of highest priority.

The "New Freedom":
A Lawyer-Senator at Work

Walsh's legal ability brought early recognition in Washington; or, as the senator himself tried to explain, he had held no intention of "cutting any figure" but soon discovered that few senators knew much about the intricate problems of constitutional and international law that came before them. Gradually he was drawn into these matters because of his interest and some facility in the law and his "industry which never lacked exercise." After demonstrating his usefulness he was speedily involved in many matters. Senator Henry F. Ashurst of Arizona observed that Walsh took a "constant interest" in the Senate's proceedings and "had pronounced views on vital subjects."[1]

One source of Senate involvement was the committee assignments, as Walsh managed to get his share of the busiest and most prestigious. Throughout the years 1913–18 he was a member of the committees on Judiciary, Privileges and Elections, Interoceanic Canals, Territories, Mines and Mining (chairman), and Pensions. He became a member of the committees on Indian Affairs, Irrigation and Reclamation, and Private Land Claims by December 1915. He joined the Naval Affairs Committee in March 1917. Eventually he served both on the Public Lands and Foreign Relations Committees.

To Walsh's mind, very little legislative work in the early Wilson years could equal, for sheer pleasure, that of the Judiciary Committee. But the Privileges and Elections Committee also gave him interesting assignments. For example, the Seventeenth Amendment to the Constitution was proclaimed in May 1913, providing for popular election of senators, and it now became necessary to frame a temporary law laying down guidelines for the new senatorial elections. Senator Jacob Gallinger of New Hampshire commented that this was a "very important matter" which was now "engaging the attention of the people all over the country." One reason for interest was the question of how far federal authority extended. Walsh argued for broad congressional power to regulate the procedures for both the nomination and the election of senators, and he took the lead in steering it through the Senate. To his law partner Walsh wrote on February 12, 1914: "I put through the senatorial election bill yesterday after a very stubborn fight." Later he and two other senators met with conferees from the House and worked out necessary agreements. Finally on June 14, 1914, the president approved this measure.

Walsh's interest in the Seventeenth Amendment was that of an ardent reformer, as well as a lawyer and student of the Constitution: he strongly believed in the desirability of popular elections. This fact became apparent in a disputed election case involving Frank P. Glass of Alabama, whom the governor of Alabama appointed to fill out the unexpired term of a senator who had died.

Walsh carefully studied the Glass appointment, along with Alabama laws and relevant documents, and decided that Frank Glass should be denied a seat in the Senate. With that view, he wrote the majority report for the Privileges and Elections Committee. During the final Senate debates, as the sentiment among senators was about equally divided, he asked, "Why were not the people of Alabama given an opportunity to elect their Senator?" He believed the governor had ample time and could have called for an election if he wanted to. However, Senator Joseph Robinson of Arkansas and most of the southern senators supported the Alabama governor and his appointee, as did President Wilson. Robinson offered a substitute motion to seat Frank Glass, which failed by only one vote, 31 to 32. Then the committee's resolution passed by 34 to 30, and the case was settled.

According to an article in the *Baltimore Sun*, Walsh's prowess as a lawyer had led to Glass's defeat. His study of the Alabama code particularly had enabled him to convince the Privileges and Elections Committee of the correctness of his interpretation. The matter then went to the Senate floor and the ultimate victory. No one seemed aware that the subject of disputed elections had been a special interest of Walsh's for some thirty years. He was an expert in these matters and added to his growing reputation as a result. Writing to his law partner, Walsh commented: "I got great credit for my successful conduct of the Glass case, . . . the debate engendered no bitterness, and I think had a tendency to heighten the regard in which I am held by even my democratic associates who, outside of the Privileges and Elections Committee, generally voted against me." To another friend Walsh wrote that he had especially appreciated "the congratulations of Henry Cabot Lodge, who said to me that it was a rare thing for a speech to change a vote in the Senate, but that I had accomplished it and saved the honor of the Senate."[2]

Walsh's membership on the Judiciary Committee was a source of pride to him and contributed to his recognition as a legal and Constitutional authority. Others on the eighteen-member committee in 1913–14 were William E. Borah of Idaho, George Sutherland of Utah, Albert Cummins of Iowa, and Elihu Root of New York. Walsh may have been the single Democrat most able to hold his own in discussions with these Republican colleagues, although several party associates, including James Reed of Missouri, were formidable. Much of the work of the committee, in fact, was essentially nonpartisan as members attended the meetings about once a month and received their assignments. Very likely Walsh's most important duty in 1913 was that of serving on the subcommittee charged with investigating the tariff lobby in Washington.

It would be a mistake to think that Thomas J. Walsh, a freshman senator, ranked with the most powerful leaders of the upper house during the Sixty-third Congress. Rather, he was a "comer," who compensated for the lack of seniority or positions of leadership by his ability and energy, by his wide interests and concerns, and by a willingness to speak out in committee or on the Senate floor. He got involved in nearly all the legislative problems of the New Freedom years, sometimes prominently.[3]

In the summer of 1913, while busy primarily with the tariff and other matters, Walsh began to spend some time on the problem of banking reform which would lead eventually to the Federal Reserve Act of 1914. At certain points he showed his inclination to believe charges of a money trust and of the necessity, therefore, to pass legislation of a type that would reduce the power of concentrated wealth. He wrote to one constituent, for example: "I appreciate how vitally necessary it is to have a banking system to avert the dangers of the control of money and credit by the great financial interests of New York, as revealed by the investigation of the Pujo Committee."

Walsh spoke on the Federal Reserve Act primarily to show the constitutionality of the measure under consideration. His argument seemed necessary because Cummins of Iowa recently had tried to uphold the opposite side of this question. The Montanan based his argument on the reserve power of Congress to create a corporation, bank, or similar establishment. He cited case after case to show the scope and power of this reserved right of Congress. There could be no question, he asserted, that the Federal Reserve Act fell within this sphere of congressional power.

One of Walsh's admirers in Montana commented, with reference to the Constitutional debate, that while he meant no disrespect to Senator Cummins, Walsh had "hung his hide on the fence," as one of their old friends used to say.[4]

Action against the trusts, along with tariff and banking reform, was a major aspect of President Wilson's call for a "New Freedom." Americans were not happy with trusts, monopolies, and tendencies toward monopoly so apparent in the early twentieth century; but to know what to do about the phenomenon has always been difficult. Woodrow Wilson was feeling his way on this question during the campaign of 1912. He emphatically opposed the views of Theodore Roosevelt, who accepted the fact of bigness and wanted to bring about a new system of *regulation* by the federal government. Roosevelt urged the establishment of a powerful commission that would be given regulatory authority in interstate commerce. Wilson, meanwhile, advised by Louis Brandeis, became increasingly knowledgeable on the trust problem, and he moved toward acceptance of the commission idea. Until 1914, however, neither he nor Congress could give much time to the trusts. But by early summer, under the influence of Brandeis, George Rublee, Senator Francis Newlands, and others, the president had come to believe more strongly in the importance of a regulatory commission, as against an attempt to specify by law certain business practices that were forbidden. He conveyed these ideas to leaders in Congress.[5]

Senator Walsh was not a newcomer to the question of monopoly and possible antitrust action. During all of his adult life he showed an interest in the evils of monopoly power, often criticizing big business, and he had tried numerous suits against a variety of business combinations. He seems never to have advocated seriously any plan to limit the size of corporations, although holding companies were to him a dangerous manifestation of the corporate system. All in all, Walsh accepted the fact of bigness, while hoping to encourage the competitive process and to help the little man as much as possible. He was a pragmatist rather than a fierce, unreconstructed antimonopoly man. He was looking for positive results of legislation introduced rather than a system that would punish the large corporations and their leaders.

One can surmise that Walsh was affected by what had happened to him and his friends in Montana. They had struggled against the copper interests politically and watched the process of corporate consolidation go on apace, as Senator Clark, F. Augustus Heinze, and others sold out to the Amalgamated interests or became associated with them. No one in the state could stop this process, nor could the federal government. In much of the country a similar trend was evident. Walsh was one who believed that the Sherman Law of 1890, prohibiting combinations in restraint of trade, was already a considerable help, if a president and his attorney general wanted to make use of it. Perhaps some improvements in the system could be made to encourage competition, or maintain it.

Practically speaking, Walsh had to achieve, if possible, a working relationship with the economic leaders of his state. At this time, in 1913–14, the Montana senator and his followers were endeavoring night and day to reduce the Amalgamated control over public affairs. To have fought the copper leaders simultaneously in Washington probably would have been futile and self-defeating. Walsh had to think about the possible effects of national antitrust legislation on the state's economy in general; on the great companies and also the smaller, striving companies; on the business organizations but also the farm and labor organizations. All of this can explain why Walsh made a rather curious statement early in 1914. He was "disposed to think," he said, "that the trust legislation is not imperative in character, and that there is no reason why we should stay up nights trying to pass it." Like other Democrats at this time, he was exhilarated over the successes they had already experienced with the tariff and banking bills and may have thought they needed a breathing spell. But he was soon involved in the antitrust debates.[6]

Three bills of an antitrust type were prepared in the House of Representatives, and two of these went on to eventual approval in the Senate. The trade commission bill went to the Interstate Commerce Committee, of which Walsh was not a member, but the Clayton measure came to the Judiciary Committee, where Walsh studied and debated it at length. Later on the floor the chairman, Charles Culberson of Texas, had the bill in charge. Walsh, however, gained recognition as a leading sponsor, defending provisions of the bill and offering amendments. His importance grew more apparent as the debates continued. "Rather reluctantly," he said, "at the solicitation of the leaders in the Senate I assumed the burden of defending the conference report against a particularly vicious attack made upon it by Senator Reed, on our side, and some strong men on the other side of the Chamber."[7]

A far-ranging debate on antitrust policy was yet to come, in August, September, and October 1914. Those who believed in specifying certain illegal acts were to have their chance in the Clayton Act. Yet the two measures of 1914 were both intended to prevent the occurrence of monopoly rather than to break up or prosecute monopolies. Senator Walsh made a succinct statement on this point during an exchange with Senator Reed. "The purpose of the legislation of which the pending bill forms a part [the Clayton bill] is to preserve competition where it exists, to restore where it is destroyed, and to permit it to spring up in new fields." Many years later an economist found this a particularly apt description.[8]

Senator Walsh, as noted, supported the trade commission and the Clayton bill, and at most points he seemed optimistic about the results to be achieved through this dual approach. He also insisted that the Sherman Act would still be available for use in clear-cut cases of monopoly and violations of legitimate trade practices. He believed that publicity through investigations of the FTC would lead to more prosecutions than in the past. As he debated with Reed, Borah, and others, Walsh kept repeating one of his main points. There was no need in the Clayton Act to try and specify all the undesirable or illegal practices that tended toward the development of a monopoly. Nor was it a good idea to list just a few of the more reprehensible practices. The judgment on these matters should be left mostly to the trade commission which would look into each case and often act in conjunction with federal courts and the Department of Justice. Walsh showed a concern about small business and what was necessary to give encouragement. He emphasized that it would be extremely difficult to frame a law with specific prohibitions and penalties and still give the freedom for legitimate trade and commerce.[9]

Walsh was also interested in the labor sections of this bill. He was among the senators who believed that labor unions should not be prosecuted as "combinations in restraint of trade" or organizations in violation of the antitrust law. His maiden speech in the Senate, on May 6, 1913, had dealt with the subject. Now he supported provisions of the Clayton Act intended to protect workers in their rights to organize, to assemble peacefully, to picket, to enjoy freedom of speech in the job situation, and to be free from arbitrary injunctions so often used in the past. He delivered a long address, as well, on the subject of jury trial in cases of indirect contempt, such as sometimes resulted from a strike. This was a speech rooted in history and replete with legal references. In essence, however, he was defending trial by jury. He declared at one point that "miscarriages of justice will sometimes occur" but that the "most perfect judicial systems ever known" were those that included the jury system. It was a good speech, as Senator Borah observed, and eventually this provision for trial by jury did become part of the Clayton Act.[10]

The last day of Senate debate was dominated by two men—Reed and Walsh. Walsh started things off and talked at length until Reed took the floor and talked even longer. Walsh may have had the better of this argument, emphasizing the purpose of the new legislation, the continued usefulness of the Sherman Act, the importance of officials whose duty it would be to carry out the law, and the good potentiality of the trade commission. Reed took the opportunity to reply and to get in some further sallies at Walsh. Finally the Missouri senator offered a motion to recommit the conference report. The vote was 25 yeas, 35 nays, and 36 not voting. Then came a vote on the conference report itself. It passed by 35 to 24, with 37 not voting. Among those who voted nay was a combination of progressives and conservatives of both parties; for example, Reed, Borah, Norris, Boies Penrose, and Elihu Root.[11]

Walsh seems not to have been happy with his role in this final debate on the Clayton bill or with the legislation. He found himself often acting as a party man selected to joust with Reed and in opposition to some of the more respected progressives in the Senate. Those who voted "nay," together with those who failed to vote at all, numbered 61 senators, far more than the 35 who had succeeded in passing the bill. Most important to Walsh probably was the fact that he simply did not like several provisions of the Clayton Act. A year and a half later when he gave a speech extolling the Democratic achievements of Wilson's administration he failed to mention the antitrust legislation of 1914; this was hardly an oversight.

Perhaps Walsh and the Democrats built better than they knew. Certainly the effort they made was a creditable one; and, in the perspective of history, the stress on fostering competition in the trade commission's work and through the Clayton Act was preferable to traditional antitrust campaigns.[12]

Antitrust policy was constantly in a condition of change and development. One of the questions that had arisen during debate over the Clayton Act was the possible vulnerability of U.S. exporters if they wanted to act through a combination, for example, in the export of copper products. John D. Ryan of the Amalgamated Copper Company was interested in seeing a measure that would reassure businessmen as to the legality of copper combinations or others effected exclusively for the purposes of export. President Wilson indicated in 1915 that he favored such an idea, and in 1917 the plan finally was adopted. Walsh gave his support in the final outcome.[13]

The Montana senator soon developed an unusual relationship with the Federal Trade Commission when his brother John joined the staff as one of its counsel. Apparently the senator was not the major influence in making this arrangement. John, who had been practicing law in Washburn, Wisconsin, was a personal and political friend of Joseph E. Davies, also a Wisconsinite, who became chairman of the FTC.[14]

Walsh's first real chance to affect the making of foreign policy came in the spring and early summer of 1914 during the Panama tolls controversy. The work of building the Panama Canal had been almost completed, and the crux of the dispute that developed was whether American vessels in the coastwise trade should be exempted from any charges. An act of Congress in 1912 had provided for such an exemption, but Great Britain asserted that the law if implemented would violate the Hay-Pauncefote Treaty of 1901, according to which its vessels and those of other nations were to have access to the Canal on terms of equality. President Wilson decided the British were correct in their view and that for several reasons the discrimination in favor of American ships must be repealed. He believed the integrity of the United States and its treaty obligations was at stake and showed a determination that the nagging matter of canal tolls should be settled in a way satisfactory to other countries.[15]

This issue cut across party lines, but a good majority of Democrats eventually rallied to the president's support. Senator Walsh did not join them. He believed there were excellent reasons for discriminating in favor of American ships, and he denied emphatically that the act of 1912 violated the Hay-Pauncefote Treaty. As a member of the Committee on Interoceanic Canals, the Montana senator studied the tolls question soon after coming to Washington in 1913 and made up his mind; nothing he heard thereafter convinced him the exemption ought to be repealed.

There is a likelihood that Walsh was affected, to some extent, by his latent bias against the English. He hinted at this motivation on May 16, 1914, as he began a lengthy Senate analysis of the issues involved. He said that those on both sides of this dispute ought to recognize that they might be affected in considerable part by "irrelevant considerations" and by "prejudice more or less deep-seated." The Montanan was especially annoyed by the Anglophile ambassador to Britain, Walter Hines Page, and wrote of him: "I should feel easier about it [the tolls question] if it appeared that we had an American at the Court of St. James. . . . I cannot feel that our minister there has any red American blood in his veins."[16]

Walsh's argument on the tolls question appeared to be affected most of all by his desire as a westerner to reduce shipping costs between the East and West. Reductions in the rates by sea might, in turn, force rates down on the transcontinental rail lines. Thus business would be stimulated, and consumers could benefit from lower prices. His position was consistent with that adopted at other points in his career, for example, during the 1920s when he was a principal advocate of the St. Lawrence Seaway. Doubtless, also, he was challenged by legal aspects of the matter. He argued forcefully that the discriminatory rates in favor of American ships were thoroughly justifiable and did not violate provisions of the Hay-Pauncefote Treaty. Regretting that he could not support the president, Walsh at the same time believed the tolls question was not so serious as to affect in a dangerous way America's relations with Britain and other countries.

He claimed that coastal trade was a domestic concern and was not included in phraseology of the Hay-Pauncefote Treaty where it declared for the equality of all nations in using the canal. Walsh cited court cases to show the historic interpretation of coastal trade as including distant voyages by ocean-going vessels.

Sensitive on the point of U.S. integrity so far as the treaty with Britain was concerned, Walsh countered with a call for political integrity. He discussed at length the Democratic platform of 1912 and its plank declaring in favor of discriminatory rates for American coastwise shipping. He said his own involvement in writing the Baltimore platform had been so intimate that he could not take lightly the promises made by his party and its leaders.

From the start of this controversy Walsh had indicated privately a disposition "to yield in a way" to the president's judgment. Along with other members of the Committee on Interoceanic Canals, he did not put serious obstacles in the path of an administration bill intended to repeal the 1912 exemption act. But the Montana senator proposed on the Senate floor a compromise measure that would retain the exemption for U.S. vessels while facilitating a challenge in the federal courts that could be taken on to the Supreme Court. Although the amendment was lost, 34 senators voted for it.[17]

During the last debate on June 11 Walsh gave further evidence of his interest in shipping costs, especially as they affected the people of Montana. He had been absent from the Senate earlier in the day, he said, presenting an argument for his state's railroad commission before the Interstate Commerce Commission. He was "asking for reduced freight rates upon the grain that we raise in our [Montana] fields to feed the people of this country." Apparently Walsh returned to the ICC to continue his argument. In any case, he was "necessarily absent" later in the day, according to his colleague Henry Myers, when the tolls question came to a final vote. By a margin of 50 to 35 President Wilson had his way in passing the repeal measure. It was Myers's understanding that if Walsh had been present he would have voted "nay."

Walsh and thirty-five colleagues had lost their fight. The Montanan's opposition to the president was so obviously based on principled argument, and conducted in such a tactful way, that his relationship with the White House was not damaged. Back in March Walsh had written to C. B. Nolan: "The tolls question is the burning topic of the hour here. I hate to do it but feel impelled to vote against the President on the matter." He went on to say he and the president had had "an hour's heart to heart talk" that afternoon and they had parted "with the very pleasant assurance from him" that Walsh could vote his own views.[18]

12

The "New Freedom" and Western Land Policy

No subject was more interesting to Walsh in the Wilson period, or consumed more of his energy, than western land policy. This was a time when western leaders were clamoring for the development of public lands, located primarily in their states, and many were convinced that the policies adopted under Theodore Roosevelt and William Howard Taft had been too restrictive. Land withdrawn from private entry, including mineral lands and water power sites, ought to be opened for development on a reasonable basis. Some of the agencies recently established, it was widely believed, showed a lack of understanding of western people and conditions; for example, the Forest Service and Reclamation Service. Reforms were overdue. The territory of Alaska was a subject of much interest in the West, and many believed its resources, too, should be opened to easy access and exploitation. The national parks were sources of interest and controversy partly because their status of being almost sacrosanct was not well established.[1]

A westerner who reflected the interests of his region, Walsh was knowledgeable on resource problems and he rose to the challenge of studying and debating these issues, often of a legal nature, in Senate committees and on the Senate floor. Another challenge was that of doing for his friends and acquaintances back home those things they most wanted done—"bringing home the bacon," in other words. There was still another aspect to this. If Woodrow Wilson's party could succeed in handling these resource problems, it could expect to make gains politically.

The "New Freedom" that one associates with Woodrow Wilson's economic reforms of 1913–14 had relevance to the western land policy of this period. Walsh tried to find practical answers involving land and conservation that would bring early results. His ideas were similar to those of the man who became secretary of the interior in 1913 and continued in that position for the next seven years, exercising a strong influence on Wilsonian policies.

Franklin K. Lane was a Californian and an honest, well-intentioned administrator. He had entered public life as a lawyer, newspaperman, and Democratic reformer in his home city of San Francisco. In 1902 he conducted a race for governor of California and almost won. Three years later, having made the acquaintance of Theodore Roosevelt, he gained an appointment to the Interstate Commerce Commission and served as a commissioner until he accepted Wilson's offer to head the Interior Department.

In his annual reports of 1913 and 1914 Lane summed up his ideas which, all in all, seemed to be those of an idealist and a reformer. The report of 1913 gave greatest prominence to "the fuller and freer use" of the natural resources. As was well known, a feeling existed in the West that its needs and problems merited more consideration in Washington than they had received. Action must be taken, with proper safeguards, to open up resources for development.

Lane was a dynamic figure who exercised his powers of executive leadership somewhat as Woodrow Wilson did. He proposed to get bills through the Congress, bringing about appropriate changes, and he looked for allies in the House and Senate. One of the most important of these by 1914 was the junior senator from Montana, Thomas J. Walsh.[2]

When Walsh arrived in Washington, he did not know Secretary Lane, but he sensed how important the secretary would be to his own interests and those of Montana. He communicated with Lane probably for the first time on March 11, 1913, as an opportunity arose: "I am enclosing herewith a letter from Mr. J. L. Cole, of Kalispell, Montana, relative to conditions on Glacier National Park. I have a summer home in the park . . . and am able to give you information at first hand upon conditions there, should you feel that you would like to talk the matter over at some future time." Lane responded by saying he would be glad to have a talk, and probably the two became acquainted shortly thereafter.[3]

One question of concern to Walsh and other Montana leaders was the state's unfinished reclamation projects. They feared for a time that Secretary Lane was going to abandon the work and the settlers at Sun River and Milk River in northern Montana. The possibility of an abandonment was more than plausible at this time because the state of Oregon was trying to get funds for reclamation purposes and made an appeal for aid to which Lane had reacted sympathetically. Since reclamation funds were scarce, one state might be sacrificed to another demonstrating greater need.

In early June 1913, Governor Stewart, former Governor Norris, and a delegation of Montanans came to Washington to plead their case with Secretary Lane and the president. The results were inconclusive, and Walsh soon after sent a long letter to President Wilson. He made these points to the president and argued much the same in a letter to Lane. He believed the secretary had demonstrated "a very earnest and a very honest desire to render the best possible service to the country." But the senator added that Lane was reported to be at the point of recommending the application of $450,000 from the Reclamation Fund for a new Oregon project although there wasn't enough money to do that, while also continuing the work at Sun River and Milk River. Meanwhile, settlers had gone into these project areas "anticipating . . . that they would have the water with which to irrigate their lands." They had made arrangements accordingly and expected the government to fulfill its part of the bargain. Walsh made this statement to the president: "The abandonment of these projects would be a disaster to our State, and would have a tendency to advertise us in a most undesirable way." He asked for an "opportunity to be heard" on the matter before any decisive action was taken. President Wilson responded reassuringly.

To his wife on June 13, the Montanan reported that he had been "horribly distressed" over the possibility that Lane might abandon the Montana projects. Ellen Walsh was traveling in the West but was soon to return to the summer home at Lake McDonald, where according to her husband she and Genevieve might have the chance to entertain Secretary Lane. Walsh thought there would be "a grand opportunity" to give Lane and his family "all necessary attention." He told Ellen to remember that "their good will is much to be desired and that our position requires something of us." Whether the visit actually happened is not clear.

Finally the case reached its climax. In September Walsh informed Ellen that he planned a short vacation during the coming recess but would remain "within call that I may return promptly on the arrival of Secretary Lane." Then, almost immediately, he had welcome news. His secretary came in with a telegram from Lane, saying he had given the order for work to resume at the Sun River project. "That relieves a very embarrassing situation," said the senator.[4]

The broader question of reclamation policy in Montana and the West demanded Secretary Lane's attention, and he undertook a thorough investigation. Walsh noted in May 1913 that the secretary was conducting "an exhaustive hearing" in one of the big rooms in the Senate office building, during which the junior senator was among those who testified on behalf of settlers.

Later Lane traveled through the West with the purpose, he said, of discovering "what the problems were that the West wanted dealt with." Walsh agreed with almost all the settlers' complaints and urged upon Lane and the Interior Department an easing of requirements so far as water users were concerned.[5]

Secretary Lane went on to alter irrigation policy, much as the westerners wanted it altered. Walsh was the author of one reclamation measure providing for homestead entries in what was formerly the Flathead Indian Reservation and he was a vigorous proponent of appropriations to carry on the reclamation work. He was a party to the meetings and discussions that resulted finally in the Reclamation Extension Act of August 1914, under whose provisions the ten-year repayment period for settlers was increased to twenty years while other concessions were made as well.[6]

One of the fights of 1913 was the Hetch Hetchy affair, which had repercussions concerning the national parks and water policy. The essence of the dispute was this: should the U.S. government give permission to the City of San Francisco to obtain part of its water supply from the Hetch Hetchy Valley, although that valley lay 150 miles away in Yosemite National Park? Leaders of a utilitarian type, including Franklin Lane, Gifford Pinchot, and Senator Walsh, believed the answer should be "yes." The need for water by the people of San Francisco was a higher need than that for the preservation of nature in a valley to be flooded, regrettable though the choice might be. Since the project proposed was a municipal one involving public power, progressives for the most part were helpful. But many friends of the parks, and naturalists such as John Muir, were outraged at the idea of invading Yosemite or any national park and setting a dangerous precedent.

Walsh supported the administration measure. His contribution was largely a legal argument. The bill was constitutional in all respects, he argued, and the interests of farmers and others with prior rights to the water would be fully protected. The only real question involved here, asserted Walsh, was "whether the water to be impounded if this bill passes shall be allowed to run idly and uselessly to the sea . . . [for the present, at least] or whether we shall devote it to the use of the city of San Francisco immediately, as is provided by the pending bill."

Walsh closed by citing the need, not only of San Francisco in this case but of all the West, for adequate supplies of water. He could not "permit the love that [he had] for the beauties of nature to outweigh for a moment the appeals for water to drink of a whole city full of people." The bill passed the Senate on the day of this speech, December 6, 1913, and soon became law.

This was an impressive performance. Other senators took note of Walsh's knowledgeability concerning water questions, and a year later a California senator-elect remembered "with a deep sense of gratitude" the Montanan's "valiant and able advocacy of the Hetch Hetchy grant." Walsh's efforts were all the more impressive because he was not even a member of the Public Lands Committee, which had the bill in charge. He was interested in this matter, knew a good deal about it, and jumped into the discussion.[7]

By the end of 1913 and early 1914, Walsh and Secretary Lane were moving into a period of collaboration. As western men they were prepared to be more generous with the federal largesse than were men of the East, such as Gifford Pinchot or Theodore Roosevelt. On the other hand, they saw the necessity for appeasing eastern opinion and for trying to achieve legislative compromises through which could occur the development of water power sites and mineral lands of the west, and the coal lands of Alaska. Much of this might be accomplished through the method of leasing federal lands rather than selling them or giving them away, as in the past.

Because of his membership on the Territories Committee, the Montana senator became deeply involved in a legislative program for Alaska, working with Key Pittman, chairman of the committee, with Secretary Lane, and others. Actually two major proposals for Alaska were inherited from the Taft administration. The first was to meet the transportation needs of the territory, then owned almost entirely by the federal government, through the building of a government railroad; and a second, closely related plan was to work out the means for developing Alaskan coal fields so that residents would have the fuel supplies they needed and coal would be available during construction of the railroad.

For two days in mid-January 1914, Walsh gave an informative speech on the Alaska railroad bill. It was historical and geographical in emphasis and was loaded with essential information, as he used a map and responded to questions from many senators. To expect the government to build a railroad in thickly settled parts of the United States was one thing; to build in a "frontier territory for the primary purpose of the development and settlement of that territory" was something quite different.

Soon the bill gained Senate approval, and Walsh received thanks and congratulations for his efforts, one telegram coming from Governor Strong of Alaska. A Seattle lawyer told the Montana senator that he had given a "masterly argument" and demonstrated an "exhaustive knowledge" of the subject. All this gained meaning as the bill received the president's signature in March 1914, and $35,000,000 was authorized to build the Alaskan railroad.

In his discussion of the related bill for leasing coal lands in Alaska Walsh gave hints of a change in ideas soon to come. Speaking in the Senate, he said: "I have insisted that the policy which has been justified by a century of our history of the absolute disposition of the public lands is the proper course to pursue. But I am ready to surrender my convictions in the hope that these rich coal lands may be made available to the people of the United States." A leasing bill for Alaska was important, and it continued to be discussed through much of 1914, but more important was the broader question of leasing water power sites and a variety of western resources. This was the direction in which Walsh was moving, as were Secretary Lane and others in the Department of the Interior.[8]

There was one western issue which chilled the relations between the Montana senator and Secretary Lane, or Lane's subordinates. This was the matter of how the national parks were to be administered. Walsh had a proprietary attitude toward Glacier Park. He and his wife first went to the area before the park was created in 1910 and built a summer home on the shore of Lake McDonald. They knew the area intimately and the people who lived in and around the park and were confident that many of their ideas would find favor with park officials. At this time, however, the modern movement for professional administration of the parks was gaining strength, and Lane found men who strongly believed in this new approach, most importantly Stephen T. Mather and Horace M. Albright. Both became famous for their pioneering role in the development of a professionally administered Park Service committed to the *preservation* of the flora, fauna, and scenery within a park's boundaries. Some of the park enthusiasts became almost fanatical in their opposition to commercialization of the parks or intrusions such as that permitted in the Hetch Hetchy grant.

Opposing the "beauties of nature" people and park enthusiasts were some powerful conservation leaders, including Gifford Pinchot, who believed in authorization for limited development of a commercial type. Secretary Lane leaned in this direction on occasion. Here was one of the famous divisions in the conservation movement—that between preservationists and utilitarians.[9]

Almost from the day he assumed office, Walsh announced that he was going to work for a "new freedom" in the parks; he would oppose the "monopolistic features" that had prevailed "more or less offensively in the past." What he referred to specifically in this case, writing to Secretary Lane, was the Yellowstone Stage Company and its transportation privileges in Yellowstone Park. He hoped to make a formal presentation in behalf of another transportation firm. Apparently he did this and won the necessary permits for this firm to carry on business in the park.

A similar situation existed in Glacier Park, and Walsh was obviously attempting to help his friends and constituents, some of whom needed help to make a living in the western country. The sincerity of Walsh's free enterprise beliefs concerning the parks cannot be doubted. In one instance in 1917, when Mather and the leaders of several transportation companies were working out a plan to consolidate the system in Yellowstone, Walsh got highly indignant, as he revealed in a letter to his law partner: "I roundly denounced such a plan to Lane and inquired of him whether he did not feel that he was traveling perilously near a violation of the Sherman act."[10]

Walsh was a hiker and an avid fisher who gloried in the beautiful surroundings at his summer home, a lodge on the shore of Lake McDonald built of cedar logs that ran the full width of the structure for a distance of forty-five feet. With such a home, at the foot of towering peaks, he was interested—not surprisingly—in preserving the beauty of the place. Thus he supported a bill in 1914 for government acquisition of a lovely stand of cedars which were in private hands and might be cut by the owners. He supported the idea of private owners selling their property in the parks if they wanted to do so but resisted the attempt to force residents to sell and get out. In the late 1920s this became an acrimonious issue.[11]

Another source of vexation between Walsh and the park administrators was patronage politics, with the senator wanting to find jobs for some of his friends. Walsh and other members of Montana's congressional delegation in 1913–14 assumed that the Republican superintendant of Glacier Park would be replaced by a Democrat. When he was not, Democrats in the vicinity of Glacier Park began to complain, exerting pressure mostly for the appointment of S. Frank Ralston, a capable man whom Walsh was already supporting. Lane's advisers on the parks were trying to put an end to patronage appointments and to find someone scientifically knowledgeable and with tastes "in a way artistic."

The Montanan continued to exert pressure, to such a point that he admitted he had made himself "offensive." Yet he believed Ralston was qualified for the job and ought to be appointed. A very able man and a progressive Democrat, he had given loyal support even against the copper interests. "I found myself at a loss," Walsh wrote to Ralston, "to think of any man in the state who would accept the place and come any more nearly meeting his [Miller's] ideal than yourself." Finally the stalemate ended:

"Mahomet concluded . . . to come to the mountain," as Walsh described the situation.[12]

Walsh used his influence forcefully on behalf of old friends and constituents who were not always qualified for the work in question. He probably believed that he was merely continuing patronage practices of the past and that in Flathead County, which was Republican, the Democrats needed help.

How Walsh came to "represent" Lane in the Senate and to be so important to his legislative program is rather amazing, considering that the Montanan was a newcomer on Capitol Hill and did not belong to the Public Lands Committee in this period. He was a member of the Committee on Mines and Mining and served in fact as its chairman, but traditionally this committee had been regarded as "one of the paper committees," in Walsh's words, when compared with those on Public Lands, Indian Affairs, and Irrigation and Reclamation. In February 1914 the Montanan became a member of the Irrigation Committee, and in December 1915 he joined Indian Affairs, while retaining his chairmanship of Mines and Mining.

Even before this time in 1913 and 1914, Walsh had been steadily enlarging his influence regarding western lands. He did it in part by demonstrating his interest and ability as in the fight over Montana reclamation projects and the Hetch Hetchy Dam. He did it by his willingness to come before committees of which he was not a member to speak on bills that interested him. Most of all, perhaps, he did it by his jurisdictional arguments, trying to get bills referred to his committee on Mines and Mining or to Irrigation and Reclamation rather than to the Public Lands Committee, where he thought prospects less favorable. He asserted that the latter committee was loaded down with bills and would not be able to act on these urgent matters for months to come, if ever; he also believed that some senators in the Public Lands Committee were hostile toward the bills in which he was interested and might prevent them from reaching the Senate floor. Reed Smoot of Utah and A. B. Fall of New Mexico were among the senators with whom Walsh occasionally tangled in these jurisdictional disputes. Another was his colleague, Henry Myers, who had become the chairman of the Public Lands Committee but was not noted for energy or efficiency.[13]

A succession of events early in 1914 brought Walsh and Lane into close collaboration on the Wilson land policy. Both men had become interested in the use of radium for cancer treatment, and they knew that the principal source of radium-bearing ore was in Utah and Colorado on government lands. Lane took note of western opposition to plans for the development of the radium lands, even though the efficacy of radium treatment was now being demonstrated. He was hopeful that the accumulating evidence would help to win support for the necessary legislation. Walsh, meanwhile, had introduced a radium bill "for the purpose of securing an adequate supply of radium for Government and other hospitals in the United States, and for other purposes." This measure called for direct sponsorship by the government in order to secure the radium supplies, and many senators and others objected. The bill ran into repeated difficulty.

In May of 1914 Walsh received this letter from the secretary:

My dear Senator:

Wont [sic] you be good enough to see senator Kern [the majority leader] and urge upon him the advisability of calling a conference of the Democratic Senators for the purpose of planning a legislative program which shall include:
1. The Alaskan Coal Leasing Bill,
2. The General Oil, Coal and Phosphate Leasing Bill,
3. The Smith-Ferris Water Power [leasing] Bill,
4. The Radium Bill.

I am urging this course at the suggestion of the President, who is anxious that these measures be enacted into law at the present session.

It is not clear whether the meeting of senators ever occurred, but Walsh assumed from this time on that he was Lane's representative in trying to bring to completion a program of the type described. What helped most in drawing the two men together, legislatively, was their acceptance of a large role for the federal government in the establishment of a land policy. Development of the public resources should be encouraged but with the proper safeguards. Gifford Pinchot, Secretary Lane, and many others now had decided that title to the public lands should stay with the federal government, and that development of coal lands, petroleum lands, and water power sites, for example, should occur through a system of leases.

In March 1914 Walsh announced on the Senate floor his conversion to this point of view: "I am willing to accede to some kind of a leasing law in relation to these valuable deposits, . . . because we recognize that we have got to have it or have no effective law for the disposition of land at all."

Walsh and Lane tried to convert a number of senators who still believed in the old system of private development and alienation of the public lands. One basis of the appeal that carried weight was monetary: public land states would share in the royalties and fees paid by leaseholders of the federal government.[14]

Walsh's letters of 1915–16 and some speeches of that period reveal that he became a genuine believer in the principles of a leasing system which, however, would never be applied to agricultural land. He believed that water power sites stood "on a different footing because power is the basis of all modern industry." In addition to water power there was, of course, coal, gas, and oil; in fact, the "nations of the earth are scouring it now for oil." Walsh said he was not troubled by a possible loss of taxes under government ownership and leasing. He was satisfied that under a good leasing law the states would share liberally in the rentals or royalties and the "local government will get infinitely more out of these lands than it ever would derive from the taxation of them if they passed into private ownership."

Writing to his law partner, Walsh commented on the social justice of a leasing system. "My opinion is that fifty years hence all of these lands, the power sites, and oil and coal lands particularly, scarcely less so the phosphate and potash lands, will be worth sums beyond the power of the human mind adequately to conceive." He wanted the public to enjoy an "unearned increment" (using Henry George's phrase) rather than letting great capitalists amass fortunes from the natural resources.[15]

Walsh became an agitator for the leasing system and was sometimes regarded by westerners as a dangerous man, or a "dangerous gentleman," in the words of Senator John D. Works. In December 1915 the Montanan delivered an address on the country's mining laws before a conference of the Mining and Metallurgical Society of America in which he vividly described the inadequacies of these laws and the need for improvement. He sent a copy to Senator Ashurst and soon had a reply, saying in part, "I have read your speech and desire to congratulate you upon the forcible way in which you present this interesting, and I may say, amazing information." Ashurst, Key Pittman, and a few other western senators had also come to accept the leasing principle.

Meanwhile, Walsh introduced in the Senate a bill for mineral leasing, whose origins he described to Senator Pittman: "it is, as you know, the result of a conference between Secretary Lane and the Director of the Bureau of Mines and the Director of the Geological Survey on the one side, and the heads of the committees on Public Lands and Mines and Mining in the Senate and the House on the other." It had the approval, he noted, of President Wilson and Secretary Lane.

The Montanan now launched a campaign for the passage of his bill or something similar. One line of his letter referred to savage attacks being made on the principle of leasing, and how he was doing everything possible to overcome this powerful opposition. Directly or indirectly Walsh communicated with the governors of Montana, Arizona, Nevada, California, Wyoming, and Washington, hoping to use their responses with good effect.

In this same period Walsh became involved in a movement of the American Institute of Mining Engineers for mining law revision and codification of the laws. He and Horace V. Winchell, a mining geologist, aimed at the establishment of a special commission, by act of Congress, to investigate the subject broadly and help bring about desired changes. Walsh served as a Washington publicist for the movement.

None of these efforts helped much. The Congress simply bogged down over Walsh's leasing bill and other measures such as that introduced by Congressman Scott Ferris of Oklahoma. One source of dissension was the naval petroleum reserves in California and Wyoming which had been set aside by executive orders of 1912 and 1915. The justification of conservationists for these reserves was that, in a time of apparent petroleum scarcity, the U.S. government should preserve in underground reservoirs on the public lands certain oil supplies for the possible needs of the Navy. Oilmen and others, however, were unhappy with this new example of government interference. Added to the broader conflict over leasing, the naval petroleum reserves helped create a stalemate that lasted until 1920, when a general minerals leasing law went through Congress.[16]

So bitter was the fight over western resources that Senator Walsh came to be regarded in some quarters, at least temporarily, as a traitor to the West. *The Mining American,* a journal published in Denver, portrayed him in a series of editorials as a collaborator with eastern exploiters and "the most dangerous man in the Senate." They made the charge partly because of "his advocacy of a federal leasing policy" but also because he represented the state of Montana, which was controlled absolutely, they said, by the Standard Oil interests (Rockefeller) in New York City.[17]

Walsh and other advocates of a leasing program were able to achieve just one notable success in the early Wilson years. This was the leasing law for Alaskan coal, mentioned earlier in connection with the Alaskan railroad. In February 1914 the Montanan introduced a bill "to provide for the leasing of coal lands in the Territory of Alaska, and for other purposes." Indicative of Walsh's prominent role was a jurisdictional argument on the Senate floor over whether his Committee of Mines and Mining should handle the bill, or whether it should go to the Committee on Public Lands. The latter finally won the argument. Some months later, however, during debates in the Senate, Walsh was taking an active part in the proceedings and Gilbert Hitchcock of Nebraska noted that the Montana senator "was practically in charge of the bill." He was one of its leading sponsors, although the measure that finally passed was not Walsh's but one similar to it introduced in the House by Scott Ferris of Oklahoma.

There seems to have been no serious threat to defeat this coal leasing bill since it was associated with, and perhaps essential to, the construction of the Alaskan railroad. The debates, nevertheless, were lively at times as the senators divided into two extremes and a middle group. Pittman, Walsh, Miles Poindexter of Washington State, and Henry Myers of Montana were prominent among the bill's supporters. The debate was far-ranging and often interesting as a number of senators talked about their own states and the extent to which their resources had been developed through leasing, rather than private ownership, and on the advantages and disadvantages of each system.

Walsh tried to rebut his colleague John Shafroth's critique of the leasing system, and he did rather well at this. He noted that the State of Minnesota had for many years leased its lands rich in iron ore and derived good revenue from the royalties; and Montana, Colorado, and Wyoming had had a similarly successful experience in the handling of coal properties. By contrast, he emphasized that the system of private development in Colorado had resulted in a wholesale appropriation of coal lands by the Colorado Fuel and Iron Company and a recent harvest of bad publicity for that Rockefeller concern.

Walsh further asserted that the government of the United States functioned on a different level than did the states and that while it could not ignore the matter of revenues its primary concern should be "the general development of the country." This argument lent itself particularly well to the main subject of discussion, the bill for the leasing of Alaskan coal lands.

Finally the measure went through and received the president's signature on October 22, 1914, shortly before the session of Congress came to an end. To Walsh, Lane, and others interested in Alaska, this was a considerable victory. But disappointments lay ahead, for the growth of population in that distant territory and the development of its resources continued to lag.[18]

Other issues of importance to the West consumed a good deal of Walsh's time. Just as he threw himself into the fight for leasing of mineral lands in order to open those areas up and achieve development, he also entered the disputes over water power sites. He became deeply involved in the power question during the Wilson administration because of the great hydroelectric potential in Montana and the western states, as well as a national fascination with this relatively new type of energy, "white coal," as it was sometimes called. Again, the Montana senator worked with Secretary Lane and others in pushing for a federal leasing policy that might win the necessary congressional approval.

As a member of the Senate Committee on Irrigation, Walsh early became active regarding legislative proposals for "the disposition of power sites on the public domain." By the spring of 1914 he was committed to a leasing system in which the federal government would retain title to its power sites and exercise supervisory authority over the lessees. The details being worked out, he said in one letter, were the result of a conference called by Secretary Lane and including representatives of the Geological Survey and Reclamation Service, along with Congressman Scott Ferris of Oklahoma, Henry Rainey of Illinois, and himself.

Walsh got deeply involved in this controversy and was, occasionally, at the center of a storm—the subject of sharp questioning and criticism by fellow senators and others. No one could ever question this senator's courage in legislative matters. He took a position out in front knowing well how bitterly some of his friends and colleagues would disapprove—those, that is, who insisted the federal government should give up the title to its land and cheer on the private developers.[19]

Both publicly and privately Walsh continually elaborated upon the argument "that power sites ought to be dealt with as cities deal with franchises"; that the public had a right which should not be surrendered in perpetuity. He made the assertion that no one "in the field of national discussion feels justified in arguing in favor of any other policy." The question then was the details. Extremely important to Walsh was an understanding that the state and federal governments would share rentals when collected and that almost all the benefits would go into the Reclamation Fund or into western development. Here was the basis of compromise and here was the means by which the "magnificent water power" of Montana could soon be developed. But compromise on water power continued to be little more than a dream, as was apparent from hard fights on the Senate floor.[20]

One other western problem ought to be mentioned here before turning to even more urgent issues concerning the nation in Wilson's first term. Senator Walsh was rather typically a man of the West in his ideas about Native Americans and their culture and reservation lands. He was affected, also, by the large number of Indians in Montana. The Dawes Act had been passed in 1887 for the apparent purpose of allotting tribal lands to individual Indians to enable them to gain economic independence and to attain full stature as citizens. In 1906 the Burke Act brought a speeding up of this process. The end result was that white men were rapidly taking over the reservation land of Native Americans who simply were not prepared by education or experience to manage their properties and compete with whites in this respect.

Walsh, a strong believer in the Dawes Act and its amendments, said to one critic in 1923 that all he was doing was to carry out the national policy. A statutory change did not come until 1934, when the Wheeler-Howard Act went through Congress.

Secretary Lane and his subordinates in the Bureau of Indian Affairs were also believers in the Dawes Act. Lane's biographer, however, has noted a certain ambivalence in the secretary's attitude: he had an appreciation of Indian culture and wished to preserve what was beautiful in it, at the same time that the Indians were expected to adapt to the whites and rise "into full fellowship with their civilized conquerors." Senator Walsh believed, in all sincerity, that he too was doing what was best for the Indians and that there was no reasonable alternative. He resisted the extreme demands of land-hungry whites in and around the Indian reservations. He worked with some of the Indian leaders and represented them legally on occasion. At the same time, the Montanan had hardly arrived in Washington before he started trying to open the Indian reservations, and in the process, to make more land available to whites. By December 1915, when he joined the Indian Affairs Committee, his influence on the question had increased. Walsh's work in the Senate contributed to a decline in Indian landholding in Montana and a weakening of their position as a race.[21]

Officials of the Wilson administration in 1915–16, increasingly turned their attention from domestic to foreign problems. The war in Europe created a situation to which the president and everyone had to adjust.

13
America and the
"War-Mad Nations of Europe"

When war broke out in Europe during the first week of August 1914, Senator Walsh had reason for concern. His wife and daughter had set sail from New York on July 4, on a German liner, the *Konig Albert*, intending to tour Europe until October. Their main problem became that of booking passage back to the United States as hundreds of others were trying to do. The tension was considerable. Ellen Walsh took pride in reporting that, within their "limited circle," the women were holding up better than the men.

Walsh's family involvement with the war came to an end in September, when the ladies of his household returned safely. Their point of view was pro-German, as revealed by Ellen's last letter from Europe: "Germany is busy getting to Paris and is having a flag prepared to fly it from the Eifel [*sic*] Tower. Success to them, though I deplore the human sacrifice."[1]

For Americans to be taking sides in the summer and fall of 1914 was nothing unusual. In a total of some ninety-two million citizens, about thirty-three million were foreign-born or had at least one foreign parent. The census of 1910 showed that eleven million persons living in the United States had been born in Germany or Austria-Hungary or had a parent who was born there. For the Irish the figures approached five million. These people, as a group, had no love for the English, and their sentiments could be understood by many whose reasons were more complex, dating back, perhaps, to the American Revolution and the War of 1812. Yet the intellectuals and "opinion-makers" were strongly pro-Ally as a group. Most Americans had a feeling that was predominantly friendly toward England and France.

President Wilson announced an official policy of neutrality toward the war, and Walsh agreed with the president that citizens of the United States should try their best to be "neutral in fact as well as in name." What concerned the senator most was the effects of the war on rights of U.S. citizens to trade with Europeans. Exports of wheat and copper from Montana had high priority in his thinking. As Britain asserted its control of the seas, and Germany responded with a submarine campaign that threatened the destruction of neutral ships as well as those of its enemies, Walsh reacted angrily.

His perspective early in the war was that of a strong nationalist and an isolationist. Thus he wrote to a constituent, telling how Senator Root the previous day had given an impressive reading on the Senate floor of Washington's Farewell Address, warning against entangling alliances. Walsh added: "Its precepts ought to be observed by every true American in this trying hour." To another correspondent the Montanan wrote expressing his "astonishment and disappointment" that so many Americans somehow let their "sympathies . . . heavily influence their thinking as to what ought to be the national policy." According to him, when the fighting first started his sympathies, "so far as they were in any way pronounced, were with the allies"; he changed somewhat because of the "arrogance with which the English sway over the seas is asserted." Walsh consciously guarded against his own tendency toward anti-English feelings apparent in many Irish-Americans. Helping him in this effort to be fair-minded was the respect he held for British achievements.

As the war continued, and the incidents of interference with American ships multiplied—in violation of international law, as Walsh saw it—he reacted strongly. To one of his correspondents he announced: "It would be unfortunate if German militarism should be imposed upon the world, but I am not sure it would be found more oppressive than is England's supremacy on the seas." He didn't believe that either nation had the "slightest regard" for U.S. rights as a neutral.[2]

Early in 1915 Walsh had a revealing exchange of letters with an attorney friend. The latter wrote deploring tendencies of American leaders to get involved in the European war and he endorsed one of the popular ideas for noninvolvement, an embargo on the sale of munitions to combatant nations. Walsh said that he agreed as to the "brutality" of selling munitions "to the war-mad nations of Europe." On the other hand, to stop the sale of munitions would play into the hands of Germany, which had become "an arsenal for the warring nations of the earth," while her opponents had not laid in adequate supplies before the war began. Walsh declared that if trade in munitions could not occur in wartime, all countries, including the United States, would have to start large military buildups in order to be prepared for the eventuality of war. Obviously this was unthinkable.

To a surprising extent the Montanan's early reactions to the war were optimistic and hopeful, largely on the basis of his anticipation that a war boom, or greatly increased trade, would soon be apparent. If he saw the outbreak of fighting as a tragedy for western civilization, as many did, it is not apparent in his letters.[3]

The trade Walsh hoped for was not to be achieved without difficulty. Gradually the administration moved in the summer and fall of 1914 toward a neutrality slanted in favor of the allies. By the spring of 1915 the process was completed. In effect, the United States acquiesced to British direction and control of neutral commerce in European waters, although officially the State Department protested time and time again over the violation of American neutral rights. Meanwhile, British warships, notwithstanding losses to enemy torpedoes, asserted their control of the seas. They prevented the shipment of goods to German ports but also stopped shipments to Holland, Sweden, and other neutral nations. Without such surveillance, argued the British, cargoes allegedly destined for Rotterdam or Stockholm would end up in Germany.

To a considerable extent, Senator Walsh was at odds with administration policy on the matter of neutral rights. Yet he asserted his views in such a manner, and with such regard for presidential prerogatives, that he did not get into serious difficulties. He also agreed with major decisions of the administration, such as that to permit the granting of loans to the allies. It was deplorable, he said, for money from the United States to be used for the purchase of munitions, but the facts had to be considered: "The allies have spent hundreds of millions on munitions of war. They are short of cash. If they do not raise the money in this country they will have no money with which to purchase the enormous quantities of wheat and cotton grown by American farmers this year."

Just a few days after the war started in Europe, Walsh announced on the Senate floor that due to the decline of the demand for copper, resulting from disruptions abroad, copper smelting in Montana had come to a halt at the Great Falls smelter and many mines had closed around Butte. He concluded: "This is one of the contingencies arising from the unfortunate hostilities in Europe that will demand, . . . some legislation from Congress." Just what he had in mind is not clear, but the Montanan would continue for more than two years to speak and agitate on the subject of copper and other Montana products—aiming to bring to an end the interference with their sale in European markets. What he objected to particularly was the British Orders-in-Council that stopped the export trade in these commodities to neutral ports.[4]

In October 1914 Walsh received an appeal from John D. Ryan, president of the Anaconda Copper Mining Company, who requested that the senator do everything he possibly could "to enable a continuance of the large export business in copper which has been carried on from this country to Holland ever since the exports from this country have been important." What he had in mind particularly was that Walsh should persuade the State Department and the president, if necessary, of the urgency of this problem. If the copper business were disrupted, thousands of men all over the country in mines, smelters, mills, and refineries would be unemployed.

Ryan had already talked with Walsh on the telephone, and he was only one of the copper magnates deeply concerned over this matter. He and Cornelius ("Con") Kelley of Anaconda, along with executives of the American Smelting and Refining Company were those principally who kept in touch with the Montana senator and fed him information. Walsh also asked for help from the Librarian of Congress, the Bureau of Mines, the ministers of all Scandinavian countries, the Department of Commerce, and the Department of State. He sought the help of the senators from other copper producing states, and he suggested to members of the legislature in Helena that they pass a resolution or memorial that would be useful to the cause: "I am seeking no bouquets myself in the matter," he said, "and feel that no other member of the [congressional] delegation is. Make it impersonal and in such form as the Secretary [of State] can take it to the English Ambassador and say to him that the people of the copper producing states are up in arms and demanding that he do something." The Montanan also asked leading newspapers of his state to give publicity and support.

Meanwhile, he was going to see Secretary of State Bryan, Robert Lansing, solicitor of the Department, and the president. Over a period of months he saw these and other government officials many times. The first results were not encouraging. In October he advised John D. Ryan that the State Department was not well informed on the "copper troubles." In early November 1914, Walsh, who was then in Helena, sent a strident telegram to Secretary Bryan: "Unless unjustifiable interferences with shipments of copper to neutral ports cease all Montana production will stop," he said, and with deplorable results.

By mid-December 1914 Walsh decided he should speak on the Senate floor, giving to his colleagues and the nation a detailed explanation of the copper troubles. To Secretary Bryan he wrote: "I have thought it wise to lay before the country a temperate statement of the facts in the expectation that Great Britain will not be unresponsive to the sentiment that will be aroused when the facts are generally known. I have thought it better that this task should be undertaken by one friendly to the administration." In the meantime, the senator had talked again with Bryan, talked briefly with the president, and had "a protracted session with Mr. Lansing." He thought Lansing was now well informed, and progress was being made.

On December 31 he gave the speech he had planned. It was an impressive performance. First, he brought together in succinct form a great deal of information about the copper business and the problems it was facing; second, he showed the importance of copper as an American export second only to cotton in its value, and he asserted that no other article of commerce had been so drastically interfered with as copper; third, he proceeded to a historical and legal examination of the question of neutral rights and contraband of war; finally, though critical of the British policy toward copper, he was temperate and fair-minded in his presentation.

Germany before the war had imported American copper in large quantities, and Walsh conceded that England acted within her rights to stop that direct trade to her enemy in contraband goods. He also admitted that British leaders had reason to worry about transshipments of copper from neutral countries to Germany.

John D. Ryan was among those who congratulated the Montana senator on his address, and, almost in disbelief, Walsh mentioned high praise from a distinguished Republican colleague. Elihu Root had paused in the course of some discussion on the Senate floor to say: "Mr. President, I will say that my attention was called to this subject by listening to the very admirable, temperate, and scholarly presentation of the law of contraband by the Senator from Montana [Mr. Walsh] a few days ago." Walsh had not been on the floor at the time, but writing to Lewis Penwell later he showed his gratification.

What Walsh had won was a small victory, at best. He grew disillusioned with the State Department and with Secretary Bryan. Yet the Montanan defended Bryan and the president against criticism considered unfair. In essence he argued that, while the administration had acquiesced to British aggression on the seas, so had Holland, Norway, Sweden, and Italy. Neutral nations generally had consented to a reduction of their rights under international law in order to "court the favor of England" and carry on as much trade as the conditions would permit. Moreover, said Walsh, public opinion supported the administration policies. He had tried in vain to arouse the public against violations of neutral rights so clearly demonstrated in the copper seizures. Secretary Bryan was a "man of peace," unwilling to take drastic action, and his ideas reflected the "astonishing apathy" of most Americans concerning British tactics on the high seas.

In the summer of 1915 Walsh expressed even more strongly his surprise at the state of public opinion. "The forebearance exhibited by the American people in the face of these arrogant aggressions [by Great Britain] is without a parallel in our past history. The newspapers seem to be in a conspiracy of silence about the matter."

But by the second week of April 1915, American copper was moving freely to neutral ports, and, in this sense, the problem of previous months had been solved. Correspondence between John D. Ryan and Walsh reveals what happened. Britain simply had the power, said Ryan, to get what she wanted. Individual companies in the United States made agreements with the British Admiralty committing their businesses to give the facts about proposed shipments of copper, and cargoes could move once permission had been granted by the British. Walsh exploded that the whole plan was "in the last degree humiliating." Eventually, he said, he would consider it his duty "to call attention to the device to which our citizens were compelled to resort in order to protect their right to trade with neutral nations." In a later comment Walsh used stronger language: "the fact is that not a pound of copper leaves the port of New York except as Great Britain permits it. . . . we are today, so far as our foreign commerce is concerned, a mere province of Great Britain."

Doubtless some of those cooperating with the British in their copper exports, and making money in the process, were happy with the situation. Montana's junior senator, meanwhile, continued to seethe with indignation, and periodically he called for appropriate action. In March 1915 he believed the combatants could be brought "to their knees" by shutting off "all intercourse with them." He wished that Congress, before it adjourned, had authorized the president to "lay an embargo." Four months later he considered the export of munitions and whether that trade might be used as a lever. He would "at the first opportunity empower the President to prohibit the export of such in order to force an abandonment of the outrages and aggressions to which our legitimate foreign commerce is daily subjected under the British Orders-in-Council, more flagrant than those which brought on the War of 1812."

The Montana senator continued through the first months of 1916 to advocate some type of embargo or strong action in the fight for neutral rights. By this time, Woodrow Wilson and many other Americans, including Walsh, had come to believe in "preparedness" for the eventualities of war—though primarily still with the hope of avoiding war. Walsh had an unusual argument in favor of naval preparedness. By increasing the size of the Navy and building dreadnaughts in large number, the United States might be in a position to send its commerce to any neutral port under the protection of its own warships. He also had the notion that Britain could be "brought to its senses" by a short-lived embargo, lasting perhaps no longer than a week, or by other vigorous action to convince the leaders in Whitehall how mistaken they had been in flagrantly violating neutral rights.

Arthur S. Link has referred to Walsh of Montana and Hoke Smith of Georgia as "powerful" senators who represented a large segment of public opinion and whose protests against British aggressions could not be ignored. They may have contributed to a stiffening of the attitudes toward British policy in both the State Department and White House. The threat of U.S. retaliatory action was, at times, a real one. Nevertheless, by the spring and summer of 1915, the problems with Germany over submarine attacks had grown far more ominous than the disputes with Britain, and the result was a deliberate effort by the president to avoid having serious differences with both sides simultaneously. In point of fact, there was not much chance that Wilson would impose an embargo on the shipment of goods to Britain.[5]

There was another losing cause in which Walsh was involved, relating to neutral rights; and, more important, the Wilson administration also failed in this effort. Almost from the day war started in Europe, a serious need of the United States became apparent—that for more ships to replace foreign vessels called into war service. The number of ships under U.S. registry was pitifully small. President Wilson called attention to the problem, and Congress quickly passed a Ship Registry bill facilitating the registry of foreign-built ships under the American flag. This was particularly easy if the owners happened to be Americans. A fight developed, however, over German ships in great number which lay at anchor in U.S. ports and which President Wilson and others hoped to incorporate into the American fleet. (If they tried to sail as German ships they would probably be captured or destroyed by the British Navy.)

Once again, England had the power to determine what happened on the high seas and to influence heavily the making of American policy. President Wilson, at the urging of Secretary of the Treasury McAdoo, decided to establish a government-owned merchant marine in which some of the ships probably would be the former German vessels caught in American ports. Leaders in London soon revealed their opposition to any sale or transfer of these German ships that could be expected to give benefit to the enemy. The French also protested.

The big fight in Congress occurred during January and February 1915, and Walsh was in the middle of it for a time. Arthur Link has referred to this affair as the "most violent congressional controversy" during the entire session.

Few members of Congress wanted the United States to get directly involved in the war, but many had sympathies with one group of belligerents or the other and saw the ship-transfer issue in this light. Of concern to many was the proposal for a government-operated merchant marine, a drastic move in the direction of socialism, said the extreme critics. Politics was important, too. Republican leaders decided to fight the shipping bill and to filibuster, if necessary.

One of the most respected GOP leaders, Senator Elihu Root, presented a legal argument against the transfer of belligerent ships in wartime, to which Walsh responded. He did so at the request of his Democratic colleagues, according to the *New York Herald* and other eastern newspapers. One can imagine, however, that the Montanan wanted this chance to argue against Elihu Root on a matter of such interest and significance.

Walsh began his address with a historical survey of the positions taken by major powers on this question, that is, on the purchase of ships belonging to a nation at war. He introduced evidence to show that for over one hundred years both England and the United States had maintained the right of a neutral to make such purchases. According to his argument, the Declaration of London in 1908 had reaffirmed the British and American stand. Elihu Root was then Secretary of State. The Montanan admitted there could be honest disagreement over certain provisions in the Declaration of London. "But what of it?" he asked. Britain had never ratified the Declaration anyway. Was the United States to abandon its historic position "simply because some or all of the warring nations may exhibit some disposition to dispute it?" Of course not. The nation should stand by its rights in a "temperate but determined" way, and American citizens should be encouraged to do the same.[6]

The Montanan was gratified at reactions to his speech. He wrote to Lewis Penwell in Helena: "The President called me up Sunday night on the telephone and complimented me very highly upon it and thanked me for the contribution it made to the fight. He seemed very much delighted that Root's [argument] had been so satisfactorily met." The president, he said, was "obdurate" on the right to buy belligerent ships and was not at all inclined to yield just to please England or some members of Congress. Senator La Follette, Vice President Marshall, and others had words of high praise for Walsh's effort, and newspapers in the Treasure State were duly impressed.

Meanwhile, the ship purchase bill was not faring well in the Senate. Walsh observed in early February 1915 that the Democrats were in "dire straits," with defections in their party, while the president was refusing to make concessions that might have won the support of several progressive Republicans.

Norris and La Follette ardently favored government operation of a merchant fleet, but Norris particularly was alarmed by the idea of buying belligerent vessels, a practice which might lead to war.

Norris also said of Walsh in a telling observation: "The Senator is so belligerent in his good-natured way that he sees here [in the ship purchases] an opportunity for a discussion and a debate and he wants the Government to get into it right away."

The Montanan was not able to convince Norris; nor was the administration able to muster the necessary votes, and it gave up trying. In spite of strenuous efforts, then, the shipping bill went down to defeat.[7]

In a sideshow to this shipping fight, Walsh served as chairman of a special Senate committee appointed by the vice president. He and four colleagues were charged with the duty of looking into an alleged ship lobby in the capital. According to rumors and reports, there were powerful, covert forces working to get the bill passed and other powerful, covert forces working to get it defeated. The most interesting matter that came to Walsh's attention was an assertion by Theodore Roosevelt in *Metropolitan* magazine of April 1915, that seemed to call for investigation. Writing on "The Need of Preparedness," the former chief executive lashed out at President Wilson and Secretary of State Bryan and leveled a specific charge: that Wilson and Bryan had "endeavored in the interest of certain foreign business firms to secure for the United States the power to purchase the interned ships of one of the belligerents."

Walsh's Ship Lobby Committee invited the Colonel to appear before it and to "answer inquiries" concerning his statement in *Metropolitan*. When he declined to come Walsh issued a statement that brought forth another blast from the Colonel.

Probably the altercation with Roosevelt was the most memorable aspect of the Ship Lobby Committee. Walsh and his committee did not turn up evidence of a conspiracy or a powerful lobby on one side or the other. The time devoted to this subject, however, did increase Walsh's knowledge of the merchant marine, and it added to his experience as a Senate investigator.[8]

The shipping bill did not die a permanent death in the winter or spring of 1915. In December of that year the president again called upon Congress to pass a shipping bill, along with other measures considered necessary for military preparedness. When the bill passed in August 1916, it had been amended to forbid the purchase of German ships. Neither Walsh nor the president had prevailed in the end on this point.[9]

The *Lusitania* sinking in May 1915, with its heavy loss of life, did not elicit detailed comments from Senator Walsh, although he deplored the tragedy.

What interested him for months to come was the administration's handling of this crisis in German-American relations. He had more confidence in Woodrow Wilson than he did in Secretary of State Bryan and found little reason to regret the latter's resignation during the policy dispute that developed.

Accounts of this disagreement in the Wilson administration have stressed the secretary's belief in "true" neutrality and fair play toward Germany whereas the president is said to have made up his mind to hold Germany responsible for its submarine policy. Walsh saw Bryan at the time as closely associated with the unneutral, pro-allied policy so firmly established by the spring of 1915. Writing to a friend, Walsh reviewed the British interferences with American trade and the State Department's passive attitude as the "aggressions" mounted, "each one serving as a precedent for others." Walsh believed that Bryan's departure would immediately give advantages to the United States: "the Germans have all along insisted that our Government was a silent ally of Great Britain because of Bryan's friendliness for that country, his daughter having married an English officer."

Walsh further believed in a tough stand toward England as well as Germany. He also believed, perhaps unrealistically, that attempts should be made to inject a little more common sense into the rules of international law. For example, ships catering to passenger traffic ought to advertise that they did not carry munitions, while those that did carry such a cargo had no right to enjoy immunity from attack.

Walsh had many friends and constituents who were German-American, and his wife and daughter may still have preferred to see a victory by the Central Powers. Whether for that reason or not, he expressed his regret that the United States had "lost the good will of the Germans which we enjoyed in such a marked degree at the beginning of the war." He feared that the consistent policy of yielding to British "aggressions" might now have gone so far that little could be done to restore the cordiality of 1914, that is, between the people of Germany and the United States. This was a reasonable concern by 1915–16. If Woodrow Wilson was to get concessions from the German leaders or to bring about a negotiated settlement, as he periodically tried to do, Germans needed to believe in Wilson's capacity for fair play. Walsh believed that the "Germanic peoples" had come to hate Americans "with an intensity that is scarcely surpassed by that which they harbor towards the English."[10]

In a few months, during the second half of 1915, the Montana senator became an advocate of military preparedness. He moved to this position reluctantly and with occasional expressions of regret such as "I think the whole country has gone crazy about the army and navy." Previously he could not believe that "by preparing for war" the United States could keep the peace; nor did he believe that the sort of influence the United States ought to exercise in world affairs depended very much, if at all, on military strength. The happiness and prosperity of Americans would hardly be served by that kind of growth. But he did concede the importance of maintaining an "adequate navy," one that would "give reasonable assurance against the landing of hostile armies on our shores."

To his mind, only one nation would have any real capacity to land troops successfully along the Atlantic coast. That was Great Britain. If the United States was to ready itself for combat with any European country, it was Britain; she had a great navy and could benefit from landing in Canada and attacking southward from there. Having stated propositions that must have seemed implausible to himself and ridiculous to not a few, he went on to say that such military preparations would "not insure peace" but, more likely, would "precipitate war." Similarly, military preparations on a large scale in the Pacific would "invite a conflict with Japan" rather than forestalling or preventing it. So he could not support the ideas for a military buildup.

Five months later, with the crises over neutral rights continuing and with the president moving to support sizeable increases of the army and navy, Walsh had changed his way of thinking. One of his constituents wrote from Butte asking that he use his influence "against the preparedness propaganda."

Walsh replied that he was strongly inclined to agree with this view, but could not: "I once had myself the profoundest faith in the efficacy of treaties and conferences, through which rules governing nations in their relations with foreign powers might be promulgated, but having seen treaties by the score regarded as mere scraps of papers . . . I am forced to modify to some extent the views I have long cherished." He described the "aggressions" of Great Britain on the high seas and how the United States had become a "province" of that country in its foreign commerce.

By the first weeks of 1916 Walsh had broadened his view somewhat. He noted, for example, how the people of France were "making a glorious fight for their national existence" and how, recalling the help they had given to America in the Revolution, they believed the United States ought to be doing more for them than it was. The Montanan seemed to be flirting at least with the ultimate possibility of full scale involvement in the war. He noted again his disillusionment over the violation of treaties, the breakdown of international law, and the "destruction of life and property" in such a prolonged conflict. He had not believed such a thing could happen, and now he had to modify his old ideas. He said he hated "the policy upon which it seems we are embarking particularly because it involves an utter abandonment of the ideals our people have long cherished." He was saddened to think of the possibilities of military indoctrination. At the same time, he was a public official and had to look "facts squarely in the face." He had "to listen to the admonitions of the men at the head of our army and navy." The country must start preparing for future eventualities.[11]

Public opinion in Montana continued to be divided on the preparedness issue, and Walsh showed caution in his expressions. For the most part he frankly stated his conversion to the preparedness position even when it might hurt him politically. In a typical exchange, one J. J. Condon of the Miles City Trades and Labor Council, affiliated with the American Federation of Labor, wrote to Walsh saying they were opposed to "preparedness" programs and believed that a standing army "would menace the very spirit of our democracy." The senator replied that he was sorry they felt the way they did. He was sending a statement of his own and hoped it would be "beneficial and helpful . . . in arriving at the viewpoint from which we are working here [in Washington]." Walsh became firmly convinced there was no turning back. The subject was "no longer debatable," he said in a letter of May 23, 1916, "except in respect to details." Three days previously, the House of Representatives had voted 351 to 25 in favor of the conference report on the Army Reorganization Bill, and the Senate had approved without a roll call. At the same time, the submarine crisis with Germany seemed to have eased, and to Walsh's mind, the possibility of war was "much more remote."[12]

One section of the Army Reorganization Bill had to do with industrial preparedness for war, and it aroused Walsh's keenest interest, as it did that of his colleague, Henry Myers, and other Montana leaders. In Walsh's words, the bill carried "an appropriation of $20,000,000 for the construction of a nitrate plant or plants by the Government." From this plant, necessarily to be located at a great power site, the United States would obtain supplies of nitrogen needed to manufacture explosives. In time of peace the nitrogen might be used to produce fertilizers. In either case, the state or section of the country with a site good enough to be chosen would experience obvious economic benefits.

Losing no time, Walsh began a campaign in behalf of Montana and the Northwest. He wrote, for example, to Louis W. Hill of the Great Northern Railroad Company, to James M. Hanaford, president of the Northern Pacific Railroad, and to others, urging that the claims of Montana be brought to the attention of the secretary of war. Community organizations, such as the Billings Chamber of Commerce, also began to agitate on the subject. But Walsh warned in one letter: "A determined effort will be made to locate . . . at the muscle shoals of the Tennessee River."

In Walsh's correspondence and the related documents one can get a sense of the excitement generated among engineers, businessmen, farmers, politicians, and others over the prospects of landing a nitrate plant. This activity continued through the spring and summer of 1916. Walsh's colleague, Henry Myers, introduced a bill "To authorize an investigation of the power possibilities near Polson, Montana, for the purpose of establishing a Government-built power plant in connection with the fixation of atmospheric nitrogen." Apparently Myers, Walsh, and the entire Montana delegation met with the president at one point to present the arguments for one or another of the Montana locations. Meanwhile, Walsh had received from Senator Oscar W. Underwood of Alabama a pamphlet on the problem of taking nitrogen out of the air in order "to manufacture powder and fertilizers." Perhaps Underwood was showing great confidence in the ability of his state to win the support of adminisration leaders; or perhaps he was showing "senatorial courtesy." Walsh did the best he could to rally support for his own state, all to no avail.[13]

While the European war seemed at times pervasive in its influence and demands, much else was happening. Certainly for Walsh, the years 1915 and 1916 were among his busiest. Deep involvement in legislative matters was only to be expected, but he also was caught up in the campaign for Wilson's re-election. This campaign included among its issues the matter of preserving the peace. Americans could not escape from the extraordinary conflict raging across the Atlantic.[14]

14

Winning the West with Wilson, 1915–16

Walsh had a part in developing the issues for Wilson's reelection. He gave support to major economic legislation of this period; for example, to the La Follette Seaman's Act, the Federal Farm Loan Act, the Child Labor Act, the Kern-McGillicuddy Workmen's Compensation Act, and the Adamson Act for interstate railway workers. Often he was an active, contributing legislator. He vigorously backed the woman suffrage amendment to the federal Constitution, which the president hesitated to endorse, and the Jones Act for Philippine independence. As a member of the platform committee in St. Louis, forcefully stating his views, Walsh had an influence on the progressive side. Eventually he managed the western campaign for Wilson's reelection, from headquarters in Chicago.

The Montanan was emerging as a figure to be watched. One of the reasons undoubtedly was his support of the president's policies. By the fall of 1915, he had moved into the preparedness camp, joining Wilson on that important issue. Perhaps a closer relationship was facilitated by the fact that the president grew increasingly critical of British tactics on the high seas while the Montana senator had been for many months a critic of Britain over this issue. Walsh also stood out among the western Democratic senators at a time when that region loomed importantly with a national campaign in the offing.

One indication of his standing came at the Jefferson Day banquet on the evening of April 13, 1916, with some 700 guests at the tables. Held at the Willard Hotel in Washington, this was a "brilliant" occasion, in Walsh's words, and according to some it was the "biggest political banquet" ever held in the capital. Among the throng were Democratic state chairmen from all sections of the United States, women leaders of the party, and dignitaries of the national government including President and Mrs. Wilson. Walsh was a featured speaker, along with Senator Henry Hollis of New Hampshire, Representative Carter Glass of Virginia, and the president, whose relatively nonpolitical address capped the occasion. "It was no small honor," Walsh commented, "to be seated . . . on one side of the master of ceremonies [Robert W. Woolley, Director of the Mint], with the President of the United States on the other." Walsh said that he had never regarded himself "as in the same class as a public speaker with President Wilson." The *Washington Post*, however, in its coverage of the affair, stated that Walsh had given an "eloquent speech" and provided arguments for his party in the approaching campaign.[1]

The Montanan's topic was one that fellow Democrats reacted to with understandable enthusiasm—"Three Years of the New Freedom." He spoke as a Jeffersonian Democrat and a Wilsonian but also as a western man who had been an active leader and a keen observer during the past twenty years. Why had his region, which was overwhelmingly Republican in 1904, turned decisively to the Democratic party since that time? He explained and predicted that this support would continue, that Montana and other states beyond the Missouri River would gladly give their electoral vote to President Wilson. Western people, he said, trusted the president and approved the administration of public lands under Secretary of the Interior Franklin Lane.

Walsh received glowing compliments from a number of those at the banquet. Printed as a public document, the speech was available for circulation during the presidential campaign.[2]

One of Walsh's closest friends in the Senate was Henry Hollis of New Hampshire, who had spoken at the Jefferson Day banquet on the subject of agricultural credits legislation. Their personal friendship contributed to a useful collaboration in the Senate's business. Hollis served on the Senate Banking and Currency Committee and was chairman of a subcommittee that in 1914 had begun to put together the elements of a farm credits bill. Walsh also was on friendly terms with Representative Robert J. Bulkley of Cleveland, chairman of a subcommittee in the House working on the same subject. These two brought him into their consultations in 1914–15 and made him a party to much of their work, partly no doubt because of his legal ability.

Walsh considered this bill extremely important, both for economic and political reasons. To a banker friend in Helena, George Ramsey, he wrote of his satisfaction in trying, with popular support, "to enact wise laws that will unloose the energies of the people and promote the general welfare." To an old friend in South Dakota he wrote, "Not only do I believe that it [the credits bill] would be the greatest boon that has been conferred upon the people in a generation through legislative action, but it would, as I think, make us impregnable in the campaign two years hence."

Walsh's best contribution in the Senate debates was to make a constitutional argument intended to meet objections raised by Cummins of Iowa and Sutherland of Utah. His argument made the necessary points: The federal government had all the power needed to establish land banks of this type, based on many precedents. Speaking to the bar association of Ohio a little later, Walsh commented that the Senate debates over the farm credits act had "presented anew the ever recurring and always interesting question of the limit of the power of the National Government as against the reserved rights of the States." The vote was 58 to 5 with 33 abstaining.[3]

Walsh was optimistic concerning Montana's potential as an agricultural state, and proud of its current achievements. Montana's growth in agriculture depended upon the federal government. Homesteaders poured into eastern Montana during this period and, using dry-farming methods, added greatly to the state's production of wheat. Rainfall proved adequate for a time, and World War I stimulated demand. The output in 1915 was more than 42,000,000 bushels, a record crop. In addition to thousands of farmers engaged in grain production there were those who benefited from government irrigation projects, who grazed their sheep and livestock on public land, and who homesteaded inside the national forest areas (when permitted to do so). Montana had a diversity of agricultural situations, and problems, too, in which Walsh as a senator got involved. He also had a personal investment in sheep and cattle ranching.[4]

Labor questions were among the most controversial of those that came before Congress in 1915 and 1916. In July 1914, during Senate consideration of labor provisions in the Clayton Act, Walsh had remonstrated with a union leader who expected him to work for the bill as it had come from the House of Representatives. He said that he felt the Democrats were entitled to "very generous approbation" for the labor measures they had been able to put through Congress. His first Senate speech in 1913 had been in opposition to using funds from the general appropriation bill for prosecution of labor unions under the Sherman law, that is, as combinations in restraint of trade. Leaders in Congress, he said, had amended the Sherman law so that labor unions were "exempted from its operation." They had acted to restrict the use of antilabor injunctions and provide for jury trial in cases of "indirect contempt." They enacted the seamen's law sponsored by Senator La Follette for the protection of workingmen on the high seas. They "put a provision in all of the appropriation bills prohibiting the stopwatch system in government works," or a labor speedup. Finally he concluded: "we have enacted more laws and more important laws demanded by the labor interests of this country than the republicans [have] for a generation."[5]

Walsh could not include at this time several important bills that would pass Congress in the next three months, during the summer of 1916. He was in touch with John B. Andrews, secretary of the American Association for Labor Legislation, who urged in July that the Senate pass, in unamended form, the Kern-McGillicuddy bill for compensation of injured federal workers. Notwithstanding Senate opposition Walsh argued for the bill and thus for making a change from the old system of "alleged contributory negligence," which "almost invariably" undermined the employee in his effort for compensation. Injuries on the job, said the Montanan, ought to be blamed on human nature and the work situation, rather than negligence. President Wilson was now pushing for the enactment of this and other progressive bills, and he found a ready response from most members of Congress.

One of the measures that Walsh debated over, hoping to support it, was the Keating-Owen Child Labor Bill. In an effort to alleviate the evils of child labor, this would ban the movement in interstate commerce of goods manufactured by children. Early in 1916 the Montanan told correspondents on the subject that he would study the measure as a member of the Judiciary Committee and would support it unless he had constitutional objections. A little later he said flatly that he would give his support to the bill. When the bill passed in August, Walsh was at his job in Chicago as the western campaign manager. He had to ask his colleague, Senator Myers, to make the announcement of his "yea" vote if he had been present.[6]

In the spring of 1916 Walsh had a part in one of the dramatic events of Wilson's first term, a fight that had significance for the labor movement and for the development of progressivism. Wilson nominated Louis D. Brandeis of Boston to fill a vacancy on the Supreme Court. If confirmed, Brandeis would be the first Jew to hold such a position. He was also known as a left-of-center lawyer who had argued for "pragmatism of the law," for reinterpreting the law and Constitution in the light of modern conditions. He was noted especially for his scientific brief that won a case for working women in *Muller v. Oregon* (1908).[7]

Walsh became involved because of his being on the Judiciary Committee and a subcommittee as well that made recommendations to the full committee and Senate. Three Democrats on the subcommittee—William E. Chilton of West Virginia, Duncan U. Fletcher of Florida, and Walsh—decided in favor of the nominee, while Republicans Albert Cummins of Iowa and John D.

Works of California voted against Brandeis. The vote in the Senate finally was 47 to 22, with only one Democrat (Francis Newlands of Nevada) opposing Brandeis, while La Follette, Norris, and Miles Poindexter of Washington State joined the Democratic majority.[8]

Walsh's contribution had been, first, to fight for Brandeis in the subcommittee (overcoming a few doubts), and, second, to write a strong report for the nominee, a brilliant analysis that was widely circulated along with Senator Chilton's. Walsh examined the disputes about Brandeis's cases and sometimes commented trenchantly or with a touch of sarcasm: "If this is professional misconduct the bar needs regeneration." He said also, "The real crime of which this man is guilty is that he has exposed the iniquities of men in high places in our financial system. He has not stood in awe of the majesty of wealth."[9]

The Brandeis appointment could have been hurtful to the Democrats politically, but they judged otherwise about its consequences. In the early months of 1916 Democrats were looking ahead to the national convention, to begin in St. Louis on June 14. Walsh anticipated with pleasure the role he would play as a Montana delegate helping to write the party platform. However, before he could actually go to St. Louis, he had to get himself elected as a delegate. In early April he and his office staff did some long distance campaigning. Letters went out to Montana Democrats, calling attention to the primary to be held on April 21 and asking their support. When the results came in, Walsh had easily gained election as one of the eight delegates.[10]

When the delegates assembled in St. Louis, Walsh assumed a position of importance in helping to shape the final draft of the platform. Senator Stone had appointed him to the subcommittee of the platform committee, along with Senators Hollis, Thomas Martin of Virginia, Atlee Pomerene of Ohio, and a few others who were not of the senatorial group. He favored a progressive appeal that would include planks on woman suffrage and child labor legislation, together with a listing of Wilson's achievements "that could be indefinitely extended"; and, according to one newspaper, Walsh said he believed that with this kind of campaign a million votes could be drawn to the president from progressive Republican voters of the country. In foreign policy he called for "strict neutrality towards the warring nations," continuing efforts to end that "sanguinary conflict," and a commitment to "all necessary measures and means" to protect the United States. He reasserted the principles of the Monroe Doctrine, which included, according to his view, a "scrupulous regard" for the rights of other countries in the Americas. His draft lauded the president for his refusal to be drawn into a war with Mexico.

His ideas closely resembled those in the platform as finally written. He and other progressives of the party exerted the largest influence in St. Louis. But the literary style, the organization, and the precise emphases found in the final document were the result of many minds and talents at work, most of all the president's. Senator Walsh did have his time of glory, however, in a stirring debate on the convention floor concerning the position to be adopted on woman's suffrage.[11]

The convention assembled at noon on Wednesday, June 14, with the atmosphere resembling a family reunion. Everyone knew the president would be nominated by acclamation. Democrats who crowded into the Jefferson Hotel, many dressed in Palm Beach suits, were freely predicting that the recent nomination of Charles Evans Hughes, in Chicago, would bring disgruntled Progressives of 1912 into the fold of Woodrow Wilson; surely the signs were encouraging. There was one note of possible disharmony. Women by the thousands were arriving in St. Louis. These suffragists had determined to exert all the influence they possibly could on members of the resolutions committee and other party leaders. Alice Paul of the Congressional Union for Woman Suffrage, along with her workers, set up headquarters in the Jefferson Hotel lobby. Women associated with the larger organization, the National American Woman Suffrage Association, were also in evidence at this meeting.

Members of the resolutions committee held long meetings of the full committee with its forty-eight members and public hearings, as well, featuring conflicts of viewpoint on the woman suffrage question; there were attempts to put the planks into final form, and arguments among the members in both the subcommittee and full committee. Sessions continued virtually all night on June 15, after the president had been renominated at midnight. After all this effort the committee members still had not settled the suffrage matter, thus assuring that a majority and a minority report would be debated on the floor of the convention.[12]

The platform was the final business to be attended to when the convention convened on Friday, June 16, and many delegates were impatient to finish and leave for home. Senators Walsh and Hollis were given the honor of reading the completed platform to the entire gathering, with Walsh leading off. "Long as it was," said an observer, "the platform was listened to attentively, with routine cheers for the principal planks." Then a fight ensued over the woman suffrage plank.[13]

Senator Stone moved that the platform be adopted as read, and he ran into vocal opposition from Governor James E. Ferguson of Texas, along with a number of his Texas delegates and others. They proposed the adoption of a substitute for the plank on woman suffrage, so that the convention would make no recommendation as the majority plank did, but simply leave the question to the states. Ferguson's group vehemently opposed the idea of woman suffrage; so did many others in the hall. The Texan said that the majority position was one of expediency only and that such a position, calling for woman suffrage, did not represent the views of a majority of American Democrats but was intended to avoid the loss of electoral votes in "three or four Western States." That would be a shameful thing, he declared, to lay aside their principles and the principles of great Democratic leaders of the past merely to win a few votes.

Senators Stone, Pittman, and Walsh responded, speaking for the majority plank. It was Walsh who spoke to the point of the dispute and made the most telling arguments, while women in the galleries "went wild," said the *New York Times* reporter.

Far from being intimidated by Governor Ferguson's charge of "expediency," Walsh declared that it was a "condition and not a theory" that confronted the convention. Twelve states had already given the suffrage to women and those states would control a total of 91 electoral votes in the coming election. "So that it becomes a simple question," he said, "as to whether you will or whether you will not incur the natural enmity that will be directed against the nominee of this Convention in those twelve states." There was no possibility of losing votes if the majority resolution was adopted. The senator went on to say that the governor of Texas had "assumed a great virtue" in this matter and deplored the sacrifice of convictions. "Oh, dear!" Walsh exclaimed ironically. "I wonder if that is the only plank upon which some of us didn't have to compromise to some extent or other." According to the columnist, "A shrill scream of laughter ran through the hall."

Walsh went on: "Why my friends, we never shall be anything but a divided and discordant and a contending party unless we surrender some of our convictions to the united wisdom of the whole. [Applause.]" He made the point that he had recently emphasized at the Jefferson Day dinner. The Democratic party had been gaining remarkably in the trans-Missouri West, rising from its depths of 1904, when only Colorado sent a Democratic senator to Washington and not a single state in that region gave its support to the Democratic presidential candidate. He reminded the delegates that, with the exception of Illinois, all the woman suffrage states were in that same western region. Now the question was, did this convention want to turn the trans-Missouri West back into the hands of their "political enemies forever. [Applause.]"

Finally, the Montana senator declared that their "great leader," the president, was in favor of the majority resolution. "I reveal no secrets when I say that it is common knowledge that the presidential candidate always is apprised beforehand of the planks that are going into the platform. [Applause.] And this has his approval. [Applause.] He deems it vital to his success that it shall stay there. [A voice: 'Good for you.' Applause.] And I ask you, and I ask you with all the fervor of my soul, who of us here is wiser or more patriotic than he? [Great applause.]" Quickly the convention voted on Ferguson's substitute and defeated it overwhelmingly, 888½ to 181½. A few minutes later the convention adjourned, having nominated its candidates, Woodrow Wilson and Thomas Marshall, and adopted a platform that emphasized peace and progressivism.

Walsh undoubtedly had made a hit with his convention speech, which was widely commented upon and praised. The *New York Times,* for example, gave a detailed account of the debate over woman suffrage and quoted Senator Walsh at length. Their columnist observed that the convention's "overwhelming vote" for woman suffrage came "on the heels of a speech by Senator Walsh of Montana, in which he swung the club of the women's vote over its head."[14]

The St. Louis convention added to Walsh's prominence in the Democratic party. His speech at the Jefferson Day dinner in mid-April had attracted wide comment and favorable attention, as had his leading role in the Brandeis confirmation fight that ended just before the convening of the national convention. Then in St. Louis in the hotel meeting rooms and in the great Coliseum itself the junior senator from Montana had demonstrated a sensitivity to the issues of this election and his loyalty to the president. Meanwhile, Woodrow Wilson and his southern and eastern advisers, including Colonel Edward House, were looking for men to run the reelection campaign. Not surprisingly, they concluded that Thomas J. Walsh should be added to their staff. Within weeks, Walsh was deeply involved in the race between President Wilson and Charles Evans Hughes.

During the convention period the president chose Vance McCormick of Pennsylvania to be Chairman of the National Committee, and before the end of June announcements were made that a strategy board for Wilson's reelection had been formed.

The president and his aides also decided that the Montana senator should manage the western campaign with headquarters in Chicago. Top-level planning was underway in June and July, although Walsh did not leave his senatorial duties in Washington until early August. Of some importance was the fact that the national chairman, Vance McCormick, and his western manager got along well together. Both represented the progressive wing of the Democratic party. McCormick was a former mayor of Harrisburg, Pennsylvania, and a nominee for governor on the Democratic ticket in 1914. He had also been chosen that year as the gubernatorial nominee of the Pennsylvania Progressives. An admirer in Philadelphia described him as a very attractive person who was "peculiarly qualified" to be the national chairman: He was a business leader and practical farmer of independent means and "one of the most public spirited men in Pennsylvania."[15]

In June and July Walsh experienced a period of uncertainty. A vacancy had been created on the Supreme Court when Charles Evans Hughes resigned after winning the Republican presidential nomination. A movement then developed in Walsh's behalf, and he mulled over his decision if the offer were received. But on July 15 he wrote to his friend Lewis Penwell in Montana that Judge John H. Clarke of Ohio had been nominated. Walsh said he was happier not to have been drafted because the temptation might have been "too great."[16]

The period after the Democratic convention was a busy one for Walsh, as it was for other members of Congress. They still had before them, for example, the child labor bill, the farm loan bill, a compensation bill for injured employees of the federal government, and the highly important revenue measure that was intended to provide new monies for national preparedness. All of these soon passed or reached an advanced stage of readiness, adding to the Democratic record for reform.

By the first week of August, the western campaign started its move west— to Chicago. A site for the Chicago headquarters had not been chosen. Walsh carried on his early business at the Blackstone Hotel, where he continued to live during his residence in Chicago. The Montanan was described by an interviewer as "a man of medium stature, a prominent mustache, and bristling eyebrows." Walsh told this reporter that the recent "drift" had been toward the president.

But the Democrats had just suffered a blow in Illinois. Raymond Robins, a prominent leader of the progressive Republicans, finally made up his mind that he would support the GOP ticket. He gave as his reason the power of southern men in the Wilson administration and their conservative influence on labor questions. Asked about this by the reporter, Walsh tactfully indicated that he didn't understand Robins's line of thinking. If Robins took the time to speak with labor leaders, he would find they were supporting Woodrow Wilson in the election.

According to the reporter, as the senator commented on some of these controversial matters his mustache "stood out militantly, and the bushy eyebrows, above a clear blue eye, bristled more intently as the eyes gleamed." The impression given was that of a strong-minded and determined western manager.[17]

Soon after going to Chicago, Walsh wrote an informative letter to Ellen Walsh, who was vacationing at the summer home in Glacier Park. "Your letter of the 2nd reached me here today and I'm snatching a few moments in a lull to write." One problem, he said, had occurred when he made the decision to hire a secretary "at hazard." Then he learned that the man would "reveal everything that went on"; so he called for his nephew, John Wattawa, to come down from Wisconsin and serve as aide and secretary. Also, his longtime personal secretary, Imogene Howell, would be coming from Washington to join him.

This was a large operation Walsh had embarked upon. For example, he and his advisers decided they should set up headquarters in the Karpen Building on Michigan Avenue, even though the rent seemed high. They were getting 8,000 square feet of floor space and had no doubt they would need all of it, and more. About a month later a newspaperman who interviewed Walsh in the Karpen Building described the headquarters as resembling a beehive, or "a mail-order house billing department." He found ninety partitions and on every glass pane of each door there was the name of the person holding the particular office and a description of the job. "You wouldn't believe how many offices it takes to elect one President, and this does not take into account post offices."[18]

The Chicago headquarters was responsible for campaign efforts west of the Mississippi River and in the State of Illinois. It had to coordinate its work with that of Vance McCormick and his staff in New York and, of course, with the activities of party leaders at the state level. The presidential campaign loomed largest in Walsh's thinking, but he and his associates had to give aid, as well, to congressional candidates and other aspiring Democrats.

By the end of August, Walsh had virtually completed his staff organization. That he ran a tight ship seems apparent. The hours of work were nine o'clock to five thirty, with only half an hour for lunch and—at first—a full day's work on Saturday. Every day the senator had a conference at noon with the heads of bureaus, and then they all went to lunch together at one o'clock. Undoubtedly Walsh and some of the policymakers put in a good many hours at night.[19]

Contemporary judgments seemed unanimous that Walsh created an excellent organization. The bureaus established were those actually needed, and the persons chosen to head them were hardworking and effective. There was, of course, some controversy over the appointment of personnel. Of all the bureaus, that concerned with financial problems and the collection of money was the most important. Without adequate funds, the Wilson campaign would obviously have failed. Francis S. Peabody, whom Walsh referred to as "one of the strong men of Chicago" and a "fine fellow," did a good job of soliciting contributions, although there was never enough money to do all that the headquarters thought they ought to do. But more and more Republicans or fence-sitters were making up their minds to support the probable winner, President Woodrow Wilson.[20]

The appointment giving Walsh his greatest difficulty was that of a director for the bureau of women voters. He wrote to his wife in mid-August: "The Woman's Bureau is still up in the air. McCormick took it out of my hands and turned it over to Mrs. [Percy V.] Pennypacker and Mrs. Borden Harriman. They got nowhere and after waiting on them until further delay was impossible he told me to go on and make a choice." Walsh then considered a number of possibilities including Mary McDowell, a settlement worker associated with Jane Addams, but finally offered the position to Mrs. George Bass, formerly president of the Chicago Federation of Women's Clubs. Complaints were heard from a few unhappy women, but the choice of Mrs. Bass turned out to be fortunate indeed compared with mishandling of the same question by Republican campaign managers.[21]

In this same period Walsh was successful in persuading another woman, his wife, Ellen, to get into the effort to win the women's vote, especially in Montana. He urged her to "go at it" when she left the lake and returned to Helena. His recommendation was that she get the ladies she knew in various places "to make up a loose kind of an organization," then to have meetings in people's homes, as they were doing successfully in Chicago. Of course, she should engage prominent local speakers, and she should work with members of the state Democratic committee, including Thomas Arthur of Billings, the chairman. With this and other advice he soon had his wife busily at work to win the women's vote for President Wilson.

The top appointments to run the western headquarters were mostly senators and representatives whom Walsh knew on Capitol Hill and whose talents he respected. A few got their assignments on the advice of Democratic leaders such as Joseph E. Davies, who had directed this same office in the campaign of 1912. For his research specialist Walsh looked to Madison, Wisconsin, where Charles McCarthy had organized a pioneering legislative reference service that gave aid to the Wisconsin legislature. At Walsh's request,

Edward Fitzpatrick of McCarthy's staff came to Chicago on temporary assignment. With the expertise of Fitzpatrick added to Walsh's scholarly interests and attention to facts, the western headquarters was well-primed for a battle over the issues in 1916.[22]

The Montanan lost no time in taking steps to rally the western Democratic forces and to improve his office's communication with them. On August 17 at the Hotel Sherman he gave what was described as a "rousing old-fashioned democratic speech." He addressed members of the Illinois State Central Committee and used the occasion to tell of his plans for organization and procedure in the western headquarters. Walsh had tried to drive home the message, as he informed his wife the next day, that "we must *tell the people* what we [Democrats] have done and not make the mistake of supposing they know it."

At the end of August he sent a long letter by Western Union to each of the Democratic state chairmen in his territory. He listed the Chicago bureaus and their heads and discussed in some detail the services his staff could provide and the kind of cooperation and united effort that was likely to bring Democrats a great victory. In part, this was a "pep talk." They had a great cause and ought to be able to prevail. The "burden of the fight," he said, must fall upon Democratic workers out in the states. But he and his staff in Chicago could supply outside speakers, for example, and wanted to know when and where they were needed.

He asked the state leaders to work with county leaders and to encourage them to be "specially vigilant and active." In this letter and in many others to Democrats individually Walsh urged his co-workers to send information about how the "battle" was going, so that decisions on the allocation of money and resources could be made more wisely in New York and Chicago. Thus writing to a friend in Great Falls, Walsh solicited information and declared: "Don't feed me on what I like to hear, but tell the truth."

Another thing Walsh needed from the local leaders was voter lists, "the preparation of which may be a tedious and perhaps burdensome task." But they had to have these lists, doubtless for mailing purposes, to give all the help they could give. Then, too, he or his staff members would be glad to write to any "inactive democrat of prominence" to try and stir the person into action, if state officials wanted them to do so.[23]

Perhaps on the same day, Walsh sent a communication to Democratic newspapers in the western states. He stressed the importance of newspapers in spreading the facts about Democratic achievements and he emphasized the services his organization was prepared to render. He declared: "our main reliance must be upon the newspapers which go daily or weekly into the homes, the shops and the offices, carrying the truth about our cause."

There was one kind of political information Walsh valued above any other—that coming from a true professional who knew the West and its people and who exhibited a wisdom based on long experience in the political wars. One such informant was Fred T. Dubois, formerly a territorial delegate and a senator from Idaho. Dubois had been a Republican, a Silver Republican, and a Democrat over the years and in 1916 served as a traveling adviser to the Democrats. He provided "ammunition" for Walsh as he tried to prevail on McCormick and others in the East to do those things that seemed necessary to win in the western states.[24]

Early in September some of the campaign leaders enjoyed a change of pace and scenery. Woodrow Wilson had to be "notified" of his nomination for the presidency, according to the ceremonial practices of the day, and he and his advisers set the date of this occasion for Saturday, September 2. The place was "Shadow Lawn," Wilson's summer home on the seashore of New Jersey, to which various party leaders and others were invited. Walsh told his wife he "had no hesitancy in leaving" Chicago for the ceremonies because he and his staff had gradually worked their way "out of chaos" and "into a somewhat systematic machine."[25]

By the time of this ceremony, the campaign was fully launched. Wilson, in fact, during the preceding weeks had forcefully exercised his leadership in the matter of a threatened railroad strike; the so-called Adamson Act was ready for his signature immediately after the notification ceremonies. Republican leaders saw in this "surrender" to the railroad unions an issue that would win the election for Charles Evans Hughes. They began to hammer away on this theme. Democrats, however, did not retreat.

Walsh followed the president's lead on economic matters in an address to the businessmen of Chicago, gathered at a banquet of the Iroquois Club. The Montana senator stated forcefully: "Mr. Wilson calls in clarion tones to the business men of America to go into the markets of the world prepared to meet all comers"; and the president was ready to give aid and encouragement in this competition. Walsh continued: "I ask, What does Mr. Hughes propose? His ingenuity, his originality, his vision exhausts itself in the suggestion of a protective tariff." This appeal for support, on the shores of Lake Michigan, naturally gave recognition to the greatness of Chicago as a producing and shipping center.[26]

As the campaign continued, there could be little doubt that Wilson's candidacy was a tremendous asset to the Democratic party while Charles Evans

Hughes, though making a strenuous effort, did not live up to his reputation. He slipped into some mistakes from the start and, most important, simply could not bridge the gap between Old Guard members of his party and the Progressives. He had to struggle also with Theodore Roosevelt and a noisy minority who wanted war with Germany, in opposition to the peace-loving sentiments of most Americans. Hughes seemed to be searching for an issue until, with the passage of the Adamson Act, he believed he had found one. The president, in contrast, had a record of achievement on which to run but deliberately chose not to do much campaigning. When he did speak, he made his efforts count.

The Democrats had some problems. These included at all times a shortage of money, restricting the number of speakers who could be sent out, the amount of literature that could be distributed, and the advertisements that could be placed. One reason for the money shortage was, as usual, the predominant business support for the GOP; another was the strength of Hughes in New York State and the Northeast where the oddsmakers predicted a victory for the Republicans.

The indications are that President Wilson and his advisers recognized more clearly by mid-September the odds against them in New England and the Northeast generally. They were prepared, as a result, to give more attention to doubtful states in the West where a groundswell seemed to be moving in their favor. Walsh continued to be optimistic. On October 11, 1916, he wrote to his son-in-law, Emmet C. Gudger, "I say briefly in answer to the inquiry of your letter that in my opinion we shall prevail whichever way New York goes. The West is ablaze with enthusiasm for Wilson. The people at home talk most confidently."[27]

Senator Walsh observed in one of the many letters he sent from Chicago that his campaign work was "an awful grind." But he also described recreational opportunities to be found in the city and its environs. One problem was a heat wave in August, from which he found relief some evenings by going to the dining room in the Blackstone Hotel, where the temperature, Walsh explained, could be kept at 65 degrees by artificial cooling. The principal sources of recreation were dining out and playing golf. These he combined at times with politics.

Walsh said his routine might sound like a holiday, but it was far from it, with "a stream of people in and out all day long so that I am obliged to cut everything short and nearly everybody." Cool weather helped when it came, and he gradually learned to be "more sensible" and stop fretting so much. He remarked in late October that he was "keeping up a tremendous gait" but fortunately had not been ill at any time, although he was "pretty anxious often."[28]

A sketch of Senator Walsh in his "beehive headquarters" came from the typewriter of Jack Lait in the *Chicago Herald*. He was impressed with the western manager's handlebar mustache and with his skill in handling "smart-Alec young men," such as himself. Walsh seemed to have no doubt that the Democrats would win this election, and he insisted that he was satisfied with his place in the Senate and expected nothing personally from a Democratic victory.[29]

Of all the issues in the campaign, Walsh took a most personal interest in woman suffrage. It could hardly be otherwise when his wife was running the women's campaign in Montana while the twelve "suffrage states" were all in his area of responsibility. Then he had been active concerning this question in the St. Louis convention. Walsh believed the Democratic appeal should be made to women voters primarily on the basis that they were good citizens and were concerned with the issues in general: with the question of peace, with the elimination of child labor, and with other matters of importance rather than the single issue of extending the vote to women in all forty-eight states. William Jennings Bryan, on the campaign trail, wrote to Walsh: "'He has kept us out of war' is our strongest slogan," and he agreed with McAdoo that the peace issue had a strong appeal to the women. Walsh wrote to a Montana lady: "I do not know how you feel about it, but knowing, as you have had abundant opportunity to know, of the horrors of war that are ravaging Europe, I reach the conclusion that in common with most women you have been profoundly gratified at the success which has thus far attended President Wilson's efforts to keep us out of the conflict." Confirmation of the effectiveness of this type of appeal came from good sources.[30]

Ethnic groups were a source of concern. Of these, the Irish-Americans and their threatened defection from the Wilson administration touched Walsh most deeply and personally, so that he gave a disproportionate amount of time to this problem. He showed no sympathy with extreme critics of the president. He wrote to one correspondent that he had rejoiced when Wilson answered the "insolent telegram" from O'Leary as he did. The senator went on to explain that, in condemning O'Leary and his type, the president was referring only to a small minority of people who "put the interests of a country beyond the seas above those of this country" and wanted public officials to act accordingly.[31]

Many of the Irish seemed as agitated about Mexico and the treatment of Catholics there as they were about Ireland and its problems. One answer came from Democratic "stars" like Bryan. They pointed to the fact that Wilson had stayed out of war with Mexico and, they argued, had succeeded generally in his policies south of the border. Of course, he had not done what the capitalist exploiters of Mexico would like him to; nor had he interfered in the religious polity of that country. Senator Walsh talked on countless occasions with members of his own faith and carried on an extensive correspondence with Catholics inside and outside the party leadership. How could they counteract the attacks on Wilson's policies? To what extent should they even try? The western manager seems to have been the center of the Democratic "brains trust" on this problem.[32]

Walsh did not get caught up in an attempt to corral the German-American vote, as he had in the situation involving the Irish-Americans. He was actively interested, however. Soon after going to Chicago he announced he was looking for a man "who stands well with the German newspapers through the country" and who would write articles or help prepare them suitably for publication in these papers. Apparently he found such a man, one Hans Rieg.[33]

One of the issues inevitably stressed by Walsh was the Wilson administration's record on land policy, under the leadership of Franklin K. Lane in the Interior Department. Lane was a westerner who appealed to Republicans as well as to the Democrats of his region. There was no doubt his programs had been, in many respects, successful by 1916. He seemed to represent a logical compromise between the Gifford Pinchot school of federal activists and those who, in strong opposition to Pinchot, would turn public lands over to private interests or to the western states.[34]

An important function of the western manager was to keep the peace among rambunctious co-workers, and he did this with a fine sense of discrimination. When Arthur Mullen complained, for example, that the needs of Nebraska were not being met, Walsh responded this way: "Our German department has not failed to recognize the value of the ideas you advance as to how to reach the Germans. They are issuing literature constantly expressing similar views." The western manager concluded that Nebraska was not being overlooked and that the "intemperance" of Mullen's language probably could be attributed to "a natural infirmity and the zealousness of your disposition." Three weeks later Nebraska went Democratic, and some of the credit was due to the western headquarters.[35]

The problems in Walsh's own state were not serious, although he was worried that GOP Progressives in Montana had nominated most of the Republican candidates. One of these was Jeannette Rankin. She ran a good race, gained some Democratic support, and had an excellent chance to become the nation's first elected congresswoman. The Republican nominee for the U.S. Senate, trying to unseat Myers, seemed a threat, but Myers managed to hold on, with aid from Walsh and the western headquarters. His senate colleague, said Walsh, like many other Democrats expected the "Big Ship" to bring them safely into port. Walsh quoted Senator Stone on Myers as a campaigner: "That fellow is as helpless as a child."[36]

Walsh combined knowledgeability and a determination to win the election with the requisite tact, sociability, and willingness to accept suggestions. When necessary, he was a "good soldier" and followed advice from the East. That he did, in fact, develop a superb organization in Chicago no one seemed to question.

Walsh's legal skills, coupled with experience in the tough school of Montana politics, served him in good stead. Near the end of September, for example, word reached Chicago that an attack had been made on the Democratic governor of Wyoming, John B. Kendrick, who was running for the U.S. Senate while still occupying the governor's chair. Allegedly he could not qualify for the Senate or any other office while he was governor; the state constitution prohibited such a candidacy. Walsh immediately sent a refutation.

The Montanan exhibited in this campaign, as he did later in the Teapot Dome affair, a scrupulous regard for political ethics; thus Walsh advised a Montanan holding federal office that he should send his campaign contribution to the Democratic National Committee in New York, not to him (Walsh). To another Montanan associated with the Myers campaign he wired: "See Section thirty-three Corrupt Practices Act and consult lawyer before doing anything further."[37]

The tide seemed to be flowing strongly in the president's favor by October and November, and Walsh dared dream of a tidal wave; so did Vance McCormick and many party leaders. They were elated over the Bull Moosers who had announced their support for Wilson and the luminaries, in politics or out, who had done likewise. There were Henry Ford, Thomas Edison, Herbert Croly, Walter Lippmann, Amos Pinchot, Jane Addams, Ella Flagg Young, and hundreds of others. Some of this crème de la crème Walsh and his Chicago staff had cultivated and helped to win over, as he often reported to his wife.[38]

But the trend was misleading. The GOP continued to show its strength and was particularly formidable in northeastern states and parts of the Midwest, such as Indiana, Illinois, Iowa, and Wisconsin. For the Democrats to win these states in 1916 would have been extremely difficult.

Early returns in the East strongly indicated that Wilson could not win, and he went to bed on election night knowing the odds were against him. But favorable returns from western states normally Republican had a strongly encouraging effect. The electoral votes for Wilson mounted and, finally, California's 13 votes put the count at 277 to 254. Wilson had carried Arizona, New Mexico, California, Nevada, Idaho, Washington, Montana, Wyoming, Colorado, Utah, North Dakota, Kansas, Oklahoma, and Texas. The exhilaration of Democrats is conveyed in Walsh's telegram to Senator Henry Hollis, on November 9: "SHAKE OLD MAN. THERE IS A GOD IN ISRAEL. PERFECT ASSURANCES FROM CALIFORNIA, NORTH DAKOTA, AND NEW MEXICO." Walsh was a hero in Chicago, and some suggested that he had done more than anyone, except the president himself, to win this election.[39]

15

From Peace to War

The high point of Walsh's career, preceding the Teapot Dome investigation, came in the fall and early winter of 1916–17. He had attained the status of a hero in the minds of many Democrats, and he savored his associations with co-workers in the Chicago headquarters and his newly extended range of acquaintances among politicos, lawyers, businessmen and other leaders of the Midwest. There was a possibility that Walsh would move into the upper echelons of Senate leadership on the basis of recent achievements.

In late 1916 and early 1917 the European war threatened more ominously to involve the people of the United States. Walsh loyally followed the president, whose policies were developing, it seemed, in accordance with the national interests and those of Montana. In the fall of 1916 Wilson made a last attempt to bring the fighting to an end by diplomatic means. He delivered a "peace without victory" speech reflecting disillusionment with both sides, and he endeavored to speak for all people everywhere, calling for a "federation of mankind," as Walsh phrased it. When Germany made its decision for unrestricted submarine warfare, the president severed diplomatic relations with Berlin and sought authority from Congress to arm merchant vessels so they could follow their accustomed routes and defend themselves. Senate opposition erupted, however, in February and March, and the measure could not be passed. But Wilson went ahead and called for arming merchant vessels.

The country entered a state of armed neutrality and moved ever closer to war, although Wilson did not rule out the possibility of peaceful solutions, based on a suspension of German submarine warfare. That did not happen. Rather, the sinking of additional ships brought cries for war. The president continued to agonize and delay over a decision being forced upon him. Finally he came before Congress on April 2 to ask for a declaration of war against "an irresponsible government which has thrown aside all considerations of humanity and of right and is running amuck."

Walsh agreed with the president in nearly every detail of his war message, the main point being that German policy on the high seas was forcing the United States to become a belligerent: the time had come for Americans to join with the entente powers and assist them in every way possible to defeat a common enemy.

The event was not long delayed. On April 6, after the House of Representatives followed the Senate's lead by a vote of 373 to 50, the United States was officially at war with the Imperial German Government.

Many aspects of mobilization demanded the attention of congressional leaders, including a military conscription bill sponsored by the administration. Secretary of War Newton D. Baker and others believed that the old system of volunteers no longer could be used; a more efficient way of building up the armed services must be found, based on the European experience. It could be argued, however, that conscription was anti-American, militaristic, and totally unnecessary in a country of patriotic young men such as the United States boasted. On this highly emotional matter Walsh listened to what his constituents had to say and revealed some of his own ideas, although he was predisposed to support the administration.

To one writer favoring the volunteer method he replied: "I have the same traditional repugnance to conscription that you voice, but I am beginning to think that may be I am wrong about it." He gave an argument for drafting men from all classes and all occupations without favor. Relying on volunteers would mean, in his view, that "the best blood in the country will enlist, the bright, the energetic, the enthusiastic, the patriotic," while others perhaps lacking in patriotism and selfish in purpose would stay home. The country, then, should move to a well planned system of conscription. Walsh resisted, however, the calls for a Universal Military Training Bill, commenting: "I am apprehensive that our youth may be filled with a military spirit"; and he added: "The army officers, as a rule, look with eagerness to a war."

Walsh believed in patriotic service and a willingness to sacrifice during the wartime emergency. His viewpoint is clearly delineated in an address of July 4, 1917, before the Bar Association of North Carolina in Asheville. Originally entitled "Who Is Afraid of a Dictator?" it later was published as "War Powers of the President." Walsh defended Congress's granting to the president great and extraordinary powers to prosecute the war. He cited the Roman example of the same practice in times of peril when a dictator had been appointed and the republic did not collapse because of temporary suspension of privileges ordinarily assumed in peacetime. Walsh also noted Machiavelli's commentary on the occasional necessity of a dictatorship.

His loyalty to the administration may have been heightened by several influences: first, he had identified with President Wilson and Democratic officials during the recent political campaign and after; second, there was his need possibly, as an Irish-American leader, to show repeatedly that he and his "people" were solidly behind the war effort.[1]

Obviously Senator Walsh was caught up in the fervor of national mobilization, along with the great majority of Americans. As a member of the Judiciary Committee, Walsh helped to write the Espionage Act of June 15, 1917, and did so enthusiastically, seeing this as a major contribution to the war effort. When the measure appeared too weak to him and others in the administration he played a role in writing an amendment called the Sedition Act of May 16, 1918, which had sweeping provisions intended to catch critics of the war. Walsh also sponsored bills aimed at the "Reds" and other radicals who allegedly advocated a violent overthrow of the U.S. government.[2]

Labor disturbances in Montana involving the Industrial Workers of the World helped to stimulate his intolerance of wartime dissenters generally. He regarded members of the IWW as "public enemies," who threatened to bring the legitimate labor organizations into disrepute. In April 1917 he was so alarmed at troubles reportedly caused by the IWW that he asked the secretary of war to send troops to the Eureka Lumber Company in Eureka, Montana, where a strike was in progress. Troops soon broke the strike.[3]

Labor problems persisted, and some officials in Montana blamed business and the government rather than the IWW. U.S. Attorney Burton K. Wheeler was unwilling to prosecute left wing workers, whom he regarded as being falsely accused of treasonable and revolutionary activities. And Federal Judge George M. Bourquin, of Butte, in *Ex Parte Jackson* stated emphatically that business interests and federal agents were trying to destroy the IWW for their own purposes, rather than to win the war in Europe.[4]

Walsh continued to advocate the suppression of the IWW. This might be achieved by broadening the Espionage Act so that Wheeler and Judge Bourquin would be compelled to move against the Montana radicals. Walsh utilized his position on the Judiciary Committee to help frame the Sedition Act of May 1918, which made liable to a $10,000 fine or twenty years imprisonment those who interfered with or criticized the war effort of the United States. To one correspondent Walsh wrote: "we have succeeded in so amending the espionage act as that it will be difficult for any one guilty of uttering disloyal sentiments to escape punishment." He went on: "I have been obliged to make a continuous fight both before the Judiciary Committee and on the floor to secure and to keep the bill as strong as it is."[5]

Far from believing that the restrictive acts of 1917 and 1918 were too harsh, Walsh sought special legislation to crush the IWW and similar groups. His unlawful associations bill, introduced in May 1918, was intended to outlaw associations that in time of war proposed to bring about any governmental, social, industrial, or economic change in the United States by physical force, violence, or injury. Violation of the act could bring ten years imprisonment and/or a fine of not more than $5,000. The Senate accepted this bill on May 6 without a roll call, but the House Judiciary Committee refused to give its approval. On June 3, 1919, the day after Attorney General A. Mitchell Palmer's home was bombed, presumably by radicals, Walsh reintroduced his unlawful associations bill. With slight modifications, the measure became known as the Sterling Bill and received much attention from Congress during 1919–20.[6]

Walsh seems to have been oblivious to possible dangers in the sedition acts. He gave no credence to the arguments that public officials were likely to misinterpret or transgress the law in their eagerness to wipe out dissent. He gave no attention to the subtleties of the question of whether an individual's membership in the IWW, or possession of revolutionary tracts, necessarily proved that the particular individual would try to overthrow the government by force and violence.

Walsh also participated in a Senate movement to investigate Robert M. La Follette and perhaps expel him from his Senate seat. The cause of this uproar was a speech by La Follette in St. Paul, Minnesota, on September 20, 1917, before the farmers' Nonpartisan League, a group lacking in enthusiasm for the war (Walsh seems not to have objected to the socialistic ideas of Nonpartisan Leaguers). The Wisconsin senator repeatedly made statements indicating that the United States did not have sufficient reason to go to war against Germany, although he admitted that the United States did have grievances and that "war was declared, and lawfully declared." Much of the address was an attack on organized wealth and war profiteers and on Congress for failing to adopt a pay-as-you-go plan of taxation. "Shame on Congress," he said. "It takes what the administration sends down, looks at it cockeyed, and swallows it!" Many in the audience cheered at this.[7]

From Walsh's point of view, La Follette was the one who was cockeyed, and he might have violated the Espionage Act by speaking so caustically of the war effort. Part of the problem was to establish exactly what La Follette had said, since newspaper reports could not be trusted. As the criticism mounted in Minnesota and Wisconsin and the Minnesota Commission of Public Safety petitioned the Senate for La Follette's expulsion, Walsh reacted with disapproval of what his colleague had apparently said. He wanted to look into the charges through the Privileges and Elections Committee. La Follette, his family, and friends thought Walsh violated the proprieties by commenting publicly on the case and by implying that the senator from Wisconsin could be guilty as charged.[8]

This affair went on from the fall of 1917 to December 1918, when the committee members by an overwhelming vote decided that "the speech in question does not justify any action by the Senate." Walsh was not persuaded. He and Chairman Atlee Pomerene believed the committee had been ordered to investigate and should carry out the charge. In Walsh's opinion, politics had much to do with the conclusion. He commented in a speech long after that some Republicans on the committee had ardently approved of the investigation until their party in 1918 obtained control of the Senate by a margin of one vote—La Follette's vote. Republicans "suddenly grew fond of La Follette," he said. Every Republican then voted to dismiss the proceedings. Although Walsh and La Follette respected each other's ability, they did not enjoy cordial relations in this period.[9]

During 1917–18 Walsh had a personal crisis that threatened his future. It began with his wife's illness and eventual death in late August, apparently of cancer. He spent many days at Ellen's bedside in Baltimore, and in a letter of mid-August, referred to his "anxiety" that he was "unable at this critical time to give more than furtive attention to public affairs." Some matters he referred to Senator Myers. Other senators offered to help, and his secretaries did much to carry the load. After Mrs. Walsh's passing, the grieving senator took a last trip with her back to Montana for the funeral services.[10]

Soon after Walsh returned to the Capital, his secretary wrote that he was "very much depressed" and seemed to be "inconsolable." He was grieving over the loss of his wife, who had contributed immensely to his success as an attorney and public man and now had been taken away. His secretary noted another factor—"that he has been a liberal contributor to the Red Cross, for the relief of the Belgians and many other things since the war started, but now feels the pinch, that others occasionally feel for money, his wife's illness having cost him thousands of dollars." Walsh tried to follow his regular work schedule during the fall before he returned to Montana with the intention of touring the state. Then he suffered, in his own words, "a severe nervous breakdown, the result of over-work and anxiety." His daughter remembered him saying at some point how nice it would be to get out of the cold of Montana and go to California. Arrangements were made. Accompanied by his personal physician, he went to Los Angeles and slowly recuperated in a hotel. By early 1918 he was sufficiently improved to sit in a little park near his hotel and talk politics. Not until March 1918, however, was he back on the job in Washington and functioning more or less normally.[11]

Much like others, Walsh had projects that he continued to work for during the war period. It seemed possible, in fact, that the charged atmosphere of 1917–18 contributed to the success of measures previously languishing. This was particularly true of leasing bills for the development of western public lands. At the opening of the Sixty-fifth Congress, Walsh introduced a mineral leasing bill which became known as the Walsh-Pittman Bill when Senator Pittman of Nevada took over its management because of the Montana senator's illness. A fight developed in which the Interior Department and its congressional allies supported the bill while representatives of the Navy and Justice Departments took the other side. Much of the dispute involved claimants to the public petroleum lands who, according to critics, were using the wartime need for oil as an excuse to push the measure through. Walsh saw this "relief" for claimants as subordinate to the broader plan for development through leasing. In any case, the bill became deadlocked.[12]

Water power development in the West, both on the public lands and navigable streams, seemed a matter of regional and national necessity to the Montana senator. The failure to utilize this natural resource was lamentable. Before and after his illness he was at work trying to get his own leasing bill passed, even though he was not on the Public Lands Committee. Often Walsh seemed to be the principal proponent of such action, and he and his allies attained some success in the second session of the Sixty-fifth Congress (1918), with the passage of bills in both houses. They did not, however, bring a measure to final approval; the effort had to be made again in 1919–20.[13]

Quite a different issue began to require Walsh's attention from 1916 to 1918, even though it did not rank near the top among his priorities. This was the prohibition movement, which until recently had been predominantly a state and local affair. One of the signs of change was a federal law of 1913, intended to restrict the interstate shipment of alcoholic beverages. Meanwhile, Montana was one of fourteen states in the West and Middle West that went dry by 1917, joining a bloc of southern states already committed to prohibition. As the dry area grew ever larger, possibilities for the passage and ratification of a federal prohibition amendment obviously improved. The Anti-Saloon League, the Woman's Christian Temperance Union, and other organizations—mostly church affiliated—mounted a campaign that seemed unstoppable, especially after the United States entered the war.[14]

From his youth, Walsh was a believer in temperance, and in later years he advised Montana acquaintances, for the sake of their lives and careers, to avoid the saloon. Thus he was one of the millions of Americans who, while having some doubts, were susceptible to prohibitionist arguments: alcohol was a poison, a threat to one's physical and moral well-being, and a destroyer of families and the home; furthermore, to produce intoxicating beverages in wartime would be a waste of essential food and resources.[15]

Walsh in 1916 noted a "remarkable" change of emphasis in the dry campaign, of which he approved: "It formerly had an aspect almost exclusively religious. Now-a-days, the basis of the propaganda is distinctly industrial, and sanitary. Even the addict in these days recognizes that indulgence in intoxicants is injurious to his health." The Montanan seemed impressed most of all with the need for action in southern states and the District of Columbia, where the women, he said, must be protected "from the assaults of drink-crazed negroes." A broad base of popular support was necessary for dry laws to work and Walsh reached the conclusion that such support had come to exist. "Nothing will meet the demand," he wrote in June 1917, "except complete prohibition, and 'bone-dry' prohibition at that." Wine and beer must come under the ban, even though this was regrettable. Repeatedly in his letters to Montana constituents who were opposing prohibitionist measures, Walsh said he was acting "under instructions" on this matter, apparently meaning that Montana had voted itself dry and that most of his constituents were in favor of prohibition. Facing the possibility of a hard fight for reelection in 1918, he was frankly taking the popular side in the controversy. The Montanan was not unusual in this respect. A historian notes that dry crusaders "had the assistance, or at least the compliance," of William E. Borah of Idaho, George W. Norris of Nebraska, Robert M. La Follette of Wisconsin, and many of the ablest men in Congress.[16]

In one aspect of the prohibitionist movement Walsh was a leader. As a member of a subcommittee of the Judiciary Committee, he helped write the provisions that ultimately became the Eighteenth Amendment, and he made arguments on the Senate floor that were considered effective and useful to the cause. On August 1, 1917, the Senate gave approval to the amendment and by the end of the year it went to the states for ratification.[17]

Several years later, after the Eighteenth Amendment had been ratified and the Volstead Act passed, with the prohibition experiment in full swing, Walsh received a letter questioning his loyalty to the cause. He could hardly believe this correspondent was unaware of the record he had made and noted his reputation as "one of the only two 'dry' Senators, that is, Senators who live as they vote."[18]

Most Americans were caught up in the unprecedented mobilization of 1917 and 1918, and they experienced a variety of problems, as revealed in Senator Walsh's correspondence of the period. Perhaps nothing caused so much difficulty for individual citizens as trying to understand and work within the maze of wartime regulations, especially as they affected economic activity. Walsh did what he was able to. There were Montana businessmen who wanted the establishment of a nitrate plant to help in the defense effort; who asked to build ships for the government somewhere on the West Coast; who wanted contracts with the military to supply shirts, caps, and other clothing; who sought permission from the War Industries Board to obtain building materials; and who needed help or relief in a hundred ways. There were unemployed workers who wanted the government to intercede for them and, in some instances, to pay transportation costs to shipyards or labor centers. One of the more serious problems, with political overtones, was that of wheat farmers, who in 1917 began to react unhappily to prices fixed by Washington on their crops—and, in their view, fixed much too low.[19]

There is no reason to doubt that Montanans wanted to serve their country and tried to do so in 1917–18. They bought war bonds if financially able to, paid their taxes, worked industriously to produce the goods of war, and entered the military service in surprising numbers. But "slackers," as they were called, could be found, too; and not a few were members of the IWW or others in the labor movement, who believed the war was a capitalist's war in which the Anaconda Copper Company and other selfish interests would principally benefit. Such views on the left played into the hands of zealots on the right, who wrapped themselves in the American flag while setting out to punish the state's dissenters. Senator Walsh, as noted earlier, played a role in this conservative reaction on the national level by helping to write the Espionage and Sedition Acts.[20]

Amid the labor turmoil of Butte, where an IWW leader was lynched in August 1917, and the Miners' Union had been broken, Anaconda ruled supreme. Its president, John D. Ryan, headed the American Red Cross for a time and went on to become an assistant secretary of war in charge of airplane production. Anaconda's friends and allies included the governor of Montana, Samuel V. Stewart, and members of the Montana legislature and the Montana Council of Defense. Senator Walsh, as usual, preferred to be independent. He believed, with many Montanans, that the Company did not pay its share of taxes and enjoyed an excessive influence in state affairs. But the indisputable fact recognized by Walsh and many in positions of responsibility was that Anaconda kept the mines and smelters running. In spite of his doubts and reservations, Walsh had a "live and let live" relationship with Company officials, whose posture was that of patriotic backing for the war effort.[21]

Opinions of the Montana voters were always important to Walsh but perhaps never more so than in 1917–18, as he looked ahead to a probable campaign for reelection. All the problems raised by mobilization were likely to have an effect in the polling booth, as would the many issues of state and national affairs. Notwithstanding some advantages that Walsh enjoyed, his reelection was by no means assured, if he decided to run. This question was answered in the sunshine of California, early in 1918. With his health restored, Walsh began to make clear his intentions to seek a second term and his belief that nowhere could he serve his country better than in the Senate of the United States.[22]

16

Reelection in 1918

The congressional elections of 1918 indicated a significant setback in the fortunes of Democrats. Walsh's prospects were threatened by his friendship for Burton K. Wheeler, U.S. attorney for Montana, whose sympathies for laborers and farmers made him anathema in the eyes of conservatives. Predictions were made that "the one issue" Walsh was going to face was "Burt Wheeler." Wheeler's personality and principles were an issue between radicals and conservatives. Walsh could not obtain the backing of mining interests if he befriended Wheeler; nor could he obtain the backing of liberals and radicals if he abandoned Wheeler. The election turned on this pivot.[1]

Walsh struggled with himself and with partisans on the question of reappointing Wheeler as U.S. attorney. Realities of economic pressure, political strategy, and personal ambition show up in the fight between the Anaconda Copper Mining Company and its friends on one side, and most farmers, laborers, and liberals on the other side. The election epitomizes the clash of forces in Montana and reveals the adaptable "organization" with which Senator Walsh remained in power.

Organized labor could not be discounted politically although it suffered reversals in Montana during the war period. Formerly strong, the Miners' Union was torn by internal dissension and beaten in strikes. IWW outbreaks led to martial law, patrolling by U.S. troops, talk of pro-Germans in Montana, shootings and lynchings, the branding of moderate labor as radical, and the complete suppression of the IWW railroad brotherhoods and various craft unions, including those in the mining towns, still constituted an important group of voters. If laborers combined politically with aggrieved farmers as they threatened to do, the big interests might lose control of the state.[2]

Farmers, like laborers, had troubles. The years 1917 and 1918 were a period of drought, harsh winters, and depression; also, people in the Northwest became incensed that the administration in Washington had set prices on wheat lower than the prices in the free market. Disgruntled and militant, the farmers entered politics with a novel and intelligently-conceived organization—the Nonpartisan League.[3]

Political party lines were shifting in 1918 although the economic groups in Montana remained unchanged. The Progressives of 1912 and 1916 looked for other political instruments: they might go into the Republican party, help to form another party, or support liberal Democratic candidates. Some Democrats were unhappy with Wilson's wartime administration and with their Montana leadership. All the parties, in fact, were in ferment.

Most striking of the political developments was the farmers' Nonpartisan League. Founded in North Dakota in 1915, this organization by 1918 aimed at winning control of Montana with tactics analogous to those employed by Anaconda. It would work within either party. "Nonpartisans," regardless of party, might agree to support candidates friendly to them in either the Republican or Democratic primary; or they might solidly support a liberal of either party in the general election; and if major party candidates were unsympathetic toward agricultural interests they might form their own party temporarily. If placed in office, they proposed to provide state credit facilities, reduce the farmer's tax burden, and in other ways better their lot through governmental action.[4]

Among the Republicans were a number of independents, or progressives, including Representative Jeannette Rankin of Missoula and her brother Wellington Rankin, ex-senator and Bull Moose leader Joseph Dixon, former mayor of Helena and unsuccessful gubernatorial candidate Frank Edwards, and State Attorney General Sam Ford. Of all these, the most important in the 1918 campaign was Jeannette Rankin. A graduate of the State University at Missoula in 1902, she continued her training at the School of Philanthropy in New York. She engaged in social work in Seattle, became active in the woman suffrage cause, and in 1915 visited New Zealand to study social conditions. Her campaign for Congress in 1916 was successful. She gained fame, but not popularity, by voting against war in 1917, and her advocacy of reforms such as federal ownership of mines did not please the copper interests of Montana.[5]

Both the Republican and Democratic parties had their conservative wings, sympathetic toward the big interests or controlled by them. Walsh in 1918 was not so clearly identified with the liberals of his party in Montana as he had been six years earlier. As an indication, however, of his independent position the conservative *Helena Independent* sometimes referred to the "Walsh men." Walsh and his closest associates in the party ran probably from the middle of the road to the extreme left. Outstanding among his friends in 1918 was, first, A. E. Spriggs, sometimes called "Governor" because in 1896 he had been elected lieutenant governor and was for a time acting governor. Spriggs was Industrial Accident Commissioner, located in Helena, and he managed the Walsh campaign. C. B. Nolan, a native of Ireland with a brogue and a keen sense of humor, was Walsh's law partner and an active assistant in the campaign. Former Congressman Tom Stout of Lewistown, editor of the *Democrat-News,* was an able writer of pleasing personality and a staunch Walsh man. Burton Wheeler of Butte represented the left wing of the Walsh crowd and played a special part in this election.

Various Democrats were considered more sympathetic toward the mining interests than the Walsh group. John D. Ryan, C. F. Kelley, and Senator William A. Clark—the mining chieftains themselves—headed this list. Governor Samuel V. Stewart was friendly toward the Company. National Committeeman Bruce Kremer of Butte was recognized by all as a "Company Man." Will Campbell edited the *Helena Independent* in a manner pleasing to business, and the same was true of Jerry Dobell, editor of Senator Clark's *Butte Miner.* Helena lawyer E. C. Day found favor with the Company in this 1918 campaign. The conservative, or reactionary, list of Democrats was a long one.[6]

It was not yet certain that Walsh would be a candidate for reelection. His wife's illness and death and his nervous breakdown kept him out of Washington for many months while the curious could do little but wait. Walsh returned to the Capital in early spring. Though delaying an announcement of his candidacy, he hinted that his health was sufficiently restored for him to make the race. One leader received word from Walsh that he was getting into his stride again and would be equal to the strain. The senator also revealed that he knew of no place where he could serve more usefully than in the Senate.[7]

Recovery came just in time to quiet the ambitions of Democrats on the left and right. Nonpartisan Leaguer O. H. P. Shelley of Helena wanted to know whether Walsh was going to run. If not, he and others intended to back Wheeler. Walsh's answer on July 1 was brief and friendly, mentioning a recent announcement of his candidacy. Conservatives in the party now offered the only opposition to an easy nomination.

Walsh's association with Wheeler caused uneasiness among the conservatives. A native of Massachusetts, Wheeler was of old New England stock. He went to the University of Michigan for his law degree and in 1906 began his practice in Butte. If Butte was tough, so was Wheeler. Big, strong, ambitious— and able—he had no intention of taking orders from the copper interests. After building a good law practice, he was elected to the state legislature for the term 1911–13. He antagonized the conservatives in part by his efforts to send Walsh to the U.S. Senate. Grateful for Wheeler's backing, and recognizing his abilities, Walsh in 1913 recommended the young lawyer's appointment as U.S. attorney for Montana.

Wheeler made his name repugnant to many conservatives and superpatriots from 1913 to 1918. His sympathies for the workers, the drought-ridden farmers, and liberals of both parties were openly expressed. He favored laborers over employers in the bloody labor strife of the war years, charging that dirty Company policies and its paid agents among the IWW caused most of the trouble. He insisted that in many cases he was not empowered to prosecute under the 1917 Espionage Act. But conservatives and hysterical patriots demanded that he punish the "traitors." A splendid opportunity existed for the corporate interests to eliminate some of their foes among the workers and liberals by damning them as disloyal in the war effort, and if Wheeler did not cooperate he might be among those eliminated. Wheeler defended himself, dared his antagonists to prove that he had not done his duty, and refused to quit under fire.[8]

Walsh considered asking his young friend to resign but reconsidered and determined to back him. His own "peace of mind," he decided, forbade him to abandon Wheeler to promote his own political prospects, when the Justice Department said there was not a blemish on Wheeler's record.[9]

The Wheeler affair became a live issue by April 1918, when Walsh recommended to President Wilson that Wheeler be reappointed. Two crucial questions appeared in the Montana senatorial picture as conservative Democrats joined Republicans in attacking Wheeler, and thus indirectly attacking Walsh. First, would Wheeler's enemies among the Democrats go so far as to oppose Walsh in the party primary? And second, how would the Republicans react to fighting among the Democrats? Would they be stimulated to run an unusually strong candidate against Walsh? A determined attack on many fronts promised trouble.

High-placed state leaders opposed the Wheeler reappointment, and Walsh's Democratic colleague in the Senate, Henry L. Myers, wanted the Helena lawyer, E. C. Day, to take over Wheeler's job. Another attack on Walsh's protégé came in an executive session of the Montana Council of Defense when the members voted 8 to 1 against Wheeler's reappointment. Among the members of this group opposing Wheeler were Governor Samuel Stewart and Will Campbell of the *Helena Independent*.[10]

These developments menaced Walsh's nomination as he searched for ways out of his trouble short of removing Wheeler. Walsh wrote to his appointee urging that he make clear his determination to enforce the Espionage Act and the Sedition Act and to cooperate with state authorities. The amended Espionage Act soon would become law, he observed, and it would be a good idea for Wheeler to send a copy of it to every sheriff and police officer and county attorney saying that the government ought to do the prosecuting, that he would be obliged for aid given, but if the state prosecuted under its own law he would be glad to help. Having in mind Wheeler's belief that many so-called traitors could not be prosecuted under the 1917 Espionage Act, Walsh concluded: "[this new law] is certainly broad enough to catch the disloyal." Wheeler replied that he would do as Walsh wished.[11]

Walsh also urged the Democrats to leave Wheeler alone. He pointed out that their internal conflict stimulated Republican ambitions to steal the Senate seat. He asserted that he had no desire to force Wheeler out and it would be bad Democratic politics to do so. Wheeler's friends obviously would be disaffected if he were dismissed and various unsuccessful seekers after the vacated job would be antagonized. He asked friends to talk with the hostile Democrats and dissuade them from their course "calculated as it is to give the republicans a Senator from Montana."[12]

It was astute of Walsh to stress the danger of a Republican victory rather than the threat to himself. He seems to have ignored the possibility of losing in the Democratic primaries. Indicating a deliberate silence on his own vital interests was his decision not to send a letter, written to Jerry Dobell of the *Butte Miner*, in which he noted Dobell's efforts to get another Democrat to run against him. Abandoning this approach, he asked a mutual friend to try and dissuade Dobell from his attacks which might give the Republicans a new senator from Montana. His appeal was to party loyalty.[13]

The big interests of the state were recognized by Walsh and his associates as the focus of anti-Wheeler feeling and the possible boosters of a primary opponent for Walsh. Tom Stout, Nolan, Spriggs, Wheeler, and Walsh all referred to these conservative activities and threats. Wheeler commented that the Clark people and perhaps the Anaconda people were anxious to get E. C. Day into the race against Walsh. Nolan sent alarming news that the conservative Democrats were holding conferences. This hostile movement, he thought, came largely from Dobell's effort to defeat Walsh, and the contenders most favored for the nomination were E. C. Day, Governor Stewart, and Bruce Kremer—all generally regarded as friendly toward the big interests.[14]

In spite of apparent threats, conservatives decided not to enter the primary race. Nolan sent the good news in late July that Walsh had crossed "the Rubicon . . . with no Caesar pursuing him." His return to the Senate now seemed likely.[15]

Two Republicans contested for the chance to oppose Walsh. A progressive-conservative split in the Republican party was disclosed by the primary fight between Congresswoman Jeannette Rankin and Doctor Oscar Lanstrum. Miss Rankin, because of her vote against war in 1917 and her economic radicalism, did not promise to run a strong race against Walsh in the event she received the Republican nomination. Lanstrum's candidacy was announced later than Miss Rankin's and was a shock to Walsh and his associates. As they had feared, the attack on Wheeler, indicating Democratic disunity, had brought a more formidable Republican than Jeannette Rankin into the contest. The Helena physician, turned politician and publisher of the *Record-Herald,* was an ex-progressive Republican who achieved a good local record and then in 1912 supported Taft against Theodore Roosevelt. In Montana he was recognized as sympathetic toward the interests and possibly vulnerable on that account.[16]

Very little was settled by the Republican primary. Lanstrum captured the nomination by a vote of 18,805 against Miss Rankin's 17,091, but she and her liberal friends refused to accept the verdict. Backed by the Nonpartisan League, Jeannette Rankin soon announced for the Senate as the National party candidate.[17]

This announcement was disturbing to the Walsh men. They could not agree as to whether Miss Rankin's third party would take more votes from Lanstrum than from Senator Walsh. The senator commented that, maybe without cause, he found no comfort in this latest development. He hoped, however, that Burt Wheeler's influence would throw radical support to him instead of Miss Rankin. This gave Wheeler an almost insuperable task—that of delivering the radical vote without further alienating the conservative vote.[18]

Writing to Wheeler on August 29, Walsh analyzed the campaign with particular reference to Wheeler's place in it. He predicted that "with the bloody shirt as a side issue" (that is, trying to associate Walsh with southern Democrats) Lanstrum would make his campaign upon the Wheeler matter. He believed Wheeler underestimated the value to the opposition of the attack being made on him. Walsh asserted that political considerations had not caused Wheeler's retention and did not, on the other hand, require his dismissal. At the same time many "good friends" throughout Montana believed the situation to be much embarrassed. He urged Wheeler to be diplomatic and to talk with moderates or conservatives of the party. Walsh further said it would be well for Wheeler to discuss with the Helena gentlemen the advisability of getting Jeannette Rankin out of the race. Wheeler should then see Wellington Rankin (Jeannette's brother) and persuade him to the course most favorable to the Walsh group.[19]

Wheeler did write about his efforts to work with all elements and averred his friendship for Walsh. But he could not bring himself, he said, to associate with editor Campbell of the *Independent*, whom he characterized as a political grafter, selling out to the interests—and for a small price. He denied that he was linked to the radicals. He and some liberal Republicans were friendly, partly because they had stuck by him in a way that Spriggs or E. C. Day had not, but the charge that he conferred only with radicals was "absolutely silly." He said Walsh could rest assured that he would do everything possible to help, regardless of what others might tell him.[20]

Nolan and Spriggs believed that the U.S. attorney was "running a bluff" by arguing that liberal support depended on his reappointment. They also disagreed with Wheeler on the impact of Jeannette Rankin's candidacy. Perhaps acting on Wheeler's advice Walsh made overtures to some of the liberals.[21]

He was more successful with the conservatives. On the advice of Nolan and Spriggs he won over men like Governor Stewart, with whom he had not been on good terms. He went so far as to dissuade one of his friends from coming to Montana to aid in the campaign because this friend was thought to be anti-Company and had incurred Governor Stewart's enmity. Also Walsh expressed delight that E. C. Day, a conservative and an old friend, might become chairman of the Democratic State Committee.[22]

Walsh wrote to C. F. Kelley of Anaconda at his New York office on the subject of a mining bill and added statements that had significance in view of the political situation: "Allow me to extend my congratulations upon your deserved promotion to the place [the presidency] vacated by the resignation of Mr. Ryan." Walsh hoped that Ryan's and Kelley's relations with the national administration would prevent their backing Lanstrum against him.[23]

These overtures brought rewards. On August 31 Governor Stewart assured Walsh that he and his friends were trying to "hit the ball" for him, rather than Dr. Lanstrum. The governor had even written a commendatory letter to the president in Walsh's behalf. Citing Senator Walsh as one who had lived up to the necessities of the times, the governor requested a presidential recommendation for him. Walsh thought this action was "more than kind," and he asked the governor to advise him from time to time about the progress of the campaign.[24]

By early September Walsh decided it would be politically advantageous to remove Wheeler and offered him another job that sounded ideal. The senator explained to "Dear Burt" on September 4 that he had that morning been asked to recommend an attorney for the Federal Trade Commission, who would prosecute the Minneapolis Chamber of Commerce on charges, preferred by farmer groups, that it carried on unfair and monopolistic practices in the marketing of northwestern grain. This grievance was giving the Nonpartisan League farmers their strongest talking point. He outlined fully the advantages that might accrue to the campaign and to Wheeler if he took this place. "Lanstrum's slogan undoubtedly is going to be, 'A vote for Walsh is a vote for Wheeler.' That may do him more harm than good, but if he is deprived of it there is nothing left for him to talk about, considering the marvelous way in which the war work is going on and the successes on the Western front." The place might be inviting for Wheeler, he continued, attracting nationwide attention, offering a real chance to make a reputation, and pleasing Wheeler's rural followers. It would be necessary, he added, to exercise caution in choosing a successor, "lest it should appear that the appointment had been dictated by the big interests."[25]

When Wheeler rejected this offer, the pressure on him and Walsh mounted. Nolan sent word to Walsh about the recent state Democratic convention that was only moderately reassuring. Governor Stewart, Hugh Wells, Kremer, and other conservatives apparently were for Walsh. Nolan believed, however, that the Company men would not receive their "instructions" until about the first of October. Senator Clark, according to another informant, was hostile to Walsh's candidacy .[26]

Many of the reports that Walsh received during September and early October indicated the campaign was not going well. Nolan grumbled that he and Spriggs and others felt Walsh did not promptly take up matters they referred to him. Richard Purcell warned that a number of Walsh's "warm supporters" were becoming lukewarm. Most of the trouble emanated from "Burt" Wheeler's determination not to surrender his job.[27]

Walsh's friends wrote in such close succession that agreement, or connivance, seems certain. After taking an automobile trip through the counties of Silver Bow, Madison, Beaverhead, Lewis and Clark, Jefferson, Powell, and Deer Lodge, Steve Cowley on September 28 wrote to Walsh that he was alarmed for his success. Hugh Wells, chairman of the Democratic State Central Committee, advised on September 30: "I find that the Wheeler matter is injuring your chances for re-election in most every portion of the State, and Colonel Nolan and myself are endeavoring to adjust this matter today."

Richard Purcell wrote a gossipy letter in which he gravely counseled: "Another thing, you had ought to arrange with John D. Ryan to have the Company quietly get in line for you because, candidly speaking, you have a hard fight on your hands with Jeanette [sic] Rankin in the field." Nolan meanwhile, after conferring with Wheeler, had wired that he, Wheeler, and Hugh Wells were leaving for Washington the following night. He believed a "change should be made." This was the showdown.[28]

All indications are that at this time Walsh's political fortunes were endangered. He believed not only that it was his duty to remain at his post in Washington but that his opponents would suffer by campaigning against him in such circumstances. A. E. Spriggs, on the scene of the battle, violently disagreed with Walsh. The people in Washington, he said, had better disabuse themselves of the notion that there was no fight on. He flatly declared that Walsh was badly beaten at this stage.[29]

The *Record-Herald* said that Walsh's friend Burton Wheeler was neither chasing the IWWs out of the state nor putting them in jail. Walsh's dogged insistence that Wheeler remain the U.S. attorney, it said, cast doubt upon the sincerity of his protests that he had at heart "the best interests and the general welfare of the people and industries of Montana." The *Missoulian* was critical, and the *Miles City Star* said that Walsh had a responsibility to the people of Montana, too. He would be an ingrate to disregard his political obligation to Wheeler, except for his obligation to the people of Montana. These papers avidly followed the climactic events in the Wheeler affair. The *Record-Herald* said current rumor had it that the Montana Democrats told Walsh flatly he must get rid of Wheeler and that Nolan, Hugh Wells, and Wheeler in consequence were speeding to Washington for a showdown. The same paper speculated about the Washington meeting and sneered at Wheeler: "The president may be induced to give Wheeler a commission in the army. It is understood that he would be satisfied with the rank of major in the non-combatant service."[30]

At first Walsh was unyielding when Nolan and Wells arrived in Washington urging him to let Wheeler go. But the two also interviewed Walsh's friends, Senator Key Pittman of Nevada and Senator Peter Gerry of Rhode Island; they went to Postmaster General Albert S. Burleson and Attorney General

Thomas W. Gregory; and arrangements were made for them to see President Wilson. They insisted that the Democrats would lose Walsh if Wheeler did not step aside.[31]

The end of the struggle had come. Walsh finally asked Wheeler to resign. In Wheeler's words: "Walsh came to see me at the Raleigh hotel [in Washington]. He said he was afraid they were going to beat him. I told him, 'I made my enemies in the first place by supporting you.' I told him I would resign though if he thought he was going to get beat." And Wheeler sent in his resignation. He was then offered a federal judgeship in Panama and a colonelcy in the army. Wheeler was contemptuous. He retorted that if he was to be deported they could send him to Siberia where the environment was more congenial. His final answer was, "I'm going back to Montana." Helena attorney, E. C. Day, inherited Wheeler's place as U.S. attorney.[32]

The campaign took a new turn. Wheeler was disgruntled and refused to make a statement for Senator Walsh. Many liberal and radical supporters were incensed at Walsh. Democratic conservatives were elated, while Republicans made the best of the whole situation.

Wheeler expressed himself as disappointed in the senator and probably gave little aid in the campaign after his resignation. He was disillusioned that his idol had been "gullible" enough to side with the conservatives, those "political pirates." A Walsh backer in Butte called on Wheeler urging him to make a statement for Walsh because his silence was injurious. Wheeler thereupon declared that his position was opposed to that of Wells and Nolan and he thought the voters without any statement from him should decide who was right. Wheeler's attitude was such that Nolan charged that he opposed Walsh in Butte and hoped to be able to say his resignation had cost Walsh the election. Nolan declared: "I believe that it is a case of 'good riddance to bad rubbish.'" Nevertheless Walsh expressed concern over the defections he was suffering. He thought "the fellows" had underestimated the disadvantages of dropping Wheeler, and insisted that he had been the victim of "merciless misrepresentation."[33]

In spite of laments from the radicals and assaults by the Republicans, in spite of rumors that the Copper Press was happy, and in the face of Walsh's own doubts about whether he had done the right thing, his campaign prospects brightened. From the day that Wheeler resigned Walsh's conservative friends took heart. On October 11 Walsh told President Wilson that his friends Nolan and Wells had been "gloomy" about the campaign but left Washington feeling that "the situation had been much improved." Spriggs wrote that the Wheeler resignation was wise, that plans were working out admirably, and that the enemy was badly disconcerted. Just as significant as the good news was the absence of bad news.[34]

A new aspect was given to the campaign by encouraging developments. Spriggs, for example, reported from Helena that they were getting out literature with much success. At the Washington end of the "literature" battle Walsh's secretary commented that the post office and the government printing office were choked, but he thought "the personal intervention of the p. m. [would] hurry things along." By the end of October Walsh had more resources at his command than Lanstrum did.[35]

One novel feature of this campaign was the influenza epidemic, which played havoc with political gatherings as well as people's health. Candidates cultivated the voters mostly through the press and by private communications as public meetings were forbidden. Walsh decided he should remain in Washington, and his physician opponent pronounced himself ready to devote his medical skills to the battle against influenza.[36]

Walsh received strong backing from administration leaders. President Wilson complied with Governor Stewart's request and on October 4 endorsed Walsh as one who had earned "a place of real distinction" in the Senate, showing "unusual legal ability and political judgment," and supporting the administration so consistently and generously that his own feeling was very warm toward him. Vice President Marshall, Secretary of the Interior Lane, Frank P. Walsh of the War Labor Board, and ex-Secretary of State William Jennings Bryan were others who sent letters lauding the senator from Montana. The principal issue in the campaign, next to the Wheeler affair, was a Republican charge that gained even more importance than it had in the 1916 presidential election. Wilson's administration was said to be southern-dominated and using its power to favor one region over the others. "Waving the bloody shirt" was the Reconstruction-era term for this type of Republican campaigning.[37]

Carl Riddick, the Republican from Montana's eastern district who was to win a seat in the House of Representatives in this election, helped start the attack on alleged administration favoritism to the South. In a letter to the editor of the *Record-Herald* he said it was unfair for Congress to fix the price of wheat but not the prices of southern products. The *Miles City Star*, the (Columbia Falls) *Columbian*, and other papers kept up this attack.

The Republicans did not like Walsh's attitude on foreign affairs, and they pounded at the president's assumption that Democrats would support the war better than Republicans. The Walsh forces emphasized Democratic achievements and called upon patriots to assure Allied victory and domestic justice with a Democratic vote. Walsh supplied his men with tens of thousands of copies of old speeches, which together with other individual communications "covered" all voters in Montana at least twice; and he advanced new arguments and rebuttals whenever his aides required them, overlooking practically nothing in his desire to win.[38]

One of those who seems to have aided Walsh considerably was Governor Stewart. Spriggs wrote on September 23 that he and other Walsh friends were contributing data for Stewart's speech in which he would "make the attack on the worthy Doctor" that the newspapers had refused to make. They planned to give this speech wide circulation. Walsh thought "the Governor's speech was great" and should prove "invaluable." A little later Spriggs wrote that the tide was turning favorably since the enormous circulation of Stewart's speech. In addition, without solicitation, the railroad brotherhoods' legislative representative in Washington informed the Montana lodges that Walsh's voting record was excellent. Each laboring man was expected to show his gratitude.[39]

On October 24 Colonel Nolan and other friends met Walsh in Billings, when he arrived from the East. Walsh expressed himself as approving the peace terms offered by President Wilson to the Germans—in effect, unconditional surrender. But the peace treaty would call for the nation's "best statesmanship." Turning to domestic matters, he defended the adminstration record on cotton and wheat prices. "It is considered in Washington as a closed affair, a troublesome war matter that has been disposed of and most loyal citizens will, I believe, regard it as patriotic to treat it as such." Walsh went on to Helena and visited with Spriggs and his wife. He made no speeches because of the influenza epidemic but issued several statements.[40]

November 5, election day in Montana, dawned cold and damp. When the votes were counted it was found that Walsh had won by a total of 46,160 to 40,229 for Lanstrum and 26,013 for Jeannette Rankin. No Democrats were elected to major positions except Walsh and John Evans, who pulled through for the House of Representatives in the western district. Walsh considered his victory a personal tribute. In truth, he had narrowly escaped defeat. His strength lay primarily in north central and western counties including the mining counties of Silver Bow, Deer Lodge, and Cascade where corporate influence was important. Lanstrum's vote was scattered but heaviest in the south central and eastern agricultural counties. Miss Rankin carried three agricultural counties in the northeastern corner of the state and received a heavy labor vote in Butte.[41]

The national defeat of Democrats which gave control of Congress to the Republicans was attributed by Walsh to public credence in the suggestion that the South was "running the government, and running it selfishly." Wilson's appeal for the election of Democrats was unfortunately phrased, Walsh declared, but he could not believe its effects were disastrous as many claimed. More important was the "bloody shirt," including the argument that the Democrats had fixed low prices for wheat but had let cotton prices soar. Walsh agreed with much of this Republican sectional argument.[42]

To establish the fact of corporate support for Walsh in 1918 is easy, but it is difficult to determine the significance of that support. Walsh's correspondence indicates that he made no "deal" involving Wheeler; he was dubious about the interests even after Wheeler resigned. When the *Record-Herald* insinuated that Walsh had corporation affiliations, Walsh told his friends to invite that paper to produce some proof. J. M. Kennedy tried to relieve Walsh's mind: "Nobody in this State seriously claims you have any corporation affiliations. You are recognized as a progressive and if anything, inclined to be with the radical rather than the conservative interests." He agreed with Walsh that Lanstrum was too vulnerable personally to charge Walsh with having gone over to the interests.[43]

The fact that Walsh indirectly was still seeking support from the Anaconda Company two weeks after Wheeler resigned seems to be proof that he had not previously made a "deal" with its leaders. Shortly after Walsh departed for Montana, Senator Charles Thomas of Colorado wrote two important letters regarding the Montana campaign. On October 24 he informed Walsh that he had talked with John D. Ryan and that Ryan promised to do what he could for the campaign. A week later Thomas wrote again, enclosing a letter from C. F. Kelley which he was sure would "please" Walsh.[44]

There is ample evidence that Walsh received corporate aid. Nolan wrote on November 7: "The election returns show most conclusively that the company did all that it possibly could do to bring about your election." Walsh thanked Kelley for "the very substantial aid" he had given and for his support of the Walsh candidacy when efforts "were made to sidetrack it." He assured Kelley of his "readiness to work with . . . [him] for the further development of . . . [their] State." Walsh thanked Dobell for his support, which he was sorry had been chilled at the beginning by the Wheeler matter.[45]

Kelley and Charles Donnelly, president of the Northern Pacific Railroad, explained their support. As Kelley looked at the matter, "It would be little less than a calamity to have deprived the nation of your counsel and service." He affirmed his "profound regard and esteem" for Walsh. Donnelly congratulated Walsh on his victory and remarked that his loss at this time "would have been an exceedingly regrettable one." This was not only his opinion, but also "that of many" whose ideas differed from Walsh's.[46]

Walsh did not become a corporate tool when he yielded on Wheeler and secured Company backing; his subsequent career proves that. He did surrender temporarily on Wheeler, so that once again the big interests of Montana showed their power. From the standpoint of the interests themselves a moderately sympathetic senator of proven abilities and good connections in Washington would be worth more than an untried stooge. From Walsh's standpoint the corporate officials did not appear as wicked in 1918 as in 1913. It was almost inevitable by 1918 that Americans should soften toward the big business magnates, fellow Americans, who were patriotically aiding in the war effort. The exigencies of war also brought Walsh into closer relations with Ryan and Kelley of Anaconda. More important, during the campaign Walsh was under inexorable pressures and faced the reality of probable defeat if he did not win Company support. He wanted to return to the Senate and was willing to make the necessary moves regarding Wheeler in order to win the election.[47]

In December 1918 Wheeler wrote to Senator Walsh about a legal matter and added a thought or two revealing his interpretation of the recent election. He was disillusioned with the senator because he had taken the conservative view in October and he was disillusioned with politics: "I . . . only hope that I may be endowed with good judgment enough to remain out of politics for the future, but have no doubt my enemies will take care of that." Walsh's reply was complacent and almost fatherly. He had never doubted Wheeler's sincerity, he said, and wished Wheeler had issued a statement during the election to show that he was not disgruntled, "but the thing came out all right."[48]

This election put to the test Senator Walsh's political acumen, his principles, and his friends. Though the evidence indicates that he made no pact with the corporate interests, this election continued the trend of closer relationships with the conservatives in Montana. As for Wheeler, he had not yet reconciled himself to the fact that in Montana anti-Company politicians seldom lasted long.

17

The League of Nations Fight

The close of the 1918 campaign and the armistice of November 11 introduced to Senator Walsh, as well as to other leaders, a new challenge—that of winning the peace. He wanted to "make universal military training unnecessary." In his opinion most American boys at the front understood that they were fighting so that, if possible, there would be no more world wars, and Walsh hoped for an international organization that could bring lasting peace.

The contest in the United States over a League of Nations, as one part of the Treaty of Versailles, was initiated with President Wilson's speeches that antedated American entrance in the European war. His "peace without victory" speech on January 22, 1917, called for an international organization. Almost a year later he appeared before Congress and announced his Fourteen Points for a just and lasting peace, including an association of nations. Other war messages repeated and expanded these idealistic war aims, which were showered upon millions of people the world over. Though this propaganda helped to win the war, it contained promises that were unattainable or, as many thought, undesirable. Wilson inevitably faced a hard struggle.[1]

On December 4, 1918, the president departed for the Paris Peace Conference where he, Lloyd George of England, and Clemenceau of France virtually made the peace terms for the entire world. President Wilson's fondest hope seemed realized when the Conference in its early deliberations accepted his League of Nations as part of the treaty.

By May 1919, when a special session of the Congress met, Wilson's foes in the Senate were organized. "Irreconcilables," including such notables as William E. Borah, Hiram Johnson, and Robert M. La Follette opposed the Leaque plan in toto. Other senators objected to portions of the League Covenant or to other treaty provisions. "Isolationism," sincere ideological disagreements about the validity of an international organization, personal enmity toward Wilson, fear of Wilson's "dictatorial" methods, politics on both sides, and the president's own mistakes—these are some of the factors that explain why Wilson and his supporters in the Senate finally suffered defeat.[2]

Senator Henry Cabot Lodge of Massachusetts, ranking Republican on the Foreign Relations Committee, assumed the chairmanship when his party took control in 1919 and proved himself a formidable antagonist to the Democrats. A friend and associate of Elihu Root and a follower of Theodore Roosevelt during his presidency, Lodge believed in "realism" in diplomacy, and he could not abide Woodrow Wilson's League of Nations and all it seemed to imply for future national policy. In addition to his ideas regarding world affairs, Lodge was an accomplished politician who sought to prevent defections to the Democratic side.[3]

Senator Walsh's role in the League fight was one of significance dating from the earliest debates in the Senate in 1918 to the final Senate defeat of Wilson's League in March 1920. In spite of the fact that he was not a member of the Foreign Relations Committee at this time, he considered himself a leader, if not *the* leader, of administration forces in the Senate. Energetic, ambitious, and highly regarded, he was a member of the Naval Affairs Committee and deeply interested in foreign affairs. Walsh asserted himself so strongly in Senate debate, in private correspondence, and among Democratic leaders, that his value to the League cause was widely recognized. The most significant aspect of his part in the Senate struggle was his shift in the last vote to the side of the reservationists on the ground that compromise was essential to save the League. He thus opposed the president and lost favor with the administration.

Senator Walsh's relation to the president as the League contest got under way was that of an admirer and supporter rather than a confidant. The Montanan's respect for the president and his references to him in November 1918 as the statesman of the hour whose career had been "marvelously successful" help to explain his ardent backing of the Wilson peace program. A few days after the armistice Walsh incited a debate in the Senate by urging that a world organization be formed by the approaching Peace Conference, with all civilized nations having membership. As a consequence of his emphatic views on the League and his status among the Democrats Walsh was often mentioned in November 1918 as a likely choice for a place on the American peace commission. But on November 29, 1918, Wilson announced his peace delegation; it did not include Walsh or any other senator.[4]

In spite of this rebuff, the Montanan tactfully attempted to advise the president. In a letter Walsh took it upon himself to commend Senator Gilbert M. Hitchcock as being "genuinely in favor of the League . . . notwithstanding past differences." That Walsh should so recommend Hitchcock of Nebraska, the ranking Democrat on the Senate Foreign Relations Committee and also acting minority leader, seems significant. Walsh considered himself rather than Hitchcock to be the president's principal supporter in the Senate. In this same letter Walsh urged the president, who had just returned from the first phase of his labors in the Peace Conference, to meet with six Democratic senators, including himself and Hitchcock, and six Democratic representatives frankly to discuss the League. "Incalculable good would result" from such a gathering of Democratic leaders.[5]

The president replied politely and cordially that the Covenant was reasonably clear and thoroughly workable and that a conference of the Democrats, while desirable, seemed impossible at the time. However, he would value any suggestions from Walsh or the gentlemen whom Walsh had named for the proposed conference, and he asked Walsh to convey that message. On February 23, 1919, the *New York Times* published a long interview with Senator Walsh on questions relating to the peace; the *Times* commented that Walsh was one of the men in Washington closest to the president.[6]

On March 3, 1919, the last day of the third session of the Sixty-fifth Congress, 39 Republican senators signed a Round Robin Resolution, condemning the League in its present form and indicating it could not have been ratified by the Senate at that moment. Woodrow Wilson meanwhile was returning to Paris aboard the *George Washington*. Walsh was one of those whom the administration urged to carry on the fight at home, and he did so, although he was disappointed in not being able to attend the Paris Conference.[7]

During a considerable portion of the recess Walsh campaigned for the League. On March 25, 1919, he spoke for more than an hour before the National American Women's Suffrage Association in Washington. Leaving Washington for a vacation in Montana, Walsh delivered several speeches before his constituents, praising the president's work and the League idea. His private correspondence further reveals that he was intensely interested in the Peace Conference in Europe and American opinion on the League.[8]

Senator Walsh's importance to President Wilson by comparison with that of Senator Hitchcock seems to have declined in the summer of 1919. Hitchcock's loyalty to the president, about which there had been some doubt, was soon proven on the League question and, as the Democratic minority leader in the Senate and ranking Democrat on the Foreign Relations Committee, the Nebraskan assumed many responsibilities that brought him to the fore. It is possible also that President Wilson became suspicious of Walsh because he championed Irish home rule. Wilson believed the Irish question to be irrelevant during the peace negotiations.

Walsh's influence upon the peace stemmed largely from the ability with which he discussed issues in the Senate. November 1918 to May 1919 was a period of skirmishing on the League issue as the president became immersed in preliminary problems of the peace. He went to Europe in December 1918, returned home for a short time in February, and then reembarked for the final phases of the Peace Conference from March to June 1919. Neither his friends nor his enemies in the Senate received an official copy of the treaty until July. Scraps of information regarding treaty provisions, over which senators could fight with relish, reached the United States from time to time, and in May the preliminary terms of the treaty were unofficially published in Germany and were soon circulated in the United States. When the special session of the Sixty-sixth Congress met on May 19, the early phase of debating over the League came to an end.

Prior to the special session Walsh's comments in the Senate were brief; first, because of the tentative nature of the League at this early stage; second, because of his poor health; and third, because he did not consider the occasion an opportune one. But Walsh had something to say for the Wilson peace objectives a number of times.[9]

On November 15, 1918, Walsh lauded the idea of an association of nations and sympathetically quoted several English proponents of the plan. He and his Senate antagonists engaged in heated exchanges upon some of the general questions that would subsequently be debated at length as details of the treaty and League became known. Boies Penrose of Pennsylvania, a high tariff Republican, asked whether this nebulous so-called League of Nations that Walsh advocated would include free-trade alliances. James Reed of Missouri protested against Walsh's apparent insinuation that opponents of the League had selfish motives. Miles Poindexter attacked H. G. Wells, whom Walsh had quoted, as a socialist who advocated class war. Poindexter observed that one of the most surprising features about this whole discussion was that a Democrat, one of that party which had formerly believed in local self-government, was setting forth these doctrines for an "international government." Walsh, he implied, was now ready to surrender the sovereign power of his country. At the outset it became evident that the way to international organization was strewn with doubts and prejudices.[10]

Before going to Florida for a vacation late in December 1918, Walsh participated in a bitter debate on the peace and the League. Joseph S. Frelinghuysen, Republican of New Jersey, began the exchange when he introduced a resolution asking that the president explain his Fourteen Points in view of Wilson's own expressed anxiety that no false interpretations be put upon them. In reply, Walsh said that Wilson had advanced his Fourteen Points on January 8, 1918, almost a year before and Walsh could not recall that any senator had expressed any divergence from the president's views until the past six weeks. In the absence of any important criticism it seemed to Walsh that "the people of the world very justly assumed that the views thus expressed by the President were indorsed by this great Nation."

This defense of the president was immediately challenged. Frelinghuysen, Poindexter, Philander Knox, and Hiram Johnson all entered the action. Hiram Johnson, for example, asserted that Wilson had departed for a foreign shore leaving his fellow countrymen "neither understanding what he meant nor knowing what he . . . [had gone] for." Responding to a question from Frelinghuysen, Walsh admitted that the United States was not irrevocably committed to the Fourteen Points, but he reiterated, "Any Senator who . . . [had] remained silent . . . ought to hesitate a little bit now about voicing his criticism."[11]

The first of a series of encounters between Walsh and the formidable William E. Borah of Idaho began on December 6 with Walsh emphasizing that the "balance of power" had been a failure and that the League promised greater security for the days that lay ahead. Obviously Borah was not convinced.[12]

The Senate reverberated with discussion of the League after May 10 when a special session of the new Sixty-sixth Congress met at the call of the president. Walsh was almost daily in the fight. He turned his energies to a painstaking analysis of the Covenant, and held his own in arguments with the opposition. This chance to draw fine constitutional distinctions, interspersed with historical and legal references and all for a noble cause, was a delightful experience for the junior senator from Montana.[13]

During May and June the Senate was denied an official copy of the Versailles Treaty although it was circulating unofficially in Europe and the United States. Senator Walsh maintained, as afterwards proved to be the case, that the representatives at Versailles probably agreed among themselves not to reveal the entire treaty. The president could not be expected to break his word. Caring nothing for the excuses Wilson or his friends might make, Senator Borah on June 9 read into the *Congressional Record* a newspaper copy of the treaty. Attacks on the president's "secret" negotiations continued.[14]

Walsh's most thorough analysis of the League Covenant was in a Senate address of June 11. He noted that among those who had implied unconstitutionality were Senators Philander Knox of Pennsylvania and Henry Cabot Lodge. But, Walsh argued, this treaty was not unique. Undoubtedly it obligated the United States to make war in certain situations, but so had other treaties and policies adopted in the past. What was the Monroe Doctrine, Walsh asked, but a voluntary obligation of the United States to preserve America against external aggression? The principle of the Monroe Doctrine, under Article X of the Covenant, was extended to members of the League. Mutual protection afforded under Article X was the very "soul and spirit" of the Covenant and the only plan ever devised as a substitute for systems of the past that had been "a colossal and . . . miserable failure, but to which some Senators still exhibit[ed] a fatuous attachment." Walsh denied Lodge's view that the boycott and tariff power of the League would run up against the U.S. constitutional provision that all revenue bills shall originate in the House of Representatives. Walsh's answer was that it was difficult to see how the League could meddle with tariffs, but at any rate a treaty could constitutionally alter tariff arrangements. Lodge himself, Walsh reminded the Senate, had voted in 1903 for the treaty with Cuba in which the tariff was affected. Whatever the limitations on the treaty-making power, they certainly did not affect Article X, which was in effect a treaty of alliance. The Covenant and Article X did not mean, however, that the United States was delegating its authority to make war.[15]

At various times Walsh's energies in debate were concentrated upon the security provisions of the Covenant, primarily Article X. He reiterated the view that if the nations would not cooperate in the League, thus keeping the peace, the United States should follow the German military system and become "the greatest military power on earth." But he hoped for peace and disarmament through the medium of a smoothly functioning League of Nations which would guarantee security to its members.

On June 25 Walsh clashed with the "lion of Idaho," William E. Borah, who held the floor unloosing his eloquence and nimble wit against a series of senators who dared defend Article X or other parts of the League Covenant. One of Borah's principal antagonists throughout the League fight was Walsh. So often, in fact, did the two clash that one might conclude that they were selected, at least tacitly, by their respective sides to argue constitutional technicalities.

As a rule Walsh handled himself creditably in his jousts with Borah. On the 25th of June, however, he was touched on a sore spot and was needled for months thereafter on that same spot. Borah referred "always with entire approval" to Walsh's statement "that there would be no escape from the obligations of the treaty." Walsh protested that the senator must read his speech of June 11 as a whole. Article X consisted of two parts, the first declaring that each member of the League guaranteed the territorial integrity and political independence of all other members. Here was the primary obligation to which Borah referred and the United States could not escape that obligation without dishonor. However, said Walsh, the second part was that the Council should "advise" on the means by which member nations should carry out their duties. There was no obligation that the member nations follow that advice. Borah hammered away at Walsh's second point. Borah concluded that Walsh and other Democrats had admitted, so far as the second clause of Article X went, that it created no moral or legal obligation for the United States to follow the advice of the Council.[16]

Borah was correct in his conclusion that Walsh's interpretations of Article X were inconsistent, although Wilson and others had a similar problem. Walsh hoped that Article X would establish law and order among nations like that existing among individuals. He employed this analogy in a speech at Helena on May 9, 1919, and again in a Senate speech of July 28. Yet as noted he also asserted that nations in the League were not bound by its decisions.[17]

One of Walsh's main objectives in the Senate debates was to prove the constitutionality of the Versailles Treaty, including the League. When Robert M. La Follette charged that President Wilson, by neglecting the Senate during negotiation of the treaty, had violated the Constitution, Walsh rallied to the defense. He read from volume one of Willoughby on the Constitution and cited former Senator John C. Spooner of Wisconsin to show that if Wilson was guilty so was practically every other president since George Washington. They too had negotiated independently and then asked the Senate to ratify treaties. This was not to deny, however, that the president might "commendably have taken the Senate more freely into his confidence."[18]

The Montana senator attempted to follow and to refute an assortment of anti-League arguments. He caustically observed that it was "quite impossible to follow all the inconsistencies" of those who fought the League: "One group attacks the League because it contemplates war; another because it is founded on wholly impractical notions of human perfection." In truth, he believed, the League recognized the inveterate character of greed, vanity, and other vices among people and nations.[19]

Walsh tried to meet an argument that Article X meant war not peace, and armament not disarmament. Borah, for example, asserted that in order to act under Article X a nation must be prepared every minute. Every war, more-over, would be a world war. George Norris of Nebraska was also skeptical about the League's chances of promoting disarmament. Walsh and other League proponents answered that thirty or forty nations banded together would wield such force that no single one would have to maintain expensive armaments and their combined threat would avert war. But why was it, asked Borah, that France had no faith in the security provided by Article X, and wanted a special security treaty?[20]

One of the principal contentions of the "irreconcilables" was that the Treaty of Versailles, with its League and its Article X, would put the world into a straitjacket. No such maintenance of the status quo by the United States could be tolerated. Walsh devoted much attention to this argument and strove to refute it. When Borah referred to Articles X, XI, and XIV as war articles "set up for the purpose of crushing insurrection" and for "settling all matters by means of force," Walsh asked him to point to anything in the Covenant call-ing for members to send troops to put down insurrection. Clearly the lan-guage of Article X forbade external aggression. If that phraseology bound governments to put down revolution, said Walsh, "as the Holy Alliance con-templated should be done . . . I am against this covenant."[21]

To show the flexibility of the League Porter J. McCumber, Republican of North Dakota, John Sharp Williams of Mississippi, and Walsh teamed up on June 18 in Senate debate. Walsh concluded "that the world would not be in a strait-jacket, by any means." In another instance Walsh said of Article X, "It was clearly intended by the language used to preserve the sacred right of rev-olution asserted in the Declaration of Independence."[22]

Walsh and his group also attacked the idea that the obligation of Article X rested on the United States alone. No little effort had been made, said Walsh, to convince people that whenever war broke out in any quarter of the globe, the United States as the general policeman of the world must go there to quell the disturbance. Resenting such implications, Walsh on June 20 spoke curt-ly to Senator Reed when he talked of American soldiers policing Europe, and they continued in sharp disagreement.[23]

The issue that most excited Walsh and stirred him to heated debate was that of England's influence in the new world order and particularly England's oppression of the Irish. Walsh was suspicious of England's power and ambi-tion. He believed that, should the League fail, the United States must have a navy superior to that of England. And yet he maintained that England's in-fluence would be restricted rather than enlarged by the League plan and ap-parently for this reason, discounted the fear of the British Empire.[24]

To bitter protests against Britain's six votes in the League Assembly as compared to one for the United States, Walsh replied that he did not originally favor this apportionment but the defect was not serious. It was indisputable, he claimed, that representatives from Panama, Haiti, Liberia, and Guatamala would be "practically controlled" by the United States in the natural order of things. By no means did it follow that representatives from England's colonies, such as Australia and Canada would always vote with England. In any controversy to which Great Britain was a party she could not vote. And finally no action was possible unless the vote of the Council (where England had just one vote) was unanimous and unless a majority of the Assembly members cast approving votes. Admitting that the League Covenant was not perfect, he said neither was the U.S. Constitution. In his view one must run certain risks because of the "inestimable benefits" which might result.[25]

Traditional Irish-American hatred of England became a serious barrier to ratification of the Versailles Treaty and affected Senator Walsh's attitude. For millions of Americans of Irish descent it was enough that England approved the treaty; good Irishmen must then oppose it. Some senators, including David I. Walsh of Massachusetts, showed an antagonism toward Great Britain and the League largely explained by their Irish lineage and Irish-American constituents. Tom Walsh's parents had emigrated from Ireland, and he also had to contend with thousands of Irish in Butte and other parts of Montana who bitterly assailed Great Britain and the League. Agreeing with much that these partisans had to say and hoping for Irish home rule, he nevertheless did not become an Anglophobe and continued for many months to support the League without reservations.[26]

Walsh replied to a Butte Irishman in June 1918 that most people were bitterly disappointed over the state of affairs in Ireland. He and Senator James D. Phelan of California, who was "intensely Celtic in his sympathies," had frequently conferred on this subject, but neither was convinced that it was wise to precipitate a discussion on this "exceedingly delicate matter." "You will realize," Walsh wrote, "that our first duty is to safeguard the interest of this country, but that being done, neither of us will omit any opportunity to promote the ambition of the liberty-loving Irish for his government."[27]

A future U.S. senator, James E. Murray of Montana, then practicing law in Butte, was one of the Irish who opposed the League. Walsh wrote to him that he was not at all moved by efforts to stir up prejudice against Great Britain. It was true that England held people subject, as was true also of the United States, but Walsh could not agree that the League sought to protect Great Britain against the future recognition of these subjects.[28]

In ways he considered supportive of the League Walsh used his influence for Irish independence. On the eve of Wilson's departure for the Peace Conference Walsh urged him to call for an independent Ireland. Finally, as if to reassure the president he wrote, "You know how earnestly I hope and pray that your mission may be successful." Wilson replied that he would do what he could on this "delicate" matter and that he felt much strengthened by Walsh's expressions of confidence.[29]

Several months later Walsh joined four other Democratic senators, Peter G. Gerry, David I. Walsh, Key Pittman, and John B. Kendrick, in calling the attention of Woodrow Wilson to the necessity of acting upon the Irish question while at the Peace Conference. They said it was difficult to appreciate the intensity of feeling in the United States on this subject. The future of the party demanded that something be done, and they all concurred in the belief that otherwise the "prospect of the early ratification of the treaty by the Senate" would be jeopardized. They averred that Great Britain was asking much more from the Conference than was the United States and ought to give assurances in some form that Ireland should obtain at least as much self-government as enjoyed by the favored colonies.[30]

Early in October 1919 Walsh initiated positive action to improve the League's image. He arranged a dinner for Saturday evening, October 11, to bring together a number of senators "who by reason of conditions prevailing in their States respectively . . . [were] particularly interested." Invited also were Homer Cummings, Gavin McNab, and Bernard Baruch. Cummings (chairman of the Democratic National Committee), in traveling about the country, had become impressed "with the acuteness of the situation."[31]

As a result of this Democratic assemblage Walsh on October 18 introduced a resolution in the Senate to the effect that when the United States became a member of the League of Nations it should present to the Council "the state of affairs in Ireland and the right of its people to self-government." Walsh came under heated attack, although he explained that his resolution was not offered in any spirit of hostility toward Great Britain and he did not anticipate any League action except to air the subject in open forum. His resolution did not pass.[32]

The Senate made little progress toward a vote on the treaty until late summer. Delay and more delay, as public enthusiasm waned for the president's plans, was good strategy for foes of the treaty. Chairman Henry Cabot Lodge read aloud the entire 268-page treaty to members of his Foreign Relations Committee, and the committee held public hearings through August and early

September. Friends of the League were increasingly alarmed. The president set out on a strenuous "swing around the circle" which began at Columbus, Ohio, included two stops in Montana, and ended abruptly at Pueblo, Colorado, on September 25. On the verge of a collapse the president was rushed from Colorado to the White House. There he suffered a stroke, and with his breakdown the chances for ratification of the treaty were diminished.[33]

Forty-five amendments to the text of the treaty and fourteen reservations finally were reported out from the Senate Foreign Relations Committee on September 10, and the struggle over these proposed changes began. Walsh fought for an unadulterated Wilson League and treaty. The focus of his arguments against change was that any qualification must be approved by Germany as well as by the Allies. Obviously textual changes would necessitate reopening negotiations with all the signatories to the Versailles Treaty, and Walsh insisted that no different result could be achieved by denominating something an amendment or an interpretation or a reservation, so long as this qualification was to be viewed as part of the Senate's ratification. The effect, he wrote to Governor Stewart of Montana, would be to force the United States to negotiate with Germany: "however trivial the reservations may be, they would afford Germany an opportunity to escape from the obligations which we have forced her to assume by signing and ratifying the treaty . . . we would have to *negotiate* a Treaty of Peace."[34]

The Senate considered first the forty-five textual amendments, and Walsh aided in defeating them all. He and nearly all the Democrats voted with a dozen Republican moderates to achieve this victory.

The Senate next considered fourteen reservations, advanced by Lodge from the Foreign Relations Committee, Walsh again argued that reservations and amendments were alike in that renegotiation must occur; but he also maintained, as the reservations were taken up individually, that various features of the reservations were unconstitutional, offensive to the president, or unnecessary. Walsh offered amendments to the reservations, trying to make them more palatable. Always he voted against each reservation in its final form.[35]

On November 10 he made a speech relating to the proposed reservation on Article X, one part of which read that only Congress had the "power to declare war or authorize the employment of the military or naval forces of the United States." Walsh contended that this reservation violated the Constitution in saying that Congress had the sole power to authorize use of the military forces. His fundamental objection, however, was that the United States escaped obligation to the League members while they were obligated to the United States. This was not only a taint on the country's honor, but probably would cause rejection of the treaty by the other nations. Walsh believed that the reservation "practically destroyed" Article X.[36]

So strongly did Walsh react to this reservation to Article X that he twice tried to amend it in a drastic manner. The reservation to Article X, eleven additional Lodge reservations, and two offered from the floor gained the Senate's approval. To this point in the debates Walsh exhibited a determination and an impatience toward the opposition similar to that shown by his "chief," Woodrow Wilson. The antagonistic relationship between Walsh and Senator Lodge resembled that between Wilson and Lodge. Walsh asserted that Lodge's reservation number seven, relating to Shantung province in North China, obviously was intended to "advertise to the whole world" the family quarrels of the United States. When Boies Penrose tried to interrupt, Walsh cut him off: "Let the Senator from Pennsylvania speak in his own time, not mine."[37]

Vehement in his feelings for the League, loyal to the president and to the Democratic party, Walsh was unlike Wilson in that he came to see the necessity of apppeasing the reservationists. On November 18 the Montanan wrote to Senator Hitchcock saying that, in his opinion, they should compromise with Lodge on his reservations. Article X, it was true, was greatly weakened by the reservation, but other articles left the League with power enough to succeed. Hitchcock enclosed Walsh's letter with one of his own sent to the White House and remarked that "many democrats" held views similar to Walsh's. Rejecting this compromise idea, the president sent instructions to Hitchcock that, at most, the Democrats should accept the administration's "interpretive" reservations.[38]

November 19, 1919, was a day of decision for the United States. The Senate at last was ready to vote on the Versailles Treaty. Directed by Hitchcock, the Democrats met in caucus in the morning and heard the president's letter requesting that they defeat the Lodge reservations. Ready, almost unanimously, to carry out the president's wishes, they went into the Senate at noon. After some debate the roll was called on the question of approving the treaty with the Lodge reservations. There was a tense wait as senators answered to their names, but the result was a one-sided vote, 39 ayes to 55 nays. The Democrats then moved for approval of the treaty without any reservations. Again the roll call and defeat: 38 ayes to 53 nays. Decisively the treaty was lost. Unavailing were Hitchcock's efforts to get a vote on his interpretive reservations. Walsh voted with the administration forces at every point: against the treaty with Lodge reservations (joining the "irreconcilables" to defeat it); for the treaty without reservations; and for the futile Hitchcock attempts to get a vote on his mild reservations. Thus bitterly a year's labor came to an end.[39]

In the second session of the Sixty-sixth Congress, in December 1919, discussion of the Treaty of Versailles resumed and Walsh now was a leader of the Democratic moderates attempting to compromise with the Republicans. This meant a political and personal parting for Walsh and Woodrow Wilson. Walsh's course as an independent Democrat is worthy of examination since those Democratic senators who differed with Wilson have, at times, been labelled "traitors" to the League and, at other times, have been hailed as farsighted friends of international cooperation whose spirit of compromise—if shared by the president—might have gained Senate ratification of the League and changed the course of world history. To find the compelling reasons for Walsh's new posture of a compromiser is difficult. On this question his motivation was particularly complex, but the various factors which led him to vote for a modified League in the Senate test of March 1920 can be examined.[40]

During the first debates in the new session of Congress the Montanan joined Lodge, Hitchcock, Irvine Lenroot of Wisconsin, and others in discussing the failure to ratify the treaty. Lodge angered the Democrats with an assertion that their votes "were not their own," at which point Walsh demanded that he withdraw his imputation. Lodge did so. Walsh went ahead to explain his motivation and to suggest why the treaty had been defeated. He was not conscious that anyone commanded his vote on the treaty or any other matter. He had opposed President Wilson, he reminded the Senate, on the Canal Tolls question. It so happened that from the beginning he had been favorable to the League and disposed to yield "some misgivings" about "the great man in the White House." Always since Lodge's speech of August 12, 1919, it had been Walsh's assumption that Senator Lodge wished to kill the treaty. He added: "I think, perhaps, unless his sentiments concerning the matter have undergone a radical change, in that fact lies the explanation of why the treaty was not ratified."[41]

But evidence accumulated that Walsh was in a compromising mood. He obviously disagreed with Wilson's idea of December 19, that not even an intimation of compromise should come from the Democratic side. Walsh in fact agitated for a bipartisan conference of senators to try and effect a compromise and subsequently claimed for himself at least as much credit as any Republican senator in initiating the conferences of early 1920. Another sign of the widening breach between Democratic leaders and the president resulted from Wilson's letter of January 8, read at the Jackson Day Dinner by Homer S. Cummings. This presidential letter was adamant against any substantial reservations; William Jennings Bryan jumped to his feet and voiced strenuous objections. He wanted compromise and early ratification. Walsh was of like mind.[42]

Senator Lodge, near the middle of January 1920, called together a bipartisan conference attended by Republican Senators Lodge, H. S. New (Indiana), Frank Kellogg, and Irvine Lenroot, and Democratic senators Hitchcock, Kenneth McKellar (Tennessee), Walsh, and R. L. Owen (Oklahoma). It would be well, Lodge said, to make an effort toward agreement in order to show that the differences were not verbal but vital. This was not a promising attitude with which to work for compromise, assuming Lodge really felt that way in January 1920.[43]

The conference met almost constantly until January 31 when it broke up without agreement on reservations and without agreement as to why it broke up. Lodge claimed that the senators had reached a number of tentative agreements but conspicuously failed to agree to any change in reservations dealing with the Monroe Doctrine and Article X.[44]

Walsh commented at length on these bipartisan negotiations and took issue with Lodge. He stated that he had proposed in the conference that the reservation to Article X written by William Howard Taft should be accepted as a substitute for Lodge's reservation on that subject. In Walsh's opinion, the Taft version left Article X with more strength than Lodge's. He and McCumber agreed that what was most needed was a reservation for which they could secure 64 votes. Walsh's explanations of the failure in the bipartisan conference did not coincide with those advanced by Lodge. Walsh remembered that they had been discussing Hitchcock's substitute reservation to Article X and had agreed sufficiently upon alterations to pass on to another matter, when Lodge took his Republican colleagues into the next room for a conference. The evidence, said Walsh, showed that pressure exerted by the "irreconcilables" forced Lodge to terminate the bipartisan conference.

Compromise ideas were not abandoned. Walsh said that he had hoped very much that the bipartisan conference would promote harmony, and if it had concluded its work he would "very cheerfully" have come to the Senate and voted in favor of every reservation and the resolution of ratification including the reservations. Since the work of the bipartisan committee had not been accepted by the Republicans he did not feel "under any obligation whatever to vote for any of the reservations."[45]

Reservations adopted in the debates of February and March 1920 were not significantly different from those of the past November. The Senate was covering old ground. Almost the only fresh notions concerned the unsuccessful bipartisan conference and the approaching political campaign of 1920. Walsh, arguing much as before that the reservations were unnecessary, enervating, or offensive to the president, voted against all but one of them, considered individually.

A completely new reservation introduced by Senator Gerry received Walsh's support. It declared that the United States adhered to a belief in self-determination and to its resolution of sympathy for Irish self-government passed in the Senate in June 1919; also that when Ireland had its own government it should promptly be admitted as a member of the League of Nations. Walsh spoke briefly for this reservation and helped to carry it by the narrow margin of 38 to 36.[46]

Walsh was not feeling well during the final weeks of debate, but his speech on the last day won deservedly wide acclaim. As an analysis of the whole treaty battle and a justification for those Democrats who voted aye on the treaty— with reservations—it merits careful attention. Walsh found himself confronted with two alternatives, both "in a high degree distasteful"; first, to vote for the Wilson League, without reservations, and swallow certain defeat; or second, to vote for the Lodge reservations. "The situation should not be misunderstood," he said. "The treaty has had no ardent support on the Republican side of the Chamber." Lodge's speech of August 12, 1919, showed that the senator from Massachusetts wished "to discredit the whole idea of a League of Nations and bring about the rejection of the treaty because of the covenant." Said Walsh, "the impassioned remarks with which he [Lodge] closed the debate last night clearly revealed that he does not now regard it with any higher degree of favor."[47]

Walsh admitted there was room for speculation as to whether the Lodge group really wished to defeat the treaty. Circumstances attending the failure of the bipartisan conference, however, indicated that the Lodge Republicans did not care overmuch. He reiterated his belief that Lodge had been on the verge of compromise but yielded under the pressure of the irreconcilables. Walsh was convinced that "the so-called mild reservationists would not proceed without the concurrence of the Senator from Massachusetts, and the Senator from Massachusetts found himself obliged to conform to the counsel or advice of the irreconcilables."

Notwithstanding these considerations Walsh had no difficulty in deciding how to vote. He would vote for ratification with reservations because "after reasonable effort" the treaty was the best that could be secured. Why was it best to take the treaty with reservations rather than to wait, as Wilson desired, and throw the issue into the coming campaign? Walsh was unable to find any good basis for hoping that "at any time in the future" the treaty could be ratified without reservations substantially like those before the Senate. There could be no real issue in the campaign of 1920. Suppose the Democrats won decisively. The best net gains they could reasonably expect would be five Senate seats, so that it would still be necessary "to go across the aisle for at least fourteen votes." And there would be little chance of getting those Republican votes without reservations.

Walsh analyzed the reservations to show that they left a League worth voting for. In so concluding he modified some of his previously expressed views. No vital principle of the treaty was seriously affected, he held, except Article X, concerning which the United States refused to assume its obligations. But the Covenant was not "a vain thing without Article 10." "Indeed," he said, "I am satisfied upon mature reflection that I myself originally attached to it undue importance. I believe it can be demonstrated that almost, if not quite all, that is or will be accomplished by article 10 is secured to the world by other provisions of the Covenant."

Walsh deplored the reservations principally because his pride as a citizen of the United States was hurt. He shrank from having his country classed with those that, even in diplomacy, found

> The good old rule
> Sufficeth them, the simple plan
> That they should take who have the power
> And they should keep who can.

And yet these reservations, said Walsh, were supported by men as highminded as he could claim to be. In moving words he expressed his final decision. "Reluctantly I yield my judgment to theirs on that point, and, having dismissed it, the path of duty is perfectly clear to me—so clear that in my conviction there is 'no variableness, neither shadow of turning.'"[48]

Unlike the vote of the year before on the Treaty of Versailles with reservations, that of March 19, 1920, was close—49 to 35, only seven votes short of the necessary two-thirds majority. Twenty-one Democrats bolted their party, voting for reservations; others were almost won away from Wilson. Two senators ventured the opinion that Walsh's speech was so powerful that it came near being decisive. In a letter to the *Louisville Courier-Journal*, which had praised his address and was printing it, Walsh said that, although he had not intended to convert anybody, perhaps he had nearly done so. "Senator Beckham [J. C. W. Beckham, Kentucky] insists . . . that if I had made the address a few days before it was delivered the result of the vote probably would have been different." Senator Charles A. Culberson of Texas also was impressed. Three of the first four Democrats voted on the roll call for the treaty. Then came Culberson, a highly respected man whose vote carried influence. It is said that he hesitated at the call of his name, but finally he voted for the administration and against the treaty. Later, in conversation with a friend, the Texan extravagantly praised Walsh's speech and said, "You know, for a minute in there I didn't know how to vote."[49]

Why did Senator Walsh change and vote for the League with reservations in March 1920? Can one accept his own reasoning at face value? Walsh's reasons as stated in his final speech were of a general type that applied to a number of Democratic senators from different parts of the country who voted independently. He emphasized the hopelessness of getting a League without reservations and therefore the distasteful but reasonable alternative of accepting the Lodge reservations. He believed it was futile to throw the League issue into the political campaign of 1920. Implicit in these views was a willingness to compromise that seemed to reflect the wishes of most Americans, though not those of Woodrow Wilson. That powerful forces for compromise were at work is clearly shown by the shift of 21 Democrats to Lodge's side. Possibly the broad influences for quick ratification, summed up by Walsh himself, adequately explain his vote.[50]

Among the influences not mentioned by Senator Walsh was the Irish question. Consistently he had been concerned about Irish antagonism toward the Wilson League and had reacted to pressures from the Montana Irish. On February 20, 1920, his law partner, C. B. Nolan, warned that the Irish in Butte and throughout the state might help to beat him as a candidate for delegate to the Democratic national convention. Walsh was doubtful but wrote to Tom Stout *confidentially* asking him whether the Irish, indeed, were so hostile toward him. No answer is available, but the facts strongly suggest an affirmative response. As mentioned, Walsh voted on March 18 for the Gerry reservation for Irish self-government. On the final vote on the entire treaty, so far as the Irish went, Walsh might have voted safely against the League or for the treaty with the Lodge reservations (now including Gerry's); but a vote for Wilson's (and England's) League would have been most unpopular among the Montana Irish.[51]

No one can be sure how much the Irish issue affected Walsh's vote. Obviously, however, he was personally sympathetic toward Gerry's reservation for Irish self-government, which was a logical culmination of Walsh's own activities in behalf of Ireland, and he was sensitive to the political pressure of 28,000 Irish-Americans in his home state. In May 1920 many of the Montana Irish were among those who gave Walsh a good complimentary vote for delegate to the Democratic national convention in San Francisco.

But cumulative differences with the president over the manner in which he conducted his peace program probably affected Walsh's final decisions. That the Senate should have been given a larger share in peace making was frequently implied in Walsh's comments. For one thing, the president neglected to take any senator to Paris with him, and Walsh was disappointed that he had not been chosen. When Wilson returned briefly to the United States in February 1919, he refused to discuss the League Covenant with Democratic members of Congress, as the Montanan had proposed. It was shortly after this rebuff that Walsh privately expressed keen disappointment: "I think the President has handled the thing most maladroitly and has evidenced a disposition to exclude the Senate from any real, active participation in the making of the treaty." After seven additional months of haggling over the League, Walsh in November advised his "Chief" to compromise with the reservationist forces. Wilson refused. Walsh subdued his misgivings temporarily, voted as Wilson requested, and with his party suffered a stunning defeat. In the fall of 1919 the Montanan took stock of all the factors before a second and final vote occurred in March 1920. Walsh sincerely believed that "half a League" was better than none and voted accordingly. Politically an acceptance of reservations was prudent in view of growing sentiment in the country against "Mr. Wilson's League" and in view of Montana public opinion. Walsh saw what seemed to be a practical course for his country, his party, and himself. He then acted in behalf of compromise on the League.

18

1920 *Politics and Issues of the Red Scare*

Walsh's Senate seat was secure until 1924, and in many respects the politics of 1920 was not crucial to him. But the fact that Warren G. Harding won the presidency by a landslide was meaningful and his own career was significantly affected by policies adopted under Harding. Walsh attended the Democratic National Convention in San Francisco and served later in Chicago as chairman of the Democratic Senate campaign committee.[1]

Of primary importance for Walsh was the Montana situation, where a bitter gubernatorial battle split the state Democratic party. Burton K. Wheeler won the Democratic nomination with support from the Nonpartisan League and many of a left-wing persuasion. He then opposed Joseph M. Dixon, formerly a U.S. senator and Bull Moose leader. Dixon won the election, partly because Senator Henry L. Myers and many Democrats refused to support their party candidate.[2]

The conservatives of Montana, with the power of corporate interests and the press behind them, conducted a bitter campaign against Wheeler and his associates. Colonel Nolan wrote that Company men were active among the opposition. "They have their shift-bosses here [Helena, the Placer Hotel], likewise their attorneys." Congressman John M. Evans and candidate Burton Wheeler agreed that National Committeeman Bruce Kremer, generally linked with the Anaconda Company, was "fighting the ticket." The *Helena Independent* was one of the Democratic papers that eagerly joined the Republicans in assailing "dangerous radicals" trying to take over Montana. Most spectacular was the conduct of Democratic Senator Henry Myers, who bolted the party. He said he was amazed to discover "that the Non Partisan Leaguers, aided by a lot of Socialists and nondescripts and some Bolshevists," had captured the Democratic party in Montana and nominated their ticket. The worst elements in the Montana Democratic party, he believed, intended to carry on the same "orgy of State Socialism" that North Dakota had suffered.[3]

Loyal Democrats reacted indignantly as Myers joined the opposition. Walsh wired Senator Pat Harrison that Myers had been reported ready to leave Washington, D.C., for Montana to take the stump. Walsh urged: "Please . . . send him to Missouri where he was reared, or elsewhere, but keep him out of Montana." Chairman George White also was requested to restrain Myers. But he went on to Montana. Colonel Nolan wrote from Helena about the contemptible way in which the bolting senator was holding forth and working with "swash-bucklers" who plied their business between the party lines. Walsh replied that Myers must feel proud to be lavishly extolled by the Republican *Record-Herald;* he "never contributed an idea toward forming any party policy, or toward the organization or direction of a campaign before, nor did anyone ever think of consulting him on such matters." Walsh refused to dignify the man by meeting him on the stump. "Whom the Gods would destroy," he said, "they first make mad."[4]

In the latter part of October Walsh returned from Chicago to Montana and delivered an important address for the Democratic state ticket. At the Miles City Opera House on October 25 he defended Governor Lynn J. Frazier of North Dakota and Wheeler of Montana, who had been backed by the Nonpartisan League. It had often been alleged that they were puppets of the League's founder, A. C. Townley. But Walsh declared that Governor Frazier was "a man of culture, college trained, no mere automaton, doing the bidding of another." By popular vote the League had gained power in North Dakota, and he would accept the judgment of the people of that state rather than "the stale stuff" being peddled around Montana. He added, "I am not half-hearted in my support of Mr. Wheeler. He has been tried as by fire."[5]

Walsh contracted laryngitis after the Miles City speech and could do little during the remainder of the campaign except issue statements and write letters expressing disappointment that he had to "sniff the battle from afar." In a long telegraphic message to John D. Tansil of the county committee in Billings, Walsh was critical of the Republican Old Guard, lauded the Democratic record under Wilson, and defended the young and able gubernatorial candidate. In a private communication Walsh stated that Wheeler's election as governor would give "new birth" to the Democratic party of Montana by attracting young and enterprising men who recognized that grievances and abuses needed to be removed. When Senator Myers and other conservatives charged that Wheeler and his supporters advocated free love, Walsh retorted in words stinging with sarcasm in the *Helena Independent.* All his efforts to stem the Republican tide were unavailing, however.[6]

Election day came, and the heavens fell on those admitting the label "Democrat." Harding swept into power with a popular vote almost twice that of Governor James M. Cox of Ohio. Republicans increased their majority in the Senate and the House. In Montana Joseph M. Dixon beat Burton K. Wheeler by approximately 35,000 votes out of a total of some 175,000; and Republicans won all the other state offices.[7]

This election had consequences other than the loss of the state to the Republicans. By breaking from his own party and fighting Wheeler, Senator Myers antagonized Walsh and other loyal Democrats and ruined his chances for another Senate term. Wheeler thus obtained his opportunity for a national career. Profiting from Myers's misfortune and from dissension in Governor Dixon's new administration, Wheeler adopted a moderate approach toward the big interests and soon went to join Walsh in the Senate.

For Walsh, as a Democratic leader, the election results meant vindication as well as defeat. He had predicted that throwing the League of Nations question into the campaign would be a blunder; Woodrow Wilson and his stubborn friends in the Senate and in the San Francisco convention had suffered the most resounding defeat of all. Their hope that this would be a solemn referendum in which the American people would declare for Wilson's League was utterly lost. Walsh, a minority senator before the 1920 campaign, continued in the Democratic minority, but within the party he was stronger than before the election. His postelection mood, however, seems to have been a melancholy one. He referred in one letter to the "avalanche" which had struck in November. A New Year's testimonial of friendship evoked the response: "Your letter . . . is of the character to restore one's confidence that life is worth living after all."[8]

Despite his support of Wheeler and his calm evaluation of the situation in Montana, Walsh became intolerant of Reds, pro-Germans, IWWs, and other dissenters—though not of traditional Socialists. He used his position on the Senate Judiciary Committee to work for the Espionage Act of 1917, the Sedition Act of 1918, and an unlawful associations bill aimed at organizations which in wartime proposed to bring about any governmental, social, industrial, or economic change in the United States by physical force, violence, or injury. He had in mind the IWW and similar radical groups.

Walsh appears to have been oblivious to any danger to civil liberties involved in the enforcement of sedition acts. In late 1919 and early 1920 he gave no credence to arguments that public officials would transgress the law in their eagerness to track down radicals. He gave no attention to the subtleties of the question of whether an individual's membership in the IWW, or possession of revolutionary tracts, necessarily proved that the particular individual would try to overthrow the government by violence. On January 8, 1920, Walsh wrote to Attorney General A. Mitchell Palmer and enclosed a telegram he had recently received from Butte asking for action against radicals. Walsh said to Palmer that he would be obliged if he conducted an investigation and advised him "of what action the Department will take." Such evidence indicates that Walsh approved the idea of strict enforcement during December 1919 and January 1920.[9]

When agents of the Department of Justice in January 1920 launched their greatest raids, swooping down on thousands of alleged revolutionaries, they aimed at efficiency rather than legality. They invaded homes and meeting places without obtaining search warrants. Immediately there were protests against the wholesale seizures and violations of personal liberties. For example, Francis Fisher Kane, U.S. attorney in Philadelphia, resigned from the Justice Department after condemning its illegal practices. In May 1920 a brochure appeared under the auspices of the National Popular Government League titled *To the American People, Report Upon the Illegal Practices of the Department of Justice.* Twelve outstanding lawyers actually prepared this report. They included Felix Frankfurter, Roscoe Pound, Zechariah Chafee, Ernst Freund, and Frank Walsh. As lawyers, whose sworn duty it was to uphold the laws and the Constitution of the United States, they felt they must bring to the attention of the American people the "utterly illegal acts which have been committed by those charged with the highest duty of enforcing the laws." Nineteen exhibits were offered as proof.

Senator Walsh became particularly interested in civil liberties after the lawyers' expose of A. Mitchell Palmer. The manner in which he shifted his position invites investigation, especially since changes occurred often in Walsh's career. In spite of his anti-Red sentiments and his early approval of the campaign against radicals by the Department of Justice, Walsh became a principal agent in bringing about a Senate investigation of the Palmer raids.

On December 10, 1920, Walsh asked for an investigation of Attorney General Palmer based upon the charges of the twelve lawyers. Harold Ickes, of the law firm of Richberg, Ickes, Davies & Lord, expressed gratification "that a Senator of Mr. Walsh's political faith should have had the courage and right feeling to initiate such action."[10]

One curious feature of the investigation was a strained relationship between the two principals before the Senate hearings began. Walsh gave two reasons for the tension between him and Palmer. First, the Attorney General had requested Bruce Kremer, the Democratic National Committeeman from Montana, rather than Walsh, to recommend a new U.S. attorney for Montana. Second, Walsh suspected that he had been bypassed because he and his brother John (a delegate from Wisconsin) had not "come across" for Palmer in the Democratic National Convention of 1920. Walsh declared that he was not alarmed that his "prerogatives" were usurped, but the facts belie his statement. During the hearings and while Palmer was testifying, Walsh was requested by the U.S. marshal in Helena to make an inquiry of the attorney general. The senator replied: "The relations between the Attorney General and myself are so strained . . . that I prefer not to make the inquiry suggested by you until after the 4th of March."[11]

The Judiciary Committee appointed a subcommittee to conduct hearings. It consisted of Thomas Sterling (Republican, South Dakota), chairman; L. B. Colt (Republican, Rhode Island); William E. Borah (Republican of Idaho); William H. King (Democrat, Utah); and Walsh. Sterling, King, and Walsh were the main participants. The most important witnesses were the attorney general, his subordinates in the Justice Department who had conducted the raids, members of the Labor Department who had been legally charged with deportation proceedings, and several of the twelve lawyers who prepared the *Report*. Senator Sterling presided, and Walsh acted as prosecuting attorney.[12]

Walsh's demeanor while interrogating the witnesses was not altogether that of a relentless prosecutor. He harmonized his past record as an antirevolutionary with his current role of investigating those who had seized the radicals. But he left no doubt that he believed the Department of Justice guilty of proceeding without warrants, holding people incommunicado, usurping duties of the Labor Department relating to deportation proceedings, and other illegal activities. Once, while the attorney general was on the stand, Walsh commented that Zechariah Chafee was the author of a book on free speech, "with all of which" he did not agree. Palmer was gratified to hear this; but Walsh then declared that Chafee was a very able lawyer. Most revealing was Walsh's reply to a remark by J. W. Abercrombie, who had been acting secretary of labor during the raids and who averred at the hearing that the laws on anarchy could not be made too rigid to suit him. Walsh retorted: "We tried hard in this committee to make them more rigid than they are now. The chairman and myself both urged it. But we trusted to you gentlemen to observe the law in enforcing it"; and yet, he said, Abercrombie's agents went on to "search residences of people, aliens, and otherwise, seizing books and papers, and rifling drawers, and that kind of thing."[13]

Unable to refute many of the charges against him, Palmer delivered an impassioned defense that had some merit. He declared that there was no criticism of his department at the time of these raids for its handling of the situation. "How soon we do forget!" He described vividly the demand for action in 1919 when Bolshevism was on the march. He pointed out that the Senate on October 19, 1919, had asked what he was doing and had demanded the enforcement of the deportation statute; there was no complaint then about his expressed plans and his close cooperation with the Labor Department. His defense embodied the idea that the Senate and the country had demanded action rather than protection of constitutional rights. Palmer would admit no wrong: "I apologize for nothing that the Department of Justice has done in this matter. I glory in it."[14]

Because the hearings ended with a sharp division of opinion in the subcommittee, its action and that of the full Judiciary Committee was slow and inconclusive. Sterling believed that the affair should be forgotten and that the Judiciary Committee should make no report to the Senate. Walsh, on the other hand, wished to condemn Palmer's raids. He insisted to the reluctant chairman of the subcommittee that they should meet and take action in order to expedite a decision in the full committee. Both senators wrote reports in line with their contradictory views. About a year after the reports were written, the Judiciary Committee rejected that of Walsh by a vote of 7 to 4. But Norris, Borah, and Ashurst sided with him. The committee then voted to make no report. A few days later, Walsh obtained consent to print his report and Sterling's and his reply to Sterling in the *Record*.[15]

Walsh's case against Palmer was convincing in so far as violation of the Bill of Rights and the laws was concerned. Noting that agents of the Department of Justice were instructed before the raids to get warrants only if "absolutely necessary," Walsh commented: "It is difficult to conceive how one bred to the law could ever have promulgated such an order." He deplored Palmer's lack of humanity. And he denied that Congress had sanctioned the drastic measures taken against the radicals, as was maintained by Palmer and Senator Sterling.[16]

Walsh ended his answer to Senator Sterling with a ringing defense of personal liberties. The public hysteria which prevailed at the time of the Palmer raids was no excuse for violations of the Constitution, he declared: "It is rare except when the public mind is stirred by some overwhelming catastrophe or is aghast at some hideous crime or otherwise overwrought, that one is required to appeal to his constitutional rights." That was precisely when the Constitution should be a "shield."[17]

Long before their insertion in the *Record* Walsh's reports were circulated and gained public recognition. He sent copies to Woodrow Wilson, Felix Frankfurter, and other important figures, as well as to the press, receiving praise in return. He called the attention of a number of Montana newspapers to an article in the *New York World* which declared "few cabinet officials have received a more humiliating rebuke from a member of their own party than that administered to A. Mitchell Palmer by Senator Walsh of Montana." The senator who from 1917 to 1920 had been in the forefront of the campaign against radicals and many dissenters now was eulogized as a defender of civil liberties.[18]

Walsh's correspondence indicates that he had political fences in mind. That he gave wide publicity in Montana to his branding of A. Mitchell Palmer seems significant. And in one letter to a Montana lady who doubted his progressivism Walsh expressed the belief that his attack on Palmer would win back old supporters. "Whatever offense I may have given in any quarter, and I can not believe that it is serious enough to deserve notice, by my advocacy of so-called sedition and syndicalist laws, I feel perfectly certain it would be regarded as extinguished by my report on the so-called 'red raids.'"[19]

Valuable though Walsh's investigation proved to be, his motives were doubtful and his attitude from 1917 to 1922 contained contradictions. Misinterpretation or misuse of such statutes as the sedition acts which Walsh endorsed and of the Deportation Act of 1918 was accurately forecast by many who cherished liberty even in wartime. Walsh's reverence for the Bill of Rights in 1922, a time of comparative calm, was newly acquired since 1919 (a time of cataclysm and hysteria). He may have indicted himself when he declared in 1922 that human rights needed protection especially in times of catastrophe and hysteria. Thomas R. Marshall, vice president during the Wilson years, was one of Walsh's contemporaries who noted this characteristic. Walsh, he said in 1925, "was, and is a politician." The Montanan stood for his convictions, "but he would have found a way to have stood for them" without being "immolated upon the altar of his ideals."[20]

Walsh was not a cold man, a thought-machine, as sometimes described. He had the advantages and suffered the failings of an emotional makeup. Energetic and ambitious, he was capable of taking in the heat of the moment a position that soon became intellectually or politically untenable, and which might be abandoned without qualm. Walsh was by no means unprincipled, but issues often were not clear-cut and posed no moral problems. His delight in close reasoning perhaps stimulated him to find a rational way out of his dilemmas, such as that over civil liberties. Whether consciously or not, he often employed his resourceful brain in justifying courses of action which at other times he deplored.

19

Walsh and Wheeler, 1922

Hardly had the Democrats lost in 1920 when they began preparations for the state and national elections of 1922. Walsh was especially interested in the approaching senatorial campaign of his state. Burton K. Wheeler, a state and local leader of Butte, was determined to find a new theater for his talents. He set out to convince the mining leaders, Walsh, and others that no longer was he a "dangerous radical," whose candidacy for high office would split the Democratic party as it had in 1920. Soon Wheeler gained the Democratic senatorial nomination and went on to obtain conservative as well as liberal backing. Wheeler was to have his "place in the sun," as he termed it. Quickly he was a national figure, as well known as his colleague, the senior senator.

In spite of the Democratic debacle of 1920, Senator Walsh was increasingly recognized as a man of stature and an outstanding Democratic leader. Mark Sullivan, for example, said in April 1921 that the Montanan was "as fine a scholar and as able a lawyer as ever sat in the Senate." In the new Sixty-seventh Congress, declared Sullivan, the outstanding Democratic senators would be Oscar Underwood (the new Democratic floor leader), Furnifold Simmons (minority leader of the Finance Committee), Pat Harrison, Carter Glass, and Walsh.[1]

Walsh was high in party councils. In November 1921 he attended the meeting of the Democratic National Committee in St. Louis, at which Cordell Hull was appointed to succeed George White as chairman. Walsh considered Hull a "high-class man, exceptionally able and wise." A short time later Walsh attended a party conference including Bernard Baruch, Harrison Nesbitt of the Democratic Finance Committee, and Chairman Hull. After this meeting Walsh expressed the view that Democratic prospects for 1922 were favorable.[2]

Troubles of the Harding administration gave hope to the Democrats. Shortly after Harding's inauguration Walsh observed that the event had not been characterized by "any marked enthusiasm," though possibly that was a result of "the general aridity with which Mr. Volstead is charged." A few months later Walsh was convinced that the Harding administration was "accumulating a peck of trouble." The farmers were "rebellious," servicemen "grievously disappointed," and the man who expected lower taxes "mad." And it was rumored that the head of the Shipping Board, A. D. Lasker of Chicago, was a "Jonah." Walsh observed that there was a "rather sullen bloc" among the Senate Republicans, including La Follette, Johnson, Borah, Norris, Davis Elkins of West Virginia, and W. S. Kenyon of Iowa. Meanwhile, he added, the president apparently was having a good time on weekend parties and "other like jollifications," with the reaction reported to be little to his credit. "A few of the faithful" Democrats were to gather the next evening at Senator Peter Gerry's home to find ways of profiting from "the rising disaster."[3]

Guided in part by that meeting at Senator Gerry's, Walsh during 1922 repeatedly assailed Republican doctrine and performance. Despite this, there were rumors in late 1922 that President Harding might appoint Walsh to the Supreme Court vacancy created by William R. Day's resignation. Walsh, as a Democratic partisan, knew better than to wait expectantly.[4]

One issue with political overtones exemplified Walsh's role as an opposition leader. He played a major part in the Truman H. Newberry contested election case. Newberry, a wealthy industrialist, defeated Henry Ford in the 1918 Republican primary for the U.S. Senate and went on to win the general election. Because of charges that he had gained his primary victory by spending hundreds of thousands of dollars, the Senate Committee on Privileges and Elections took the case under review. Investigation was accompanied in 1921–22 by furious debate in the Senate. Walsh, Pat Harrison, and Claude Swanson attacked the Republicans on November 16, 1921, after the majority report of the Privileges and Elections Committee to seat Newberry was presented by Senator Selden Spencer of Missouri. Walsh later wrote that he was not trying to put Henry Ford in the Senate; he was attempting to keep Newberry out.[5]

Early in 1922 Walsh was trying to line up the anti-Newberry vote and received assurance from Robert M. La Follette that he would be on hand. On January 10 Walsh delivered a long speech, citing Newberry's expenditures, and asserted that "if this violation of the fundamental rights of the American people" went unrebuked the government of the United States might be regarded as in "peril." The Republicans succeeded in passing a resolution which seated Newberry though deploring the expenditures of his campaign. Walsh was satisfied with the "good fight" in which he had helped, and Newberry soon resigned.

In Montana, meanwhile, Joseph M. Dixon's victory over Burton Wheeler in the gubernatorial race of 1920 was the key to the times. Having gained support from the big interests or benefited from their opposition to Wheeler, Governor Dixon turned against those interests and inaugurated a progressive program. His chief issue was based on his belief that the mining interests failed to pay their share of the taxes. Conservatives were startled if not infuriated when Dixon raised taxes on mining companies and pressed for further increases. The press assailed him. Many Democrats who had voted for Dixon as a moderate in 1920 were disillusioned by his "radicalism" and were anxious to prove their loyalty to the Democratic party in the hope that a party victory in 1922 would be followed by the defeat of Dixon two years later.[6]

Walsh had an ability to view this state situation objectively while located in distant Washington. Though interested in Democratic victories, he was sympathetic with Dixon. Like the governor, he had been compelled to reckon with the Anaconda Company and its allies. Walsh's secretary, Miles Taylor, had formerly been secretary to Dixon and still corresponded with him. One detects a note of sympathy in Walsh's observation that the governor was "being violently assailed by all the newspapers of the State generally believed to be more or less under the influence of the Anaconda Company." However, as Walsh considered the controversies raging in Montana, he attempted to find Democratic advantage in the situation.

The task of Montana Democrats in 1922 was to put the broken party together again, and a critical question was the senatorial nomination. Senator Myers might desire renomination, but he was unqualified by being one of the bolters of 1920. Walsh wrote to Tom Stout that he had been in consultation with Cordell Hull trying to get him to go to Montana "with a view to getting the fellows to agree on a Congressional ticket, . . . which would command the respect and support of the people of the State." In Walsh's opinion Myers could not get the nomination and would be overwhelmingly defeated if he ran in the general election. Furthermore, Walsh opposed giving any bolter of 1920 a commanding position in the party. He believed that Democratic chances were excellent if qualified Democrats were nominated.[7]

Walsh had decided that the senatorial nomination ought to go to one of two men, Tom Stout or Burton Wheeler, and he was committed to Stout. Bruce Kremer would not do because the campaign would take on "the char-

acter of a contest between the Anaconda Company, on one side, supported
by the Democratic party, and the rest of the State on the other." Bruce was
"a very capable, genial fellow" but could not get the nomination or win if he
did get it. Walsh thought either Stout or Wheeler would make a good senator. Tom would be popular and "Wheeler would be virile, if not outstanding
by reason of his ability."[8]

Chairman Hull yielded to Walsh's "importunities" and met with about two
hundred leading Montana Democrats on April 14, in Helena. State Chairman
J. E. Erickson presided and read to the assemblage a message from Walsh in
which the senator assailed the national Republican policies. Shortly before the
meeting Walsh suggested to Nolan that the group might pass up any expression of approval of the senators and thus avoid praising Myers. If one can
believe the *Helena Independent,* the meeting was a great success. It reported
that many Democrats who had bolted in 1920 were repentant because of the
deception practiced by Governor Dixon as a gubernatorial candidate and were
now ready to present "a solid front to the opposition." Hull's talks with Wheeler
and others promoted harmony, although the meeting did not determine the
Democratic senatorial nominee.[9]

Burton K. Wheeler faced the decision of his life in 1922. He had been kicked
around by the Anaconda Company and the conservatives in 1918, with a re-
peat performance in 1920. Should he now withdraw from politics? The defeat of 1920 had left him bitter and defiant. In January 1921, he had a fist fight
with an Anaconda man and wrote to Walsh averring it was no wonder that
people disliked the Anaconda Copper Company when its officers kept men
in their employ who browbeat and intimidated people. For himself, he refused to take beatings from Kelley's and Ryan's "gun men and thugs"; eventually they would lose the respect of all right-thinking people.[10]

Wheeler's course may have been determined by the similar decision earlier
forced upon Walsh. It will be recalled that Walsh abandoned Wheeler, the
"radical," in 1918 and sought Company support in order to be reelected.
Wheeler thought frequently and bitterly upon Walsh's decision and must have
scrutinized the effects upon the senator before determining what his own
future should be. What did he observe? Walsh, first of all, enjoyed prestige
such as Wheeler craved. Second, Walsh cooperated with regular Democrats
in Montana but appeared to many people to be a liberal; and in 1920 he had
met the test of dealing with Kremer, Myers, and other conservatives of the
party. Finally, Walsh considered himself independent of the big interests and
experienced few pangs of conscience over needing to consult with them.

By 1922 Wheeler had decided that further struggle against the Company was futile, and that without conservative backing or sufferance he could never reach the high political places to which he aspired. Walsh got an inkling of this change in Wheeler when the latter visited him in Washington in February 1922, and they had "a long and frank talk," in the course of which Wheeler manifested "a very keen desire" to get into the Senate. Walsh doubted Wheeler's assertions that the "Company forces and their allies" had become more friendly toward him, knowing how prone Wheeler was "to transform meaningless expressions of courtesy into promises of support."[11]

Wheeler's assertions were soon corroborated. Charles Kelly, banker and friend of C. F. Kelley, paid Walsh a visit and actually expressed a desire to see Wheeler running for Myers's Senate seat. Letters from Wheeler soon showed plainly that this ex-bad boy of Montana politics had made his peace with the "interests." On April 20 Wheeler wrote Walsh that it might seem "egotistical" but he was sure he could get the nomination. As if in explanation he said that he had a long talk with Jerry Dobell of the *Butte Miner*, who was primarily interested in the composition of the state legislature. Wheeler suggested to Dobell that they might "compromise" the matter. Wheeler wrote Walsh that he had it "upon good authority" that if he won the nomination the *Butte Miner* would support him and that the fight of 1920 against him would not be renewed. Wheeler also told Walsh that he had talked with members of the Nonpartisan League at Great Falls and told them that under no circumstances would he run if they endorsed him. They agreed to support him without endorsing him. Thus Wheeler quietly angled for the backing of both conservatives and radicals, while avoiding the label of either.[12]

Wheeler strove to prove to Senator Walsh the disappearance of old animosities, as well as his positive advantages over his rivals, so that Walsh would support him. The Butte man charged that it was generally recognized among old line Democrats that Tom Stout failed to take a definite stand on any issue at any time.[13]

Hating to see his two friends competing for the nomination and believing that Stout stood the better chance, Walsh tried to dissuade Wheeler from running. To Stout he explained that Wheeler was bent on seeking the Democratic nomination in this year when there was such a grand opportunity and it was difficult to turn him from his purpose. By May 15 Walsh recognized also that he had greatly overestimated the extent of the opposition to Wheeler. "Fuller information," he wrote, "some of a rather direct character," was convincing. The change in attitude toward Wheeler, Walsh said, was due in large

Walsh and Burton K. Wheeler. (Walsh-Gudger Collection, Illinois
Historical Survey, University of Illinois at Urbana-Champaign)

measure to disappointment with Wheeler's Republican rival of 1920; the antipathies engendered by Governor Dixon quickly "made many people wondrous kind to Wheeler." Walsh kept his commitment to Stout even though Wheeler's chances were improved. While advising both men during the campaign, he chiefly aided Stout.[14]

Wheeler swept to victory over three opponents in the Democratic primary of August 29. His vote was 20,914 to 6,550 for Tom Stout, 6,296 for James F. O'Connor, and 4,500 for Hugh Wells. An excellent campaigner, Wheeler apparently obtained most of the liberal vote while conservatives waged no fight against him as they had in 1920. In the general election he would face Representative Carl Riddick of Lewistown, who had defeated Wellington Rankin and two other candidates for the Republican senatorial nomination.[15]

Early in September Senator Walsh arrived in Montana for a vacation and for the Democratic state convention which met in Helena on September 13 at the Placer Hotel, where he and Wheeler were the principal speakers. Walsh also delivered numerous speeches during October in the Montana campaign.[16]

A severe cold forced him to abandon his schedule for the last ten days in October; early in November he returned to the fight, although hampered by nervous indigestion. On November 2, Walsh presided at a rally for Wheeler in Helena. Several days later he closed the campaign in Helena praising the Democratic ticket and criticizing President Harding's "solicitous care" for the railroads and his ship subsidy bill by which a "magnificent merchant fleet" that had cost billions was to be handed over to private corporations for "a few paltry hundred millions."[17]

On November 7, Wheeler easily defeated Carl Riddick just as Walsh had predicted in spite of the fact that the state was "unquestionably Republican by a decided majority." Wheeler's vote was 88,205 to 69,464 for Riddick, and he almost trebled the vote on his opponent in Silver Bow County, where the Anaconda influence was strong. The only other Democrat elected was John M. Evans in the First Congressional District. Democrats, however, had reason to be jubilant, having taken possession of another Senate seat and one of two in the House of Representatives.[18]

Throughout the United States, Democrats made encouraging gains. A Republican majority of 172 in the House was reduced to 20 and that of 22 in the Senate was reduced to 8. Prospects for 1924 looked good.

Especially because of success at home, Montana Democrats showed their pleasure. Walsh observed that there was "glory" for everyone interested in the "cause of democracy" and that Wheeler's victory was especially "pleasing." Anaconda's friend, Bruce Kremer, also saw Wheeler's election as "a great

Democratic victory." The *Helena Independent* held that whatever his past affiliations Wheeler was a smart man, a shrewd businessman, a scholar, and a good lawyer. He and Walsh would work together to give the state its best representation in history.[19]

The team of Walsh and Wheeler was an able one, soon to become famous, and was based upon a long and close relationship. These Helena and Butte lawyers had helped each other to the top, while having views and ambitions that sometimes clashed. Their careers were so closely related that it is difficult to visualize one without the other.

20

Public Lands, Native Americans,
and Campaigns for (Honest) Leasing

E arly in his Senate career Walsh became active in matters involving public lands of the United States, particularly after he joined the committees on Public Lands and Indian Affairs. His reputation regarding complicated land questions was most firmly established in the oil investigation of
1923–24. Although he was not the initiator of the investigation, once started
he carried on almost singlehandedly a Senate inquiry which uncovered flagrant corruption and incompetence in President Harding's cabinet and eventually caused fraudulently granted oil leases to be restored to the U.S. government. His probe reached into every segment of society. Of particular
importance were these aspects: the manner in which Walsh, not previously
noted as a conservationist, took over this investigation and relentlessly pursued the enemies of conservation; Walsh's views and tactics as an investigator and cross examiner; his connection with the investigation from a political standpoint; and the matter of public opinion and the investigation. This
chapter is concerned, first, with Walsh and reservation lands of American
Indians; second, with his advocacy of the leasing principle under which the
oil scandals occurred; and finally with the influences that made him the chief
investigator who exposed the corrupt oil leases.

One fact stands out in trying to understand official policy toward the Native Americans: whites were almost unanimous in wanting the reservations
opened, with tribal land made available to whites as well as the Indians. "Indian policy," as it was usually referred to, evolved over the years but was heavily
affected by the Dawes Act of 1887, providing for allotments to Indians allegedly to enable them to gain economic independence and to attain full status
as citizens. One complicating factor was that Indians who obtained land and
the right to lease their land were often drawn into a leasing system that won

the support of many people of both races. Educated Indians who had achieved some success in farming and business were those most likely to support the policy of land allotments and assimilation. The complexities were many, and they varied from tribe to tribe, from the Crow to the Blackfeet, to the Flathead, the Crees, the Rocky Boy, and the Northern Cheyenne.[1]

Montana legislators and nearly all of the Montanans elected to Congress wanted reservations opened. If they were opened only in part, later action should be taken to open the remaining land. This was not a partisan issue. It was one's duty, almost a patriotic duty, to do the necessary legislative work, and to spread the word, in order to get something accomplished in the opening process. Occasionally homesteaders, irrigators, businessmen or others went too far in making crass demands on their political leaders, and the effort to "open things up," with large profits in mind, was a failure. Members of Congress did not wish to be known as crudely or cruelly anti-Indian. Eastern senators and representatives tended to be more solicitous of the Native American, and they raised points and made arguments in his defense. But many of the westerners as well, including Senator Walsh, had a paternalistic attitude or a kindly streak. Politics was involved, too: by 1924 many Indians were voting and their votes might gain importance in a particular election.

When Thomas J. Walsh came to the Senate in 1913, he was assertive in trying to open the reservations, much as Joseph M. Dixon had been ten years earlier. In 1918 Walsh introduced a bill "to change the communal system" on the Crow Reservation, where a dwindling Indian population, he said, showed the "tragic" failure of the old system. Shortly before his bill received President Wilson's signature, Walsh, writing to a member of the Billings Commercial Club, disclosed another aspect of the measure: large tracts of reservation land would be placed on the market. Walsh was once singled out by Robert Yellowtail of the Crow Indians as a stern foe who had to be resisted. Yellowtail and others mistakenly said that Walsh had started a battle against them in 1910 (three years before he came to the Senate), and Yellowtail told his story in the form of a morality play that was entertaining but unreliable factually. Yellowtail, however, came to look upon Walsh as a friend of the Crow Indians who with his newfound fame in the Teapot Dome inquiry of 1924 could be a champion of the tribe.[2]

Walsh unquestionably was interested in the well-being of Native Americans and often tried to help them. He held, however, the usual attitude that Indians were inferior to white men and almost inevitably must yield. Writing to a Wisconsin woman who had inquired anxiously about the welfare of the Indians, Walsh suggested no improvements: "I must confess that, in the multiplicity of duties which devolve upon me, I have not had time to study any plan for the regeneration or reclamation of the Indians." The problem was not a simple one, he added, and he was inclined to agree with a missionary to the Indians who, upon reflecting on past efforts to civilize and Christianize them, remarked, "We can only go on and pray for results."[3]

As noted earlier, Walsh is especially remembered for his role in the Teapot Dome affair and for his legislative work that contributed to a new system of leasing on the public domain. The mineral Leasing Act and the Water Power Act of 1920 capped a long period of controversy stemming from the Roosevelt and Taft conservation program, particularly the withdrawal of great tracts of public land from sale. When Walsh went to Congress in 1913, water power sites and rich deposits of oil, coal, and other minerals were "hermetically sealed up," as Walsh described the situation. This natural wealth, publicly owned, could neither be bought nor leased until a new governmental policy was formulated. In 1913 and 1914 Walsh ranged himself with the advocates of leasing, believing that if any agreement could be reached it would be in that direction.[4]

In 1919 Walsh stated his general position in a letter to Senator Charles S. Henderson. He said those still wedded to the policy of alienation rather than leasing public lands did not understand the situation. It was a "condition and not a theory" which confronted the western senators, who had almost to a man protested "loud and long and often," but futilely, against the government withdrawals. The Supreme Court decision in the case of the *United States* v. *Midwest Oil Company*, upholding withdrawal of mineral lands, and "a strong public sentiment" throughout the eastern part of the country forced westerners to conclude reluctantly that the withdrawal policy would continue. Only leasing could open up the public lands.[5]

From the beginning of the Wilson administration Walsh worked closely with Secretary of the Interior Franklin Lane for leasing legislation. Lane called for leasing of reserved lands in such a way that western states would share the royalties, thus mollifying western opposition, and, as he saw it, guarding against federal monopoly. Walsh, as chairman of the Senate Committee on Mines and Mining, was one of those selected by Secretary Lane to draft appropriate leasing legislation, and Walsh asserted in 1914 that he was representing Lane in connection with the "whole conservation program."[6]

The advocates of leasing ran into much opposition from 1913 to 1920. Most powerful in opposition, said Walsh, were westerners who blocked leasing because they continued to believe in government alienation of public lands. Included in this group were Senators Reed Smoot, Albert B. Fall, C. S. Thomas, C. D. Clark, John F. Shafroth, and for a time William E. Borah. Several in this number, and others, insisted on government relief to those having claims on withdrawn lands. At the other extreme were staunch conservationists, led in the Senate by Robert M. La Follette, ever on guard, distrusting the big interests, and suspicious that there was more to the leasing agitation than met the eye. Walsh declared that he did not favor alienation and that he took no part in efforts to afford relief to oil locators in Wyoming and California.[7]

Several bills to lease oil lands were introduced by Walsh between 1915 and 1918, one of which received serious attention before being defeated in March 1919, during the closing hours of the Sixty-fifth Congress. He was disappointed, if not embittered, over the fate of this measure, "the result of four years' labor." The man he blamed was Senator La Follette, who talked the conference report "to death" when only a few hours had been set aside for its consideration. Again Walsh grumbled that the filibuster which beat the oil leasing bill was "a rather expensive piece of partisan politics for Montana."[8]

More than that, Walsh charged that a far-reaching plot existed to delay action so that by default the government would eventually obtain the opportunity to develop and operate the public lands. "Doctrinaires and theorists socialistically inclined," according to him, were working industriously to defeat "any practical measure" of handling the public resources. He asserted, apparently with La Follette in mind, that filibustering was their method of delaying action. There was some justification for Walsh's apprehensions. Senator Borah of Idaho, sometimes anticonservation and certainly antisocialist, was one of those who gradually had swung over to approve of government development.[9]

La Follette, the former forester Gifford Pinchot, and others who opposed the Montana senator's bill advanced reasons sometimes at variance with Walsh's, although there was no clear division between conservationists and anticonservationists in the fight over the bill. Some thought it too liberal to the oil land claimants and other "exploiters" and not a conservation measure, while others thought it unfair to the "pioneers" who were developing the country. Pinchot, now a private citizen who retained great influence on conservation matters, argued against the bill with telling effect. He disliked the concessions made to oil trespassers and the provisions for granting absolute patents which might prevent unified government control of an area. He believed, furthermore, that Secretary Lane's administration had been antipublic and could not be trusted. La Follette, like Pinchot, believed that under the measure the public lands would be turned over to exploiters such as the Standard Oil Company.[10]

Senator Walsh is probably less vulnerable than Lane to charges of favoritism, although he too talked conservation and at times, in practice, seemed to oppose it. Walsh, however, was especially interested in helping the small businessmen of the West rather than oil giants. When faced with the charge that his oil leasing bill would help the large companies instead of the little fellow, Walsh replied, "absurd." The very purpose of the bill, he said, was to prevent absorption of oil properties by such companies.[11]

At last in 1920 a general bill providing for the leasing of mineral lands passed Congress and became law. Senator Smoot introduced it in August 1919, some of the old controversies were fought out anew, and the end product was regarded as a victory for the conservationists. Walsh favored the bill as a whole. As in the case of his own bill defeated in 1919, he denied any sympathy for oil prospectors who had intruded on reserved areas and averred that he tolerated provisions for their relief "only because to combat them would imperil and probably defeat the bill."[12]

The Leasing Act of 1920 was long and complicated. It provided in part for government leasing of oil, gas, coal, phosphate, and sodium lands. In the case of proven oil lands not subject to a preferential lease, the secretary of the interior could lease to the highest bidder for twenty years at a minumum royalty of $12\frac{1}{2}$ percent, and a minimum rental annually of a dollar per acre. No such leasehold was to be larger than 640 acres. Claimants on public land outside the naval reserves might surrender the claims and then secure a lease upon them. Those who asserted claim to the naval reserves could relinquish such claims and lease only their producing wells, unless the president, at his discretion, authorized leasing of the whole claim. An important stimulus to passage of the bill was a provision that each state was to receive $37\frac{1}{3}$ percent of all royalties accruing within its borders.[13]

Another phase of the leasing campaign took shape at last in the Federal Water Power Act of 1920, by which the Federal Power Commission was established with authority to issue licenses for power development and for improvement of navigation on U.S. lands or on navigable streams. Walsh toiled for this act as he had for mineral leasing.[14]

Walsh was so sensitive to western problems and needs that he hardly qualifies as a conservationist of the Roosevelt-Pinchot-La Follette breed. He emphasized utilization of resources more than their conservation and apparently was not alert to the dangers of leasing legislation. He showed naiveté in a discussion on this subject when he cited in Senate debate and attached "very great importance" to the expert opinion of E. L. Doheny that the naval oil reserves should be leased. Doheny was one of the most successful oilmen in the world, Walsh said, and was not influenced on this question by selfish considerations. The possibility that Doheny himself might obtain a lease of naval oil reserves and thus stand to profit immensely was not mentioned by Walsh. It seems at times that Walsh did not regard special interests with the distrust that generations of land spoliation should have inculcated.[15]

Advocates of leasing had no direct responsibility for the corrupt oil leases under Warren G. Harding. Causes of that affair date back to President Taft, who in 1912 created naval oil reserves number one and two in California, sometimes designated respectively as Elk Hills and Buena Vista Hills. President Wilson three years later made the Teapot Dome field in Wyoming a third naval petroleum reserve. Each of these covered several thousand acres and was considered proven oil land (whether true or not) whose riches would be preserved for the future use of the navy. Such a policy by no means seemed desirable to ambitious oilmen or to others who demanded that the government sell or lease its lands. The Leasing Act of February 1920 permitted leasing of land in the naval reserves under certain restricted conditions. In June 1920 another act having to do with the reserves passed Congress at the instance of Secretary of the Navy Josephus Daniels, who was worried because new private gushers near the Elk Hills reserve might drain the government oil. Authority therefore was granted the secretary of the navy definitely to take possession of that portion of the reserves where there were no pending claims or applications under the Leasing Act and to conserve, develop, and exchange the oil thereof directly or by lease. His power seemed unlimited—except for a clause apparently making him dependent upon Congress for funds.[16]

Much of the testimony in the hearings which began in 1923 revolved around the above two laws. Had they been disregarded, misinterpreted, or flagrantly violated by A. B. Fall and others in leasing naval reserves? If so, why? Walsh later declared that the real subject of the inquiry was the possibility of bribery and fraud and that never was there any doubt that the laws and the Constitution had been flouted.[17]

Activities of President Harding and Secretary Fall in 1921–22 were enough to fill informed people with wonder if not suspicion. The president's executive order of May 31, 1921, transferred administration of the naval reserves to the Interior Department. This seemed strange in view of Fall's known anticonservation views and the previous determination of the navy to hold on to its petroleum reserves. Then word spread in 1922 that Secretary Fall had leased the Teapot Dome reserve to Harry F. Sinclair of the Mammoth Oil Company. Later it was discovered that the Elk Hills reserve had been leased to E. L. Doheny, president of the Pan-American Oil Company.

Senators John B. Kendrick and Robert M. La Follette were the first to demand facts concerning the alleged leasing of the naval reserves. Some of Kendrick's constituents in Wyoming heard of the lease of Teapot Dome and sought information. He tried unsuccessfully to answer their questions by inquiring at the Navy Department and the Department of the Interior and then on April 15, 1922, introduced a resolution in the Senate calling upon the secretary of the interior to explain the status of Teapot Dome. Had a lease been granted or was one contemplated? The official reply from Edward C. Finney (acting secretary of the interior since Fall's resignation) and Secretary of the Navy Edwin Denby was affirmative. They elaborated on the good contract made by the government with the Mammoth Oil Company. Their report did not satisfy La Follette. Since March he had been receiving tips about Teapot Dome, and he set inquiries going in many directions. On April 21, the same day that Secretary Finney's letter arrived, La Follette introduced Senate resolution 282, calling upon the secretary of the interior to supply the Senate with all documents concerning leases of naval reserves number one, two, and three; and furthermore authorizing the Senate "to investigate this entire subject of leases upon naval oil reserves, with particular reference to the protection of the rights and equities of the Government of the United States and the preservation of its natural resources."[18]

Robert M. La Follette was the first to expose Secretary Fall's defenses. His resolution prepared the way for a full investigation, which was delayed, however, until the fall of 1923. Meanwhile, in late 1922 and early 1923, La Follette incidentally gathered information about Teapot Dome while conducting a Senate inquiry into gasoline prices. Among the witnesses before his subcommittee of the Committee on Manufactures were Harry Sinclair and R. W. Stewart, chairman of the board of directors of the Standard Oil Company of Indiana. Their testimony showed the close connections between Standard Oil of Indiana and Sinclair. Fall's argument that he had reduced monopoly by giving the Teapot Dome lease to Sinclair was exploded.[19]

The interest of the La Follette Committee in Teapot Dome was revealed pointedly by its probing into the terms of Sinclair's lease wherein he promised to build an oil pipeline from Missouri to Wyoming. Allegedly his new pipeline, constructed at great cost in an area where none existed before, would constitute an important service to the nation. But Gilbert Roe as counsel for the La Follette Committee skilfully led R. W. Stewart to admit that the pipeline was warranted by business prospects even before the Teapot Dome Lease. A pipeline would have been built anyway, in the opinion of this oilman whose associations with Sinclair were close. After examination on this subject, Stewart exclaimed that he had learned more about "the Teapot" during this inquiry than he ever knew before. While Stewart seemed disconcerted by his disclosure, the investigators were jubilant. One of their informants, Chester Washburne, an oil expert, congratulated La Follette and declared the pipeline testimony destroyed "the last of the reasons given by Secretary Fall for leasing Teapot [Dome] to Sinclair." More proof was necessary, however.

Thus in early 1923, nine months before the first hearings actually were conducted on the naval oil leases, La Follette, Gilbert Roe, and others found evidence that Secretary Fall had been duped or had lied about his activities. Some of this evidence was turned over to Walsh for his use.[20]

By his own testimony, Walsh took a hand in the Teapot Dome matter at the request of Senators La Follette and Kendrick. He had no other reason, he explained, except that he was a member of the Public Lands Committee, which conducted the investigation, and La Follette was not a member. The chairman, Reed Smoot of Utah, was a conservative Republican. It was possible, therefore, "to divine" why La Follette wanted someone to see that the investigation "was prosecuted with vigor." As La Follette suspected, the ranking Republicans, Smoot and Irvine Lenroot, were hostile toward the investigation. Most others on the committee were apathetic. It was fortunate that La Follette recognized Walsh's aptitude for the job at hand, in spite of previous disagreements with the Montanan on U.S. entry into the war, Indian policy, leasing legislation, and other matters.[21]

Indications are that Walsh interested himself in this affair with some reluctance. Walsh was a busy man, as always, with more committee assignments than any other senator. "I can't do everything," he told Burton K. Wheeler, who at La Follette's suggestion urged Walsh to take hold of the investigation. Walsh, a westerner, was more sympathetically disposed toward A. B. Fall and his ranching and prospecting enterprises than was La Follette. Walsh, an advocate of leasing, was more inclined to tolerate questionable leases than was La Follette, a conservationist who had battled the leasing principle from the beginning. Certainly, however, Walsh did not advocate fraudulent and crooked leasing. The probability is that he became suspicious by early 1923 that Fall was guilty of misconduct. Wheeler told him that a Montana oilman thought the leasing was crooked. La Follette and others were saying or insinuating the same thing. Walsh decided this case demanded investigation.[22]

While Walsh expressed interest in Teapot Dome by early 1923, the events from then until the beginning of the hearings indicate that he expected no sensations and considered other matters of greater importance. In March 1923 he left Washington for a trip to the Orient, primarily to visit his daughter in the Philippines, and did not return to Capitol Hill until September. He had "a most delightful summer" in Asia and in Montana on his return, "renewing old acquaintances and making many new ones." On the occasion of his embarkation at San Francisco he was quoted as saying his chief domestic concern was to increase the world production of silver. Walsh's daughter remembers that he did not expect any sensational results in the oil inquiry. She was surprised in January 1924, upon returning to the United States, to learn from ship's officers about her father's revelations in Washington.[23]

Apparently not until he returned to Washington did Senator Walsh really get the "scent." He then took the trouble to inform himself of the general situation and to study intensively the leases and the laws applicable to them. Finding that Fall's whole procedure was an "usurpation," he concluded that it was "fraudulent." By now Walsh had done much more than join the probe. He was stirred to fever pitch by the scent of corruption in the leases. And he could not be driven from the trail.[24]

The Investigator

Sherlock Holmes could not have been presented with a more tantalizing case than that facing Senator Thomas J. Walsh in September 1923. One big question was which petroleum reserves or portions of reserves had been leased. The surreptitious lease of reserve number one to E. L. Doheny was not discovered until October 23, 1923, although the lease was dated December 11, 1922.[1]

Various smaller but complicated leases had been granted on the naval reserves and had to be studied. Another and most important task was that of analyzing the excuses made by Secretaries Fall and Denby and others for their leasing policy. In summary they were that subsurface drainage out of the reserves into private wells nearby would have destroyed the reserves; that fuel oil for the navy must be stored at readily accessible spots, and the lessees would be required to exchange fuel oil for government crude oil obtained and to provide storage tanks for the navy wherever needed along the coast; that Sinclair would be required to build a pipeline, a common carrier, from Wyoming eastward to connect with other lines and thus stimulate competition among producers in Wyoming; that different bids were considered or conferences were held with oilmen competing for the contracts; that royalties and terms for the government were good; and that due regard had been shown the laws and the Constitution by consulting the president, talking of the contracts in cabinet meetings, and seeking legal advice. Secretary Fall wrote to President Harding in June 1922 a 25-page letter which was forwarded to the Senate, explaining his policies. He wrote this merely to give an explanation, "frankly and freely," he said, for he recognized "no necessity for . . . defense."[2]

In order to save the naval reserves, said one expert, it was necessary to prove that they had been leased under false pretenses. But to prove that Fall and Denby exaggerated drainage from the naval reserves or were mistaken concerning other technicalities of the oil business would not be easy, for experts disagreed. To show that laws had been loosely interpreted or violated would be easier.[3]

Limitations on the investigatory powers of the Senate might hamper Walsh. He had in his favor a long history of congressional inquiries based on the theory that a knowledge of the facts about a particular subject was essential to passage of desirable legislation. The power to subpoena witnesses, compel attendance, and ask pertinent questions was taken for granted. Witnesses in contempt of Congress might be turned over to the district attorney of the District of Columbia. But a congressional investigator found it hard to know just what questions were pertinent, just what documents could be subpoenaed, and precisely what rights a person possessed who pleaded fear of self-incrimination. He often had to proceed by indirection, trying to build up a mass of facts, which, when assembled, had significance, or to trick the witness into making statements that were damaging.[4]

The long lapse of time between La Follette's resolution in April 1922 and the actual investigation was expected to dampen the proceedings. A. B. Fall had resigned long since, and some thought that people would not like to "kick a dog after he was down."[5]

For these and other reasons Walsh's first month or two of preparation and cross-examination were disappointing in results. One difficulty was that neither on the Public Lands Committee nor elsewhere did he find strong support for the investigation. Republicans Smoot and Lenroot, each of whom served as chairman in the course of the proceedings, made absolutely no preparation for the inquiry, according to Walsh, and for a time showed a "decidedly hostile attitude," no doubt because their "political friends were under fire." Lenroot's biographer, however, noted that his subject had reason to question in this early period whether a scandal actually had occurred. Among those who at least gave "moral support" and whose vote could be counted upon were E. F. Ladd of North Dakota, Peter Norbeck of South Dakota, George Norris, and A. A. Jones of New Mexico. But Walsh wrote, "the work of ferreting out the facts and assembling the witnesses to establish them was all mine."[6]

Walsh eagerly sought aid from two of his fellow Democrats on the Public Lands Committee, Kendrick and A. A. Jones, who were vacationing in the West when Walsh returned to Washington. He informed Kendrick that he had returned to prepare for the investigation and was counting on seeing him soon, as his counsel would be invaluable. Kendrick replied that his livestock business and other pressing matters would keep him away from Washington in the near future. Senator Jones did better. He received a letter from Walsh, similar to that written to Kendrick, returned to Washington for the first hearing, and gave Walsh considerable aid from time to time.[7]

Assistance from other people of prominence was inadequate. Ex-Secretary of the Navy Josephus Daniels expressed regret in early October that business engagements would keep him from conferring with Walsh in Washington for several weeks. Walsh was much disappointed that Daniels could not come. Most of the work had fallen on him, largely because "no one else" was "giving himself any concern about it." In spite of aid soon forthcoming from Daniels and various naval officers or their families, Walsh complained on November 5 that he was "struggling along with little help from any source except that extended by Mr. [C. W.] Washburne and Mr. [Harry] Slattery." (The latter was a counsel of the National Conservation Association and thus affiliated with Gifford Pinchot.) Another door was closed when Ex-Secretary of the Interior John Barton Payne declined, because of the "press of other matters," to look into public land regulations drawn during his administration of the Department of the Interior.[8]

Periodicals, even those considered staunchly Democratic, paid slight attention to early developments in the investigation. Walsh wrote to ask Herbert Swope of the *New York World* why it had not given its readers an adequate idea of the disclosures, "more or less startling" in nature. One good reason for this indifference was advanced by magazine writer Christopher Connolly, when invited by Walsh to write on the "real live topic" of Teapot Dome. Connolly noted what was undoubtedly in other minds beside his own: "muckraking" had become "extremely unpopular" among magazine editors. Because of financial dependence on advertising, the punishment for magazines "attacking big interests" was "death." His answer, therefore, was no, even though he would like very much to pursue this subject.[9]

Walsh had to move on primarily with his own staff, relying especially upon John G. Holland, a law student from Georgetown University employed in his office as a clerk. Holland did much of the tedious work of examining leases and other documents in the Land Office, the Bureau of Mines, and elsewhere. Masses of materials had to be studied—any page of which might give an all-important clue. Walsh was the driving force. Yet aid and comfort from Slattery, La Follette, Gilbert Roe, Chester Washburne, Josephus Daniels, Bernard Baruch, Cordell Hull, Scripps-Howard investigators, the *St. Louis Post-Dispatch,* the newspaper *Labor,* and other people and organizations was hardly insignificant. Walsh perhaps overemphasized his lack of assistance.

The first phase of the hearings lasted from October 22 to November 2, at which time two senators left the city and the committee adjourned for almost a month. Senators Smoot (chairman), Ladd, Jones of New Mexico, and Walsh conducted the investigation with Walsh acting in the role of prosecuting attorney. About twenty witnesses came to room 210 of the Senate Office Building, in some cases more than once, to offer testimony. By comparison with later hearings the number of senators and spectators in attendance was small. The room was small. Developments were unspectacular but not lacking in importance.[10]

Among the principal witnesses were A. B. Fall, Edwin Denby, Harry Sinclair, and Theodore Roosevelt Jr., the assistant secretary of the navy. Witnesses of this period may be divided roughly into "defendants," headed by Fall and Sinclair, oil experts, and naval men who had some knowledge of the naval reserve policy. Walsh particularly probed into the executive order placing naval reserves under the Interior Department, the nature of Fall's leases, reasons for them and for their secret negotiation, and alleged pressure exerted by Fall and Denby on naval officers opposing their changes in policy.

These hearings were informative for those in attendance. Albert B. Fall, ex-senator, ex-secretary of the interior, rancher, man of big affairs, was not at all intimidated by the proceedings. Sometimes he apparently feigned ignorance, mocking the committee. At other times he erupted "frankly" with a surplus of details on involved subjects. Walsh asked him questions, and Fall fired questions back in exchanges that were sometimes caustic. Nothing incriminating was pinned on Fall, but he expressed convenient enthusiasm for an extra-loose interpretation of the Constitution and the laws. Walsh pressed him on the constitutionality of President Harding's executive order which transferred the reserves to the Interior Department. Finally Fall replied: "The President has a different and superior authority as the Chief Executive rather than simply as an administrative officer; yes sir." Thus President Harding by an executive order could nullify the act of June 4, 1920, wherein petroleum reserves were placed under the Navy Department. Walsh also pressed the ex-secretary on the secret bidding, citing a general statute that required open and competitive bidding. Secret leasing, in Walsh's view, was the cause of this whole trouble. He admitted privately, however, that the language of the general statute was "somewhat ambiguous" and that the leasing act of June 4 did not require competitive bids.[11]

Secretary of the Navy Denby, Theodore Roosevelt Jr., E. C. Finney, and Harry Sinclair were other figures of high connections who came to defend themselves. Denby's testimony showed a remarkable lack of knowledge about the naval reserves.

Walsh had corresponded and conferred with a number of naval people and oil experts on the subject of the leases, and some of them came to testify. One highlight of the remarks by naval personnel was Commander H. A. Stuart's testimony that Secretary Fall very likely got him transferred from the Navy Department Bureau of Engineering in Washington to Charleston, South Carolina in April 1922 because he (Stuart) was hostile to plans for leasing the reserves.[12]

In spite of all the impressions made in the first two weeks of the hearings, Secretary Fall had been damaged only slightly. The most objective person following the proceedings might still adjudge him innocent. Walsh observed that important "though not altogether sensational" disclosures had come from the inquiry but he predicted there would be "front-page stuff" soon. It was exceedingly difficult at this point to prove Fall guilty of anything worse than misinterpretation or overzealousness. On October 30 Walsh wondered if and how it could be proven that Sinclair had bought off Teapot Dome competitors in order to obtain a lease. On November 6 he was "particularly desirous" that some experienced oilman should analyze the Teapot Dome contract, since those who made it had "quite elaborately and fully" set forth its virtues. Ten days later he reported an inability to find an experienced oilman who would give an "unfavorable" conclusion on the royalty schedule in the lease. In December he wished for someone competent to prove what he strongly suspected, that a pipeline would have been built from the Teapot Dome region, without Sinclair's promise in his lease to build one. Such proof would eliminate a principal excuse for the lease. The technical case of a bad lease obviously still was unproven.[13]

Walsh's cross-examination technique is illuminated by his reply to one critic. Chester Washburne insisted on bringing out all the facts, since truth was on their side. Walsh explained that he had no desire "to exhibit" himself "as Smoot did" by propounding questions prepared by someone else and whose significance he did not fully comprehend. Washburne argued further, and the senator explained further. Walsh was willing to yield to Washburne on geological problems, "but an active experience in trial work as a lawyer extending over a period of twenty-five years" and all the writings on cross-examination of witnesses with which he was familiar made him prefer his own judgment on this matter. Questions prepared by Washburne would be of no avail unless they were accompanied by a statement of the facts to be elicited. With that information he was confident that he could formulate the questions himself. Yes, they wanted the truth, but one rarely got "the truth out of the camp of his adversary" without advance information enabling him to draw it out.[14]

During November while the committee was adjourned Walsh prepared to launch a new attack where Fall's defenses seemed weakest. Scrutinizing documents, writing to "aides" and prospective witnesses, organizing and digesting material, he was ready by November 30 to expose the ex-secretary's interesting financial arrangements. This new strategy had been evolving for some time as a result of various rumors brought under investigation.[15]

Information of the utmost importance reached Walsh in late October 1923, through friends of W. B. Colver, editor of the *Washington Daily News*. Colver's connections in Denver, Colorado, were most helpful. One of them, Editor Sidney B. Whipple of the *Denver Express*, wired Walsh that D. F. Stackelbeck, a reporter on the *Denver Post*, had made an investigation and discovered one of the worst scandals in history. Empowered by Walsh, Whipple served a subpoena on Stackelbeck and sent him on to Washington. From Stackelbeck, who had investigated Fall's financial status for his newspaper in the summer of 1922, Walsh learned about a number of witnesses and what they could be "expected to tell." Thus Carl C. Magee, G. V. Clayton, Will Ed. Harris, and others from New Mexico told their stories in the hearings of late November and December 1923. By letter, meanwhile, Walsh urgently requested official figures from New Mexico on the subject of Fall's financial situation.[16]

Carl C. Magee was the first witness to get Fall into serious trouble. On November 30 he took the stand and told a dramatic story of how, making arrangements in 1920 for the purchase of the *Albuquerque Morning Journal*, in which Fall had a small interest, Magee visited Fall's ranch at Three Rivers, New Mexico. Fall explained that he was so straitened financially that he would have to resign from the Senate to rehabilitate himself. His ranch was dilapidated, as Magee had observed, and he said he could not even pay the taxes on it. Chairman Smoot at one point exclaimed, "a great deal of this testimony of yours is politics anyhow?" To which Magee replied: "Well, I did not ask to come here, Senator, and I said what I have said here under oath with reference to it." Walsh interrupted Magee's account to submit Senator Fall's tax assessments for 1921–23 and a certificate from the treasurer of Otero County, New Mexico. These showed, in brief, that A. B. Fall paid no taxes assessed against his property from 1912 to 1922, but that in June 1922 he paid all taxes for the preceding ten years. Magee continued that three years after this conversation with Fall he passed through Three Rivers on a trip. Fall's "dilapidated" ranch was supposed to be in view, but he could not locate it. So many improvements had been made that he "couldn't recognize" the place. He talked with an electrician, moreover, who said he was doing a $40,000 electrical job on Fall's property. Testimony showing that Magee and Fall were political enemies in New Mexico did not seriously weaken Magee's account. The inevitable question was, Where did Fall's money come from?[17]

Others from New Mexico took the stand. They gave new evidence and differed on interpretations but substantiated the charge that Fall was suddenly prosperous. Senator Walsh continued to introduce corroborative documents. G. V. Clayton, former treasurer of Otero County, where Fall's ranch was situated, testified about the delinquency in tax payments, suddenly paid in June 1922. He commented further on "quite a few improvements" and Fall's purchase of an adjoining ranch. Chairman Smoot's hostility to the investigation is indicated by the fact that Walsh proceeded without trusting him with information. Smoot asked Clayton whether the owner of the ranch now sold to Fall was still living and, if so, where? Walsh answered the question: "He is here."

Will Ed. Harris testified that he sold his adjacent ranch to Fall for $91,500. He also told of a new power plant and other improvements on the Fall holdings. The manager of Fall's ranch, J. T. Johnson, defended his boss as best he could, saying for example that Magee was all wrong about the transformation of the scenery. He admitted, however, that Harry Sinclair had visited Fall for several days in December 1921, that Sinclair gave them a thoroughbred horse and sold them some Holstein cows and five or six registered hogs, that they had taken over the Harris ranch, and that the new power plant cost at least $35,000.[18]

Harry Sinclair told the committee, after much questioning, that he had paid the freight charges on livestock sent to Fall's ranch. Sinclair asserted that Fall did not profit from their agreement, except possibly on the livestock, although few were likely to believe that.[19]

Walsh, meanwhile, was receiving tips on Sinclair's financial manipulations and decided to probe into that subject. He heard of Bernard Baruch's suspicion that considerable Mammoth Oil stock was distributed among magazine writers and newspapermen to keep them friendly toward Sinclair. After trying to communicate by telephone with Baruch, he dispatched his able assistant, John G. Holland, to confer with the New York magnate. They had no right, explained Walsh, to go indiscriminately through the Sinclair stock books, but perhaps Holland could be given definite information, such as names and details, with which to start. H. S. Reavis added rumors that Sinclair and his friends created a million dollar fund to secure Fall's appointment as secretary of the interior in 1920 and that Sinclair's Mammoth Oil stock which was put on the New York curb by Jesse Livermore in October 1922 was accepted as collateral at the Chase National Bank, in spite of the fact that it was a mere "prospect." If true, why was Sinclair thus favored? Other rumors circulated concerning gifts of Sinclair stock to important persons, and of speculation in his stock by those "in the know."[20]

Information of this type opened a line of inquiry which Walsh and others pursued intermittently for months, in fact, years. At first only a few hints of the involved and unsavory story emerged. Jesse Livermore talked freely about his stock operations for the mysterious Sinclair "group," selling and repurchasing stock to keep the price up. He confirmed what H. S. Reavis said about this new stock's having no collateral value. Assistant Cashier of the Chase National Bank Carl P. Biggerman testified about loans which his bank had granted on the Mammoth Oil stock. Walsh could not get him to admit, however, that this stock had no collateral value. Sinclair also came to the stand and was interrogated about his stocks. He was not a willing witness, insisting that he should not have to disclose "internal, delicate, and complicated operations" of his oil enterprises. Walsh showed little sympathy for this point of view. He did not concede defeat and ultimately the infamous Continental Trading Company Limited was brought into daylight as a result of further inquiry.[21]

E. L. Doheny testified and proved to be a hard witness to handle. Pressed by Walsh on December 3, he flared back: "I claim my lease was made in the interest of the United States Government, of which you are a senator and I am a citizen." He was concerned about matters of honor, declaring, for example, that in 1920 he contributed $75,000 to the Democratic party and then gave $25,000 to the Republicans to help them refute base charges against Warren G. Harding's ancestry [that he had Negro blood]. He now "felt very badly," in fact was "greatly outraged," at reflections on the character of his old friend Judge Fall. Asked point-blank by Lenroot if Fall had profited in any way by making the contract with him, Doheny replied: "Not yet." Walsh drew an admission from Doheny that his contract covering Elk Hills was a "special" one, rather than one based upon competitive bidding. He admitted further that he expected to make $100,000,000 profit from his lease—unless his luck was poor.[22]

Walsh called other witnesses who added to the growing mass of evidence that Fall and the naval reserves lessees were, at the very least, guilty of anomalous practices. Three representatives of the navy cast no honor upon that organization. Secretary Denby could give scarcely any information upon returning to the stand but repeatedly said he was willing to "consult the records of the Navy Department" and answer in writing or personally. The chairman finally turned to Walsh and asked if this would be acceptable.

"No," was his reply. "That will not do me any good at all. I wish the record to show that the Secretary does not know anything about it." Assistant Secretary Roosevelt showed more ability than his chief to answer questions but confessed he knew practically nothing about details of the leasing. Former Marine officer George K. Shuler, on the other hand, was able to testify from intimate experience about some singular activities of the Navy Department. In the summer of 1922, after conferring with Secretary Fall and the major general commandant of the Marine Corps, General LeJeune, Shuler was assigned a special mission—that of going to the Teapot Dome reserve in the Wyoming desert, just leased to Sinclair, with orders to drive off a competing oil outfit. Accompanied by four marines, Shuler accomplished his mission by threatening to use pistols and rifles on some thoroughly intimidated oil operators. Walsh pointed out that this was a strange procedure. The legal way to stop oil trespassers was by getting an injunction from the federal court in the state of Wyoming. Implied was this question: Why did Secretary Fall go to such lengths to keep the case out of the courts?[23]

Meanwhile A. B. Fall's self-assurance began to sag under the weight of testimony. On December 27 Senator Lenroot, now chairman, announced the receipt of a letter from Albert Fall and placed it in the record. Fall wrote that because he had been "seriously ill" for more than a week, he must dictate this information. It was difficult for him to understand the curiosity about his personal finances. As to the matter of delinquent taxes, he had long tried to get the authorities to make a correct description of his properties in order that payment would be possible. He suggested that his efforts to perform his duty as U.S. senator in Washington made him somewhat negligent of this local matter. Most important, the ex-secretary said that he had borrowed $100,000 from Edward B. McLean of Washington, D.C., so that he might reorganize his New Mexico holdings. Some "evil-minded persons" suspected him of taking money from Sinclair or Doheny. It should be needless for him to deny that. The whole subject was "more or less humiliating even to refer to."[24]

What would "Ned" McLean, playboy owner of the *Washington Post,* now say? Many Washingtonians who knew McLean's ways and his close friendship with Fall believed that a personal loan was in character and that the investigation would now collapse. Walsh, however, was curious to hear a version of the loan from McLean's lips, especially when he tried to dodge the committee. McLean allegedly was recuperating from an illness in Palm Beach, Florida. Through A. Mitchell Palmer, as his attorney, McLean notified the committee that he lent A. B. Fall $100,000 and would testify accordingly in writing. On January 3 Walsh wrote to Palmer that after serious reflection he had decided McLean should appear before the committee rather than submit an ex-parte affidavit. McLean's employees at the *Post* meanwhile pleaded with Senators Charles Curtis, Oscar Underwood, and others to use their influence so that McLean might remain in Florida, for he was unwell and a sudden change of climate might delay his recovery. Also his son recently had undergone an operation.[25]

Two days after Walsh's letter to Palmer the committee heard Wilton J. Lambert, another McLean lawyer, and then voted on the question of a subpoena for McLean. Lambert's testimony about the piteous condition of McLean, suffering from a sinus infection, did not greatly impress Walsh. He ventured the opinion, "as a mere layman, that the possible result in an operation for a sinus trouble . . . [was] not necessarily or usually serious." A few weeks before he went through the operation himself "without any very disastrous results." Other committee members sympathized with McLean's suffering; the majority voted that he might remain in Florida and answer Walsh's questions in writing.[26]

Even so, Chairman Lenroot proposed that Walsh travel to Florida and interrogate McLean. Walsh finally decided that he would go south and was appointed a subcommittee of one to take the testimony of Edward B. McLean or other witnesses in Florida or elsewhere. Walsh had never ceased to want a cross-examination, and this matter of the $100,000 seemed of the utmost importance. McLean's story, he thought, bore intrinsic evidence of inaccuracy. The "knowing ones" doubted that McLean had such a large sum to lend Fall. Since McLean would not come to Walsh he would have to go to McLean.[27]

Both McLean and Fall were at Palm Beach waiting frantically for Walsh's arrival. According to McLean, Fall at this time was "an awfully ill man . . . shot to pieces." They conferred with each other; they conferred with their lawyers; they tried to confer with new lawyers. Attorney William A. Glasgow Jr., of Philadelphia, was vacationing in Palm Beach and played golf with McLean, with C. Bascom Slemp (President Coolidge's secretary), and others, and talked with Fall. Glasgow refused to act as attorney for either Fall or McLean. When McLean and his lawyer Lambert asked him what they should do, he replied that they had better tell Walsh the truth and the whole truth.[28]

McLean's story, related under oath to Walsh in Palm Beach, was sensational.

Senator WALSH. Mr. McLean, did you loan $100,000 to Mr. Fall?
Mr. McLEAN. I did, yes, sir, in checks.
Senator WALSH of Montana. Whose checks?
Mr. McLEAN. My own checks.
. . .
Senator WALSH of Montana. Have you got the checks?

Mr. McLean. I do not think so—I am not positive.

Senator Walsh of Montana. Were they returned? What became of them?

Mr. McLean. Senator Fall returned them to me.

Senator Walsh of Montana. When?

Mr. McLean. In the last part of December 1921, sir—the last week—I am not positive as to date.

Senator Walsh of Montana. So that so far as you are concerned you did not give him any cash?

Mr. McLean. Cash? No, sir.

The remainder of his testimony was superfluous. Fall had lied; McLean had lied; and the reason almost certainly was discreditable. This outcome left Walsh "dumbfounded." He had expected some subterfuge rather than a frank admission that McLean had lent no money.[29]

Walsh then addressed a communication to Senator Fall summarizing the testimony just taken and asking Fall if he wished to testify orally or to make a written statement. When the manager of the Breakers Hotel refused to deliver the message to Fall, who he said was not registered, Walsh threatened to let the sheriff rummage through and look for him. The manager thereupon agreed to deliver the letter through McLean. Almost immediately McLean and Lambert came to see the senator and told him that Fall wanted very much to talk with him, but was too ill. They arranged for a conference the next morning. Apparently Fall was on the verge of confessing everything, then lost his nerve, for a short time after the conference was arranged McLean and Lambert returned with a letter from Fall which verified McLean's testimony. Fall asserted that the source from which he actually obtained the $100,000 "was in no way connected with Mr. Sinclair or in any way involved in any connection regarding the Teapot Dome, or any other oil concession." Although not at this time "in anything like the physical condition to stand the ordeal of an examination," he might later desire to amplify this statement.[30]

Senator Walsh now kept the unhappy ex-secretary under surveillance. From the Breakers Hotel in Palm Beach Fall moved to the Hotel Roosevelt in New Orleans, where he was watched by law officers under orders from Governor John M. Parker and Walsh. The governor wrote that they would be ready for "quick action."[31]

Events rushed to a climax as McLean's confession set a warm pot to boiling and the implicated ones scrambled out as best they could. Sinclair mysteriously departed for Europe while his employees and friends began to talk. So involved, however, were the Sinclair transactions that pieces of the puzzle slowly had to be fitted together. Not so the case of Doheny.

E. L. Doheny was forced out of his pose as an aggrieved citizen of upstanding character. He and his attorney, Gavin McNab, rushed from California to New Orleans for a conference with Fall. From the St. Charles Hotel in New Orleans, McNab wired Walsh on January 21 that he had been trying to reach him by telephone. He appealed to Walsh to issue no more subpoenas and postpone the hearings until he could reach Washington and give Walsh "most important facts" which he could then use according to his own "judgement."[32]

It is difficult to escape the conclusion that Doheny was trying to use his position in the Democratic party to stop the investigation. William G. McAdoo, leading aspirant for the Democratic nomination, later told of Doheny's unsuccessful attempt through him to exert pressure on Walsh at this crucial moment. Doheny and McNab from New Orleans then pleaded with Walsh by telegram and perhaps by telephone to hold up the hearings. Did they mean to delay for a few days only? Hardly. What argument could they possibly use on Walsh, however, that might deter him from his course? It is possible that Doheny either threatened or hinted that, if he were exposed, the Democratic party would be sorry. His vengeful and damaging testimony about McAdoo and other prominent Democrats lends weight to this theory.[33]

Doheny and McNab came on to Washington immediately, communicated with Walsh, and decided to give voluntary testimony. If they tried the political argument on Walsh, it failed. On January 24, 1924, before a swelling committee and a crowd of expectant newspapermen and others, E. L. Doheny revealed that it was he who "loaned" A. B. Fall $100,000.

It was a curious and poignant turn of fate that brought Doheny and Gavin McNab before their friend now become inquisitor, T. J. Walsh. Contacts for a number of years had placed Walsh and Doheny in a friendly relationship. In 1920 Doheny urged Walsh to drop down to Los Angeles for a visit after the Democratic convention in San Francisco, and either then or at other times Walsh visited the Dohenys and became indebted to them "for many kindnesses."[34]

On December 21, 1923, in the middle of the oil inquiry, Doheny wrote to invite Walsh and his brother John to join him in an oil proposition. He wished Walsh a merry Christmas and mentioned having received a Christmas card from Walsh's daughter in the Philippines. Walsh's return expression of "kind regards" to Mrs. Doheny and his "warmest greetings of the season" indicate a cordial relationship at this time. Something else in his reply, however, was more important than the niceties. Walsh turned down Doheny's business proposition, tactfully mentioning another instance when he refused to participate with friends in an enterprise based on a government lease. He explained: "This may be squeamishness on my part, but I prefer rather to be thought oversensitive than to be under suspicion of having utilized the position to which my people have elevated me for my own profit." Thus Walsh passed one of the greatest crises of his life. It is at least possible that Doheny deliberately tried to trap the friend who unwittingly was close to exposing him.[35]

Doheny's excuses for his "loan" were plentiful. He and Secretary Fall had been warm friends since they prospected together when "Indian troubles were still on the country," and he was glad to lend him $100,000. The amount was a mere "bagatelle." It was not strange that his son delivered the $100,000 cash to Fall in a satchel, Doheny told a skeptical committee. His business transactions were often conducted that way rather than by check. Asked why he failed to correct Fall's statement in December that the money came from Edward McLean, Doheny replied: "Well, that is a difficult question to answer, I will say, Senator. I was willing to await developments and see what they were going to develop." There was no impropriety in this whole affair, he said—no connection between the loan and the contracts which Fall awarded him.[36]

Walsh was fair and even kind in his triumph. He assured Doheny at one point that he wanted to hear "any explanation" he could make and again declared: "Mr. Doheny, I want to give you a perfect opportunity to make any statement in connection with the matter you wish to make." In spite of the disclosures Walsh retained a "very warm regard" for his old friend.[37]

But this Walsh of warmth and mercy was the same man who declared when investigating A. Mitchell Palmer in 1922, "a crime is a crime, by whomsoever committed." Possibly his allegiance to God and the law was such that, regardless of personalities, he was determined to get the facts. It is true also that at this point he might have had difficulty in turning back. Whatever the reason, he got the essential facts from Doheny and at times showed toughness. He demanded to know, for example, whether Doheny had communicated with any member of the committee since arriving in Washington. Doheny and Senator Smoot had to admit that they exchanged a note, but Smoot explained he merely wished to ask Doheny about some friends' oil property. Senator Smoot, cool toward this investigation from the beginning, was on the defensive.[38]

That there had been "impropriety," to say the least, was now admitted by almost all members of the committee. Conservative Republicans like Irvine Lenroot and Robert N. Stanfield as well as the Democrats and liberal Repub-

licans were convinced of this fact. The knowledge that Doheny was nominally a Democrat perhaps contributed to a sense of nonpartisanship.[39]

Paul Y. Anderson, crack correspondent in Washington for the *St. Louis Post-
Dispatch*, gave a vivid description of the change in attitude toward Walsh's
investigation by the end of January. Cynical Washington and most newspapers had paid little attention until Fall was caught lying. Then "four-column
headlines leaped to the first page of the haughty New York Times. . . . At once
the inquiry was transferred from the cosy committee room to a spacious caucus hall, and the air became redolent of costly perfumes. Larger press tables
were hastily dragged in, and Senators, after introducing themselves to the
chairman as members of the committee, took their seats at the table for the
first time, wearing an air of stern resolve. Senator Smoot left off scoffing, and
Senator Lenroot went into action with a ferocity which made Senator Walsh's
tactics seem mild by comparison."

Anderson also paid tribute to Walsh, "a hard-boiled lawyer from the Montana copper country, who, in the face of killing apathy and less passive hin-
drances . . . [had] made one of the most brilliant, resourceful and persistent
fights ever carried out against the private plundering of the public wealth."[40]

Startling testimony against Sinclair and Fall developed just before Doheny's
"big day," then continued on January 25, and trickled in thereafter. On January 21 Assistant Secretary of the Navy Theodore Roosevelt and his brother
Archie took the stand. An employee and director of the Sinclair Consolidated Oil Corporation, Archie Roosevelt said that after talking with his brother
about certain suspicions they had he decided he must turn in his resignation.
He was "in the wrong place." "Amazing testimony" before the committee was
partly corroborated by occurrences in the Sinclair office. The final piece of
evidence, said Archie, was when Sinclair told him to get him a ticket on the
first ship departing for Europe and to see that "his name was not put in the
passenger list." Both Roosevelt and Sinclair's private secretary, G. D. Wahlberg, testified to their unhappiness in the Sinclair organization. Wahlberg, like
Roosevelt, was suspicious of certain occurrences and had decided to resign.
He maintained stoutly, however, that Archie Roosevelt's choicest bit of information—that Wahlberg mentioned a payment of $68,000 to Fall—was er-
roneous. He possibly spoke of "six or eight cows" going to Fall, but Roosevelt
could not have heard him say $68,000. Wahlberg's testimony about Sinclair
loans in securities and the possibility of such a loan to Fall was provocative.
Specifically he mentioned a loan of Sinclair stock and of $25,000 in liberty
bonds to Colonel J. W. Zevely, Sinclair's private attorney.[41]

Colonel Zevely's testimony on January 25 was revealing about the Fall-Sinclair relationship. In the summer of 1923, Sinclair planned a trip to Russia in connection with leases he was seeking there, and he wanted the "advice and counsel of Secretary Fall." Zevely traveled to New Mexico to ask Fall to accompany Sinclair to Russia. Why the long trip instead of a telegram or letter? asked Walsh. Perhaps because they did not want to write on the subject, was the reply. Most important was Zevely's statement that Fall agreed to go "but would need some money." Subsequently in Fall's name he sent $25,000 in liberty bonds to an El Paso bank. This was a loan, he said. Fall did not give him a note for six or seven weeks—until after he returned from Russia—but this was a loan. Fall also received $10,000 from Sinclair for expenses.[42]

Months of correspondence and extended testimony enabled Walsh and the committee to piece together the story of Sinclair's leasing of Teapot Dome. Its essence was that Sinclair, almost certainly with Fall's knowledge, handed out payments totaling more than $1,000,000 in order to get the Teapot Dome lease without competitive bidding and to silence "blackmailers." Walsh put on the stand three who were paid off by Sinclair. F. G. Bonfils of the *Denver Post,* John C. Shaffer of the *Rocky Mountain News,* and oil adventurer John Leo Stack told a great deal about their activities. When Harry Sinclair returned from Europe he denied any wrongdoing, denied that the committee had any further jurisdiction to examine him, and refused to answer as Walsh sharply questioned him on a series of transactions. Two days later, on March 24, the Senate voted to declare Sinclair in contempt of the Senate and to certify the case to the district attorney of the District of Columbia for action.[43]

On the day that Doheny admitted "lending" Fall $100,000 Walsh expressed the opinion that the investigation had reached a climax. One week later when damaging testimony against Sinclair had been added to that against Doheny, A. B. Fall arrived in Washington to testify again. This was surely the climax. Fall on this occasion contrasted tragically with the jaunty westerner of a year before. Wearing wrinkled and baggy clothes, he leaned on a cane, almost tottered at the witness chair, looked at no one, and dully read his statement. The burden of it was that the committee lacked authority to conduct this investigation; also, he said, he refused to answer on the ground that he might incriminate himself.[44]

Walsh and his supporters on the floor of the Senate demanded that the government take action to protect its property and punish criminals. President Coolidge was moving slowly. Senator Caraway of Arkansas proposed that Congress simply annul the leases, but Walsh suggested as an alternative that the president employ special counsel to institute suit to cancel the leases.

Refusing to trust Attorney General Daugherty, Walsh commented upon the widespread public suspicion of his department. Under some pressure Coolidge now announced that he would act when facts of sufficient importance were revealed to him, and since men belonging to "both political parties" were involved he would appoint two special prosecutors, one from each party. Another reason for the special prosecutors that he did not mention was a lack of public confidence in Harry Daugherty's Department of Justice.[45]

Walsh determined to oust the delinquent members of Coolidge's cabinet and led what he termed a "somewhat spectacular fight." On January 28 he addressed the Senate for hours, marshaling his facts and answering questions on the oil scandal. Fellow senators and packed galleries listened closely. In closing, Walsh spoke of Secretary Denby's negligence and incompetence and declared that unless Denby's resignation was in the hands of the president by sundown he would take the necessary steps in the Senate to deal with the matter. About one week later he spoke again. As James O. Bennett of the *Chicago Tribune* described it, "Lean Walsh of Montana carved his way into the Denby fat on the floor of the senate this afternoon . . . his method was not spectacular. It was dryly desolating." Walsh denied any feeling of malice toward the navy secretary, but charged him with ineptness and stupidity worse than crime. Denying improper invasion of the province of the executive, he inquired whether they should just sit back and wait. Were they invading the president's province by asking him to do what his "sense of duty" should have caused him to do two months earlier? He finished with a fierce call for Denby's dismissal as a lesson for the Republic: "I desire to see him driven from public office with all the odium and ignominy that the occasion possibly can demand, in order that his fate may serve as warning to anyone who may come after him and who might otherwise fail the Republic as he has failed it." The president and his secretary of the navy did not act as quickly as Walsh wished, but on February 18 Denby's resignation, to be effective on March 10, was announced. Vacationing in Pinehurst, North Carolina, Walsh hailed this announcement as "a consummation devoutly wished."[46]

Attorney General Daugherty also attracted attention. As a friend and confidant of Harding, Fall, McLean, and others his name was mentioned often in the hearings. Leslie C. Garnett and Charles D. Hamel, former special assistants to Attorney General Daugherty, testified to certain irregular procedures of Daugherty and Fall by which the Standard Oil Company of California retained control of rich oil lands within the Elk Hills reserve. Garnett testified that while in the Justice Department he received a message from his chief, Daugherty, that action against Standard Oil's claim on two fabulously rich sections of oil land was to be suspended, and that the man who delivered Daugherty's notice was the vice president of the Standard Oil Company of California.[47]

At times Walsh could hardly restrain his contempt for Daugherty and his friends. When questioning Edward McLean about his meetings in Daugherty's house with Daugherty, Jess Smith, and Secretary Fall, Walsh commented that this was apparently "a kind of rendezvous." To William J. Burns's assertion that Walsh did not ask the Justice Department for assistance, Walsh retorted that he had not understood that the Justice Department must be requested to stop notorious corruption; furthermore he wondered who was "so simple minded" as to expect him to seek support from Burns when he was Daugherty's assistant. "No man can serve two masters." Walsh did what he could to aid Burton K. Wheeler's Senate investigation of Harry Daugherty, and they were rewarded on March 28 when Daugherty followed Denby out of the cabinet.[48]

Walsh gave anxious attention to the matter of the two special prosecutors whom Coolidge decided to appoint. Objections to several men on the basis of alleged oil connections led finally to the appointment of Atlee Pomerene, former Democratic senator from Ohio, and Republican Owen J. Roberts of Philadelphia. Before Pomerene and Roberts were confirmed in the Senate Walsh protested that they lacked the necessary experience. Roberts, he said, made a favorable impression upon him but had a purely local reputation. Roberts had been recommended to Coolidge by the conservative Senator George Wharton Pepper of Pennsylvania. Privately Walsh wrote of this affair: "Strange as it may seem . . . I have not the slightest influence in the selection of counsel, as I have not been consulted in any way." He believed that Coolidge had treated him "contemptuously." George Norris commented on the Senate floor that he was "dumbfounded," "amazed," and "humiliated" when he learned that President Coolidge had not consulted Senator Walsh in the selection of special counsel.[49]

Walsh believed that the capacity of Coolidge's appointees to combat Doheny and Sinclair and their armies of skilled lawyers could seriously be questioned, but as they began their difficult assignment, they obtained Walsh's full cooperation. After many delays and disappointments they won their main objectives in 1927. By Supreme Court decision the reserves were restored to the control of the secretary of the navy and judgments totaling $15,000,000 for oil extracted were obtained against the two leasees. The criminal proceedings were less successful, but Fall and Sinclair went to jail for short terms and Fall had to pay a fine of $100,000.[50]

In the spring of 1924 Walsh directed his attention increasingly toward rumors of an oil conspiracy in the Republican convention of 1920 which some informants insisted placed Harding in the White House on condition that Fall and others got places in the cabinet. As early as December 1923 he was inquiring about the possibility that Sinclair raised a million dollars to elect Harding so that Fall could get the Interior Department. Through February, March, and April he kept up a volume of correspondence about a possible conspiracy.[51]

This was a legitimate course of inquiry, Walsh maintained, since the oil leases perhaps stemmed from this early arrangement. Legitimate though his probe might be, principal Republicans did not "remember" what occurred back in the 1920 convention, at least not about a conspiracy. Will Hays, William Cooper Proctor (chairman of the General Leonard Wood campaign), Robert F. Wolfe of Columbus, Ohio, and James G. Darden, an associate of Harding and Daugherty, were among the many who testified on this subject. Through the mail Gifford Pinchot and Nicholas Murray Butler politely denied knowledge of a plot in the convention.[52]

Walsh found enough evidence nevertheless to become "convinced that Mellon and Fall were appointed pursuant to a deal made at the Chicago convention, which likewise contemplated the appointment of Daugherty as Attorney General." He had no doubt that Senator James E. Watson of Indiana "could tell quite a little" or that George Harvey "could tell the whole story," but he felt their memories would prove as "treacherous" as Colonel Proctor's if called to the witness stand.[53]

On May 14 at Walsh's request the Public Lands Committee suspended its hearings. He had not exhausted all his leads but found himself at last circumvented. Republicans were secretive, or uninformed, about the alleged 1920 conspiracy, and Sinclair escaped further investigation at this time by refusing to show his books. The scene of the inquiry now shifted to the federal courts, although Walsh's revelations were in the news and bound to be a political factor in the campaign of 1924.[54]

22

New Prospects for the Democrats

I t was inevitable that Walsh's revelations from the oil leasing investigation in 1924, a presidential year, should draw attention. The Democrats blamed the Republicans for unprecedented corruption, and leaders of the GOP searched for a way out of their predicament. They were aided by the implication in the scandals of several Democrats. Walsh became famous or infamous according to one's point of view, although the investigation seems to have been appreciated by most people. Recognition of his leadership in the oil probe made him a likely choice for chairman of the Democratic National Convention in 1924. There were those who accused Walsh of playing politics in 1924, particularly when he demanded Denby's resignation and criticized the president. But the evidence is that the Coolidge administration was unfriendly toward the oil investigation until disclosures grew so threatening they could not be ignored. Coolidge lauded the deceased Harding—who had appointed Fall, Denby, and Daugherty—as a president eminently fitted for service in a difficult period of the nation's history. Coolidge's friends on the Public Lands Committee, including Senators Smoot and Lenroot, led an attempt to thwart Walsh's efforts. The president's appointees as special counsel were not conspicuously qualified for the task, while some officials associated with the fraudulent leases were permitted to remain in office. Walsh probably was justified in placing blame for the "delay and disappointments" upon the Coolidge administration.[1]

It appears that in early 1924 President Coolidge was willing to overlook the transaction involving Fall and Edward McLean or to give aid and comfort to those questionable characters. The president's positive opposition to the investigation is apparently indicated by a telegram sent to McLean in Florida on January 29, 1924, by the editor of the *Washington Post:* "Saw principal.

Delivered message. He says greatly appreciates and sends regards to you and Mrs. McLean. . . . He expects reaction from unwarranted political attacks." Walsh had a "very definite belief" as to who the "principal" was. He consistently held that President Coolidge opposed the investigation and failed in his duty. He would not be deterred, he wrote privately at one point, "by the thunderous, though senseless, fulmination from the White House." To an old friend who said he would vote for Walsh for president if he ran, otherwise for Coolidge, Walsh responded: "Will you not please tell me why you would be inclined to vote for Coolidge as against *any* Democratic candidate?"[2]

The presence in the hearings of an additional senator, a Republican "sniper" who had replaced Lenroot, was one reason that relations between Walsh and the administration worsened. Selden Spencer of Missouri began to impugn Walsh's motives and methods. One of the bitter incidents in this committee fight occurred when Spencer brought John Walsh, brother of the senator, before the committee and interrogated him about his work as attorney for some oil companies. As Senator C. C. Dill remarked, if all lawyers connected with any oil companies were called before the committee, they might number into the thousands. Senator Walsh was frank and incisive: "Of course, we understand perfectly well that this witness is called here for the purpose of casting some suspicion on me, and you [Spencer] are a party to that." Spencer rejoined that the anxiety and solicitude his colleagues showed for "this particular witness" was a matter of great interest to him. He was only trying to get information.[3]

Administration leaders tried more extreme measures in an effort to smear Burton Wheeler, who had driven Daugherty from the cabinet. The Department of Justice and the Republican National Committee were most active in this smear campaign. Walsh noted that the Republican organization apparently had abandoned its effort to show him up as "a public enemy" in order to "direct its guns" against his colleague. Agents of the Department of Justice and of the Republican National Committee investigated Wheeler in Montana and then advanced the charge that he had accepted a fee (while a senator) to use his influence for a client in obtaining oil concessions. A Senate investigating committee headed by Senator Borah cleared Wheeler of the charge, and in 1925 a federal jury in Montana did likewise. Walsh served as an attorney for his friend and colleague in the latter trial.[4]

Walsh conducted a fair-minded investigation, although he was a good Democrat. With reason he condemned the effort to "instil the idea that the whole affair was a political gesture." He was not unwilling for his party to enjoy political advantages resulting from the revelations, he said, but those who knew him would believe that the desire to "render a public service was not lacking." He defended himself against charges of politics and challenged any fair-minded person to produce proof of such action. He concluded that, whatever people believed, the culpability of those who disposed of the national resources, "either corruptly or stupidly," was indisputable.[5]

Some charged that Walsh's methods deteriorated and that, most of all, his witnesses in the latter stages were a bunch of rogues. Walsh was willing to admit that some of his witnesses were unreliable. "It is not strange that, handicapped as I was, witnesses should be brought here from time to time of whose worth or lack of worth I could have no very exact knowledge."[6]

He seems to have tried honestly to obtain witnesses with legitimate information. In the middle of March, as in the beginning of the probe, he rejected prospects who presumably knew something but of whom he possessed no inside knowledge.[7]

The Republicans were handed a splendid opportunity in the testimony of E. L. Doheny, a California Democrat, which eventually forced Walsh and others into an apparently hypocritical position. Doheny besmirched high-placed Democrats, one of whom was William G. McAdoo, leading contender for the presidential nomination, who had been endorsed by Senator Walsh as the Democrats' best hope for victory in 1924. Prodded by Senator Lenroot, Doheny asserted that since the war he had employed ex-Secretary Lane for $50,000 a year, ex-Secretary Gregory, ex-Secretary Garrison, and ex-Secretary McAdoo. Doheny said that McAdoo had received a retainer of $50,000 yearly and a total of about $250,000. McAdoo soon showed that Doheny's figures were inflated and objected in Los Angeles to "a continued effort to make my private law practice a political issue"; obviously he was damaged.[8]

Regular Republicans now argued plausibly that the corruption was bipartisan. George B. Lockwood, secretary of the Republican National Committee, stressed Doheny's career as "one of the nation's most distinguished democrats" and his employment of Wilsonian leaders "at fabulous salaries." President Coolidge in a speech of February 12 in New York avowed that the guilty would be punished, whether Democratic or Republican. As the *Philadelphia Record,* a Republican paper, noted, party leaders were trying to put a nonpartisan aspect on the oil scandal.[9]

The fallacy in Republican arguments designed to smear Democrats with oil was clearly identified by Senator Walsh. Though a Democrat, Doheny was a private citizen. Of what political significance, Walsh asked, was the bribery of a Republican official by a Democratic private citizen? "No one was ever so

foolish as to deny that some democrats are scoundrels." The party, he pointed out, was not liable for acts of individual, unofficial Democrats.[10]

Democrats soon recognized that the Doheny-McAdoo episode weakened
their position. McAdoo had been secretary of the treasury and now was running for the highest office in the land. On February 18, 1924, Walsh sent a
telegram to a McAdoo conference at Chicago referring to McAdoo as a "progressive" and pledging support for his nomination. The ex-secretary's character, said Walsh, was "untouched by any revelation" made before the Senate
committee investigating the naval oil leases. Later, when McAdoo had crossed
the continent to Los Angeles and made additional statements, Walsh changed
his mind. In a number of letters he said that McAdoo was no longer a "clean
government" candidate as a result of disclosures that a Mexican oil arrangement with Doheny carried a million dollar contingent fee and that McAdoo's
firm appeared in tax cases before the Treasury Department shortly after he
had resigned as secretary of the treasury. McAdoo continued briefly to be the
outstanding Democratic contender for the nomination, showing strength that
was surprising, as Walsh noted.[11]

Some writers have held that more aspersions were heaped upon Walsh, the
investigator, than upon the criminals whom he exposed and that the public was
apathetic to corruption in this period of poor taste and materialism. Coolidge's
victory of 1924 is sometimes cited as proof that the people were unwilling to
turn out the guilty ones. But other factors were involved in the Democratic
defeat—the convention split dramatized by McAdoo's and Smith's long fight
for the nomination, La Follette's third party movement, and Coolidge prosperity—which show the danger of assuming that those who failed to vote Democratic were thereby indifferent to corruption. A deeper cause for the Democratic
defeat was the feeling that both parties were implicated in the scandals. Some
observers noted quite early that the Democrats were not gaining much from
the exposures. Various factors help to explain why Coolidge almost doubled
the vote on John W. Davis and why La Follette obtained a third party vote of
nearly 5,000,000.[12]

Walsh found consolation in support by such papers as the *St. Louis Post-
Dispatch* and in hundreds of letters from admirers. On February 16, 1924, he
commented: "It has been a long, hard and up-hill fight, but the developments
have amply repaid me for the arduous work connected therewith." One remark, "I have become famous or infamous as the case may be considered,"
was evoked by the mixture of praise and abuse heaped upon him. And on
April 1 he said his friends' letters were doubly appreciated since newspaper
supporters of the rascals were abusing him. Walsh thanked the *Philadelphia*

Inquirer on June 10, 1924, for its praise of his work and stated that he believed it expressed the "sentiment of the plain people."[13]

By 1926 Walsh began to show disillusionment. With one friend he agreed that one of the first sins of the times was the toleration of the Harding scandals. Three years later, in declining to deliver an address on public morals, he explained that a Jeremiah was an ungracious role, and this was "a stiff-necked generation."[14]

Amid their hopes for the coming campaign, Democrats in early 1924 were shaken by ominous developments. There were the revelations touching McAdoo, which, in the opinion of Senator Walsh and many others, eliminated him as a good government candidate, although the self-assured Californian plunged ahead with his campaign, asserting he was the only progressive in the race. Walsh privately was puzzled that McAdoo should show so much strength in the preferential primaries. Meanwhile, the efficient governor of New York, Alfred E. Smith, forged ahead with his campaign. Lacking McAdoo's strength, Smith piled up what might be sufficient votes to block the McAdoo drive. It took no political wizard to see the explosive possibilities of this clash between the New York Catholic and "wet" and the Georgian turned Californian with his Protestant-"dry"-Klan following.[15]

As Democrats readied themselves for the big show in New York, the opposition gave a smooth performance in Cleveland. Calvin Coolidge was now the businessman's hero and, as the apparent embodiment of honesty in politics, the redeemer of his party's soiled reputation. It was a lucky day for the Republican party when Warren G. Harding passed away and "Puritan" Calvin Coolidge moved into the White House. Coolidge's friends at Cleveland steamrollered his nomination, notwithstanding the La Follette Progressives who futilely tried to get their platform adopted, worked to nominate their "Bob," and left the convention to form a third party.

On June 21 Walsh left Washington for the convention in New York. He stayed in the home of Charles R. Crane, a former Wilson supporter and minister to China. Walsh and others of the Montana delegation played an important role in the proceedings at Madison Square Garden, as Bruce Kremer helped to manage the McAdoo campaign, and S. V. Stewart was a member of the Resolutions Committee, while Walsh won higher honors.[16]

Walsh of Montana became a familiar sight or "voice" to millions of Americans in the campaign of 1924. He presided over the convention in Madison Square Garden which lasted a record two weeks and produced one of the ugliest brawls in American political history. Day after day as the delegates orated, shouted, perspired, and voted they saw before them the figure of the senator from Montana—the Teapot Dome investigator. An outside audience, made possible by the recent development of the radio, came to know his voice well. Walsh's slight figure moved with quick steps on the speakers' platform to and from a lectern banked with four large microphones. When speaking at the lectern, he habitually lifted and dropped his pince-nez, suspended on a ribbon around his neck. He talked, he shouted, he pounded with his gavel trying to bring order to the disorderly mob. An appearance of dignity and power was imparted by his thick gray hair, a heavy mustache (now cropped), bushy eyebrows, large piercing eyes, and rugged features set firmly, perhaps in a scowl. But the convention routine, his occasional slips, and his struggle with the crowd helped to reveal the human side of his nature. Sometimes in an idle moment Walsh was observed in a corner of the platform munching on a banana.[17]

Symbolic of the plight of the Democratic party in this campaign was Walsh's pounding gavel—pounding, pounding, pounding—trying to silence the discordant voices, the anger, and the hatred which threatened to tear the party to pieces. References to the much-used gavel were many and sometimes humorous. Heywood Broun thought Walsh's technique could be improved, since he brought the gavel down—crash, bang, zing—at the moment he opened his mouth to speak. The Associated Press reported on July 5 that one Herman Shoerstein "suffered concussion of the brain . . . when he was struck on the head by Chairman Walsh's gavel head as it flew off the handle and bounced into the delegate space." One suggestion at the close of the convention was that "all those delegates who escaped being hit by Tom Walsh's gavel" should meet in a telephone booth "to adopt a resolution of thanksgiving." It was good to discover some humor in the spectacle of Catholics against Protestants, drys against wets, Crackers against Tammanyites, white against blacks, and wrongheaded people against the welfare of their country.[18]

The explosive issue in the convention was the Ku Klux Klan. Since 1915 the hooded order had been terrorizing blacks and others whom it considered "unAmerican," multiplying rapidly in numbers, and wielding a growing influence in politics. But Klan activities were repugnant to many. Because the Democratic party drew its strength from all parts of the nation, including the big cities, where anti-Klan sentiment was strong, as well as from the Klan strongholds of the South and West, it was apparent that delegates might fight bitterly over the Klan question.

A row ensued over the Klan plank in the platform. Delegates disputed whether they should condemn the Klan by name or settle on a general and inoffensive statement, deploring intolerance and injustice. Al Smith's friends in northern cities determined to call the Klan by name, whereas the McAdoo forces, who counted upon backing from the South and West where the Klan was strong, preferred a general plank which would not alienate that organization. A struggle occurred first in the Resolutions Committee, where the McAdoo men won. The defeated minority then carried the issue to the convention floor for a final decision. Personal and emotional appeals and angry heckling from the floor characterized the speeches. When Andrew Erwin, a Georgian, finished his appeal to the best traditions of the South, a great demonstration occurred. Most of Erwin's fellow southerners sat in silence while Yankees hoisted Erwin to their shoulders and paraded to the band's rendition of "Marching Through Georgia."[19]

Walsh of Montana—a Catholic, but a westerner and a dry—presided through this uproar and attempted to avert the worst that he had feared was coming. Writing to McAdoo on November 28, 1922, he had referred to the Klan as that "evil institution," with headquarters in Atlanta and tentacles reaching into his own state of Montana. Something, he said, had to be done by southern Democrats to refute the notion that the Klan represented the dominant sentiment of the South and was an index of that region's "liberality of thought." McAdoo expressed surprise that Walsh regarded the Klan as being so strong. He attempted to impress upon Walsh his impatience with intolerance or bigotry of any kind.[20]

The Montanan's attitude in the convention apparently was similar to that of McAdoo and Bryan. He was quoted just prior to the convention as saying: "I would vote for a very strong, straight religious freedom plank, and think we should adopt one, but would not name the Ku Klux Klan." He revealed subtle sympathy during the proceedings for this point of view. When Bryan arose at the close of the bitter debate over the Klan, he was introduced by the permanent chairman as a "revered Democrat." Bryan then shouted among other things that "the use of three words [Ku Klux Klan]" meant more to the minority than "the welfare of a party." As Bryan was booed and hissed, Walsh thundered that he would clear the galleries. Division of the party and perhaps its destruction promised no end to racial and religious intolerance or to rule by the Republicans. Walsh worked for compromise.[21]

At last the delegates voted on the Klan plank. From Alabama through the long roll call every vote was answered by applause until the Garden filled with a continuous and deafening roar. Only the presence of the New York City Police prevented a riot. The convention secretary polled individual members of some delegations to obtain an accurate count, and so close was the vote that Chairman Walsh ordered the secretary to recapitulate the totals by state. Various delegates challenged the totals of their states, screaming simultaneously for recognition by the chair. Walsh was forced to make decision after decision as Saturday night passed away and Sunday morning "found the crowd . . . a vast, unmanageable personification of chaos." The voice that had "thundered" at Teapot Dome witnesses was swallowed up in the rumble from the galleries and from the floor of Madison Square Garden. A reporter described Walsh at 1:55 A.M. as looking "ill and bewildered," his face "alternately a flaming red and the drawn gray of exhaustion." Finally the plank to condemn intolerance in a general way was declared to have carried by one vote, Walsh's gavel came down "in a final crash," and "the tired petulant mob that had been a democratic convention" drifted out into a rainstorm breaking over New York City.[22]

After resting on Sunday the delegates met again on June 30 to battle over a presidential nominee, and the expected happened. McAdoo could not amass the necessary two-thirds majority over Smith and others. Ballot after ballot was futilely taken for more than a week as tension mounted. Neither Smith nor McAdoo could win the nomination, but neither would withdraw and allow his rival to win. A way out of this deadlock was sought by Walsh and other party leaders. According to one report, Walsh was instrumental in bringing about a personal meeting between Smith and McAdoo, the result being an announcement by Franklin D. Roosevelt, Smith's floor manager, that they would withdraw when McAdoo did.[23]

Walsh believed that he was the logical compromise choice to break the deadlock, even though he did not say so forthrightly. He emphasized in one of the party conferences that differences must be composed and that it was long past time when delegates should be released to vote as they pleased.[24]

Ever since he had exposed Fall and his associates in January 1924, Walsh had been often in the headlines and was mentioned as a possible presidential nominee. He gave little or no encouragement to his boosters.[25]

Lacking an organization and having expressed no desire for the presidency, Walsh nevertheless came to New York as a "dark horse." Political commentators like Arthur Krock placed him among the twenty most likely contenders. Discussion of compromise choices was stimulated by each turn of events in the convention. One line of reasoning was that, as a Catholic, Walsh would be acceptable to the Smith forces and as a western dry he would be popular in the West and the South. As the balloting went on day after day, Walsh constantly moved before the delegates, introduced speakers, and delivered rulings generally regarded as fair and able. Occasionally he won mention from the delegates as a good man to head the ticket. William Jennings Bryan, for example, listed his favorites for the nomination and included the man from

Montana. "As a lawyer he has no superior; as a statesman he has few equals, and as an investigator he is above them all."[26]

Walsh hardly figured in the balloting until after Smith and McAdoo released their delegates. He then came up strong, however, and apparently had a chance to win. On the 102d ballot he was up to 123, in third place. John W. Davis of West Virginia now had 415½ votes and Oscar Underwood of Alabama followed with 317. Reportedly Walsh was about to gain the large vote of the Smith forces, who had temporarily backed Underwood in order to stop Davis. The patience of the delegates had worn thin, however. They jumped on the Davis bandwagon, and the Walsh boom was over.[27]

Walsh said he regarded Davis as being splendidly equipped for the presidency. No one, he said—except one alternative that he modestly refrained from mentioning—would have been a better compromise choice than Davis.[28]

Walsh believed he would have won the nomination if he had not been a Catholic. This reason was annoying to him, because, as he explained to Arthur Brisbane, Catholicism of itself would not handicap a good nominee: "I have always felt that if a man otherwise possessing the confidence of the country were nominated for the presidency, the fact that he happened to be a Catholic would not militate seriously against him."[29]

Although he failed to receive the highest honor the convention might bestow, Walsh was spontaneously complimented in a dramatic way when the question of the vice presidency arose. Shortly after John W. Davis won the presidential nomination on Wednesday afternoon, July 9, Josephus Daniels of North Carolina moved that the convention adjourn until 8:30 that night in order to consider "solemnly" what "great American" should get the second place. The delegates already knew whom they wanted. Cries of "Walsh," "Walsh," "Walsh," filled the Garden, "constant, persistent and innumerable cries, approaching unanimity and acclamation." Finally Walsh thanked the delegates for their compliment, and assured them he had given the matter careful consideration and was not available. He then adjourned the convention until 8:30 in the evening.[30]

Party leaders in the next few hours put pressure on Walsh to change his mind. John W. Davis wanted Walsh as his running mate and immediately set out to persuade him to take the place. According to Burton Wheeler, party chieftains assembled with the convention chairman slumped in a chair. Among those present were Josephus Daniels, Senator Peter Gerry, and Senator Key Pittman. Relentlessly these leaders pressed Walsh to take the honor and aid his party. Walsh was inclined to keep his relatively secure Senate seat and, after hearing Wheeler's advice, apparently determined to do so. "Gentlemen," he said, turning to the party leaders, "that settles it." Finally the leaders were convinced that Walsh would not yield.[31]

Acting Chairman Alben Barkley in the evening session read Walsh's letter declining the vice presidential nomination. Although profoundly appreciative of the honor paid him, Walsh said that neither from a party nor a personal standpoint would it be wise for him to accept the nomination. It would be best to select another equally competent person whose nomination would not entail a sacrifice for the party. The convention then unenthusiastically nominated Governor Charles W. Bryan of Nebraska. The ticket therefore was one of Davis and Charles Bryan.[32]

On July 10 the Democratic convention of 1924 came to an end. Walsh survived "the whirlwind," as he termed it, "without serious damage" of a physical nature, and he climbed in party esteem and that of the public at large. He had resisted pressure to join a nominee doomed to defeat, but remained on cordial terms with John W. Davis and campaigned vigorously for him. He had added to his reputation for fairness and political sagacity. Those present at this convention were likely to remember the mustachioed man from Montana who had presided ably through the tumult.[33]

23

Winning a Third Term in 1924

Political patterns of Montana were more bizarre than usual in 1924 chiefly because of the La Follette-Wheeler Progressive party. A Democratic candidate for reelection, Walsh was endorsed by the Progressive leaders while working also with the party regulars. Walsh and Wheeler, the vice-presidential candidate on the Progressive ticket, joined conservative Democrats to help defeat Joseph M. Dixon for a second term as governor of Montana. While the Progressives backed Walsh for the Senate, he did not support them in the presidential race but rather campaigned for John W. Davis, whom he defended as a liberal. Strange though the pattern might be, it offered more evidence that Walsh and Wheeler on the state level had become "stand-patters." Political ambition and loyalty to the forms of party facilitated corporation control, or leverage, in Montana, although two powerful senators were now among the players.[1]

On August 11 Walsh led in the notification ceremonies at Clarksburg, West Virginia, in which John W. Davis formally learned of his nomination. In his address Walsh hailed the party nominee as a liberal. Some lawyers, Walsh said, unfitted themselves for public office by constant service to great corporations. "Happily," John W. Davis's vision was not thus restricted.[2]

Many Democrats, Republicans, and independents could not accept these views repeatedly expressed by Walsh and other Davis supporters. Dissatisfaction with both the Republican and the Democratic leadership resulted in the new Progressive party of 1924, headed by Robert M. La Follette and Burton K. Wheeler and consisting of various farmer-labor-liberal elements.

Senator Walsh was invited to participate in this new insurgency. In November 1922 he had received a joint letter from La Follette and Representative George Huddleston of Alabama as well as a personal letter from La Follette inviting him to attend a conference of progressive members of Congress. Now was an opportune time, they said, for a conference in which progressive members of Congress might decide on a definite plan of cooperation.[3]

Walsh's reply to La Follette helps reveal why he did not associate with this conference, nor with the farm bloc, nor with the La Follette Progressives of 1924. He was "highly gratified" that his career in the Senate was such that La Follette and his friends extended the invitation, but he could not accept it. This progressive protest had developed, he said, because of a reactionary Republican administration. To be effective it had to show formidable discontent among both Republicans and Democrats. The attendance of Democrats at the meeting would not be helpful since his own "unstinted support" and that of the great majority of Democrats would be given to most progressive measures anyway.[4]

Burton Wheeler felt no inhibitions about associating with Republican progressives. He came to Washington and attended the progressive conference in December 1922, talked briefly at a banquet held in conjunction with the meeting and made "a very decidedly favorable impression." Wheeler continued to work with the La Follette group. He added distinction to his name in 1924 by leading in the exposure of Attorney General Daugherty. Then, a few days after the Democratic National Convention on July 10, 1924, he bolted the party ticket, saying he could not and would not support Davis, whom he called an attorney for the "principal interests of Wall Street." Robert La Follette now asked Wheeler to run with him on the Progressive ticket and quickly received his consent.[5]

This startling development might have caused angry words between the two Montana senators, but instead they continued their friendly relationship. Walsh's attitude a few days after his colleague bolted the party was typical of that he maintained during the campaign: Senator Wheeler was "a man of strong convictions and of earnest purpose" and had taken the course which he considered his duty "as a public spirited citizen." Emphatically Walsh concluded that he did not agree with Wheeler. For his part, Wheeler announced that he would support Walsh and other Democratic candidates in Montana. On October 1, speaking at Billings, Wheeler gave specific reasons for backing the senior senator from Montana: "The defeat of Senator Walsh in this campaign would be looked upon by the country at large as a repudiation of his magnificent fight against corruption. He has aligned himself with the progressives on almost every issue during the last term of congress."[6]

La Follette was not so sure about Walsh's progressivism but he also endorsed him: "I trust that the progressives of Montana will unite in their support of

your candidacy for reelection to the United States senate. . . . your signal service in prosecuting the Teapot Dome investigation transcends all other issues
in this campaign."[7]

The gubernatorial race revealed most clearly the complexity and hypocri-
sy of Montana politics. Republican Joseph M. Dixon had been the laborer's
and the farmer's friend since becoming governor in 1921. After four years in
office he, along with Walsh and Wheeler, won high praise from the Labor
Conference for Progressive Political Action. But Dixon's efforts to raise corporate taxes and to alleviate farm distress helped to convince conservatives
and corporate interests that he must be defeated in 1924.[8]

Senator Walsh at one point mentioned the governor's popularity with the
farmers, but he also said that, "if common report" were true, extravagance
and high taxation had almost unbearably burdened the people of Montana.[9]

Thus a progressive Republican governor was defeated by Montana conservatives with the help of Walsh and Wheeler. Walsh, in fact, had much to do
with selecting J. E. Erickson to run against Dixon. In September 1923 Walsh
and Jerry Dobell of the *Butte Miner* agreed that Erickson of Kalispell might
make a good man for the gubernatorial race. Dobell observed that Erickson
lived far enough from Butte to avoid suspicion of being under Anaconda
influence, made a fairly good speech, had a "commanding appearance" that
should appeal to the farmers, and probably could swing the Scandinavian vote
in the eastern part of the state. Walsh had a conference with C. F. Kelley of
Anaconda and then expressed his belief that the "Butte forces" favored Erickson. So Erickson obtained conservative backing as well as some "progressive"
backing and the victory in November.[10]

Montana's senior senator had become a national figure of such renown that
his reelection seemed virtually assured. When he arrived in Helena from the
East on August 15, merchants of the city placed flags in front of their places
of business, the State Capital band heralded his arrival, and a parade of automobiles escorted him to the Marlow Theatre, where he was to give his address. Before this admiring audience, Walsh spoke with frankness and warmth:
"I should indeed be the cold, unemotional, reserved and unsocial creature
which tradition perpetuated by political rivalry makes me if I were not stirred
to the depths by this manifestation of your esteem." He continued that he
felt like a "regular fellow" when called "Tom" and believed that his popularity outside the state which had prompted the use of the diminutive was shared
fully by the people of Montana. He hoped that his own people, whom he
loved best, found him growing "mellow rather than acrid with age."[11]

Walsh did not make the fatal mistake of trying to coast on his reputation.

He waged a vigorous campaign against Frank Bird Linderman, a newspaper-man and author who had defeated Wellington Rankin for the Republican nomination. Thousands of Native Americans were to vote for the first time as a result of being made citizens in 1924, and as early as mid-June Walsh wrote to a number of his friends asking their advice about the Indian vote. His brother "Jack" urged him to cultivate the 2,500 Flathead Indians who would gain the suffrage. Walsh appreciated this suggestion, for shortly after his ar-rival in Montana, when setting out for his summer home in Glacier Nation-al Park, he chose a route through the Flathead Reservation. Walsh contin-ued to cultivate the Native Americans' friendship. One of his speeches was delivered at the Crow Agency in Hardin before a large audience of Indians and whites.[12]

A threat to Walsh of some consequence came from the Ku Klux Klan, or manifestations of a related type. Walsh fought back. In the State Democratic Convention of September 10, for example, he led an attack on the Klan and other organizations that applied racial or religious tests to candidates for public office. An apparent threat was money sent in by conservatives from outside the state for the purpose of defeating Walsh, the Teapot Dome investigator. Alarmed, Walsh asked the special U.S. Senate Committee on Campaign Expenditures to investigate rumors of large and unreported contributions. Meanwhile during the last month of the race he spoke almost every day.[13]

Walsh enjoyed advantages over Linderman. His career had given him pub-licity and prestige that Linderman could not match. He could depend upon a large liberal following because of his record and because the Progressive leaders had announced in favor of him. At the same time Walsh and the con-servative forces in the Democratic party worked together, assuring a conser-vative turnout.[14]

Walsh swept to victory on November 4 by a majority of about 10,000 votes in a total of 170,000. Erickson also won in the gubernatorial race. But Coolidge carried the state, and Republicans won most Montana offices. Linderman, a strong Coolidge supporter, benefited from the national swing to Coolidge and from his own popularity as a successful Montana writer of fiction.[15]

Linderman received letters of particular interest concerning his campaign. A friend and supporter in Lincoln, Nebraska, wrote: "Considering that you were pitted against the 'peerless investigator,' you made a wonderful show-ing." This writer and many others in 1924 seemed to believe that Walsh's Teapot Dome inquiry was mostly politics.[16]

With respect to John W. Davis's crushing defeat, Walsh observed that once again the Democratic party had been taught that it could not take a candidate out of a Wall Street background and elect him. On his own victory, Walsh commented, "the prayers of the righteous availed much on election day." His reelection was necessary, he believed, to encourage honest citizens and to rebuke the Ku Klux Klan element. It would have been a shock if voters of Montana had rejected their senior senator in the year of his most brilliant achievements.[17]

Walsh's position as a leader in the minority Democratic party was assured by his successes of 1924. Until that time he had not been a truly national figure. His career as an exceptionally able lawyer who often sided with the underprivileged in Montana had enabled him to ride a wave of progressivism into the Senate in 1913. But his support of nearly all the Wilson measures, his reelection in 1918, his notable part in the League contest, his enviable reputation as a constitutional lawyer, and his record for political astuteness left him still unknown among the "general public." Walsh became famous in 1924 with his oil investigation. Repercussions from the early disclosures and a renewal of the investigation in 1928 kept him in the news, as did his work in the Senate.[18]

24
Abiding the Coolidge Administration

When Calvin Coolidge acceded to the presidency following the death of Warren G. Harding, he and Senator Walsh enjoyed a friendly relationship. The same was true later when the former president was quietly living in retirement. Walsh wrote to him in 1932 asking for a photograph, to be given to a friend, and also requested that Coolidge be "good enough to present my compliments to Mrs. Coolidge, whose gracious friendship while in the White House we all remember with pleasure." Coolidge noted in his reply that it was just eight years earlier that his father in Vermont listened on the radio as Walsh announced from the Democratic National Convention in New York "the death of my son." He said he would try to find a picture for Walsh.[1]

No such harmony existed in the major part of Coolidge's presidency, as the two men were virtually at war. They each viewed the other as politically motivated in large part, and Walsh had little respect for Coolidge's ability. The senator believed that Coolidge represented the Republican Old Guard in crucial matters of taxation and the tariff, that he gave aid and encouragement to monopoly interests and strove to undermine federal regulatory agencies, and that he afforded halfhearted support at best in the oil investigations. According to Walsh, Andrew W. Mellon, secretary of the treasury and one of the richest men in America, was the real brains of this reactionary administration. Thus by attacking Mellon, as he frequently did, Walsh believed he was essentially attacking Coolidge and his policies.[2]

Notwithstanding his assaults on the GOP, the Montanan was by no means an economic radical. In private correspondence and speeches he sometimes revealed himself as a great booster for America, tinged a little with "Golden Twenties" optimism. Thus in 1928 he wrote enthusiastically regarding economic opportunities for young people, if they were only "willing to toil and live uprightly." In the same year an interviewer came away strongly impressed with Walsh's essential optimism and "mildness." Even the oil scandals were to him "a blot and not a cancer on the national government."[3]

Walsh never escaped the Teapot Dome scandal that had made him famous, and he never wanted to. He was busy with many things from 1925 to 1933—working indefatigably, for example, to get the United States into the World Court (and cooperating with the administration)—but matters pertaining to the oil leases of the Harding administration continued to arise. He had "started it all," and his reputation was involved in continuing discussions on the subject and in events such as the Supreme Court decision of 1927, cancelling the corrupt leases. In January 1928 the Public Lands Committee of the Senate resumed its hearings suspended four years earlier and now paid special attention to the mysterious Continental Trading Company Limited and the uses made by its organizers of the illicit profits in oil. Senator Walsh felt impelled repeatedly to counter the arguments that he and his party were playing politics or that he was "grandstanding." With his mastery of detail and an innate sense of fair play, Walsh simply overwhelmed diehards on the scandals who were foolhardy enough to take the floor against him. By the end of the decade his fame was enhanced. He was widely regarded as an authentic hero of the Washington scene, a legend in his lifetime.

In a Senate speech of March 17, 1925, Walsh showed his determination to keep the record straight regarding Teapot Dome and the findings of the Public Lands Committee. Walsh was responding to the minority report, written by Seldon Spencer of Missouri, a bitter foe in later phases of the committee's 1924 hearings. By a Senate vote of 41 to 30, the Spencer report had been rejected in favor of Walsh's majority view, and the Montanan might have rested on that success. But he did not. Some weeks later on the Senate floor he showed that the Spencer report was inaccurate. It was, he said, "so fantastic in its distortion of the facts revealed, so flatly contradicted in many important features by the record," that it was hard to believe the senators who signed it had actually taken the time to read it.[4]

Walsh seized this opportunity to defend his own investigation, as well as others, since they frequently came under attack. Secretary Mellon was one of many who objected to "government by investigation." But Walsh emphasized that they were trying in Congress to perform a necessary and useful function: "It is my view that as great a public service may be rendered by a demonstration through searching inquiry that rumors touching the integrity of public officials and public men are unfounded as though it had been revealed that there was too much truth in them. How shall the investigator, . . . know in advance that the rumors are or are not well founded, and how shall the public be assured that they are without foundation except upon inquiry?" These were not the words of a probing mudslinger.[5]

Walsh believed that the Teapot Dome inquiry had revealed "a regrettable episode in our national life if not . . . a decadence in public morals," and therefore he had been impelled to comment upon the strictures of the minority report. There was no rebuttal or Senate debate. A few months later Seldon Spencer died, and it was not until 1928 that another Republican emerged in the Senate who devoted a good deal of energy to sniping at Walsh and the Democrats in a style reminiscent of Spencer's. This new antagonist was Arthur R. Robinson of Indiana, appointed to the Senate in 1925 and elected in his own right the following year. These matters relating to government oil lands always seemed to be in some unfinished state, awaiting the action of presidents, the Justice Department, the special prosecutors, and members of Congress, as well as decisions of judges and juries.[6]

Walsh was pleased at any opportunity, by contrast with the oil matters, to achieve a quick, decisive solution to a problem before the Senate. Such occurred in March 1925, in a debate and parliamentary struggle over a cabinet appointment. The *Philadelphia Record* described this as "one of the most sensational fights in history against the President of the United States." James O'Donnell Bennett in the *Chicago Tribune* asserted there had been "nothing like it since the Dempsey-Firpo fight," and "Walsh was the Dempsey."[7]

It all began when Coolidge nominated Charles Beecher Warren of Michigan, a lawyer, businessman, and political friend, to be his new attorney general, replacing Harlan Fiske Stone. Ordinarily such a nomination would have been confirmed easily. No cabinet nominee had been rejected since 1868. Coolidge, however, ran into opposition from disgruntled progressives in his own party who saw an opportunity, while taking high ground, to oppose the man in the White House. But it was the Democrats, led by Walsh, who carried this fight initially and did the most to bring about a victory.[8]

Probably Walsh was suspicious of Warren from the start. He had a previous acquaintance with him, having helped to interrogate him during the Senate lobby hearings of 1913. But the decisive influence on the Montanan which sent him into a determined fight against Warren came from Basil Manly and his People's Legislative Service, a public service lobby. Manly had learned from an "accurate and reliable source" of Warren's trust associations that would indicate a conflict of interest, should he become head of the Justice Department. The senator did research of his own, wrote a report for the Senate Judiciary Committee, and reached the conclusion that this nomination was a bad one and must be opposed. To have any chance of succeeding, Walsh and his early supporters, notably Senator Reed of Missouri, had to make an argument that rallied the Democratic senators. They also had to win votes from progressives across the aisle.[9]

Newspapermen reacted with surprise and excitement to the Warren fight. There was speculation among some as to Walsh's motives. The *New York Evening Bulletin* may have guessed correctly that the Montana senator was thinking, in part, of the Wheeler trial just ahead and of Warren's probable antagonism in that affair if he were confirmed. Walsh knew from experience that the head of the Justice Department had a powerful influence on public questions, and he regretted the practice of appointing men who were strongly partisan or legally undistinquished.[10]

Shortly before opening the Senate debate, Walsh explained to a conference of the Democratic senators the crux of his case against Warren; namely, that Warren had been a friend of the "Sugar Trust" in Michigan. They were "startled" by the evidence, he said, and most were willing to be helpful. As the arguments continued, Democrats who were at first disinterested or absent from the Chamber also entered the fracas, and progressives in the Republican ranks became more active.[11]

The Montanan made two principal arguments against Warren, the first of which by itself would never have prevailed. He asserted that the nominee had no real standing as a lawyer and thus owed his appointment primarily to personal and political considerations. Walsh was implying that Warren might be another Harry Daugherty.[12]

Turning to his second and more promising argument, Walsh said that Warren had been for years "a representative in his state of the Sugar Trust." Walsh had opened a subject which the senators discussed for some 300 pages of the *Record,* from March 7 through March 16. Many knew a great deal about the American Sugar Refining Company and its notorious operations. Now they heard in detail how Charles Beecher Warren had helped H. O. Havemeyer as he gained control in Michigan.[13]

In assailing the credentials of the nominee, Walsh also got in whacks at Secretary of the Treasury Andrew Mellon, whose aluminum company was constantly being charged with antitrust violations. "Just imagine," Walsh said, "the Aluminum Co. of America being brought to book by Charles B. Warren for having violated the Sherman Antitrust Act!" Why, if Warren were confirmed as attorney general they might as well repeal the Sherman law. Walsh said that Republicans had to consider and explain the many letters placed in the *Record* in which Warren was obviously functioning as agent and organizer—as part and parcel—of the sugar trust. Their position was weakened by the fact that both senators from Michigan and apparently nearly all of the House delegation from that state declined to speak in favor of Warren. But regular Senate Republicans were ready to support the president's nominee.[14]

Late on the afternoon of Tuesday, March 10, the first vote occurred amid "scenes of tense excitement," according to the *New York Times* reporter. President pro tempore George Moses of New Hampshire suddenly called the question, apparently thinking that Democrats Lee Overman of North Carolina and Oscar Underwood of Alabama would join the Republicans to provide a margin of victory. But Underwood did not vote, and the first test was a 40 to 40 tie. If Vice President Charles Dawes had been in the chair, he could have broken the tie in Warren's favor, settling the question once and for all; but he did not reach the Chamber in time. The vote was 41 to 39 in favor of Walsh's motion. Thus the Coolidge administration sustained a defeat of historic proportions.[15]

Refusing to admit defeat, Coolidge resubmitted the nominee's name. Walsh challenged the authority of the president to do such a thing, arguing that according to established principles of parliamentary law a question once having been disposed of could not be reconsidered during the same session of a legislative body. His arguments won the support of the Judiciary Committee's majority. Nevertheless, on the floor of the Senate the debate continued, mostly in repetition of the old ideas. Finally, on Monday, March 16, the decision went against Coolidge by a larger margin than ever—46 to 39. Thus the Senate, as stated in the *Record*, "refused to advise and consent to the nomination."[16]

Furious at opponents in the Senate and unhappy with his party leadership, Coolidge threatened to give Warren an interim appointment. When better judgment won out, he called upon an old friend from Vermont, John Garibaldi Sargent, to come to Washington and head the Justice Department.[17]

While the Warren affair ended, the repercussions continued. Walsh had enhanced his position as a senator who fought ably and stubbornly on matters of principle. Perhaps most important, the Montanan and many admirers saw his political leadership and parliamentary skill as evidence of presidential stature. It should be remembered that Franklin D. Roosevelt was a near invalid in 1925, holding no political office, and John W. Davis, William G. McAdoo, and Alfred E. Smith were uncertain quantities nationally. Many Democrats were searching for a new leader. Walsh's own interest had been

whetted by his rise to importance while the party was having so many problems. He was willing to advertise himself more than usual and, in a preliminary way, to test the political waters.

Writing to a friend in Helena, the day before the final vote on Warren, Walsh
revealed his excitement and not a little vanity: "The papers will have advised
you that I have been active since the extra session began. I am sending to the
Montana papers James O'Donnell Bennett's account [in the *Chicago Tribune*]
of the most hectic hour I have known in the Senate when we defeated the
confirmation of [Charles B.] Warren by a tie vote—the Vice President being
temporarily absent. . . . I had to convert most of my democratic associates on
the question as well as enough on the republican side to give us the narrow
margin shown by the vote."[18]

Walsh overemphasized his part in "converting" the progressive Republicans.
Usually, however, he acknowledged that without the support of that group
the Warren struggle would have been in vain. In this instance, as in many
others, the Democrats and progressives from across the aisle had to work
together to defeat the regular Republican organization.[19]

Meanwhile, a celebrated legal battle of the mid-1920s involved Walsh, along
with his Montana colleague, Burton Wheeler. The latter was indicted by a
federal grand jury for allegedly misusing his senatorial office in representing
a Montana oil promoter. Wheeler at the time was leading the investigation
of Attorney General Daugherty that eventually drove him from office. Walsh
was then running the Teapot Dome inquiry. The attorney general, it seems,
tried to "get" the probers before they got him, assisted by the Republican
National Committee. After Daugherty's resignation, subordinates in the Justice Department persisted with plans for legal action against Wheeler, cul-
minating with a trial in the federal court at Great Falls, Montana, in April
1925. The principal attorney for the defense was Senator Walsh, who had
himself been investigated by agents from the Department of Justice.[20]

Walsh never doubted, he said, that the action against Wheeler was intended to disrupt his investigation. Along with many Senate colleagues, Walsh
believed the Wheeler indictment was an intolerable attempt by the executive
branch of government to interfere with legitimate functions of the legislative
branch.[21]

Walsh rose in the Senate to express confidence in the integrity of his colleague and to ask for the appointment of a select committee to look into the
charges. The justification for this procedure was simple—that the Senate had
the power to judge of the qualifications of its own members and should not
wait for the decision of a jury, although in other circumstances that would

be proper. Walsh stressed that Wheeler was doing work of "exceptional value to the country" in the Daugherty investigation and ought not to have it disrupted. The select committee, headed by William E. Borah and containing two additional Republicans and two Democrats, decided within weeks that Wheeler was innocent and had at all times observed the letter and the "spirit of the law."

Disagreeing with the majority, Senator Thomas Sterling said the matter should have been left to a federal court in Montana, and he gave essentially the administration point of view: there had been no "frame-up," and Wheeler might have acted carelessly or illegally as charged. Walsh replied that they all knew the "circumstances" of Wheeler's indictment: he was innocent, and the country was indebted to him for his services in the Daugherty investigation. Walsh presented this case as one of broad significance, noting recent charges that the Senate was engaged in a "usurpation" of power. It was ridiculous, he said, to maintain that the Senate should drift along for months with an accused colleague in its midst and take no action regarding his alleged fitness or unfitness, merely waiting for a court to render its verdict.

Chief Justice William Howard Taft revealed quite a different view of the Wheeler episode, writing privately: The Senate was "showing itself in its usual disgraceful attitude," now trying to "shield" a member from "prosecution for crime."

The federal case was still pending against Wheeler, and in 1925 Walsh served as his attorney versus the U.S. attorney and staff in Great Falls. The government's charges against Wheeler were much the same as those considered by the Senate select committee; that is, that he had violated federal law by representing a Montana client before the Interior Department. The U.S. attorney developed an elaborate argument and produced a star witness who told improbable stories about the defendant's actions. Walsh asserted in reply that the government really had no case. "There is no evidence on which you would condemn a jail bird or a street walker. Senator Wheeler is not asking sympathy; he is asking justice, and acquittal of a baseless charge." Walsh said one had to remember that all this began while Wheeler was conducting his Senate probe of the former attorney general and exposing "infamy" in the Justice Department.[22]

There was cause for celebration by Senators Walsh and Wheeler and many others who believed in Wheeler's innocence and resented the suit that had been brought against him. One of the telegrams Walsh received came from Senator Robert M. La Follette, not long before his death in 1925: "Congratulations on your magnificent work. You have added another score to your great record. Our first concern was to see Wheeler exonerated. But back of that as you clearly perceived the integrity of the public service was at stake."[23]

Wheeler still faced the possibility of a "conspiracy trial" in the District of Columbia. In January 1926, however, the government abandoned its case, and Walsh commented in the Senate: "Thus there is brought to an inglorious end the effort of the Department of Justice to punish a Member of this body for daring to assail it in the discharge of his official duties." Walsh noted that doubts about Harry Daugherty's conduct had been dispelled when "that gentleman declined to testify before a grand jury concerning his official acts on the ground that his evidence might incriminate him."[24]

Congratulatory telegrams were in order, following Wheeler's acquittal in the Montana trial, but the big celebration was delayed a year until the government abandoned its case in the District of Columbia. The Wheeler Defense Committee, headed by Norman Hapgood, Basil M. Manly, and Mercer G. Johnston, arranged for a "Civic Victory Dinner," held at the City Club of Washington, D.C., on April 15, 1926, with 300 in attendance.[25]

That the Wheeler affair had significance cannot be doubted. Above all, it saved Wheeler's reputation and Senate career and provided an additional basis for good relations with his senior colleague from Montana. Also, dragging on as it did in the mid-1920s, it helped to keep alive the issues involved in recent congressional investigations: How serious had the scandals and abuses of power really been? Had the investigators in fact performed a notable public service, notwithstanding the frequent criticism or lack of appreciation? Certainly the outcome of Wheeler's exoneration was a liberal triumph, and one of the few that could be claimed in this period. So far as Walsh is concerned, *Time* magazine captured the essence of his position in the Senate with its cover photograph of Walsh on May 4, 1925, captioned "Unforgetting." He was indeed unforgetting—alert to every development regarding Teapot Dome, and also to similar abuses in the government service or in government-business relationships.

Walsh followed closely all the legal maneuvers and the actual trials relating to the allegedly corrupt leases of oil lands. He did this in part through his frequent communication with the special prosecutors whom Coolidge had appointed in 1924—Atlee Pomerene, the former senator from Ohio, and Owen J. Roberts, a Philadelphia lawyer (who later became a Supreme Court Justice). Notwithstanding the fact that Walsh originally questioned their qualifications for the exacting task, they soon impressed him favorably, and the three cooperated surprisingly well. In part, they simply shared information relating to the oil cases and congratulated each other when the decisions went their way. Walsh, however, was in a position to help the prosecutors appreciably. Besides giving advice, he pressed for the passage of laws, and even the negotiation of a treaty, that would facilitate their task of bringing alleged oil criminals to justice. Walsh was determined to do everything in his power to substantiate, through court verdicts, his own findings in the Senate probes of 1923–24 and 1928.[26]

The court proceedings began inauspiciously for the government when, in April 1925, the suit against Fall and Sinclair which charged them with fraud and conspiracy in the Teapot Dome lease was quashed on a technicality. Walsh and others saw confirmation of their fears that the special prosecutors were not qualified for their difficult assignment. Soon thereafter, in the civil suit against Sinclair's Mammoth Oil Company, in the federal district court in Wyoming, Judge T. Blake Kennedy dismissed a bill to cancel the Teapot Dome lease. Kennedy held that the lease appeared to be a good one and might actually result in the conservation of oil. Writing in the *National Democrat*, Walsh expressed his keen disappointment. Judge Kennedy, he said, had accepted all the excuses and pretexts intended to justify the leasing, even though that "transaction was so marked with fraud as to shock the conscience and to galvanize an otherwise listless public into rapt attention." Fortunately, Walsh added, there was an appellate tribunal, and they could afford to wait for the judgment of the four jurists comprising the Circuit Court of Appeals for the Eighth Circuit. Some were so incensed at Judge Kennedy's apparently illogical decision that they assumed he had been bought outright. Walsh, however, believed that Kennedy had merely been influenced by his surroundings in the Wyoming oil country.[27]

In September 1926 Judge William S. Kenyon in the Circuit Court of Appeals at St. Paul held that Sinclair's Teapot Dome lease had been obtained by fraud, thus reversing Kennedy's decision in the district court. Walsh, Pomerene, and others were greatly pleased. Pomerene observed that he could make good use of Kenyon's decision in arguing the parallel case against Doheny's Pan American Oil Company.[28]

This Pan American or Elk Hills suit had started well when the District Court at Los Angeles, presided over by Judge Paul J. McCormick, found that the Elk Hills lease had been obtained by fraud and ordered that it be cancelled. Walsh wrote to William G. McAdoo soon after the ruling, in 1925: "The very natural gratification which the decision of Judge McCormick brought me was tinged with regret that Mr. Doheny, for whom I entertain a very warm regard, had permitted himself to become involved in so shady a transaction." Walsh expressed his concern about the public's perception of the "integrity of the courts" and believed McCormick's decision would have a wholesome effect in this regard.[29]

In February 1927 the Supreme Court handed down a decision of momentous importance. Large headlines in the *New York Times* announced: "DOHENY OIL LEASES VOIDED FOR FRAUD BY HIGH COURT; HIS LOSS OVER $10,000,000." This was a unanimous decision in which the Court assailed former Secretary Fall as a "faithless" public servant and concluded that the lease he had granted Edward Doheny was a fraudulent transaction from start to finish. The justices held that the secrecy in which the two men had acted was convincing evidence of corruption, even omitting from consideration the $100,000 that Doheny had "lent" to the former Secretary. With this decision, the *Times* noted, one judge of the district court, six circuit judges, and eight justices of the Supreme Court had all agreed that the Doheny contract was fraudulent and must be voided.[30]

After Judge Kenyon's decision some months earlier in the Teapot Dome case, Owen Roberts had written to Senator Walsh: "I think you are entitled to congratulations as well as counsel, because the decision is a vindication of your legal judgment as well as ours." The same logic applied to the Supreme Court decision in the Doheny case, only more strongly. Walsh's hard work in the oil leases investigation, and his findings in that affair, had now been vindicated completely. A succession of events added to his feeling of achievement. In March 1927 an executive order transferred the naval petroleum reserves from the Interior Department to the Navy Department, thus revoking a similar order of 1921 under which former Secretary Fall had taken over the reserves and proceeded to lease them; the Navy now physically resumed control. And on October 10, 1927, the Supreme Court found Sinclair's lease of Teapot Dome to be fraudulent, much as it had in the case against Doheny and the Pan American Company.[31]

Letters and telegrams of congratulation poured into Senator Walsh's office in March 1927, and after; and he responded with understandable gratification, along with thanks for the support he had received. McAdoo wired as soon as the Doheny decision was handed down: "MY SINCERE CONGRATULATIONS ON YOUR GREAT VICTORY IN THE SUPREME COURT OF THE UNITED STATES STOP IT NOT ONLY VINDICATES YOU BUT EMPHASIZES THE MAGNIFICENT PUBLIC SERVICE YOU HAVE PERFORMED STOP." Perhaps the most complimentary lines came from Josephus Daniels, who scribbled in longhand: "My congratulations. If you lived in Europe you would be knighted."[32]

Walsh's letters at this time revealed a good deal about himself. To one correspondent he wrote: "All patriotic citizens ought to rejoice in the decision of the Supreme Court enforcing the truth of the biblical maxim that the 'way of the transgressor is hard.' I rejoice not only at having rendered a signal service . . . , but as well in the improvement in official standards likely to result from it. I cannot doubt that the affair will be a warning not only to public officials but to those who might out of avarice otherwise be moved to attempt [tempt] them." In Walsh's opinion, he was not given the recognition by newspaper writers that he should have received (perhaps they had "forgotten" him), and he mentioned one commentator so poorly informed as to give credit to the Coolidge administration "for its vigorous and relentless prosecution of the offenders." Much of the Republican press was, of course, hostile to him. Walsh observed, however: "He laughs best who laughs last."[33]

Government prosecutors and their supporters, such as Walsh, actually found little to laugh about concerning one category of trials that continued through the 1920s—the criminal suits. In the tangled history of the oil cases, from 1925 to 1929, no jury ever voted a conviction. Harry Sinclair escaped, as did E. L. Doheny. Thus there was the anomalous situation of a failure to convict the men who paid bribes, although the official who accepted their money (Secretary Fall) ultimately was found guilty and served a short term in the penitentiary. Disappointed at the miscarriages of justice, some concluded it was almost impossible to convict a multimillionaire, with his battery of attorneys. Others blamed the juries. Not so Senator Walsh. He pointed to the fact that a federal judge in Wyoming had sided with Fall and Sinclair. Judges could err as well as individuals in a jury, and the jury system had so much value that "the weaknesses, such as they may be, may well be overlooked." Walsh observed in 1926, after one setback in a criminal trial, that he would not "regard the investigations as fruitless unless the Supreme Court shall restore the lands involved to Doheny and Sinclair, a result I do not anticipate." Soon after came the Court's strong and decisive ruling against Fall and Doheny in the Pan American case.[34]

Walsh did not receive any thanks or congratulations from Calvin Coolidge but probably would have admitted that Coolidge, under pressure, had appointed the special prosecutors and permitted them to do their work. Meanwhile, Walsh and the administration were able to cooperate on prohibition enforcement and not a few matters foreign and domestic.

25

Oh! for a Jefferson

B y the fall of 1918 many factors contributed to a weakening of the old
Wilson coalition. After Coolidge's landslide victory in 1924, events were
especially discouraging, even for an optimist such as Senator Walsh. The continuing prosperity and a popular Republican administration left the Democrats almost moribund nationally. To be sure, the party did well in some states
and areas of the country. Montana had two Democratic senators, a Democratic congressman in the western district, and a Democratic governor. Western Democrats were notably successful in getting their senatorial candidates
elected. "Unterrified Democrats," as they sometimes called themselves, kept
trying.[1]

It will be remembered that Walsh was a contender briefly for the presidential nomination at the Democratic National Convention of 1924 in Madison Square Garden. A few thought well enough of him to support his bid,
and almost everyone eulogized his performance as the convention chairman
during two arduous weeks. From that time to 1928 Walsh believed he was a
legitimate contender for the party's top honor, a unifying influence and a
leader whose idealistic aims could serve the nation well. At the same time he
was sensible enough to know that he was unlikely ever to be nominated for
president. What the party needed, he believed, was another Thomas Jefferson—not Thomas J. Walsh, Alfred E. Smith, William G. McAdoo, John W.
Davis, or anyone else in sight; but after Smith's defeat for president in 1928
and Franklin D. Roosevelt's election as governor of New York, Walsh began
to realize that this confident young man might be the hope of the next generation.[2]

Walsh was active in the unity movement of the Democrats from 1924 to
1927, along with Roosevelt, Cordell Hull, and others. They were attempting

to heal the wounds of 1924 by stressing liberal themes and party "fundamentals," while avoiding current differences. No one could forget, however, the political enemies of 1924: Smith and McAdoo. The New Yorker had not abandoned his presidential aspirations, nor had McAdoo shown signs of forgiving and forgetting.

A recuperating Franklin Roosevelt took the lead as party peacemaker. He hoped leaders could agree upon a conference for the spring or early summer of 1925 and wrote to Walsh as permanent chairman of the recent convention, seeking his support. The Montanan replied that he was "in entire harmony" with the idea of a conference, and he also agreed that the Democratic party was "the only political agency that reflects the aims and aspirations of the great mass of the people." Walsh and Roosevelt were overly optimistic. For many reasons, the unity efforts fell flat.[3]

One positive result of their efforts was a continuing correspondence and occasional talks over a period of years. In June 1925, for example, Roosevelt wired the senator that he was "anxious" to see him, and they arranged for a meeting in New York City during the first week of July. Seven months later Walsh hosted a Democratic dinner at his Washington apartment with Roosevelt and a number of congressional leaders in attendance. Ostensibly they were meeting with the elections of 1926 in mind. Senator Joseph T. Robinson and Representative Finis Garrett were there as floor leaders of their respective houses and also Peter Gerry and William A. Oldfield as chairmen of the Senate and House campaign committees. Senator Pat Harrison of Mississippi attended, as did Representative Cordell Hull, a "tariff and taxation expert." FDR's political aide, Louis Howe, also came to the dinner and was involved in the discussions.[4]

Walsh made his own special efforts. He wrote to a number of prominent Democrats, urging them to write articles on "critical or quasi-political questions, with a view to overcoming the sordidness with which unfortunately they are now looked at." This idea had "taken possession" of him, Walsh told Professor William E. Dodd.[5]

To understand the discouragement and frustration of Senator Walsh and his party associates one must look to overwhelming Republican majorities in the elections of 1924 and 1928; also to GOP victories in Congress, often the result of Democratic defections. Only occasionally, as in the Charles Beecher Warren affair, did Democrats stand together and win an important battle.

Senator Walsh was much involved in legislative affairs of the twenties, partly in his capacity as assistant minority leader, working with "Joe" Robinson of Arkansas. Robinson, thirteen years younger than the Montanan, had entered the Senate in 1913, as Walsh did, and he too was a Wilson admirer and critic of Republican policies. Both were fighters who nevertheless tried to be fair-minded in their politics. Walsh had the better reputation as lawyer and logician and tended to be more progressive, while Robinson was admired as a good fellow, an able organizer, and a pleasing speaker.[6]

Starting in 1927 and continuing for many months, Walsh found an issue of interest, that of public utility companies and the apparent power they were exercising. They should be investigated, said Walsh, agreeing with Senator Norris and others of both parties. The question was, Could these progressives muster the votes to authorize a new Senate investigation? Norris in 1925 had obtained passage of a resolution leading to an investigation of utilities by the Federal Trade Commission that proved inadequate. One powerful advocate of a new probe was the former forester Gifford Pinchot, who talked with Senator Walsh and sent letters to many in the Senate.[7]

In February 1927, Walsh introduced a resolution reading in part: "That a committee of five members of the Senate be appointed by the President thereof . . . empowered and directed to inquire into the growth of the capitalization of public-utility corporations supplying either electrical energy in the form of power or light, or both, however produced, . . . and of corporations holding the stocks of such corporations." Three days later he spoke at length in the Senate on the possible evils occurring in the development of the electrical industry and of the need for investigation. He cited a book by Professor William Z. Ripley of Harvard University as one of his principal sources of information. Senator Norris also spoke, giving support to Walsh in his call for an investigation.[8]

Months later Walsh's resolution was resubmitted in amended form, and it caused an outcry that continued through the year and into 1928. One newspaper commented that "when Senator Walsh touched the public utilities button he summoned a bigger army of lobbyists to Washington than Napoleon took soldiers to Moscow." Another wrote of Senator Henrik Shipstead's remark that a group of "reactionary" Democrats, possibly in combination with a similar group of Republicans, might defeat Walsh's resolution. One possibility was that it would go to the Senate Committee on Interstate Commerce and there experience a quiet burial. This, in fact, seemed about to happen, and the Montanan spent time before the committee arguing his cause. He wrote that he was spending each morning before the Commerce Committee trying to get the resolution voted out and also was preparing to proceed in the Continental Trading Company affair.[9]

Walsh succeeded in his efforts before the Commerce Committee and then faced another challenge, that of having the utility investigation turned over to the Federal Trade Commission. Paul Y. Anderson, writing in the *St. Louis Post-Dispatch,* saw this as a "sly maneuver" and a plan that would weaken the power survey. Another friendly interpretation in the *Louisville Courier-Journal* said that Walsh was one who "has earned the implicit confidence of the American people." His probe would be based on facts.[10]

A major reason for opposition to the Federal Trade Commission was that President Coolidge had appointed William Humphrey as chairman of the agency and it was considered to be probusiness in outlook. At the same time, Walsh was attacked and defended as one who might lead in the probe. Senator William Cabell Bruce of Maryland went so far as to accuse the Montanan of loving to investigate, of being "like a tiger who tastes human blood and then becomes a man-eater for the rest of his life," while Senators Clarence C. Dill of Washington, Robert Howell of Nebraska, and David Walsh of Massachusetts rose to the defense of their colleague, and Frank Kent of the *Baltimore Sun* stated that utilities interests were making an "almost desperate effort" to keep this inquiry out of the hands of Walsh. The Senate finally voted to turn the investigation over to the Trade Commission.[11]

Surprisingly, by February 1928, as if to prove that it had the capacity to run an effective investigation, the commission began to do just that. During April 1928 it revealed much about utility propaganda in the schools, giving attention to an organization known as the Illinois Committee of Public Utility Information which was engaged in propaganda adverse to public ownership of utilities. Walsh indicated his pleasure at the commission's work and promised "to call the attention of the Senate and the country to similar revelations which are coming out every day." Privately he indicated his belief that the utility associations that had opposed him had won "but a pyrrhic victory in switching the investigation to the Federal Trade Commission."[12]

That Walsh had a continuing interest in the power question is apparent, one indication being an address entitled "Tampering With Education," which he delivered in Bozeman on August 4, 1928, before the Montana Bar Association. It seems probable that he, Senator Norris, and others who called for action on this matter made a lasting contribution that led finally to the Public Utility Holding Company bill of 1935. Walsh wrote in 1932 that he believed his work regarding power and utilities was no less important than his conduct of the Teapot Dome investigation.[13]

26

Prohibition and Politics

Booze" or "No Booze" did not rank in Walsh's mind with the great economic problems of the day or with issues of honesty in government and American adherence to the World Court. Countless matters of governmental policy were to him inherently more important than the liquor question. The Montanan may have been correct theoretically, but he badly underestimated the strength of popular opposition to the Eighteenth Amendment and the Volstead Act. It was ironic that strong feelings about prohibition in the 1920s, pro and con, should have done so much to prevent the Democratic party's rehabilitation nationally, about which Walsh cared greatly, and his personal identification with the dry cause cost him support as a Democratic leader and possible presidential candidate.

How Walsh developed into a prohibitionist is reasonably clear. Early influences in Wisconsin, including those of church and family, led him toward temperance if not total abstinence. Walsh did a little recreational drinking in Wisconsin and in Montana, usually on camping or biking trips with "the fellows." He was especially fond of beer. Gradually his observations convinced him that the saloon, where many became addicted to drink and injured their lives and careers in the process, ought to be outlawed. His letters contain frequent references to hard-drinking friends and acquaintances. C. B. Nolan, later his law partner, was one of them, and another friend according to Walsh had wasted five years of his life in Butte, ending up "a physical and moral wreck." Having a similar abhorrence of such tragedies, Walsh's pastor in Helena, the much admired Bishop John Patrick Carroll, led a fight in the early twentieth century to eliminate the all-night saloon in the state capital. Carroll along with Walsh became a strong prohibitionist.[1]

In 1916 Walsh congratulated a doctor for his educational efforts regarding alcohol and commented: "It is not a little remarkable that the lines along which the campaign for prohibition is carried on have so shifted in recent years. It formerly had an aspect almost exclusively religious. Now-a-days, the basis of the propaganda is distinctly industrial, and sanitary." Notwithstanding some doubts that John Barleycorn should be attacked through national prohibition, Walsh moved in that direction in the early 1900s, along with millions of others.[2]

The Montanan came to believe that prohibition was a logical extension of "progressivism"—trying to improve people's lives through the elimination of a social evil and using government power to do so. Walsh was not alarmed over a loss of personal freedom when that was compared with threats to the family and the loss of control often related to drinking. He accepted as credible the argument that women in the South and the District of Columbia must be protected from black men crazed by drink. This was an idea often repeated. In the 1920s, discussing the subject of cocktail parties in Washington and the insidious influence of alcohol, he urged that young people be warned to abide by "the old rule 'touch not, taste not, handle not.'" Total abstinence was best. The sincerity of Walsh's concerns cannot be doubted, and he practiced what he preached, as he noted: "I got the reputation of being one of the only two 'dry' Senators, that is Senators who live as they vote." Former Senator Henry Hollis, who had moved his law practice to Paris, France, remembered that Walsh did not drink even when he visited wine-imbibing Paris.[3]

In supporting wartime prohibition, the Eighteenth Amendment, and the Volstead Act that followed, Walsh was joining a popular movement that had caused most states to go dry or partially dry by their own action; Montana was one of those states in 1916. The Anti-Saloon League, particularly, became a well-organized and powerful force in public affairs, and politicians in large number joined the parade. Doubtless Walsh was affected by political concerns but, sympathizing as he did, he probably gave more help to the organized prohibitionists than politics alone would have required him to give.[4]

From the days of his youth Walsh felt a kinship with reformers of the Protestant churches whose interest in temperance, prohibition, woman suffrage, honesty in government, and various measures for civic betterment often coincided with his own. Looking back in 1913, Walsh said of one of his Two Rivers teachers, John Faville, who had become a Congregational minister and a social activist, "There is no man with whom I was ever brought in contact for whom I entertain a higher regard than for the Reverend Faville." Religious idealists such as Faville, including a minority of Catholics, worked to make prohibition a success in the 1920s and to further other causes close to Walsh's heart, including world disarmament and U.S. adherence to the World Court.[5]

The theory has been advanced that prohibitionists did not make a strong effort to enforce the Volstead Act, having won a "symbolic" victory in 1919–20. This view will find little corroboration in Senator Walsh's personal attitudes or his correspondence. He was greatly incensed that Andrew Mellon, an owner of distilleries, was placed in charge of the Treasury Department in 1921, and thus of prohibition enforcement, and that the new policy was also the responsibility of the attorney general, Harry Daugherty, of "unsavory memory." Walsh became deeply involved with continuing attempts at enforcement. First, as a member of the Senate Judiciary Committee, he helped write the legislation needed, and periodically thereafter he gave consideration to possible amendments. Second, like other members of Congress, he dealt with complaints by the hundreds from his constituents, often vehemently stated, and he tried to satisfy them concerning the details of administration and enforcement. And finally, Walsh gave his backing to the Coolidge administration in its largely ineffectual efforts.[6]

The Montanan entered a new phase of identification with prohibition in April 1926, as he served on a judiciary subcommittee considering how well the "great experiment" was working. Following a few days of the hearing, Walsh wrote to a friend: "I have had membership on the booze committee wished upon me—an annoying kind of duty—which makes me subject to communications innumerable from people afflicted with the propensity to provide legislators with ideas." One of these was a letter that began: "Until now, I have always looked upon you as a great big brainy man, but when you accepted the appointment on the one sided (4 to 1) committee . . . I lost faith in you."[7]

The five-man subcommittee was chaired by Rice W. Means (Republican, Colorado) with Guy Goff of West Virginia and John W. Harreld of Oklahoma as the other Republican members. Jim Reed of Missouri and Walsh, the two Democrats, found little to agree upon concerning prohibition. Reed was the only wet on the subcommittee. This hearing was arranged to permit an equal amount of testimony first by the "antis" and then by prohibition supporters. Approximately 200 witnesses appeared, giving 1,700 pages of testimony or "evidence."[8]

As the hearing was about to begin, Walsh wrote members of the Catholic hierarchy believed to be favorable to prohibition and tried to induce them to testify. This, he said, would be particularly desirable since "in the light of some recent expressions it would reasonably be inferred otherwise, that the church as a whole is opposed to the policy represented by the 18th amendment." James J. Keane, the Archbishop of Dubuque, Iowa, indicated that he could not come, for reasons unstated, and Cardinal Dougherty of Philadelphia replied similarly: "I do not see my way to accepting your courteous invitation." The posture of the Catholic Church at this time seemed fairly apparent. One Catholic pastor in New York state, an admirer of Walsh's, stated his belief that their coreligionists in the East were "overwhelmingly opposed to prohibition." About this time Walsh received another letter saying, "The sober Catholics are proud of you."[9]

Walsh had predicted that the inquiry would "resolve itself into a general discussion of the merits and demerits of the policy of prohibition." That is about what happened, and few minds were changed as a result. Certainly the Montana senator did not change his opinion that, while prohibition was not working well and in some places came near being a disaster, no one knew how to improve the situation appreciably. As for public opinion, he had figures to show that Congress was dry by a lopsided majority and showed no signs of changing. Observing that great causes always had their "ups and downs," he simply could not believe that prohibition would "ever be repealed."[10]

Evidence of Walsh's support for the president's policy on prohibition enforcement occurred soon after the Senate hearing. Coolidge had issued an executive order giving federal officers the right to empower state officers as prohibition agents, and his authority to do so was immediately defended on the one hand and challenged on the other. The Senate Judiciary Committee, with Walsh and Borah as leading spokesmen, upheld the presidential authority. The Montanan received a letter of commendation from the legal department of the Anti-Saloon League for his "very able exposition of the constitutional and legal principles involved." He had other complimentary letters, including one from a Butte resident that touched him deeply. J. J. Haggerty wrote to express his gratitude and that of his family for all Walsh had done and was "still doing for this United States of America." He thanked Walsh for standing with the president on prohibition enforcement and expressed his hope that *Walsh* would "fill the President's chair at our next election."

Walsh replied: "It is peculiarly gratifying to have the approbation of my home folks, and particularly of the old friends whose supremely generous attitude toward me I cherish. I may often be wrong in the stand I take toward public questions, but most of those who know me well I am sure will give me credit for voting, as a rule, my convictions and pursuing the path that seems to me the duty of an American Senator."[11]

It seems that nothing had prepared the Montana senator for a shocking initiative result in his home state during the November 1926 elections. Voters of Montana had the opportunity to repeal the state's prohibition enforcement laws, with the exception of a provision relating to drinking by minors. They voted decisively in favor of repeal and thus took a position similar to that of the electorate in several other states. Walsh felt rebuffed and refused to speak at a prohibitionist meeting.[12]

So far as national politics was concerned, Walsh did not think the wets in the Democratic party were anywhere close to settling the issue. He knew of no senator who had changed on the amendment since it was adopted, and said that only five members of the Senate in the first session of the Sixty-ninth Congress had been on the wet side. In other words, noise and agitation had failed to convert the members of Congress, whose attitude seemed critical to any hopes of repeal. He said publicly on occasion that, while many in the Democratic party disagreed with him, the nomination of a leader espousing the wet cause in 1928 would be a serious error.[13]

Having this conviction, Walsh pondered the possibilities for 1928 and whether to give encouragement to his supporters. The 1926 congressional elections, in which he took an early and continuing interest, probably fostered his presidential hopes. Walsh sounded out politicians regarding the strongest potential candidates for Congress in several western states and gave advice as best he could, and he was active as a campaigner.[14]

Walsh was often in touch with Senator Claude Swanson of the Democratic Speakers' Bureau, and after an exchange with Bernard Baruch in late October the New Yorker wired Walsh: "Would you object to coming east of Chicago if private car were arranged to insure you greater comfort Stop You are certainly entitled to most comfortable conditions when you speak." Baruch made the assertion in one of his communications that the issue had become "corruption instead of prosperity," hence Walsh's growing importance. Democrats had not lost hope involving an issue that had failed badly just two years before.[15]

One of Walsh's best receptions was in Portland, Oregon, at the Civic Auditorium on October 4. Governor Walter M. Pierce introduced the visitor, saying it was a pleasure to present "the brilliant Senator from Montana, America's outstanding leader for clean, honest, efficient government." As Walsh rose to speak, turning to Governor Pierce and the audience, he said that he was "overwhelmed."

His address ranged widely on issues of the day but was essentially an indictment of the "Old Guard" Coolidge administration, hardly to be mentioned in the same breath with those of authentic leaders of the people such as Jefferson, Lincoln, and Theodore Roosevelt. He showed little charity toward the trust-oriented Coolidge administration as he ran through a recital of its wrongheaded economic policies, emphasizing the damaging effects of the high tariff. He also gave attention to big-spending Republican candidates of recent years such as Truman Newberry of Michigan and Frank L. Smith of Illinois.[16]

Most exciting to Walsh was a trip to California to give several speeches, followed at the campaign's end by a visit with William G. McAdoo. Arriving in San Francisco on October 30, Walsh talked optimistically to the press about Democratic chances for winning control of the Senate. He had come to the state specifically to campaign for John B. Elliott, a McAdoo supporter who was dry and progressive, against the incumbent "standpat" Republican Samuel M. Shortridge. The visiting "celebrity," as Walsh was styled by the *San Francisco Chronicle*, delivered an address at the Scottish Rite Hall that was also carried over the radio. Walsh then proceeded by rail to Los Angeles. On Monday, the day before the election, he gave a luncheon address in Elliott's behalf at a Democratic gathering in the Biltmore Hotel. Walsh was trying, in part, to unite the McAdoo faction and other Democrats by speaking from a progressive perspective and by attacking Coolidge Republicanism. He suggested, also, that the GOP's vaunted prosperity was a "snare and delusion."[17]

Hampered by party divisions, Elliott did not win, but nationally the Democrats vindicated Walsh's confidence, coming within one seat of gaining control in the Senate. This was a very encouraging election, both for the Democrats and progressive Republicans in the western states. Democrats gained notably in urban areas, as reflected in a twelve-member increase in the House of Representatives. In Massachusetts, former Governor and Senator David I. Walsh won Henry Cabot Lodge's old seat, while Robert Wagner in New York defeated James W. Wadsworth Jr., a conservative Republican. The urban trend might or might not be helpful to the ambitions of Senator Walsh, whose most loyal following seemed to be located in western and southern states, where Democrats also gained, including the Senate seats won by Congressmen Alben Barkley of Kentucky and Carl Hayden of Arizona.[18]

Soon after the election Walsh spent three days in Los Angeles as the houseguest of William G. McAdoo, reporting later that McAdoo had "every desire to block the Smith candidacy [in 1928] if he can." Walsh wanted to block it, too, by his own alternative candidacy, although he knew that his chances were not very good.[19]

Privately Walsh had doubts about McAdoo's judgment and leadership that dated back to the Teapot Dome revelations of 1924. McAdoo's association with Doheny in the postwar years had hurt the Democrats badly and, somehow, he never was able to admit he had done anything wrong. Walsh believed, nevertheless, that the Californian was a progressive on the economic issues and a right-thinking man with respect to prohibition enforcement.[20]

The McAdoo association had an effect, ultimately, upon Walsh's decision to enter the presidential race in 1927–28. Ever since the Teapot Dome investigation there were friends and admirers who by word and action encouraged him to run. Little attention was given at that time to his quietly held prohibitionist views. In early June 1925, for example, Montana friends held a testimonial dinner for him in Helena, with Governor Erickson serving as master of ceremonies and toastmaster. The *Missoulian* saw this statewide "complimentary dinner" as an effort to launch Walsh's presidential bid for 1928. The *Butte Miner* agreed, running a headline on page one: "WALSH ACCLAIMED OF PRESIDENTIAL SIZE." The guest of honor was pleased at the affair. He began his speech: "Since, like Byron, I woke up one morning and found myself famous—the route in my case via the Teapot Dome, I have been the recipient of attention from various communities, . . . of the most flattering kind." But nothing had stirred him as did this occasion, with most of those present knowing him well, the "good and the bad that is in me—the strength and the weakness."[21]

From 1924 to the fall of 1927 Walsh was frequently reminded of his presidential stature and assured of support when he decided to seek a higher office. Writing to a friend in Helena he told of his "delightful trip to Texarkana" to deliver an address and how he had been compelled to decline many other invitations, "the last today to a deputation of members of the House from Ohio who want me to speak at their state convention insisting that my kind of democracy is popular in that state." In closing Walsh wondered about Montana: How was his kind of democracy out there?[22]

The senator had his answer a few months later, after the November elections. Montana's Democrats were divided, as they were in much of the nation, and a strong trend toward wets of the party was apparent. Winning the nomination would be difficult indeed for Walsh, not to mention the problems in a fall campaign.

Nevertheless, he inched his way toward a decision to run. Most of the influences can be summarized briefly. As noted before, Walsh was a fighter who often disdained the odds. He believed that ever since the Smith-McAdoo imbroglio of 1924, and in the absence of "a Jefferson," he was a logical candidate. In all probability, McAdoo would not run, while Smith was hurt by his

Tammany connections, his overt wetness, and his Catholicism. Despite Smith's excellent record as governor and his popularity in certain parts of Montana, such as Butte, it was hard to believe he could win on a presidential ticket. Walsh's vanity was obviously involved. He resented what he saw as the dogmatism of wet forces and their downplaying of economic and good government issues that to Walsh were so important. The Montanan competed with Smith as a coreligionist who believed he could better represent the West and South and perhaps the entire nation than could the New Yorker.[23]

Not so apparent was another factor in Walsh's thinking. By campaigning for president he could broaden his plea for idealism in government and possibly give encouragement to the disillusioned ones in both political parties. He himself was deeply discouraged and said repeatedly that his feelings verged on despair over corruption in government, the growth of monopoly, and tariff raids on the treasury. To one correspondent he wrote: "I can recall no period during my lifetime, nor has my reading acquainted me with any period in our history, when there was such widespread and deplorable indifference to sound government." This was the period in which Walsh urged the writing of articles by friends and associates, including Congressman Cordell Hull and President Glenn Frank of the University of Wisconsin, to try to "overcome the sordid tendencies so much in evidence."[24]

Walsh would not have tried for the nomination if forced to compete with McAdoo. The latter opened the way in September 1927 by announcing that he had no intention to run in 1928—news that may have been communicated privately to Walsh before then. In any event, in October 1927, for the first time, the Montanan showed a genuine interest in running and toured several states where friends feted him and gave assurances of support. He understood, however, that Governor Smith was leading as a presidential aspirant and that others, too, such as his colleague Jim Reed of Missouri, might beat him in a campaign. Holding little hope that he could win, the Montanan decided to sally forth, campaigning out of a sense of duty and a certain "plaguey ambition" that had to be appeased.[25]

27

The Continental Trading Company Limited
and Senate Revelations of 1928

In January 1928 Walsh again became "the Teapot Dome investigator," acting as prosecutor during hearings conducted by the Senate Public Lands Committee. This was a resumption of the hearings suspended in May 1924, when Harry F. Sinclair refused to give testimony relating to his lease of Teapot Dome, leaving much unclear about his payments to Interior Secretary Albert B. Fall.

The new inquiry became possible after the special prosecutors, Owen Roberts and Atlee Pomerene, uncovered evidence concerning the Continental Trading Company Limited of Canada, a dummy corporation of which Sinclair was one beneficiary. Specifically they found that $230,500 in Liberty bonds had been deposited to the account of Secretary Fall in Pueblo, Colorado, and they traced these bonds back to the Continental Company. Over a period of months, while preparing cases against Fall and Sinclair, the prosecutors examined this escapade further. The company was organized in November 1921, and contracted immediately to buy 33,000,000 barrels of oil at $1.50 a barrel from Colonel A. E. Humphreys of Denver. At the same time a small group of the oilmen involved, including Sinclair, planned a resale to their own companies at 25 cents above the purchase price, thus permitting a profit running into the millions. It was learned that some $3,000,000 in illicit gains were converted into 3½ percent Liberty bonds of the United States. To trace the bonds, however, or pinpoint their location was difficult. A possibility existed that they were used entirely as a slush fund for corrupt purposes and that the Republican party had become involved.[1]

By the fall of 1927, "alert representatives" of the *St. Louis Post-Dispatch*, wanting to know what had happened to the Continental Company bonds, urged Senator Walsh to inaugurate an investigation. He, too, wanted the probe and believed it justifiable but "for reasons of a personal nature" did not want to introduce the resolution, suggesting rather that Senator Norris be invited to do so. Walsh probably hesitated because of attacks made on him to the effect that he just loved to investigate. The Montanan promised that if this investigation were ordered he would interest himself in it and "prosecute it with such vigor" as he could command. Norris's resolution passed in early January 1928 without a dissenting vote, and soon the Public Lands Committee was at work, looking into "the transactions and activities of the said fraudulent [Continental] corporation" and its buying and dealing in Liberty bonds of the United States, in some connection to the leasing of the naval petroleum reserves six years earlier.[2]

From January to May the committee met thirty-two times and interviewed about 150 witnesses, some of whom were recalled for additional testimony. Gerald P. Nye (Republican, North Dakota) served as chairman. All of the fifteen members, except two, came from western states. Among the more active in interrogating witness were Chairman Nye, Key Pittman (Democrat, Nevada), Sam G. Bratton (Democrat, New Mexico), and Bronson Cutting (Republican, New Mexico). Walsh, however, was the acknowledged leader in the public hearings and also in making the principal decisions, such as those on evidence to follow and witnesses to subpoena. He functioned much as he had in 1923–24 and exercised greater authority because of his knowledgeability and the committee's relatively inexperienced members. One early decision was to have a conference of the committee members with Pomerene and Roberts, the special counsel.[3]

The probe can be divided into several phases, all of which were important to the committee. One aspect concerned those associated with the Continental Company who left the United States and had to be investigated indirectly. H. S. Osler, a Toronto attorney and president of the Continental Company, was one of three in this category. Apparently he was paid well in fees for his part in arranging the lucrative oil deal of 1921. Harry M. Blackmer, president of the Midwest Refining Company, worked mightily to accomplish the sale, claimed his share of the profits, and fled to France when the deal was uncovered in 1924. James O'Neil, president of the Prairie Oil & Gas Company, also shared in the profits and sojourned in Europe to escape interrogation or prosecution. Seeking assistance from the State Department, Walsh tried to get these men extradited, but never succeeded.[4]

Another of the adventurers, Colonel Robert W. Stewart, chairman of the board of the Standard Oil Company of Indiana, threatened to remain in Cuba and Mexico rather than return to testify, but he changed his mind under pressure from Walsh and the committee. They also sought assistance from John D. Rockefeller Jr., a leader of the Standard Oil group who, it was believed, would try to bolster the reputation of the petroleum industry by exerting his influence on Stewart. Harry Sinclair, the fourth of the oilmen, remained in the United States at this time but did not testify as the hearings opened because he was under indictment and about to come to trial. Absent though Sinclair was until the end of the hearing, his largesse in the matter of Liberty bonds occupied much of the committee's time.[5]

Walsh opened the way for important testimony regarding Sinclair by sponsoring legislation that guaranteed immunity to a witness. Thus the first person to testify was M. T. Everhart, a rancher from Pueblo, Colorado, and son-in-law of former Secretary Fall. Everhart had refused to answer questions in 1924 and in the civil and criminal suits as well. Coming before the committee now on a subpoena and with immunity Everhart proved cooperative.[6]

Suddenly the hearing was on page one. The *New York Times* ran a long article describing the committee's setting and procedure and Everhart's testimony. The room in the Senate office building, wrote the reporter, was "the same one in which Senator Walsh labored so long in the effort to get at the facts attending the leasing of the Elk Hills and Teapot Dome oil reservations to Doheny and Sinclair interests." But the committee was not the same, except for Walsh and three additional "veterans of the old investigation," all Democrats: John B. Kendrick of Wyoming, Henry F. Ashurst of Arizona, and Key Pittman of Nevada.

Senator Nye administered the oath to Everhart in the "crowded" room, after which "Walsh took command." With surprising rapidity, he and the committee members were able to establish that Harry Sinclair was the source of Liberty bonds previously traced to Secretary Fall, in the amount of $233,000. Everhart had served as messenger, picking up the bonds in Washington and New York, from Sinclair, and sending them west to his father-in-law's account. He had done so without personal knowledge of the Continental Trading Company and apparently in the belief that Sinclair was buying an interest in the Fall ranch in Three Rivers, New Mexico. His testimony was precise and highly useful.

It was possible now to draw some firm conclusions about the money Fall had received. Sinclair made two contributions to Fall of $36,000 and $35,000 as well as the larger amount, thus producing a total of $304,000. If E. L. Doheny's "loans" were added in, Fall had garnered a grand total of more than $400,000 from the two oilmen during the period of 1922 in which he granted them leases of naval reserves at Teapot Dome and Elk Hills.[7]

Walsh at his Senate office desk. (Photographer: Underwood & Underwood, Washington, D.C. Walsh-Gudger Collection, Illinois Historical Survey, University of Illinois at Urbana-Champaign)

A number of witnesses appeared before the committee and performed generally in a manner protective of their interests. Colonel Stewart and Sinclair were evasive and unrepentant and others, too, proved difficult. A good example was A. L. Carlson, secretary and treasurer of the Sinclair Crude Oil Purchasing Company of Tulsa, Oklahoma. Carlson knew about the 25 cent "differential"; that is, that his company paid 25 cents more to purchase millions of barrels of oil than did the Continental Trading Company, according to the arrangement of November 17, 1921. His board of directors had sanctioned this purchase at $1.75 a barrel, he said; there was nothing wrong with that. Walsh and Carlson had sharp exchanges, as when Walsh said, "Are you merely dummy directors, Mr. Carlson, or are you supposed to consider seriously these business propositions?"

When Carlson indicated some doubt as to Walsh's facts, the senator responded, "the contract is here, is it not?" Carlson then tried to make the excuse that "Mr. Sinclair and Mr. Stewart signed for the directors."[8]

Colonel Robert Stewart's testimony, beginning in early February, was of interest to the committee and to the public. He was the only oilman of the four leading conspirators to testify prior to Sinclair's May appearance. Also, he presided over the giant Standard Oil Company of Indiana, in which John D. Rockefeller Jr. had a very substantial interest through its identification with the family name and the ownership of stock.

Stewart was not a cooperative witness. He claimed that because he might have to appear in the Sinclair criminal trial he should not be interrogated on related matters before the Senate committee. When this excuse disappeared as Sinclair's trial ended with an acquittal, Stewart was only slightly more cooperative. Essentially he denied that he had knowledge of the Continental Trading Company and its activities, even though he participated in the meetings in New York which led to the Continental's purchase of oil and the resale to Standard of Indiana and other companies, from which the profits ran into millions. Stewart insisted that he never "made a dollar" out of the transactions. He had acted responsibly on behalf of his company and made the best deal he could make.[9]

Two days later Stewart was arrested by the Senate for his refusal "to answer certain questions relative and pertinent" to the inquiry, as a result of a resolution introduced by Senator Walsh and approved without objection. A legal battle ensued, with Stewart applying for and receiving a writ of habeas corpus, thus staying out of jail. Walsh declared on the Senate floor: "I think that the time has come when the dignity of the Senate of the United States ought to be recognized and it ought to be appreciated that it is no trifling affair to defy its authority, however high the recusant witness may stand."[10]

Another means of exerting pressure upon Stewart was to bring John D. Rockefeller Jr. before the investigating committee. This event made front page news, excited the public, and provided some pertinent information. In response to a question from Senator Walsh, Rockefeller said that he personally owned 402,280 shares of stock in the Standard Oil Company of Indiana, while the Rockefeller Foundation held 460,760 shares; and other substantial holdings were in the name of his two sisters and the University of Chicago. But he emphasized that even if he owned 100 shares his sense of obligation would be "exactly the same"—to try and help concerning this "unfortunate situation, this national scandal which this committee is seeking to uncover." In practical terms, Rockefeller appeared unable to do very much since he expressed repeatedly his "confidence in the integrity of Colonel Stewart" as well as a reluctance to try and give advice to the colonel. He admitted his disappointment in Stewart's failure to answer questions put to him by the committee. Chairman Nye thanked Rockefeller for the "measure of cooperation" that had come from him "in this entire controversy."[11]

Some two weeks later the *Baltimore Sun* announced that Colonel Stewart, who had "defied" the Senate, was "Reelected by Standard Oil"; elected again, that is, as chairman of the board of his company. Chairman Nye now showed unhappiness with Rockefeller, as did Senator Walsh, who wrote that he had failed miserably to "meet the standard of business of which he preaches."[12]

Feeling some pressure, perhaps including that of Rockefeller, Colonel Stewart decided to give additional testimony before the committee. He admitted to Senator Walsh almost immediately that he knew of the disposition of $759,500 in Liberty bonds that had been passed on to him by Osler of the Continental Company. But he maintained that the bonds were a surprise to him, for he never had expected "any of these profits," and that he did not really know their source. He claimed the bonds were now being held in trust for his company. Gradually, however, in the course of a day's testimony on April 24, the committee members wrung information out of the colonel until there was little doubt of what had happened. Senators Walsh, Bratton, Cutting, Wagner (Democrat, New York), and Nye all had a turn at the stubborn and sometimes irascible oilman. Walsh raised questions about Stewart's answers past and present and hinted at the later charges of perjury. Chairman Nye was perhaps most effective of all in the final interrogation, pinning Stewart down on his knowledge of Osler, the Continental contract, and other details, and chiding him on his continuing effort to withhold information. This last session with Stewart was a success for the committee and, according to one description, ended in a rout.[13]

In a number of letters Walsh showed his indignation over Stewart's lack of integrity as a business leader and his failure to speak truthfully to the committee. To an editorial writer of the *Boston Herald,* he said, "in my judgment no other theory is tenable than that he perjured himself like a gentleman when he first testified before the Committee. . . . It is absurd for any one to think that he participated in the [New York] meetings of November 16 and 17, 1921, without knowing that he . . . was to share in the loot." Walsh kept hoping some stockholder of Indiana Standard would sue for restitution of the funds that had been lost through the Continental transaction.[14]

Another phase of committee action was the continuing attempt to run down the 3½ percent Liberty bonds, wherever they might be located, and to identify them by number, place of purchase, and person to whom they were delivered. Questioning bankers, bond dealers, U.S. Treasury Department officials, and others, Walsh and the committee compiled a composite list of bonds that covered sixty-four pages of the hearings, along with a wealth of supporting material. The senators and their staff had a stunning success in this endeavor. There could be no doubt that the Liberty bonds were delivered to Blackmer, O'Neil, Stewart, and Sinclair, although the use they made of them was difficult to determine.[15]

With the appearance of Will H. Hays before the committee on March 1, the hearings assumed a new political emphasis. Hays, an attorney from Sullivan, Indiana, was a former chairman of the Republican National Committee and postmaster general under President Harding until he left that position to go into the movie industry. Hays's law firm had often represented the interests of Harry Sinclair, and the two men were longtime friends. Hays and Walsh, on the other hand, were political adversaries. They had faced each other in the first Teapot Dome investigation when Hays, as former national chairman of the GOP, testified on Sinclair's financial contributions to the party and claimed he had little specific knowledge of the subject.[16]

News had been spreading that Continental bonds had come into the possession of Hays or other Republican party leaders. The Indiana man apparently decided that he had better appear before the committee and set the record straight, as far as that was possible. In a prepared statement Hays admitted he had received from Sinclair, in 1923, a total of $260,000 in government bonds, and he acknowledged that they might be Liberty bonds of the Continental Company. He stated he had never heard of the Continental bonds until the committee made its disclosures. The money he had received from Sinclair was a legitimate gift of $75,000, he said, along with other bonds intended as a loan, all for the purpose of reducing the debt incurred by Republicans in the campaign of 1920. Soon he admitted that the gift mentioned was actually $160,000.[17]

Hays went on to tell a confusing story of how he had employed the bonds for debt reduction. In essence he passed them around among prominent Republicans with the idea that they would use them quietly and efficiently to raise money. They might contribute to the party an amount equal in value to the bonds received and eventually return the bonds, as well; or they could substitute other bonds and securities of like amount. Some of the Liberty bonds, however, were not returned, at least not to Hays. How he delivered them, what instructions he gave in making delivery, and many other details of the deficit campaign had slipped from Hays's memory, and he did not possess correspondence or records to help on the subject.[18]

In conducting his interrogation, "in the fiery way for which he is famous," Walsh first tried to find out just what it was that Hays had done with the Sinclair bonds; but after hours of cross examination he and his fellow committee members still were not entirely sure. Concerning the delivery of $60,000 to Fred W. Upham of Chicago, Walsh suggested the following: "didn't Mr. Upham take those bonds and distribute them around to various people in the city of Chicago, in amounts from $1,000 to $10,000, and did not those people take those bonds out into the market and sell them . . . , and then pretend to make contributions to the Republican campaign fund?"

"Certainly not to my knowledge," Hays replied.

An editorial writer for the *New York Times* had an explanation similar to Walsh's: "It was simply a way of doctoring the party accounts."[19]

Walsh challenged Hays on discrepancies between his testimony in 1924 and 1928. In the earlier appearance Hays had placed Harry Sinclair's contribution to the Republican party at a mere $75,000 and failed to mention the receipt of any bonds. "Well, I did not volunteer about these Government bonds," Hays said. "I was not asked about that."

"You were asked about contributions made by Sinclair," Walsh replied. Hays always had an answer and was difficult to pin down, but his evasions, half-truths, and lies were not difficult to discern.[20]

After Hays had testified on March 1, 1928, the committee made a discovery that promised "further sensation." According to a memorandum made available to the committee, Secretary of the Treasury Andrew Mellon was a possible recipient of Sinclair Liberty bonds, via Hays, and so was Chairman of the

Republican National Committee William Butler. Arrangements were made for both to appear before the committee to tell what they knew. Neither had accepted the bonds, it was learned, although Hays did offer them. Mellon explained that he preferred simply to make a contribution of his own to help on the party deficit and had done so, to the amount of $50,000. He also had suggested to Hays that the bonds should be sold and the receipts used for the deficit campaign. In Walsh's view, expressed during the testimony, Mellon had behaved "altogether credibly" in this matter, and Walsh thanked him as he prepared to leave the stand.[21]

The *Baltimore Sun*, a strong critic of Mellon and the Republicans, believed Walsh had gone too far in praising the secretary. In this friendly disagreement, the *Sun* editor apparently had the last word and the best of the argument. He mentioned Walsh's service to the country in this affair and went on to say: "I think the only thing in our minds was that in your desire to credit Mr. Mellon with having done the decent thing in refusing to take Hays' bonds, you allowed your generosity and kindliness to give color to your words, which gave Mr. Mellon's defenders an opportunity to use you unfairly."[22]

Certainly, in Walsh's view, Mellon was still culpable. The latter did not have to wait until March 1928 to tell the committee about suspicious circumstances involving Sinclair, of which he had knowledge, dating from December 1923. The *New York Times* in an editorial decided that Mellon may have been a "fine example of fidelity to party" but not of faithfulness to the "larger interests of the country," and thus it took a position similar to Walsh's.[23]

Will Hays returned to give further testimony and Walsh treated him about as brusquely, and sarcastically, as he ever treated anyone. He asked, early on, "Do you care to say anything, Mr. Hays, as to why you did not tell the committee about these transactions [with Mellon and Butler] when you were last on the stand?" Hays replied: "Because in my opinion they were entirely irrelevant," that is, neither Mellon or Butler had taken the bonds. Following a little more discussion on this point, Walsh suddenly asked: "If you had attempted to bribe a public official with the bonds, and he had rejected your offer, you would not have considered that relevant either, would you?"[24]

Walsh pressed the Indiana man, as he had before, on the uses he had made of the Sinclair bonds, which no one on the committee fully comprehended. Once Walsh exclaimed, "Will you just explain that thing to us, so that the ordinary mind can grasp it?" He questioned Hays insistently about the contradictions between his testimony of 1924 and 1928, and strongly implied that he had lied. One of the points Walsh had raised with Mellon he also brought to Hays's attention—how the "prima facie" case of bribery in November and

December 1923, made by the committee against Secretary Fall, synchronized with Sinclair's delivery of Liberty bonds to Hays, for the benefit of the Republican National Committee. How did Hays associate these two events? he asked. Walsh noted that if it had become public knowledge at the time that Sinclair was delivering $260,000 in Liberty bonds to the Republican party, after having connived with Secretary Fall to get his Teapot Dome lease, the news would have been sensational.[25]

Political controversies were predictable as a byproduct of the hearings, especially after Hays and Mellon had testified and involved the Republican party to an extent only suspected before. Much of the initial reaction, however, was personal rather than partisan. Republican members of the investigating committee were remarkably supportive of Walsh in his endeavors. There was no effort to defend the Continental Trading Company deal, the Sinclair slush fund, and the devious uses that Hays had made of the Liberty bonds. Senator Norris, who was not a member of the committee but had an intense interest in its work, suggested that Secretary Mellon should leave the cabinet. Senator Borah declared in a speech that all Republicans should feel a sense of "humiliation" over the Sinclair gifts and loans and related activities of Will Hays; he therefore started a fund with which to try and repay Sinclair. While some called his plan foolish or misguided, there was widespread encouragement and financial support, including a contribution from Senators Walsh and Cutting of the committee. Senator Arthur Capper of Kansas, meanwhile, made front page news with a cry for the Republican party to purge itself. The Teapot Dome scandal, he said, was a "slimy, odorous" mess and the worst scandal in history. Many idealists among the Republicans found the party entanglement with Sinclair and the burgeoning oil scandals a shameful matter, for which they could not evade responsibility.[26]

A counterattack by loyalist Republicans was inevitable; even Senator Nye defended his party. William V. Hodges of Denver, Treasurer of the Republican National Committee, declared that the Republican house was "clean," in spite of Senator Capper's lament—and that there was "no more work for the cleaners." Other Republicans said, in effect, that their party was not without sin but neither was the Democratic party. Allegedly, the Democratic National Committee had taken Sinclair money, and Governor Alfred E. Smith, leading Democratic contender for the presidential nomination, was indebted to Sinclair and had placed him on the New York state racing commission. Senator Walsh, it was said, as another Democratic contender for the nomination, ought to have his record scrutinized. Leading the attack in the Senate was Arthur R. Robinson of Indiana, who hurled accusations at Smith

and also delivered a running critique of Walsh and the Democrats with respect to the origins of the Teapot Dome Scandal.[27]

Robinson made his charges on the floor of the Senate during late March
and early April, as the hearings continued. What he said was, in Walsh's view,
mostly "old stuff," sounding like the Republican campaign speeches of 1924
and the minority report of the Public Lands Committee, written by Seldon
Spencer. These arguments, however, had to be dealt with seriously, for they
had helped to nullify the Democrats' clean government issue in 1924 and
threatened to do the same in 1928, despite the new revelations concerning the
Continental Company. Most important to Walsh was the fact that he would
not let someone "snatch away" from him "the gratitude of the American people," which he believed he had earned by his work as prosecutor.[28]

Often lacking in knowledge or solid evidence, Robinson did not hesitate
to proceed by inference and innuendo; he would, he said, let the people judge
for themselves. The Democrats, he charged, had tried to inaugurate, as early
as 1913, an iniquitous oil leasing policy which led to many scandals, and he
questioned the judgment and the integrity of Franklin K. Lane, Walsh, and
other leaders of the Wilson administration. Robinson had a problem, however: he faced the most knowledgeable man in the country on the subject
under discussion, and Senator Walsh's credibility had never been higher. As
this debate went on Walsh was sometimes mild-mannered, sometimes caustic, and not infrequently was boldly assertive in his viewpoint. Colleagues on
both sides of the aisle gave him support, although usually they were Democrats.[29]

When Senator Robinson expatiated on his view that Democrats had associated with oilmen and profited from the relationship, Walsh replied that, yes,
it was true that Democrats had worked for E. L. Doheny after they left office.
But had they given favors to Doheny while still in official positions? And had
they taken any money? Of course, they had not. Robinson tried to argue that
Walsh himself, during debates on the general minerals leasing bill, had depended on Doheny as an unbiased expert and that this kind of information
ought to come out now, since Walsh was a presidential contender. To this
Walsh responded that in 1919 he had indeed believed Doheny to be a disinterested person and had cited his opinion on the question of drainage from
the California petroleum reserves. He went on: "I want to call attention to
the fact that what the Senator is endeavoring to convey, if I am not in error,
is that I relied upon the judgment of Mr. Doheny concerning the wisdom of
that legislation. That is not true."[30]

On April 5 Walsh delivered a comprehensive speech intended to put to rest Senator Robinson's various charges and "misrepresentations of fact." He was perfectly willing, however, to be interrupted by Robinson or other colleagues and to engage in give and take. Walsh started by paying tribute to Governor Smith of New York and noting that the "heinous offense" he had supposedly committed was that of appointing Sinclair to the Racing Commission of New York or of letting him continue in that position. Walsh went on: "Just exactly what virtue or what lack of virtue is required in a racing commissioner I am not advised." He thought this whole thing was "piffle."[31]

Walsh went on to dismember much of Robinson's argument, showing the employment of half-truth and incomplete evidence in many instances. This involved an intricate review of the history of the oil legislation, and Walsh's role therein, which Robinson had implied was part of a Democratic conspiracy. As to Robinson's attacks on him, Walsh noted that by his labors in the Teapot Dome investigation he had helped to restore the naval petroleum reserves to government control and to save the nation an estimated one billion dollars in property. Other senators occasionally interrupted to add to Walsh's arguments or compliment him for his services. The Montanan finally concluded: "I know of no protection that anyone has against aspersions, so freely indulged in by the Senator from Indiana in his various addresses upon this subject, except in the self-respect and gentlemanly instincts of Members who speak on this floor under the privilege of the Constitution to be exempt from being called to answer in any other place for what they say here." And he referred to "indisputable facts disclosed in the [oil] investigation."[32]

The Senate hearings, which had continued during the political debates on the floor, finally came to an end with the testimony of Harry Sinclair on May 1 and May 2. Sinclair was perhaps jauntier than usual. About a week earlier, in the Supreme Court of the District of Columbia, he had gained an acquittal on the charge of conspiracy in obtaining his 1922 Teapot Dome lease, and thus improved his legal position somewhat. At this time, however, he was under two jail sentences, one of three months for contempt of the Senate, and another of six months for having the jury shadowed in his conspiracy trial. When Walsh asked him why he had given the Republican party so much money, about three times what Andrew Mellon gave, Sinclair replied: "I can only answer your question by saying that Mr. Mellon was much more sensible than I was." When Senator Cutting tried to question him about the Continental Trading Company, Sinclair responded: "I can only give you what I think. . . . I will agree with you, if you wish me to."[33]

Sinclair's answers were so loaded with memory lapses, denials, evasions, and outright lies that one wonders at times why the senators continued to talk or fence with him. Hearing his version of events seemed necessary, however, and often it was revealing in the context of previous testimony and the accumulated evidence. He did admit that he had received $757,000, a one-fourth share of the Liberty bonds, though not really for himself. He also corroborated Will Hays's story regarding gifts and loans to the Republican party. Generally Sinclair followed the pattern of other principals who tried to establish, at least belatedly, that they had never intended to gain personal advantage but had been acting for the benefit of their own companies. But Walsh emphasized in his "Report" that these men were "conspirators" and "freebooters" who would never have used the Continental Company device as they did, taking the risks they took, if their purposes had been legitimate.[34]

At the conclusion of the hearings, the committee members were in sufficiently close agreement that Walsh wrote a report "for the committee." His report was a summary of the committee's probe in connection with the "mysterious Continental Trading Co." but it related their work to earlier investigations, to findings of the special prosecutors, and to court decisions. He could not resist a reference to "the associates of [Harry] Daugherty caught red-handed in the most stupendous piece of thievery known to our annals or, perhaps, to those of any other country." He reminded his readers that the Supreme Court had found A. B. Fall to be a "faithless public officer." So far as the Continental Company was concerned, Walsh expressed his belief that its bonds were the "ill-gotten gains of a contemptible private steal" and that only in the case of Harry Sinclair had they been used as a slush fund. Because many of Sinclair's bonds went to Will Hays and through him to others in the Republican party, at the very time in which the Teapot Dome lease was being exposed, Walsh dared to speculate about the connection of events: "This synchrony suggests at once that the extraordinary sum yielded up at that critical time by Sinclair was not altogether voluntarily donated, . . . In the predicament in which he found himself at that juncture he stood in dire need of friends at court."[35]

Both Walsh and Nye believed their investigation had been successful. Walsh cited, for example, the $2,000,000 that the government had now recovered in taxes, with more to come, while the expense of the inquiry had been $14,165. So far as national politics was concerned, the election of 1928 revealed in a matter of months that the GOP had been damaged only slightly if at all. Once again Walsh and many Democrats were too hopeful of gains based on charges of corruption.

28

The Campaign of 1928

By October 1927, Walsh was a determined seeker after the presidential nomination. Walsh probably believed as did William E. Dodd of the University of Chicago, Josephus Daniels of North Carolina, and many admirers that he was among the best qualified men in the United States for the office of president. Of immediate concern, however, was the growing influence of Al Smith enthusiasts nationally and in the Democratic National Committee including Montana's own committeeman, Bruce Kremer. Walsh commented that "everyone is entitled to boost for his favorite," but he was sorry to learn that "state pride" was so lacking among some of his erstwhile supporters.[1]

At the Jackson Day Dinner in Washington on January 12, it was obvious that the friends of Governor Smith were gaining strength. Without even attending the affair, Smith exhibited greater popularity than other leaders and presidential hopefuls gathered at the Mayflower Hotel. "Harmony" was the key word of this meeting. McAdoo was included among the speakers, but not Walsh. No one, however, received a finer tribute than did the Montanan in the keynote address delivered by Claude G. Bowers, an editorial writer of the *New York World,* who commented on the "leadership of the brilliant senator from Montana." As Walsh reviewed the affair: "The Jackson Day dinner here was the supreme event of last week, the speech of my friend Claude Bowers . . . the supreme event of the occasion." But the senator knew that words and clapping did not translate into convention delegates.[2]

A subject of engrossing interest to the Jackson Day Democrats was Governor Smith's growing appeal. One theory reported in the *New York Times* went this way: it was better to lose the election with Smith than to deny him the nomination. By taking this course, Democrats could hold the "Roman Catholic vote which is essential to Democratic success and harmony" in such states as New York, New Jersey, Massachusetts, Rhode Island, and Illinois.[3]

The phenomenon of a dry western Catholic opposing a wet eastern Catholic stirred interest in the spring of 1928. Many writers (especially of the McAdoo connection) were suspicious of Walsh's motives and even questioned his ability to do more than "run down thieves," as stated in a *New York Times* editorial. There could be no doubt that his state and his age (69) were handicaps. On the other hand, quite a number, including L. C. Speers in a feature article for the *Times,* attested to the Montanan's character and ability and found little to criticize. Henry Cabot Lodge Jr., writing for the *New York Tribune,* referred to Walsh as a Democrat of "majestic bearing" and "the grand inquisitor of the Senate." Charles Merz did a "portrait" for the *Independent* that was highly complimentary. Despite the scalps he had collected, this senator was respected as a fair-minded man, and he was "the outstanding leader of his party in the capital." Merz believed that Walsh, who was not a radical on economic matters, had mostly insisted "that the game be played according to the letter and spirit of its rules."

A writer for *Christian Century* turned directly to the subject of Walsh's religion, saying he was the best possible Democratic nominee and would "lay the spectre of religious bigotry in his party." When the Montanan went to Boston in mid-April for two speeches that did not seem to be campaign-related, he received much attention and favorable comment.

A good analysis came from Louis M. Lyons, in the *Boston Globe.* After meeting Walsh's daughter in Boston, Lyons was able to arrange an interview with the senator at the Newport Naval Station, where he was visiting Mrs. Gudger and her family. Lyons saw the "grim prosecutor" transformed into a "benign 'Baba'" entertaining chubby grandchildren. His "mildness" was surprising. In the talk that followed Lyons succeeded in describing major differences between Walsh and Governor Smith. He said that the senator spoke of the rise of reform in the United States, of how Jefferson, Jackson, and Lincoln—men from rural America and the frontier—had been great popular leaders, and how even in the twenties the persistence of this rural idealism could be felt.

Lyons wrote: "I suggest that he distrusts the city fellow. He does not deny it. Like his political patron saint, Jefferson, he seems to distrust the city and the men produced by precinct politics."

In Lyons's view, Al Smith was the product of a new kind of frontier and was trying to bring Americans of the cities to a "full political recognition in the democracy." Lyons wondered how differently things might have looked to Walsh if he had been born under the Brooklyn Bridge. As it was, he could hardly be elected president: "He's too independent."

Walsh's quiet campaign for the presidential nomination, and its early termination, can be briefly described. He and his friends in Montana worked to get an endorsement from the Democratic State Committee and succeeded after a fight. The chairman of the committee, W. W. McDowell of Butte, became Walsh's campaign manager. In March and April 1928, McDowell traveled in the East and West. Denying that the campaign was merely a front for McAdoo, he obtained favorable statements from senators as widely separated as C. C. Dill of Washington and W. N. Ferris of Michigan, and many endorsements. Two days after the Montanan's candidacy became known, Smith barely nosed him out in a South Dakota preference primary.[4]

Walsh tried without success in this period to win the approval of former Senator James D. Phelan of California and allied Democrats now fighting grimly with the McAdoo forces of their state. He was absolutely convinced that Al Smith would be defeated if he became the party candidate, and he did not like what he saw as the bulldozer tactics of Smith adherents. His own chances, he knew, were slight. It was apparent to Walsh as to others that the California primary on May 1, in McAdoo's home state, might be decisive.[5]

The Montanan made statements in private that caused him to sound like a noncandidate, for example: "I am making no effort to become the standard bearer and have little apprehension that the honor and burden will be thrust upon me." That he was a stalking-horse, as charged, is a possibility, although the likelihood is that he had consented to a low-key campaign for his own reasons, not those of McAdoo or anyone else.[6]

On May 1 in California Al Smith not only won the election, his vote far exceeded the combined figures for Walsh and Jim Reed. Several days later the Montanan, who had remained in Washington, wrote to Mark Sullivan, the columnist, "Smith is certainly some vote-getter." Walsh announced publicly that he was dropping out of the race, assuming that Democratic voters ardently favored the New York governor and would give him the nomination in Houston.[7]

Withdrawing from the race without recriminations, the Montanan enhanced his reputation. Reactions were almost universally appreciative. The Brooklyn Daily Eagle said, for example: "Senator Walsh has accurately foretold the outcome of the Houston convention and has himself made that outcome inevitable."[8]

Having made his try for the nomination, Walsh acted quickly to get his "presidential" experience behind him. He told Senator Phelan that he was "enjoying a sense of relief at being out of the contest," and later wrote that any presidential ambitions he may have harbored had "been buried deeper than plummet ever sounded."[9]

Economic differences of 1928 may have counted more with Walsh than personalities and political parties. During the 1920s he became the leading congressional advocate of the St. Lawrence Seaway, a project he deemed of great importance to struggling farmers of Montana and the Northwest who would benefit from a reduction in shipping costs. Of all the states, New York had most lacked enthusiasm for the Seaway, fearing a loss of commerce. Secretary of Commerce Herbert Hoover was a Seaway advocate who might win votes on this issue as the Republican presidential candidate. Walsh cautioned Governor Smith on the political dangers and received a measure of reassurance.[10]

As Walsh watched from the distance in Montana, his friend, Senator Joseph T. Robinson of Arkansas, received the nomination for vice president, thus balancing the Houston ticket with a well-known and respected southern Protestant. The platform also contained a dry plank written by Senator Carter Glass of Virginia. Unfortunately, in the view of many Democrats, Governor Smith unnecessarily antagonized drys by announcing, at the convention's end, that he believed "there should be fundamental changes in the present provisions for national prohibition." Smith also selected John J. Raskob as the national chairman. A Republican recently turned Democrat, Raskob was a crusader against the prohibition experiment and a self styled "capitalist" holding high office in the Du Pont Company and the General Motors Corporation; he was chosen, Walsh said, "from the very heart of Big Business."[11]

Walsh was almost certain, nevertheless, to give his support to the national ticket. A loyal Democrat for fifty years, he would do nothing to keep in power the GOP of Harding, Coolidge, and Hoover. It will be remembered, too, that the Smith Democrats in Montana were organized and enthusiastic, and that Walsh probably thought of his next Senate campaign in 1930.

One aspect of Smith's candidacy almost compelled active support: the fact that both he and Walsh were Catholics and passionately believed in the right of non-Protestant citizens to aspire to the presidency. This right was questioned in many places. Walsh congratulated Smith on his views and, believing the subject not open to debate anyway, refused invitations for public discussion.[12]

Soon Governor Smith invited Walsh to Albany, asking him to come in mid-August, if possible, and to be his guest at the Executive Mansion. Other "dry leaders" were invited during the same week. Following Walsh's visit, the governor's office released a statement by the Montanan making the case for Smith's candidacy on the basis primarily of human qualities and fundamental democracy. Walsh said: "His geniality is irresistible and his intellectual processes refreshingly clear. His quick mastery of problems of State signifies a genius for such." They had not agreed on all issues, and Democrats could not expect such agreement. "The most that can be hoped for is that he shall be with them on fundamentals—that on the whole he shall be found more satisfactory to them than his opponent."[13]

Walsh alluded critically to Republican machines such as those of Vare and Mellon in Pennsylvania and "Big Bill" Thompson in Illinois. It should not be forgotten, he said, that Hoover "sat in the Cabinet with Fall and Daugherty without ever raising his hand to thwart their villainies," and other iniquities "had escaped his notice." Walsh agreed with a comment that if Hoover "didn't know in a general way what was going on, he hasn't sagacity enough to be President of the United States."[14]

Walsh's role in the Smith campaign exemplified the loyal Democrat who saw many things in Smith's career that ought to be lauded and much in the Republican opposition to be censured. At the urging of former Congressman Scott Ferris of Oklahoma, an old friend, Walsh created a document listing ten reasons why he was supporting Smith for president. Ferris was "delighted" with the statement and one can imagine that the Smith managers in New York were pleased too.

The Montanan pointed to how Smith had dared to oppose the "gigantic power combinations," much as Andrew Jackson had fought the Bank of the United States. He noted that Smith had been "repeatedly honored by the electorate," while Hoover had filled his official positions "by grace of the appointive power."[15]

The theme of Republican corruption was one that frequently appeared in Walsh's speeches and in those of Governor Smith as well. At Smith's request, the Montanan sent what he termed "a short story of the oil leases" and another on the Continental Trading Company and its bond deals. Copies of Walsh's speeches on the subject were circulated by the thousands. When the governor came to speak in Helena in late September, and was introduced by Senator Walsh, Smith's remarks prompted a column by Will Rogers:

"'Al' spoke in Montana on oil corruption. That subject can get more applause and less votes from an audience than any subject ever invented during our time. . . ."

"Corruption and golf is two things we'd just as well make up our minds to take up, for they are both going to be with us."[16]

Walsh did not, apparently, make any speech in October or November solely intended to boost Governor Smith; rather he aimed to assist all the Democratic candidates, while chastising the opposition. In passages picked up by the national press he hailed Smith as a second Andrew Jackson, who had struggled against poverty and was a spokesman for the common man—a leader very different from Herbert Hoover with his Hamiltonian approach to government. Walsh was obviously putting the best face on the presidential race from a Democratic standpoint. He also did his best for Wheeler in the senatorial race against Dixon, and for Erickson in the gubernatorial contest.[17]

The most important address of this tour occurred at the Parkway Theater in Butte on Thursday evening, October 25, when Walsh dealt at length with major aspects of the campaign. After referring to the privilege of voting that every citizen ought to exercise, Walsh went on the attack. The Republican party, he said, liked to assume credit for all the blessings of America, as in Hoover's recent acceptance speech in which he mentioned the increase under Harding and Coolidge in the number of children and young people attending schools and colleges. He observed: "The republican party has been accustomed in the past to take credit for good crops and it now broadcasts claims to include the fecundity of our people."[18]

Turning to another Republican boast, that of a "superior patriotism," Walsh said that Charles Curtis, the vice presidential candidate, had remarked that Democrats were "marching to the tune of the 'Sidewalks of New York,'" while the Republicans were marching to the 'Star Spangled Banner.'" This parading of patriotism by anybody, or by any political party, made him sick. Mentioning Albert B. Fall's claims to patriotism in leasing the navy's oil reserves and the support given him by many Republicans, including Charles Curtis, Walsh finished on this point: "We distrust the man who proclaims his honesty, the woman who protests her virtue, and we may justly suspect the political party that boasts its patriotism."

The Montanan spent most of his time discussing Republican corruption that he said had been an issue in every election since Harding came to office, starting with the Newberry scandal of 1922 and continuing with the latest revelations on the Continental Oil Company Limited. He included under this heading the high tariff favoritism and robbery and the GOP's reluctance to do anything to stop the growth of monopoly power. Agricultural policy had been, in his view, almost a total failure, as the GOP was primarily Hamiltonian in viewpoint and "dominated by the industrial east." But he praised the minority of Senate Republicans, the progressives who had voted so frequently with the Democrats.

Herbert Hoover, admittedly, was a man of "intellectual strength" and admirable "personal character." Nevertheless, Walsh said, Hoover's "long residence in London and in the English dependencies naturally inclined him to look favorably upon the British system of government." Furthermore, Hoover had spent his business life "as the representative of associations of capitalists operating the world over under concessions obtained for the exploitation of natural resources"; and his antecedents naturally inclined him to work amicably with men such as Andrew Mellon, "the dominating figure in the great aluminum trust." Walsh could not forgive Hoover for his apparent failure during the last seven years to take any action (public or private) regarding the scandals occurring under Harding and Coolidge or to express any criticism whatever.

Walsh worked into his address words of praise for Al Smith, similar to those expressed earlier. And then he turned to the subject of his Senate colleague, Wheeler, and went beyond a routine endorsement. Wheeler was an independent man, "able and fearless in debate," and "one of the foremost" of the liberal group active on both sides of the aisle in the Senate.

In closing, Walsh talked of Governor Erickson's campaign and the often repeated charge that the governor was a "Company man." Walsh praised Erickson as an honest person of "equable temperament, sound judgment, business capacity, and a matter-of-fact mind" (unlike his opponent, Wellington Rankin, often regarded as eccentric).

The address concluded in a statement that Walsh probably felt compelled to make for Erickson's benefit and to put himself on record: "The governor of Montana should be a man without prejudices either for or against the company or any other interest or individual in it—for the company when it is right and everlastingly against it when it is wrong—with a balanced judgment, enabling him to know when it is right and when it is wrong. Justice to all is what the people of Montana require of their governor. They have had it from Governor Erickson in the past and they will get it unadulterated in the future."[19]

In October Walsh spoke in Utah for his Democratic colleague, William H. King, and after writing eulogistic letters earlier, the Montanan did his best for Senators Kendrick of Wyoming and Dill of Washington. All three prevailed, thus bucking the Republican trend nationally.[20]

The victories of Wheeler and Erickson, together with other scattered successes, gave Walsh his only satisfaction in the national results. Of Hoover's victory he wrote on November 8: "Whatever may have been the merit of my efforts toward the election of Governor Smith, I regret that they were so fruitless." The Montanan and his friends and fellow Democrats were looking mostly to the future—to Walsh's expected bid for another term in 1930 and to the next presidential election. Yet it was difficult not to think briefly of what might have been. If Walsh had run in Smith's place, could he have won at least some of the southern states in which the New Yorker lost? Was it conceivable that he could have been elected?

In looking at Smith's defeat, Walsh told former Senator Hollis in Paris: "I was convinced from the beginning that Smith, laboring under the handicap of being a Catholic, a wet and a Tammany man, never could make the grade." The wets had been too confident of their position, and the result demonstrated that "however the nation drinks it votes dry." Meanwhile, every Democratic senator in the West—Wheeler, Dill, Kendrick, King, Ashurst, and Pittman— had "triumphed." They were all considered to be dry.[21]

Walsh probably agreed with Hollis that no Democrat could have defeated Hoover in 1928. The Montanan showed disillusionment with the voters of 1928, tending to accept the "three 'P's'" explanation of the outcome: It was the result of "'Prejudice,' 'Prosperity,' and 'Prohibition.'" He wrote Hollis: "We are to proceed at once to revise the tariff upward. The utilities pillagers are boasting that the result is a rebuke to those who sought to restrain them."[22]

Immediately after the returns were in, Walsh sent a telegram to Franklin Roosevelt congratulating him on his election as governor of New York. Roosevelt, in turn, writing from Warm Springs, Georgia, thanked "Dear Tom" for his telegram, said he was "anxious" to see him, and solicited his views regarding the recent presidential election. The New Yorker was quickly taking the lead nationally to strengthen party organization. He was buoyantly optimistic, noting "the tremendous increase in the popular vote for the Democratic National Ticket . . . significant of the virility and future success of the Party."[23]

There was no attempt on the Montanan's part to hide his very different point of view. He saw no "silver lining," although this would not affect his "determination" in attacking problems that came before him. He could find "little comfort" in Smith's large vote, for the population had grown and voter turnout was "extraordinarily high." Nothing could be gained, he thought, from neglecting the fact that the election was "a rout." He feared "the defection of thousands of Catholics in the North, the mainstay of the party." They were "convinced that bigotry in its principal stronghold [the South] was the principal cause of his [Smith's] failure." Walsh blamed Smith, too, for running a "near-wet campaign" even though the country was "overwhelmingly dry" and for accepting a tariff platform in Houston that abandoned tariff traditions of the party. Republican leaders now assumed, he said, that the country favored high tariffs. They were calling for raises already and could count on strong support in the farm sections and elsewhere.[24]

Walsh believed that people by the millions, now investing in stocks and bonds, feared Democratic success would threaten their investments. A surge of materialism was to him the general explanation for Republican victories. Always "an optimist" before, Walsh saw "no reason to plod on except that our duty to ourselves, to our party and to the country requires that we do so." To another correspondent who had asked about Democratic prospects, Walsh replied: "I have been too dazed by the returns to give any thought to the future of our party, if it has any."

The Montanan was hopeful in one respect: There might be "some turn in events quite unexpected" that would "overturn a ministry or government," as had happened before. Roosevelt was even more confident on this point: the GOP was "headed for trouble." He also emphasized to Walsh that the Democratic party had "recuperative powers" and would be all right.[25]

Roosevelt proved the better prophet. Soon after their correspondence of November–December 1928, the Great Crash occurred in the stock markets, and Democrats were making gains almost everywhere. Walsh's pessimism disappeared, as he continued with his Senate career while a successful campaign for reelection in 1930 gave him a tremendous boost.

29

A Gratifying Victory in 1930

The election of 1928 had scarcely ended when Senator Walsh and his re-election prospects for 1930 began to draw attention. One faithful supporter, now moved to Los Angeles but assuming Walsh would run again, recalled "You once remarked to me that a Senator never quit—he had to die or be defeated." By June 1929, the senator had "quite determined" to run again, although he asked that the information be kept confidential.[1]

Walsh confidently expected that Governor Erickson and Senator Wheeler would come to his support as he had to them in previous campaigns. He was secure, as well, in the expectation of backing from Democratic leaders such as Jouett Shouse, the national chairman, who assured the Montanan that his reelection was a foremost task of the campaign.[2]

Much of Walsh's campaigning in 1929 and early 1930 (from Washington) was done with the aid of two Helena friends and neighbors, "Lew" Penwell and J. Burke Clements. The latter, while chairman of Montana's Industrial Accident Board, took on the task of circulating publicity materials for the senator. In September 1930 Clements had a different mission, as Walsh sent him to the Northeast for fund-raising purposes, introducing him as "a de-voted friend and neighbor . . . with a deep interest in my re-election."[3]

Penwell had a different function to perform. Walsh's longtime friend and business associate, who often traveled the state, served as the senator's eyes and ears and as a political handyman. He was the key person in Montana in moving gradually toward "a campaign committee or board of strategy."[4]

Looking ahead in 1929 and early 1930, Walsh had a number of concerns about his reelection, one of which mounted in importance—a lack of campaign funds. This problem was rooted in the depressed economy of the times, especially in Montana, making solicitation of contributions in that state more difficult. An associate wrote to the senator describing a trip he had taken by automobile to Los Angeles and aspects of hard times wherever he stopped. He mentioned a drop in the price of copper notably affecting Butte, Anaconda, and Great Falls, and problems for wheat farmers and the producers of wool. No relief was in sight. When Walsh wrote to James W. Gerard in New York City, soliciting funds, he mentioned the "rather desperate state of business in all lines in Montana just now"; local money, he said, would be hard to get, and he personally was limited to a contribution of $1,000. Toward the end of September, Gerard (a former Montanan) gave $1,000.[5]

The Montanan turned to his nephew, John Wattawa, now practicing law in Washington, for assistance in the fund-raising enterprise. Wattawa became an agent, to whom the senator often sent suggestions. They had to function at a minimal level, compared with many campaigns of the day. When one supporter, a Chicagoan, regretfully explained that he could not contribute because of financial problems, Wattawa replied that he understood very well, for his finances also were "at a low ebb."[6]

Walsh worried over a damaging primary fight. The person often mentioned as a possible opponent was Bruce Kremer, the Democratic national committeeman, who had support among wets and conservatives of the party. Writing to James E. Murray of Butte (the future senator), who had assured Walsh of his backing, the latter unburdened himself on this subject. It was not only Bruce Kremer who was a problem but one Paddy Wallace, who had been trying to stir up trouble. Walsh wrote: "Very naturally I should dislike to have Bruce come out for the nomination, . . . Montana is a republican state, and a Democrat who wins must get the solid democratic vote and anywhere from 5,000 to 10,000 republican votes besides."

In this and other letters Walsh talked of Wallace, a "graceless fellow," who had spent time in Washington, D.C., as well as the West, trying "to drum or conjure up something that could be urged against me." He closed: "I never could understand why either he or Red Flag Taylor [a radical of Plentywood, Mont.] should make me the object of their wrath unless, in the intensity of their hatred of Wheeler, they involve me because of the friendship which has subsisted between me and my colleague." As the deadline for filing approached (June 4), neither "Beautiful Bruce" Kremer (known as a dandy) nor any other Democrat was contesting the mat with Walsh.[7]

One other concern was apparent. Walsh feared the possibility of a third party candidate who would take away some of his progressive support in both parties. He wrote to Amos Pinchot in New York City regarding a story from Butte that the League for Independent Political Action, a national organization of which John Dewey was president and Oswald G. Villard a director, was moving to organize in Montana. He asked that Pinchot open the subject with Dewey. Pinchot did as requested, writing both Dewey and Villard, and he sent the reassuring words that Walsh had hoped for.[8]

Some three months later Walsh still showed concern over candidates of the Socialist party. He wrote to Wade Parks, a lawyer of Plains (in a valley north of Missoula) whom he considered a supporter, but who was rumored to have been nominated for Congress on the Socialist ticket. Parks replied that he was not a Socialist and had not consented to his name being used; moreover, while he did not "shout a hallelujah for everything that you or Senator Wheeler have stood for and voted for," he was proud of Montana's senators.[9]

The Republican choice to oppose Walsh became a subject of comment early in 1930 as regular Republican senators George Moses and Frederick Steiwer, of the GOP's Senate Campaign Committee, moved to control or strongly influence the selection process. The GOP's State Central Committee, meeting at Great Falls, drafted Albert J. Galen, an associate justice of the Montana Supreme Court, formerly the state's attorney general, for the Senate race. Many believed that Galen was about the strongest man who could have been drafted to run against the senior senator. Galen almost had to be dragged into the fray, contending that Walsh was the "brains" of the Democratic party and would be strongly supported financially; he demanded similar backing from Washington and Montana Republicans. Galen retained his position on the Montana Supreme Court. This, to Walsh, was an admission of weakness.[10]

Galen had liabilities along with his assets. A brother-in-law of the late U.S. Senator Thomas Carter, he had been associated with Old Guard politics both at the state and national level. Fifteen years younger than Walsh, Galen was educated in the East and Middle West, with degrees from Notre Dame University and the University of Michigan. He was popularly known by the 1920s as a Legionaire, a wet, and a good fellow. Walsh described him as "something of a vote-getter and a pretty good all-round back-slapping politician." But he was not a good public speaker.[11]

The Montanan stayed busy in Washington with more than the usual number of duties, including the tariff debate and lobby inquiry. For four months in early 1930 he served as acting minority leader of the Senate, in the absence of Joe Robinson, who had joined the American delegation to the London Naval Conference. As Senate spokesman for his party, Walsh engaged in a bit of jousting with the GOP opposition. Notably, at the end of March he responded to a statement of accomplishments by the Hoover administration coming from the Republican leader in the House, John Q. Tilson of Connecticut. Walsh was caustic on several points. He claimed the administration had failed to prepare adequately for the London Conference and thereby increased the risk of failure, also that Tilson's recitation of "great feats" primarily concerned routine actions carried on from previous administrations, for example, a continuation of tax reductions first inaugurated after World War I. Walsh wondered if Tilson's "statement" had come originally from Hoover's press bureau.[12]

One subject that never went away was prohibition. Walsh had been moving toward a modification of his prohibitionist stance, and in May 1930 committed himself to change with a public statement from Washington. The *New York Times* ran a headline on page three: "WALSH WOULD AGREE TO DRY REFERENDUM[.] Montana Senator, Long Foe of 'Wets,' Would Abide by Vote of His State." The article noted that Senator Wesley L. Jones of Washington State had issued a statement of a similar type and that Senator Morris Sheppard of Texas, "author of the Eighteenth Amendment," had revealed his sensitivity to constituent opinion on this subject. Drys of both parties were feeling the stress and were responding to mounting evidence that prohibition enforcement had been a failure. It appears that Walsh was motivated largely by political concerns in this election year and by pressure from a powerful lobbying group, the Association Against the Prohibition Amendment.[13]

Probably few in Montana doubted that Walsh was still a prohibitionist at heart. He had bettered his image, however, as one who was not a militant on this subject and was trying to be fair. He often stated that he hoped constituents who disapproved of his position on the wet and dry issue would remember the range of contributions he had been able to make, or might make in the future.[14]

Meanwhile, the senators entered upon their deliberations over the London Naval Treaty, notwithstanding the desire of many to get away from Washington's humidity and out on the campaign trail. President Hoover, a strong advocate of disarmament, determined to keep the Senate at work after Congress had adjourned its general session, and the senators remained through most of July. Secretary of State Stimson and other delegates had returned from London at the end of April, satisfied as to the agreements achieved with Britain and Japan on naval disarmament and hoping to find bipartisan support. Senator Robinson took this position, speaking as one of the delegates and the Senate's minority leader, and Walsh agreed. Thus the Democratic party played a part in getting the treaty ratified.[15]

The London Treaty extended arms limitation to cruisers, destroyers, and submarines much as had been done for capital ships in the Washington Conference of 1922. It was "the first time in history," Walsh said, that such a broad agreement had been achieved. He deeply regretted that there would still be the financial burden of "competitive naval construction," with each country trying to build to the limits allowed; but, on the whole, the treaty had the Montanan's active support as a means to prevent an arms race of the sort that led to war in 1914.[16]

Walsh did not go straight home, even though advisers had been "hollering" that he was needed in Montana. He went first to Wisconsin to deliver a speech and meet with friends from his childhood and youth.[17]

Walsh then went on to eastern Montana in a Northern Pacific car. He was scheduled to speak in Billings on the London Naval Treaty and apparently intended to use a week or more in political talks and discussions, while yearning to get to his mountain home in Glacier Park. A few days after the Billings radio talk, yielding to his need for a rest (and perhaps to the near certainty of his reelection) he went to Glacier for a month's vacation. This did not mean that he put politics out of his head or neglected his correspondence. Longtime secretary Imogene Howell was with him at the Park to open the mail, read the newspapers (including the *Washington Post* and *New York Times*), take dictation, and maintain communication with their Washington office. Walsh had time for hiking with family and friends, for "huckleberrying," and for eating trout "right out of the brook."[18]

This was the period in which Walsh's campaign organization took shape, with former Lieutenant Governor W. W. McDowell as leader. McDowell, an old friend, had been giving advice for some time. As an example, when the Senate's Lobby Committee haled before it the renowned Bishop James Cannon of the Methodist Church, McDowell sent a six-word telegram: "There are many Methodists in Montana."[19]

Toward the end of August Walsh completed his preparations for a Labor Day address at Havre and also gave attention to the Democratic convention about to meet in Helena. By this time the Republicans in their primary had chosen Albert Galen for the Senate nomination.[20]

On September 1 Walsh went to Havre in north-central Montana to deliver the principal address at a Labor Day picnic. His appearance in this labor center on the Great Northern Railroad line was not surprising, for the Montanan had long been regarded as a friend of labor and he had added to that reputation in the spring by opposing the confirmation of Judge John J. Parker as associate justice of the Supreme Court. Walsh's speech of perhaps forty minutes dealt with the risks and rewards of a new industrial age and with the sound economic reasons for thinking of workers as human beings and American citizens. More pointedly, he spoke of two labor measures he was supporting in Congress: first, a pension plan for railroad workers, and second, a bill aiming to eliminate abuses in the use of court injunctions against labor. In closing, he reiterated his theme that "Freedom's battle once begun . . . though often lost, is ever won."[21]

The Democratic State Convention met in Helena on Saturday, September 6, at the Placer Hotel, where leaders confidently expected to retain control of the seats in Congress occupied by Walsh and John Evans (in the western congressional district), for they knew that depression conditions across the country would help politically. Adding to the glow of ambitious Democrats, including Governor Erickson and Bruce Kremer, was a statement Walsh made in opening his address, that he did not expect to run for a fifth term.[22]

Walsh believed that no two senators from Montana had ever brought the state more attention and greater honors than he and his Democratic colleague had in the past seven years. To be sure, it was "whispered about" that their work as critics of the administration had hurt Montana by discouraging capital investment. Not so, said Walsh. He spoke briefly of developments in oil, water power, and railroads. He asked, What issues did the opposition have? And he replied: "Failing any other ground upon which to make an appeal the sacred tariff is invoked in the hope that it will help to keep wavering republicans in line."[23]

After the convention there was time for a little touring and sampling of political opinion; also for a speech to Helena Rotarians on the Constitutional Convention of 1787. Walsh took a reassuring trip to Butte, where he stayed at the Hotel Finlen and welcomed many visitors. W. W. McDowell, James E. Murray, and others apparently believed that the campaign presented no difficulties.[24]

In mid-September Senators Moses and Steiwer of the GOP Senatorial Campaign Committee visited Montana for the purpose of determining whether to finance Galen's campaign. Writing to Frances Parkinson Keyes, the novelist and wife of Senator Keyes of New Hampshire, Walsh said the visiting senators were "mixing medicine for my political demise." However, he gave his colleagues from Washington an automobile ride around Helena and showed no animosity toward them. He believed, as did his advisers, that Moses's visit would produce a reaction against the Galen campaign.[25]

Walsh also remarked to Mrs. Keyes that he would be starting his campaign tour soon with his daughter Genevieve as "guide, philosopher and friend." He was to be accompanied, as well, by Fred Martin, an able young writer, serving as publicity man. Fairly often they combined forces at rallies with

Governor Erickson or other Democratic leaders. From his headquarters in Helena, Walsh went north to Havre for his first address on September 25. The route was clockwise from there with addresses at Malta, Glasgow, Scobey, and Plentywood. As Fred Martin remembered, they went into "every nook and corner" of the state.[26]

The Walsh campaign was a positive one that placed emphasis on his services to the state and nation. This was in response to GOP charges that the senior senator had been neglecting Montana while seeking broader recognition and pursuing his "hobby" of international affairs. By early October his staff had put together a summary of "What Walsh Has Done for Montana" that covered more than a page in the *Great Falls Tribune* and other papers.[27]

As indicated earlier, Walsh went on the attack against GOP economic policy and, above all, against the high tariff, which allegedly was doing serious damage to Montana's economy. This case was made on the evidence of policies effected essentially by eastern economic interests. By fighting Walsh on dubious grounds, the Republicans of Montana added to their own difficul-

Walsh and his daughter, Genevieve Walsh Gudger. (Walsh-Gudger Collection, Illinois Historical Survey, University of Illinois at Urbana-Champaign)

ties as bad times undermined the old arguments that higher tariffs meant prosperity for the owners of farms and factories and for the people at large.[28]

Walsh noted denunciations of the 1930 tariff by "the most influential newspapers of the Northwest" and by a majority of western farm journals, as well as a protest against it by more than 1,000 economists in the nation's colleges and universities. He confidently asserted that he and Senator Wheeler, in opposing the bill, had acted in conformity with the "enlightened opinion" of Montana.[29]

Walsh had not been able to satisfy all of Montana's wheat growers, wool producers, oil producers and others who showed concern over allegedly inadequate protection. Yet his explanation almost certainly gained votes: "the consciousness was always with me that I represented 600,000 people of varied interests and that stern duty required of me that I consult their interests as a whole rather than the immediate pecuniary advantage of any individual or group."[30]

Walsh spoke on a variety of issues and did not fail to mention matters of importance to Montana on which he was currently taking action. He had recommended to the president the appointment of Federal Judge George Bourquin of Butte to the Circuit Court of Appeals of the Ninth Circuit. Bourquin, a progressive Republican, was highly regarded as a jurist and a man of integrity. The senior senator often conveyed his enthusiasm for the St. Lawrence Seaway and how much it would mean to Montana, essentially agreeing with Herbert Hoover on that subject.[31]

Much of the campaigning in 1930 was done *for* Walsh rather than by him. His celebrity status assured a broad spectrum of support and eulogies whose sincerity could not be doubted. When he spoke in Bozeman, for example, his friend Walter G. Aitken, a local attorney, had words of introduction that included the statement: "He has done more to spread the good name of Montana than any other individual or organization."[32]

Several fellow senators made personal appearances in Montana or communicated their high regard. William H. King of Utah wrote a letter of four pages to tell authoritatively of Walsh's services in the Teapot Dome affair and to quiet any doubts of those who thought he might have been politically motivated or a publicity seeker. David I. Walsh of Massachusetts spoke in Butte and Anaconda, obviously aiming to help his colleague's cause with Irish-Americans who might be disgruntled.[33]

The enthusiastic support of both state and national labor organizations was an element in Walsh's growing strength. One of the finest tributes came from Edward Keating, the former Colorado congressman and editor of *Labor* in

Walsh and former Massachusetts governor and veteran senator David I. Walsh. (Photographer: Harris & Ewing. Walsh-Gudger Collection, Illinois Historical Survey, University of Illinois at Urbana-Champaign)

Washington, D.C.: "A volume might be written about Walsh's work in the Senate. The most spectacular single feature was, of course, his exposure of the oil grafters, but he is always fighting for some worthy cause. His industry is limitless."[34]

Endorsements of Walsh from all over the country were picked up and printed in Montana newspapers or incorporated in the campaign literature. Mercer G. Johnston of the Peoples' Legislative Service in Washington said that he had been reviewing the history of Congress since its beginning in 1789 and he did not doubt that Senator Walsh ranked high among American statesmen for his character, intellect, and faithful endeavors to serve the people. "He would have graced any Congress." The *St. Louis Post-Dispatch,* noting that Walsh's opponent, Albert Galen, was "an outspoken wet," said they would prefer to see a wet elected, "other things being equal." But other things were not equal.[35]

Walsh ended his campaign with meetings in Great Falls on a Friday night, in Butte on Saturday night, and Helena on Monday night (Oct. 31–Nov. 3). He rested on Sunday as had been his habit during the tour. In Great Falls at the Grand Theater Walsh and Governor Erickson were the principal speakers, and their voices were broadcast over KFBB radio. The *Montana Standard* remarked that Walsh's entire tour, starting back in September, had been "a grand ovation from one end of the state to the other"; and that Butte would welcome him, "the state's most illustrious public man, . . . with feasting, music, song and a grand parade." After a banquet at the New Finlen Hotel (planned for "Jeffersonian simplicity" at one dollar a plate), he spoke to an overflow crowd at the Broadway Theater. It was a "rousing" time.[36]

The *Helena Independent* advised people to come early on Monday night to the Marlow Theatre in view of the big meeting in Butte that had left hundreds standing outside. The "home folks" in Helena did come to see and hear their senator, along with a hundred veterans from Fort Harrison, and many others who "completely filled" the theater, "crowding the seating capacity and overflowing into the aisles and the foyer."[37]

By Tuesday, November 4, the only doubt about Walsh's reelection was the size of his vote. The next day, in thanking his Washington staff, he called it a "smashing victory" and soon after commented that he ought to win by 40,000 and would carry his own precinct, ward, and county (all normally Republican), where Galen also resided. To John W. Davis, Walsh exulted that he had received "a larger majority than was ever before accorded to any candidate for public office in Montana." E. C. Day of Helena marveled at Walsh's going over 100,000 in his vote total. The final tally gave Walsh 106,274 to Galen's 66,724; while the Farmer Labor candidate, the Socialist, and the Communist together collected a little over 3,000. It was gratifying to the senator that all the "boys who stood steadfastly" with him back in the electoral fights of 1910–11 were still with him in this latest campaign.[38]

It was amazing to some that Walsh was not hurt by the wet-dry issue, but he and his aides had skillfully kept this matter in the background and after November could not help gloating a little over eastern "experts," such as Mark Sullivan, who had proven mistaken in their forecasts.[39]

Walsh undoubtedly failed to hold some Irish-Americans who were angry with him, first, over the liquor question and, second, over his support of the League of Nations and World Court. One friend of Irish origins wrote from Anaconda that he was ashamed of "the fact that this normally democratic County only gave you a little more than 800 votes to the good—whereas it should have been 1800 to 2000, but our tempermental [*sic*], vengeful, Irish contingent of the usual democratic vote in Deer Lodge County was against you." The vengeful ones had some success in Silver Bow (Butte) and elsewhere, but for the most part they failed, to the delight of Walsh's friends.[40]

Walsh believed that the big corporations of Montana did not interfere in this campaign, as he wrote to Charles Donnelly of the Northern Pacific Railroad, and he was highly gratified that such was the case. He also felt kindly toward Senator George Moses and the GOP National Campaign Committee, for he believed they had actually helped his cause by trying to interfere.[41]

On Friday, November 7, Walsh was still responding to congratulatory letters and telegrams, as he would be for weeks to come, but in the evening on the mezzanine floor of Helena's Placer Hotel he was host at a reception and was felicitated by friends from around the state. Along with Governor and Mrs. Erickson, Walsh headed the receiving line. "Light refreshments" were served by volunteers from among the Helena women, and an orchestra added to the conviviality. Republican friends attended this celebration, including Albert Galen. He and Walsh "shook hands warmly and chatted for a few minutes exchanging pleasantries," as observed by a reporter. Nothing had happened to disrupt this old friendship.[42]

Soon Walsh returned to Washington for the Senate session that began on December 1, still excited over the size of his victory and reflecting over the elections just ended and problems that lay ahead.

30

The Rule of Law at Home and Abroad

Felix Frankfurter, while at Harvard Law School, wrote that Walsh was one of the "most powerful lawyers in the Senate." His interest and expertise were notably apparent, first, in a long controversy over rules of procedure for state and federal courts, in which the Senate Judiciary Committee was heavily involved, and, second, in an effort by Walsh to get the United States into the World Court, or Permanent Court of International Justice, as the Senate Foreign Affairs Committee took the lead.[1]

Soon after coming to the Senate and joining the Judiciary Committee, Walsh took sides concerning a bill intended to turn over to the Supreme Court the task of writing rules of procedure for federal courts of the United States. He became deeply involved in this controversy in 1926, when he delivered a paper on the subject at a meeting of the Tri-State Bar Association at Texarkana, Arkansas-Texas, and he circularized members of the Supreme Court and many district judges, asking their views. Speaking in Texarkana, Walsh said that the Senate bill in question "proposes to abandon the system dating from the Judiciary Act of 1789, by which it was provided that 'the practice, pleadings, and forms and modes of proceeding in civil causes . . . shall conform, as nearly as may be, to the practice, pleadings, and forms and modes of proceeding existing at the time in like causes in the courts of record of the State within which such circuit or district courts are held.'" In other words, it had been considered important that proceedings in the state courts and the federal courts of the same area or jurisdiction should stay in as close conformity as possible. Walsh believed lawyers benefited from that type of "uniformity" more than they would from having uniform procedure in the many federal courts all over the country. "I am for the one hundred [lawyers] who stay at home as against the one who goes abroad."[2]

"Under the existing system," Walsh said, "the lawyer who has mastered the practice prescribed by the legislature of his State or developed by the decisions of its courts upon the foundation of the common law is equally equipped to institute, prosecute, and try actions at law in the Federal courts, save that in certain particulars arising from the difference in the organization of them, a matter of relatively little consequence, the State practice can not be followed." Walsh believed that the new system proposed would be more of a burden than a benefit, both for the new, young lawyer and the older practitioner. The Senate bill was tied up in the Judiciary Committee year after year and Walsh, as a prominent fighter for his side on the issue, had to put up with criticism that occasionally turned sour or vitriolic.[3]

He denied that he had held up the bill or conducted a filibuster against it. Rather, he said, "I have repeatedly agreed to its being set for hearing and, appearing at the time fixed to present whatever arguments I could advance against it, found there was no quorum present or, if there were, members [of the committee] were absent who had never heard the bill discussed and were unaware of any objections to it." Partly the problem was frequent changes of membership on the committee. Writing, however, to a district judge who agreed with him, Walsh said in 1921: "The bill would have gone through years ago had it not been for my consistent opposition to it."[4]

Taking into account accusations directed his way, Walsh decided to solicit opinions from federal judges and justices of the Supreme Court, relating to the Senate bill that was pending in 1926; as a result, he counted a clear majority of the federal judges in his favor. One of the exceptions was Judge Learned Hand of the U.S. Circuit Court in New York State, who said: "I have always been in favor of a uniform practise at common law like that in equity, the same to be within the control of the Supreme Court and promulgated by it. I do not share your fears that this would prove too much for the Supreme Court to do, but in any event that is a matter which we may safely leave to them." He also commented, "The truth is that judicial procedure is like history and that nation is happiest which has the least."[5]

Among the judges who spoke strongly against the proposed change, agreeing with Walsh, were Louis Brandeis of the Supreme Court, Judge Joseph L. Bodine of New Jersey, Judge J. Whitaker Thompson of Pennsylvania, Judge James M. Morton Jr. of the Boston District Court, Judge George W. McClintic of West Virginia, and Judge David C. Westenhaver of Northern Ohio. With them "laconically," as Walsh phrased it, was Oliver Wendell Holmes of the Supreme Court. And Walsh was pleased to receive the comments of Montana Judges Bourquin and Pray, both Republicans.

Politics does not appear to have had an effect on ideas about this question, nor did age or section of the country. Some of the ablest lawyers opposed the change, but some also strongly favored it. There was occasional fear of "centralization," and a lawyer might react strongly against or in favor of the system in the state in which he was practicing. Thus Learned Hand spoke of the "barbarous" practice in New York State where efforts at reform seemed to have failed. The pros and cons seemingly were of greatest concern to those deeply interested in the practice of law and the study of law, while others seem to have paid attention only on a practical, day-by-day basis. Walsh's interest made him better known among lawyers in the bar associations, state and national, and in the Senate. He continued to have a powerful influence on this question throughout his tenure in Washington.[6]

Walsh's view of foreign affairs in the 1920s was heavily influenced by World War I and postwar problems. He spoke favorably of the League of Nations and especially of the Permanent Court of International Justice (the World Court), which he believed the United States should join, notwithstanding critics who claimed that it was tied to the League. He favored disarmament agreements and in 1928 supported the Kellogg-Briand Pact intended to outlaw war. His attitude can be described as "legalistic" but not uncritical, for he was aware of economic influences and much else in addition to the legal aspects of world disagreements. He was trying to make the best of a bad situation and was, of course, reacting against isolationists in the Senate, on the Foreign Relations Committee, and elsewhere. World War I had made Walsh into an internationalist who believed that war was the scourge of mankind and must be avoided at almost any cost.[7]

Walsh said repeatedly in the 1920s that France was the key to the peace and that by promising to support that country against a German invasion the United States could have assured European stability. Woodrow Wilson had pointed the way, he believed, but the U.S. Senate had rejected the Treaty of Guaranty with France, as well as the Treaty of Versailles. Although he realized after 1920 that the United States would not join the League of Nations, Walsh believed the organization was doing well generally and deserved at least the good wishes of American internationalists such as himself.[8]

Walsh did not see the urgency of cancelling debts owed to the United States by former allies of World War I, believing that the reduction of interest owed by those countries was in itself a major concession. His position was similar to that of presidents and diplomats whose official stand created no end of ill will among the former European allies and their creditor, Uncle Sam.[9]

The two subjects that most clearly showed Walsh's "legalism" were the

Kellogg-Briand pact of 1928 and the long-continuing struggle to get the United States into the World Court. As a senator and member of the Foreign Relations Committee, Walsh was privy to a movement to outlaw war, and by 1928 he was one of many supporters of what came to be called the Multilateral Treaty or Kellogg-Briand Pact. In a speech of September, he assessed the possible value of "outlawry," beginning with the statement that it would be "vain to imagine" that because of a treaty outlawing war this "greatest of curses to which mankind has been subject has been banished from the earth"; too many treaties had been "violated and disregarded" for one to believe that. But treaties might exercise a "restraining influence," and such could be hoped for. "In the past a nation committed no breach of international law in making war upon a neighbor." Hereafter a war-making nation would be "without honor and without shame, an outlaw, deservedly despised and detested." Walsh was optimistic on the subject.[10]

In March 1923, before sailing to Manila to visit his daughter, Walsh said he approved of efforts by President Harding and Secretary of State Hughes to secure a role for the United States in the World Court to be established at the Hague. He said the United States always had committed itself to the principle of international justice and this latest move would be no departure from established American policy. "I am not prepared to carry the idea further than this, however," he said. "I believe that the public sentiment in the United States does not favor American participation in a League of Nations or an association of nations similar to the League." Walsh recognized the opposition that would be stirred among Irish-Americans and others to even a modest move toward international cooperation. Over a period of years he received innumerable warnings and complaints from organizations such as the Thomas Francis Meagher Council of Anaconda, Montana, and the Phil Sheridan Club of the same city. Perhaps the most important single organization opposing the Court was the Friends of Irish Freedom.[11]

Among the many in support were the World Alliance for International Friendship, the Federation of Women's Clubs, the American Association of University Women, the American Council of Churches, the League of Nations Non-Partisan Association, the National Commission on the Cause and Cure of War (with Carrie Chapman Catt as chairperson), the Women's International League for Peace and Freedom (with Jane Addams as president), and the Woman's Christian Temperance Union, Inc.[12]

The problem faced by Walsh and others was not so much a lack of support as the expression of powerful opposition in certain places, such as the *Chicago Tribune,* and in the Senate Foreign Relations Committee. After all,

Presidents Harding, Coolidge, and Hoover gave their backing, as did leaders of both party organizations in the Senate, and the much respected former Senator Elihu Root of New York, who helped write the original statute of the World Court. William E. Borah, however, was chairman of the Foreign Relations Committee and continued to assert his isolationist views, as did a number of others on the committee. Even to bring the question of Court adherence to a vote required patience and skill.

Walsh and other friends of the Court would have loved to treat the Court as fundamentally separate from the old League of Nations which had provoked such a fight from 1918 to 1920. Such proved to be impossible, because there was a connection in the beginning, and almost all friends of the League tried to give support to the World Court, thus providing an excuse for criticism. But Walsh insisted on more than one occasion that "the Court . . . stands on its own bottom."[13]

Walsh explained that the Court had eleven judges, from as many countries, one of whom (John Bassett Moore) was an American and a highly esteemed jurist. The Montanan believed that the work of the Court was above criticism and that its results left no doubt that small as well as large countries could expect to be treated justly. Of course, the problems considered were legal and justiciable, rather than political. Miracles could not be expected from the World Court, but it was a source of encouragement internationally, with which the United States should be affiliated. Walsh declared emphatically that the Court was not intended to carry out its decisions by force; quite the opposite.[14]

The last months of 1925 and the first month of the next year was an important time for the Court, so far as U.S. adherence was concerned. It also was a time in which Walsh emerged as a foremost friend of the Court, particularly through his work in the Foreign Relations Committee and speeches on the Senate floor. Senator Frederick Gillett, a Republican of Massachusetts, wrote to Elihu Root on January 27 saying that Walsh of Montana, he believed, had "really contributed more . . . to the elucidation of the problems than any one else." The snags mostly concerned reservations that had been attached by Secretary of State Hughes in 1923 or others discussed as possibilities to be added by the Senate. Thus Senator George Moses proposed an amendment or reservation, and he was sarcastic in discussing the League and Court as war agencies. When Walsh had his chance on the floor he argued there would be no military enforcement of Court decisions. Finally, the vote on Moses's amendment was 22 Yeas and 69 Nays, although Borah, Norris, and a number of able people went down to defeat with Moses.[15]

Finally the Senate voted for adherence to the World Court, with five "reservations and understandings" that Walsh optimistically thought would be acceptable to the Court. The vote totals were 76 Yeas and 17 Nays, as most Democrats and Republicans voted in favor. The opposition came primarily from the progressive group of Republicans who essentially feared involvement in world affairs.[16]

The Senate's fifth reservation read as follows: "That the Court shall not render any advisory opinion except publicly after due notice to all States adhering to the Court and to all interested States . . . ; nor shall it, without the consent of the United States, entertain any request for an advisory opinion touching any dispute or question in which the United States has or claims an interest." The Court, however, refused to accept adherence of the Unites States. A few months later President Coolidge expressed his hope that the Court members would accept the fifth reservation and "admit the United States to membership," quoting the *New York Times*. Coolidge claimed that all the reservation was intended to do was to "put the United States on a parity with members of the League of Nations who have a seat in the League Council."[17]

Walsh visited Europe in 1925 and 1927 and continued to be deeply involved with the Court question. Early in 1929 he was hopeful that Secretary of State Kellogg's support of Elihu Root's "proposal for getting us into the World Court" would have good results, particularly since statesmen assembled at Geneva seemed to have reacted "cordially." Walsh gave a speech at Rollins College in Florida which was published in *Review of Reviews* as "We Approach the World Court." An editor of the magazine wrote to Walsh: "We have today mailed a marked copy to each member of the Senate. We are sure that you know how much Dr. Shaw [Albert Shaw, the editor] appreciates the opportunity to print your views, and we feel a little bit conscious of helping in a good cause by placing them before nearly two hundred thousand readers." The dilemma of gaining "adherence" continued.[18]

During the Hoover administration, from 1929 to 1933, Walsh kept up his efforts and hoped that the new administration would exert the necessary pressure on the Senate and the Foreign Relations Committee. There was also the possibility, as the Montanan noted, that adverse pressure from isolationist senators would discourage the president from calling a special session to take needed action. New issues intruded, as well, notably those of unemployment and hard times generally. The Japanese invasion of Manchuria was a distressing setback to those who believed in the possibilities of a new structure of international law. Walsh's optimism regarding the rise of the Democratic party under

Franklin Roosevelt's leadership was counteracted by worrisome trends on the international scene. He found some solace, however, in comments such as the following from the president of Whitman College in Walla Walla, Washington: "Will you permit me, a Republican by inheritance, . . . to express to you my deep appreciation of your unflagging service to the cause of the World Court? It must have been at times discouraging to realize the steadfast and irreconcilable opposition of members of the Foreign Relations Committee, but you have persevered with admirable determination." Many, he said, were aware of Walsh's services—a conclusion supported by letters and documents in the Walsh Papers.[19]

Chairman of the National Convention, Chicago, 1932

Walsh's reputation as a Democratic leader was higher in 1931–32 than it ever had been. Along with Senate minority leader Joseph Robinson of Arkansas and Senator Cordell Hull of Tennessee he did much to establish the legislative agenda for a rising Democratic party. Walsh wrote in November 1931 of how the parties lined up in Congress and how "after a year and a half of Hoover the Republican majority of 96 in the House was [almost] wiped out, . . . and in the Senate reduced from 18 to 2." The GOP had hoped the Hawley-Smoot tariff would "arrest the downward plunge." But Walsh concluded that "the trend exhibited by the 1930 elections" had persisted and even gained momentum.[1]

Walsh was an "idea man" who had exchanges with Bernard Baruch, a Democratic financier and would-be policy maker, and with Senator Robinson concerning the party's legislative program. The Montanan said he could not agree with Baruch's proposal to cut expenditures, an idea which perhaps reminded him of President Hoover and the "bunk character" of his "economy program." His recommendation was to raise income taxes on those who were best able to pay, and he tried to show there were many individuals and corporations that could afford to pay. He believed, as did leading economists of the time, that an unequal distribution of wealth during the 1920s had contributed to an "inability of the consuming masses to buy," thus bringing on the depression. Baruch scoffed at "Walsh's economists" while admitting it might be possible to get money by taxing those who had been taxed lightly if at all. He emphasized, however, that nothing must be done to kill initiative. In one of his letters Baruch quoted the historian Macaulay, and Walsh replied: "Macaulay puts eloquently, as always, the laissez-faire doctrine which was accepted as gospel in his time. Since then legislation in all countries has done violence to that theory of government . . . and it has been rejected or accepted with reservations by most present-day economists."[2]

On the subject of organizing the House of Representatives, Walsh wanted the Democrats to do as they did under Taft. If they had policies in which they believed they ought to "seize the opportunity to give them expression . . . in the branch of Congress which we control." He mentioned to Baruch that he and Cordell Hull were "trying to outline a scheme of legislation" for the House "so that the party might be said to have a real constructive program and not be merely a party of negation."[3]

Senator Robinson solicited Walsh's ideas and said he would "consult" with him when they both returned to Washington. He thought that neither party would have "decisive partisan control in either House." Should the Senate Democrats "agree upon and announce a program"? He would be glad to have Walsh's views on whether they should propose "a general program of the Minority Conference in the Senate" and on what measures should be included. Walsh sent back three single-spaced pages of suggestions. His tone seemed deferential and friendly while implying that he (Walsh) was knowledgeable concerning the issues, as they both knew.

Number one on his agenda was "immediate relief for the unemployed," and the choice before the American people was "a program of public works or a dole." Thinking of President Hoover and his opposition to a dole, Walsh said further: "If we shun the dole and advocate public works we almost drive the President to join with us." He was hopeful that the political situation would bring concessions from Hoover. It seemed wise to begin by avoiding controversy over the order of public works to be undertaken, and that might be done by asking each department to submit a list of projects "for which plans are ready or could be furnished within ninety days." Obviously one of the senators to be consulted on this matter was Robert Wagner of New York, and his advice would be particularly important regarding "plans . . . to avoid unemployment in the future."[4]

Walsh said the budget should be balanced and funds for that purpose collected (1) by increasing income tax rates "in the higher brackets," (2) by "increasing the inheritance tax in the higher brackets," (3) by "gift taxes," (4) "possibly by a luxury sales tax," and (5) by bonds "for the public works proposed." He also had suggestions concerning the tariff, "Gambling on the Stock Exchange," banking, and Farm Relief, although on the last he said "I confess my inability to propose anything, but we would be well advised, I think, to follow if possible any proposals of the general farm organizations." As to the debts of foreign governments, he thought they might appropriately offer a "resolution declaring against any reduction of the debts owing the [U.S.] government . . . without reliable assurances that the relief afforded will not be utilized to increase armaments or maintain military establishments."[5]

Busily involved in legislative matters and interested in national problems, Walsh as early as September 1931 had announced for Franklin Roosevelt for the presidency. And he firmly but politely rejected those who thought of him for the same position, or for the vice presidency. Inevitably Walsh was involved in the developing friction between Roosevelt men and those who had controlled the party since 1928; namely, Al Smith, John J. Raskob, the national chairman, and Jouett Shouse, chairman of the Executive Committee of the Democratic National Committee. By February 1932, Smith, who had earlier indicated his lack of interest, announced that he was available for the party's nomination; thus he brought the contest into the open.[6]

Though not approving of Roosevelt in all respects, Walsh believed he was essentially progressive and much the best prospect to defeat Hoover and lead the country toward an economic recovery. This friendly relationship is to be found in the two men's personal correspondence and in Walsh's replies to inquiries and various letters and statements from 1930 to 1932. It will be recalled that Walsh was looking for "a Jefferson" during the 1920s. In Roosevelt he believed the nation had found someone nearly measuring up to that standard. When FDR won election as governor of New York State and pushed through most of his legislative program the Montanan was impressed. Particularly impressive was "the magnificent endorsement" given Roosevelt for a second term "by the astounding majority of nearly three-quarters of a million votes." Walsh added in one letter: "I know him to be [a] man of ability and high-minded views."[7]

Many around the country were announcing for Roosevelt, and Walsh in May 1932 took a step which figured importantly as the national convention loomed just ahead. He wrote a letter to W. W. McDowell, chairman of the Democratic State Central Committee in Montana, intending that it be read at a meeting of the Democrats scheduled for Helena on May 17, a meeting at which delegates to the national convention would be chosen. He did not believe he should leave the Capital at this time, he explained, and therefore had to write. Walsh warned that they must avoid another disaster of the sort that occurred in Madison Square Garden in 1924. He was asking, therefore, that the Helena convention send delegates instructed for Roosevelt. There was, he recognized, a stop-Roosevelt movement, that would benefit by keeping the delegates divided. Only a blunder of this sort, he said, speaking as the chairman who had presided in 1924, could prevent the party's winning by a landslide in November.[8]

Walsh emphasized the plight of the country, "bordering on desperation," and the need for decisive action to fight the depression. Franklin Roosevelt had shown his ability as governor of New York in pushing his program through a legislature that was "politically adverse"; and he had been reelected in 1930 by the "astounding majority of approximately three quarters of a million votes." In closing, Walsh referred to "the able and eminent gentlemen" who might be nominated in a deadlocked convention. But the dangers were too great, he said, and Democrats knew they could win in November after quickly nominating Roosevelt. Soon Walsh in Washington received a telegram from FDR in Warm Springs reading: "I am grateful to you my old friend for your letter to McDowell Period It is in many ways the best message that has appeared this year and it clears the air greatly Period My warm regards."[9]

Walsh and many other Democrats were doing what they could to counter the stop-Roosevelt forces, for the dangers were real, since the winning nominee in Chicago would need a two-thirds majority. Walsh commented to Governor Erickson: "If we could nominate Governor Roosevelt without any serious contest, say before as many as 5 ballots have been taken, his [nomination and] election would be assured. If the thing drags out our chances wane with every succeeding ballot."[10]

Walsh indicated his happiness with the Helena Democratic convention that chose him, Senator Wheeler, McDowell, and other delegates and alternates and also "instructed" them to support Governor Roosevelt for president. There was only one thing to worry about regarding the forthcoming national convention and that was the continuing efforts by Chairman Raskob, Jouett Shouse, and others of their group to carry the argument that Shouse—by dint of his hard work as chairman of the executive committee of the National Committee—deserved to become permanent chairman of the National Convention of 1932. Meanwhile, Walsh learned that Roosevelt, James A. Farley, and their group favored him for the permanent chairmanship and that a sharp fight on this matter was looming; the Montanan was ready for such a fight.[11]

When the Democratic Convention met in Chicago on June 27 at the Chicago Stadium, with Chairman Raskob of the National Committee presiding, preliminaries had to be attended to. Raskob, speaking at length, referred to the radio audience and to the "master mind" of Jouett Shouse, who had worked for the party and its interests through the campaign of 1928 and since, without pay, except as the party "may register its approval and appreciation

Walsh, Gov. Franklin D. Roosevelt, and Jim Farley, in a strategy session on a train in Montana, September 20, 1932. (Photographer: International News. Walsh-Gudger Collection, Illinois Historical Survey, University of Illinois at Urbana-Champaign)

of his accomplishments." He thus hinted that Shouse ought to become permanent chairman of this convention, and he urged that Democrats "rededicate the party to those principles of government enunciated by its founder, Thomas Jefferson." The most important address of the afternoon and one that conveyed the mood of most delegates was that of the temporary chairman, Senator Alben Barkley of Kentucky.[12]

Barkley spoke for two hours with all the skills of an old-fashioned orator, reviewing the successes of the Democrats—and the failures of the opposition—and declaring that this gathering of Democrats was preliminary to a larger gathering "on the fourth of next March," when the Democratic nominee would be "inaugurated President." Barkley rallied the forces and helped to convince cautious ones that they should break sharply with Republican policies.[13]

On the second day of the convention, with Barkley presiding as temporary chairman, delegates turned their attention to the election of a permanent chairman, Walsh having been recommended for that post by the Committee on Permanent Organization. A minority report called for the election of Jouett Shouse of Kansas, and a sharp contest followed. This was an important day of the convention. If Walsh, the choice of Roosevelt delegates, were defeated by Shouse, the Smith-Raskob candidate, even before the presidential balloting began, the tone of the convention would have changed. Senators Clarence Dill of Washington and James Byrnes of South Carolina spoke glowingly in behalf of Walsh, emphasizing his long and illustrious career. A case was made for Shouse on the basis of his service to the National Committee in 1928 and thereafter. One of those speaking for Shouse was John W. Davis, the Democratic presidential nominee in 1924. It was a close contest that made Roosevelt aides nervous. Finally the states voted through the long roll call, with several major states voting for Shouse; but Walsh won, 626 to 528.[14]

Senator Barkley presented Walsh to the convention and the latter took his position with a brief speech. Walsh thanked the delegates and said that he would be "guided by a frail judgment but an honest purpose." After complimenting Shouse for his "fidelity and devotion" to the party, Walsh said he might well cease his remarks, in view of Senator Barkley's "stirring address . . . in which all was said that need be said, touching the prospects of our party and of the brighter future for our country"; besides, he said, "I am no orator, as Barkley is." Actually, Walsh gave a good speech, less blunt than Barkley's concerning failures of the GOP but caustic at points and calling for a change from the theory that "the national well being is to be looked for by giving free rein to the captains of industry and magnates in the field of finance." (In his typed speech he had called for a "new deal.") One of his quotable passages was: "Too late it has been learned, if learned at all, that our prosperity is intimately bound up in that of the whole world."[15]

Walsh then moved on to the work of the convention including a report from the Committee on Rules and Order of Business. This committee, chaired by Bruce Kremer of Montana, offered a recommendation gladly received by Walsh and many in the convention: namely, that the next convention should abandon the two-thirds rule for a presidential nomination and recognize that each convention should be the "sole judge of its own rules."[16]

Walsh and the delegates succeeded in two objectives regarding the party platform: first, to keep it as brief as possible (less than half as long as the Republicans') and, second, to avoid a fight over prohibition repeal on the convention floor that might prove disastrous to hopes of harmony. Struggling with the crowd, Walsh was able at last to call for the "Ayes" and "Nays" on the majority report on the platform and to announce that the "Ayes" had won. The next order of business was the calling of the roll for nominations for president.[17]

The key to the nomination in this convention was the two-thirds rule, one hundred years after it had been adopted in quite different circumstances. Roosevelt was far ahead in the delegate count, including states under the unit rule, but a simple majority might easily disappear, placing great pressure on Jim Farley and other Roosevelt leaders to fashion deals that would give them a two-thirds majority. This became apparent during the first roll call and continued on the second and third roll calls.

Although Roosevelt had over 600 votes, his victory was delayed by Smith having about a third of that and Garner somewhat less, with a scattering among other contenders. It seemed that the fourth roll call would determine the outcome—if Roosevelt were to win—and that was what happened. Changes in the vote for California and Texas were decisive, with McAdoo of California, Garner of Texas, and William Randolph Hearst exercising an influence, the last because Hearst stopped fighting Roosevelt as an internationalist. McAdoo stood up as a delegate from California to say that he would explain the vote of his state: they were not going to have a futile convention this time as in 1924 (when he and Smith were deadlocked). California switched its vote from Garner to Roosevelt, and Texas did the same (Garner approving): the logjam was broken.

As permanent chairman, Walsh announced that the total votes cast were 1,148½, and that Roosevelt had received 945 of those. "Franklin D. Roosevelt having received more than two-thirds of all the delegates voting, I proclaim him the nominee of this convention for President of the United States." Al Smith never released his New York votes to make the nomination unanimous; there was a residue of bitterness.[18]

Soon Chairman Walsh announced the receipt of a communication from Governor Roosevelt in Albany requesting that he be permitted to come the following day (July 2) for a notification ceremony, rather than waiting to be "notified," as had been customary; this was not a time for waiting or for the additional expense of a separate ceremony, said FDR. Walsh, agreeing, arranged for the necessary action in the convention and a day later the nominee arrived by air, accompanied by his wife, sons John and Elliott, and others; diehard partisans of Al Smith apparently showed their displeasure by tearing up Roosevelt posters in the hotels.[19]

The next step for delegates on the sixth day of the convention, July 2, 1932, was to consider the nominee for vice president, although that question presumably had been settled in determining that Roosevelt would receive votes of Texas and California formerly pledged to John Nance Garner. Garner was put in nomination with many delegates offering seconds until Matt A. Tinley of Iowa made a motion that "the rules be suspended and John Garner be nominated by acclamation." This motion was said to be adopted "unanimously," and Garner was "declared nominee of the convention for vice-president of the United States." "Applause, cheering, and parading" came next.

Walsh announced that the airplane "bearing Governor Franklin D. Roosevelt to the convention" would be arriving in "fifteen minutes." This was a period, also, when delegates were preparing to return home and entertaining telegrams and resolutions of appreciation to the permanent chairman, the Chicago Police Force, the Parliamentarian, and others. Garner sent a wire which was read by Sam Rayburn of Texas thanking the convention for Garner's nomination to run with FDR and declaring that, "Under his banner and leadership the people of the United States will have their government restored to them on March 4, 1933." Walsh expressed his gratitude for "the recognition you have given to the poor services I have been privileged to render you in this convention."[20]

By this time, T. J. Walsh was one of the better-known men in America because his voice was continually going over the air. Perhaps the high point for him was his notification address as he introduced the recently nominated Franklin D. Roosevelt.

Walsh lauded FDR's "devotion to the public weal" and the success he had had, especially as governor of "the Imperial State of New York."

In closing, Walsh declared: "I venture to pledge you, on behalf of this great convention and the constituencies represented by the delegates comprising it, their loyal, cordial, and enthusiastic support in the coming election in which even our political adversaries admit we cannot fail except we blunder. . . . we greet you now as our leader for the restoration of wise government on the lines the founder of our party [Jefferson] conceived it. (Cheers and applause.)"[21]

In a small surprise, Roosevelt spoke briefly of the Wilson era: "Let us now and here highly resolve to resume the country's interrupted march along the path of real progress, of real equality for all of our citizens great and small."

Admitting some fault on his part and others' in the "era of selfishness" through which the country had come, and saying it was not the fault of governments alone, he went on to declare: "I pledge you—I pledge myself to a new deal for the American people. (Applause and cheering). . . . Give me your help, not to win votes alone, but to win in this crusade to restore America to its own people. (Applause and cheering, ending in an ovation.)"

Walsh as chairman then thanked Mayor Cermak of Chicago for the "excellent arrangements" of the convention and the "many courtesies" shown the delegates, at which point on the motion of Arthur F. Mullen of Nebraska the convention adjourned sine die at 6:52 P.M., July 2.[22]

The convention had ended for most of the delegates but not for Chairman Walsh. He stayed on in Chicago several days, at the Blackstone Hotel, with a secretary assigned to him to answer letters and telegrams that had accumulated; and then traveled to his summer home in Glacier Park, where he continued to deal with correspondence, while also vacationing. One of Walsh's old friends wrote from the Los Angeles area, on July 5: "What a great thing is radio!" Another reported that his "11 Tube Philco brought me the proceedings of every session of the convention." Most of the communications were written in excitement over the radio broadcasts and convention sessions because the writers were listening to Walsh and the proceedings over the radio. Most flattering was the letter from a woman who said he had converted her and "four other Republicans" to the Democratic party. She referred to him as helping instill confidence by exemplifying the "Intelligensia of your party and its chosen leaders who will, we hope, control the country for the next four years, at least." Walsh and the convention had a positive impact on many millions of Americans and helped get Roosevelt off to a fine start in the campaign.[23]

FDR sent a letter to Walsh on July 26 speaking of campaign plans and congratulating the Montanan on his convention role: "I think you know of my very deep and affectionate regard for you; this was only added to by your splendid loyalty and unselfish devotion, not only to me but to the cause of Democracy during those racking days in Chicago. There is literally no man in America who could have conducted that Convention as fairly, as patiently and as brilliantly as you did. I recognize what a great strain it must have been and I trust that you will devote definite time and purpose to building up your strength during the next few weeks for the even larger task ahead of all of us."

Walsh indicated his willingness to help in the campaign and his belief that the convention assignment had not been so fatiguing for him as it seemed to others.[24]

32

Campaigning for Roosevelt in 1932

Walsh was one of many Roosevelt advisers in 1932, but he had attained distinction as a senior leader and chairman of the recent convention that nominated FDR; also it soon became apparent that he would join the president-elect's cabinet. While Roosevelt vacationed briefly and entered upon his campaign in the East, Walsh relaxed at his lodge in Glacier Park. FDR wrote to him on July 26, asking for Walsh's "thought" as to whether he should take a western trip. The candidate soon received from Walsh the advice he wanted to hear, that he should take the trip west to answer the "line of argument" that he was "physically unequal to the task to which we would call you."[1]

Democratic leaders believed they had chosen a man who could win, and perhaps win easily, against the incumbent party and president. Governor Roosevelt and Senator Walsh felt confident while being aware at the same time that they needed to run a good campaign and avoid mistakes that could antagonize large blocs of voters. Walsh had boundless confidence in the governor since his smashing reelection in 1930.[2]

Roosevelt started the presidential campaign in a radio broadcast from his state capital and next at a political gathering in Columbus, Ohio, on August 10, delighting the crowd with an "Alice in Wonderland" parody on the Republican party. Walsh continued to vacation, though busy with correspondence. Not until September did the Montanan get into action, and apparently he was well rested and enjoying the best of health.[3]

The biggest news of this period was that Franklin Roosevelt's campaign train would soon be arriving in Montana and that the Democratic State Convention was to meet in Helena on September 15. Walsh by mid-September was seeing various party leaders, and he served as chairman of the state convention's platform committee. When he spoke to the gathering he declared that Roosevelt's nomination was "a triumph of the plain people," and he predicted "a sweeping victory" for the candidate and his party in the November elections.

Starting on a note of appreciation for the faith manifested in him, Walsh went on to sound like the state and national leader that he was. He paid tribute to the nominee they had chosen, to his "indomitable spirit" and other qualities that helped explain his reelection in 1930 by a majority of almost 750,000 votes. There were those who tried to say that his winning New York State in a gubernatorial race did not mean he could win in the presidential election, but Walsh asked, Why not? Of course, he would be opposed by the power interests and others, but the times looked "unusually propitious" for FDR and the Democrats. Suppose they did lose New York? They might win California again as in 1916, and good sources were predicting that such would be the case. He also noted the news of Democratic success in the Maine elections as a happy omen. "The depression is not over," he said, and obviously Democrats were benefiting from hard times.[4]

He took pride in the Democratic candidates for Congress and the ticket generally but warned of the need for "rigid economy" and the use of volunteer workers "more than ever." He closed by saying, "With the active cooperation of those present we shall somehow get on and all rejoice in a sweeping victory in November."[5]

In Butte with the Roosevelt party, Walsh said it was "gracious" of their guest to come to Montana, particularly when "in the judgment of all impartial and informed observers there is not the slightest doubt that its electoral vote will be cast for him." Voters of the Treasure State, Walsh claimed, were known for political decisions based on "reason and reflection," and if a special argument were needed to give support to the "distinguished guest" of this occasion the people of Butte had one.[6]

Walsh proceeded to discuss an issue of particular interest to Butte and western mining country, on which he said Hoover had failed badly, while Governor Roosevelt stood with them and with the Democratic party. He believed that Roosevelt would favor the calling of an international conference on silver. President Hoover had "remained obdurate," and seemed to be in the "class that worship the gold standard."[7]

The meeting in Butte was not the most formal or one burdened with long speeches. The *Helena Independent* had a caption implying as much: "U.S. Democratic Leader Swings Crowd At Butte." FDR said in opening, "This is a Roosevelt town—the boys and girls have proved that." Seated in his presidential car, before joining a procession in the parade, the governor "was surrounded by boys and girls from the Butte schools . . . and conversed and shook hands with them for a few minutes." Later he spoke highly of Governor Erickson and of Senator Walsh, saying he had stood beside him "on a speaker's platform" for the first time since July 2, at the Democratic National Convention in Chicago.

FDR paid Walsh a tribute, as noted in the *New York Times:* "No American can stand in the presence of Senator Walsh without feeling deeply, not only a sense of gratitude for the unselfish service of this man throughout his whole life, to his state and to his country, but also a deep sense of the innate greatness of the man himself," said the candidate.

Roosevelt added: "He voices the aspirations and hopes of many people, and it is this same hope that is recognized by the platform of the democratic party and as you know I have accepted that platform without equivocation and without reservation." Responding to Walsh's suggestion that the president be host to an international conference on silver, he promised that if elected he would immediately call for such a conference "to consider the rehabilitatation of silver."

The gathering at Butte was a success for Roosevelt and a great occasion for Senator Walsh, Governor Erickson, James E. Murray (chairman of the county committee), and others in the crowd estimated to number 7,000 to 8,000. In a matter of hours, the Roosevelt special train moved out for Missoula, intending to reach Seattle sometime that night.[8]

Walsh arranged to stay with the Roosevelt train much of the time during its western trip. Before it arrived at Butte he had gone by airplane to join the train at Salt Lake City, from which it went to Butte, and he rode on to Missoula with the Roosevelt party. Later he flew from Helena to San Francisco to meet the train as it was going south from Seattle. He was with the nominee in San Francisco and continued with him to Los Angeles, San Diego, and Williams, Arizona; and, finally, it seems, all the way back to the Middle West and Northeast.[9]

Speaking in Denver on September 28, Walsh said he was confident that Roosevelt would win. As to Montana he had no doubt, "and if enthusiastic crowds can be taken as an indication the rest of the West will go for Roosevelt." He commented that Roosevelt was a candidate "who fits the ideas of this section of the country."[10]

Walsh was one of a group of Democrats chosen to be major spokesmen for Roosevelt during the campaign, and his assignments were to cities of the Midwest in late October; this was in addition to a short tour in Montana

Democratic council of war at the Greenway Ranch in Williams, Arizona, September 26, 1932: (*seated left to right*) C. C. Pettijohn (New York), Sen. Key Pittman (Nevada), Gov. Franklin D. Roosevelt (New York), Walsh, Sen. John S. Cohen (Georgia); (*standing left to right*) Judge Robert Marx (Ohio), J. Bruce Kremer (Montana), Breckenridge Long (Missouri), W. F. Githens (New York), Carl T. Hayden (Arizona). (Franklin D. Roosevelt Library, Hyde Park, N.Y. NPx48-22:3704[277])

during early November intended to give a boost primarily to Governor Erickson and other candidates for state offices. The senator thus had an opportunity to go to his office in Washington and to visit his daughter and her family in Virginia before leaving for a final, busy period of campaigning in late October and early November.[11]

Walsh delivered a radio address from Chicago on October 22, which was released from Democratic headquarters. He called on the nation to repudiate the Republicans for a "failure to get action." He said that Democrats in Congress had been those who pushed for relief for the unemployed. Now, he said, "Startlingly incomprehensible" as it might seem, "the President takes credit to himself for the legislation."[12]

In Milwaukee on October 24 Walsh continued his attack on Hoover's relief and unemployment policies. The *Great Falls Tribune* quoted him as saying: "Following fatuously his notion that the needy could be cared for through private charity, the president promoted two successive organizations to 'coordinate'—whatever that may mean—the relief work, making unheard of demands upon the charitably inclined." These organizations vanished, Walsh said, having accomplished almost nothing and "appalled at the magnitude of the task with which they had been charged." Walsh mentioned the Democratic relief legislation sponsored by Robert Wagner in the Senate and John N. Garner in the House, for which Hoover now had the audacity to claim credit. Walsh also blasted Hoover's tariff policies, which he said had caused European nations to raise their duties on U.S. farm products, bringing "near beggery to . . . the great grain growing sections of the country," and "with the result that eventually all lines of business became involved in a common ruin."[13]

Walsh took pride, he said, in being invited to speak in the "metropolis of the state in which I was born and in which I lived until I grew to manhood." And he took more pride in the fact that Wisconsin, though a Republican state, had been known a generation or more for its progressivism. Thus it was not surprising to him that progressive leaders of the Republican party, "to a man," opposed the reelection of Herbert Hoover and that most of them, including Robert M. La Follette Jr. and the state's junior senator, John J. Blaine, were "openly and actively supporting the candidacy of that sterling progressive democrat, Gov. Franklin D. Roosevelt for President of the U.S."[14]

Walsh then launched into one of his arguments regarding legislative battles in the Senate, namely, that the Democrats and progressive Republicans often had worked together and badly needed each other as in the oil scandal controversies, the fight against the nomination of Charles Beecher Warren for attorney general, and "in the struggle to expose the iniquities of the Power Trust." The Montanan could hardly say enough in praise of the two La Follettes and John J. Blaine, with whom he had served.[15]

Walsh spoke in Duluth the night of October 25. He assured his audience that, reports to the contrary notwithstanding, FDR was a staunch backer of the St. Lawrence Seaway. In years past, Walsh explained, there had been opposition to the Seaway in New York State, the fear being that its export business would suffer. But it was now recognized that any such loss would be compensated for by the power development of the Seaway. Roosevelt as governor, Walsh said, was well aware of the need to prevent "selfish private interests" from controlling the state's water power, including the St. Lawrence. "Indeed," Walsh continued, "the fight has centered about that potentiality."[16]

On October 27 an editorial titled "The Man From Montana" appeared in the *Omaha World-Herald.* It began: "A distinguished guest of Omaha today is Senator Thomas J. Walsh of Montana who will speak tonight at the city auditorium." The editorial described him as "truly a tribune for the people" and a "veteran of many a hard campaign for the public good."[17]

Walsh lived up to his billing, for he spoke vigorously of Republican failings in several areas of interest to ordinary people. He said that the "ever increasing tariffs" had been "obviously ruinous to the farmers" and cited a recent report which stated that farm income had shrunk from 16 to 5 billion dollars annually. Hoover's federal farm program, he said, was no more than an effort to quiet farmer demands for relief. Speaking in Nebraska as he was, he dwelled on Senator George Norris and his contributions, and declared: "His devotion to the cause of the common man amounts to a passion."[18]

Walsh spoke in Denver on the 28th. He said the "standpat policy" of the Republicans had "brought ruin upon the country." He again flayed Hoover's relief policies. As to Hoover's assertion that federal aid would undermine the moral fiber of its recipients, Walsh stated that "it was never made clear how the receipt of aid from the national treasury would be any more deadly than from that of the state or local relief organizations, private or public." Walsh said that economists were generally agreed that the primary cause of the depression was the excessive concentration of wealth. "But has anyone heard a word of warning from the White House or from anyone speaking for or close to this or either of the two preceding administrations?"[19]

That the voters of Colorado, even as those of Montana, were drawn to "that sterling progressive Democrat, Franklin D. Roosevelt" was one of Walsh's assumptions; and he noted that prominent progressives on the Republican side, as well as the Democratic, were strongly supporting the governor. He was glad to speak out for his friend and former U.S. senator, Alva Adams, who was seeking to return to the Senate. As a member of the Senate Public Lands Committee, Adams had helped him in the Teapot Dome probe and now was opposing a Republican who had been on the wrong side of that issue. Though talking mostly of issues in 1932, the Montanan obviously found it difficult to forget his "historic inquiry" of the 1920s.[20]

Soon Walsh was back in south-central Montana doing his best for the Montana Democratic ticket, as well as for Roosevelt, although the latter did not need much help. By railway if possible and automobile elsewhere, Walsh made his way from town to town, always finding a welcome as one of the Democratic party's notable leaders. The task on this Montana tour was to help reelect Governor Erickson and to defeat if possible the formidable Scott Leavitt, who had represented the eastern district in Congress since 1923.[21]

The first stop was Hardin on the Crow Indian Reservation in what was said to be "one of the largest political gatherings ever held in this little town." On November 1 Walsh spoke at a Democratic rally in Billings emphasizing his theme of the need for relief legislation and Hoover's "pretense of authorship" of Democratic legislation.[22]

A day later, Walsh, along with Governor Erickson, spoke before a large crowd in Livingston. Previously Walsh was the "honor guest at a dinner attended by more than 150." The senator in his address remarked about failures of agricultural policy in the Hoover administration, although, he gibed: "Our economic policies are perfect, in the opinion of those who have guided and directed our government for the past twelve years."[23]

At Harlowton on November 3, Walsh's themes were similar as they were at Lewistown where voters filled the hall to hear his address. The next stop was Stanford to the west of Lewistown where Walsh predicted that "REPUBLICANS WILL JOIN IN VOTING FOR ROOSEVELT." He was speaking primarily of Republicans who were progressive in viewpoint. When Walsh arrived in Helena soon thereafter he was reported to have said (not surprisingly) that Montana was for Roosevelt and for Governor Erickson's reelection. An article of Sunday, November 7, stated that, notwithstanding Walsh's strenuous schedule of addresses, "the senior senator presents a picture of health." He was tanned by "autumnal winds and much driving" on his trips.[24]

Walsh closed his tour at the Marlow Theatre on Monday night, the day before the election, and received an "ovation," according to the *Helena Independent*. "From the orchestra pit came the strains of 'Row, Row, Row With Roosevelt' and 'Happy Days Are Here Again' and the rhythm of campaign music was caught up by the happy crowd and flung in reverberations from back stage to gallery heights."

"When [county] chairman Hugh Adair grasped the arm of Senator Walsh and escorted him to the speaker's table, the orchestra struck up 'Auld Lang Syne.' The crowd arose en masse to pay merited homage."[25]

Headlines on November 9 and November 10 suggested the political avalanche that had occurred. "ROOSEVELT AND GARNER SWEEP NATION"; "MAJORITY OF ROOSEVELT IS NEW RECORD." Hoover had managed to carry only one county in Montana—Sweetgrass—and that by 22 votes. One can imagine the feelings of satisfaction with which Walsh greeted his friends in Helena and set out to return to his Washington office. The long fight to restore Democratic rule at the state and national level had succeeded, notwithstanding near hopelessness at times. Erickson and the state Democratic ticket had been successful.[26]

When Walsh arrived at his office on Capitol Hill he found a letter from Governor Erickson: "Thank you for your telegram of congratulations. I want to thank you for your very fine support and I assure you it is greatly appreciated, and I bespeak the sentiment of my associates on the ticket who were successful. It was a glorious victory from President down." Neither man could possibly realize that Governor Erickson would soon be in Washington to occupy Walsh's Senate seat.[27]

33

The "New Deal" Begins, Remarriage, and Death

W alsh led a dramatic life, and the final months were no exception. From Washington, he wrote to an editor in December 1932: "I am driven so hard here that you must excuse me from furnishing the article for which you ask." The Montanan had a busy time inside the Senate and out from December 1932 to March 1933, as he tried to maintain his usual pace regarding legislative matters and the problems that included a cabinet position which FDR urged upon him.[1]

Returning to Washington after his fall campaign efforts, Walsh attended to duties in the second session of the Seventy-second Congress and hoped for action on the World Court protocols and the St. Lawrence Seaway. The *New York Times* noted that he was "assistant Democratic floor leader of the Senate," and, further, that he was one of the senators "closest to the President-elect and at the same time a member of the committee on foreign relations." His correspondence makes clear that he was most interested in the Seaway and the Court though anticipating difficulty in getting them through the Senate.[2]

Walsh had something to say about the repeal of the Prohibition Amendment as a member of the Judiciary Committee's subcommittee concerned with the subject. He showed no signs of retreating on repeal, while indicating he had not changed his mind on the desirability of moderation where alcohol was concerned.[3]

Along with Senators Robinson, Borah, and others on the Foreign Relations Committee, Walsh was prepared to urge "recognition of the Soviet Government." He was quoted as saying: "I am now and long have been in favor of the recognition of the existing government of Russia." Commercial advantages were the main consideration with him, he said. The Montanan participated in discussions of the Glass-Steagall banking bill, Philippine independence, unemployment relief (which concerned him greatly), loans to the states through the Reconstruction Finance Corporation to help in the building of highways, and many other matters.[4]

In early January 1933, Walsh visited the president-elect at Hyde Park and announced his support for a proposed increase in the income tax that had been agreed upon by Democratic congressional leaders. "We have to have the money," he said, and there was not "any better way" to get it; the budget ought to be balanced. He expressed his opposition to a sales tax. Walsh said he had discussed with Roosevelt "the balancing of the budget, beer, repeal of the Eighteenth Amendment, and the St. Lawrence Seaway." Another subject that came up was Walsh's joining the cabinet and which position he probably would occupy if he decided to leave the Senate.[5]

The Montanan wrote to his daughter on this matter a few days after seeing the president-elect: "There isn't much to tell about my visit with Governor Roosevelt. He wrote saying he wanted me to come to talk with him about the St. Lawrence seaway. Most gratifyingly I found him for it if New York does not have to pay too much for the power to be developed. He remarked as I was about to leave that he wanted me in the cabinet (this is on the q.t.) and that we would talk further about the subject and the particular place when he comes here next week." In closing, Walsh said "obviously there are only three places thinkable—state, justice and interior."

The Montanan told his daughter in another letter that the State Department was really out because, "I couldn't hold up that place on the salary and my meager income otherwise." Practically speaking, he and others were thinking that, if he went to the cabinet, it would be to the Justice Department.[6]

A number of complimentary letters came to Walsh's office in the Senate office building, hailing the idea of his joining the cabinet as attorney general or secretary of state or—even better—of his gaining a seat on the Supreme Court. Some of these letters, particularly if written in February or early March, he never had an opportunity to answer. A Washington lawyer, Charles A. Douglas, wrote: "We will sorely need just such an Attorney General as I know you would make, and then again, it will be an easy and natural thing for you to move up to the place that God made for you." The journalist Herbert Bayard Swope of New York City wrote: "I think you have a real contribution to make to any position you hold, in the way of character, dignity, intelligence, and human sympathy." Justice of the Supreme Court Pierce Butler said that, assuming Walsh was to be the attorney general, "I hasten to extend my best wishes to you and to congratulate the President-elect and the country."

Former Attorney General Thomas W. Gregory sent a telegram: "Your selection fulfills my hopes." He congratulated Walsh "and the nation." The *Nation* magazine declared: "Senator Walsh's selection as Attorney General puts at the head of that department for the first time in much more than a decade a man who is not a reactionary and a trusted friend of the 'interests' but a relentless and brilliant prosecutor." Surveying the cabinet selections near the end of February, The *Washington Daily News* declared: "The outstanding individual among Mr. Roosevelt's selections is Sen. Walsh, the prospective Attorney General, the one member who on his public performance to date might be considered of presidential caliber."

Two comments seemed most pertinent because they were similar to what Roosevelt himself had said in urging Walsh to join the cabinet (or so Walsh recalled in writing to his daughter). Leo S. Rowe, Director General of the Pan-American Union in Washington, stated: "Few men in public life enjoy, to quite the same extent as you, the complete confidence of the entire country." And Finis J. Garrett, Associate Judge of the U.S. Court of Customs and Patent Appeals in Washington, wrote to Walsh: "Personally I have the feeling that no single act of the President-elect has done more to inspire public confidence in the genuine success and historic greatness of his administration than this."[7]

On January 20 Senator Walsh reported to Genevieve that "Governor Roosevelt today asked me—in fact urged me to take the Attorney Generalship and sweetened the offer by proposing to appoint me to the Supreme Court—vacancies being anticipated." Walsh added: "My very strong preference is to stay where I am, but if it be true, as the Governor insists, that no one in the country commands public confidence in the same measure as I and that no appointment he can make would be so generally acclaimed it is hard to resist. . . . There could not fail to be embarrassment and possibly estrangement should I at this juncture fail him." He invited his daughter's comment.[8]

In his letter to the president-elect of January 24, 1933, and other letters as well, Walsh discussed his concerns about retirement from the Senate. He worried most of all over the World Court, which was obviously in "peril." Even his colleague Wheeler might vote with progressive Republicans who opposed. Hugo Black of Alabama, "an able young man," had declined to commit himself, and Senator Walter George of Georgia, another "high class lawyer," might be "adverse." Walsh discussed other opponents, or possible opponents, and said that he feared "the case for adherence will be but feebly presented in my absence." The Montanan concluded: "Defeat would be a sorry blow to the prestige of the administration both at home and abroad."[9]

As to the Canadian Treaty, or St. Lawrence Seaway, he said the situation was "scarcely less serious," with opposition coming from the railroads, the power interests, the exporting interests in many cities, and others. So far Walsh had "pulled the laboring oar" and he feared that others interested, such as Borah, Vandenberg, and La Follette, would not make this a "major consideration." Walsh stated: "I should like to be remembered by the people of that section [the northwest], to whom it would be a boon, as one who contributed conspicuously in its consummation."[10]

Walsh thought that the outlook for the Senate in other respects, too, was "disturbing," for one thing because Huey Long had an "evident purpose to rule the place" and because some colleagues might be "driven to extremes by the desperate plight of their constituents." He gave examples of these tendencies and of one colleague who came over to his desk a few days before and said that Walsh's presence in the Senate was badly needed just now. Others seemed to feel the same way. The Montanan also expressed concern about who would be named to replace him, particularly since the person chosen must stand for reelection in 1934 and he should be a Democrat who came from east of the mountains (not Butte, since Wheeler resided there) and who could win in the Republican state of Montana.[11]

When Roosevelt replied to "Dear Tom" on February 3, he made a strong argument for Walsh joining the cabinet. He had delayed answering, he said, because he knew that he should "give real consideration" to the questions raised. FDR argued that he might be able to "swing quite a number of our friends such as Black, George and others"; and the use of a caucus in the Senate might help. He thought that Walsh, too, would still have "a great influence among your old colleagues." So far as the Seaway was concerned, he mentioned his "own influence in New York and the Eastern Seaboard." He complimented Walsh concerning "the practically unanimous national acclaim of your appointment as the Head of the Department of Justice" and continued: "Countless people have already told me—Republicans and Democrats of great prominence—that your appointment will restore a great measure of faith on the part of the public in the administration of justice." And, he said: "For all of these reasons I am made personally really jubilant that you will be in this important 'key' post in the 'family'—not only because of my personal happiness at having you at my side, but also because of the importance of the position to the Country as a whole." Finally he concluded: "Take care of yourself. You have made me very happy. Cordially and affectionately yours."[12]

It is apparent why Walsh decided that, notwithstanding his doubts, he should accept the cabinet appointment. He wrote to Governor Erickson on

February 22 saying: "I hereby tender my resignation as United States Senator from the State of Montana, for the term ending March 4, 1937, to take effect at noon on the fourth day of March, 1933." If he had known the governor's ambitions Walsh might have held on to his Senate seat. For Erickson likely thought of resigning from his post and having the lieutenant governor appoint him to fill Walsh's place when he moved to the cabinet.[13]

No one could know what would happen next. Walsh had been seeing a widow named Señora Nieves Peres Chaumont de Truffin (Mina) occasionally when in Cuba. A trip to Florida for a rest and some rounds of golf turned into a wedding trip as announced by newspapers on February 25 or thereabouts when the senator flew from Miami to Havana and was married at Mina's country home on Saturday, February 25. The wedding was speeded up, Walsh said, to avoid publicity and to enable him to get back to his work in Washington. First pictures revealed a comely "Bride of Sen. T. J. Walsh" who appeared to be in her twenties or thirties. Later pictures and information made clear that the bride was closer to sixty than thirty. A vivacious woman who spoke English adequately, she often was in New York or Washington, and Walsh had seen her over a period of years. Probably her Catholic faith made her more appealing to the senator. As a father without a son, or a grandson, Walsh must have liked the idea of gaining two foster sons. He also was a strongly individualistic man yielding to a romantic streak that some had failed to recognize in him. Contrary to newspaper accounts, Mina was not a wealthy woman, having suffered with her family and others from a collapse in sugar prices.[14]

After the wedding, Walsh and his bride traveled to Miami by plane and briefly honeymooned in Florida. Walsh went to the Jackson Memorial Hospital in Miami to see the wounded Mayor Cermak of Chicago, injured in the attack on president-elect Roosevelt; then the two honeymooners went up the east coast to Daytona Beach, where Walsh probably had stayed before, and remained about 24 hours. Almost immediately he was suffering from indigestion or some condition that could have been a heart problem, as his wife remembered soon after. The attending physician said that he advised Walsh to stay in bed and not to try to go to Washington, but the senator declared that he "had to go on." Those who saw Walsh in Daytona Beach or on the Seaboard Airline train that he boarded with Mina, remembered that he did not look well. On the night of March 1 he seemed ill but wanted to go to sleep, his wife said. So she tucked him in his bunk.[15]

When she awoke the next morning Walsh was lying on the stateroom floor, face down, and could not be revived by Mina, the porter, or a physician-passenger who came in and tried to help. Briefly, the stricken man had a faint pulse and then was declared dead. A priest among the passengers administered the rite of extreme unction. At Rocky Mount, North Carolina, the body was removed from the train and prepared for burial, while Mrs. Walsh, suffering herself from a mild heart condition, had to be attended by a physician in the city, although she was said to have borne up well after her first "hysteria." The next train did not leave for Washington until 3 P.M.. Walsh was gone, and it was a long grim day for his widow.[16]

According to accounts in the *New York Times*, Mina's maid, Rosalie, who spoke only Spanish and that rapidly, had added to the confusion. Several hundred people gathered quietly at the funeral parlor in Rocky Mount to pay their respects. Captain Emmet Gudger, Walsh's son-in-law, arrived by airplane from the naval base at Hampton Roads, and soon went on to Washington to try and make arrangements. Genevieve Walsh Gudger, meanwhile, telephoned her friend, Frances Parkinson Keyes, to arrange for escorting Mina Walsh to the apartment at Crescent Place where she was to have lived with Senator Walsh. Genevieve soon arrived in Washington with her two daughters.[17]

Much had happened, meanwhile, in the capital. When the Senate convened on March 2, the morning Walsh died, Minority Leader Joseph Robinson was said to have had "tears in his eyes" as he announced the passing of their colleague, "one of our ablest and most beloved members." Walsh, he said, had served for twenty years in the Senate with "exceptional ability and constant loyalty to duty." After Vice President Charles Curtis had named a delegation of senators to act as pallbearers, the Senate and House adjourned almost immediately, "as a gesture of respect," said the *New York Times*, while many others including President Hoover and President-elect Franklin Roosevelt, also paid their respects.[18]

Members of the Senate and Walsh's family decided there should be a State Funeral in the Senate on Monday, March 6, and another service in Helena, Montana; Walsh would be laid to rest beside his first wife, Elinor, in the Resurrection Cemetery. Mina Walsh decided she would not make the trip to Helena, and Genevieve believed that, all things considered (especially Mina's near hysteria), this was a good decision. An odd result of Walsh's death was the belief by some, especially in Montana, that the senator had been murdered. One theory was that a Cuban faction hostile to the dictator, Machado Morales, with whom the de Truffins had been friendly, induced or paid Mina's maid, Rosalie, to poison Senator Walsh. According to a second theory, someone in the business world, fearing Walsh's antimonopoly proclivities as the new attorney general, had found a way to murder him. It is noteworthy that Mina de Truffin Walsh expressed her willingness to have an autopsy performed and that Genevieve Walsh Gudger did not take the rumors seriously.[19]

For those who loved and admired Walsh some satisfaction could be found in the tributes paid him by newspapers across the political spectrum; for example, by the *New York Times*, notably on March 3, 1933, and by the *New York Sun* on that day, in an editorial and in a poem that read, in part:

> Senator Thomas J. Walsh
> A sudden darkness fills the scene
> And dims the eye.
> A penetrating light, long seen,
> Fades into night—

Rather remarkably, the *New York Times*, which had treated Walsh skeptically during most of his early career in the Senate, gave him on March 3 a first-page column, almost a full page inside concerning his career and death, and a tribute on the editorial page that was probably unsurpassed for anyone below the presidential level.

Afterword

Walsh's successes came from great skill as a lawyer and a determination to achieve. This ability and determination enabled him after years of struggle to rise to the top in Montana and to give legal advice to men such as Joseph M. Dixon, who preceded Walsh in the Congress. By 1910 Walsh was ready to try for the Senate and did so by traveling the state and campaigning for the election of qualified men to the legislature who would in turn vote for him for the position of senator. The Democrats won the legislature, but under pressure from the Anaconda Copper Mining Company did not elect Walsh to the Senate. Rather, with his concurrence, Democrats elected one of their own, Henry L. Myers. Walsh, however, was recognized as a martyred leader in the long and bitter struggle and two years later was elected in his own right. From that time to 1946 no Republican was elected to the Senate from Montana, although they had dominated the office previously.

When Walsh gained a Senate seat and a place on the Judiciary Committee, he had succeeded almost beyond his dreams. Other successes followed, such as that to confirm the nomination of Louis D. Brandeis for a seat on the U.S. Supreme Court. Walsh's effectiveness and reputation for "progressivism" led to his becoming President Wilson's western manager in the campaign of 1916 and to giving major assistance in a dramatic "winning of the West."

That Walsh should love the Senate and wish to remain there was hardly a surprise, particularly when by 1924 he had become a hero of the Teapot Dome investigation, using all of his skills as interrogator and investigator. By the fall of 1928 he abandoned any idea of a presidential nomination for himself and looked with new respect to the recently elected governor of New York, Franklin D. Roosevelt. Among the Montanan's accumulating honors was that of assistant minority leader of the Senate and permanent chairman of the Democratic National Convention in Chicago in 1932, that nominated Roosevelt for president. Although his position in the Senate was a precious one to him, and he loathed the thought of leaving to become attorney general, eventually he yielded to Roosevelt's blandishments, intending to become the nation's chief law officer; doubtless, at times, he relished the thought of this honor.

If Walsh had lived to join the cabinet of Franklin Roosevelt in 1933, he would have been a progressive influence, probably of the Brandeisian (or individualistic) school. He would have been the senior cabinet officer and a strong influence. Whether he would have advised Roosevelt against the "Court packing" scheme remains a question, but this much can be said: He was virtually certain to support FDR's economic programs and to disapprove of a Court that seemed to stand in the way of progress. He was not in awe of the Justices and could well have backed the FDR plan much as Homer E. Cummings did as the new attorney general.

Notes

Abbreviations

Cong. Rec.	*Congressional Record*
E.M.	Elinor McClements
E.W.	Elinor McClements Walsh
GFT	*Great Falls Tribune*
HI	*Helena Independent*
LC	Library of Congress, Washington, D.C.
NYT	*New York Times*
NYW	*New York World*
Walsh Mss	Thomas J. Walsh Papers, LC
W-G Mss	Walsh-Gudger Collection, Illinois Historical Survey, University of Illinois Library, Urbana-Champaign

Chapter 1: An Irish-American Family

1. William Hard, *Washington Star,* Nov. 2, 1930, Cavanaugh to Walsh, June 13, 1931, Walsh Mss. A copy of the original manuscript of this study (1996) may be found in the Manuscript Division of the Library of Congress and in the Illinois Historical Survey at the University of Illinois Library, Urbana-Champaign.

2. John Walsh to Genevieve Walsh Gudger, July 2, 1933, Katherine Walsh Wattawa to Genevieve Gudger, n.d. (but 1933), W-G Mss.

3. Carl Wittke, *The Irish in America* (Baton Rouge: Louisiana State University Press, 1956), 10, 36–37, and passim; Rowland Tappan Berthoff, *British Immigrants in Industrial America* (Cambridge: Harvard University Press, 1963), 212. See also William V. Shannon, *The American Irish: A Political and Social Portrait* (New York: Collier Macmillan, 1963).

4. Sister M. Justille McDonald, *History of the Irish in Wisconsin in the Nineteenth Century* (Washington, D.C.: Catholic University Press, 1954), 7–8, 46–53, 88–89, and passim.

5. A good account of the Walsh family in Two Rivers is Joseph Schafer, "Thomas James Walsh: A Wisconsin Gift to Montana," *Wisconsin Magazine of History* 23 (June 1940), 448–73.

6. J. F. Wojta, "The Town of Two Creeks, Manitowoc County," *Wisconsin Magazine of History* 25 (Dec. 1941), 138, 146–47; Louis Falge, ed., *History of Manitowoc County, Wisconsin*, 2 vols. (Chicago: Goodspeed Historical Association, 1912); Reuben Gold Thwaites, *Wisconsin: The Americanization of a French Settlement* (Boston: Houghton Mifflin, 1908).

7. Reminiscences of John Walsh and Katherine Walsh Wattawa, passim, statement by Mr. Vandril, Two Rivers, Wis., June 1933, Walsh diary, Apr. 18, 1923, W-G Mss; Two Rivers, Wis., City Ledger, vol. I.

8. Walsh to E.M., Dec. 19, 1885, in J. Leonard Bates, ed., *Tom Walsh in Dakota Territory: Personal Correspondence of Senator Thomas J. Walsh and Elinor C. McClements* (Urbana: University of Illinois Press, 1966), 63. See also Katherine Walsh Wattawa reminiscences, W-G Mss.

9. Walsh to E.W., July 9, 1906, and passim, W-G Mss. Personal correspondence for the 1890s and thereafter consists of original manuscripts.

10. Walsh to Peter Scharrenbroich, Helena, Oct. 1, 1912, W-G Mss.

11. Schafer, "Walsh," 449; Wittke, *Irish in America*, 106; "Felix Walsh—Obituary," *Manitowoc County Chronicle* (Two Rivers, Wis.), Sept. 8, 1891; John Walsh reminiscences, W-G Mss.

12. McDonald, *History of the Irish in Wisconsin*, passim; Katherine Walsh Wattawa reminiscences, W-G Mss; Schafer, "Walsh," passim.

13. Katherine Walsh Wattawa and John Walsh reminiscences, W-G Mss; Bates, ed., *Tom Walsh in Dakota*, 23, 265, and passim.

14. Walsh to E.W., Aug. 18, 1898, W-G Mss; clipping on Mrs. Elizabeth Martin Harris, *Chronicle* (Two Rivers, Wis.), n.d. (but 1933), John Walsh reminiscences, W-G Mss.

15. Lyman J. Nash et al., *Pioneer Courts and Lawyers* (Manitowoc, Wis.: Manitowoc Pilot, 1921), 7–8; Walsh quoted in "The John Nagle Memorial," *Wisconsin Magazine of History* 14 (Dec. 1930), 223; John Walsh reminiscences, W-G Mss; J. S. Anderson to Sen. Walsh, Aug. 31, 1923, Walsh to Anderson, Sept. 13, 1923, Walsh Mss.

16. Walsh to E.M., Oct. 9, 1887, Bates, ed., *Tom Walsh in Dakota*, 140.

Chapter 2: The Young Intellectual

1. *Cong. Rec.*, 63d Cong., 2d Sess. (Oct. 5, 1914), 16151; Walsh to E.M., Aug. 24, 1884, Bates, ed., *Tom Walsh in Dakota*, 4; interview with former Sen. Henry F. Ashurst, Sept. 9, 1949, Washington, D.C.

2. Walsh to Patrick J. Haltigan, Sept. 20, 1929, Walsh Mss.

3. Walsh diary, Oct. 7, 1923, W-G Mss; Walsh to E.M., July 18, 1886, Dec. 10, 1888, Bates, ed., *Tom Walsh in Dakota*, 87–88, 207–8; address at Eureka, Dakota Terr., July 4, 1889, W-G Mss.

4. Papers and certificates, Katherine Walsh Wattawa reminiscences, W-G Mss.

5. Address to the graduating class, Montana Agricultural College (Montana State University at Bozeman), June 5, 1910, W-G Mss.

6. Walsh to E.M., Dec. 11, 1881, Feb. 5, Mar. 9, Apr. 5, 1882, Bates, ed., *Tom Walsh in Dakota*, 258–64.

7. Wittke, *Irish in America*, 164–65; McDonald, *History of the Irish in Wisconsin*, 242–46; Walsh to the Door County Auxiliary Land League, Mar. 17, 1882, W-G Mss; Walsh to E.M., Apr. 5, 1882, Bates, ed., *Tom Walsh in Dakota*, 263–64.

8. Walsh to E.M., May 14, 1882, Bates, ed., *Tom Walsh in Dakota*, 265.

9. E.M. to Walsh, Nov. 20, 1881, Walsh to E.M., Nov. 26, 1881, Feb. 24, 1889, W-G Mss.

10. Walsh to E.M., Apr. 1, 1883, and passim, W-G Mss.

11. Walsh to E.M., Apr. 1, 1883, Oct. 9, 1887, Mar. 9, Nov. 12, 1882, E.M. to Walsh, Mar. 25, Nov. 19, 1882, W-G Mss; Bates, ed., *Tom Walsh in Dakota*, passim.

12. Undated paper on Byron from the Dakota period (1884–90), W-G Mss.

13. Walsh to E.M., July 7, 1889, Bates, ed., *Tom Walsh in Dakota*, 242–43; Larry Gara, *A Short History of Wisconsin* (Madison: State Historical Society of Wisconsin, 1962).

14. Interview with former Sen. Henry F. Ashurst, Sept. 9, 1949; Walsh to E.M., Oct. 23, 1883, W-G Mss.

15. *The Badger*, Nov. 29, 1883, Jan. 17, 24, 1884, Nov. 8, 1883. On Chief Justice Ryan see Alfons J. Beitzinger, *Edward G. Ryan: Lion of the Law* (Madison: State Historical Society of Wisconsin, 1960).

16. Correspondence in May–June, 1884, passim, W-G Mss.

Chapter 3: On the Dakota Frontier

1. "Dakota's Vote," editorial, *Chicago Tribune*, Nov. 28, 1884; Howard R. Lamar, *Dakota Territory, 1861–1889* (New Haven: Yale University Press, 1956); Herbert S. Schell, *History of South Dakota*, 3d ed. (Lincoln: University of Nebraska Press, 1975); Dana D. Harlow, ed., *Prairie Echoes: Spink County in the Making* (Aberdeen, S.D., 1961).

2. Schell, *History of South Dakota*, 211; Walsh to E.M., Aug. 17, 1884, W-G Mss. Almost all of this correspondence for 1884–90 is in Bates, ed., *Tom Walsh in Dakota*.

3. See Robert S. Sampson, "History of Spink County Economy and Agriculture," in Harlow, ed., *Prairie Echoes*, and ibid., passim.

4. Bates, ed., *Tom Walsh in Dakota*, 14, 17; *Pioneer Press* (St. Paul and Minneapolis), Dec. 13, 1884.

5. Bates, ed., *Tom Walsh in Dakota*, 14, 17; Schell, *History of South Dakota*, 203–4.

6. See David Lindsey, *"Sunset Cox": Irrepressible Democrat* (Detroit: Wayne State University Press, 1959), 195–99.

7. *Redfield Observer,* Oct. 4, 11, 18, 1888; George W. Kingsbury, *History of Dakota Territory,* 2 vols. (Chicago, 1915), 2:1531–32, 1536; Lamar, *Dakota Territory,* 274–76.

8. Sen. James E. Murray of Montana later described Walsh's style of advocacy: "In court he was very austere, clear, cold, precise, inspiring confidence." Interview with Sen. Murray, Aug. 27, 1949, Washington, D.C.

9. *Redfield Observer,* Oct. 18, Nov. 1, 15, 1888; *Ashton Argus* quoted in ibid., Aug. 30, 1888.

10. John P. Frank, *Lincoln as a Lawyer* (Urbana: University of Illinois Press, 1961), 4–5.

11. Christopher P. Connolly, "Senator Thomas J. Walsh," *The Devil Learns to Vote: The Story of Montana* (New York: Covici, Friede, 1938), 295–303; Frank, *Lincoln as a Lawyer,* 3; Walsh to E.M., Mar. 29, 1885, W-G Mss; Bates, ed., *Tom Walsh in Dakota,* 33.

12. *Harris v. Watkins,* 5 Dakota Terr., 374–78 (1888); Walsh to E.W., Sept. 13, 1899, W-G Mss.

13. See Bates, ed., *Tom Walsh in Dakota,* 243, n.3; *Redfield Observer,* July 25, Aug. 8, 29, 1889.

14. *Redfield Observer,* May 9, 16, 1889.

15. Ibid., May 16, 1889; *Doland Times-Record* quoted in ibid., June 13, 1889; Lamar, *Dakota Territory,* 174–75.

16. Walsh to Henry T. Scudder, Feb. 18, 1913, Walsh Mss; Walsh's comments in a political debate at Townsend, *Montana Record-Herald* (Helena), Oct. 29, 1906.

17. See especially Walsh to E.M., Jan. 2, 9, 20, 1889, E.M. to Walsh, Jan. 6, 14, 1889, Bates, ed., *Tom Walsh in Dakota,* 209–15; speech by Walsh, Eureka, Dakota Terr., July 4, 1889, W-G Mss.

18. See Walsh to Mary McClements, Aug. __, 1890, Walsh to E.W., Sept. 17, 18, 1890, and notes, Bates, ed., *Tom Walsh in Dakota,* 250–54.

Chapter 4: A Helena Lawyer and Democrat

1. Walsh to E.W., Sept. 17, 1890, W-G Mss. See Michael P. Malone, Richard B. Roeder, and William L. Lang, *Montana: A History of Two Centuries,* rev. ed. (Seattle: University of Washington Press, 1991); Joseph Kinsey Howard, *Montana: High, Wide, and Handsome* (New Haven: Yale University Press, 1944); Paula Petrik, *No Step Backward: Women and Family on the Rocky Mountain Mining Frontier, Helena, Montana, 1865–1900* (Helena: Montana Historical Society Press, 1987).

2. "Mines: Montana's Contribution to Eastern Wealth," *Rocky Mountain Magazine* 1 (Jan. 1901), 395–411; C. P. Connolly, "The Story of Montana," *McClure's Magazine* 27 (Sept. 1906), 451.

3. See *Helena Weekly Herald,* Feb. 6, 13, Dec. 18, 1890, and passim for valuable in-

formation; Walsh to E.W., Sept. 17, 1890, W-G Mss; Willard B. Robinson, "Helena's Fabulous Business Blocks," *Montana: The Magazine of Western History* 18 (Jan. 1968), 46–59.

4. Petrik, *No Step Backward,* 51–53 and passim.

5. U.S. Census, 1890; Carter to Mrs. Carter, Nov. 9, 1890, Thomas Henry Carter Mss (hereafter Carter Mss), LC; *Helena Weekly Herald,* Apr. 24, July 8, Oct. 16, Dec. 18, 1890; G. L. Foster in *Red Bluff Daily News* (Calif.), Mar. 15, 1924, W-G Mss; *Muller v. Buyck,* 12 Mont., 354–57 (1892); C. P. Connolly, "The Man Who Blew the Lid Off Teapot Dome," *Hearst's International* 46 (Sept. 1924), 57.

6. For Walsh's office location and home address, see the Helena City Directory for 1891.

7. Connolly, "Walsh," *Devil Learns to Vote;* Connolly, "Teapot Dome," 57; Foster in *Red Bluff Daily News,* Mar. 15, 1924.

8. Thomas J. Walsh account book, 1891–99, W-G Mss; Connolly, "Walsh," *Devil Learns to Vote; HI,* Oct. 28, 1894.

9. Walsh to John Walsh, Sept. 2, 1891, W-G Mss.

10. Carter to Mrs. Carter, Dec. 15, 1892, box 1, Carter Mss, LC; Walsh to E.W., Dec. 19, 1893, W-G Mss.

11. Walsh to E.W., Apr. 13, 1896, Mar. 31, 1903, W-G Mss; interview with Wellington Rankin, May 24, 1961, Helena; interview with Mrs. Raymond Wine, May 22, 1961, Helena.

12. Address at the Montana Agricultural College, Bozeman, June 5, 1910, W-G Mss; address to the graduating class of Suffolk Law School, Boston, June 6, 1929, in *Cong. Rec.,* 71st Cong., 1st Sess. (June 19, 1929), 3161–64.

13. Walsh speech, n.d. (but 1892), Walsh speech of Oct. 13, 1892, address by Walsh on contingent fees, at a meeting of the American Bar Association, Seattle, Wash., Aug. 25–28, 1908, W-G Mss; Arnold M. Paul, *Conservative Crisis and the Rule of Law: Attitudes of Bar and Bench, 1887–1895* (Ithaca: Cornell University Press, 1960), 39–60.

14. Connolly, "Walsh," *Devil Learns to Vote;* interview with Sen. James E. Murray, Aug. 27, 1949; Justice William H. De Witt in *Sanford* v. *Gates,* 18 Mont. 398 (1896).

15. E.W. to Walsh, quoting Judge _____ Bennett, Apr. 19, 1893, W-G Mss; interview with Judge Jeremiah Lynch, May 22, 1961, Helena.

16. Address in Seattle, W-G Mss; Walsh to E.W., Sept. 10, 11, Dec. 15, 1895, May 13, 1898, W-G Mss.

17. E.W. to Walsh, Feb. 21, 1890, Bates, ed., *Tom Walsh in Dakota,* 248–50; Walsh to E.W., Feb. 26, 1896, July 27, 1899, W-G Mss.

18. Walsh to E.W., Aug. 10, 11, 23, Sept. 17, 21, 1895, E.W. to Walsh, Sept. 10, 1895, W-G Mss.

19. Walsh to E.W., Sept. 11, 1895, Feb. 7, 1896, Aug. 22, 1898, and passim, W-G Mss; J. Leonard Bates, "Thomas J. Walsh: His 'Genius for Controversy,'" *Montana* 19 (Oct. 1969), 2–15.

20. *Zickler* v. *Deegan et al.*, 16 Mont. 198 (1895); Walsh to E.W., Apr. 25, 1893, W-G Mss.

21. *Kelley* v. *The Fourth of July Mining Company*, 16 Mont. 484 (1895); *Charles Kelley* v. *Joseph K. Clark*, 21 Mont. 291 (1898); Walsh et al., Collected Briefs, vol. 1, Montana State Law Library, Helena; Walsh to E.W., Sept. 5, 21, 24, 1895, Aug. 11, 1898, Apr. 11, 1899, W-G Mss; *Engineering and Mining Journal* 66 (July 16, 1898), 78; Connolly, "Teapot Dome," 148–49.

22. *Helena Herald*, Jan. 16, 17, 1895; Connolly, "Teapot Dome," 148.

23. *Helena Herald*, editorial, Jan. 16, 1895; *Cameron* v. *Kenyon-Connell Commercial Co.*, 22 Mont. 312 (1899); Walsh et al., Collected Briefs, vol. 1; Walsh to E.W., Dec. 15, 1895, Feb. 28, 1896, and passim, W-G Mss.

24. Walsh's letters to E.W., early Jan. 1894, W-G Mss.

25. Merrill G. Burlingame and K. Ross Toole, eds., *A History of Montana*, 3 vols. (New York: Lewis Historical Publishing Co., 1957), 1:193.

26. Walsh speech, n.d. (but before the campaign of 1892 had entered its decisive phases), W-G Mss; Helena City Directory for 1892.

27. See "Ghost Town," in John K. Hutchens, *One Man's Montana: An Informal Portrait of a State* (Philadelphia: J. B. Lippincott, 1964).

28. Address at Marysville, Sept. 24, 1892, and at East Helena, Oct. 13, 1892, W-G Mss.

29. Speeches at Granite, East Helena, and Marysville, passim, W-G Mss; John Higham, *Strangers in the Land: Patterns of American Nativism, 1860–1925* (New Brunswick: Rutgers University Press, 1955), 80–87.

30. See speech at Marysville, Sept. 24, 1892, and passim, W-G Mss.

Chapter 5: Politics, Law, and the Copper Kings

1. Walsh speech at Fargo, N.D., Jan. 18, 1912, E.W. to Walsh, Aug. 27, 1898, W-G Mss; Connolly, "Story of Montana," 452. See also Michael P. Malone, *The Battle for Butte: Mining and Politics on the Northern Frontier, 1864–1906* (Seattle: University of Washington Press, 1981), 80, 110, and passim; Clark C. Spence, *Territorial Politics and Government in Montana, 1864–89* (Urbana: University of Illinois Press, 1975), 309.

2. U.S. Congress, Senate, *Montana Senatorial Election* (hereafter *Mont. Sen. Election*), 1899, Report of the Committee on Privileges and Elections, Senate Report 1052, in 3 parts, ser. 3891–93 (Washington, D.C.: Government Printing Office [hereafter GPO], 1900), William A. Clark's testimony, 3:1756 and passim; report of the majority, 1:1–15; testimony of C. B. Nolan in "Memorial of Citizens of Montana," 1:70 and passim; Malone, *Battle for Butte*, passim.

3. *Mont. Sen. Election*, Daly's testimony, 3:2204–39 and passim; Malone, *Battle for Butte*, 18–19 and passim.

4. Sarah McNelis, *Copper King at War: The Biography of F. Augustus Heinze* (Mis-

soula: University of Montana Press, 1968), 186–89 and passim; K. Ross Toole, *Twentieth-Century Montana: A State of Extremes* (Norman: University of Oklahoma Press, 1972), 112 and passim.

5. Connolly, "Story of Montana," 463.

6. A. J. Steele to Samuel Hauser, Oct. 10, 1892, Samuel T. Hauser Mss, Montana Historical Society, Helena; Connolly, "Story of Montana," 464–65; *Helena News,* Jan. 4, 1894.

7. Correspondence between Walsh and E.W., passim, W-G Mss.

8. Walsh to E.W., Nov. 4, 1894, W-G Mss; *HI,* Nov. 4, 1894; Walsh, speech or portion of speech given in Butte or nearby, n.d., W-G Mss.

9. *Anaconda Standard,* Nov. 8, 1894, 1.

10. *HI,* Sept. 25, 1894, 1.

11. Walsh speech in ibid., Oct. 27, 1906; Thomas A. Clinch, *Urban Populism and Free Silver in Montana* (Missoula: University of Montana Press, 1970), 140, 153, and passim.

12. Clinch, *Urban Populism in Montana,* passim; E.W. to Walsh, Sept. 2, 1896, W-G Mss; *Helena Weekly Herald,* Sept. 10, 1896, 4.

13. Connolly, *Devil Learns to Vote,* 297; Walsh to E.W., Dec. 23, 1896, W-G Mss.

14. Walsh to E.W., Dec. 23, 1896, Aug. 11, 1898, July 18, 1899, W-G Mss.

15. Walsh to E.W., Aug. 16, 1898, E.W. to Walsh, Aug. 22, 27, 1898, W-G Mss; *Mont. Sen. Election,* testimony by Charles W. Clark, 3:2048–49 and passim.

16. *Mont. Sen. Election,* testimony by Fred Whiteside, 1:89 and passim; Ralph E. Owings, ed., *Montana Directory of Public Affairs, 1864–1960* (Ann Arbor: Edwards Brothers, 1960), 103–4; Malone, *Battle for Butte,* 111ff.

17. Brief by Jesse B. Roote, *State of Montana ex rel. Fred Whiteside* v. *First Judicial District Court,* 24 Mont. 539 (1900), in Walsh et al., Collected Briefs, 15 vols. (microfilmed as Montana Supreme Court, *Briefs Submitted to the Court,* 7 reels, University of Illinois Library, Urbana-Champaign), 3:525; Malone, *Battle for Butte,* 195–200.

18. Walsh to E.W., Nov. 15, 1899, W-G Mss.

19. Walsh to E.W., June 20, 1900, W-G Mss.

20. Walsh to E.W., July 30, 1899, Feb. 24, 1901, and passim in 1901, W-G Mss; Walsh to B. K. Wheeler, Jan. 21, 1921, Walsh Mss.

21. C. P. Connolly, "The Fight of the Copper Kings," *McClure's Magazine* 29 (June 1907), 221; Malone, *Battle for Butte,* 150–79 and passim.

22. Walsh to E.W., Sept. 21, 1902, W-G Mss.

Chapter 6: Lawyer, Progressive, and Public Man

1. See Sidney Fine, *Laissez Faire and the General-Welfare State: A Study of Conflict in American Thought, 1865–1901* (Ann Arbor: University of Michigan Press, 1956) and Russel B. Nye, *Midwestern Progressive Politics: A Historical Study of Its Origins and Development, 1870–1950* (East Lansing: Michigan State College Press, 1951); Dewey

W. Grantham, "The Progressive Era and the Reform Movement," *Mid-America* 46 (Oct. 1964), 227–51; Walsh speech at Fargo, N.D., Jan. 18, 1912, W-G Mss.

2. Walsh to E.W., Mar. 31, 1905, June 5, 1907, W-G Mss; *HI*, editorial, Sept. 26, 1906, 4.

3. Brief by Jesse B. Roote, in *State ex rel. Whiteside* v. *First Judicial District Court,* in Walsh et al., Collected Briefs, 3:525; Walsh to E.W., Oct. 20, 1912, W-G Mss; Bates, "T. J. Walsh: His 'Genius for Controversy,'" 10–14; *Montana Lookout,* Aug. 8, 1908, 8; *HI,* Aug. 22, 1906, 4, Oct. 1906, passim; Walsh address in Seattle, W-G Mss.

4. *Helena Democrat and Insurgent,* Sept. 15, 1910; *Montana Lookout,* July 24, 1909, 9, Oct. 30, 1909, 9; Walsh to E.W., July 19, 22, 27, 1897, W-G Mss; Walsh address at the Montana Agricultural College, Bozeman, June 5, 1910, W-G Mss; address by Walter S. Hartman at the memorial service for Walsh, Helena, Mar. 4, 1934, W-G Mss.

5. E.W.'s activities in "The Ideal Scrapbook," W-G Mss; Petrik, *No Step Backward,* 123; E.W. to Sen. Thomas Carter, Feb. 10, 1910, box 9, Carter Mss, LC; *HI,* Jan. 29, 1903, 5; ibid., Mar. 12, 1916, Walsh Mss, Scrapbooks; Walsh to E.W., Feb. 25, 1901, W-G Mss; *Montana Lookout,* May 14, 1910, 9.

6. *Montana Daily Record* (Helena), Dec. 13, 14, 1905; *HI,* Dec. 15, 1905. On the national movement for railroad regulation see George E. Mowry, *The Era of Theodore Roosevelt, 1900–1912* (New York: Harper & Row, 1958), 198–99. Some of Walsh's early mining cases, such as the fight over the Minnie Healey, have been omitted in this account (but see the writings of Christopher Connolly). The full text of Walsh's railroad address was printed in the *Montana Record,* Dec. 14, 1905.

7. Lee Mantle quoted in *Butte Evening News,* Dec. 16, 1905; *Butte Miner,* June 21, 1900; Walsh to E.W., June 20, 1900, July 29, 1906, W-G Mss.

8. Walsh to E.W., June 15, July 7, 1906, W-G Mss; Jules A. Karlin, *Joseph M. Dixon of Montana: Senator and Bull Moose Manager, 1867–1917* (Missoula: University of Montana Publications in History, 1974), passim.

9. Walsh to E.W., July 29, 1906, Sept. 5, 1906, W-G Mss; Charles Pray in *Montana Daily Record,* Oct. 3, 1906; *HI,* Aug. 22, 1906, 4, and Sept.–Oct. 1906, passim.

10. *HI,* Sept. 21, 1906, 1–2, and Sept. 26, 1906, 1–2; *Butte Miner,* Sept. 26, 1906, 1, 9; *Anaconda Standard,* Sept. 26, 1906, 1, 6, 9.

11. See "The Peerless Bryan," editorial, *Daily Missoulian,* Nov. 2, 1906, 4; *Butte Inter Mountain,* Oct. 31, 1906.

12. Walsh to E.W., June 21, 1906, Walsh to Genevieve Walsh, June 22, 1906, W-G Mss; *Montana Daily Record,* Oct. 3, 1906; *Daily Missoulian,* Oct. 8, 1906, 4; *HI,* Oct. 9, 1906, 4.

13. *HI,* Oct. 14, 1906, 1. See *HI* and *Butte Miner* for articles generally favorable to Walsh and *Missoulian* and *Record* for articles almost inevitably on the other side.

14. *Daily Missoulian,* Oct. 8, 1906, 4, and Oct. 28, 1906, 1, 8; *HI,* Oct. 28, 1906, 1, 5.

15. *Daily Missoulian,* Oct. 28, 1906, 1, 8; *HI,* Oct. 28, 1906, 1, 5; Karlin, *Joseph M. Dixon of Montana, 1867–1917,* 70–71 and passim; H. Samuel Merrill and Marion G.

Merrill, *The Republican Command, 1897–1913* (Lexington: University Press of Kentucky, 1971), passim.

16. Quoted in *Fort Benton River Press*, Nov. 14, 1906; Walsh to E.W., Oct. 13, 1907, W-G Mss.

17. Walsh to E.W., Feb. 10, 1907, W-G Mss.

18. Walsh to E.W., Feb. 20, 1907, W-G Mss.

19. Walsh to E.W., Oct. 17, 1907, W-G Mss.

20. Walsh to E.W., June 19, 1908, July 2, 1908, and passim, W-G Mss; *HI*, July 2, 1908.

21. *HI*, July 9, 1908.

Chapter 7: The Emergence of a Leader

1. Carter Mss, LC. See also Jerre C. Murphy, *The Comical History of Montana: A Serious Story for Free People* . . . (San Diego: E. L. Scofield, 1912), 49, 70–71, and passim; Malone, *Battle for Butte*, 204 and passim.

2. Carter to Sen. Winthrop Crane, July 11, 1910, Crane to Carter, July 11, 14, 1910, Aug. 19, 1910, John D. Ryan to Carter, May 10, 1910, Carter to Ryan, May 11, 1910, box 10, Carter Mss, LC.

3. Walsh to E.W., Mar. 21, 1910, W-G Mss.

4. See Walsh correspondence for 1910, passim, W-G Mss; Murphy, *Comical History of Montana*, 147 and passim; Robert M. La Follette, *La Follette's Autobiography: A Personal Narrative of Political Experiences* (Madison: Robert M. La Follette Co., 1913).

5. Carter to Arthur S. Henning, *Chicago Tribune* (Washington, D.C., Bureau), Apr. 25, 1910, Carter to E. A. Morley, May 28, 1910, Carter to Charles G. Burk, July 2, 1910, boxes 10, 11, Carter Mss, LC. See also Walsh correspondence for 1910, W-G Mss.

6. Karlin, *Joseph M. Dixon of Montana, 1867–1917*, 86–96 and passim.

7. See E. W. Beattie to Carter, July 17, 1909, Carter to J. H. Carroll, July 23, 1909, Carter to Louis W. Hill, Aug. 29, Sept. 5, 1910, Oscar Lanstrum to Carter, May 23, 1910, John D. Ryan to Carter, May 10, 1910, boxes 7, 10, Carter Mss, LC.

8. Laws of Montana, Legislative Assembly (1911), 120–24; editorial, *Montana Lookout*, Jan. 9, 1909, 4; E. W. Beattie to Carter, Jan. 20, 1909, Carter Mss, LC; Walsh to Carl H. Mote, Jan. 9, 1915, box 365, Walsh Mss.

9. Walsh speech at Fargo, N.D., Jan. 18, 1912, W-G Mss.

10. Walsh to E.W., Mar. __, 1910, Walsh to E.W., Apr. 1, 1910, Walsh telegram to E.W., Apr. 4, 1910, W-G Mss.

11. Walsh to E.W., Aug. 8, 14, 1910, W-G Mss.

12. Walsh to E.W., Aug. 14, 1910, W-G Mss.

13. Harold Blake to Sen. Carter, Mar. 15, 1910, box 9, Carter Mss, LC.

14. "The People's Choice, Limited," in *Montana Lookout*, June 4, 1910, 5; ibid., July 23, 1910, 4–5, Aug. 20, 1910, 1, 13, Sept. 10, 1910, 12–13, and Oct. 1, 1910, 5.

15. Carter to Crane, Aug. 26, 1910, Carter to Norton, Sept. 20, 1910, Carter to

Dawes, Oct. 10, 1910, Carter to McKenzie, Oct. 10, 1910, W. W. Taylor, Republic Coal Co., to Carter Oct. 17, 1910, boxes 11, 12, Carter Mss, LC.

16. T. A. Marlow to Carter, Feb. 27, 1910, Carter to Howard Elliott, Oct. 31, 1910, box 12, Carter Mss, LC.

17. Carter to Mark Sullivan, Sept. 6, 1910, Carter Mss, LC.

18. Carter to Crane, Nov. 17, 1910, Carter to Henry L. West, *Washington Herald,* Nov. 17, 1910, box 12, Carter Mss, LC; Walsh to W. J. Bryan, Dec. 26, 1910, box 386, Walsh Mss.

19. *Montana Lookout,* Nov. 26, 1910; *Cutbank Pioneer Press* in ibid., Dec. 10, 1910, 6.

20. *Montana Lookout,* Nov. 26, 1910, 4.

21. *HI,* Jan. 11, 1911, 1; *Montana Daily Record,* Jan. 10, 1911, 1, Feb. 21, 1911, 1.

22. *Anaconda Standard,* Jan. 13, 1911, 8, 11.

23. *Montana Lookout,* Jan. 14, 1911, 4, and Feb. 4, 1911; *Anaconda Standard,* Feb. 27, 1911, 1; *Montana Directory of Public Affairs,* 108–9.

24. Walsh to Bryan, Dec. 26, 1910, box 386, Walsh Mss; Dr. A. P. Rooney to Bryan, Jan. 20, 1911, W-G Mss; Clarence Darrow to Walsh, Jan. 18, 1911, enclosing copy of letter to Charles R. Moyer, Jan. 18, 1911, W-G Mss.

25. Will H. Smith to Carter, Jan. 25, 1911, Rt. Rev. John Ireland to Carter, Feb. 2, 1911, box 14, Carter Mss, LC.

26. Carter to W. F. Meyer, Mar. 17, 1911, box 14, Carter Mss, LC.

27. Walsh quoted in *HI,* Mar. 3, 1911, 1; ibid., Mar. 2, 1911; Walsh to A. E. Spriggs, Mar. 3, 1911, Spriggs to Walsh, Mar. 4, 1911, box 386, Walsh Mss.

28. "Senator Stout Serves Notice," *Fergus County Democrat,* in the *Montana Lookout,* Apr. 1, 1911, box 386, Walsh Mss.

Chapter 8: To the Senate at Last

1. Walsh speech at Fargo, N.D., Jan. 18, 1912, W-G Mss.

2. Walsh, "Growth of Democracy in the West," Jefferson Day address in Walla Walla, Wash., Apr. 13, 1912, W-G Mss. See also "Call of the West," *Walla Walla Bulletin,* Apr. 14, 1912, W-G Mss.

3. Walsh speech at Fargo, N.D., Jan. 18, 1912, W-G Mss.

4. Ibid.

5. Ibid.; Walsh to E.W., Feb. 4, May 10, 1912, W-G Mss.

6. Walsh speech at Walla Walla, Wash., Apr. 13, 1912, W-G Mss.

7. Ibid.

8. Walsh to E.W., Feb. 4, 1912, W-G Mss.

9. Walsh to E.W., Mar. 17, 1912, W-G Mss.

10. Burton Wheeler to Walsh, May 16, 1912, Walsh to Frank Woody, Mar. 21, 1912, miscellaneous correspondence, box 387, Walsh Mss.

11. Walsh to E.W., May 30, 1912, W-G Mss; *Montana Daily Record,* May 23, 1912, 5, editorials, May 23, 27, 1912.

12. Walsh to E.W., May 30, 1912, W-G Mss; *Montana Daily Record,* May 30, 1912, 1; Walsh to *Montana Daily Record,* May 31, 1912, Walsh to Tom Stout, June 6, 1912, box 387, Walsh Mss.

13. Walsh to E.W., Oct. 20, 1912, W-G Mss.

14. Walsh to Genevieve Walsh, Aug. __, 1912, Walsh to E.W., Aug. 18, 1912, Walsh to Genevieve Walsh, Aug. 23, 1912, W-G Mss.

15. *GFT,* Oct. 30, 1912, 1, 2, 9, and passim.

16. Walsh to Genevieve Walsh, Aug. __, 1912, W-G Mss; Karlin, *Joseph M. Dixon of Montana, 1867–1917,* 174.

17. Walsh to E.W., Sept. 6, Oct. 2, 1912, W-G Mss; Karlin, *Joseph M. Dixon of Montana, 1867–1917,* 172–74 and passim.

18. Walsh to E.W., Sept. 6, 1912, W-G Mss.

19. Walsh speech of Sept. 23, 1912, in *Billings Gazette,* Sept. 24, 1912, 1, 8; Josephine O'Keane, *Thomas J. Walsh: A Senator from Montana* (Francestown, N.H.: Marshall Jones, 1955), 44–46.

20. Walsh to E.W., Oct. 4, 13, 1912, W-G Mss.

21. Walsh to E.W., Oct. 13, 1912, W-G Mss.

22. See Walsh to E.W. and Genevieve Walsh, summer and fall, 1912, passim, W-G Mss.

23. E.W. to Mary D. McClements, Nov. 6, 1912, W-G Mss; *Missoulian,* Nov. 6, 1912, 1, Nov. 7, 1912, 1.

24. Wheeler to Walsh, Nov. 9, 1912, and passim, box 389, Walsh Mss.

25. Wheeler to Walsh, Nov. 9, 1912, Walsh to Wheeler, Nov. 12, 1912, box 389, Walsh Mss.

26. Miles Taylor to Walsh, Dec. 12, 1912, Political: Montana, Walsh Mss; Walsh to Dixon (alluding to Dixon's congratulations of Nov. 14 and offers of assistance), Nov. 19, 1912, Dixon to Walsh, Nov. 25, 1912, box 389, Walsh Mss.

27. *Montana Daily Record,* Jan. 14, 1913.

28. Walsh address, *Helena Daily Independent,* Jan. 16, 1913, 3. See also "Mr. Walsh's Election," editorial, ibid., Jan. 15, 1913, 4.

29. "Walsh Is Host of 1,000 Guests," ibid., Jan. 16, 1913, 5; banquet of Feb. 18, 1913, invitation and menu, W-G Mss.

Chapter 9: The Tariff Fight of 1913

1. Donald Bruce Johnson and Kirk H. Porter, comps., *National Party Platforms, 1840–1972,* 5th ed. (Urbana: University of Illinois Press, 1975), 168–69.

2. Arthur S. Link, *Wilson: The New Freedom* (Princeton: Princeton University Press, 1956), 178–81.

3. Walsh to J. S. Alling, May 20, 1913, Walsh to John Stanton, July 15, 1913, box 317, Walsh Mss.

4. Walsh to E.W., May 4, June 13, 1913, W-G Mss.

5. Walsh to E.W., June 13, 1913, W-G Mss.

6. Evans C. Johnson, *Oscar W. Underwood: A Political Biography* (Baton Rouge: Louisiana State University Press, 1980), 198–202; Link, *Wilson: The New Freedom*, 179–81.

7. Walsh to C. L. Merrill, Jan. 29, 1913, box 364, Howard Elliott, Northern Pacific Railroad, to Walsh, Apr. 1, 1913, Walsh to Elliott, Apr. 9, 1913, box 316, Walsh Mss.

8. Walsh to E.W., Aug. 9, 1913, W-G Mss.

9. Walsh to Pres. Wilson, Apr. 5, 1913, Wilson to Walsh, Apr. 7, 1913, box 316, Walsh Mss.

10. Walsh to A. L. Stone, May 22, 1913, box 317, Walsh Mss.

11. Walsh to Otis Mellon, Department of the Interior, Apr. 22, 1913, box 314, Walsh to Judge C. C. Hurley, May 30, 1913, box 317, Walsh Mss.

12. Walsh to S. O. C. Brady, Apr. 28, 1913, Walsh to J. S. Alling, May 15, 1913, box 317, Walsh Mss.

13. Walsh to Penwell, Apr. 16, 1913, Penwell to Walsh, Apr. 23, 1913, box 317, Walsh Mss; Link, *Wilson: The New Freedom*, 184–86.

14. Walsh to E.W., ca. May 24, 1913, W-G Mss.

15. Walsh to E.W., ca. May 10, 1913, W-G Mss; *Cong. Rec.*, 63d Cong., 1st Sess. (May 7, 1913), 1606–8.

16. Link, *Wilson: The New Freedom*, 186–90; Walsh to E.W., June 13, 1913, and passim, W-G Mss; Thomas J. Walsh, "Lobbies and Lobbyists as Walsh Sees Them," *NYT,* Oct. 13, 1929, 10:3.

17. Walsh to Genevieve Walsh, June 22, 1913, W-G Mss.

18. Walsh to E.W., June 13, 22, 1913, W-G Mss.

19. Walsh to E.W., ca. July 10, 1913, W-G Mss; Karl Schriftgiesser, *The Lobbyists: The Art and Business of Influencing Lawmakers* (Boston: Little, Brown, 1951), 35–43.

20. Walsh to E.W., ca. June 28, July 10, 1913, Walsh to F. A. Krieger, June 4, 1913, W-G Mss.

21. Walsh to E.W., ca. July 10, 1913, W-G Mss; Walsh to S. W. McClure, Aug. 11, 1913, Walsh Mss.

22. Walsh to E.W., July 24, 1913, W-G Mss; Walsh to John Sharp Williams, May 29, 1913, Walsh Mss.

23. *Cong. Rec.*, 63d Cong., 1st Sess. (Aug. 2, 1913), 3032–41, (Aug. 19, 1913), 3496; Walsh to E.W., Aug. 3, 9, 1913, W-G Mss; Walsh to J. M. Kennedy, July 23, 1913, box 314, Sec'y of the Librarian of Congress to Walsh, June 19, 1913, box 316, Walsh Mss.

24. Walsh to E.W., ca. Aug. 3, 1913, W-G Mss; *Cong. Rec.*, 63d Cong., 1st Sess. (Aug. 2, 1913), 3032–41 and passim.

25. Link, *Wilson: The New Freedom*, 192–94; Walsh to E.W., Aug. 9, Sept. 8, 1913, W-G Mss.

26. Link, *Wilson: The New Freedom*, 193–97; Walsh to E.W., Sept. 1913, passim, W-G Mss.

27. W. Y. Pemberton, Librarian of the State Historical and Miscellaneous Library, to Walsh (longhand letter), Feb. 19, 1914, box 392, Walsh Mss.

Chapter 10: The "New Freedom" in Montana

1. *Cong. Rec.,* 63d Cong., 2d Sess. (Jan. 15, 1914), 1705. See also Richard Brown Roeder, "Montana in the Early Years of the Progressive Period" (Ph.D. diss., University of Pennsylvania, 1971), passim.

2. Walsh to James C. McReynolds, Aug. 27, 1913, Subject File A, Walsh Mss.

3. Malone et al., *Montana,* 259–60; *Cong. Rec.,* 63d Cong., 2d Sess. (Aug. 20, 1914), 14028; Malone, *Battle for Butte,* 210–11; editorial, *Missoulian,* Nov. 10, 1912, 4; M. McCusker, sec'y-treas., People's Power League, to Walsh, Oct. 26, 1913, Sept. 19, Sept. 21, 1914, Walsh to McCusker, Oct. 31, 1913, Sept. 29, Oct. 6, 1914, boxes 364, 365, Walsh Mss.

4. Malone et al., *Montana,* 262–66; Jeannette Rankin to Walsh, Oct. 14, 1914, Walsh to Rankin, Oct. 19, 1914, box 365, Walsh Mss.

5. Walsh address at the Montana Agricultural College, Bozeman, June 5, 1910, W-G Mss.

6. Malone et al., *Montana,* 362–63; Walsh to Paris Gibson, May 27, 1914, box 392, Gibson to Walsh, June 2, 1914, box 393, Craighead to Walsh, May 16 (with enclosure from the *Daily Missoulian*), May 7, Dec. 1, 1914, box 392, Walsh to Craighead, May 27, Dec. 7, 1914, box 394, Walsh to Penwell, Oct. 23, 1914, box 365, Walsh Mss; Stewart in *Butte Miner,* Nov. 1, 1914, Walsh Mss, Scrapbooks.

7. See Richard T. Ruetten, "Anaconda Journalism: The End of an Era," *Journalism Quarterly* 37 (Winter 1960), 3–12, 104; Malone et al., *Montana,* 366–68; *Montana Lookout,* Aug. 15, 1908, 12; Walsh speech at Walla Walla, Wash., Apr. 13, 1912, W-G Mss.

8. Walsh to W. A. Clark (not the Butte capitalist), Feb. 1, 1913, Walsh to Wm. Wallace Jr., Feb. 25, 1914, box 364, Walsh to Penwell, Dec. 23, 1914, box 394, Walsh Mss.

9. Walsh to Jerre C. Murphy, Apr. 6, 1916, Penwell to Walsh, Oct. 16, 1914, box 393, Walsh Mss.

10. Walsh to B. K. Wheeler, Aug. 3, 1914, box 365, Walsh Mss.

11. J. W. Farrell to Walsh, July 18, Sept. 14, 1914, box 365, Walsh to True W. Child, Sept. 23, 1913, box 391, Walsh Mss.

12. Frank T. Hayes to Walsh, Mar. 18, 1913, S. V. Stewart to Walsh, Jan. 29, 1914, box 364, Penwell to Walsh, Oct. 7, 1914, box 393, B. K. Wheeler to Tom Stout, Oct. 13, 1914, box 365, Walsh Mss; Karlin, *Joseph M. Dixon of Montana, 1867–1917,* 229–30.

13. W. B. Rhoades to Walsh, Jan. 7, 1914, box 95, Walsh Mss.

14. Walsh to James O'Connor, Sept. 10, 1913, box 96, C. B. Nolan to Walsh, Apr. 14, 1913, box 391, and passim, Walsh Mss.

15. See *HI,* Oct. 26, 1920; Walsh to Wheeler, June 13, 1922, Walsh Mss.

16. Kirschwing to Walsh, Aug. 27, 1914, Walsh to Kirschwing, Aug.–Sept. 1914, box 365, Walsh Mss; newspaper accounts in Walsh Mss, Scrapbooks.

17. D. J. Donohue to Walsh, Apr. 30, 1914, box 364, Walsh Mss.

18. Stewart to Walsh, Apr. 21, 1914, Walsh to Stewart, Apr. 27, 1914, Walsh to Penwell, Apr. 30, 1914, box 364, and passim, Walsh Mss.

Chapter 11: The "New Freedom": A Lawyer-Senator at Work

1. Walsh quoted in *HI*, Aug. 3, 1924; interview with former Sen. Henry F. Ashurst, Sept. 9, 1949.

2. *Cong. Rec.*, 63d Cong., 2d Sess. (Jan. 28, 1914), 2414–21, (Feb. 3, 1914), 2793–98, 2800–810, (Feb. 4, 1914), 2882–86; Walsh to E.W., n.d., W-G Mss; Walsh to J. S. Alling, Feb. 2, 1914, Walsh to Nolan, Feb. 12, 1914, Walsh to Stephen J. Cowley, Feb. 18, 1914, box 392, Walsh Mss; J.F.E. in *Baltimore Sun*, Mar. 23, 1914, Walsh Mss, Scrapbooks.

3. See minutes of the Senate Judiciary Committee, 63d Cong., 1st Sess., National Archives, Washington, D.C.

4. Walsh to "Gentlemen" in Montana, July 1, 1913, Walsh to Sam H. Wood, Aug. 11, 1913, Walsh to H. H. Pogue, Oct. 15, 1913, Walsh to John G. Morony, Oct. 27, 1913, Walsh to *Anaconda Standard* and other Montana newspapers, Nov. 24, 1913, Judge Sydney Sanner, Montana Supreme Court, to Walsh, Jan. 1, 1914, and passim, box 220, Walsh Mss; *Cong. Rec.*, 63d Cong., 2d Sess. (Dec. 13, 1913), 825–26, (Dec. 16, 1913), 959–62, (Dec. 17, 1913), 1054.

5. Arthur S. Link, *Wilson: The Road to the White House* (Princeton: Princeton University Press, 1947), 476–77, 488–91, 509; Link, *Wilson: The New Freedom*, 423–27; George Cullom Davis Jr., "The Federal Trade Commission: Promise and Practice in Regulating Business, 1900–1929" (Ph.D. diss., University of Illinois at Urbana-Champaign, 1969), 110–13, 124–26, and passim.

6. Walsh to A. L. Stone, Feb. 25, 1914, box 313, Walsh Mss.

7. Walsh to Thomas Arthur, Oct. 6, 1914, Walsh Mss; Link, *Wilson: The New Freedom*, 425–27; *Cong. Rec.*, 63d Cong., 2d Sess. (July 23, 1914), 12531 and passim, (Aug. 5, 1914), 13306–7, 13317–18, (Aug. 17, 1914), 13844–51, (Aug. 18, 1914), 13897–902, (Aug. 25, 1914), 14224–25.

8. Walsh in *Cong. Rec.*, 63d Cong., 2d Sess. (Oct. 5, 1914), 16145; Benjamin J. Klebaner, "Potential Competition and the American Antitrust Legislation of 1914," *Business History Review* 38 (Summer 1964), 163–85.

9. *Cong. Rec.*, 63d Cong., 2d Sess. (Aug. 21, 1914), 14098–99, (Aug. 26, 1914), 14267, (Aug. 27, 1914), 14323 and passim, (Sept. 30, 1914), 15954–58.

10. Ibid. (Sept. 29, 1914), 15863, (Aug. 17, 1914), 13851–56, (Aug. 18, 1914), 13898–902, 13906–7, (Aug. 28, 1914), 14367–70, 14377, and passim.

11. Ibid. (Oct. 5, 1914), 16142–62, passim, 16168–70.

12. Walsh to Thomas Arthur, Oct. 6, 1914, Walsh Mss; Walsh, *Three Years of the New Freedom*, speech delivered at the Jefferson Day Banquet, Apr. 13, 1916, Senate Doc. 410, 64th Cong., 1st Sess., Senate Docs., vol. 42, ser. 6952 (Washington, D.C.: GPO, 1916), 3–7; John Perry Miller, "Woodrow Wilson's Contribution to Antitrust

Policy," in Earl Latham, ed., *The Philosophy and Policies of Woodrow Wilson* (Chicago: University of Chicago Press, 1958), 142–43.

13. Walsh to Ryan, June 10, 1914, Ryan to Walsh, July 27, 1914, C. F. Kelley to Walsh, Aug. 3, 1914, box 160, Walsh to *Butte Daily Post,* Feb. 10, 1915, box 185, Joseph E. Davies, Federal Trade Commission, to Walsh, May 27, 1916, box 223, Walsh Mss.

14. Walsh to Charles G. Heifner, Jan. 30, 1915, Walsh to Hollis, Apr. 1, 1915, box 333, Walsh Mss.

15. Link, *Wilson: The New Freedom,* 304–11.

16. Walsh to H. J. Burleigh, Feb. 19, 1914, box 364, Walsh Mss; *Cong. Rec.,* 63d Cong., 2d Sess. (May 16, 1914), 8694; Walsh to James J. Murphy, Oct. 19, 1914, box 365, Walsh Mss.

17. *Cong. Rec.,* 63d Cong., 2d Sess. (May 16, 1914), 8704–5, (June 11, 1914), 10211, 10226–28; Walsh to H. J. Burleigh, Feb. 19, 1914, Walsh to John Walsh, May 19, 1914, box 364, Walsh to Nolan, Mar. 25, 1914, box 392, Walsh Mss.

18. *Cong. Rec.,* 63d Cong., 2d Sess. (June 11, 1914), 10227, 10247–48; Walsh to Nolan, Mar. 25, 1914, box 392, Walsh Mss; Link, *Wilson: The New Freedom,* 309–14.

Chapter 12: The *"New Freedom" and Western Land Policy*

1. Cf. Roy M. Robbins, *Our Landed Heritage: The Public Domain, 1776–1936* (Princeton: Princeton University Press, 1942), 380–82; Elmo R. Richardson, *The Politics of Conservation: Crusades and Controversies, 1897–1913* (Berkeley: University of California Press, 1962), 145–47 and passim.

2. *Reports of the Department of the Interior . . . 1913,* 2 vols. (Washington, D.C.: GPO, 1914), 1:3–5, 15–18; J. Leonard Bates, *The Origins of Teapot Dome: Progressives, Parties, and Petroleum, 1909–1921* (Urbana: University of Illinois Press, 1963), 34–36, 44, 47, and passim; Keith W. Olson, *Biography of a Progressive: Franklin K. Lane, 1864–1921* (Westport, Conn: Greenwood Press, 1979), 3–4, 52–53, and passim.

3. Walsh to Lane, Mar. 11, 1913, Lane to Walsh, Mar. 14, 1913, box 95, Walsh Mss.

4. Walsh to Wilson, June 16, 1913, Wilson to Walsh, June 17, 1913, Walsh to Lane, June 16, 1917, box 221, Lane to Walsh, June 21, 1913, box 149, Walsh Mss; Walsh to E.W., June 13, 1913, and passim, W-G Mss. See also John G. Morony to Walsh, May 20, 1913, Stewart to Walsh, May 26, June 30, 1913, Walsh to Stewart, May 27, June 26, 1913, boxes 149, 364, Walsh Mss; *Montana Daily Record* (Helena), Washington, D.C., dateline, June 4, 1913, Walsh Mss, Scrapbooks.

5. Walsh to E.W., ca. May 10, 1913, W-G Mss; Lane, *Water Power Bill,* Hearings before the Committee on the Public Lands, House of Representatives, 63d Cong., 2d Sess., on H.R. 141893 (Washington, D.C.: GPO, 1914), 287; R. M. Trafton to Walsh, Mar. 6, 1913, and passim, boxes 149, 221, Walsh Mss. See Samuel P. Hays, *Conservation and the Gospel of Efficiency: The Progressive Conservation Movement, 1890–1920* (Cambridge: Harvard University Press, 1959), 248 and passim.

6. Walsh to Congressman W. R. Smith of Texas, Jan. 21, 1914, Walsh to C. C.

Hurley, Jan. 21, 1914, Walsh to B. S. Adams, Feb. 19, 1914, and passim, boxes 149, 221, Walsh Mss.

7. *Cong. Rec.*, 63d Cong., 2d Sess. (Dec. 1, 1913), 6–10, (Dec. 2, 1913), 50, 52, 53, 68–71, (Dec. 6, 1913), 353–57, 385–86; James D. Phelan to Walsh, Nov. 14, 1914, box 365, Walsh Mss; Hays, *Conservation and the Gospel of Efficiency,* 189–98; Olson, *Biography of a Progressive,* 94–97.

8. Walsh to E.W., ca. May 10, 1913, W-G Mss; *Cong. Rec.*, 63d Cong., 2d Sess. (Jan. 14, 1914), 1634–44, (Jan. 15, 1914), 1696–705, (Jan. 24, 1914), 2223–25; Gifford Pinchot to Walsh, May 21, 1913, Walsh to Key Pittman, May 28, 1913 (enclosing copy of Pinchot letter), Walsh to Maurice D. Leehey, n.d. (but 1913), John F. Strong to Walsh, Jan. 26, 1914, and passim, box 155, Walsh Mss.

9. See Robert Shankland, *Steve Mather of the National Parks* (New York: Knopf, 1954), passim; Donald C. Swain, *Wilderness Defender: Horace M. Albright and Conservation* (Chicago: University of Chicago Press, 1970), 26–29, 34–36, 38–46, and passim; John Ise, *Our National Park Policy: A Critical History* (Baltimore: Johns Hopkins University Press, 1961), 193–99 and passim.

10. Walsh to Lane, Mar. 20, 1913, box 364, Lane to Walsh, Apr. 5, 1913, box 96, Walsh to Helen P. Clarke, July 14, 1916, Walsh to Mather, July 14, 1916, box 95, Walsh to J. E. Swindlehurst, Apr. 14, 1913, Walsh to Nolan, Apr. 9, 1917, box 96, Sec'y of the Park County Chamber of Commerce to Walsh, Nov. 6, 1915, and passim, box 223, Mather to Walsh, May 25, 1916, Walsh to Penwell, May 27, 1916, box 95, Walsh to W. E. Estill, May 20, 1916, Mather to Walsh, May 29, 1916, box 96, Lane to Walsh, Sept. 24, 1919, Walsh to Walter C. Shaw, Sept. 25, 1919, box 97, Walsh Mss.

11. Walsh to James L. Galen, superintendent, Glacier Park, Mar. 28, 1913, Walsh to Robert D. Heinl, Sept. 8, 1913, box 391, Walsh to Fred Whiteside, July 15, 1914, Walsh to Scott Ferris, Feb. 5, 1915, box 220, Walsh to John E. Lewis, July 25, 1916, box 223, Walsh to Mather, July 25, 1927, and passim, box 96, Walsh Mss; *Cong. Rec.,* 63d Cong., 2d Sess. (Apr. 29, 1914), 7414, (June 5, 1914), 9840.

12. Walsh to Genevieve Walsh, June 22, 1913, W-G Mss; Walsh to Albert Galen, Mar. 19, 1913, Dave Browne to Walsh, Feb. 14, 1913, Judge J. E. Erickson to Walsh, May 28, 1913, and passim, box 95, Walsh Mss; editorial, *Western News* (Hamilton, Mont.), May __, 1914, Walsh Mss, Scrapbooks.

13. Walsh to S. F. Ralston, Apr. 29, 1914, box 95, Walsh to Stephen J. Cowley, Feb. 18, 1914, box 392, Walsh Mss; *Missoulian,* Dec. 19, 1915, Walsh Mss, Scrapbooks; *Cong. Rec.*, 63d Cong., 2d Sess. (Feb. 19, 1914), 3654–57, (Feb. 20, 1914), 3696–701, (Mar. 31, 1914), 5905–6.

14. Lane to Walsh, Jan. 12, Apr. 6, May 7, 1914, box 125, Walsh Mss; *NYT,* Apr. 6, 1914, 1; Walsh to *HI,* Aug. 11, 1914, Personal File, Walsh Mss; *Cong. Rec.*, 63d Cong., 2d Sess. (Feb. 7, 1914), 3103, (Mar. 23, 1914), 5275–77, 5299, (Mar. 31, 1914), 5905–6, (July 23, 1914), 12519–21.

15. Walsh to G. L. Sheldon, Jan. 6, 1915, box 221, Walsh to Nolan, n.d., box 225, Walsh Mss. See also Walsh address before the Mining and Metallurgical Society of

America, Dec. 16, 1915, Senate Doc. 233, 64th Cong., 1st Sess., Senate Docs. vol. 41, ser. 6951 (Washington, D.C.: GPO, 1916), 68–80.

16. Sen. John D. Works to Walsh, Jan. 4, 1916, Walsh to Works, Jan. 14, 1916, Ashurst to Walsh, Jan. 3, 1916, Walsh to Gov. Stewart, Dec. 28, 1915, Walsh to Pittman, Dec. 29, 1915, Walsh to Winchell, Jan. 31, 1916, and passim, box 225, Walsh to Nolan, Mar. 25, 1914, box 392, Walsh Mss. See Bates, *Origins of Teapot Dome*, 22–25, 156–65, and passim.

17. Editorials, *The Mining American* (Denver), Dec. 18, 1915, Mar. 25, Apr. 8, Apr. 29, and Oct. 7, 1916, Jan. 5, 1918; Works to Walsh, Jan. 4, 1916, box 225, Walsh Mss.

18. *Cong. Rec.*, 63d Cong., 2d Sess. (Feb. 9, 1914), 3203, (Feb. 18–19, 1914), 3592, 3654–57, (Feb. 20, 1914), 3696–701, (Feb. 24, 1914), 3821–25, (Aug. 15, 1914), 13764–65, (Sept. 22, 1914), 15529–39, (Sept. 23, 1914), 15574–88, (Sept. 24, 1914), 15622–37, (Sept. 25, 1914), 15664–92, (Oct. 9, 1914), 16347–76, (Oct. 10, 1914), 16406–12, (Oct. 23, 1914), 16964; Ernest Gruening, *The State of Alaska* (New York: Random House, 1968), 187–88 and passim.

19. *Reports of the Department of the Interior . . . 1914*, 2 vols. (Washington, D.C.: GPO, 1915), 1:15; *Reports of the Department of the Interior . . . 1915*, 2 vols. (Washington, D.C.: GPO, 1916), 1:17–18; Walsh to Charles W. Helmick, Dec. 12, 1913, Gov. E. M. Ammons of Colorado to Walsh, Apr. 14, 21, 1914, and passim, box 335, Walsh to F. H. McDermont, May 1, 1914, Walsh to Frank J. Edwards, May 5, 1914, box 221, Walsh Mss.

20. *Cong. Rec.*, 64th Cong., 1st Sess. (Feb. 15, 1916), 2572–84, (Feb. 16, 1916), 2638 and passim, (Feb. 29, 1916), 3300–301, (Mar. 2, 1916), 3415, (Mar. 8, 1916), 3744, 3755–58; Jerome G. Kerwin, *Federal Water-Power Legislation* (New York: Columbia University Press, 1926), passim.

21. Walsh to Judson King, director, National Popular Government League, Mar. 3, 1923, Legislation: Indians, D. D. LaBreche to Walsh, Mar. 13, 1913, Walsh to LaBreche, Mar. 26, 1913, box 220, Walsh to Att'y Gen. James C. McReynolds, Oct. 17, 1913, McReynolds to Walsh, Oct. 22, 1913, box 391, Walsh Mss; Janet A. McDonnell, *The Dispossession of the American Indian, 1887–1934* (Bloomington: Indiana University Press, 1991), 2–5 and passim; Olson, *Biography of a Progressive*, 91–94; Malone et al., *Montana*, 355–58.

Chapter 13: America and the "War-Mad Nations of Europe"

1. E.W. to Walsh, July 5, Aug. 2, Sept. 3, 1914, and passim, W-G Mss; Walsh to John Walsh, July 2, 1914, box 333, Walsh Mss; Genevieve Walsh, "Germans Gain Sympathy of American Tourists in War Zone Owing to Courteous Treatment," *HI*, Oct. 4, 1914.

2. Walsh to Jim O'Connor, Feb. 23, 1915, Walsh to John M. Hiner, Mar. 11, 1915, Walsh to J. E. Engstad, Apr. 1, 1915, box 185, Walsh to S. W. McClure, Mar. 17, 1915, box 334, Walsh to M. W. O'Shea, Feb. 14, 1916, box 341, Walsh to Lady Anna Barlow, Dec. 29, 1915, box 322, Walsh Mss.

3. O'Connor to Walsh, Feb. 18, 1915, Walsh to O'Connor, Feb. 23, 1915, Carl Albert Gerken to Walsh, Aug. 11, 1914, Walsh to Gerken, Aug. 17, 1914, Walsh to G. E. Snell and George Arnott Jr., Aug. 10, 1914, Walsh to E. J. Blair, Aug. 21, 1914, box 185, Walsh Mss. See John M. Hiner to Walsh, Feb. 27, 1915, F. G. Ellis to Walsh, Feb. 19, 1915, box 185, Walsh Mss.

4. Walsh in *Cong. Rec., 63d Cong.*, 2d Sess. (Aug. 7, 1914), 13438. See Ernest R. May, *The World War and American Isolation, 1914–1917* (Cambridge: Harvard University Press, 1959); Arthur S. Link, *Wilson: The Struggle for Neutrality, 1914–1915* (Princeton: Princeton University Press, 1960); idem, *Wilson: Confusions and Crises, 1915–1916* (Princeton: Princeton University Press, 1964).

5. Ryan to Walsh, Oct. 2, 1914, Walsh to Ryan, Oct. 9, 1914, box 165, Walsh telegram to Bryan, Nov. 8, 1914, and passim, Correspondence with State Department, Walsh Mss; *Cong. Rec., 63d Cong.*, 3d Sess. (Dec. 31, 1914), 795–802, (Jan. 6, 1915), statement by Root, 1015. Box 165 in Walsh Mss contains copious correspondence and information. Walsh to E. J. Clapp, May 25, 1915, box 165, Walsh to W. B. E. Shufeldt, June 25, 1915, Walsh to Floyd Bushnell, Nov. 27, 1915, box 322, Walsh to John M. Hiner, Mar. 11, 1915, Walsh to Lady Anna Barlow, Dec. 29, 1915, box 185, Walsh to P. A. O'Farrell, Feb. 9, 1916, Walsh to John Treland, Dec. 19, 1916, box 338, Walsh Mss; *Cong. Rec., 64th Cong.*, 1st Sess. (Jan. 28, 1916), 1671–79; Link, *Wilson: The Struggle for Neutrality,* 341, 594ff.; Link, *Wilson: Confusions and Crises,* 90–92 and passim.

6. See Link, *Wilson: Confusions and Crises,* 339; *Cong. Rec., 63d Cong.*, 2d Sess. (Aug. 5, 1914), 13291–92, 3d Sess. (Jan. 25, 1915), Root address, 2208–18, (Jan. 28, 1915), Walsh address, 2434–43; *New York Herald* and *New York Commercial,* Walsh Mss, Scrapbooks.

7. Walsh to Penwell, Feb. 3, 1915, Walsh to Nolan, Feb. 1, 1915, box 394, Walsh Mss; *Butte Miner,* Feb. 1, 1915; *HI,* Jan. 29, 1915, Walsh Mss, Scrapbooks; *La Follette's Magazine* quoted in *Cong. Rec., 63d Cong.*, 3d Sess. (Feb. 16, 1915), 3873, (Jan. 29, 1915), Norris speech, 2538–49. See also ibid. (Feb. 8, 1915), 3400–406.

8. *Cong. Rec., 63d Cong.*, 3d Sess. (Feb. 15, 1915), 3773–77; Walsh telegram to Theodore Roosevelt, Mar. 24, 1915, Walsh to Sen. George Sutherland, Mar. 26, 1915, box 221, and passim in shipping corrrespondence for 1915, Walsh Mss. See also *NYT,* Mar. 25, 1915, 7, Mar. 27, 1915, 13, Mar. 28, 1915, 10.

9. Link, *Wilson: Confusions and Crises,* 339–41.

10. Walsh to O'Connor, June 12, 1915, Walsh to Judge Charles L. Crum, box 322, Walsh Mss. See also Walsh to Alex Steinberg, May 17, 1915, Walsh to Joseph Oker, June 11, 1915, Walsh to W. B. E. Shufeldt, June 25, 1915, Walsh to Sen. William J. Stone, Dec. 27, 1915, Walsh to A. L. Stone, Jan. 4, 1916, box 322, Walsh Mss.

11. Walsh to P. N. Bernard, Oct. 26, 1915, box 223; Walsh to the *New York American,* June 10, 1915, Walsh to Floyd Bushnell, Nov. 27, 1915, Walsh to A. L. Stone, Jan. 4, 1916, box 322, Walsh Mss; signed article by Walsh, *Redwater Valley Pioneer,* Feb. 12, 1916, Walsh Mss, Scrapbooks.

12. Condon to Walsh, Feb. 26, 1916, Walsh to Condon, Mar. 7, 1916, and passim, box 341, Walsh to Edgar Phinney, May 23, 1916, Walsh to Lewis Penwell, Apr. 26,

1916, box 311, Walsh Mss; *Cong. Rec.*, 64th Cong., 1st Sess. (May 20, 1916), 8406, (May 17, 1916), 8139; Link, *Wilson: Confusions and Crises,* 332.

13. Walsh to Louis W. Hill, May 17, 1916, Walsh to James M. Hanaford, May 17, 1916, Underwood to Walsh (with enclosure), Apr. 3, 1916, Myers to Walsh, May 31, 1916, Chief of Ordnance to Walsh, Aug. 7, 1916 (sending copy of "Requirements for a Site for the New Army Powder Factory, July 24, 1916"), and passim, box 339, Walsh Mss.

14. C. H. Spanuth to Walsh, Jan. 6, 1915, Walsh to Spanuth, Jan. 13, 1915, box 185, Heinrich Charles, sec'y, Chamber of German-American Commerce, Inc., to Walsh, Feb. 22, 1916, box 341; Edmund von Mach, chairman, Citizens' Committee for Food Shipments, to Walsh, Jan. 18, 1916 (with enclosures), Nov. 17, 1916, Walsh to von Mach, Jan. 19, 1916, box 338, Walsh Mss.

Chapter 14: Winning the West with Wilson, 1915–16

1. Walsh to John R. Faulds, May 2, 1916, Walsh to Woolley, Apr. 19, 1916, box 405, Walsh Mss; *Washington Post,* Apr. 14, 1916, 1, 5; "The Nation's Capital," *Harper's Weekly,* Apr. 29, 1916, 456; passim, Walsh Mss, Scrapbooks.

2. Walsh, *Three Years of the New Freedom;* Woolley to Walsh, Apr. 18, 1916, Walsh to Woolley, Apr. 19, 1916, box 405, Franklin Lane to Walsh, n.d., Walsh to Lane, Apr. 18, 1916, box 400, Adolph C. Miller, Federal Reserve Board, to Walsh, Apr. 14, 1916, Walsh to Miller, Apr. 17, 1916, box 401, Walsh Mss.

3. Penwell to Walsh, Feb. 28, 1914, Hollis to Walsh, Dec. 9, 1914, Walsh to George Ramsey, May 20, 1914, Walsh to True Child, Feb. 1, 1915, and passim, box 221, Walsh Mss; *Cong. Rec.,* 64th Cong., 1st Sess. (Mar. 13, 1916), 4016, (May 4, 1916), 7372–77, 7412. See Walsh, *Federal Farm Loan Act,* Senate Doc. 524, 64th Cong., 1st Sess., Senate Docs., vol. 43, ser. 6953 (Washington, D.C.: GPO, 1916), 3.

4. Walsh to James F. O'Connor, Mar. 10, 1915, box 337, Walsh to Sec'y of Agriculture David Houston, Mar. 23, 1915, Walsh to A. D. Melvin, chief, Bureau of Animal Industry, May 21, 1915, boxes 334, 338, Walsh to McAdoo, Sept. 14, 1915, box 225, L. M. Rheem, Helena Commercial Club, to Walsh, Oct. 21, 1915, box 339, Walsh Mss. See Walsh to Henry S. Graves, chief forester, June 5, 1915, and passim, box 338, Walsh Mss; Malone et al., *Montana,* 241–52.

5. Walsh to J. L. Duffy, Brotherhood of Railroad Trainmen, July 16, 1914, Walsh to Marcus A. Beeman, New Jersey State Chamber of Commerce, Aug. 3, 1914, box 160, Walsh to George Lodge, June 13, 1916, box 228, Walsh Mss.

6. Andrews to Walsh, July 18, Aug. 1, 1916, Walsh to Andrews, July 19, 1916, box 224, Walsh to J. C. Lucey, Central Labor Council, June 20, 1916, box 223, Walsh Mss; *Cong. Rec.,* 64th Cong., 1st Sess. (Aug. 5, 1916), 12166–67, (Aug. 19, 1916), 12896, 12902, and passim; Walsh to Mr. and Mrs. Joseph C. Tope, Mar. 7, 1916, and passim, box 222, Walsh Mss; *Cong. Rec.,* 64th Cong., 1st Sess. (Aug. 8, 1916), 12312–13.

7. A. L. Todd, *Justice on Trial: The Case of Louis D. Brandeis* (New York: McGraw-

Hill, 1964), is a readable account. See also Alpheus T. Mason, *Brandeis: A Free Man's Life* (New York: Viking Press, 1946); Melvin I. Urofsky and David W. Levy, eds., *Letters of Louis D. Brandeis*, vol. 4: *Mr. Justice Brandeis* (1916–21) (Albany: SUNY Press, 1975).

8. U.S. Congress, Senate, *Nomination of Louis D. Brandeis*, Hearings before the Subcommittee of the Committee on the Judiciary, 64th Cong., 1st Sess., 2 vols., ser. 6926–27 (Washington, D.C.: GPO, 1916), 1:5, 75, 171, 682ff., and passim; Todd, *Justice on Trial*, 141–43 and passim.

9. Reports of the subcommittee members are in *Nomination of Louis D. Brandeis*, 2:176–211 (Chilton), 212–34 (Walsh), 307–23 (Cummins), 325–71 (Works).

10. Walsh to Penwell, June 9, 1916, box 415, Walsh to Nolan, Mar. 10, 1916, box 400, Walsh to Montana Democrats, Apr. 10, 1916, box 366, Walsh to Thomas Arthur, Apr. 18, 28, 1916, and passim, box 366, Walsh Mss.

11. Walsh to Burleson, June 7, 1916, Walsh to A. J. McKelway, June 9, 1916, box 400, Walsh draft of a platform, June 1916, box 252, Walsh Mss; *New York Evening Telegram*, June 10, 1916, *Anaconda Standard*, June 14, 1916, and passim, Walsh Mss, Scrapbooks; Arthur S. Link, *Wilson: Campaigns for Progressivism and Peace, 1916–1917* (Princeton: Princeton University Press, 1965), 38–42. See also Sen. Robert Owen to Pres. Wilson, June 3, 1916, microfilm, reel 79, Woodrow Wilson Mss, LC (hereafter Wilson Mss).

12. *NYT*, June 14, 1916, 1–2, and June 16, 1916, 1, 3; "Women Return from St. Louis Meeting," *Butte Miner*, June 22, 1916, Walsh Mss, Scrapbooks. See Link, *Wilson: Campaigns for Progressivism and Peace*, 41–42, 48.

13. See J. Bruce Kremer, comp., *Official Report of the Proceedings of the Democratic National Convention . . . St. Louis . . . 1916*, 120–48; *NYT*, June 17, 1916, 1–2.

14. *NYT*, June 17, 1916, 2; *Proceedings of the Democratic National Convention, 1916*, 142–48; Walsh to Mrs. C. B. Nolan, Oct. 15, 1918, W-G Mss.

15. *NYT*, June 16, 1916, 3 (two articles), June 28, 1916, 8; *The Examiner* (Atlanta, Ga.), June 29, 1916, and passim, Walsh Mss, Scrapbooks; Vance McCormick to Walsh, July 11, 1916, box 172, Walsh Mss; Roland S. Morris to McAdoo, June 12, 1916, box 161, William G. McAdoo Mss, LC. See also Leonard Bates, "Mr. Wilson's Campaign: Winning the West with Wilson in 1916," *Journal of the West* 34 (Apr. 1995), 16–23.

16. Walsh to Penwell, July 15, 1916, Walsh Mss; Norman Hapgood to Wilson, July 6, 1916, file 6, 510, box 351, Wilson Mss; Kenneth Romney in *HI*, June 28, 1916, and passim, Walsh Mss, Scrapbooks; Walsh to Nolan, June 22, 1916, Walsh Mss; *Anaconda Standard*, July 21, 1916, Walsh Mss, Scrapbooks; Bates, ed., *Tom Walsh in Dakota*, 223.

17. *Chicago Daily Journal*, Aug. 2, 1916, 4, Aug. 7, 1916, 1, 3; Richard J. Finnegan to Walsh, July 18, 1916, Roger Sullivan to Walsh, July 30, 1916, Walsh telegram to Gov. Dunne, Aug. 5, 1916, and similar wires to others in Illinois, box 175, Walsh Mss. See Richard Allen Morton, *Justice and Humanity: Edward F. Dunne, Illinois Progressive* (Carbondale: Southern Illinois University Press, 1997).

18. Walsh to E.W., ca. Aug. 9, 1916, W-G Mss; Walsh to McCormick, Aug. 10, 1916, box 172, Walsh Mss; Jack Lait interview with Walsh, *Chicago Herald,* Sept. 14, 1916.

19. Walsh to Mrs. O. F. Barnes, Oct. 19, 1916, box 167, Walsh to McCormick, probably Aug. 28, 1916, McCormick to Walsh, Aug. 29, 1916, box 172, Walsh to William J. Gleason, Sept. 8, 1916, box 170, Walsh to heads of bureaus, Sept. 9, 1916, box 167, Walsh Mss; Walsh to E.W., ca. Sept. 23, 1916, W-G Mss.

20. Walsh to Genevieve Walsh Gudger, ca. Aug. 25, 1916, W-G Mss; Walsh to Peabody, Sept. 6, 19, 1916, Peabody to Walsh, Sept. 18, Nov. 6, 1916, box 173, Walsh Mss. See boxes 167–68 and Subject File B: Democratic Campaign, 1916, Walsh Mss.

21. Walsh to E.W., Aug. 16, 1916, W-G Mss; Walsh to Mrs. B. W. Dickson, City Health Office, Butte, Aug. 24, 1916, box 169, Mrs. Elizabeth Bass to Walsh, Aug. 9, 1916, box 167, Mrs. Bass telegram to Walsh, Aug. 12, 1916, Walsh to Vance McCormick, Aug. 18, 1916, box 172, Walsh Mss. See also the statement concerning Mrs. Bass from the Western Democratic Headquarters, n.d., Walsh Mss; *Chicago Daily Journal,* Aug. 29, 1916; *HI,* Aug. 24, 1916, 1, 4; clippings, Walsh Mss, Scrapbooks.

22. Walsh to Lewis Penwell, Aug. 21, 1916, box 173, Walsh to Charles McCarthy, Aug. 9, 1916, Walsh's sec'y to McCarthy, Aug. 11, 1916, Walsh to McCarthy, Aug. 20, 1916, McCarthy to Walsh, Aug. 10, 18, 1916, box 172, Walsh Mss; Walsh to E.W., Aug. 9, 1916, W-G Mss; T. A. Larson, "Montana Women and the Battle for the Ballot," *Montana* 23 (Winter 1973), 25, 34–36, 41, and passim.

23. Walsh address, Aug. 17, 1916, box 255, Walsh Mss; Joe D. Salkeld in *Chicago Daily Journal,* Aug. 17, 1916, 1; "To Committeeman," Aug. 29, 1916, "To Newspapers," box 170, Walsh to Joseph Kirschwing, Sept. 12, 1916, box 171, Walsh to Charles E. Bowers, Sept. 6, 1916, box 167, Walsh Mss; Walsh to E.W., Aug. 18, 1916, W-G Mss.

24. Fred Dubois to Walsh, Oct. 1, 1916, box 169, Walsh to Vance McCormick, Oct. 5, 1916 (quoting Dubois and a telegram from S. G. Hopkins, Democratic state chairman in Wyoming), box 172, Walsh Mss.

25. McCormick to Walsh, Aug. 19, 29 (telegram), 1916, box 172, John Wattawa to Charles F. Davis, Sept. 1, 1916, box 168, Walsh Mss; Walsh to E.W., ca. Aug. 29, 1916, W-G Mss; *Chicago Daily Journal,* Sept. 2, 1916, 1, 2; Link, *Wilson: Campaigns for Progressivism and Peace,* 94.

26. *Chicago Daily Journal,* Sept. 4, 1916, 12; Democratic National Committee and Democratic Congressional Committee, *The Democratic Text Book, 1916,* 29–40. See Link, *Wilson: Campaigns for Progressivism and Peace,* 83–92, for an examination of the railroad settlement; Louis Seibold, "Care of Children Not Wilson's Idea,"*NYW,* Sept. 3, 1916, 6. Iroquois Club Address, Sept. 28, 1916, box 252, Walsh Mss; Walsh to E.W., ca. Sept. 9, 1916, W-G Mss; Seward W. Livermore, *Woodrow Wilson and the War Congress, 1916–1918* (Seattle: University of Washington Press, 1968), 44–45. See also Thomas W. Marshall, "The Constructive Work of the Wilson Administration," *The Forum* 56 (July 1916), 46–62.

27. Taft to Hughes, Nov. 10, 1916, in Merlo J. Pusey, *Charles Evans Hughes,* 2 vols.

(New York: Columbia University Press, 1963), 1:364; *Chicago Daily Journal,* Sept. 29, 1916, 6. See also W. J. Bryan, "Hughes and Fairbanks," *The Commoner* (Lincoln, Nebr.) 16 (June 1916), 1; Robert E. Hennings, *James D. Phelan and the Wilson Progressives of California* (New York: Garland Publishing, 1985), 134–45 and passim; Walsh to Emmet Gudger, Oct. 11, 1916, Select File, Walsh Mss.

28. See Walsh to E.W., Aug. 18, ca. Aug. 29, ca. Sept. 9, ca. Sept. 30, ca. Oct. 1, ca. Oct. 10, ca. Oct. 24, 1916, Walsh to Genevieve Walsh Gudger, ca. Aug. 25, 1916, W-G Mss.

29. Jack Lait, *Chicago Herald,* Sept. 14, 1916.

30. Walsh to Genevieve Walsh Gudger, ca. Aug. 25, 1916, W-G Mss; Bryan to Walsh, Oct. 6, 1916, Walsh to Bryan, Sept. 30, 1916 (sending copy of letter from McAdoo to McCormick, Sept. 24, 1916), box 167, Walsh to Mrs. Mary E. Morony, July 24, 1916, H. A. Davee to Walsh, Aug. 12, 1916, box 168, Walsh Mss; McAdoo to Att'y Gen. Thomas W. Gregory, Sept. 15, 1916, General Correspondence, box 166, William G. McAdoo Mss, LC.

31. *Irish World and American Industrial Liberator* (New York City), Sept. 29, 1916, editorial and 12, Oct. 7, 1916, 3, Oct. 28, 1916, editorial; John D. Moore to Walsh, June 21, 1916, Walsh to Moore, June 19, 1916, box 400, Walsh to J. E. Engstad, Oct. 2, 1916, box 169, Walsh Mss; Link, *Wilson: Campaigns for Progressivism and Peace,* 104–5.

32. Claude Bowers to Walsh, Sept. 5, 1916, Walsh to Bowers, Sept. 8, 1916, box 167, Walsh Mss. S. D. Lovell, *The Presidential Election of 1916* (Carbondale: Southern Illinois University Press, 1980), shows no awareness of a western headquarters. Link, *Wilson: Campaigns for Progressivism and Peace,* 130–34; Louis Seibold, *NYW,* Oct. 16, 1916, 1, 2. Walsh subscribed to radical Protestant publications such as *The Menace* (Aurora, Mo.). Walsh to *The Menace,* Aug. 24, 1916, box 173, Walsh Mss.

33. Walsh to Kent E. Keller, Aug. 29, 1916, box 171, Walsh to McCormick, Oct. 5, 1916, McCormick to Walsh, Oct. 6, 1916, box 172, Walsh to Peter Scharrenbroich, Oct. 28, 1916, box 174, and passim in Walsh campaign boxes, Walsh Mss. See also Walsh to Pres. Wilson, Aug. 18, 1916, microfilm, reel 82, Wilson Mss; *Chicago Daily Journal,* Aug. 25, 1916, 4, Sept. 5, 1916, 6, Oct. 2, 1916, 4, Oct. 11, 1916, 4; *The Commoner* 16 (Aug. 1916), 4; Seibold, *NYW,* Sept. 3, 1916, 6, Oct. 1, 1916, 2E; *NYT,* Oct. 1, 1916, 1:2.

34. See Bates, *Origins of Teapot Dome,* 88–92; Harlan G. Palmer, *Hollywood Citizen,* to Chicago Headquarters, Sept. 29, 1916, Walsh to *Citizen,* Oct. 4, 1916 (with enclosure), box 170, Walsh Mss.

35. Walsh to Arthur Mullen, Oct. 13, 1916, box 173, Walsh Mss; Arthur F. Mullen, *Western Democrat* (New York: Wilfred Funk, 1940), 180–83.

36. Walsh to McCormick, Sept 20, 1916, box 172, Spriggs to Walsh, Sept. 13, 1916, box 366, Dave Browne to Walsh, Sept. 18, 1916, box 167, and passim, Walsh campaign correspondence, Walsh Mss. The allusions to Myers appear in Walsh to E.W., ca. July 30, ca. Sept. 16, ca. Sept. 30, 1916, W-G Mss. See also Karlin, *Joseph M. Dixon of Montana, 1867–1917,* 165, 224–27.

37. Walsh to S. G. Hopkins, Sept. 29, 1916, Walsh to J. T. Hamilton, Miles City Land Office, Oct. 10, 1916, box 170, Walsh telegram to Sen. Henry Myers, Oct. 24, 1916, Walsh telegram to J. B. Mulcahy, Oct. 25, 1916, box 173, Walsh Mss.

38. Louis Seibold, "Wilson Is Cheered by 90,000 in Mid-West Towns," *NYW,* Oct. 5, 1916, 1, Oct. 7, 1916, 1, Oct. 22, 1916, 1; *Chicago Daily Journal,* Oct. 13, 1916, 5, and passim; *NYT,* Oct. 18, 1916, 4, Oct. 19, 1916, 3.

39. Link, *Wilson: Campaigns for Progressivism and Peace,* 156–64 and passim; Walsh to Hollis, Nov. 9, 1916, box 170, Walsh Mss; *Chicago Tribune,* Nov. 12, 1916, 5; Joe D. Salkeld, "Cabinet Place for T. J. Walsh . . . Won West for President," *Chicago Daily Journal,* Nov. 10, 1916, 3, Nov. 11, 1916; Medill McCormick to Sir Horace Plunkett, Sept. 13, 1917, Hanna-McCormick Family Mss, LC; Meyer Jonah Nathan, "The Presidential Election of 1916 in the Middle West" (Ph.D. diss., Princeton University, 1965), 63–64.

Chapter 15: From Peace to War

1. Link, *Wilson: Campaigns for Progressivism and Peace,* passim; May, *World War and American Isolation,* passim; Walsh, "War Powers of the President," *Case and Comment* 24 (1917), 279–89. See Sen. John Sharp Williams to Sen. Charles S. Thomas, Dec. 5, 1916, John Sharp Williams Mss, LC; Sidney Fine, *Frank Murphy: The Detroit Years* (Ann Arbor: University of Michigan Press, 1975), 35–37, 41, and passim.

2. *Cong. Rec.,* 65th Cong., 1st Sess. (May 11, 1917), 2111–14, 2119–20, 2122, and passim, 2d Sess. (Apr. 4, 1918), 4559–61, (Apr. 5, 1918), 4648–49.

3. Walsh to Newton D. Baker, Apr. 17, 1917, C. A. Weil, Eureka Lumber Co., to Gov. Stewart, Apr. 25, 1917, Walsh Mss; *HI,* Apr. 26, 1917.

4. Penwell to Walsh, Aug. 2, 1917, Walsh Mss; *HI,* Oct. 3, 1918; Judge Bourquin quoted in Zechariah Chafee Jr., *Free Speech in the United States* (Cambridge: Harvard University Press, 1941), 227. See also Paul F. Brissenden, *The I.W.W.: A Study of American Syndicalism* (New York: Columbia University Press, 1919), 10; Melvyn Dubofsky, *We Shall Be All: A History of the Industrial Workers of the World* (New York: Quadrangle, 1969), 391–93 and passim; Herbert E. Gaston, *The Nonpartisan League* (New York: Harcourt, Brace and Howe, 1920), 211–13.

5. Walsh to Richard Lockey, Apr. 29, 1918, Walsh Mss. See also Walsh to Att'y Gen. Gregory, Mar. 26, 1918, Gregory to Walsh, Mar. 29, 1918, and passim, Walsh Mss.

6. *Cong. Rec.,* 65th Cong., 2d Sess. (May 2, 1918), 5933, (May 6, 1918), 6082–83, 6091, (Aug. 19, 1918), 9238.

7. This version of the speech was printed, with other documents, in *Senator from Wisconsin,* on S. Res. 360 recommending dismissal of resolutions favoring expulsion of Robert M. La Follette, 65th Cong., 3d Sess., Senate Report 614, Dec. 2, 1918. See also Belle Case La Follette and Fola La Follette, *Robert M. La Follette, June 14, 1855–June 18, 1925,* 2 vols. (New York: Macmillan, 1953), 2:761–69.

8. Walsh longhand ms, n.d., "Inquiries La Follette Examination," Walsh to Mrs.

F. H. Knoble, Oct. 13, 1917, box 188, Walsh Mss; *Senator from Wisconsin; HI,* Oct. 28, 1917 (news dispatch from Wibaux, dated Oct. 27), Nov. 7, 1917 (dispatch from Livingston, dated Nov. 1), Nov. 7, 1917 (dispatch from Bozeman, dated Nov. 6); La Follette and La Follette, *Robert M. La Follette,* 2:803–4 and passim.

9. *Senator from Wisconsin;* Walsh speech at Great Falls, Sept. 23, 1924, reported in *HI,* Sept. 24, 1924. See also passim in box 188, Walsh Mss.

10. Walsh to E. E. Esselstyn, Aug. 16, 1917, box 161, Sen. James Hamilton Lewis to Walsh, Aug. 25, 1917, box 343, Walsh's sec'y to former Sen. T. C. Power, Sept. 1, 1917, box 161, and passim, Walsh Mss.

11. Walsh's sec'y to Wm. C. Liller, Sept. 28, 1917, Walsh to Bankers Life Co., May 14, 1920, Walsh to George W. Randall, Nov. 5, 1917, sec'y to Nolan, Feb. 8, 1918, box 99, Walsh Mss; interview with Genevieve Walsh Gudger, Feb. 16, 1950, Washington, D.C.

12. See Bates, *Origins of Teapot Dome,* 116–17 and passim; Walsh and Pittman in *Cong. Rec.,* 65th Cong., 2d Sess. (Sept. 17, 1918), 10382, 10385.

13. See *Cong. Rec.,* 64th Cong., 2d Sess. (Jan. 15, 1917), 1412–22, 65th Cong., 1st Sess. (May 2, 1917), 1684–85, (Sept. 23, 1918), 10636–42; Walsh to John J. Harris, Dec. 12, 1918, Walsh Mss; Walsh to Mrs. A. E. Spriggs, Sept 24, 1918, Walsh to *Montana Equity News* (Great Falls), Oct. 9, 1918, W-G Mss.

14. James H. Timberlake, *Prohibition and the Progressive Movement, 1900–1920* (Cambridge: Harvard University Press, 1966), 162–66 and passim; Norman H. Clark, *Deliver Us from Evil: An Interpretation of American Prohibition* (New York: W. W. Norton, 1976), 127–30 and passim; K. Austin Kerr, *Organized for Prohibition: A New History of the Anti-Saloon League* (New Haven: Yale University Press, 1985), 2–3, 205–6.

15. Walsh to D. J. Donahue, Dec. 2, 1915, Walsh Mss. See Walsh to E.W., Oct. 18, 1894, Oct. 25, 1895, Mar. 16, 1897, Aug. 11, 1899, W-G Mss.

16. Walsh to W. H. Griffin, Feb. 8, 1916, box 302, Walsh to Dr. Gustavus Werber, Aug. 5, 1916, box 223, passim in prohibition boxes, Walsh to J. E. Hamilton, May 29, 1917, Walsh to George L. Ramsey, June 15, 1917, box 302, Walsh to W. F. Doonan, July 1, 1918, box 303, Walsh Mss; Clark, *Deliver Us from Evil,* 129.

17. Walsh to Klara Winsor, Feb. 16, 1917, box 302, Sen. Morris Sheppard to Rev. Joseph Pope, July 19, 1918, Pope to Walsh, July 30, 1918, Walsh to Pope, Aug. 3, 1918, box 303, Walsh Mss. See, for example, Walsh to Mrs. William Tocher, Nov. 23, 1921, Walsh Mss.

18. Walsh to Mary O'Neill, Mar. 1, 1923, Walsh Mss.

19. See Walsh to T. E. Richardson, Oct. 2, 1917, box 183 (on wheat) and passim, Walsh Mss; Livermore, *Woodrow Wilson and the War Congress,* passim.

20. Malone et al., *Montana,* 268–79; Arnon Gutfeld, *Montana's Agony: Years of War and Hysteria, 1917–1921* (Gainesville: University Presses of Florida, 1979), passim; Walsh to Norman B. Holter, June 8, 1917, box 412, Walsh Mss.

21. Malone et al., *Montana,* 273–75; "The Rustling Card," *Big Timber Pioneer,* Jan. 19, 1918, Walsh Mss, Scrapbooks; Walsh to Will Campbell, Sept. 15, 1913, Lowndes

Maury to Walsh, Aug. 24, 1917, box 206, Walsh to John D. Ryan, Aug. 28, 1918, box 344, and passim in Walsh-Ryan correspondence, July 1917, box 343, Walsh Mss. See also Walsh to C. F. Kelley, Nov. 18, 1919, Walsh Mss.

22. Livermore, *Woodrow Wilson and the War Congress,* chap. 9 and passim.

Chapter 16: Reelection in 1918

1. *HI,* Oct. 22, 1917.

2. See Federal Writers' Project, Work Progress Administration, *Montana: A State Guide Book* (New York: Viking Press, 1939), 72–75; John A. Fitch, "A Union Paradise at Close Range, *The Survey* 32 (Aug. 29, 1914), 638–39; Louis Levine, "Politics in Montana," *The Nation* 107 (Nov. 2, 1918), 507–8.

3. Federal Writers' Project, *Montana,* 61; Carl Riddick, *Helena Record-Herald,* July 29, 1918; *Helena Record-Herald,* Oct. 24, 28, 1918; Walsh to W. M. Johnston, Nov. 12, 1918, Walsh Mss.

4. See Samuel P. Huntington, "The Election Tactics of the Nonpartisan League," *Mississippi Valley Historical Review* 36 (Mar. 1950), 613–16.

5. Tom Stout, ed., *Montana: Its Story and Biography,* 3 vols. (Chicago and New York: American Historical Society, 1921), 1:480; Levine, "Politics in Montana," 507–8.

6. For short biographical sketches, Stout, ed., *Montana,* is helpful. See also *HI,* July 19, 1921, June 24, 1922, Nov. 5, 1920.

7. Interview with Genevieve Walsh Gudger, Feb. 16, 1950; Nolan to Miles Taylor (Walsh's sec'y), Jan. 2, 1918, Taylor to Sen. Henry Ashurst, Jan. 22, 1918, Walsh to Bruce Kremer, Apr. 11, 1918, Walsh to Spriggs, July 5, 1918, O. H. P. Shelley to Walsh, June 13, 1918, Walsh to Shelley, July 1, 1918, Walsh Mss.

8. Wheeler to Walsh, Nov. 26, 1917, Walsh to Wheeler, Apr. 23, 1918, Walsh Mss; *Helena Record-Herald,* Sept. 30, Oct. 3, 1918; Stout, ed., *Montana,* 2:7; Kenneth Campbell MacKay, *The Progressive Movement of 1924* (New York: Columbia University Press, 1947), 136–38. Bourquin quoted in Chafee, *Free Speech in the United States,* 227.

9. Walsh to Stephen J. Cowley, July 23, 1918, Walsh Mss. See Walsh to Nolan, Apr. 30, 1917, Walsh Mss; Burton K. Wheeler with Paul F. Healy, *Yankee from the West* (Garden City, N.Y.: Doubleday, 1962), 157–58 and passim.

10. *HI,* Apr. 15, 1918; *Helena Record-Herald,* May 4, June 5, 6, 1918; Walsh to Tom Stout, May 17, June 27, 1918, Stout to Walsh, June 9, 1918, Walsh Mss.

11. Walsh to Wheeler, Apr. 23, 1918, Wheeler to Walsh, Apr. 29, 1918, Walsh Mss.

12. Walsh to McDowell, July 22, 1918, Walsh Mss. See also Walsh to Nolan, June 26, 1918, Walsh to Richard Purcell, June 27, 1918, Walsh to Stout, May 17, 1918, Walsh Mss.

13. Undated and unsigned letter intended for Jerry Dobell, Walsh to McDowell, July 22, 1918, Walsh Mss.

14. Stout to Walsh, June 9, 1918, Walsh to Stout, June 27, 1918, Wheeler to Walsh, July 9, 1918, Nolan to Walsh, July 8, 1918, Walsh to Spriggs, July 5, 1918, Walsh Mss.

15. Nolan to Taylor, July 30, 1918, Walsh Mss; State of Montana, Certificate of Official Returns for the Primary Election Held on Aug. 27, 1918.

16. *Anaconda Standard* quoted in *Helena Record-Herald,* Aug. 14, 1918. See Wheeler to Walsh, Aug. 23, 1918, Walsh to Richard Purcell, June 27, 1918, Spriggs to Walsh, Aug. 28, 1918, J. M. Kennedy to Walsh, Oct. 20, 1918, Walsh Mss; Murphy, *Comical History of Montana,* 75–84.

17. State of Montana, Certificate of Official Returns for the Primary Election Held on Aug. 27, 1918; *Helena Record-Herald,* Aug. 31, Sept. 12, 1918.

18. Walsh to Spriggs, Sept. 14, 1918, Walsh Mss.

19. Walsh to Wheeler, Aug. 29, 1918, Walsh Mss.

20. Wheeler to Walsh, Aug. 23, Sept. 3, 1918, Walsh Mss.

21. Wheeler to Walsh, Oct. 2, 1918, Nolan to Walsh, Sept. 9, 1918, Spriggs to Wheeler, Sept. 21, 1918, Walsh Mss; interview with Wheeler, July 7, 1949.

22. Walsh to Edward Horsky, Sept. 3, 1918, Walsh to Nolan, Sept. 3, 1918, Wheeler to Walsh, Oct. 2, 1918, Walsh Mss.

23. Walsh to Kelley, Sept. 11, 1918, Walsh to Spriggs, Sept. 28, 1918, Walsh Mss.

24. Stewart to Walsh, Aug. 31, 1918 (enclosing copy of letter to Woodrow Wilson, Aug. 31, 1918), Walsh to Stewart, Sept. 7, 1918, Walsh Mss. See also Gov. Stewart's speech at Bozeman (endorsing Walsh for a second term), Oct. 14, 1918, Montana State University Library, Bozeman.

25. Walsh to Wheeler, Sept. 4, 1918, Walsh Mss.

26. Nolan to Walsh, Sept. 14, 1918, James Donovan to Walsh, Dec. 11, 1918, Walsh Mss.

27. Nolan to Walsh, Sept. 9, 1918, Purcell to Walsh, Sept 3, 1918, Walsh Mss.

28. Cowley to Walsh, Sept. 28, 1918, Wells to Walsh, Sept. 30, 1918, Purcell to Walsh, Oct. 2, 1918, Nolan to Walsh, Sept. 30, 1918, Walsh Mss.

29. Spriggs to Walsh's sec'y, Oct 3, 1918, Walsh Mss.

30. *Helena Record-Herald,* Oct. 2, 4, 9, 1918; *Missoulian* quoted in ibid., Oct. 8, 1918; *Miles City Star* quoted in ibid., Oct. 10, 1918.

31. Walsh made a "humiliating confession" to the president: he had forgotten to tell Nolan and Wells of their appointment. Walsh to Wilson, Oct. 11, 1918, Walsh Mss.

32. Interview with Wheeler, July 7, 1949.

33. Wheeler to Walsh, Dec. 17, 1918, Nolan to Walsh, Nov. 7, 1918, Walsh to Spriggs, Oct. 16, 1918, Walsh Oct. 1918 political letters, passim, Walsh Mss.

34. Walsh to Woodrow Wilson, Oct. 11, 1918, Spriggs to Walsh, Oct. 15, 1918, Spriggs to Imogene Howell (in Walsh's office), Oct. 25, 1918, J. M. Kennedy to Walsh, Oct. 20, 1918, Walsh Mss.

35. Spriggs to Walsh, Oct. 20, 1918, Walsh's sec'y to Nolan, Oct. 15, 1918, Walsh Mss.

36. Walsh's sec'y to Patrick H. Loughran, Oct. 19, 1918, Walsh Mss; *Helena Record-Herald,* Oct. 14, 1918.

37. Wilson to Stewart, Oct. 4, 1918, quoted in *HI,* Oct. 18, 1918; Thomas R. Marshall to Hugh Wells, Oct. 25, 1918, quoted in ibid., Oct. 28, 1918; Franklin Lane to Nolan, quoted in ibid., Oct. 25, 1918; Frank P. Walsh quoted in ibid., Nov. 3, 1918; W. J. Bryan to Walsh, quoted in ibid., Nov. 5, 1918; Walsh to Spriggs, Oct. 4, 1918, Walsh Mss; *Helena Record-Herald,* Oct. 5, 1918.

38. Carl Riddick quoted in *Helena Record-Herald,* July 29, 1918. See also *Record-Herald,* Oct.–Nov. 1918, for its own editorials and many quoted from other newspapers; Walsh to L. H. Turner (University of Wisconsin alumnus), Oct. 18, 1918, Walsh to John B. Densmore, Oct. 8, 1918, and other campaign letters, Walsh Mss.

39. Spriggs to Imogene Howell, Oct. 21, 25, 1918, Spriggs to Walsh, Sept. 23, 1918, Walsh to Spriggs, Oct. 16, 1918, Walsh Mss; *HI,* Oct. 25, 1918; Gov. Stewart speech, Oct. 14, 1918; letter from railroad representatives quoted in *HI,* Oct. 31, 1918.

40. *HI,* Oct. 25, 27, 1918.

41. State of Montana, Certificate of Official Returns for the General Election Held on Nov. 5, 1918; Walsh to Adolphus Ragan, Nov. 11, 1918, Walsh to M. J. Hutchins, Nov. 14, 1918, Walsh Mss; *Helena Record-Herald,* Nov. 11, 1918; Walsh to W. M. Johnston, Nov. 12, 1918, Walsh to C. F. Morris, Nov. 19, 1918, Walsh Mss.

42. Walsh to Johnston, Nov. 12, 1918, Walsh Oct.–Nov. 1918 political letters, passim, Walsh Mss.

43. Walsh to W. Napton, Oct. 10, 1918, Walsh to Mrs. F. S. Lusk, Oct. 14, 1918, Walsh to Spriggs, Oct. 10, 1918, J. M. Kennedy to Walsh, Oct. 20, 1918, Walsh Mss.

44. Sen. Thomas to Walsh, Oct. 24, 30, 1918, Walsh Mss.

45. Nolan to Walsh, Nov. 7, 1918, Walsh to Kelley, Nov. 22, 1918, Walsh to Dobell, Nov. 22, 1918, Walsh Mss.

46. Kelley to Walsh, Nov. 25, 1918, Donnelly to Walsh, Nov. 12, 1918, Walsh Mss.

47. Donnelly to Walsh, Nov. 12, 1918, Walsh Mss; interview with Genevieve Walsh Gudger, Feb. 16, 1950.

48. Wheeler to Walsh, Dec. 17, 1918, Walsh to Wheeler, Jan. 28, 1919, Walsh Mss.

Chapter 17: The League of Nations Fight

1. Walsh to C. F. Turner, July 1, 1918, Walsh Mss; Mark Sullivan, *Our Times: The United States, 1900–1925,* 6 vols. (New York: Charles Scribner's Sons, 1926–35), 5:423–56.

2. See Ralph Stone, *The Irreconcilables: The Fight against the League of Nations* (Lexington: University Press of Kentucky, 1970), 4–23, 58, and passim.

3. William C. Widenor, *Henry Cabot Lodge and the Search for an American Foreign Policy* (Berkeley: University of California Press, 1980), 310–23 and passim; Warren F. Kuehl, *Seeking World Order: The United States and International Organization to 1920* (Nashville: Vanderbilt University Press, 1969); Lloyd E. Ambrosius, *Woodrow Wilson and the American Diplomatic Tradition: The Treaty Fight in Perspective* (Cambridge: Cambridge University Press, 1987).

4. Walsh to D. J. O'Hern, Nov. 22, 1918, Walsh Mss; *Cong. Rec.,* 65th Cong., 2d

Sess. (Nov. 15, 1918), 11561; Walsh to M. J. Hutchins, Nov. 14, 1918, Walsh to D. D. Dotson, Nov. 23, 1918, Walsh Mss; *HI,* Nov. 22, 26, 1918; Thomas A. Bailey, *Wilson and the Peacemakers* (combines *Woodrow Wilson and the Lost Peace* and *Woodrow Wilson and the Great Betrayal*) (1945; New York: Macmillan, 1947).

5. *Cong. Rec.,* 65th Cong., 3d Sess. (Feb. 4, 1919), 2658; Walsh to Wilson, Feb. 25, 1919, Walsh Mss; Gilbert M. Hitchcock to Wilson, Mar. 29, 1917, Gilbert M. Hitchcock Mss, LC; Bailey, *Woodrow Wilson and the Great Betrayal,* 54–55.

6. Wilson to Walsh, Feb. 26, 1919, Walsh Mss; *NYT,* Feb. 23, 1919.

7. Walsh to Lewis Penwell, Mar. 11, 1919, Walsh Mss.

8. *Washington Post,* Mar. 26, 1919; *HI,* May 5, 9, 12, 13, 1919; Walsh to R. R. Purcell, Apr. 22, 1919, Walsh to F. S. Lusk, Mar. 10, 1919, Walsh to C. M. Kutzner, Mar. 17, 1919, Walsh to Dr. Robert E. Layton, Apr. 2, 1919, Walsh Mss.

9. Walsh to Norman Hapgood, Jan. 15, 1919, Walsh to R. R. Purcell, Apr. 22, 1919, Walsh Mss.

10. *Cong. Rec.,* 65th Cong., 2d Sess. (Nov. 15, 1918), 11555, 11561–67; Walsh to Mrs. M. W. Alderson, Nov. 18, 1918, Walsh Mss; Ambrosius, *Woodrow Wilson and the American Diplomatic Tradition,* chap. 4.

11. *Cong. Rec.,* 65th Cong., 3d Sess. (Dec. 4, 1918), 69–71; Walsh to Hapgood, Dec. 5, 6, 1918, Hapgood to Walsh, Dec. 13, 1918, Walsh Mss.

12. *Cong. Rec.,* 65th Cong., 3d Sess. (Dec. 6, 1918), 191–92; Borah in *Cong. Rec.,* passim.

13. See Bailey, *Woodrow Wilson and the Lost Peace,* 205.

14. *Cong. Rec.,* 66th Cong., 1st Sess. (May 23, 1919), 157–58; *HI,* July 11, 1919.

15. *Cong. Rec.,* 66th Cong., 1st Sess. (June 11, 1919), 955–60; *Philadelphia Record,* June 13, 1919.

16. *Cong. Rec.,* 66th Cong., 1st Sess. (June 25, 1919), 1744–47; Stone, *Irreconcilables,* 144–47.

17. *HI,* May 9, 1919; *Cong. Rec.,* 66th Cong., 1st Sess. (July 28, 1919), 3229.

18. Westel Woodbury Willoughby, *The Constitutional Law of the United States,* 2d ed., 3 vols. (New York: Baker, Voorhis, 1929), 1:520–25; *Cong. Rec.,* 66th Cong., 1st Sess. (Nov. 6, 1919), 8010–11.

19. *Cong. Rec.,* 66th Cong., 1st Sess. (July 28, 1919), 3229.

20. Ibid. (June 25, 1919), 1742–44, (June 18, 1919), 1271; Marian C. McKenna, *Borah* (Ann Arbor: University of Michigan Press, 1961), 150–71.

21. *Cong. Rec.,* 66th Cong., 1st Sess. (June 30, 1919), 2077–78.

22. Ibid. (June 18, 1919), 1269, (July 28, 1919), 3223.

23. Ibid. (Oct. 6, 1919), 6447, (June 20, 1919), 1447–48.

24. Walsh to Hugh Thomas Carter, Oct. 9, 1919, Walsh Mss; *Cong. Rec.,* 66th Cong., 1st Sess. (Oct. 6, 1919), 6446, (Sept. 29, 1919), 6086–87.

25. Walsh letter to citizens of Butte, Mont., quoted in *HI,* Oct. 28, 1919.

26. David M. Emmons, *The Butte Irish: Class and Ethnicity in an American Mining Town, 1875–1925* (Urbana: University of Illinois Press, 1989), 292–332 and passim.

27. Walsh to John Bribben, pres., Robert Emmet Literary Association, June 29, 1918, Walsh Mss.

28. Walsh to John J. McHatton, Mar. 26, 1919, Walsh to James E. Murray, Apr. 1, 1919, Walsh Mss.

29. Walsh to Woodrow Wilson, Dec. 2, 1918, Walsh Mss; Wilson to Walsh, Dec. 3, 1918, quoted in Joseph P. Tumulty, *Woodrow Wilson as I Know Him* (Garden City, N.Y.: Doubleday Page, 1921), 401.

30. Walsh and others to Wilson, Mar. 28, 1919, Walsh Mss.

31. Walsh to Gov. Stewart, Oct. 8, 1919, Walsh Mss. See also Sen. Peter Gerry to Walsh, Oct. 9, 1919, Walsh Mss.

32. *Cong. Rec.,* 66th Cong., 1st Sess. (Oct. 18, 1919), 7109–15.

33. Walsh helped to plan the president's itinerary, although the latter did not stop in Glacier Park. See Walsh to Joseph Tumulty, July 19, 1919, Walsh to Mrs. Wilson, Aug. 27, 1919, Walsh Mss.

34. *Cong. Rec.,* 66th Cong., 1st Sess. (Aug. 7, 1919), 3696, (Oct. 2, 1919), 6273–76, (Sept. 26, 1919), 5978–80, (Nov. 7, 1919), 8064–66; Walsh to S. V. Stewart, Oct. 8, 1919, Walsh Mss.

35. *Cong. Rec.,* 66th Cong., 1st Sess. (Oct. 29, 1919), 7680–82, (Nov. 7, 1919), 8063–66.

36. See ibid. (Nov. 15, 1919), 8564–69, (Nov. 17, 1919), 8633–34, (Nov. 18, 1919), 8703–4, (Nov. 10, 1919), 8194–96, (Nov. 13, 1919), 8423–24.

37. Ibid. (June 11, 1919), 960, (Nov. 13, 1919), 8425–27, (Nov. 15, 1919), 8569.

38. Walsh to Sen. Hitchcock, Nov. 18, 1919, Hitchcock to Mrs. Wilson, Nov. 18, 1919, Wilson Mss; Stone, *Irreconcilables,* 128–46.

39. *Cong. Rec.,* 66th Cong., 1st Sess. (Nov. 19, 1919), 8786–803.

40. Stephen Bonsal, *Suitors and Suppliants: The Little Nations at Versailles* (New York: Prentice-Hall, 1946), 196–97; Bailey, *Woodrow Wilson and the Great Betrayal,* 182–86; interview with Genevieve Walsh Gudger, Feb. 16, 1950.

41. *Cong. Rec.,* 66th Cong., 2d Sess. (Dec. 13, 1919), 535–37.

42. Ibid. (Feb. 20, 1920), 3178–79; Walsh to A. E. Spriggs, Jan. 22, 1920, Walsh Mss; Henry Cabot Lodge, *The Senate and the League of Nations* (New York: Charles Scribner's Sons, 1925), 192–95.

43. Lodge, *Senate and the League of Nations,* 192–95.

44. Statement made to the press, quoted in *Cong. Rec.,* 66th Cong., 2d Sess. (Jan. 31, 1920), 2285–87.

45. Ibid. (Mar. 4, 1920), 3861–63, (Feb. 21, 1920), 3232; Stone, *Irreconcilables,* 156–57.

46. *Cong. Rec.,* 66th Cong., 2d Sess. (Mar. 18, 1920), 4499, 4505, 4522.

47. Walsh in ibid. (Mar. 19, 1920), 4581–85; Walsh to Clarence D. Clark, Mar. 16, 1920, Walsh Mss.

48. *Cong. Rec.,* 66th Cong., 2d Sess. (Mar. 19, 1920), 4581–85.

49. Walsh to Wallace T. Hughes, May 6, 1920, Walsh Mss; Culberson quoted in Bailey, *Woodrow Wilson and the Great Betrayal,* 267.

50. Walsh and other senators may have been influenced by John Maynard Keynes, *The Economic Consequences of the Peace* (New York: Harcourt, Brace and Howe, 1920). See Walsh to Reinhardt Rahr, Feb. 26, 1920, Walsh Mss.

51. Nolan to Walsh, Feb. 20, 1920, Walsh to Tom Stout, Feb. 26, 1920, Walsh to Will Campbell, Mar. 15, 1920, Walsh Mss.

Chapter 18: 1920 Politics and Issues of the Red Scare

1. On Harding and the Republican presidential campaign see Robert K. Murray, *The Harding Era: Warren G. Harding and His Administration* (Minneapolis: University of Minnesota Press, 1969), 69–70 and passim.

2. Stout to Walsh, Dec. 12, 1919, Walsh Mss; Associated Press report in *HI*, June 24, 1920. See Spriggs to Walsh, Sept. 11, 28, 1920, Walsh to Stout, Feb. 28, 1922, Nolan to Walsh, May 29, 1919, Stout to Walsh, Dec. 12, 1919, Walsh Mss.

3. Nolan to Walsh, Oct. 8, 1920, Wheeler to John M. Evans, Oct. 1, 1920, Walsh Mss. Walsh believed that Campbell of the *Independent* was "richly paid" for abusing the Nonpartisan League. Walsh to George H. Pew, Nov. 1, 1920, Raymond Nagle to Miles Taylor (Walsh's sec'y), Nov. 4, 1920, Walsh Mss. See Edward G. Hoffman, comp., *Official Report of the Proceedings of the Democratic National Convention . . . San Francisco . . . 1920,* 4–6.

4. Walsh to Pat Harrison, Sept. 29, 1920, Walsh to George White, Oct. 2, 1920, Nolan to Walsh, Oct. 8, 1920, Walsh to Nolan, Oct. 18, 1920, John E. Erickson, chairman, Democratic State Central Committee, to Walsh, Oct. 8, 1920, Walsh to Erickson, Oct. 9, 1920, Walsh Mss.

5. *HI*, Oct. 26, 1920; Judge Charles Amidon of North Dakota to Walsh, Oct. 23, 1920, Walsh Mss.

6. Walsh to J. Bruce Kremer, Oct. 30, 1920, Walsh to John D. Tansil, sec'y, Democratic County Committee, Billings, Oct. 29, 1920, Walsh to Herbert M. Peet, Nov. 1, 1920, Walsh to George H. Pew, Nov. 1, 1920, Walsh Mss; *HI*, Nov. 2, 1920.

7. *HI*, Nov. 6, 1920; interview with Wheeler, July 7, 1949; Raymond Nagle (Walsh's staff) to Miles Taylor, Nov. 4, 1920, Walsh Mss; Jules A. Karlin, *Joseph M. Dixon of Montana: Governor versus the Anaconda, 1917–1934* (Missoula: University of Montana Publications in History, 1974), 45–61 and passim.

8. Jerry W. Farrell to Walsh, Jan. 1, 1921, Walsh to Farrell, Jan. 10, 1921, Walsh to William Jennings Price, Envoy to Panama, Dec. 10, 1920, Walsh Mss.

9. Walsh to Richard R. Kilroy, Jan. 8, 1920, Walsh to A. Mitchell Palmer, Jan. 8, 1920, Walsh Mss.

10. *Cong. Rec.,* 66th Cong., 3d Sess. (Dec. 10, 1920), 149–50. See also Robert W. Dunn, ed., *The Palmer Raids* (New York: International Publishers, 1938), 38; Louis F. Post, *The Deportations Delirium of Nineteen-Twenty* (Chicago: Charles H. Kerr, 1923), 302–4, for praise of Walsh's role; Harold Ickes to Walsh, Jan. 19, 1921, Walsh

Mss; Robert K. Murray, *Red Scare: A Study in National Hysteria, 1919–1920* (Minneapolis: University of Minnesota Press, 1955), 256–57 and passim.

11. Walsh to Nolan, Sept. 16, 1920, Walsh to Joseph L. Asbridge, Department of Justice, Helena, Feb. 21, 1921, Walsh Mss.

12. U.S. Congress, Senate, *Charges of Illegal Practices of the Department of Justice*, Hearings before a Subcommittee of the Committee on the Judiciary, U.S. Senate, 66th Cong., 3d Sess., Jan. 19–Mar. 3, 1921 (Washington, D.C.: GPO, 1921), passim.

13. Ibid., 85–86, 134, 414, 648.

14. Ibid., 578–82; Walsh quoted in *NYT,* Feb. 23, 1919.

15. Walsh to Thomas Sterling, Jan. 27, 1922, Walsh notes on the Judiciary Committee minutes, Walsh Mss.

16. *Cong. Rec.,* 67th Cong., 4th Sess. (Feb. 5, 1923), 3008; U.S. Congress, Senate, *Charges of Illegal Practices,* 3011, 3026.

17. U.S. Congress, Senate, *Charges of Illegal Practices,* 3027. In a review of Post, *Deportations Delirium,* Walsh maintained the same liberal point of view. See Thomas J. Walsh, "The Red Deportations of 1920," *The New Republic* 37 (Feb. 20, 1924), 340–41.

18. See Felix Frankfurter to Walsh, Mar. __, 1922, Frank P. Walsh to Tom Walsh, Mar. 16, 1922, Edwin Borchard to Walsh, Mar. 23, 1922, Walsh Mss; *NYW,* Mar. 16, 1922; Walsh to *HI* and other newspapers, Mar. 16, 1922; Post, *Deportations Delirium,* 302–4; Oswald Garrison Villard, "Thomas J. Walsh: A Great Prosecutor," in *Prophets True and False* (New York: Knopf, 1928), 146–47.

19. Walsh to Mary O'Neill, Mar. 1, 1923, Walsh Mss.

20. Thomas R. Marshall, *Recollections: A Hoosier Salad* (Indianapolis: Bobbs-Merrill, 1925), 315.

Chapter 19: Walsh and Wheeler, 1922

1. *New York Evening Post,* Apr. 9, 1921; Sullivan, "Republican Leaders in the Senate," *The World's Work* 42 (June 1921), 142–52.

2. Walsh to James T. Finlen, pres., Silver Bow National Bank, Nov. 3, 1921, Walsh to Tom Stout, Feb. 28, 1922, Walsh Mss.

3. Walsh to Nolan, Mar. 7, 1921, Walsh to S. V. Stewart, Aug. 1, 1921, Walsh Mss. See Alice Roosevelt Longworth, *Crowded Hours* (New York: Charles Scribner's Sons, 1933), 320–25; Murray, *Harding Era,* 113–28.

4. *HI,* Oct. 25, 1922; Walsh to Nolan, May 18, 1921, Walsh to Laura Mohun, Nov. 7, 1922, Harding to Walsh, Sept. 6, 1922, Walsh Mss.

5. *HI,* Nov. 17, 1921; Walsh to Grace Chapman, Nov. 28, 1921, Walsh Mss; *Cong. Rec.,* 67th Cong., 1st Sess. (Nov. 19, 1921), 7956.

6. Walsh's sec'y to E. O. Pace, Dec. 23, 1921, Walsh and Atlee Pomerene to John B. Kendrick, Jan. 6, 1922, La Follette to Walsh, Jan. 7, 8, 1922, Walsh to J. C. Hooker,

Jan. 14, 1922, Walsh Mss; *Cong. Rec.*, 67th Cong., 2d Sess. (Jan. 10, 1922), 993–97, (Jan. 12, 1922), 1115–16; Spencer Ervin, *Henry Ford vs. Truman H. Newberry* (New York: Richard R. Smith, 1935), passim; Louis Levine, *The Taxation of Mines in Montana* (New York: B. W. Huebsch, 1919); idem, "Are the Great Montana Mines Deliberately Dodging Taxes?" *Current Opinion* 66 (May 1919), 335–36. See Walsh to William Hard, Aug. 24, 1922, Walsh Mss; interview with Sen. James E. Murray, Aug. 27, 1949.

7. Walsh to Stout, Feb 28, 1922, Walsh to Nolan, Mar. 22, 1922, Walsh to C. P. Greenfield, Aug. 26, 1922, Walsh Mss; Wheeler, *Yankee from the West*, 185–97.

8. Walsh to Nolan, Feb. 13, 1922, Walsh to Stout, Feb. 28, 1922, Walsh to A. L. Stone, Feb 27, 1922, Walsh Mss.

9. Walsh to Dobell, Mar. 27, 1922, Walsh to Nolan, Apr. 10, 1922, Wheeler to Walsh, Apr. 20, 1922, Erickson to Walsh, Apr. 18, 1922, Walsh Mss; *HI*, Apr. 15, 16, 1922.

10. Wheeler to Walsh, Jan. 7, 1921, Walsh to Wheeler, Jan. 21, 1921, Walsh Mss. Walsh replied expressing his sympathy and gratification that he had not gone to work for the company.

11. Walsh to Stout, May 22, 1922, Walsh to Nolan, Feb. 13, 1922, Walsh Mss.

12. Walsh to Nolan, Apr. 3, 1922, Wheeler to Walsh, Apr. 20, May 10, 1922, Walsh Mss. Wheeler stated, in his letter of May 10, that he would destroy copies of letters from Walsh.

13. Wheeler to Walsh, Apr. 20, May 10, 1922, Stout to Walsh, May 6, 1922, Erickson to Walsh, Apr. 18, 1922, Stout to Walsh, July 24, 1922, Walsh Mss.

14. Walsh to Wheeler, Apr. 28, June 19, 1922, Walsh to Stout, May 22, Aug. 24, 1922, Walsh to J. A. Lovelace, May 15, 1922, Walsh Mss.

15. Interview with Wheeler, July 7, 1949; State of Montana, Certificate of Official Returns for the Primary Election Held on Aug. 29, 1922.

16. *HI*, Sept. 10, 14, Oct. 6, 8, 10, 13, 14, 19, 1922; *Butte Miner* quoted in *HI*, Oct. 24, 1922.

17. *HI*, Oct. 21, 1922. Bruce Kremer and Tom Stout took over part of Walsh's itinerary. Ibid., Oct. 22, Nov. 3, 7, 1922; Walsh to George Randall, Nov. 7, 1922, Walsh Mss.

18. Walsh to Laura Mohun, Nov. 7, 1922, Walsh Mss; State of Montana, Certificate of Official Returns for the General Election Held on Nov. 7, 1922.

19. Walsh to A. B. Melzner, Nov. 23, 1922, Bruce Kremer to Walsh, Nov. 10, 1922, Walsh Mss; *HI*, Nov. 9, 1922; Wheeler, *Yankee from the West*, 194–97.

Chapter 20: Public Lands, Native Americans, and Campaigns for (Honest) Leasing

1. McDonnell, *Dispossession of the American Indian*, passim; John Collier, *Indians of the Americas: The Long Hope* (New York: New American Library of World Literature, 1947), passim.

2. Karlin, *Joseph M. Dixon of Montana, 1867–1917*, 55–59; Burton M. Smith, "The Politics of Allotment: The Flathead Indian Reservation as a Test Case," *Pacific North-*

west Quarterly 70 (July 1979), 131–40; Walsh to Philip Ironhead, Apr. 8, 1919, Walsh to Fred T. Lincoln, May 20, 1920, Walsh Mss; *HI,* Sept. 26, 1919; Robert Summers Yellowtail Sr.'s "story" in *Black Jack* (Albuquerque, N.Mex.: Wowapi, 1973).

3. Judson King to Walsh, Mar. 2, 7, 1923, Walsh to King, Mar. 3, 9, 1923, Walsh to Mrs. E. T. Baillie, Dec. 19, 1922, Walsh Mss.

4. Robbins, *Our Landed Heritage,* 372ff.; John Ise, *The United States Oil Policy* (New Haven: Yale University Press, 1926), 337.

5. Walsh to Sen. Charles S. Henderson, Sept. 2, 1919, Walsh Mss; J. Leonard Bates, "The Midwest Decision, 1915: A Landmark in Conservation History," *Pacific Northwest Quarterly* 51 (Jan. 1960), 26–34.

6. Portland *Oregonian,* Dec. 26, 1913; Walsh to *HI,* Aug. 11, 1914, Walsh Mss. See also Walsh quoted in *HI,* Aug. 3, 1924, on his leasing work; Olson, *Biography of a Progressive,* 12–13, 103–10, and passim.

7. Walsh to J. M. Kennedy, Oct. 12, 1918, Walsh Mss; Ise, *United States Oil Policy,* 333–34; Bates, *Origins of Teapot Dome,* passim.

8. Walsh to J. S. Warner, Mar. 5, 1919, Walsh to J. E. Logan, Mar. 11, 1919, Walsh to Hattie Grace, Mar. 26, 1919, Walsh Mss.

9. Anonymous "Interview," Mar. 12, 1919, included among Walsh addresses and speeches (in his language for the most part and expressing his views), Walsh Mss; *Cong. Rec.,* 65th Cong., 2d Sess. (Jan. 4, 1918), 648, (Sept. 17, 1918), 10382.

10. *Cong. Rec.,* 65th Cong., 3d Sess. (Feb. 18, 1919), 3705–6, 66th Cong., 1st Sess. (Sept. 3, 1919), 4758–61. See also Ise, *United States Oil Policy,* 336–40; Olson, *Biography of a Progressive,* 174–75.

11. Spriggs to Walsh, June 19, 1919, Nolan to Walsh's sec'y, June 12, 1918, sec'y to Nolan, June 17, 1919, Walsh to R. S. Hamilton, Oct. 19, 1918, Walsh to James F. O'Connor, Oct. 12, 1918, and passim, Walsh Mss.

12. Ise, *United States Oil Policy,* 352; Walsh quoted in *HI,* Aug. 3, 1924.

13. *U.S. Statutes at Large* (1919–21), 41:437–45.

14. *U.S. Statutes at Large* (1919–21), 41:1063–77. See Walsh to John J. Harris, pres., Big Horn Canyon Irrigation & Power Co., Dec. 12, 1918, Harris to Walsh, Dec. 16, 1918, Walsh to Scott Ferris, June 9, 11, 1920, clipping from *Hardin Tribune,* Aug. 20, 1920, Walsh to Sec'y of State Bainbridge Colby, June 8, 1920, Colby to Walsh, June 8, 1920, Walsh to Edward Lawlor, June 19, 1920, Walsh to John J. Harris, June 10, 1920, Walsh's sec'y to Harris, June 29, 1920, Walsh Mss; Walsh quoted in *HI,* July 13, 1920; Robbins, *Our Landed Heritage,* 396–97.

15. *Cong. Rec.,* 66th Cong., 1st Sess., 4770 (Sept. 3, 1919).

16. U.S. Congress, Senate, *Leases upon Naval Oil Reserves,* Hearings before the Committee on Public Lands and Surveys Pursuant to S. Res. 282, S. Res. 294, and S. Res. 434, 67th Cong., and S. Res. 147, 68th Cong., 3 vols. with continuous pagination (Washington, D.C.: GPO, 1924), 1, passim (hereafter *Leases upon Naval Oil Reserves* [1924]; also in *The Teapot Dome Documents,* microfilm, 7 reels, listed in John Moscate, ed., *A Guide to the Teapot Dome Documents* [Arlington, Va.: University

Publications of America, 1975], 8 pp., reels 6–7). See also Ise, *United States Oil Policy,* especially chap. 25; Robbins, *Our Landed Heritage;* Bates, *Origins of Teapot Dome;* Burl Noggle, *Teapot Dome: Oil and Politics in the 1920's* (Baton Rouge: Louisiana State University Press, 1962); *U.S. Statutes at Large* (1919–21), 41:813–14.

17. Walsh to Ray Harris, Apr. 7, 1932, Walsh Mss.

18. Interview with Fola La Follette, July 13, 1949; Fola La Follette, "Teapot Dome: 'A Portrait in Oil,'" in La Follette and La Follette, *Robert M. La Follette,* 2:1041–54. See *Leases upon Naval Oil Reserves* (1924), 1–27.

19. U.S. Congress, Senate, *High Cost of Gasoline and Other Petroleum Products,* Hearings before a Subcommittee of the Committee on Manufactures, 67th Cong., 2d Sess. and 4th Sess., Pursuant to S. Res. 295 (Washington, D.C.: GPO, 1923), 1, 763, 786–87.

20. Ibid., 797–98. See also Chester Washburne to Robert M. La Follette, Jan. 27, 1923, Walsh to Alan D. Reynolds, Dec. 10, 1923, La Follette correspondence, passim, Walsh Mss.

21. Walsh to Albert F. Demers, *Record* (Troy, N.Y.), Nov. 28, 1924, Walsh to D. F. Pugh, Dec 13, 1927, Walsh Mss.

22. Interview with Wheeler, July 7, 1949; Walsh to Bruce Dutton, May 7, 1920, Walsh to Hamilton Holt, Mar. 12, 1923, Walsh to Albert Demers, Nov 28, 1924, Walsh Mss.

23. Walsh to Sen. A. A. Jones, Sept. 21, 1923, Walsh Mss; *HI,* Mar. 28, 1923; interview with Genevieve Walsh Gudger, Feb. 16, 1950.

24. Walsh to D. F. Pugh, Dec. 18, 1927, Walsh Mss.

Chapter 21: The Investigator

1. *Leases upon Naval Oil Reserves* (1924), 330–35, 356–63. See also La Follette and La Follette, *Robert M. La Follette,* 2:1041–54; Bates, *Origins of Teapot Dome,* 219–35.

2. *Leases upon Naval Oil Reserves* (1924), especially a letter by A. B. Fall, 27–53. See also Ise, *United States Oil Policy,* chap. 25; David H. Stratton, "New Mexican Machiavellian? The Story of Albert B. Fall," *Montana* 7 (Oct. 1957), 2–14.

3. Chester Washburne to La Follette, Jan. 3, 1923, Walsh Mss.

4. See George H. Haynes, *The Senate of the United States: Its History and Practice,* 2 vols. (Boston: Houghton Mifflin, 1938), 1:507–67 and passim; Walsh in *Cong. Rec.,* 68th Cong., 1st Sess. (Mar. 24, 1924), 4788–89; Thomas J. Walsh, "The Senate as Censor," *The Forum* 78 (Oct. 1927), 593–604.

5. Chester Washburne to La Follette, Jan. 3, 1923, Walsh Mss.

6. Walsh to D. F. Pugh, Dec. 13, 1927, Walsh to Roy E. Reed, Feb. 4, 1926, Walsh Mss; Herbert F. Margulies, *Senator Lenroot of Wisconsin: A Political Biography, 1900–1929* (Columbia: University of Missouri Press, 1977), 371–73; Noggle, *Teapot Dome,* 43–63 and passim.

7. Walsh to John B. Kendrick, Sept. 27, 1923, Oct. 6, 1924, Kendrick to Walsh, Oct. 1, 1923, Walsh to A. A. Jones, Sept. 21, 1923, Walsh Mss; *Leases upon Naval Oil Reserves* (1924), 1.

8. Walsh to Daniels, Nov. 5, 1923, Payne, chairman, Central Committee, American Red Cross, to Walsh, Oct. 25, 1923, Walsh Mss.

9. Walsh to Swope, *NYW,* Nov. 15, 1923, Walsh to Washburne, Nov. 8, 1923, Walsh to Connolly, Nov. 6, 1923, Connolly to Walsh, Nov. 8, 1923, Walsh Mss.

10. See *Leases upon Naval Oil Reserves* (1924), passim; Frederic J. Haskin in *HI,* Feb. 19, 1924.

11. *Leases upon Naval Oil Reserves* (1924), 178–82, 186–91; Walsh to Joseph Zimmerman, *Daily Metal Reporter,* Mar. 10, 1924, Walsh to Alan Reynolds, Dec. 10, 1923, Walsh Mss.

12. *Leases upon Naval Oil Reserves* (1924), 767–78; Walsh to Chester Washburne, Nov. 7, 1923, Adm. Griffin to Walsh, Oct. 23, 1923, Frank Scofield to Walsh, Oct. 31, 1923, Daniels to Walsh, Nov. 1, 1923, and passim, Walsh Mss.

13. Walsh to Ernest A. Hardcastle, Nov. 8, 1923, Walsh to Leslie Parker, Oct. 30, 1923, Walsh to W. H. Gray, pres., National Association of Independent Oil Producers, Nov. 6, 1923, Walsh to Edward Keating, Nov. 16, 1923, Walsh to Alan D. Reynolds, Dec. 10, 1923, Walsh Mss.

14. Washburne to Walsh, Nov. 3, 5, 1923, Walsh to Washburne, Nov. 5, 6, and 7, 1923, Walsh Mss; *Leases upon Naval Oil Reserves* (1924), 502–3.

15. Walsh to Sen. Jones, Sept 21, 1923, Byron O. Beall to Cordell Hull, June 8, 1922, Walsh to Beall, Sept 23, 1923, Walsh Mss.

16. Thomas J. Walsh, "The True History of Teapot Dome," *The Forum* 72 (July 1924), 7–8; Whipple to Walsh, Oct. 30, 31, 1923, Walsh to Whipple, Oct. 31, 1923, Walsh to Andrew H. Hudspeth, Nov. 16, 1923, Walsh to Justiniana Baca, land commissioner, Santa Fe, N.Mex., Dec. 1, 1923, Walsh Mss.

17. Walsh informed Magee that a subpoena was being served entitling him to mileage and per diem and asked him to report early for a conference if possible. Walsh to Carl C. McGee [*sic*], Nov. 23, 24, 1923, Magee to Walsh, Nov. 24, 1923, Walsh Mss.

18. *Leases upon Naval Oil Reserves* (1924), 846–49, 861–90.

19. Ibid., 1017–39.

20. Walsh to Baruch, Dec. 4, 5, 1923, Walsh Mss. See also John Carson, Scripps Service, to Walsh, n.d., H. S. Reavis to Walsh, Dec. 11, 1923, Walsh to Seymour Cromwell, pres., New York Stock Exchange, Feb. 8, 1924, Gordon F. Hull to Walsh, Feb. 20, 1924, Walsh to Hull, Feb. 22, 1924, Walsh Mss.

21. *Leases upon Naval Oil Reserves* (1924), 1371–415, especially 1373–74, 1414–15, 1421–28, 1435–51. After Walsh's investigation of 1923–24 had ended, special government prosecutors Owen D. Roberts and Atlee Pomerene discovered the Continental deal. Walsh and other senators then conducted a second investigation.

22. Ibid., 973–1016.

23. Ibid., 1283–87, 1298–305, 1054–60.

24. Ibid., 1429–34.

25. Sullivan, *Our Times,* 6:305–6 and passim; Ise, *United States Oil Policy,* passim; Walsh to Palmer, Jan. 3, 1924, Walsh Mss.

26. *Leases upon Naval Oil Reserves* (1924), 1546–50.

27. Walsh, "True History of Teapot Dome," 10.

28. *Leases upon Naval Oil Reserves* (1924), 2715–16; William A. Glasgow Jr. to Walsh, Feb. 26, 1924, Walsh to Glasgow, Feb. 27, 1924, Walsh Mss.

29. *Leases upon Naval Oil Reserves* (1924), 1693–97; Walsh, "True History of Teapot Dome," 11.

30. *Leases upon Naval Oil Reserves* (1924), 1698–99; McLean's testimony in ibid., 2719–20.

31. John M. Parker to Walsh, Jan. 20, 21, 1924, Walsh Mss.

32. McNab to Walsh, Jan. 21, 1924, Walsh Mss; *Leases upon Naval Oil Reserves* (1924), 1775, 1787–90.

33. McAdoo to Walsh, June 23, 1925, Walsh Mss; *Leases upon Naval Oil Reserves* (1924), 1775, 1787–90. See also on this general subject Sullivan, *Our Times,* 6:318–35.

34. Walsh to Doheny, Dec. 24, 1923, Walsh to Thomas M. Hodgens, Apr. 11, 1918, Walsh to T. P. Cullen, June 11, 1920, Walsh to John Francis O'Keefe, Mar. 31, 1926, Walsh Mss.

35. Walsh to Doheny, Dec. 14, 1923, Doheny to Walsh, Dec. 21, 1923, Walsh to Doheny, Dec. 24, 1923, Walsh Mss. In Walsh's letter to Doheny of Dec. 14 he enclosed a letter from T. S. Hogan, Great Falls, concerning Montana oil development. Walsh introduced his correspondence with Hogan and Doheny into the record. *Leases upon Naval Oil Reserves* (1924), 2479–82.

36. *Leases upon Naval Oil Reserves* (1924), 1771–823, especially 1771–80, 1809.

37. Ibid., 1776, 1781; Walsh to James D. Phelan, Jan. 24, 1924, Walsh to Frank B. Moore, Dec. 10, 1926, Walsh to McAdoo, June 23, 1925, Walsh Mss.

38. *Leases upon Naval Oil Reserves* (1924), 1790, 1799; Walsh to Warren S. Blauvelt, Mar. 22, 1922, Walsh Mss.

39. See, for example, *Leases upon Naval Oil Reserves* (1924), 1798, 1807, 1817.

40. Paul Y. Anderson, "The Scandal in Oil," *The New Republic* 37 (Feb. 6, 1924), 277–79.

41. *Leases upon Naval Oil Reserves* (1924), 1712–18, 1726–28.

42. Ibid., 1825–45.

43. Ibid., 2894–900; *Cong. Rec.,* 68th Cong., 1st Sess. (Mar. 24, 1924), 4790–91. The case went through the courts and finally, in 1929, the Supreme Court decided against Sinclair. See Haynes, *Senate of the United States,* 1:519–21.

44. Walsh to F. B. Linfield, Jan. 24, 1924, Walsh Mss; *Leases upon Naval Oil Reserves* (1924), 1961–63; Sullivan, *Our Times,* 6:327–29.

45. *Cong. Rec.,* 68th Cong., 1st Sess. (Jan. 7, 1924), 583, (Jan. 23, 1924), 1313–14,

(Jan. 28, 1924), 1520; James N. Giglio, *H. M. Daugherty and the Politics of Expediency* (Kent, Ohio: Kent State University Press, 1978), 166–69.

46. Walsh to Connolly, July 21, 1932, Walsh Mss; *Cong. Rec.,* 68th Cong., 1st Sess. (Jan. 28, 1924), 1518–38; *HI,* Jan. 29, 1924. See Walsh, "Senate as Censor," 594; Bennett quoted in *HI,* Feb. 12, 1924. Walsh thought Bennett's description was "lovely." Walsh to Connolly, July 21, 1932, Walsh Mss; *Cong. Rec.,* 68th Cong., 1st Sess. (Feb. 8, 1924), 2055–65; Associated Press report quoting Walsh, *HI,* Feb. 19, 1924.

47. *Leases upon Naval Oil Reserves* (1924), 1248–79.

48. Ibid., 2703–4; *Brooklyn Eagle* to Walsh, Mar. 1, 1924, Walsh to *Brooklyn Eagle,* Mar. 1, 1924, Walsh Mss. See also various letters, "Legislation Department of Justice, 1924," Walsh Mss; Wheeler, *Yankee from the West,* 213–45.

49. *Cong. Rec.,* 65th Cong., 1st Sess. (Feb. 16, 1924), 2555–56, 2559–60, (Feb. 26, 1924), 3169; Edward Keating to Walsh, Feb. 6, 1924, Anonymous to Walsh, Jan. 31, 1924, Walsh's sec'y to Pres. Coolidge, Jan. 31, 1924, Walsh to Thomas C. Spelling, Apr. 7, 1925, Walsh to Sigmund Zeisler, Feb 16, 1924, Walsh to Charles Lobingier, Mar. 3, 1924, Walsh Mss; Ise, *United States Oil Policy,* 383–88; George Wharton Pepper, *Philadelphia Lawyer: An Autobiography* (Philadelphia: J. B. Lippincott, 1944), 197.

50. See correspondence with Atlee Pomerene and Owen J. Roberts, Walsh Mss. First, Walsh found confirmation of his fears that Pomerene and Roberts were not qualified for their assignment, but a short time later Judge Paul J. McCormick of Southern California held against the Doheny contracts. Thomas C. Spelling to Walsh, Apr. 5, 1925, Walsh to Spelling, Apr. 7, 1925, Walsh Mss. Upon appeal to the circuit court, Doheny lost again. This time Walsh congratulated Pomerene and Roberts for their "very able conduct of the case." Walsh to Pomerene, Jan. 22, 1926, Walsh Mss. When this decision finally was affirmed by the Supreme Court, one of Walsh's comments was, "he laughs best who laughs last." Walsh to E. Ben Johnson, Mar. 21, 1927, Walsh Mss. See also Francis X. Busch, *Enemies of the State . . .* (Indianapolis: Bobbs-Merrill, 1954), 91–170.

51. Walsh to Scott Ferris, Dec. 13, 1923, Walsh Mss.

52. Walsh to S. B. Fairbank, Apr. 16, 1924, Walsh Mss; *Leases upon Naval Oil Reserves* (1924), passim; Walsh to Pinchot, Feb. 16, 1924, Pinchot to Walsh, Feb. 25, 1924, Walsh to Butler, Apr. 3, 1924, Butler to Walsh, Apr. 7, 1924, Walsh Mss.

53. Walsh to H. F. Alderfer, Nov. 10, 1927, Walsh to J. J. Baumgardner, Apr. 19, 1924, Walsh to Harriette Goldsmith Osborn, Apr. 21, 1924, Walsh to Warren W. Price, Apr. 1, 1924, Walsh Mss.

54. Walsh's principal findings were embodied in a report submitted by him for the majority of the Public Lands Committee on June 6, 1924. *Leases upon Naval Oil Reserves,* Senate Report 794, 68th Cong., 1st Sess., Submitted by Mr. Walsh of Montana from the Committee on Public Lands and Surveys Together with Minority Views (Washington, D.C.: GPO, 1924), also in *Teapot Dome Documents,* reel 6.

Chapter 22: New Prospects for the Democrats

1. Coolidge quoted in *HI*, Dec. 11, 1923; Walsh to August F. Herrman, Nov. 8, 1929, Walsh Mss. A balanced evaluation of Harding and Coolidge policies is Murray, *Harding Era*, 498–506 and passim.

2. *Leases upon Naval Oil Reserves* (1924), 2699, 2343–56, 2679–722, 2699–701. *HI*, Sept. 29, 1924. Walsh to B. S. Osborn, Apr. 14, 1924, Walsh to W. M. Buckles, Sept. 10, 1924, George Randall to Walsh, June 13, 1924, Walsh to Randall, June 19, 1924, Walsh Mss. See also Ise, *United States Oil Policy*, 377–87.

3. *Cong. Rec.*, 68th Cong., 1st Sess. (Mar. 17, 1924), 4315; *Leases upon Naval Oil Reserves* (1924), 3004–15.

4. Walsh to Gertrude Maynard, Apr. 4, 1924, Walsh to Albert F. Coyle, Mar. 29, 1924, Walsh Mss. On Walsh's legal aid, see Wheeler to Walsh, Aug. 25, 1924, Walsh to J. F. Buchheit, Feb. 24, 1925, ibid.; Associated Press report in *HI*, May 2, 1924; *Washington Evening Star*, Apr. 25, 1925, *HI*, Apr. 25, 1925; Wheeler, *Yankee from the West*, 235–45.

5. Walsh to Charles N. Kessler, June 16, 1924, Walsh Mss; *Cong. Rec.*, 68th Cong., 1st Sess. (Feb. 8, 1924), 2055.

6. Anonymous "Woman Voter" to Walsh (enclosing cartoon of rogues waiting to testify), Apr. 2, 1924, Walsh to Phil B. Baer, May 7, 1924, Warren W. Price to Walsh, Mar. 28, 1924, Walsh to Price, Apr. 1, 1924, Walsh to J. D. Joseph, Mar. 24, 1924, Walsh Mss.

7. Sen. Kenneth McKellar to Walsh, Mar. 14, 1924, Walsh to McKellar, Mar. 19, 1924, ibid.

8. *HI*, Aug. 16, 1923; Phelan to Walsh, Jan. ___, 1924, Walsh to Phelan, Jan. 24, 1924, Walsh Mss; *Leases upon Naval Oil Reserves* (1924), 1937–49, 1969–72, 2059–72; McAdoo quoted in *HI*, Feb. 24, 1924.

9. Lockwood quoted in *HI*, Feb. 1, 1924; Pres. Coolidge quoted in ibid., Feb. 13, 1924; *Philadelphia Record* quoted in ibid., Feb 6, 1924; Amos Pinchot to Wheeler, Feb. 21, 1924, Walsh Mss.

10. Walsh speech at Great Falls, quoted in *HI*, Sept. 24, 1924.

11. Patrick Quinn to Walsh, Feb. 1, 1924, Walsh to Jim O'Connor, Mar. 27, 1924, Walsh to Hugh R. Wells, Apr. 4, 1924, Walsh to Walter Aitken, May 29, 1924, Walsh Mss; Walsh quoted in *HI*, Feb. 19, 1924.

12. See, for example, Frederick Lewis Allen, *Only Yesterday: An Informal History of the Nineteen-Twenties* (New York: Harper & Bros., 1931), 136–42; Ise, *United States Oil Policy*; Noggle, *Teapot Dome*, passim. See also Henry Scudder to Walsh, Apr. 10, 1924, Walsh Mss; J. Leonard Bates, "The Teapot Dome Scandal and the Election of 1924," *American Historical Review* 60 (Jan. 1955), 303–22.

13. Walsh to editor, *Philadelphia Inquirer*, June 10, 1924, Walsh Mss.

14. Walsh to Alfred Brandeis, Dec. 23, 1926, Hamilton Holt to Walsh, Feb. 18, 1929, Walsh to Holt, Feb. 22, 1929, Walsh Mss.

15. See Walsh to Jim O'Connor, Mar. 27, 1924, Walsh to S. V. Stewart, May 21, 1924, Walsh Mss; Sloane Gordon in *NYW,* June 22, 1924; David Burner, *The Politics of Provincialism: The Democratic Party in Transition, 1918–1932* (New York: Knopf, 1970), 86–114 and passim; Robert K. Murray, *The 103rd Ballot: Democrats and the Disaster in Madison Square Garden* (New York: Harper & Row, 1976), passim; Johnson, *Oscar W. Underwood,* chap. 14.

16. Walsh to Charles R. Crane, June 20, 1924, Walsh Mss; interview with John Wattawa, Aug. 23, 1949; *HI,* June 23, 1924; Sloane Gordon and Arthur Krock in *NYW,* June 22, 1924.

17. Interviews with Genevieve Walsh Gudger, Feb. 16, 1950, and John Wattawa, Aug. 23, 1949; *HI,* June 24, 28, July 13, 1924; *NYW,* June 26, 27, 29, July 1, 1924.

18. Heywood Broun in *NYW,* July 3, 1924; Associated Press report in *HI,* July 5, 1924; *NYW,* July 10, 1924.

19. Alfred E. Smith, *Up to Now: An Autobiography* (Garden City, N.Y.: Garden City Publishing, 1929), 284–85; Charles A. Greathouse, comp., *Official Report of the Proceedings of the Democratic National Convention . . . New York . . . 1924,* 279–309; Associated Press report in *HI,* June 28, 1924; Heywood Broun in *NYW,* June 29, 1924.

20. Walsh to McAdoo, Nov. 28, 1922, McAdoo to Walsh, Dec. 13, 1922, May 7, 1923, Walsh Mss.

21. H. E. C. Bryant in *NYW,* June 23, 1924; Walsh to Suzanne Murrell, Apr. 18, 1924, Walsh to W. C. Robertson, Nov. 13, 1924, Walsh Mss; Associated Press report in *HI,* June 28, 1924; Oliver H. P. Garrett in *NYW,* June 29, 1924. See also *Proceedings of the Democratic National Convention, 1924,* 304; Charles Michelson in *NYW,* July 3, 1924.

22. Associated Press report in *HI,* June 30, 1924. See also *Proceedings of the Democratic National Convention, 1924,* 309–34; Oliver Garrett in *NYW,* June 30, 1924.

23. Associated Press report in *HI,* July 9, 1924. See also Charles Michelson in *NYW,* July 6, 7, 1924.

24. See, for example, Walsh to Arthur Brisbane, *New York Evening Journal,* Oct. 1, 1925, Walsh to Mrs. George Barnett, July 24, 1924, Walsh Mss; Charles Michelson in *NYW,* July 7, 1924.

25. See Arthur Brisbane in *Washington Herald,* quoted in *HI,* Feb. 2, 1924; Gould Lincoln in *Washington Star,* quoted in *HI,* Feb. 10, 1924; Charles Michelson in *NYW,* quoted in *HI,* Mar. 2, 1924; Frederick J. Haskin in *HI,* Mar. 28, 1924; Walsh to M. M. Lyter, Apr. 7, 1924, W. B. George to Walsh, n.d., Walsh Mss; Walsh quoted in *HI,* Feb. 2, 1924.

26. Arthur Krock in *NYW,* June 22, 1924; Charles S. Hand, Charles Michelson, and George Wood in ibid., June 30, 1924; Michelson in ibid., July 10, 1924; Arthur Sears Henning in *Chicago Tribune,* quoted in *HI,* June 30, 1924; *Proceedings of the Democratic National Convention, 1924,* 530; Associated Press report in *HI,* July 3, 1924; Oliver Garrett in *NYW,* July 3, 1924.

27. William Randolph Hearst in *New York Evening Journal,* quoted in *HI,* July 2,

1924; J. Burke Clements in *HI*, July 8, 1924; Charles Michelson in *NYW*, July 10, 1924; *Proceedings of the Democratic National Convention, 1924*, 935, 946, 955, 958–63. For signs of cumulative Walsh strength, see Arthur Krock in *NYW*, July 1, 1924; Charles Michelson in ibid., July 2, 1924; John J. Leary Jr. in ibid., July 3, 1924; Justin Stewart, *Wayne Wheeler, Dry Boss* (New York: Fleming H. Revell, 1928), 220.

28. Mrs. George Barnett to Walsh, July 5, 1924, Walsh to Mrs. Barnett, July 24, 1924, Walsh Mss.

29. Walsh to Arthur Brisbane, *New York Evening Journal*, Oct. 1, 1925, Brisbane to Walsh, Oct. 9, 1925, Walsh Mss; P. H. Callahan to *New Republic*, Mar. 24, 26, 1924, copies in box 50, William Jennings Bryan Mss, LC. See Paul A. Carter, "The Other Catholic Candidate: The 1928 Presidential Bid of Thomas J. Walsh," *Pacific Northwest Quarterly* 55 (Jan. 1964), 1–8.

30. *Proceedings of the Democratic National Convention, 1924*, 972–73; *NYW*, July 10, 1924; Murray, *103rd Ballot*, 207.

31. Charles Michelson in *NYW*, July 10, 1924; interviews with Wheeler, July 7, 1949, and Genevieve Walsh Gudger, Feb. 16, 1950; Wheeler to J. Leonard Bates, Feb. 8, 1952.

32. *Proceedings of the Democratic National Convention, 1924*, 993–94, 1026–39; MacKay, *Progressive Movement of 1924*, 108–9; Burner, *Politics of Provincialism*, 125–29; La Follette and La Follette, *Robert M. La Follette*, 2:1116–20 and passim.

33. Walsh to Mrs. George Barnett, July 24, 1924, Walsh Mss.

Chapter 23: Winning a Third Term in 1924

1. Murphy, *Comical History of Montana*, 48–49.

2. Walsh quoted in *HI*, Aug. 12, 1924.

3. La Follette and Huddleston to Walsh, Nov. 24, 1922, La Follette to Walsh, Nov. 24, 1922, Walsh Mss; La Follette and La Follette, *Robert M. La Follette*, 2:1066–67, 1175.

4. Walsh to La Follette, Nov. 27, 1922, Walsh Mss.

5. Walsh to Stout, Jan. 2, 1923, Walsh Mss; Wheeler quoted in Associated Press report in *HI*, July 17, 1924; MacKay, *Progressive Movement of 1924*, passim

6. Walsh quoted in Associated Press report in *HI*, July 18, 1924; Walsh quoted in ibid., Aug. 16, 1924; Wheeler quoted in Associated Press report in ibid., Oct. 2, 1924. The *HI* was not kind to Wheeler, referring to him as "unable to keep his word on anything." Ibid., July 20, 1924.

7. La Follette to Walsh quoted in *HI*, Oct. 26, 1924.

8. Ibid., Mar. 17, 1924. For anti-Dixon articles see ibid., Oct. 24, 1922, Aug. 5, Sept. 25, 1924; *Flathead Monitor* quoted in ibid., Mar. 10, 1924.

9. Walsh to J. R. Wine, Dec. 7, 1923, Walsh to Hugh R. Wells, Apr. 4, 1924, Walsh Mss; Walsh in *HI*, Sept. 11, 1924; Karlin, *Joseph M. Dixon of Montana, 1917–1934*, 171–208 and passim.

10. Dobell to Walsh, Sept. 13, 1923 (replying to letter in which Walsh had raised

question of gubernatorial candidate), Walsh to Erickson, Sept. 28, 1923, Erickson to Walsh, Oct. 8, 1923, Walsh Mss; interview with Wheeler, July 7, 1949.

11. Walsh quoted in *HI*, Aug. 16, 1924.

12. Walsh to H. G. Young, June 18, 1924, Young to Walsh, June 25, 1924, John Walsh to T. J. Walsh, Aug. 2, 1924, Walsh to M. D. Woodson, Aug. 16, 1924, Walsh Mss; dispatch from Hardin in *HI*, Oct. 29, 1924.

13. Walsh quoted in *HI*, Nov. 2, Sept. 11, 1924; Associated Press report in ibid., Oct. 24, 1924; *HI*, Nov. 19, 1924, and passim.

14. See Walsh to Bruce Kremer, Dec. 13, 1924 (thanking him for "generous" aid in campaign), Walsh Mss.

15. State of Montana, Certificate of Official Returns of the Secretary of State for the Election Held on Nov. 4, 1924. See Linderman speech, June 14, 1924, in box 6, Frank Bird Linderman Mss, University of Montana at Missoula.

16. Samuel McKelvie to Linderman, Nov. 7, 1924, Sen. Reed Smoot to Linderman, Dec. 2, 1924, boxes 3, 6, Linderman Mss.

17. Walsh to Alva B. Flood, Dec. 3, 1924, Walsh to Rev. V. Day, Nov. 6, 1924, Walsh Mss; Associated Press report in *HI*, Nov. 7, 1924.

18. Walsh to Christopher Connolly, July 21, 1932, Walsh Mss.

Chapter 24: Abiding the Coolidge Administration

1. Coolidge to Walsh, Sept. 26, 1923, Walsh to Coolidge, Dec. 19, 1923, June 22, 1932, Coolidge to Walsh, July 2, 1932, Walsh Mss; Murray, *103rd Ballot*, 194–95.

2. Walsh to Charles S. Lobingier, Mar. 3, 1924, Walsh address in Portland, Oreg., Oct. 4, 1926, box 254, Walsh Mss; Donald R. McCoy, *Calvin Coolidge: The Quiet President* (New York: Macmillan, 1967), 213–14, 220–21; Sen. George Norris in *Cong. Rec.*, 69th Cong., 1st Sess. (Jan. 16, 1926), 2187–89.

3. Walsh to "Our Heroes Class," First Methodist Church, Ranger, Tex., Dec. 1, 1928, Walsh Mss; Louis Lyons in *Boston Globe*, Apr. 22, 1928, W-G Mss.

4. *Cong. Rec.*, 68th Cong., 2d Sess. (Jan. 20, 1925), 2133–41, 69th Cong., Special Sess. of the Senate (Mar. 17, 1925), 312–17; *Washington Post*, Jan. 20, 1925, in Walsh Mss, Scrapbooks.

5. *Cong. Rec.*, 69th Cong., Special Sess. of the Senate (Mar. 17, 1925), 312–17; Mellon to Coolidge, Apr. 10, 1924, in ibid., 68th Cong., 1st Sess. (Apr. 11, 1924), 6087–88.

6. Ibid., 69th Cong., Special Sess. of the Senate (Mar. 17, 1925), 317.

7. *Philadelphia Record*, Mar. 22, 1925, Walsh Mss, Scrapbooks; James O'Donnell Bennett, *Chicago Tribune*, Mar. 11, 1925, 1, 5.

8. *NYT*, Jan. 11, 1925, 1, Feb. 10, 1925, 3; Walsh to J. T. Carroll, Mar. 23, 1925, box 371, Legislative Reference Service memo to Walsh, box 328, Walsh Mss; McCoy, *Calvin Coolidge*, 278–81. Cf. LeRoy Ashby, *The Spearless Leader: Senator Borah and the Progressive Movement in the 1920's* (Urbana: University of Illinois Press, 1972), 185–94.

9. Manley to Walsh, Feb. 3, 1925, memo on "Relations of Charles B. Warren with the Sugar Trust," n.d., box 328, People's Legislative Service news release, Washington, D.C., Feb. 11, 1925, Walsh Mss; *NYT,* Feb. 10, 1925, 3; Walsh in *Cong. Rec.,* 69th Cong., Special Sess. of the Senate (Mar. 7, 1925), 18–19.

10. *Bulletin,* Mar. 15, 1925, Walsh Mss, Scrapbooks. See also *NYT,* Mar. 11, 1925, 1, 5.

11. Walsh to J. Burke Clements, Mar. 23, 1925, box 328, Walsh Mss.

12. *Cong. Rec.,* 69th Cong., Special Sess. of the Senate (Mar. 7, 1925), 18–19; Bennett in *Chicago Tribune,* Mar. 11, 1925, 1, 5.

13. *Cong. Rec.,* 69th Cong., Special Sess. of the Senate (Mar. 7, 1925), 18–20, 21–40 passim, (Mar. 10, 1925), 74–102 passim, (Mar. 14, 1925), 227–45 passim, (Mar. 16, 1925), 250–75 passim.

14. Ibid. (Mar. 7, 1925), 28–32, (Mar. 10, 1925), 84–92, (Mar. 16, 1925), 254–55, 272–73.

15. *NYT,* Mar. 11, 1925, 1, 5; Walsh to Mrs. C. B. Nolan, Helena, Mar. 15, 1925, W-G Mss; *Cong. Rec.,* 69th Cong., Special Sess. of the Senate (Mar. 10, 1925), 101–2; McCoy, *Calvin Coolidge,* 278–79; Bascom N. Timmons, *Portrait of an American: Charles G. Dawes* (New York: Henry Holt, 1953), 246–47.

16. *Cong. Rec.,* 69th Cong., Special Sess. of the Senate (Mar. 14, 1925), 228–29, 230–45 passim, (Mar. 16, 1925), 255, 272–75; *Chicago Tribune,* Mar. 16, 1925, 1.

17. Walsh to George Fort Milton, Apr. 4, 1925, box 328, Walsh Mss; Bennett, *Chicago Tribune,* Mar. 17, 1925, 1, 5; McCoy, *Calvin Coolidge,* 279–81.

18. Walsh to Mrs. C. B. Nolan, Mar. 15, 1925, Walsh Mss. The front-page article in the *Chicago Tribune,* Mar. 11, 1925, featured Walsh as the victor in this Senate struggle.

19. Walsh speech in *Montana Standard* (Butte), Oct. 26, 1928, 16, 18.

20. *Christian Science Monitor,* Apr. 16, 1924, quoted in *HI,* Apr. 16, 1924; Burton Wheeler, "Personal Explanation," in *Cong. Rec.,* 68th Cong., 1st Sess. (Apr. 9, 1924), 5946–48; Giglio, *H. M. Daugherty and the Politics of Expediency,* 170–75; Wheeler, *Yankee from the West,* 237–45.

21. Walsh to Albert F. Coyle, Mar. 29, 1924, Walsh Mss; Walsh to Claude C. Gray, Apr. 28, 1925, W-G Mss; *Cong. Rec.,* 68th Cong., 1st Sess. (Apr. 9, 1924), 5946–51, (May 22, 1924), 9144–57 passim; *Senator Burton K. Wheeler,* Senate Report 537, in *Cong. Rec.,* 68th Cong., 1st Sess. (May 14, 1924), 8524; Bartlett Sinclair to Sen. Borah, Apr. 24, 1924, box 242, William E. Borah Mss, LC; *Cong. Rec.,* 68th Cong., 1st Sess. (May 22, 1924), 9144–57; Frank J. Burns to Walsh, May 22, 1924, Walsh to Burns, May 24, 1924, Walsh Mss; Richard T. Ruetten, "Burton K. Wheeler of Montana: A Progressive between the Wars" (Ph.D. diss., University of Oregon, 1961), 43–44; Taft to Elihu Root, Jan. 26, 1925, box 284, Elihu Root Mss, LC (hereafter Root Mss).

22. This account of the trial is drawn mostly from the *GFT,* Apr. 25, 1925, 1, 2, 6, W-G Mss. See also *Chicago Tribune,* Apr. 25, 1925, 1; "Oil: Fizzle," *Time,* May 4, 1925, 2–3; "Senator Wheeler's Acquittal," *NYW,* Apr. 27, 1925, W-G Mss.

23. Robert M. La Follette telegram to Walsh, n.d. (but 1925), Robert M. La Follette Mss, LC.

24. For later aspects of the Wheeler affair, see *Cong. Rec.*, 69th Cong., 1st Sess. (Mar. 15, 1926), 5594–603, (Mar. 25, 1926), 6222; Walsh "In Defense of the Senate" (Apr. 6, 1925), *The Nation* 120 (May 6, 1925), 519.

25. Mercer Johnston to Walsh, Mar. 31, 1926, Walsh to Johnston, Apr. 2, 1926, box 405, Walsh Mss; *Washington Post*, Apr. 16, 1926, 2; Elizabeth Wheeler Colman, *Mrs. Wheeler Goes to Washington: Mrs. Burton Kendall Wheeler, Wife of the Senator from Montana* (Helena, Mont.: Falcon Press, 1989), 100–103. See congratulatory telegrams of April 1925, dispatched after the Montana trial had ended with Wheeler's acquittal, W-G Mss.

26. Pomerene to Walsh, June 17, 1925, Walsh to Sen. Morris Sheppard, June 7, 1926, Walsh to Sen. George W. Norris, Dec. 11, 1927, correspondence with Pomerene and Roberts, 1924–29, passim, Walsh Mss. See also Roberts and Pomerene, Special Counsel for the U.S., to Walsh, Apr. 7, 1930, in *Cong. Rec.*, 71st Cong., 2d Sess. (Apr. 7, 1930), 6562, 7029, concerning a settlement with the Sinclair Crude Oil Purchasing Co.

27. T. C. Spelling to Walsh, Apr. 5, 1925, Walsh to Spelling, Apr. 7, 1925, Walsh to H. B. Henderson, Apr. 6, 1925, Walsh to William G. McAdoo, June 23, 1925, Walsh Mss; Walsh in *The National Democrat* (Washington, D.C.), June 27, 1925; T. Blake Kennedy, "Memoirs" (ms, Western Historical Collection, University of Wyoming at Laramie), 522–40; Busch, *Enemies of the State*, 118–22; Rita Dielmann, comp., "Chronology of Events in the History of the Naval Petroleum Reserve, No. 3, Teapot Dome," Apr. 25, 1928, in *Cong. Rec.*, 70th Cong., 1st Sess. (May 29, 1928), 10523–29.

28. Pomerene to Walsh, Sept. 29, 1926, Walsh to Otis Mellon, Nov. 30, 1926, Walsh Mss; Busch, *Enemies of the State*, 122; Dielmann, "Chronology in the History of Teapot Dome."

29. Section on court decisions in R. G. Tracie, "History of the Naval Petroleum Reserves" (ms, 1937), copy in box 264, Josephus Daniels Mss, LC; Busch, *Enemies of the State*, 117–18; Walsh to McAdoo, June 23, 1925, Walsh Mss.

30. *NYT*, Mar. 1, 1927, 1.

31. Roberts to Walsh, Oct. 1, 1926, box 164, Walsh Mss; Dielmann, "Chronology in the History of Teapot Dome." See also Atlee Pomerene to Josephus Daniels, Apr. 21, 1925, box 591, Daniels Mss; Pomerene to Walsh, Sept. 29, 1926, Walsh Mss.

32. McAdoo to Walsh, Feb. 28, 1927, Daniels to Walsh, Mar. 2, 1927, Teapot Dome file, passim, Walsh Mss.

33. Walsh to George F. Blackburn, Mar. 4, 1927, Walsh to John Cohen, editor, *Atlanta Journal*, Mar. 8, 1927, Walsh to E. Ben Johnson, Mar. 21, 1927, Walsh Mss.

34. Walsh to L. L. Cowen, June 13, 1928, Walsh to G. D. Ball, Dec. 21, 1926, Walsh Mss. See also Walsh to Mrs. Jean Rushmore Patterson, Nov. 5, 1927, *Pittsburgh Press*, Mar. 2, 1930, clipping, box 163, Walsh Mss; *NYT*, Oct. 26, 1929, 1, 8; Noggle, *Teapot Dome*, passim.

Chapter 25: Oh! for a Jefferson

1. Walsh to Mrs. C. B. Nolan, Dec. 7, 1928, W-G Mss; Livermore, *Woodrow Wilson and the War Congress;* Burner, *Politics of Provincialism;* Murray, *103rd Ballot;* Burl Noggle, *Into the Twenties: The United States from Armistice to Normalcy* (Urbana: University of Illinois Press, 1974).

2. Miles Taylor to Walsh, July 9, 1924, box 376, Walsh Mss; Walsh to Mrs. C. B. Nolan, Aug. 4, 1924, W-G Mss; Murray, *103rd Ballot,* 291–92 and passim.

3. Roosevelt to Walsh, Feb. 28, 1925, General Correspondence, Roosevelt Mss, Roosevelt Library, Hyde Park, N.Y.; Walsh to Roosevelt, Mar. 7, 1925, copy of Roosevelt to Clem Shaver, Mar. 10, 1925, copy of Louis Howe to Walsh, Mar. 11, 1925, box 376, Walsh to George Fort Milton, Mar. 23, 1925, box 328, Walsh to Madge V. O'Neill, national committeewoman from Iowa, Mar. 23, 1925, box 376, Walsh Mss; *Washington Post,* Apr. 5, 1925, Walsh Mss, Scrapbooks; Walsh speech to Women's National Democratic Club, Washington, D.C., Nov. 14, 1927, box 256, Walsh Mss.

4. Roosevelt to Walsh, June 25, 1925, Walsh to Roosevelt, June 27, 1925, Louis Howe to Walsh, Feb. 2, 1926, copy of Howe to Sen. Robinson, Feb. 2, 1926, box 376, Walsh Mss; Roosevelt to Walsh, Feb. 22, 1926, General Correspondence, Roosevelt Mss; Richard V. Oulahan, "Democrats Map Out Congress Campaign," *NYT,* Feb. 1, 1926, 1.

5. Walsh speech to Women's National Democratic Club, Nov. 14, 1927, box 256, Walsh to Dodd, July 22, 1927, and passim, box 376, Walsh Mss, Hull to Scott Ferris, Dec. 6, 1926, and passim in Cordell Hull Mss, LC.

6. Beryl E. Pettus, "The Senate Career of Joseph Taylor Robinson" (M.A. thesis, University of Illinois at Urbana-Champaign, 1952), 6–14 and passim; Walsh to Board of Governors, Chevy Chase Club, May 28, 1921, box 407, Walsh Mss, Thomas W. Gregory to T. W. Davidson, Mar. 4, 1925, Thomas W. Gregory Mss, LC.

7. Davis, "Federal Trade Commission," 273–74 and passim; *Cong. Rec.,* 69th Cong., 2d Sess. (Feb. 28, 1927), 4991–93, 4996, 70th Cong., 1st Sess. (Dec. 17, 1927), 788.

8. *Cong. Rec.,* 69th Cong., 2d Sess. (Feb. 25, 1927), 4740, (Feb. 28, 1927), 4991–93, 4996–5009.

9. Rodney Dutcher, "By the Way in Washington," *Pensacola Journal* (Fla.), Jan. 2, 1928, editorial, *Wichita Eagle,* Jan. 28, 1928, Walsh Mss, Scrapbooks; Walsh to Mrs. C. B. Nolan, Jan. 19, 1928, W-G Mss.

10. *St. Louis Post-Dispatch,* Jan. 30, 1928, 1, "Here Is No Demagogue," *Louisville Courier Journal,* Jan. 20, 1928, Walsh Mss, Scrapbooks; Walsh in *Cong. Rec.,* 70th Cong., 1st Sess. (Feb. 13, 1928), 2893. The *Electrical World* was a semiofficial mouthpiece of the electric industry. See, for example, issues of Jan. 21, 1928, 133, 163; Feb. 4, 1928, 235; Feb. 11, 1928, 287; Feb. 25, 1928, 389; May 5, 1928, 897–98; June 16, 1928, passim.

11. *Cong. Rec.,* 70th Cong., 1st Sess. (Feb. 13, 1928), 2896, (Feb. 14, 1928), 2954, (Feb. 15, 1928), 3006, 3009–16, 3021–23, 3045, 3054; *Baltimore Sun* quoted in ibid. (Feb. 15, 1928), 3025; *NYT,* Feb. 16, 1928, 22, Feb. 18, 1928, 28, Feb. 26, 1928, 4.

12. *Cong. Rec.,* 70th Cong., 1st Sess. (Apr. 27, 1928), 7330–33, (May 11, 1928), 8366, 8368; *HI,* Feb. 17, 1928, Walsh Mss, Scrapbooks; Walsh to Mrs. C. B. Nolan, Mar. 16, 1928, W-G Mss, Walsh to John H. Roemer, May 16, 1928, box 403, Walsh Mss; "The Million Dollar Lobby," *The Nation,* 126 (May 16, 1928), 554–55.

13. Walsh address on "Tampering with Education," relating to Public Utility Corporations in Disseminating Propaganda in the Public Schools and Otherwise; *Cong. Rec.,* 70th Cong., 2d Sess. (Dec. 5, 1928), 47–52; Forrest McDonald, *Insull* (Chicago: University of Chicago Press, 1962), 267–68, 336–37, and passim; Walsh to Christopher Connolly, July 21, 1932, box 396, Walsh Mss; Wheeler, *Yankee from the West,* 306–10 and passim.

Chapter 26: Prohibition and Politics

1. Walsh to E.W., Oct. 18, 1894, Aug. 15, 24, Sept. 9, Oct. 25, 1895, Jan. 6, 1896, Mar. 16, July 19, 1897, Aug. 11, 1899, W-G Mss; Walsh to D. J. Donahue, Dec. 2, 1915, Walsh telegram (with statement on news of Carroll's death) to *HI,* Nov. 5, 1925, Walsh to James W. Remick, Nov. 24, 1926, box 303, Walsh Mss.

2. Walsh to Dr. Gustavus Werber, Aug. 5, 1916, box 223, Walsh to S. S. Berry, Nov. 30, 1926, box 303, Walsh Mss.

3. Walsh to W. H. Griffin, Feb. 8, 1916, Walsh to J. J. McGraw, Feb. 9, 1916, box 302, Walsh speech to parent-teacher association (probably in Helena), 1928, Walsh to Mary O'Neill, Mar. 1, 1923, box 254, Henry Hollis to Walsh, Nov. 10, 1930, box 397, Walsh Mss. See also Timberlake, *Prohibition and the Progressive Movement;* Clark, *Deliver Us from Evil;* Paul A. Carter, "Prohibition," in *Another Part of the Twenties* (New York: Columbia University Press, 1977); Louis J. Bahin, "The Campaign for Prohibition in Montana: Agrarian Idealism and Liquor Reform, 1883–1926" (M.A. thesis, University of Montana, 1984).

4. Walsh to Mrs. A. C. Herbst, pres., Montana WCTU, Apr. 1, 1918, box 183; Walsh to Joseph Pope, Anti-Saloon League, Billings, Oct. 4, 1918, Walsh Mss; Timberlake, *Prohibition and the Progressive Movement,* 125–48; Kerr, *Organized for Prohibition,* 3–9.

5. Walsh to A. E. Spriggs, July 7, 1913, Walsh to Faville, Oct. 8, 1925, box 14, Faville to Walsh, Nov. 10, 1926, Walsh to Faville, Nov. 30, 1926, box 15, Walsh to Vincent Fortune, Sept. 28, 1931, box 415, Walsh Mss; John Walsh reminiscences, W-G Mss; Robert Moats Miller, *American Protestantism and Social Issues, 1919–1939* (Chapel Hill: University of North Carolina Press, 1958), 31–35, 120–21.

6. Joseph R. Gusfield, *Symbolic Crusade: Status Politics and the American Temperance Movement* (Urbana: University of Illinois Press, 1963); Walsh to Rev. Jacob Mills, June 14, 1919, Walsh statement on prohibition enforcement, n.d., box 254, Walsh Mss; Andrew Mellon, as told to W. G. Shepherd, "Prohibition Is Up to You," *Collier's* 77 (Jan. 30, 1926), 7–8; McCoy, *Calvin Coolidge,* 303; John J. Travis to Walsh, May 26, 1926, Walsh to Travis, June 7, 1926, box 303, passim, box 122, Walsh Mss.

7. Walsh to Mrs. C. B. Nolan, ca. Apr. 18, 1926, W-G Mss; James W. Meers to Walsh, Apr. 22, 1926, Walsh to Sid Coffee, May 17, 1926, box 303, Walsh Mss.

8. U.S. Senate, *The National Prohibition Law*, Hearings before the Subcommittee of the Committee on the Judiciary, on Bills to Amend the National Prohibition Act, Apr. 5–24, 1926, 2 vols. (Washington, D.C.: GPO, 1926), 1:iii–vii, 1–10, and passim.

9. Walsh to Rev. Keane, Apr. 1, 1926, Keane to Walsh, Apr. 5, 1926, Walsh to Cardinal Dougherty, Apr. 7, 1926, Dougherty to Walsh, Apr. 8, 1926, Rev. George Zurcher to Walsh, Apr. 3, 1926, J. Gallagher to Walsh, June 10, 1926, Walsh to J. W. Remick, Nov. 24, 1926, box 303, Walsh Mss.

10. "After the Wet-Dry Battle," *Outlook* 143 (May 5, 1926), 6–7; Walsh (taking the negative side of "Shall the Nation Ballot on Prohibition?") in *NYT*, June 13, 1926, 8:5; Walsh, "Why I Am in Favor of Prohibition," *Extension Magazine* (Chicago), Nov. 1926, box 254, Walsh to Rev. John Faville, Nov. 30, 1926, box 15, Walsh Mss.

11. Edward B. Dunford to Walsh, May 26, 1926, Wayne Wheeler to Walsh (enclosing memo for possible use), June 1, 1926, Walsh to Sen. Borah and Sen. Cummins, June 3, 1926, J. J. Haggerty to Walsh, May 28, 1926, Walsh to Haggerty, June 3, 1926, box 303, Walsh Mss; Ashby, *Spearless Leader*, 256–59 and passim.

12. Walsh to Fred B. Smith, Citizens Committee of One Thousand, Nov. 30, 1926, box 403, Walsh Mss; Bahin, "Campaign for Prohibition in Montana," 102–9 and passim; Walsh to C. H. McKinney, Nov. 24, 1926, "How the Nation Views the Wet and Dry Vote," *Literary Digest* 91 (Nov. 13, 1926), clipping, box 303, Walsh Mss.

13. Walsh in *NYT*, June 13, 1926, 8:5; Walsh to S. S. Berry, Nov. 30, 1926, box 303, Walsh to Cordell Hull, Mar. 22, 1927, box 376, Walsh Mss.

14. Walsh to Bernard Baruch, Sept. 25, 1926, J. T. Carroll to Walsh, Nov. 14, 1926, Walsh to Carroll, Nov. 20, 1926, box 371, Walsh Mss; *GFT*, Oct. 6, 1926, *HI*, Oct. 7, 1926, Walsh Mss, Scrapbooks.

15. Baruch to Walsh, Oct. 23, 1926, Baruch telegram to Walsh, Oct. 22, 1926, Walsh telegram to James H. Moyle, Oct 25, 1926, and passim, box 376, manuscript of speech in Idaho, Oct. __, 1926, box 252, Walsh Mss.

16. Manuscript text of speeches and audience reactions, box 254, Walsh Mss; *Oregon Journal*, Oct. 5, 1926, Walsh Mss, Scrapbooks; Walsh's sec'y to McAdoo, Oct. 11, 1926, box 376, Walsh Mss.

17. McAdoo to Walsh, Oct. 6, 1926, Elliott to Walsh, Oct. 28, 1926, box 376, Walsh Mss; *San Francisco Chronicle*, Oct. 31, 1926, 11; *Los Angeles Times*, Nov. 2, 1926, 7.

18. *St. Louis Post-Dispatch*, Nov. 3, 1926, 4; Burner, *Politics of Provincialism*, 154–57.

19. Walsh to McAdoo, Dec 2, 1925, Walsh to Samuel V. Stewart, Nov. 17, 1926, box 371, Walsh Mss; Burner, *Politics of Provincialism*, 148–49, 154–55, and passim.

20. "A Slander upon Montana," *Anaconda Standard*, Jan. 30, 1927; Walsh to W. H. Maloney, Feb. 3, 1927, and passim, box 122, Walsh to Mark Sullivan, July 25, 1927, Walsh to Ellen N. Colleran, Nov. 27, 1927, box 376, Walsh Mss.

21. *Butte Miner*, June 3, 1925, 1–2, June 4, 1925, 4, *Missoulian*, May 31, 1925, *Butte Miner*, May 2, 1925, Walsh Mss, Scrapbooks.

22. Samuel Small to Walsh, Feb. 20, 1926, Walsh to Small, Feb. 23, 1926, box 403, Walsh Mss; Walsh to Mrs. C. B. Nolan, May 6, 1926, W-G Mss.

23. Walsh to J. T. Carroll, Apr. 7, 1927, box 371; Walsh to Dr. W. L. Bywater, Apr. 26, 1927, Walsh to Prof. William E. Dodd, July 22, 1927, Walsh to John W. Dodge, July 25, 1927, Walsh to Mark Sullivan, July 25, 1927, box 376, Walsh Mss; Burner, *Politics of Provincialism,* 180–83 and passim.

24. Walsh to Edward H. Potter, Apr. 29, 1927, Walsh to H. T. Scudder, Apr. 28, 1927, Walsh to Dodd, July 22, 1927, Walsh to Glenn Frank, July 22, 1927, box 376, Walsh Mss.

25. *NYT,* Sept. 11, 1927, 22, Sept. 18, 1927, 1; Walsh's sec'y to True Child, Sept. 3, 1927, Walsh to Mrs. W. M. Sheldon, Jan. 10, 1928, box 376, Walsh Mss; Walsh to Mrs. C. B. Nolan, Mar. 16, 1928, W-G Mss.

Chapter 27: *The Continental Trading Company Limited and Senate Revelations of 1928*

1. *Leases upon Naval Oil Reserves,* Hearings before the Committee on Public Lands and Surveys, 70th Cong., 1st Sess., Pursuant to S. Res. 101, Senate Report 1326 (Washington, D.C.: GPO, 1928) (hereafter *Leases upon Naval Oil Reserves* [1928]; also in *Teapot Dome Documents,* reel 7): Walsh, Report, 1171–84; Sen. Gerald P. Nye, Supplemental Report, 1185ff.

2. Walsh to *St. Louis Star,* Nov. 22, 1927, Walsh to *St. Louis Post-Dispatch,* Nov. 26, 1928, box 254, Walsh Mss; *NYT,* Jan. 6, 1928, 9; *Cong. Rec.,* 70th Cong., 1st Sess. (Feb. 15, 1928), 3006 and passim; *Montana Record-Herald,* Feb. 15, 1928, 1; *Leases upon Naval Oil Reserves* (1928), 2–3; Noggle, *Teapot Dome,* 189–93, 197, and passim.

3. *Leases upon Naval Oil Reserves* (1928), 3–48 passim; *NYT,* Jan. 12, 1928, 5, Jan. 26, 1928, 1, 8.

4. Walsh to Sec'y of State Frank B. Kellogg, Mar. 22, 1928, Kellogg to Walsh, Mar. 27, 1928, box 164, Walsh Mss; Walsh, Report, in *Leases upon Naval Oil Reserves* (1928).

5. *Leases upon Naval Oil Reserves* (1928), 71–74; *NYT,* Jan. 26, 1928, 1.

6. Walsh to Norris, Dec. 11, 1927, Walsh Mss; Walsh, Report, in *Leases upon Naval Oil Reserves* (1928), 1174; Walsh, *The Oil Scandals,* address before the Harvard Democratic Club, Boston, Apr. 12, 1928, in *Cong. Rec.,* 70th Cong., 1st Sess. (Apr. 16, 1928), 6497–500.

7. *NYT,* Jan. 25, 1928, 1–2. See also *Leases upon Naval Oil Reserves* (1928), 48–68 passim.

8. *Leases upon Naval Oil Reserves* (1928), 110–23.

9. Ibid., 184–98 passim; Walsh, Report, in ibid., 1175–77; *NYT,* Feb. 3, 1928, 1, 14.

10. *Cong. Rec.,* 70th Cong., 1st Sess. (Feb. 3, 1928), 2439–40, (Feb. 4, 1928), 2468; *NYT,* Feb. 4, 1928, 1, 2.

11. *Leases upon Naval Oil Reserves* (1928), 311–23; *NYT,* Feb. 12, 1928, 1, 26.

12. *Baltimore Sun,* Mar. 2, 1928, 1, 2; Walsh to E. A. Bowers, Mar. 3, 1928, box 163,

Walsh Mss. Rockefeller soon decided that Stewart should resign as board chairman of Indiana Standard. *NYT,* May 10, 1928, 1.

13. *Leases upon Naval Oil Reserves* (1928), 973–80, 984–1005 passim, 1026–47; *NYT,* May 13, 1929, 1, 14. The *Times* article describes Paul Y. Anderson of the *St. Louis Post-Dispatch,* winner of the 1928 Pulitzer Prize for journalism because of his exploit in passing questions to Chairman Nye of the Senate committee, which, when asked, helped expose Colonel Stewart during a final appearance before the committee.

14. Walsh to F. L. Bullard, May 7, 1928, box 163, passim, boxes 163–64, Walsh Mss.

15. *Leases upon Naval Oil Reserves* (1928), 1211–75 and passim.

16. *Leases upon Naval Oil Reserves* (1924), 2900–913 passim; *NYT,* Mar. 2, 1928, 21.

17. C. G. Poore, "Wider Spreads the Elusive Film of Oil," *NYT,* Feb. 19, 1928, 9:1; Mar. 2, 1928, 1, 20; *Leases upon Naval Oil Reserves* (1928), 459–61.

18. *Leases upon Naval Oil Reserves* (1928), 459–81 passim.

19. Ibid., 477; "'Using' Sinclair Bonds," editorial, *NYT,* Mar. 10, 1928, 16.

20. *Leases upon Naval Oil Reserves* (1928), 471, 475.

21. Frank Kent, "The Great Game of Politics," *Baltimore Sun,* Mar. 2, 1928, 1; Richard P. Whiteley to Walsh, Mar. 11, 1928, Walsh to Whiteley, Mar. 12, 1928, box 164, Walsh Mss; *Leases upon Naval Oil Reserves* (1928), 569 and 549–77 passim.

22. Walsh to *Baltimore Sun,* Mar. 15, 1928, *Baltimore Sun* (John W. Owens) to Walsh, Mar. 22, 1928, box 164, Walsh Mss; "The Mellon Exposé," *Baltimore Sun,* Mar. 12, 1928, Walsh Mss, Scrapbooks.

23. Walsh, Report, in *Leases upon Naval Oil Reserves* (1928), 1178–80; Walsh to *Baltimore Sun,* Mar. 15, 1928, box 164, Walsh Mss.

24. *Leases upon Naval Oil Reserves* (1928), 577–78.

25. Ibid., 577–614 passim; Walsh to William Allen White, Mar. 10, 1928, box 164, Walsh Mss.

26. "Political Corruption," editorial, *NYT,* Mar. 4, 1928; Richard V. Oulahan, in ibid., Mar. 11, 1928, 3; "Republican 'Humiliation,'" editorial, ibid., Mar. 11, 1928, 3; "Republican 'Humiliation,'" editorial, ibid., Mar. 12, 1928, 20; Ashby, *Spearless Leader,* 263–66; Richard Lowitt, *Bronson M. Cutting: Progressive Politician* (Albuquerque: University of New Mexico Press, 1992), 139–40; *NYT,* Mar. 13, 1928, 1, Mar. 17, 1928, 1, 2, Mar. 19, 1928, 1, 2; Walsh to Borah, Mar. 21, 1928, box 163, Walsh Mss.

27. *NYT,* Mar. 19, 1928, 2, Mar. 20, 1928, 1, 2, Mar. 15, 1928, 1, Mar. 17, 1928, 1; *Cong. Rec.,* 70th Cong., 1st Sess. (Mar. 19, 1928), 4976–79, (Mar. 24, 1928), 5302.

28. *Cong. Rec.,* 70th Cong., 1st Sess. (Apr. 5, 1928), 5933, 5938.

29. See, for example, ibid. (Mar. 19, 1928), 4977–84 passim, (Mar. 21, 1928), 5096–97, (Mar. 24, 1928) 5298–304 passim.

30. Ibid. (Mar. 21, 1928), 5104.

31. Ibid. (Apr. 5, 1928), 5932–33.

32. Ibid., 5932–44 passim.

33. *Leases upon Naval Oil Reserves* (1928), 1086, 1143; "Jury Shadowing Case a Maze of Sensations," *NYT,* Feb. 26, 1928, 9:5.

34. *Leases upon Naval Oil Reserves* (1928), 1057–124 passim, 1129–55 passim; Walsh, Report, in ibid., 1182–83; *NYT,* May 2, 1928, 1, 12.

35. *Leases upon Naval Oil Reserves* (1928), 1171–93 passim.

Chapter 28: The Campaign of 1928

1. Walsh to former Sen. James D. Phelan, Feb. 4, 1928, May 21, 1928, James D. Phelan Mss, Bancroft Library, University of California at Berkeley (hereafter Phelan Mss); Dodd to Walsh, June 5, Aug. 4, 1927, box 376, Walsh Mss; Daniels to John B. Elliott, Apr. 11, 1928, quoted in *NYT,* Apr. 12, 1928, 1; Hennings, *James D. Phelan,* 216–17; Walsh to Mrs. C. B. Nolan, Oct. 21, 1927, W-G Mss; *NYT,* Jan. 9, 1928, 2, Mar. 4, 1928, 1; Walsh to J. E. Swindlehurst, Jan. 4, 1928, box 15, Walsh Mss.

2. *NYT,* Jan. 9, 1928, 1–2, Jan. 11, 1928, 4, Jan. 12, 1928, 1, 2, Jan. 13, 1928, 1, 12; *Washington Post,* Jan. 13, 1928, 1, 4, 5; Walsh to Mrs. C. B. Nolan, Jan. 19, 1928, W-G Mss.

3. *NYT,* Jan. 12, 1928, 2; Burner, *Politics of Provincialism,* 188–93.

4. *NYT,* Mar. 5, 1928, 2; Speers, in ibid., Mar. 11, 1928, 9:3, 11; Merz, "Walsh of Montana," *Independent* 120 (Feb. 11, 1928), 128–30; Lodge, "A Democrat, a Catholic, and a Dry," *New York Tribune,* Mar. 11, 1928, Walsh Mss, Scrapbooks; editorial, *The Christian Century* 45 (Mar. 5, 1928), 335–36; Carter, "Other Catholic Candidate"; *Boston Evening Globe,* Apr. 12, 1928, 1; Louis Lyons, in ibid., Apr. 22, 1928, Walsh to Mrs. C. B. Nolan, Mar. 16, Apr. 19, 1928, Lewis Penwell to Walsh, Apr. 2, 1928, W-G Mss. See also *HI,* Apr. 1, 1928, 1, miscellaneous clippings, W-G Mss; *NYT,* Mar. 3, 1928, 1, 3, Mar. 4, 1928, 1, 17, Mar. 9, 1928, 3; *Baltimore Sun,* Mar. 4, 1928, 1.

5. Walsh to Phelan, Dec. 19, 1927, Feb. 4, May 21, 1928, Phelan Mss; *NYT,* Mar. 24, 1928, 3; Edmund A. Moore, *A Catholic Runs for President: The Campaign of 1928* (New York: Ronald Press, 1956).

6. Walsh to Frederic Hinrichs, Feb. 25, 1928, box 302, Walsh to Mrs. W. M. Sheldon, Jan. 10, 1928, Walsh Mss.

7. Walsh to Mark Sullivan, May 4, 1928, box 164, Walsh Mss; *NYT,* May 1, 1928, 10, May 3, 1928, 1, May 5, 1928, 1; clippings, Walsh Mss, Scrapbooks.

8. *NYT,* May 5, 1928, 1–2; clippings, Walsh Mss, Scrapbooks; *Outlook* 149 (May 16, 1928), 99; "The Walsh Hat Out of the Ring," *Literary Digest* 97 (May 19, 1928), 11.

9. Walsh to Phelan, May 21, 1928, Phelan Mss; Walsh to James H. McCrahon, Mar. 4, 1920, box 371, Walsh Mss.

10. *Cong. Rec.,* 70th Cong., 1st Sess. (Apr. 6, 1928), 6024–27; Walsh telegram to Smith, June 4, 1928, Smith to Walsh, June 6, 1928, Walsh to Herbert Hoover, Mar. 22, 1924, box 25, Walsh-Erickson Mss (John E. Erickson's papers were added to Walsh's); Walsh to Claude Bowers, July 2, 1928, Bowers to Walsh, July 12, 1928, W-G Mss; Walsh "Radio Talk," Jan. 29, 1929, typescript, box 252, Walsh Mss.

11. *NYT,* June 29, 1928, 1, June 30, 1928, 1; Walsh to Bowers, July 2, 1928, Bowers to Walsh, July 12, 1928, W-G Mss; Robinson to Walsh, July 3, 1928, box 377, Walsh

Mss; Burner, *Politics of Provincialism*, 198–201; Walsh to Kent Keller, July 19, 1928, W-G Mss.

12. *Atlantic Monthly* 139 (Apr. 1927), 540–49, (May 1927), 721–28; Walsh to Smith, Apr. 18, 1927, Smith to Walsh, Apr. 28, 1927, box 403; Walsh to James F. O'Connor, Apr. 15, 1927, box 376; Walsh to George W. Oakes, *Current History Magazine*, Dec. 19, 1927, box 377; Walsh to Leigh-Emmerich Lecture Bureaus, Inc., Mar. 10, 1928, box 399, Walsh Mss.

13. Walsh to Alva B. Adams, June 12, 1928, box 163, Walsh Mss; Walsh to Kent Keller, July 19, 1928, W-G Mss; Walsh statement (released from the Executive Chamber, Albany, N.Y.), Aug. 17, 1928, box 377, Walsh Mss; *NYT*, Aug. 18, 1928, 1, 3.

14. Walsh statement, Aug 17, 1928; Smith statement and letter to Walsh, Aug 31, 1928, box 377, Walsh Mss.

15. Walsh "list," Sept. 13, 1928, in box 254, Walsh Mss; Walsh to J. J. Canavan, director, Publicity Bureau, National Democratic Committee, Sept. 13, 1928, W-G Mss; Scott Ferris to Walsh, Aug. 21, Sept. 19, 1928, box 377, Walsh Mss; "Walsh Tells Basis for Smith Support," *NYT*, Oct. 5, 1928, 2.

16. Walsh to Smith (with enclosures), Sept. 6, 1928, Smith to Walsh, Sept. 13, 1928, Walsh's sec'y to Edwin A. Halsey, Sept. 19, 1928, Mrs. J. E. Mullowney telegram to Walsh, Sept. 24, 1928, Walsh to Mrs. Mullowney, Sept. 29, 1928, box 377, Walsh Mss; Will Rogers, in *Evening Star*, Sept. 26, 1928, Walsh Mss, Scrapbooks.

17. Walsh to J. E. Swindlehurst, Sept. 7, 1928, Walter L. Pope to Walsh, Aug. 16, 1928, Walsh to Sen. Pat Harrison, Nov. 8, 1928, box 377, Walsh to Douglas Gilbert, *New York Evening Telegram*, Mar. 4, 1931, newspaper articles folder, Walsh Mss; *Montana Standard*, Oct. 26, 1928, 16; *NYT*, Oct. 29, 1928, 11; Karlin, *Joseph M. Dixon of Montana, 1917–1934*, 219–37; interview with Wellington Rankin, May 24, 1961.

18. Typescript of address, 22 pp., box 254, Walsh Mss; *Montana Standard*, Oct. 26, 1928, 1, 2, 16, 18.

19. Typescript of address, box 254, Walsh Mss; press release in *NYT*, Oct. 29, 1928, 11; *HI*, Oct. 16, 1928, 4, Oct. 17, 1928, 10, Oct. 18, 1928, 3; *Montana Standard*, Oct. 31, 1928, 1.

20. Walsh to Howard F. Vickery, Sept. 14, 1928, Walsh to King, Oct. 4, 1928, Dill to Walsh, Nov. 8, 1928, Kendrick telegram to Walsh, Nov. 10, 1928, King to Walsh, Nov. 8, 1928, and passim, box 377, Walsh Mss.

21. Walsh to Nicholas Thomas, Nov. 8, 1928, box 377, Walsh to Sen. Hollis, Dec. 6, 1928, box 399, Walsh Mss.

22. Walsh to Hollis, Dec. 6, 1928, Hollis to Walsh, Dec. 20, 1928, box 399, Walsh Mss.

23. Roosevelt to Walsh, Nov. 13, 22, 1928, box 377, Walsh Mss; Burner, *Politics of Provincialism*, 246–52; Frank Freidel, *Franklin D. Roosevelt: The Ordeal* (Boston: Little, Brown, 1954), 266–69 and passim; idem, *Franklin D. Roosevelt: The Triumph* (Boston: Little, Brown, 1956), 1–15 and passim.

24. Walsh to Roosevelt, Nov. 27, 1928, box 377, Walsh Mss.

25. Walsh to G. W. Hardy, Nov. 13, 1928, Walsh to Roosevelt, Nov. 27, 1928, Roosevelt to Walsh, Dec. 3, 1928, box 377, Walsh Mss.

Chapter 29: A Gratifying Victory in 1930

1. J. T. Carroll to Walsh, Nov. 26, 1928, box 377, Walsh to Herbert Peet, *GFT,* Nov. 26, 1928, Walsh to Stout, June 12, 1929, box 380, Walsh Mss.

2. Walsh to Peet, Nov. 26, 1928, Penwell to Walsh, Dec. 1, 1928, Walsh to Penwell, Dec. 5, 1928, Nov. 26, 1929, box 380, Walsh Mss.

3. Walsh to Clements, Feb. 13, 1929, box 377, Walsh to Thomas C. Colton, Mar. 7, 1930, Walsh to Charles R. Crane, Sept. 24, 1930, box 378, Walsh Mss.

4. "'Tom' Walsh: The Saintly Senator," in Ray Tucker and Frederick Barkley, *Sons of the Wild Jackass* (Boston: L. C. Page, 1932), 123–47; Purcell to Walsh, June 10, 1930, box 411, Walsh Mss.

5. Stout to Walsh, Apr. 18, 1930, Walsh to Stout, Apr. 24, 1930, box 379, Walsh to Gerard, June 19, 1930, box 378, list of "Contributions," box 381, Walsh Mss.

6. Wattawa to Walsh, Aug. 6, 1930, box 443, Walsh to Wattawa, Sept. 11, 1930, Boetius H. Sullivan to Wattawa, Sept. 19, 1930, Wattawa to Sullivan, Sept. 20, 1930, and passim, box 381, Walsh Mss.

7. Murray to Walsh, Oct. 31, 1929, Walsh to Murray, Nov. 5, 1929, box 379, Walsh to Gifford Pinchot, Apr. 24, 1930, box 380, Walsh Mss; Thomas F. Corbally to Walsh, Jan. 30, 1930, W-G Mss.

8. Walsh to Amos Pinchot, Apr. 24, 1930, Pinchot to Walsh (with copies of May 14 letters to Dewey and Villard), May 14, 1930, Walsh Mss.

9. Walsh to Parks, Aug. 11, 1930, Parks to Walsh, Aug. 15, 1930, box 380, Walsh Mss.

10. Corbally to Walsh, Jan. 30, 1930, L. K. Devlin to Walsh (enclosing copy of Feb. 8 letter to Tom Stout, *Lewistown Democrat News*), Mar. 22, 1930, Walsh to Devlin, Apr. 2, 1930, C. C. Guinn to Walsh, Apr. 15, 1930, Walsh memo, n.d., W-G Mss; Walsh to Daniel L. O'Hern, Apr. 17, 1930, box 380, Walsh Mss; Reifenrath to Dixon, Mar. 21, 1930, box 67, F. C. McWilliams to Dixon, June 7, 1930, box 75, Joseph M. Dixon Mss, University of Montana at Missoula (hereafter Dixon Mss).

11. Walsh to A. U. Marvin, May 27, 1930, box 401, Stout to Walsh, Apr. 18, 1930, box 379, Walsh Mss.

12. *NYT,* Jan. 12, 1930, 9:3, 7; "Tilson Party Boost Assailed by Walsh," ibid., Apr. 1, 1930, 3; Joseph T. Robinson to Walsh, Jan. 3, Feb. 19, 1930, Walsh to Robinson, Feb. 13, 1930, box 183, Walsh Mss.

13. *NYT,* May 29, 1930, 3; Walter Aitken to Walsh, Jan. 15, 1930, box 377; copy of Daniel L. O'Hern to Burton Wheeler, Apr. 11, 1930, box 381, R. R. Purcell to Walsh, May 20, 1930, Walsh Mss; Fletcher Dobyns, *The Amazing Story of Repeal: An Exposé of the Power of Propaganda* (Chicago: Willett, Clark, 1946), 69–70, 337–38; Kerr, *Organized for Prohibition,* passim.

14. Walsh to Francis Crowley, May 16, 1930, Walsh to L. K. Devlin, June 2, 1930,

box 378, Walsh to George L. Peddison, Sept. 20, 1930, box 380, Walsh Mss; Lee Bennett to Walsh, June 15, 1930, Walsh to Bennett, June 20, 1930, W-G Mss.

15. *NYT,* Apr. 30, 1930, 1, 14; "Parties and the Treaty," editorial, ibid., July 10, 1930, 24; Robert H. Ferrell, *American Diplomacy in the Great Depression: Hoover-Stimson Foreign Policy, 1929–1933* (New Haven: Yale University Press, 1957), 5, 87–105; Alexander DeConde, "Herbert Hoover and Foreign Policy: A Retrospective Assessment," in *Herbert Hoover Reassessed: Essays Commemorating the Fiftieth Anniversary of the Inauguration of Our Thirty-First President* (Washington, D.C.: GPO, 1981), 322–23.

16. Typescript of Walsh radio talk (on London Naval Treaty), July 30, 1930, box 254, Walsh telegram to T. C. Armitage, July 24, 1930, box 377, Walsh Mss; "Foes of the Naval Treaty Overwhelmed," *Literary Digest* 106 (Aug. 2, 1930), 5–6.

17. Walsh to True Child, July 14, 1930, box 378, Walsh to Judge Emil Baensch, July 23, 1930, box 404, Walsh Mss; *Manitowoc Herald-News,* July 26, 1930, 1; Walsh to Katherine Walsh Wattawa, Nov. 21, 1930, box 381, Walsh Mss; Baensch and Walsh quoted in "John Nagle Memorial," 219–23.

18. Walsh radio talk, July 30, 1930, box 254, P. E. Burke, *Montana Standard,* to Walsh, Aug. 2, 1930, Walsh to Burke, Aug. 13, 1930, box 377, Walsh Mss; Imogene Howell to Miles Taylor, Aug. 10, 1930, box 5, Walsh-Erickson Mss.

19. McDowell to Walsh, June 7, 1930, Walsh to McDowell, June 18, 1930, McDowell to Walsh, July 10, 1930, box 379, Penwell to Walsh, Aug. 7, 1930, Mary O'Neill to Walsh, Aug. 11, 1930, Walsh to O'Neill, Aug. 18, 1930, box 380, Walsh Mss; *HI,* Sept. 7, 1930, 1, 7.

20. Walsh to J. D. Ferguson, *Milwaukee Journal,* May 27, 1930, box 378, Walsh to Mrs. R. C. Battey, Democratic State Central Committee, Aug. 15, 1930, box 377, Walsh to Sen. Robert Wagner, Aug. 24, 1930, box 381, Walsh Mss.

21. Typescript of address, Sept. 1, 1930, box 253, Walsh Mss; "Special" from Havre, Sept. 1, in *HI,* Sept. 2, 1930, 1, 2; *GFT,* Sept. 2, 1930, 1; Walsh to Sen. C. C. Dill, Aug. 11, 1930, box 378, Walsh Mss; Walsh to William Green, pres., American Federation of Labor, Sept. 19, 1930, W-G Mss.

22. *HI,* Sept. 6, 1930, 1–2; typescript of address, Democratic State Convention, Sept. 6, 1930, box 254, Walsh Mss; cf. *HI,* Sept. 7, 1930, 6, *GFT,* Sept. 7, 1930, 11.

23. Walsh to Roy Ayers, Sept. 10, 1930, box 377, Walsh Mss. In 1930 Walsh gave his approval to private development of the important Flathead project in western Montana, seeing no prospects of public development. *Cong. Rec.,* 71st Cong., 2d Sess. (Apr. 11, 1930), 6943–50; H. L. Maury to Walsh, May 20, 1930, Walsh to Maury, May 26, 1930, box 379, Walsh Mss; O. A. Bergeson to Joseph M. Dixon, Feb. 5, 1930, Dixon Mss.

24. *HI,* Sept. 15, 1930, 9, Sept. 16, 1930, 5, Sept. 18, 1930, 2; Walsh to Borah, Sept. 20, 1930, box 377, Walsh to Wheeler, Sept. 23, 1930, box 381, Walsh Mss.

25. Walsh to Mrs. Keyes, Sept. 18, 1930, W-G Mss; *GFT,* Sept. 18, 1930, 1.

26. *HI,* Sept. 18, 1930, 1; Walsh to Mrs. Keyes, Sept. 18, 1930, W-G Mss; *HI,* Sept.

19, 1930, 1; Fred Martin, editor's note, *Park County News* (Livingston, Mont.), Sept. 4, 1969, 10.

27. Walsh to M. P. Diamond, Feb. 24, 1930, box 378, Walsh Mss; "Senator Walsh and Montana," editorial, *HI*, Sept. 6, 1930; excerpt from speech by Gov. Erickson at Malta, Sept. 26, 1930, W-G Mss; *GFT*, Oct. 5, 1930, 2:1, 5; *Montana Standard*, Oct. 5, 1930, 6, 14–15.

28. Statements by Dan J. O'Hern at Miles City, Oct. 4, 1930, *GFT*, Oct. 5, 1930, 7; James F. O'Connor to Walsh, Nov. 7, 1930, box 380, typescript of Walsh speech, n.d. (but 1930), box 254, Walsh Mss.

29. *Montana Standard*, Nov. 2, 1930, 1, 2, 19.

30. Typescript of Walsh speech, n.d. (but 1930 campaign), box 254, Walsh Mss; *Montana Standard*, Oct. 30, 1930, 1, Oct. 31, 1930, 1; *GFT*, Oct. 30, 1930, 4, 6, Oct. 31, 1930, 10.

31. See especially *GFT*, Oct. 1–28, 1930, passim.

32. Ibid., Oct. 14, 1930, 13.

33. Copy of Sen. King to W. S. Young, Oct. 4, 1930, W-G Mss; *Montana Standard*, Oct. 6, 1930, 1–2, Oct. 7, 1930, 1, 13; *GFT*, Oct. 23–31, 1930, passim.

34. *GFT*, Oct. 5, 1930, 14; Walsh to William Green, Sept. 19, 1930, W-G Mss; Imogene Howell to H. E. Miles, Jan. 27, 1932, box 314, Walsh Mss.

35. Johnston, "Senator Walsh of Montana," *The People's Business,* issued for the People's Legislative Service (Washington, D.C., Sept. 1930), Mercer Johnston Mss, LC; "Montana, the Nation and Senator Walsh," editorial, *St. Louis Post-Dispatch*, Oct. 24, 1930, reprinted in *HI*, Nov. 2, 1930, 15, and *GFT*, Nov. 3, 1930, 4; Democratic ad, ibid., Nov. 2, 1930, 2.

36. *GFT*, Oct. 31, 1930, 20, Nov. 1, 1930, 1–2, Nov 2, 1930, 13; *Montana Standard*, Nov. 1, 1930, 1–2; *HI*, Nov. 3, 1930, 1.

37. *HI*, Nov. 4, 1930, 1, 10.

38. Walsh to Miles Taylor and Alice Engle, Washington office, Nov. 5, 1930, Walsh to Joseph Tumulty, Nov. 6, 1930, box 381, Walsh Mss; E. C. Day to Walsh, Nov. 7, 1930, W-G Mss; Walsh to John W. Davis, Nov. 28, 1930, box 16, Walsh to W. B. George, Dec. 26, 1930, box 378, Walsh Mss; Ellis L. Waldron, *Montana Politics since 1864: An Atlas of Elections* (Missoula: Montana State University Press, 1958), 232–33.

39. Louis Wiley, *NYT*, to Walsh, Nov. 5, 1930, Walsh to Wiley, Nov. 20, 1930, Jerome Williams, *Big Timber Pioneer*, to Walsh, Nov. 2, 1930, and passim, box 381, Walsh Mss.

40. James J. O'Connell to Walsh, Nov. 5, 1930, box 380, D. H. Morgan to Walsh, Nov. 6, 1930, and passim, box 379, Walsh Mss.

41. Walsh to Donnelly, Oct. 9, 1930, box 378, Walsh to Walter Aitken, Nov. 7, 1930, box 377, Walsh Mss.

42. "Home Folks Crowd about Walsh to Congratulate Him," *HI*, Nov. 8, 1930, 1, 10; Genevieve Walsh Gudger to Walsh, Nov. 6, 1930, Walsh letters, Nov. 5–7, 1930, W-G Mss; Albert Galen to Walsh, Nov. 5, 1930, box 378, Walsh Mss.

Chapter 30: The Rule of Law at Home and Abroad

1. Frankfurter, "The Business of the Supreme Court of the United States: A Study in the Federal Judicial System," *Harvard Law Review* 39 (June 1926), 1072; Tom Stout to Walsh, Feb. 3, 1926, box 122, Walsh Mss; Walsh Senate eulogy on Philander Knox, 67th Cong., 4th Sess. (Jan. 28, 1923), 2644.

2. Thomas J. Walsh, *Reform of Federal Procedure* (address), Apr. 23, 1926, 69th Cong., 1st Sess., Senate Doc. 105, Senate Docs., Misc., vol. 2, ser. 18558 (Washington, D.C.: GPO, 1926), 1–2; Thomas W. Shelton to Walsh, Oct. 25, 1924, box 405, Walsh to Shelton, Feb. 26, 1925, box 403, Walsh Mss.

3. Walsh, *Reform of Federal Procedure*, 2; Charles E. Clark, "Procedural Reform and the Supreme Court," *American Mercury* 8 (Aug. 1926), 445–49, box 302, Walsh Mss; Roscoe Pound, "Senator Walsh on Rule Making Power on the Law Side of Federal Practice," *American Bar Association Journal* 13 (Feb. 1927), 84–86.

4. Walsh to Charles B. Letton, May 27, 1926, box 302, Judge Frank S. Dietrich to Walsh, July 20, 1921, Walsh to Dietrich, July 25, 1921, Legislation: Judiciary, Walsh Mss.

5. Judge Learned Hand to Walsh, May 25, 1926, box 302, Walsh Mss.

6. Ibid., and passim, box 302, Walsh Mss. Soon after Walsh died the measure he had opposed gained approval in committee and in Congress as well.

7. Walsh open letter to J. E. Erickson, in *HI*, Apr. 15, 1922, 1, 10; Walsh to Rev. John Helmer Olson, July 5, 1922, Walsh to T. M. Hill, Dec. 1, 1922, Disarmament file, Walsh Mss; Walsh speech to American Legion, Billings, Aug. 10, 1923, quoted in *HI*, Aug. 11, 1923, 1, 6; Walsh diary (on trip to Geneva), Sept. 5–13, 1925, W-G Mss; Walsh statement for *NYW*, Apr. 6, 1927, box 256, Walsh Mss.

8. Walsh to Judge George W. Anderson, U.S. Circuit Court, Boston, Apr. 14, 1924, Walsh to Sec'y of State Charles Evans Hughes, Apr. 17, 1924, Walsh Mss.

9. Walsh to Frederick H. Allen, July 2, 1926, box 243, Walsh Mss; Walsh in *Cong. Rec.*, 69th Cong., 1st Sess. (Apr. 19, 1926), 7734–35; Charles DeBenedetti, *Origins of the Modern American Peace Movement, 1915–1929* (Millwood, N.Y.: KTO Press, 1978), 186–87 and passim.

10. Speech delivered in Sept. 1928, box 254, Walsh Mss, "The Outlawry of War Treaty," commencement address, Loyola University (Chicago), June 6, 1928, Walsh Mss; *Cong. Rec.*, 70th Cong., 2d Sess. (Jan. 5, 1929), 1187.

11. Walsh quoted in *HI* Mar. 28, 1923, 1; John D. Murphy et al., Phil Sheridan Club, Anaconda, to Walsh, Dec. 30, 1925, James Hamill et al., Thomas Meagher Council, to Walsh, Dec. 30, 1925, box 14, Walsh Mss.

12. See R. D. Crowder to Walsh, n.d., Walsh to Crowder, Jan. 26, 1926, box 15, Walsh Mss.

13. Walsh to S. R. Logan, Jan. 30, 1925, John J. Rooney to Walsh, Oct. 2, 1925, Walsh to Rooney, Oct. 8, 1925, box 14, Walsh Mss.

14. *Cong. Rec.*, 69th Cong., 1st Sess. (Dec. 18, 1925), 1067ff., (Jan. 27, 1926), 2813–

14, (Jan. 9, 1926), 1754–66; Walsh to Oswald G. Villard, Dec. 11, 1924, box 14, Walsh Mss; Walsh, "Commemoration of Birth of Woodrow Wilson," speech at Louisville, Ky., Dec. 28, 1926, in *Cong. Rec.*, 69th Cong., 2d Sess. (Jan. 10, 1927), appendix.

15. Gillette to Root, Jan. 27, 1926, box 125, Root Mss; *Cong. Rec.*, 69th Cong., 1st Sess. (Jan. 27, 1926), 2795–2803, 2814–16, 2824–25, (Jan. 26, 1926), 2747–49.

16. *Cong. Rec.*, 69th Cong., 1st Sess. (Jan. 27, 1926), 2824–25; Walsh in ibid. (Jan. 9, 1926), 1754–66; Walsh, "Address at Dinner Given by National League of Women Voters," Feb. 13, 1926, box 253, Walsh Mss.

17. *NYT,* Sept. 4, 1926, 1; document from Geneva, Apr. 2, 1929, quoting "Resolution Adopted by the Senate of the United States of America on January 27th, 1926," box 16, Walsh Mss; *Cong. Rec.*, 69th Cong., 1st Sess. (Jan. 9, 1926), 1758–59; Henry C. Ferrell Jr., *Claude A. Swanson of Virginia: A Political Biography* (Lexington: University Press of Kentucky, 1985), 176–77.

18. Howard Florance to Walsh, May 1, 1929, Walsh Mss; Walsh, "We Approach the World Court," *Review of Reviews* 79 (May 1929), 43–46.

19. Stephen B. L. Penrose to Walsh, May 3, 1932, box 17, Walsh Mss. See also Walsh to Kate Trenholm Abrams, Non-Partisan Association, League of Nations, May 19, 1928, Carrie Chapman Catt, National Committee on the Cause and Cure of War, to Walsh, Dec. 16, 1929, correspondence, 1928–35, passim, box 15, Walsh Mss.

Chapter 31: Chairman of the National Convention, Chicago, 1932

1. Walsh article, unpublished, written for McNaught Syndicate, Inc., Nov. 17, 1931, Walsh to George W. Beardsley, Jan. 21, 1932, box 414, Walsh Mss; Sen. Tom Connally of Texas, in *Cong. Rec.*, 71th Cong., 2d Sess. (Mar. 24, 1930), 5995–96; J. T. Carroll to Walsh, Sept. 22, 1931, box 382, Walsh Mss; Albert U. Romasco, *The Poverty of Abundance: Hoover, the Nation, the Depression* (London: Oxford University Press, 1965), 180–201 and passim.

2. Walsh to Bernard Baruch, Oct. 6, 22, 1931, Baruch to Walsh, Oct. 10, 1931, box 382, Walsh Mss; Albert U. Romasco, "Herbert Hoover's Policies for Dealing with the Great Depression: The End of the Old Order or the Beginning of the New?" in *Herbert Hoover Reassessed,* 292–309; Jordan A. Schwarz, *The Speculator: Bernard M. Baruch in Washington, 1917–1965* (Chapel Hill: University of North Carolina Press, 1981), passim.

3. Walsh to Bernard Baruch, Oct. 16, 22, 1931, Baruch to Walsh, Oct. 7, 1931, box 382, Walsh Mss.

4. Walsh to Sen. Robinson, Nov. 7, 1931, box 382, Walsh Mss; J. Joseph Huthmacher, *Senator Robert F. Wagner and the Rise of Urban Liberalism* (New York: Atheneum, 1968), 62–69, 107–29.

5. Walsh to Sen. Robinson, Nov. 7, 1931, box 382, Walsh Mss; "Democrats in New Congress Outline the Task before Them," *NYT,* Dec. 6, 1931, 9(2):8.

6. *NYT,* Sept. 17, 1931, 5; Walsh to P. J. Geraghty, *Butte Daily Post,* Aug. 26, 1931,

box 383, Albert S. Burleson to Walsh, July 28, 1931, Walsh to Burleson, Aug. 6, 1931, Walsh to Mayor James M. Curley, Sept. 25, 1931, James W. Gerard to Walsh, Oct. 1, 14, Walsh to Gerard, Oct. 9, 1931, Walsh to E. G. Worden, Nov. 17, 1931, Joe Swindlehurst to Walsh, Nov. 14, 1931, Walsh to Swindlehurst, Nov. 19, 1931, box 384, Walsh Mss; Freidel, *Franklin D. Roosevelt: The Triumph*, 228, 240, and passim.

7. Walsh to Roosevelt, Dec. 20, 1930, and passim, box 382, Walsh to Mrs. Martin H. Gerry Jr., Apr. 31, 1932, box 383, Walsh Mss; Wheeler, *Yankee from the West*, 294–95.

8. "Senator T. J. Walsh Out for Roosevelt," *NYT*, May 15, 1932, 27.

9. Ibid.; Franklin D. Roosevelt telegram to Walsh, May 16, 1932, box 384, Walsh Mss; Bernard Bellush, *Franklin D. Roosevelt as Governor of New York* (New York: Columbia University Press, 1954), 282–85 and passim.

10. Homer Cummings to Thomas L. Chadbourne, May 20, 1932, box 382, Walsh to J. E. Erickson, Mar. 9, 1932, box 383, Walsh Mss; Freidel, *Franklin D. Roosevelt: The Triumph*, 268–71.

11. Walsh to Kenneth Romney, Montana House of Representatives, May 19, 1932, box 384, Walsh Mss; "Sketches of Democratic Delegates to Convention," *GFT*, June 21, 1932, 4; Robert Jackson to Walsh, June 11, 1932, box 385, Walsh Mss; Arthur M. Schlesinger Jr., *The Crisis of the Old Order, 1919–1933* (Cambridge, Mass.: Houghton Mifflin, 1957), 298, 301.

12. Ewing LaPorte, comp., *Official Report of the Proceedings of the Democratic National Convention . . . Chicago . . . 1932*, 121–36.

13. Ibid., 17–39.

14. Ibid., 121–35; R. G. Tugwell, *The Brains Trust* (New York: Viking Press, 1968), 213; Freidel, *Franklin D. Roosevelt: The Triumph*, 302 and passim; Frank Freidel, "Election of 1932," in Arthur M. Schlesinger Jr., *The Coming to Power: Critical Presidential Elections in American History* (New York: Chelsea House, 1971), 331, 342, and passim; Eleanor Roosevelt, *This I Remember* (New York: Harper & Bros., 1949), 69.

15. *Proceedings of the Democratic National Convention, 1932*, 136–38; cf. Tugwell, *Brains Trust*, 213, 475–79, and passim.

16. *Proceedings of the Democratic National Convention, 1932*, 140.

17. Ibid., 145–206; David E. Kyvig, *Repealing National Prohibition* (Chicago: University of Chicago Press, 1979), 155–59.

18. *Proceedings of the Democratic National Convention, 1932*, 287–329; Freidel, *Franklin D. Roosevelt: The Triumph;* 291–311; Roosevelt, *This I Remember*, 69–71 and passim.

19. *Proceedings of the Democratic National Convention, 1932*, 332; Roosevelt, *This I Remember*, 70–71; Schlesinger, *Crisis of the Old Order*, 311.

20. *Proceedings of the Democratic National Convention, 1932*, 337–73.

21. Ibid., 374–83.

22. Ibid., 383.

23. J. T. Carroll to Walsh, July 5, 1932, box 382, Walsh to Frank C. Walker, July 21, 1932, box 385, Mrs. Frances Rowse Sammons to Walsh, July 3, 1932, box 384, Wil-

liam E. Dodd to Walsh, June 19, 1932, Walsh to Dodd, July 5, 1932, and passim, boxes 382–84, Walsh Mss.

24. Roosevelt to Walsh, July 26, 1932, Walsh to Roosevelt, Aug. 3, 1932, W-G Mss.

Chapter 32: Campaigning for Roosevelt in 1932

1. Roosevelt to Walsh, July 26, 1932, Walsh to Roosevelt, Aug. 3, 1932, W-G Mss; papers of the Democratic National Committee, box 357, Roosevelt Library, Hyde Park, N.Y.; Freidel, *Franklin D. Roosevelt: The Triumph*, 338–39.

2. John Snure, "Party Leaders in Both Camps Feel Uncertain," *New York Herald Tribune*, July 10, 1932, 4; Mark Sullivan, "Slump as Issue Viewed Pitfall for Democrats," ibid., July 10, 1932, 1, 4, box 397, Walsh Mss; Freidel, *Franklin D. Roosevelt: The Triumph*, 338–42; Schlesinger, *Crisis of the Old Order*, 413–39.

3. Freidel, *Franklin D. Roosevelt: The Triumph*, 339–41; Joseph P. Tumulty to Walsh, July 16, 1932, Walsh to Tumulty, July 21, 1932, box 404, Walsh to Jim Farley, July 18, 1932, Farley to Walsh, July 27, 1932, box 383, Walsh to T. J. Lloyd, pres., Roosevelt-Garner Club, Twin Falls, Idaho, July 29, 1932, box 400, Walsh Mss; James Harbert quoted in *GFT*, Aug. 11, 1932, 4; ibid., Sept. 2, 1932, 6.

4. "Address of Senator Thomas J. Walsh . . . Democratic State Convention at Helena, Sept. 15, 1932," box 385, Walsh Mss; *GFT*, Sept. 16, 1932, 2.

5. "Address of Senator Thomas J. Walsh, Sept. 15, 1932," box 385, Walsh Mss.

6. Walsh, "Introducing Governor Roosevelt" (address), Sept. 19, 1932, box 385, Walsh Mss.

7. Ibid.; *GFT*, Sept. 20, 1932, 1.

8. *Helena Daily Independent*, Sept. 20, 1932, 1, 2, Sept. 21, 1932, 5; James A. Hagerty in *NYT*, Sept. 20, 1932, 1, 4; ibid., editorial, Sept. 21, 1932, 20.

9. *Helena Daily Independent*, Sept. 24, 1932, 1, 2, Sept. 29, 1932, 7; *GFT*, Sept. 24, 1932, 1, Sept. 25, 1932, 5, Sept. 28, 1932, 2, Oct. 4, 1932, 1; Walsh to Mr. and Mrs. Isaac Edinger, Sept. 13, 21, 1932, box 397, Walsh Mss.

10. *HI*, Sept. 29, 1932, 1.

11. *GFT*, Sept. 2, 1932, 2, Oct. 11, 1932, 6, Oct. 12, 1932, 2; Sen. Claude Swanson telegram to Walsh, Oct. 20, 1932, box 384, Walsh Mss; Ferrell, *Claude A. Swanson of Virginia*, 197–98.

12. *HI*, Oct. 23, 1932, 1; *GFT*, Oct. 23, 1932, 2.

13. *GFT*, Oct. 25, 1932, 2.

14. Box 385, Walsh Mss.

15. Ibid.

16. *GFT*, Oct. 26, 1932, 9.

17. *Omaha World-Herald*, editorial, Oct. 27, 1932, 1, 10.

18. Ibid., Oct. 28, 1932, 1, 6; speech in Omaha, Oct. 27, 1932, box 385, Walsh Mss.

19. *GFT*, Oct. 29, 1932, 2; *HI*, Oct. 29, 1932, 1, 2; speech in Denver, box 385, Walsh Mss.

20. Speech in Denver, box 385, Walsh Mss; *GFT,* Oct. 29, 1932, 2.

21. This account is drawn largely from the *HI* and *GFT,* late Oct.–early Nov. 1932.

22. *HI,* Nov. 1, 1932, 10, Nov. 2, 1932, 1, 2; *GFT,* Nov. 1, 1932, 2, Nov. 2, 1932, 1.

23. *HI,* Nov. 3, 1932, 1; *GFT,* Nov. 3, 1932, 6.

24. See *HI* and *GFT,* Nov. 1–7, 1932.

25. "Helena Jam Hears Walsh Score G.O.P.," *HI,* Nov. 8, 1932, 1, 2, Nov. 9, 1932, 1; "Speech Delivered by Senator Thomas J. Walsh during National Campaign of 1932," typescript, 24 pp. (from which he probably drew for part of the Helena address), box 385, Walsh Mss.

26. *HI,* Nov. 9, 1932, 1, Nov. 10, 1932, 1; *GFT,* Nov. 29, 1932, 3.

27. Erickson to Walsh, Nov. 15, 1932, box 371, Walsh Mss.

Chapter 33: The "New Deal" Begins, Remarriage, and Death

1. Walsh to Richard J. Finnegan, *Chicago Daily Times,* Dec. 21, 1932, box 398, Walsh Mss.

2. "Democrats Expect Soviet Recognition," *NYT,* Dec. 4, 1932, 1; Walsh to Roosevelt, Jan. 24, 1933, W-G Mss.

3. *Cong. Rec.,* 72d Cong., 2d Sess. (Feb. 16, 1933), 4231 and passim; Walsh to Mrs. W. C. Dawes, pres., Montana WCTU, July 19, 1932, box 382, Walsh Mss.

4. *NYT,* Dec. 4, 1932, 1; Walsh to O. S. Warden, Feb. 9, 1933, box 21, Walsh-Erickson Mss; Walsh in *Cong. Rec.,* 72d Cong., 2d Sess. (Feb. 18, 1933), 4418 and passim.

5. "Rise in Income Tax Backed," *NYT,* Jan. 9, 1933, 3.

6. Walsh to Genevieve Walsh Gudger, Jan. 12, 20, 1933, W-G Mss; Charles A. Douglas to Walsh, Dec. 16, 1932, box 382, Walsh Mss; *GFT,* Dec. 4, 1932, 1.

7. Douglas to Walsh, Dec. 16, 1932, box 382, Swope to Walsh, Jan. 26, 1933, box 384, Butler to Walsh, Jan. 29, 1933, box 382, Gregory to Walsh, Jan. 31, 1933, box 383, Walsh Mss; *The Nation* clippings in W-G Mss; John F. Fitzgerald to Walsh, Feb. 24, 1933, box 383, Walsh Mss; *Washington Daily News,* Feb. 23, 1933, W-G Mss; Rowe to Walsh, Jan. 27, 1933, box 384, Garrett to Walsh, Feb. 27, 1933, box 383, Walsh Mss.

8. Walsh to Genevieve Walsh Gudger, Jan. 20, 1933, W-G Mss.

9. Walsh to Roosevelt, Jan. 24, 1933, W-G Mss.

10. Ibid.

11. Ibid.; Walsh to Gov. Erickson, Feb. 22, 1933, Erickson to Walsh, Jan. 24, 1933, box 383, Walsh Mss.

12. Roosevelt to Walsh, Feb. 3, 1933, Walsh to Genevieve Walsh Gudger, Jan. 20, 23, 1933, W-G Mss.

13. Walsh to Erickson, Feb. 22, 1933 (two letters, one the brief tender of a resignation to take effect later), Jan. 21, 1933, box 443, Walsh Mss. What happened later leaves little doubt that the governor was thinking of himself as a possible replacement for Walsh. Cf. Wheeler, *Yankee from the West,* 300–302, Samuel Stewart, Associate Jus-

tice of the Montana Supreme Court, to Walsh, Feb. 1, 1933, and passim, box 383, Walsh Mss.

14. *GFT,* Feb. 24, 1933, 1, Feb. 25, 1933, 1, Feb. 26, 1933, 1; *HI,* Feb. 28, 1933, 1; *Virginian Pilot,* Feb. 27, 1933, W-G Mss; Walsh to Regis de Truffin, Jan. 7, 1931, box 404, Walsh Mss; Ruth Reynolds in *New York City News,* Mar. 5, 1933, W-G Mss; Mina de Truffin Walsh to Roosevelt, Apr. 16, 1933, Roosevelt Library, Hyde Park, N.Y.; John Walsh to Louise Pearson Blodget, Mar. 7, 1936, W-G Mss.

15. *NYT,* Mar. 3, 1933, 1, 8, 9.

16. Ibid.; newspaper clippings and pictures, W-G Mss.

17. *NYT,* Mar. 3, 1933, 1, 8, 9, 16.

18. Ibid., 8, cols. 6–7, and passim.

19. Ibid., Mar. 4, 1933, 5, Mar. 6, 1933, 13; *GFT,* Mar. 10, 1933, 1; Genevieve Walsh Gudger to J. Leonard Bates, July 18, 1971, W-G Mss; Coleman, *Mrs. Wheeler Goes to Washington,* 138–40. For material on the settlement of Walsh's estate, see box 443, Walsh Mss.

Bibliographical Essay

Of greatest importance in the writing of this book were the letters and papers of Thomas J. Walsh in two locations: first, the Walsh manuscripts in the Manuscript Division of the Library of Congress; second, the Walsh-Gudger Collection in the Illinois Historical Survey, University of Illinois Library, at Urbana-Champaign. The first and larger collection is predominantly Walsh's senatorial correspondence from 1910 to 1933. The second consists of letters and miscellaneous papers related to Walsh's career and collected by his daughter, Genevieve Walsh Gudger. These include personal correspondence of Walsh and his first wife, Elinor McClements Walsh, dating from the 1880s to 1917, and a few letters and documents by other family members. The collection continued in the 1930s and 1940s as Mrs. Gudger sought information after her father's death and contemplated writing his biography.

When I first began this research I worked in Walsh's papers at the Library of Congress in hundreds of boxes that were not numbered or clearly identified. During later research I found the boxes had now been classified and numbered, and I began to give complete citations in my writing. Readers can expect to find, therefore, some variation in the form of citation. The subject at hand such as legislative matters or Montana politics will often help in finding a particular box.

About twenty interviews were conducted between 1949 and 1969 in the Washington, D.C., area and in Montana, the most important of which are listed below (other references will be found in the notes): former Senator Henry F. Ashurst in Washington, Sept. 9, 1949; Genevieve Walsh Gudger, Feb. 16, 21, 1950 (and occasionally thereafter), mostly in Washington; Senator James E. Murray in the Senate Office Building, Washington, on Aug. 27, 1949; former Senator Burton K. Wheeler, July 7, 1949, in his Washington law office; former Judge Jerre Lynch in Butte, May 22, 1961; Frieda Fligelman, friend of the Walsh family, in Helena, on Feb. 25, 1968; Fred Martin, newspaperman and aide who accompanied Senator Walsh on his 1930 campaign tour around Montana, on March 6, 1968.

Numerous manuscript collections were indispensable; for example, the Papers of Franklin D. Roosevelt at Hyde Park and of Woodrow Wilson at the Library of Congress. Also helping at the Library of Congress were the Papers of Calvin Coolidge, William G. McAdoo, Thomas H. Carter, John Sharp Williams, Gilbert Hitchcock, Robert M. La Follette, Josephus Daniels, Thomas W. Gregory, William Allen White, William E. Borah, George Norris, Gifford Pinchot, and Elihu Root. At the University of Montana in Missoula insights were provided by the Papers of Joseph M. Dixon, Charles N. Pray, and Frank Bird Linderman, as was true also of the Albert Fall Papers at the Huntington Library, the Samuel T. Hauser Papers at the Montana Historical Society, the Warren G. Harding Papers at the Ohio Historical Society, and the James D. Phelan Papers at the Bancroft Library.

During my work on land policy of the United States in the period I made extensive use of files in the National Archives, especially minutes of the Senate Judiciary Committee, which proved important to this book.

Obviously such a book would be impossible without the *Congressional Record* from 1913 to 1933 and all the related hearings and government reports, including the Teapot Dome hearings in 1923–24 and 1928. Almost as useful were official reports of the proceedings at national political conventions, scrapbooks, clippings, and newspapers. As to the last, the *New York Times* with its index and the *Helena Independent* and *Great Falls Tribune* were perhaps most important.

Published works and miscellaneous sources probably can be found without difficulty in the notes, chapter by chapter. For example, there is Michael P. Malone et al., *Montana: A History of Two Centuries,* rev. ed. (Seattle: University of Washington Press, 1991), an excellent book that includes an extensive bibliography.

Index

At the time of his death in October 1998, J. Leonard Bates was professor emeritus of history at the University of Illinois at Urbana-Champaign. His publications include *The Origins of Teapot Dome: Progressives, Parties, and Petroleum, 1909–1921* (1963), *Tom Walsh in Dakota Territory: Personal Correspondence of Senator Thomas J. Walsh and Elinor C. McClements* (1966), and *The United States, 1898–1928: Progressivism and a Society in Transition* (1976).

Typeset in 11/13 Adobe Garamond
with Centaur display
Designed by Dennis Roberts
Composed by Celia Shapland
for the University of Illinois Press
Manufactured by BookCrafters

University of Illinois Press
1325 South Oak Street
Champaign, IL 61820-6903
www.press.uillinois.edu